WITHDRAWN
UTSA LIBRARIES

RENEWALS 458-4574

# Classificatory Particles
## in
## Kilivila

**OXFORD STUDIES
IN
ANTHROPOLOGICAL
LINGUISTICS** William Bright, *General Editor*

**Classificatory Particles in Kilivila**

Gunter Senft

# Classificatory Particles
# in
# Kilivila

## Gunter Senft

New York Oxford
**OXFORD UNIVERSITY PRESS**
1996

**OXFORD UNIVERSITY PRESS**

Oxford  New York
Athens  Aukland  Bangkok  Bombay
Calcutta  Cape Town  Dar es Salaam  Delhi
Florence  Hong Kong  Istanbul  Karachi
Kuala Lumpur  Madras  Madrid  Melbourne
Mexico City  Nairobi  Paris  Singapore
Taipei  Tokyo  Toronto

*and associated companies in*
Berlin  Ibadan

---

Copyright © 1996 by Gunter Senft
Published by Oxford University Press, Inc.
198 Madison Avenue, New York, New York 10016

Oxford is a registered trademark of Oxford University Press

All rights reserved. No part of this publication may be
reproduced, stored in a retrieval system, or transmitted,
in any form or by any means, electronic, mechanical,
photocopying, recording, or otherwise, without the prior
permission of Oxford University Press.

**Library of Congress  Cataloging-in-Publication Data**

Senft, Gunter 1952-
Classificatory Particles in Kilivila / Gunter Senft
    p.  cm, - (Oxford Studies in Anthropological Linguistics)
    Includes bibliographical reference and index.
    ISBN 0-19-509211-2
    1. Kiriwinian language-Particles
    2. Kiriwinian language-Classification
    3. Trobriand Islands (Papua New Guinea-Languages-
Grammar)
    I. Title    II. Series
PL6252. K5S38  1995
499'. 12-dc20

Printing (last digit) : 9 8 7 6 5 4 3 2 1

Printed in the United States of America
on acid free paper

**Library
University of Texas**
at San Antonio

pela minana sinebada namanabweta
nakabitam ula kwava nabweliguee

BARBARA

... Cassirer 1923 behandelt im ersten Teil seiner *Philosophie der symbolischen Formen* die menschliche Sprache, wobei auch die "Grundrichtungen der sprachlichen Klassenbildung" besprochen werden... Das Wort "Philosophie" möchte vielleicht Namen, wie die eines MAUTHNER und HOOGVLIET und andere mehr in Erinnerung rufen, hier aber ganz zu unrecht. Dieses Buch ist reich an Gedanken und Einsichten, äußerst suggestiv und lehrreich.

Es sei nicht die Aufgabe der Sprachphilosophie "die verschiedenen Formen der Begriffs- und Klassenbildung, die in den Einzelsprachen wirksam sind, zu beschreiben, und sie in ihren letzten geistigen Motiven zu verstehen... Die Wege, die die Sprache hier einschlägt, sind so vielfältig verschlungen und so dunkel, daß es nur durch die genaueste Versenkung und durch die feinste Einfühlung in das Detail der Einzelsprachen gelingen kann, sie allmählich zu erhellen. Denn gerade die Art der Klassenbildung macht ein wesentliches Moment jener "inneren Form" aus, durch welche sich die Sprachen spezifisch voneinander unterscheiden".

Man sieht, daß sich CASSIRER visionärer Flüge in das Reich der erphantasierbaren Möglichkeiten enthält und dauernde Fühlungnahme fordert mit der reichen Mannigfaltigkeit der sprachlichen Tatsachen. Aber wenn auch die verschiedenen Klassifikationssysteme in verschiedenen Varianten wechselten, so könnten doch in dieser großen Mannigfaltigkeit "gewisse allgemeine Gesichtspunkte" entdeckt werden. Zweifellos sei es möglich, diese Gesichtspunkte so anzuordnen, "daß man dabei jenen ständigen Fortgang vom "Konkreten" zum "Abstrakten", der die Richtung der Sprachentwicklung überhaupt bestimmt, als leitendes Prinzip benutzt". Aber, so fügt CASSIRER... hier richtig hinzu, man dürfe nicht vergessen, "daß es sich hier nicht um eine zeitliche, sondern um eine methodische Schichtung handelt, und daß demnach in einer gegebenen historischen Gestalt der Sprache die Schichten, die wir hier gedanklich zu sondern versuchen, neben- und miteinander bestehen und sich in der mannigfachsten Weise übereinander lagern können".

Gerlach Royen (1929:254–255)

---

... wer auf der Studierstube ein System zimmert, ohne es der Welt anzupassen, der lebt entweder seinem System all Augenblick schnurstracks zuwider, oder er lebt gar nicht.

Jakob Michael Reinhold Lenz (1774)

# Preface

We shall deal in this article with a single phenomenon, namely, the *classificatory formatives* in the language of Kiriwina, Trobriand Islands, an archipelago lying due north of the eastern end of New Guinea.

Bronislaw Malinowski (1922:37)

---

Classification is certainly a basic fact of life. That classification abilities are necessary for the survival of every organism is an important insight of biology. Human beings classify consciously and unconsciously—and subconsciously, of course—in all situations. When we confront a scientific problem, we try to solve it by first classifying the various parts of the problem. Thus it is not surprising that the history not only of philosophy but of all branches of science is also the history of how these sciences have classified their research subject. Classification always implies selection because, as Koestler (1978:201) stated,

> (our) minds would cease to function if we had to attend to each of the millions of stimuli which—in William James's classic phrase—constantly bombard our receptor organs in a "blooming, buzzing confusion." Thus the nervous system and the brain itself function as a multilevelled hierarchy of filtering and classifying devices, which eliminate a large proportion of the input as irrelevant "noise," and assemble the relevant information into coherent patterns before it is represented to consciousness.

If we want to communicate about this perceived, classified, and filtered input, we have to classify once more: We have to transform this input into classes and categories provided by the systems that organize our communicative verbal and nonverbal faculties. With our systems of language and gesture, we again classify and filter on various levels while communicating. On one of these levels, we decide, for example, on the grammatical structure we want to use to refer to what we want to communicate about; on another level, we also have to classify the referents of our communication. Linguistics is the science that tries to describe, illuminate, and explain the processes of classification that are relevant for communication—and this goal is the reason that many linguists find their discipline so fascinating. Indeed, human beings have developed a number of different linguistic techniques to apprehend the world, providing an enormous database for the analysis of this problem. This book deals with a classification technique used by the speakers of an Austronesian language, Kilivila.

In August 1982, I entered for the first time the district that was to be the future site of my linguistic fieldwork—the Trobriand Islands in Milne Bay Province of Papua New Guinea. I did so with, I suppose, almost the same feelings of intense interest and suspense that Malinowski felt (Malinowski 1922:51). However, I had the enormous advantage of having read Malinowski's masterpieces on the Trobriand Islanders' culture. Nevertheless, there is a difference between having read about a completely foreign world and actually confronting it. The aim of my research project was to describe and explain aspects of ritual communication. To achieve this aim, it was necessary to acquire a certain competence in the language, of course. Since there was no existing grammar of the Trobrianders' language, writing a grammar was one of the prerequisites (G. Senft 1986:3–5). Among the few linguistically reliable sources on Kilivila was Malinowski's fascinating article "Classificatory Particles in the Language of Kiriwina," published in 1920. Working on this system of classifiers became one of my preoccupations as soon as I was able to master the language. After fifteen months of field research, I returned to Germany with a great deal of data on classifiers, knowing that I would concern myself for a long time with the analysis of these data and with an attempt to understand this system and its importance for the language as well as for the culture. This concern is documented in a number of publications (G. Senft 1983, 1985a, 1985b:133–134, 1986:68–72, 1987a, 1989, 1991c, 1993).

In this book, I present the results of almost ten years' work on the system of classificatory particles in Kilivila. However, I am not at all sure whether this means that I am really "through" with my Trobriand friends' classifier system.

The work is offered as a contribution to the research on classifiers and classifier languages.

It is an empirical work, based on data gathered during a period of fifteen months of field research in 1982 and 1983 and four months of field research in 1989. It is extremely data-oriented and emphasizes the use of classifiers in social contexts. The aim of this work is to describe (1) the functions of the system of Kilivila classifiers; (2) the acquisition of the classifier system; (3) the inventory of Kilivila classificatory particles (produced in actual speech); (4) the processes of language change that affect the system; and (5) the semantics of the Kilivila classifier system.

The introductory chapter—based on a broad survey of the relevant literature—gives a general definition of the concepts "classifier languages" and "classifiers" and presents the aims and methods pursued in traditional studies on the classifier systems of classifier languages in general and on the Kilivila language in particular. Chapter 2 presents a description of the grammatical and discourse functions of the system of classificatory particles (CPs) in the Kilivila language.

The third chapter is the central chapter of this book. After a description of the aims and methods used in data collection, the CP data gathered in a specially developed elicitation test, as well as CP data documented in my overall corpus of Kilivila speech, are presented in detail. First, the CP production data are presented and preliminarily interpreted separately for each of the five age groups into which I divided my consultants. This data presentation is meant to give the reader a first impression and a general account of CP production in each of the five age groups. Second, the data gathered in the CP elicitation test are presented in two ways: (1) the CP types and the respective tokens produced by all consultants during the elicitation test are given, including a description of which consultant produced how many tokens of the respective CP type; and (2) the CP types produced by all consultants in the elicitation test are given, allocating the tokens of the CP type produced to the CP type or types actually expected. Finally, the CP types and tokens documented in my overall corpus of Kilivila speech data are presented.

This kind of data presentation serves as an empirical, checkable basis for the analyses necessary to reach the aims of this study. I am aware that this large-scale presentation requires space; however, it allows the critical reader to check (and countercheck) all the analyses and all the inferences made using these data. Moreover, it is hoped that this large-scale data presentation makes it easier for the reader to understand the train of thought that starts with the empirical datum elicited (on the basis of theoretical reflection and ideas presented in the relevant literature) and leads to the description, interpretation, and evaluation of this empirical datum, resulting in theoretical conclusions.

Following the data presentation, the results of the CP research are given. First, the question of how the CP system is acquired by Trobriand children is considered. Here, all but one of the many side issues of this complex question are answered. The subquestion of why the individual CPs are acquired in the order found is the last question addressed in this chapter, because the answer requires the information provided by the answers to the other two main questions raised in the study. The question of how the individual CP types are produced in actual speech is considered next. The third and last question answered in chapter 3 is that of the semantic domains constituted by the CP system. The headings of the sections and subsections in chapter 3 should make it easy for readers to find the answers to aspects of this study that may be of special interest to them.

Chapter 4 presents the results of a restudy I did in the Trobriand Islands in 1989, in which I reconsidered the results of my analyses of the Kilivila CP system based on data gathered in 1982 and 1983.

Chapter 5 is an excursus; it discusses—with all necessary caution—possible interdependencies between language, culture, and cognition based on an analysis of the CP system.

Chapter 6 summarizes the results of the study and presents a "network" model for the description of classifier systems.

Appendix A lists the individual consultants used in gathering CP data in 1982 and 1983; appendix B lists which consultant produced which CP in what text category in my overall corpus of Kilivila speech data; appendix C lists the consultants I worked with during my restudy in 1989; and appendix D presents some hypotheses on the origin of classifiers.

I would like to mention here two concepts that are central in understanding the research and the arguments that I present.

First, I speak of the "system" of CPs in Kilivila and of "systems of classification" in general. I do this not only because I follow the general usage in the literature, but especially because I am convinced that my analyses of the CPs in Kilivila justify the use of the term "system." One of the aims of this research is to describe a set of elements—that is the set of CPs in Kilivila—and the set of relations existing among these elements (Klaus 1968:634). I try to describe the internal order among linguistic elements and to present the functional relation that can be found on various levels of description and in relation to social and other subsystems (Bussmann 1983: 489).

Second, I speak of "referents" and of the "act of referring." A referent is an object or a fact in the extralinguistic reality to which noun phrases as verbal signs "refer." By "act of referring," I understand on the one hand the verbal reference to language-internal and language-external contexts and on the other hand the relation between the verbal expression (name, word, etc.) and the object in the extralinguistic reality to which the expression refers (Bussmann 1983:428).

I would like to end this preface with a warning to my readers: much of this book contains rather dry linguistic descriptions. However, I hope that the results presented help readers forget some of these long hauls and that they may get at least an impression of the fascination I experience in dealing with the complex linguistic phenomenon of classifier systems in general and in particular the system of classificatory particles in Kilivila.

June 1995
Nijmegen, The Netherlands                                    G.S.

# Acknowledgments

During my work in Tauwema in the Trobriand Islands and during the writing of this book, I received the help of many people and institutions. First, I want to thank the Deutsche Forschungsgemeinschaft (DFG: Ei-24/ 10-1-5; Se-473/2-1-2), especially Ursula Far Hollender and Manfred Briegel; the Research Unit for Human Ethology of the Max-Planck-Society; and the Cognitive Anthropology Research Group at the Max-Planck-Institute for Psycholinguistics for their support during my field research.

I am also indebted to Penelope Brown, Bernard Comrie, Volker Heeschen, Stephen C. Levinson, Bernd Nothofer, Roland Posner, and Barbara Unterbeck for their critical reading of first drafts of this monograph; their extensive comments were extremely valuable to me in the preparation of this book.

I would like to thank William Bright and two anonymous referees for their insightful comments, and I thank the team at Oxford University Press for their helpfulness and expertise.

I want to thank the National and Provincial Governments in Papua New Guinea and Milne Bay Province for their assistance with, and permission for, my research projects. I also thank the Departments of Linguistics and Anthropology of the University of Papua New Guinea, the Institute of Papua New Guinea Studies, the Council of Chiefs of the Trobriand Islands, and the Embassy of the Federal Republic of Germany in P.N.G. for their support of my research.

I especially thank the people of the Trobriand Islands, and above all the inhabitants of Tauwema and my consultants for their hospitality, friendship, and patient cooperation. Without their help, none of my work on the Kilivila language and the Trobriand culture would have been possible.

Although I typed the manuscript myself, finishing touches have been made by Edith Sjoerdsma and Gertie de Groen. All the problems I had with the various computers I used were competently solved by Gertie de Groen, Caroline Rek, Herbert Baumann, and Karl Grammer. Many thanks to all of them.

A German version of this manuscript was accepted as my Habilitationsschrift at the Fachbereich 1 of the Technische Universität Berlin. I would like to thank all the people involved in the process of my Habilitation for their support and for helpful comments on my research.

Last, but by no means least, I want to thank my wife for her patience and perseverance in discussing my research with me, criticizing it, and living and working with me in the field. I dedicate this monograph to Barbara Senft.

# Contents

## Chapter

## 1

### Introduction      3

## Chapter

## 2

### Classificatory Particles in Kilivila: Grammatical and Discourse Functions      16

## Chapter

## 3

### The System of Classificatory Particles in Kilivila      24

Chapter
## 4

**On the Validity of Some of the Presented Results:**
**Six Years Later—A Restudy**          **295**

Chapter
## 5

**Excursus: Language, Culture, and Cognition?**          **312**

Chapter
## 6

**Closing Remarks: Using Network Models to**
**Describe Classifier Systems**          **323**

# Classificatory Particles
## in
## Kilivila

# Chapter

# 1

# Introduction

Kilivila (also known as Kiriwina and Boyowa) is one of the 40 Austronesian languages spoken in the area of Milne Bay Province in Papua New Guinea. It belongs to the "Papuan Tip Cluster" (Capell 1976:6, 9; Ross 1988:25–27), and typologically is classified as having verb-object-subject (VOS) word order (G. Senft 1986:107–112). The Kilivila language family comprises Budibud (also known as Nada), Muyuw (also known as Murua), and Kilivila. Kilivila has about 25,000 speakers, most of whom live on the Trobriand Islands.

Bronislaw Malinowski's ethnographic work on the Trobriand Islands has made this area rather well known, even outside the field of anthropology. In fact, Malinowski first reported the phenomenon that is the subject of this book. As a result of his classic article, "Classificatory Particles in the Language of Kiriwina" (Malinowski 1920), Kilivila is known to linguists as a so-called classifier language (Allan 1977:286–288).

The present chapter first defines the concepts "classifier" and "classifier language". It then gives an overview of the structure and function of classifier systems and the methods and aims of traditional classifier studies, including those on classifier languages in general and those on Kilivila in particular.

## 1.1 WHAT ARE CLASSIFIER LANGUAGES?

John Lyons (1977b:463) notes an important feature of classifier languages:

Languages which grammaticalize the distinction between entity-denoting nouns and mass-denoting nouns tend to draw a sharp syntactic distinction between phrases like "three men" on the one hand, and "three glasses of whisky,'' on the other. Classifier languages do not: they treat enumerable entities and enumerable quanta in much the same way.[1]

Classifier languages also show the following three characteristics (Allan 1977:286–8):

1. They have a system of classifiers.

2. They follow the almost universal principle that "A classifier concatenates with a quantifier, locative, demonstrative or predicate to form a nexus that cannot be interrupted by the noun which it classifies" (Allan 1977:288; but see also Adams 1989:12, 24).

3. They belong to one of the following four classifier language types: numeral, concordial, predicative, or intralocative.

Classifier languages are distributed around the world and are found in such different language families as Malayo-Polynesian, Mon-Khmer, Austro-Asiatic, Sino-Tibetan, Altaic, Dravidian, and Indo-Aryan (see, among others, Adams and Conklin 1973:9; Foley 1968:77–91; Greenberg 1975:18).[2] Numeral classifier languages are considered the paradigmatic type, and Kilivila belongs to this class.[3]

Languages with numeral classifiers differ from other languages primarily with respect to the following characteristic feature: in counting inanimate as well as animate referents, the numerals obligatorily concatenate with a certain morpheme, which is the so-called classifier.[4] This morpheme classifies and quantifies the respective nominal referent according to semantic criteria (see Serzisko 1980:1, 1982a:147; Hundius and Kölver 1983:166).[5] Moreover,

---

[1] For further examples where one noun takes over similar classifying functions with respect to a second noun in the noun phrase, see Adams and Conklin (1973); Allan (1977:292–293, 301); Burling (1965:260); Clark (1976:449–450); Denny (1976:129); Greenberg (1975:22); Hla Pe (1965:167), Hoa (1957:125–126); Katz (1982); Kölver (1982c:162); Lee (1988:225, 242); Löbel (1986); Harweg (1987a); Jackendoff (1968); Parsons (1970); Plank (1984); Verhaar (1986, 1987:503, 1988:21–23); Zubin and Köpcke (1986); and Jacob (1965); for a formal logical discussion of count terms, mass terms, and quantification, see Lonning (1987); for the difference between noun classes and classifiers, see Dixon (1982: Part D:157–159); Silverstein (1986); Chin (1989, 27–29); but see also Gomez-Imbert's (1982) thesis on nominal classification in Tatuyo, a language that has features characteristic of classifier systems as well as features characteristic of noun class systems; for an interesting discussion of levels of semantic structuring in Bantu noun classification, see Spitulnik (1988).

[2] Moreover, we find classifiers in American Sign Language (ASL); Egyptian hieroglyphics and Mesopotamian cuneiform use graphemic classifiers (see, e.g., Klima and Bellugi 1979: 13–15, 191–192; Kantor 1980; Newport and Supalla 1980; Kegl and Schley 1986; Supalla 1986; Rude 1986).

[3] This book deals with the classificatory system of Kilivila; thus, I will not discuss the other three types of classifier languages mentioned. For a discussion of these types, see Allan (1977:286–287) and Craig (1986:3–4).

[4] As the example of Kilivila shows, this morpheme may also be a so-called zero morpheme (G. Senft 1986:75; see also Mufwene 1980c:246). Moreover, due to processes of language change, it may well be that in some languages and some contexts the classifier is no longer obligatory, but becomes optional (see Chin 1989:4–6), Stolz (1991) presents data for classical Nahuatl, where the classifier is optional (see also Adams 1989).

[5] What Seiler and his research team call *Das sprachliche Erfassen von Gegenständen* (and living beings, I would add) by means of numeral classification is, by the way, just one of nine different techniques this linguist defines as *Sprachhandlungsprogramme* describing the dimension "apprehension" within the framework of the so-called Kölner Universalienprojekt (see Seiler 1982).

in numeral classifier languages, we find classifier morphemes in anaphoric (see, e.g., Downing 1986) and deictic expressions. Therefore, the term "numeral classification" is somewhat inaccurate (see also Asmah 1972:90; Berlin and Romney 1964:79; Unterbeck 1990b:90). Nevertheless, I will adhere to this technical term as it is used in the general linguistic literature (see, e.g., Allan 1977:286; Becker 1975:114–115; Greenberg 1975:19; Haas 1942).

Greenberg (1978:78) has answered the question of why such classifying systems apply only to nouns:

> . . . it is the noun par excellence which gives rise to classificational systems of syntactic relevance. It is not so much that the noun designates persisting entities as against actions or temporary states of persisting entities. It is that nouns are continuing discourse subjects and are therefore in constant need of referential devices of identification. As soon as we wish to talk about an action as such, we nominalize it; classification is a help in narrowing the range of possible identification.[6]

In sentence analysis, the syntactic description of the phenomenon of classification in numeral classifier languages is restricted to the noun phrase level (see Kölver 1983:55).[7] The order in which the three constituents—classifier, numeral, and noun—appear varies across languages; however, according to the principle formulated by Allan (1977:288), in general the noun does not interrupt the nexus formed by the numeral and the classifier (see also Adams and Conklin 1973:1; Adams 1989:12, 24).

The morphological/syntactic role of classifiers is generally neglected in the literature in favor of their semantic functions. However, Goral's statement that "in [classifier] systems, syntax and semantics are inextricably intertwined" (Goral 1978:5; see also Friedrich 1970:381) holds for all classifier languages and confirms the definitions proposed for the concept classifier.

## 1.2 WHAT ARE CLASSIFIERS?

We have defined classifiers as morphemes that classify and quantify nouns according to semantic criteria.[8] Because of the twofold function of classifiers, Serzisko (1980:7)—following Hla Pe (1965:166) and Bloomfield (1933:237)—proposes the generic term "Numerativ" to denote the "obligatorische Konstituente in Quantifizierungskontexten" (see also Hundius and Kölver

[6] See also Mufwene 1980a:1025 and Broadfield 1946:25.

[7] On the other hand, Schafer (1948:413) states the following about classical Chinese: "Classifiers are also used with numbers accompanying verbs …."

[8] For general definitions of classifiers, noun classifiers, and nominal classifiers, see Allan 1977:285; Becker 1975:114–115; Benton 1968:137; Berlin 1968:20; Burling 1965:249; Denny 1979:97; Hoa 1957:124; see also the contributions in Craig (1986). Mufwene (1980a:1025) characterizes classifiers as "delimitative markers"; see also Mufwene 1984:200, 202.

1983:167–169). The term numerative subsumes classifiers proper and quantifiers.

Classifiers classify a noun inherently, that is, they designate and specify semantic features inherent to the nominal denotatum and divide the set of nouns of a language into disjunct classes (see Cholodovic 1954:49; Unterbeck 1990b:43).

Quantifiers classify a noun temporarily, that is, they can be combined with different nouns rather freely and designate a specific feature of a noun that is not inherent to that noun. Thus, quantifiers are predicative (see Serzisko 1980:17, 68–69, 1982a:152; Berlin 1968:175; Friedrich 1970:397; Denny 1986:302–307).

Contrary to one of Greenberg's (1975:25) language-universal postulates, not all but only the majority of nouns in numeral classifier languages lack a marking with respect to the category 'number'; in these languages, number is usually marked with nouns denoting persons (see, e.g., Barz and Diller 1985:170; Goral 1978:15; Miram 1983:36–37; Rausch 1912; Serzisko 1980:13, 48, 70; G. Senft 1986:45–46; Stolz 1991:18). Numeratives can take over the syntactic function of marking number for the nouns to which they refer.

Referentially, nouns in classifier languages can be characterized as having generic reference (see Royen 1929:775). With their referential function, numeratives individualize nominal concepts; they can mark a noun as obligatorily nongeneric in reference (see H. Seiler 1982:6, 8; Serzisko 1980:15, 86–87; also Carpenter 1992:147).

The functions that numeratives or classifiers fulfill are succinctly summarized by Adams et al. (1975:2):

Besides their function in numeral noun phrases, classifiers in various languages function as nominal substitutes, nominalizers of words in other form classes, markers of definiteness, relativizers, markers of possession, and as vocatives; serve to disambiguate sentences; establish coherence in discourse and regularly mark registers and styles within a language.

These functions will be discussed in detail in chapter 2.

So far we have differentiated classifiers and quantifiers (see also Adams 1989:3–5, 194) or, to use Lyon's (1977b:463) terms, "sortal classifiers" and "mensural classifiers" (see also Unterbeck 1990b:40). However, along with the definition of classifiers proper and quantifiers one generally finds a third category, the so-called repeaters. A repeater is a noun that serves as its own classifier, that is, the noun is repeated in the classifier slot. Hla Pe (1965:166) defines the terms classifier (proper), repeater, and quantifier as follows:

A classifier is a word for an attribute of a specific object, some of which may have more than one; a repeater is the specific object itself or part of it, used as numerative; whilst a quantifier concerns itself with the estimating of things by some sort of measure—size, extension, weight or number *especially* of ten or multiples of ten.

---

Repeaters are defined by Burling (1965:249) as "echo classifiers", Fischer (1972:69) calls them "identical classifiers", and Kölver (1982c:178, 183, 1979:34) characterizes them as "semantischer dummy"; finally, Goral (1978:33) defines repeaters as "autoclassifiers ... filling a syntactic slot ..." (see also Adams and Conklin 1974:3–4, 7; Benton 1968:116; Smith 1979:88; Carpenter 1992:132). In connection with this phenomenon, Lehmann (1979:169) hints at the possibility of studying this problem from a different point of view; he notes: "... a classifier can also function as an independent noun ...". Whether this repeater category of numeratives, which probably has to be assigned to the category classifier, carries the principle of classification to the point of absurdity, as Kölver (1982c:178) claims, must be doubted after a closer inspection of the numeratives within the individual languages. Allan (1977:295) discusses the problem of repeaters with all necessary caution and offers some hypothetical answers to the question of why this category develops in languages.[9] I shall not discuss this problem in detail here,[10] but I want to emphasize that as far as I know there is no language described so far where all nouns can be used as repeaters to classify themselves. Thus, in all languages that have them, repeaters represent a relatively closed category; they form—in principle—a finite set of formatives.

Moreover, most if not all classifier languages have, in the words of Lyons (1977b:461), at least one "semantically neutral classifier, which may be employed ... with reference to all sorts of entities .... In many languages the semantically neutral classifier is restricted to non-personal, or even inanimate, entities ...." (see also Asmah 1972:95). This general classifier (see Serzisko 1980:24) has to be assigned to the category of classifiers, too (see also Schafer 1948:410–411).

Finally, I want to note here that Malinowski (1920) does not differentiate between classifiers proper, quantifiers, and repeaters, but refers to these formatives as "classificatory particles". I will use Malinowski's general term (abbreviated as CP) for these formatives to pay tribute to the master of Trobriand ethnography.[11]

---

[9] Jones (1970:2) states "It is interesting to speculate on the possibility that such usage arises from an inadequate supply of classifiers once their use becomes firmly established". See also Adams (1991) and Adams (1989:1).

[10] Goral (1978:8) and Denny (1976:130) emphasize the strong affinity between nouns and numeratives (see also Schafer 1948:410–411). However, keeping in mind Dixon's (1968:114) admonition that we know very little about the development of such systems, I do not want to indulge in speculation on this topic here; but see appendix D of this volume and Dixon (1986); Mithun (1986); Delancey (1986); Demuth et al. (1986); Royen (1929:58, 63, 78, 141, 254, 266–268, 543, 705, 780); G. Senft (1993).

[11] Royen (1929:iii, 37, 68, 185, 192, 305, 364, 889) emphasizes repeatedly that an interdisciplinary approach is not only necessary but also inevitable for an analysis of nominal classifier systems. See also Berlin et al. (1973:214). I want to mention for the sake of completeness that Berlin

(*continued on page 9*)

Figure 1 summarizes this system—or classification—of CPs or numeratives and the technical terms found in the literature to refer to them.

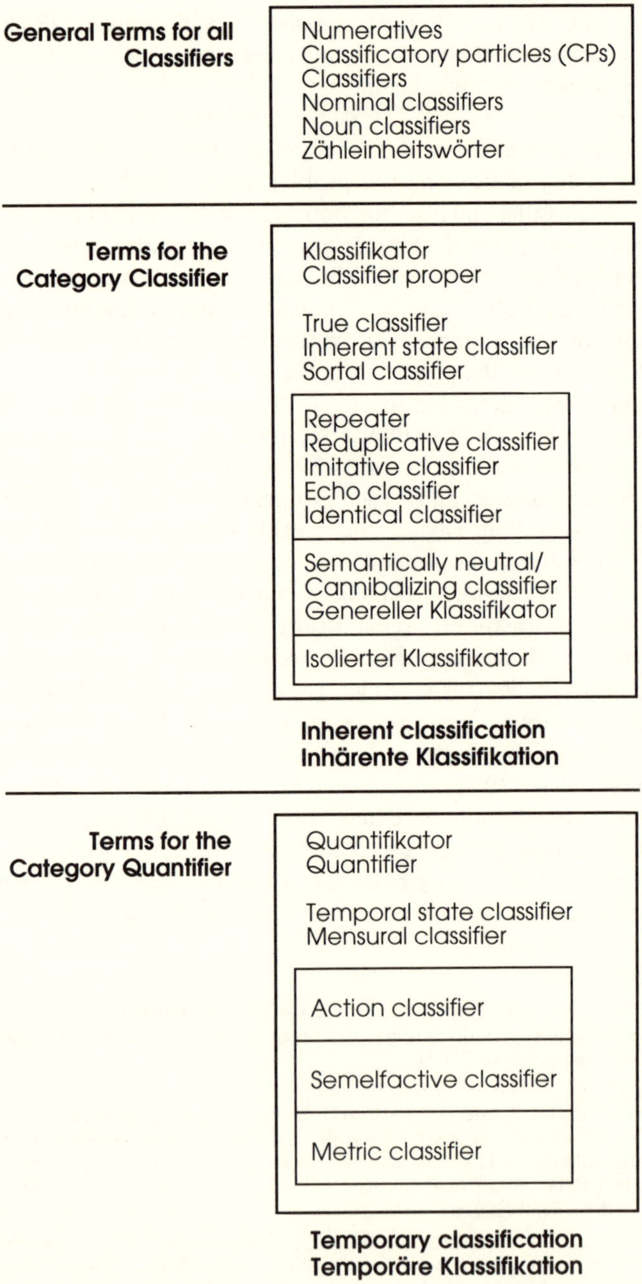

**General Terms for all Classifiers**

> Numeratives
> Classificatory particles (CPs)
> Classifiers
> Nominal classifiers
> Noun classifiers
> Zähleinheitswörter

**Terms for the Category Classifier**

> Klassifikator
> Classifier proper
>
> True classifier
> Inherent state classifier
> Sortal classifier
>
> > Repeater
> > Reduplicative classifier
> > Imitative classifier
> > Echo classifier
> > Identical classifier
>
> > Semantically neutral/
> > Cannibalizing classifier
> > Genereller Klassifikator
>
> > Isolierter Klassifikator

**Inherent classification
Inhärente Klassifikation**

**Terms for the Category Quantifier**

> Quantifikator
> Quantifier
>
> Temporal state classifier
> Mensural classifier
>
> > Action classifier
> >
> > Semelfactive classifier
> >
> > Metric classifier

**Temporary classification
Temporäre Klassifikation**

**Figure 1.** Classification of Classifiers.

## 1.3 STRUCTURE AND FUNCTION OF CLASSIFIER SYSTEMS

In classifier languages, nouns are classified and categorized according to characteristics of their referents. This classification is based on semantic principles and results in the ordering of objects, living beings, concepts, actions, and events. In other words, it leads to a categorization of all the nominal denotata, of all nominal "conceptual labels" (Hundius and Kölver 1983:182; see also Denny 1986) coded in the language. We can refer to the units of this classification as "semantic systems" (Denny 1979:97) or as "semantic domains" (Berlin 1968:34; Tyler 1969:8). Thus, CPs can be regarded as indices or as "Exponenten von nach inhaltlichen Merkmalen geschiedenen Nominalklassen" (Kölver 1979:1); they represent the semantic (sub) structures of a (classifier) language (see Friedrich 1970:379).

The critical questions to be answered are, What are the semantic criteria and principles this kind of classification is based on? and, Are the classifications in different languages culturally determined?

Before I attempt to answer these questions, I want to emphasize that the classificatory systems of the various numeral classifier languages are usually not comparable to folk taxonomies, but must, more often than not, be regarded as paradigms (see Becker 1975:111; Berlin 1968; Berlin et al 1973; Burling 1965; Conklin 1962:124; Ellen 1979:7–9; Foucault 1966:108, 110; Frake 1969:34; Haas 1942; Barz and Diller 1985:176; Hundius and Kölver 1983:204; Miram 1983; Saul 1965; G. Senft 1987b; Tyler 1969:7–9). In taxonomies, the respective nominal referents are classified on the basis of the objectively perceptible and verifiable features. In paradigms, the single nominal referents are categorized in contrastive relation to other nominal referents. Mixed forms of taxonomic and paradigmatic classification do exist, but they are exceptional; moreover, such mixed forms of classification depend on the inventory of CPs these languages display. The inventory of CPs in classifier languages ranges from 2 to 528 (or even 730) (see Adams and Conklin 1973:9; Berlin 1968; Miram 1983:103).

Descriptions of the criteria that structure classifying systems generally give the following features: ± human; human and social status; human and kinship; ± animate; sex; shape/dimension; size; consistency; function; arrangement; habitat; number/amount/mass/group; measure; weight; time; action; ± visible (see Adams 1989; Adams and Conklin 1973; Allan 1977; Becker 1975; Benton 1968; Burling 1965; Denny 1979; Friedrich 1970; Haas

---

(*continued from page 7*)

(1968) also describes "action classifiers" in Tzeltal; that Harweg (1987b) uses the term *Zähleinheitswörter* as a synonym for *Numerativ*; that Hoa (1957:128) introduces the term "semelfactive classifier" for a "type of classifier which indicates single action", referring to certain numeratives in Vietnamese; that Adams (1989):177, 182 describes "the general or cannibalising classifier"; that Hiranburana (1979:39–40) uses the terms "reduplicative classifier" and "imitative classifier"; that Fischer (1972:69, 77) speaks of "*isolierte Klassifikatoren*" (i.e., one classifier classifies only one noun) and mentions "metric classifiers" (i.e., classifiers for numerical and temporal units); and that Craig (1992:285–286) mentions "genitive classifiers" that are also called "relational" or "possessive classifiers". See also Seiler (1986).

1942; Hiranburana 1979; Hoa 1957; Kaden 1964; Miram 1983; Royen 1929:82–83, 125–137, 142, 256, 396–397).[12]

Classificatory systems are usually described by feature lists that give the features in a relatively free order; however, there have been a few attempts to order the features hierarchically (see, e.g., Goral 1978:38; cf. Craig 1986:5–6). Becker (1975) describes the Burmese system of CPs hierarchically in the form of concentric circles; Miram (1983) proposes functional diagrams—*Fluss-diagramme*—to describe the system of Yucatecan Maya (I will discuss this approach in more detail in section 1.4.1). What must be emphasized here is the fact that most, if not all, of these features represent semantic categories that are fundamental in all languages. For example, Friedrich (1970:404) characterizes the feature "shape" as the "ultimate semantic primitive" (see also Allan 1977:302). Moreover, it should also be noted that—at first sight, at least—these features seem to be universal (Lyons 1977b:466). However, a closer look at the CPs that constitute the semantic domains in individual languages on the basis of these features reveals that these general, probably universal, categories are defined in culture-specific ways (Berlin 1968:35). It is also evident that the boundaries between the individual semantic domains are rather fluid (Rosch 1978:36, 1977:4, 15, 18, 21). Thus, Craig (1986:1), on the basis of prototype theory, claims rightly that "... categories ... should be described as having fuzzy edges and graded membership ..." (see also Posner 1986; Givón 1986).[13]

Therefore, the description of semantic domains within any numeral classifier language requires a sound analysis of how these domains are constituted, that is, which features are relevant for the definition of the semantic domain (see Lenneberg 1953:468; Rosch 1978:28). This ethnosemantic descriptive and analytical research is rather complex and presupposes the linguist's thorough knowledge of the language described. This may explain why, at least in my opinion, typological, comparative studies on classifier languages, which necessarily use a general approach, neglect this microlevel of ethnosemantic analysis.[14] In these studies, relating the general results of the description of semantic domains to a specific language is possible only in a rather indirect, intermediate way. Moreover, it may well be that the complexity of ethnosemantic analysis is the reason that most descriptions of classificatory systems thrust the equally important morphological/syntactic role of CPs into the background.

Now, what about the actual use of the CPs that constitute such complex

---

[12] Apparently no classifier language makes use of a color classifier (see Adams 1989:5; Allan 1977:297; Asmah 1972:94; Berlin and Romney 1964:80; Carroll and Casagrande 1958:27–29, 31; Lee 1987:397; but see also Royen 1929:151).

[13] With respect to prototypes, see Rosch (1988); see also Mufwene (1980b:30, 31, 33, 36; 1980c;1983) who describes prototypes as "underlying principles of cognitive classification" and discusses possible ambiguities because of their "metaphorical extension(s)". For a critical discussion, see MacLaury (1991); see also Fischer (1972:68), who pleads for a historical foundation for the structure of so-called *semantische Felder*.

[14] Here the eminent exception is Royen (1929)!

systems?[15] As mentioned previously, the inventory of CPs in classifier languages varies from 2 to 730 lexemes. In languages with many CPs, it must be emphasized that some CPs can refer to any nominal denotatum. That is, even with inherent classification, CPs can be used to specify special aspects of relatively general nominal concepts. In other words, complex systems of CPs allow the possibility of referring to a noun within its semantic domain either by the general, characteristic, "unmarked" CP or by a more specific CP.[16] The choice of the appropriate CP occurs on the semantic level. It can be independent of the intended speech act, and thus attains stylistic denotation, meaning, and significance (see Becker 1975:113; Burling 1965:259; Goral 1978:26). Individual speakers use these options in their choice of CPs.[17] They may even be innovative by using a certain CP in a metaphoric way. Some linguists (e.g., Becker (1975:113), in his work on Burmese CPs) even claim that the actual "use of classifiers ... is in part an art" (see also Rosch 1977:42). This implies that analyses of CP systems must take into account the function of CPs as sociolinguistic variables (Labov 1972:237; see also Hla Pe 1965:170). Thus, we can conclude that *all* CPs do have meaning (Allan 1977:290; see also Adams 1989:7–8, 192; Adams et al. 1975:14, 17; Berlin and Romney 1964:79, 82; Mufwene 1984: 201, 203–204, 214; Schafer 1948:412). The problem of how to describe this meaning leads us to basic linguistic methodological considerations.

## 1.4 METHODS AND AIMS OF TRADITIONAL CLASSIFIER STUDIES— A BRIEF SURVEY

This section discusses studies on classifier languages in general, as well as studies on Kilivila in particular.

### 1.4.1 Studies on Classifier Languages

The literature cited so far includes typologically oriented comparative studies, on the one hand, and empirical descriptive studies of individual languages, on the other. A discussion of the methods that typological comparative studies use is unnecessary here. Rather, methodological techniques used in

---

[15] With the exception of Downing (1986) and Erbaugh (1986) this question is not answered in any of the literature cited here.

[16] Benton (1968:111) states, "The 'characteristic' or unmarked meaning of a form is generally that which is most likely to be encountered in a particular context and may not have any direct connection with a specific set of inherent features", and (Benton 1968:137), "Within a domain, a change in classifier generally signals a change of meaning. That is, certain semantic features of the noun ... are highlighted by a particular classifier ...." See also Adams (1986:241–243) and Lehmann (1979:171), who mentions "... the semigrammatical (e.g., sarcastic or insulting) deliberate choice of a 'wrong' classifier ...." See also Allan (1977).

[17] With respect to the topic "frequency of usage", see for example, Rosch (1977:38). See also Mufwene (1980a) who notes the discrepancy between CP inventory and actual CP usage.

empirical descriptive studies of individual languages will be described, based on Berlin's (1968) and Miram's (1983) monographs; other studies will then be discussed in light of the questions raised by these monographs.

In his work on the system of CPs in the Mayan language Tzeltal, Berlin presented two literate, Spanish-speaking, native Tzeltal speakers with 4,410 "phonemically possible forms". Using these forms, he elicited from the two consultants 528 numeral classifiers, which were counterchecked with the help of three more consultants in "informal and nonsystematic checks of reliability" (Berlin 1968:13, 19–20; see also Berlin and Romney 1964:80–81). The elicited CPs are described according to their features. Using the same consultants and a questionnaire, Berlin ordered the CPs hierarchically and according to the semantic domains they constituted. Thus, the Tzeltal CPs were described on the basis of the judgments of only two—or, if we include the three counterchecking Tzeltal speakers, five—consultants.

In her study on the CPs in Yucatecan Maya, Miram (1983) also worked with a literate and bilingual consultant, Edilberto Ucan Ek; he became her assistant and also did transcriptions for her. Miram's data are based on observations of ordinary language spoken in a natural context, as well as on interviews with consultants. During these interviews, she (or her assistant) checked lists of possible or already described CPs and elicited further, "new" CPs. It is unclear, however, which kind of data she is referring to in her study. Miram elicited 730 CPs; on the basis of clearly defined criteria, she reduced these CPs to 225 forms that were semantically analyzed. Her assistant grouped 194 of these CPs into 47 semantic domains. What is decisively new in her approach is her use of functional diagrams based on these data. The diagrams are intended to simulate a native speaker's decision processes in choosing a certain CP. This form of data presentation allows a description of the semantic domains as "open" systems that may be linked with each other in various ways (see Ellen 1979:17).

The value of Miram's novel approach is unfortunately partially diminished by the somewhat unclear description of her consultants' contributions and by the important role her assistant played in the processes of data collection and data processing. Linguists experienced in field research will probably agree that Miram's assistant falls into the category of the so-called marginal native (Freilich 1970). This is true of Berlin's consultants, too. In general, all data gathered with the help of such consultants must be looked upon with a certain amount of skepticism.

Although I am critical of the databases used in both of these studies because they resulted mainly from work with only a few consultants, it should be pointed out that Berlin and Miram at least reveal the methods of their data collection. Although there are a few exceptions (e.g., Carpenter 1991), many other investigators either do not mention the methods used in data collection or claim that theirs is a comparative study, which need not use empirical data gathered by the author. Some studies are based on data presented in already published papers and on judgments of native speakers and (foreign) trained linguists. Kölver's excellent study on Central Thai is an example (Kölver 1979; see also Unterbeck 1990b:3–4, 61). Nevertheless, in general descriptive studies of the CP systems of individual classifier languages have a number of significant methodological shortcomings.

The research interests of published CP studies can be summarized as follows:

1. Descriptions of the syntactic role of CPs.
2. Descriptions of the semantics of CPs.
3. Descriptions of CPs with respect to their constitutive function for semantic domains, as well as lists of these semantic domains.
4. Comparisons of semantic domains constituted by CPs in different classifier languages, with respect to the question of language universals.

To my knowledge, only nine empirically founded studies deal with the question of first-language acquisition of CP systems (Carpenter 1986, 1991; Chin 1989; Erbaugh 1986; Gandour et al. 1984; Luke and Harrison 1986; Matsumoto 1985; Sanches 1977); Clark (1976) unfortunately indulges in sheer speculation.[18] However, the studies of Allan (1977:295), Burling (1965:261), Goral (1978:4), Haas (1942:201–202), and Tversky (1986:72–73) provide some hints toward possible answers to the question of how the CP system is acquired by native speakers.

With respect to data showing CPs in actual speech, the currently available CP studies—with the exception of Becker 1986, Downing 1986, and Erbaugh 1986—only present isolated sentences as examples to support the syntactic and/or semantic description of the CP systems. Context influence (Rosch 1978:42; Strawson 1950:334; cf. Levinson 1983:172–177) on the speaker's choice of a certain CP is a problem sometimes mentioned but not illustrated by relevant data. Symptomatic of the state of the art with respect to this question is Berlin's (1968:23) statement (which he does not indicate is a hypothesis) that "The actual occurrence of numeral classifiers in recorded texts is relatively low ...." He then concludes that the occurrence of CPs in various contexts can be ignored in analyzing the CP systems of individual languages, and supports this conclusion with the statement that "... only systematic elicitation for classifiers *per se* ... can hope to claim partial exhaustiveness" (see also Craig 1986:8). Thus, Berlin supports Burling's (1965:264) guiding methodological principle for the analysis of CP systems:

> Seeing the problems which arise in the attempts to bring order into the set of classifiers, one may feel that the best available "analysis" so far is simply the list of classifiers with their definition.

---

[18] For the acquisition of Niger-Congo noun class and agreement systems, see Demuth et al. (1986:463–465). Noun classes and agreement in Sesotho acquisition are discussed in Demuth (1988) and Demuth (1992). For a discussion of how and when number and countability distinctions are acquired in English, see Mufwene (1984:207–208). This criticism and some of the other statements presented here do not hold for studies on the ASL classifiers; see, for example, Kantor (1980). For a criticism of Clark (1976) see Goral (1978:4), also Chin (1989:156–158).

For the lexicology of a classifier language, this is an important conclusion, of course; however, for a CP analysis that tries to penetrate into the microlevels of the CP system, the static listing of CPs is certainly not entirely satisfactory.[19]

Finally, there is virtually no information about processes of language change in progress affecting CP systems.[20]

### 1.4.2 Studies on Kilivila

The previous section surveyed rather briefly publications on numeral classifier languages other than Kilivila, the Austronesian language whose CP system is the focus of the analyses presented here.[21]

Milner (1963:66) poses the following question:

---

Is an Oceanic linguist to concentrate on one language at a time to treat it with the same searching analysis that is now taken for granted in the study of, say, Latin or French, at the risk of too great a degree of specialisation, or is he to be content with general surveys and comparative work founded generally on second-hand and superficial knowledge of his material?

---

Faced with these alternatives, (see also Vachek 1976:225–226), I decided on the first course, the analysis of the CP system of one language, namely, Kilivila.

Kilivila CPs are first mentioned by Fellows (1901) and Ray (1907). Baldwin (no date), who worked as a missionary on Kiriwina Island, lists 75 classifiers in his unpublished fragment of Kilivila grammar, translates them into English, and describes aspects of their morphological role and function. Malinowski (1920) describes 42 CPs with respect to their morphological, syntactic, and semantic functions. Capell (1969:61) lists 44 CPs in his description of noun class division in Kiriwina.[22] Capell (1971:273–274) and Lithgow (1976:461, 465–467, 480, 488–490) also refer briefly to the Kilivila CP system.

Ralph Lawton's unpublished Master's thesis "The Kiriwinan Classifiers" (Lawton 1980) is the most comprehensive description of Kilivila CPs so far, and thus warrants a brief review. After a description of the morphological

---

[19] That it is possible to describe the semantic domains constituted by the CPs as dynamic, open systems is convincingly demonstrated by Miram's (1983) monograph.

[20] As far as I know, only Asmah (1972:96); Becker (1975:120); Demuth et al. (1986); Dixon (1986:110–111); Erbaugh (1986); Jacob (1965); and Kölver (1982a:107, 115, 120) discuss possible processes of language change affecting CP systems.

[21] The CP system of Kilivila is mentioned briefly in the following publications: Allan (1977:285, 288, 290, 295–296, 299, 300, 303–305); Chin (1989:24–25); Friedrich (1970:401–403); Greenberg (1975:18–19; 1978:78).

[22] However, the CP *ukdu* that Capell mentions is not (or no longer?) known to Kilivila native speakers; one explanation for this may be that this CP does not agree with Kilivila syllable patterns (see G. Senft 1986:20–22).

role the CPs fulfill and a discussion of the special relationship between CPs and nouns, Lawton presents a semantic description of 147 CPs. He divides these into two groups: Group 1 comprises 34 CPs, which "specify whole items in terms of their features or properties" (Lawton 1980:80). Group 2 comprises 113 CPs, "which classify items in terms of some modification they have undergone. Modification of items is conveniently divisible into three categories labelled activity, partition and arrangement" (Lawton 1980:81).

Lawton then subdivides the CPs of group 1 into the following three classes:

1. Basic property specifiers which are subclassified according to the features ± animate, ± human, dimension, and residue.

2. Subclassifying CPs within the semantic domains constituted by the basic property specifiers.

3. Residue.

The individual CPs are listed and described, and a phrase or sentence is given as a reference for the use of the respective CP.

In his semantic description of the CPs of group 2, Lawton subclassifies the partitive classifiers according to the features "topographical, parts within wholes, pieces, multiple reference", and the arrangement classifiers according to the features "inherent/non-inherent arrangement"; the feature non-inherent arrangement is itself further subcategorized according to the features "distributional", "configurational", and "quantitative". The individual CPs of group 2 are presented in the same way as the CPs of group 1.

Lawton then discusses the CPs in connection with adjectives, verbal expressions, associations, and metaphors; the appendix presents a list of the 147 CPs according to Lawton's classification principles and in alphabetical order.

Some of Lawton's expositions are problematic, but the whole topic is complex. Thus, I shall not criticize Lawton (1980) in detail here. However, I want to note that almost all the points of criticism mentioned in the discussion of the studies of classifier languages in general hold for Lawton's thesis as well.

# Chapter

# 2

# Classificatory Particles in Kilivila: Grammatical and Discourse Functions

In this chapter, we will look at the grammatical and discourse functions[1] of the Kilivila system of CPs, including the morphological relevance of CPs with respect to Kilivila inflectional morphology and the functions that are assigned to CPs in Kilivila.

## 2.1 MORPHOLOGICAL RELEVANCE

The Kilivila system of CPs contains at least 177 formatives. (Section 3.3.1 lists these CPs in detail.) I assume that with all the subtle and very specific differentiations possible, there are probably more than 200 CPs in Kilivila. Moreover, if we keep in mind all the pragmatic functions CPs can serve, the Kilivila CP system can even be regarded as basically open; here it has to be noted, however, that at least so far no loanword has been incorporated completely or in part into the inventory of Kilivila CPs (see G. Senft 1991a, 1992a).

The system of noun classification in Kilivila is an important means of word formation with (1) all but one of the demonstrative pronouns, (2) one

[1] Kilivila has a fourfold series of possessive pronouns, partly realized as free pronominal forms, partly realized as pronominal affixes. One of these series is produced in a specific semantic context, referring to food only; the other three series are used to distinguish different degrees of possession: one series marks inalienable possession and two series mark nonedible alienable possession (G. Senft 1986:47–54). These possessive pronominal forms classify the Kilivila noun, too, of course (see also Royen 1929:186; Wurm 1981). However, I do not deal with this kind of nominal classification in this book, but rather present research on the specific system of formatives that consists of quantifiers, repeaters, and noun classifiers proper, which all are referred to with the general term—classificatory particles—that Malinowski coined for them. Finally, I am sure that Kilivila has verbal derivational classificatory prefixes similar to those described by Ezard (1978) for languages of the Massim cluster; however, as stated elsewhere (G. Senft 1986:28), I have omitted all consideration of derivational morphology in my description of Kilivila.

form of (numerical) interrogative pronouns/adverbs, (3) two classes of adjectives, and (4) numerals. These word classes require concord with the class of the noun to which they refer. This concord is secured by the CPs, which are infixed or prefixed to the respective word frame or word stem. I have described these processes of word formation and the syntactic aspects of constituents with CPs in detail elsewhere (G. Senft 1985a:374–379, 1986); however, I will give a rather general account of the processes of word formation here.

With the exception of the purely exophoric demonstrative pronoun *besa* or *beya* 'this' (with a deictic gesture), all other demonstrative pronouns consist of a fixed morphological frame, formed by the word-initial morpheme *ma-* (or, according to phonological rules, *m-* or *mi-*), the word-final morpheme *-na*; and an infixed morpheme, which is the CP. To distinguish between singular and plural, there is also a plural marking morpheme *-si-*, which is infixed between the CP and the word-final morpheme *-na*. Demonstrative pronouns formed in this way express the concept of 'this/these'. To express the deictic concept of 'that/those', the morpheme *-we-* is infixed in singular forms between the CP and word-final *-na* and in plural forms between the plural marker *-si-* and word-final *-na*. To express the kind of deictic concept that comes close to the English demonstrative 'yonder', the Kilivila speaker takes the forms of the demonstrative pronouns expressing the concept of 'that/those' and changes the final vowel /a/ of the word-final morpheme *-na* to an /e/ that is lengthened and has a minor accent.

There are three classes of adjectives in Kilivila. One class must be used without CPs, the second may be used with or without CPs, and the third must always be used with CPs that are prefixed to the word stem.

The numerals or, more precisely, the cardinal numbers in Kilivila consist of the word stem and a prefixed CP.

There is also one form of an interrogative adjective or adverb that consists of the word stem *-vila* and a prefixed CP (for CPs with an interrogative quantifier see de León 1988:65–66).

I conclude this brief account of the processes of word formation in Kilivila with the presentation of two sentences containing all four word classes involved in the system of noun classification (see G. Senft 1989):

(1) *Kevila waga lekotasi?*
    *ke-vila*                    *waga*    *le-kota-si?*
    wooden-how many     canoe    3Ps.Past-arrive-Plural[2]
    'How many canoes arrived?'

---

[2]I tried to use as few abbreviations as possible for glosses and in the Kilivila orthography (see Senft 1986). Here is the list of abbreviations used for these purposes:

| | |
|---|---|
| Ps | person |
| PP-IV | fourth series of possessive pronouns |
| | (see note 1 to this chapter) |
| ' | glottal stop |

**(2)** *Keyu waga makesina kemanabweta (lekotasi).*
*ke-yu*            *waga*     *ma-ke-si-na*
wooden-two     canoe     this-wooden-Plural-this

*ke-manabweta*          *(le-kota-si).*
wooden-beautiful     (3Ps.Past-arrive-Plural).
'These two beautiful canoes (arrived).'

The speakers of these sentences in referring to canoes must indicate the noun class of 'canoe' with the CP for 'wooden things'—*ke*—in the interrogative pronoun, in the numeral, in the demonstrative pronoun, and in the adjective.

Concerning the morphological relevance of the CPs in Kilivila, I have already mentioned one function of these formatives, namely, to secure concord between the noun and the four word classes involved. The next section describes the functions of CPs in Kilivila in more detail.

## 2.2 FUNCTIONS OF CPS IN KILIVILA

I have already mentioned some functions CPs fulfill in classifier languages in general. I will now describe the functions of CPs in Kilivila. I will illustrate these functions by isolated phrases or sentences (see G. Senft 1989); however, I refer anyone interested in the actual realization of CPs in Kilivila speech production to the already published parts of my Kilivila text corpus (Eibl-Eibesfeldt et al. 1987; B. Senft and G. Senft 1986; G. Senft 1985c–f, 1986, 1987c,d, 1991b,d, 1992b).

### 2.2.1 Referential Function—Concord

As mentioned previously, CPs perform the referential function of securing concord between the nouns and the word classes that use CPs in their word formation. This concord, of course, creates redundancy in the information conveyed by a sentence, as was illustrated in examples (1) and (2). The reference of the various word classes is unequivocal, and the redundancy is obvious: Trobriand canoes are made of timber; they are "wooden things" (this aspect of redundant information will be discussed in section 2.2.3).

The complex inventory of CPs allows speakers to classify a noun "temporarily" (Berlin 1968:175), that is, to emphasize certain characteristics of the referent of the noun. This is illustrated by the following examples (from G. Senft 1985a:380–387):

**(3)** *natala yena*
     *na-tala*        *yena*
     animal-one     fish
     'one fish'

**(4)** *kevalalima yena*
    *kevala-lima*         *yena*
    batch drying-five   fish
    'five batches of smoked fish'

**(5)** *oylalima yena*
    *oyla-lima*    *yena*
    string-five   fish
    'five strings with stringed-on fish'

**(6)** *makupona yena*
    *ma-kupo-na*         *yena*
    this-two string-this   fish
    'these two strings of fish'

**(7)** *mapwasasina yena*
    *ma-pwasa-si-na*     *yena*
    this-rotten-Plural-this   fish
    'these rotten fish'

These examples first represent the CP *na* meaning 'animals' and then illustrate a set of the noun-modifying group of CPs that specify the noun with respect to quantity, order, arrangement, and condition or state.

Example 8 presents the two gender-specifying CPs *to/te* and *na* (now meaning 'persons of female gender') and the age-subclassifying CP *gudi*.

**(8)** *Bibodi tetala natala guditala*
    *bi-bodi*         *te-tala*    *na-tala*     *gudi-tala*
    3Ps.Fut.-benefit   male-one   female-one   child-one
    'It will benefit each man, woman, and child.'

The noun phrase in example (9) (see Lawton 1980:49) illustrates the semantic power of CPs.

**(9)** *kai mabubosina kwelatolu*
    *kai*    *ma-bubo-si-na*              *kwela-tolu*
    wood   this-cut across-Plural-this   potlike-three
    'these three potlike sawed-off sections of timber'

Example (10) shows that CPs can also be used metaphorically. Here, a speaker refers to a 'dinghy' as a 'child-canoe':

**(10)** *Kugisi magudina waga kekekita okopo'ula waga dimdim!*
    *ku-gisi*    *ma-gudi-na*    *waga*    *ke-kekita*
    2Ps.-look   this-child-this   canoe   wooden-small

    *okopo'ula*    *waga*    *dimdim*
    behind    canoe   white man
    'Look at this small dinghy behind the motorboat!'

All these examples illustrate the referential function of CPs and their semantic power. A closer look at some of these examples shows other (grammatical) functions that CPs perform, as described in the next section.

## 2.2.2 Nominalization, Plural Marking, Numeralization, and Verblike Expressive Functions

In example (8), the numerals *tetala, natala, guditala* are translated as nominal expressions. This is legitimate, especially if we assume that the nouns of the three noun phrases (*tetala tau* 'one man', *natala vivila* 'one woman', and *guditala gwadi* 'one child') were omitted. This analysis—which is possible because of redundancy conveyed by CPs—assigns proper nominal status to the numerals. We also find this kind of nominalization with demonstrative pronouns and adjectives (see G. Senft 1985a:384).

The noun phrases in (11) and (12), as well as those in (4)–(6), illustrate the plural-marking function of CPs.

**(11)** *makena nuya bwaveaka*
     *ma-ke-na*         *nuya*     *bwa-veaka*
     this-wooden-this   coconut   tree-big
     'this big coconut tree'

**(12)** *mapo'ulana nuya bwaveaka*
     *ma-po'ula-na*      *nuya*     *bwa-veaka*
     this-plantation-this   coconut   tree-big
     'this plantation of big coconut trees'

Besides plural marking, we also find some CPs that quantify numeralization, a function independent of that of numerals proper. The noun phrase in example (6), given previously, illustrates this function.

In examples (4), (5), (7), and (9), it is clear that some CPs take over the function of verblike expressions within a noun phrase. This is especially true for CPs that specify or refer to certain activities (see G. Senft 1985a:385).

So far we have dealt with CPs only on a sentence or phrase level. In the next section we look at CPs as they are used in actual discourse.

## 2.2.3 Redundancy, Ellipsis, and Discourse Coherence

Example (8) shows that noun phrases can be composed of numerals without the respective nouns to which they refer. I explained this type of noun phrase construction by proposing that the noun is omitted and that the other word class (in this case, the numeral) acquires nominal status.

Malinowski (1920:59–60) hinted at such an interpretation and compared this type of sentence with elliptical utterances in English. Sentences that are constructed like example (8) are, indeed, quite frequently produced in Trobriand discourse. Trobriand Islanders introduce a certain nominal denotatum explicitly. If they then want to further refer to this noun in discourse, using numerals, demonstrative pronouns, and adjectives, they usually omit the noun. This is only possible because the CPs represent the omitted nouns in a quasi-fragmentary way and the anaphoric reference of CPs secures semantic concord beyond sentence boundaries. Now we can explain why we sometimes find redundant information within the noun phrase: the information redundancy given by the CPs within a Kilivila noun phrase enables the omission of the noun without any loss of information, even beyond sentence boundaries.

Thus, CPs perform the important function of securing coherence in discourse. As a general rule, a noun can be elided as long as it is not reclassified (e.g., for stylistic reasons) by another CP. If this occurs, the noun must be overtly realized again as a constituent of the noun phrase to ensure unequivocal and unambiguous reference. In my sample of transcribed Kilivila speech data, I have one (rather extreme) example where a speaker (Tomalala, Consultant No. V16) introduces a nominal referent to which he then refers 16 sentences (78 words, 113 morphemes) later with the appropriate CP; nevertheless, the reference is unequivocal.

Examples (13)–(15) illustrate these functions of CPs.

**(13)** *Atatai tataba. Tauwau Tabalu mtosina makena si koni.*

| | | | |
|---|---|---|---|
| *a-tatai* | *tataba* | *tauwau* | *tabalu* |
| 1Ps.-carve | tataba-board | men | Tabalu-subclan |

| | | | |
|---|---|---|---|
| *m-to-si-na* | *ma-ke-na* | *si* | *koni* |
| this-male-Plural-this | this-wooden-this | their | sign of honor |

'I carve a tataba-board. These men belonging to the Tabalu-subclan, this is their sign of honor.'

Here, the speaker refers to a certain board with carved patterns that marks houses, food houses, and canoes as the personal property of men belonging to the Tabalu-subclan. The reference of the two demonstrative pronouns is unequivocal because in this context the CP *to* can only refer to the noun *tauwau*, and the CP *ke* can only refer to the noun *tataba*.

**(14)** *Tauwau pela emesi bilebusi. Ekokwa'usi kebila mabudanaga ekugwasi emesi.*

| | | | |
|---|---|---|---|
| *tauwau* | *pela* | *e-me-si* | *bi-lebu-si* |
| men | for | 3Ps.-come-Plural | 3Ps.Fut.-take-Plural |

| | | |
|---|---|---|
| *e-kokwa'u-si* | *kebila* | *ma-buda-na-ga* |
| 3Ps.-weave-Plural | stretcher | this-group-this-Emphasis |

| | |
|---|---|
| *e-kugwa-si* | *e-me-si* |
| 3Ps.-first-Plural | 3Ps.-come-Plural |

'The men have come to take him with them. They have woven a stretcher, the men belonging to this group who were the first to arrive.'

Here, the speaker uses the CP *buda* with the demonstrative pronoun in the second sentence to refer unequivocally to the noun *tauwau* in the first sentence (see G. Senft 1985d:481).

**(15)** *O davalusi esisusi tommota topaisewa. Vivila nasalau, tauwau tobugubagula Tommota gala todubakasala, kena kumwedona enukwalisi bubunesi bwena.*

| *o* | *da-valu-si* | *e-sisu-si* | *tommota* |
|---|---|---|---|
| in | 1Ps.incl-village-Plural | 3Ps.-live-Plural | people |

| *to-paisewa* | *vivila* | *na-salau* | *tauwau* |
|---|---|---|---|
| human beings-work | woman | female-busy | men |

| *to-bugubagula* | | *tommota* | *gala* | *to-dubakasala* |
|---|---|---|---|---|
| male-work in the garden | | people | not | human beings-rude |

| *kena* | *kumwedona* | *e-nukwali-si* | *bubune-si* | *bwena* |
|---|---|---|---|---|
| but | all | 3Ps.-know-Plural | manners-their | good |

'In our village live people taking pleasure in their work. The women are busy, the men are good gardeners. The people are not rude, but all have good manners.'

Example (15) illustrates that, in general, reclassification of a noun does not allow it to be omitted. To emphasize the different characterization of men and women, on the one hand, and all villagers, on the other, the nouns can hardly be omitted. The speaker uses the CP *to* to refer to 'human beings' and to 'persons of male sex'. The CP *na* is used to refer to 'persons of female sex'. If the speaker did not use the noun *tommota* in the last sentence again, then this sentence would refer to 'persons of male sex' only (see G. Senft 1985a:387–388).

## 2.3 SUMMARY

The grammatical and discourse functions CPs perform in Kilivila are following (see G. Senft 1991c):

1. They play an important role in the word formation of all numerals, all demonstrative pronouns (with the exception of the general demonstrative *besa*), some adjectives (see G. Senft 1986:85–88), and one interrogative adverb or numerical interrogative pronoun.

2. They mark concord between nouns classified and the word classes containing the CP.

3. They classify and specify their nominal referents, inherently as well as temporarily, in many different ways and with much semantic power.

4. They can nominalize all numerals, some adjectives, and all demonstrative pronouns (with the exception of *besa*).

5. Being collective terms (*Kollektiva*, see Royen 1929:595, 597, 601, 612, 251, 512), they can mark plural on the nouns to which they refer (see also Adams and Conklin 1973:8–9).

6. Some can perform verblike functions within noun phrases in a sentence.

7. With their anaphoric referential function, they can constitute noun phrases that are comparable to elliptical utterances: once a noun has been introduced, as long as it is not reclassified, the following references to this nominal denotatum may consist of numerals, adjectives, and/or demonstrative pronouns only, that is, the noun itself is then no longer realized; it is ellipsed in the noun phrases (see also Adams et al. 1974:1, 10–12; Bühler 1978:155–158).

8. With their anaphoric referential potential, they can perform the function of preserving coherence in discourse (see also Hopper 1986).

# Chapter

# 3

# The System of Classificatory Particles in Kilivila

In this chapter, an analysis of the Kilivila CP system is provided. Section 3.1 describes the research aims and methods; section 3.2 presents the data collected, as well as a first interpretation of the data; and section 3.3 presents the results of my research, answering the questions raised in section 3.1.

The tables presented in this chapter are numbered according to the following logic:

Tables 3.1.1 and 3.1.2 present the consultants and the questionnaire used to elicit CPs.
Tables 3.2.0–3.2.216 present the data on which the analyses are based.
Tables 3.3.1–3.3.7 present ordered data for, and results of, analyses with respect to the inventory, the acquisition, and the production of CPs.
Tables 3.4.1–3.4.22 present ordered data for, and results of, the CP semantics as well as the semantic domains constituted by the CPs.

The table numbers do not correspond to numbered sections and subsections within this chapter.

## 3.1 AIMS AND METHODS

In carrying out linguistic research in the Trobriand Islands, one of my main interests—stimulated by reading Malinowski's 1920 article—was to work on the system of classificatory particles, as soon as I was able to master the language in an appropriate way (this is, in my opinion, a necessary prerequisite for performing such a study). I wanted to answer the following questions:

1. Number of CPs.
    a. *Which formatives constitute the Kilivila CP system?* Malinowski (1920:44) discusses 42 CPs, Capell (1969:61) lists 44 CPs, and Lithgow (1976:480) mentions more than 50 noun classes.
    b. *What is the actual occurrence of CPs in recorded texts?*

**2.** Acquisition.
  **a.** *What is the general temporal progress of the CP acquisition process?*
  **b.** *Are there any differences in the CP acquisition process with respect to the production of demonstrative pronouns, adjectives, and numerals that use CPs as morphemes in their word formation?*
  **c.** *Are there any gender-specific differences in the CP acquisition process?*
  **d.** *What is the order in which the individual CPs are acquired, and why are the individual CPs acquired in this order?*
  **e.** *Are there any parallels between Kilivila CP acquisition and CP acquisition data for other classifier languages?*
  **f.** *Are there any parallels between the Kilivila data and acquisition data with respect to demonstrative pronouns, adjectives, and numerals for such Indo-European languages as English and German?*

**3.** Realization of CP types in actual speech.
  **a.** *Can a classification of the CP system be devised?*
  **b.** *How do consultants realize the individual CP types, and can we observe any processes of language change in progress?* If I had an opportunity to observe language change, I wanted to answer the following questions:
  **i.** *Why are CP types affected by processes of language change, and who opposes and who fosters language change?*
  **ii.** *What are the possible consequences of language change for the grammar of Kilivila?*

**4.** Semantic domains.
  **a.** *What semantic domains are constituted by the Kilivila CP system?*
  **b.** *What are the dynamics of the semantic domains constituted by the CPs and what rules do speakers use in their production of a certain CP?* This was of special interest to me because I assume that a complete description of a classifier system must explain why a speaker produces a certain CP to refer to a certain nominal concept. Thus, the linguist's description should predict which CPs a speaker will produce (and with what relative frequency) to refer to certain nominal concepts.

After answering these questions, my goal was to discuss possible interdependences between language, thought, and culture (see chapter 5).

To achieve these aims, some basic methodological decisions had to be made, especially concerning the method of data gathering. My overall corpus of recorded and transcribed Kilivila speech data had to be checked with respect to the CP types produced when I returned from my fieldwork. However, I also wanted to do a study in the field on the system of CPs. Thus, I started my first informal pretests on how to elicit CP data in January 1983, after having lived in Tauwema village for five months. Of course, my corpus then was not as extensive as it was at the end of my fifteen months of field research (see: G. Senft 1985b:131–134); therefore, it could only serve an auxiliary function with respect to this specific research interest.

My first aim was to make an inventory of Kilivila CPs. Using Malinowski's (1920) list, and Baldwin's list in his unpublished (and undated) manuscript "Biga Boyowa" (see G. Senft 1987a:102, 119), as well as writing down all the CPs I heard in everyday conversation in the Trobriand Islands and checking my transcriptions, I arrived at a total of seventy formatives. I checked these with my main consultants and then compiled a list of CPs to be used as a basis for further data gathering with other consultants.

At this point, a decision had to be made with respect to consultants: I could have worked either with consultants living in different villages scattered all over the Trobriand Islands or with consultants living in Tauwema village, my place of residence during my field research. I chose the latter alternative because of transportation problems and because working with people in various locations would have meant a serious neglect of other interests I wanted to pursue during my field research. Thus, I conducted my research on CPs using the language variety of Kilivila that is spoken by the inhabitants of Tauwema village on Kaile'una Island (see G. Senft 1986:6–8).

At the time of my research, Tauwema had 239 inhabitants (120 adults: 58 women, 62 men; 119 children; 52 girls, 67 boys). I decided on a random sample of 60 consultants (30 female and 30 male), representing five different age groups ranging from approximately 4 to 75 years. Table 3.1.1 shows the age and gender of the consultants with whom I worked (appendix A presents the individual consultants with their consultant number, name, age, and clan). This sample included 20% of the children and 30% of the adults living in Tauwema. Because there is no official or reliable registration of dates of birth on the Trobriand Islands, the age of all consultants had to be estimated. Pretesting had shown that there was no point in trying to elicit CPs from children younger than 4 years of age; children start to acquire these formatives around the age of 4 ($\pm 6$ months). Within all five age groups, I tried to balance the consultants according to gender and age, especially in the two adult groups that spanned ages 14 to 39 years (in the actual test: 11 to 38 years; see appendix A). As demonstrated elsewhere (B. Senft and G. Senft 1986, Senft 1987b), the size of this sample is adequate to meet all the requirements that the aims of studies like the one presented here demand.

**Table 3.1.1.** Consultants

| | Age group | Female | Male | All |
|---|---|---|---|---|
| I. | Children, approximately 4–7 years | 6 | 6 | 12 |
| II. | Schoolchildren, approximately 8–14 years | 6 | 6 | 12 |
| III. | Adolescents, approximately 15–20 years | 6 | 6 | 12 |
| IV. | Adults, approximately 21–35 years | 6 | 6 | 12 |
| V. | Adults, approximately 36–75 years | 6 | 6 | 12 |
| | Total | 30 | 30 | 60 |

Regarding an appropriate method of data gathering, I decided to compile a questionnaire to elicit data on CPs. The questionnaire used the 70 CPs in my inventory. To elicit these formatives, I asked my main consultants in various sessions for typical nouns or noun phrases that are classified most appropriately and unequivocally by the respective CP and thus would elicit the production of this CP. These typical nouns and noun phrases, the qualities they described, and the class indicated by the particular CP were noted. The stimuli for the CPs elicited by the questionnaire were presented in random order. Table 3.1.2 presents the questionnaire with the CPs in alphabetical order, together with the then known meaning(s) of the respective CPs (for all meanings of the CP types found in this study, see Table 3.3.1 in section 3.3.1) and with the eliciting nouns or noun phrases and their translation. The actual order in which the CPs were elicited in the test is indicated by a number (in the third column in Table 3.1.2).

**Table 3.1.2.** The questionnaire

| CP to be elicited | Eliciting noun/noun phrase | No. in test |
|---|---|---|
| *bobu* 'block cut off' | *bobu* 'log, round timber' | 65 |
| *bogi* 'night' | *bogi* 'night' | 45 |
| *bubwa* '(parts) cut off' | *babwabutou kai* 'I will cut off wood' | 20 |
| *buda* 'group, team' | *boda* 'group, team' | 55 |
| *bukwa* 'fruit cluster' | *budubadu nuya* 'many coconuts' | 17 |
| *bwa* 'trees, wooden things' | *kai* 'wood, tree' | 44 |
| *deli* 'group, company on the move' | *deli* 'group' | 56 |
| *duli* 'cluster, bundle' | *duli* 'cluster, bunch, bundle' | 57 |
| *duya* 'door, entrance' | *duyava* 'door, entrance, window' | 47 |
| *gili* 'row' | *vakala* 'belt of spondylus shell discs' | 38 |
| *giwi* 'cut' | *giwi* 'cut' | 66 |
| *gudi* 'child' | *gwadi* 'child' | 43 |
| *gula* 'heap, group' | *budubadu tetu* 'many yams' | 39 |
| *gum* 'bit, small piece' | *gum* 'bit, small piece' | 67 |
| *iga* 'name' | *yegila* 'name' | 58 |
| *kabisi* 'compartment of a foodhouse' | (drawing)[†] | 25 |
| *kabulo1* 'protuberances, point' | *tasisia matala peni* 'one has the point of a pencil' | 22 |
| *kabulo2, kabulu* 'village sector' | *kabuluyuvela* 'village sector' | 48 |
| *kada* 'road, track' | *keda* 'road, track, way' | 11 |
| *kaduyo* 'door, entrance' | *vaya* 'door' | 12 |
| *kai* 'stone blade' | *beku* 'stone (axe) blade' | 7 |

[†]A drawing was used, rather than verbal elicitation.

**Table 3.1.2.** *(continued)*

| CP to be elicited | Eliciting noun/noun phrase | No. in test |
|---|---|---|
| *kala* 'day' | *yam* 'day' | 31 |
| *kapwa* 'bundles (wrapped up), parcel' | *luba* 'bundle' | 32 |
| *kasa* 'row, line' | *kasa* 'row' | 37 |
| *kavi* 'tool' | *kavi* 'tool' | 49 |
| *ke* 'wooden things' | *kai* 'wood, tree' | 3 |
| *kila* 'cluster, hands of bananas' | *usi amakala beya* (gesture) 'bananas like this' (arms crossed before the breast) | 15 |
| *kova* 'fire' | *kova* 'fire, fireplace' | 68 |
| *kubila* 'large land plot' | *kwabila* 'ground, land' | 28 |
| *kudu1* 'band of fibers' (at the waistband of a skirt) | *doba* 'grass skirt' | 35 |
| *kudu2* 'tooth' (noted as *kuduu*)[‡] | *kudu* 'tooth' | 59 |
| *kumla* 'earth oven' | *kumkumla* 'earth oven' | 50 |
| *kwe* 'thing, anything unknown' (unmarked form for inanimates) | *dakuna* 'stone' | 4 |
| *kweya* '(severed) limb' | *imitabogu* 'my finger' | 8 |
| *kwoila* 'clay pot' | *kwena* '(Amphlett) pot'[§] | 10 |
| *kwoya* 'mountain, hill' | *koya* 'mountain, hill' | 51 |
| *liku* 'compartments of a foodhouse' | *liku* 'foodhouse' | 24 |
| *lila* 'bough, branch' | *keyala deli kelima ketolu* 'spear with nine off-branching heads' | 13 |
| *lilo* 'walk, journey' | *lola* 'journey, trip' | 52 |
| *luva* 'wooden dishes' | *kaboma* 'plate, bowl' | 9 |
| *meila* 'part of a song' | *wosi* 'song' | 27 |
| *mmwa* 'conical bundle (of taro)' | *budubadu uli* 'much taro' | 34 |
| *na1* 'persons of female sex' | *vivila* 'girl, woman' | 2 |
| *na2* 'animals' (noted as *\*bunu*) | *bunukwa* 'pig' | 46 |
| *nina* 'parts of a song' | *wosi kwetala biga* 'one word of a song' | 26 |
| *nunu* 'corners of a garden' | *nunula bagula* 'corner of a garden' | 23 |
| *nutu* 'kneaded things, dot, drop' | *notu* 'kneaded things, dot, drop' | 69 |
| *oyla* 'string, fish on strings' | *wela* 'string of fish' | 60 |
| *pila* 'part, piece' | *akatui nuya* 'I cut a coconut' | 18 |
| *pona, pwanina* 'punctured, hole' | *pwanana* 'hole' | 53 |
| *po'ula* 'plantation, grove' | *po'ula* 'plantation, grove' | 61 |

[‡]With "noted as" I refer to the fact that I noted down *kudo2* as *kuduu* to differentiate it from *kudo1* (which was noted as *kudu*) in my data. The same holds for the notation of *na2* (as *bunu*).

[§]The gloss "(Amphlett-)pot" for *kwena* refers to the fact that these pots come from the Amphlett Islands.

**Table 3.1.2.** *(continued)*

| CP to be elicited | Eliciting noun/noun phrase | No. in test |
|---|---|---|
| *sa* 'nut bunch' | *budubadu buva* 'many betel nuts' | 16 |
| *si* 'small bit' | *tasisia pikekita tobaki* 'one has a bit of tobacco' | 42 |
| *sipu* 'sheaf' | *sipu* 'sheaf' | 62 |
| *sisi* 'bough, cut off, part of a tree' | *sisila* 'branch' | 6 |
| *siva* 'time' | *tuta* 'time' | 30 |
| *siwa* 'sea portions' | *bwalita* 'sea' | 29 |
| *ta* 'basket' | *peta* 'basket' | 63 |
| *te/to* 'persons of male sex' | *tau, tauwau* (drawing)[†] 'man, men' | 1 |
| *utu* 'scrap, parts (cut off)' | *babwabutou pikekita tou igau, tasisia ...* 'I will cut off a bit of sugar cane, then one has ...' | 21 |
| *uva* 'span' | *kuvi amakala* (gesture) '(long) *kuvi* yams tuber like this' (gesture: extending the arms) | 41 |
| *vili* 'untwisted' | *tobaki amakala* (gesture) 'tobacco like this' (gesture: straightening a stick of tobacco) | 19 |
| *vilo* 'place, village' | *valu* 'village' | 14 |
| *wela* 'batch/string of fish' | *basuya yena* 'I will string fish' | 33 |
| *ya* 'flexible, thin things' | *yoyu* 'palm branch' | 5 |
| *yam1* 'day' | *yam* 'day' | 54 |
| *yam2/yuma* 'hand' | *yama* 'her/his hand' | 70 |
| *yulai* 'bundles of four things' | *tasisia kwevasi buva* 'one has four betel nuts' | 36 |
| *yuva* 'shoal' | *boda (kena yena kena avaka)* '(a) group (of fish or so)' | 64 |
| *0* 'a basketful of yams' (zero classifier) | *tetu* 'yams' | 40 |

I approached potential consultants to find out whether they would like to cooperate in the study, using the following statement:

**(1)** *magigu kupaisewa deli yegu*
    *magi-gu*        *ku-paisewa*        *deli*        *yegu*
    wish-my      2Ps.-work      with        I
    'I want you to work with me.'

I then showed them a drawing of two men and elicited an adjective, a numeral, and a demonstrative pronoun in combination with the word for either 'man' or 'men'. I received responses like the following:

**(2)** *tomanabweta tau (tauwau)*

| *to-manabweta* | *tau* | *(tauwau)* |
|---|---|---|
| male-beautiful | man | (men) |

'beautiful man (men)'

**(3)** *mtona (mtosina) tau (tauwau)*

| *m-to-na* | *(m-to-si-na)* | *tau* | *(tauwau)* |
|---|---|---|---|
| this-male-this | (this-male-Plural-this) | man | (men) |

'this (these) man (men)'

**(4)** *tetala tau (teyu tauwau)*

| *te-tala* | *tau* | *(te-yu* | *tauwau)* |
|---|---|---|---|
| male-one | man | (male-two | men) |

'one man (two men)'

Having elicited the CP *te/to* in this way, I explained that I would like to continue along the same lines, presenting to them different nouns that they would then use with an adjective, a numeral, and a demonstrative pronoun. I did this in the following way:

**(5)** *Alivala makala tomanabweta tau, tetala tau, mtona tau. Igau alivala dakuna (...), igau yokwa bukulivala ...*

| *a-livala* | *makala* | *to-manabweta* | *tau* | *te-tale* | *tau* |
|---|---|---|---|---|---|
| 1Ps.-say | like | male-beautiful | man | male-one | man |

| *m-to-na* | *tau* | *igau* | *a-livala* | *dakuna (...)* | *igau* |
|---|---|---|---|---|---|
| this-male-this | man | then | 1Ps.-say | stone (...) | then |

| *yokwa* | *buku-livala ....* |
|---|---|
| you | 2Ps.Future-say .... |

'I say, beautiful man, one man, this man; then I say, stone (etc.); then you will say ...'.

At this point, I wanted to hear the adjective, numeral, and demonstrative with the CP that agreed with the class of the noun presented (in this example, *dakuna kwemanabweta* 'beautiful stone', etc.). If the consultant did not react, I said the following:

**(6)** *Gala tomanabweta dakuna kena ...*

| *gala* | *to-manabweta* | *dakuna* | *kena ....* |
|---|---|---|---|
| not | male-beautiful | stone | but .... |

'It is not male-beautiful stone, but ...'.

I then would pause. If the consultant reacted, the CP he or she produced in connection with the noun was noted down for all three word classes on a separate list; if the consultant did not react, I noted that, too.

This method was tested in some informal pretests where it became evident that the best way of eliciting data was the following:

1. To ask for one word class after the other and not attempt to obtain a combination of adjective, numeral, and demonstrative pronoun together with the noun within just one utterance (although such utterances are documented in naturally produced phrases such as *mtona doketa tetala toveaka* 'this one fat medical doctor').

2. To ask for the adjective first, then for the numeral, and finally for the demonstrative pronoun.

The second point was quite important, especially in working with children.

This way of gathering data, using a questionnaire and lists to note the consultants' responses (some of the tests were also tape recorded to document the data collection), as well as the standardized introduction, marked the situation as being quite formal. Nevertheless, my consultants did not seem to be bothered by this; on the contrary, they were highly cooperative and gave no sign of losing interest. Even the children, to whom the test seemed to be a new kind of game, cooperated enthusiastically and attentively. This is quite surprising, considering that it took some consultants up to forty minutes to complete the questionnaire. All sixty tests were done in one session with each consultant.

These data constitute the first CP sample for my analyses. The second CP sample consists of all the CPs I found in my overall transcribed corpus of Kilivila language production. I noted who produced the CP, the word class, and the context (see appendix A and appendix B); I also noted the complete noun phrases in which the CPs were produced.

The data elicited in the test were ordered and processed for analysis using an IBM PC and ordering programs supplied by the Max-Planck-Institute for Psycholinguistics, Nijmegen, The Netherlands.[1]

After the analyses were computed (1987–1989), I returned to the field in 1989 to confirm the main results. This restudy, including its aims, methods, and results, is presented in chapter 4.

Before presenting the data, I want to make a final, rather general, remark: It should be clear from the methods used to gather the data that the emphasis of my research was on actual language production with respect to the system of CPs in Kilivila. The data and the results presented in the following sections show the system of CPs used in actual speech production by a relatively high percentage of the inhabitants of Tauwema village on Kaile'una Island.

## 3.2 THE DATA

In section 3.2.1, the data are first ordered according to the age group of the consultants, and first interpretations are given. Section 3.2.2 then presents

[1] I want to thank Wolfgang Klein, Pim Levelt, Peter Wittenburg, Gerd Klaas, and especially Kees van der Veer for their friendly and generous support. I tried a scalogram analysis (Guttmann) on my data, but recording the data did not produce a typical Guttmann pattern.

the CP types and their tokens as they were produced by all consultants during the elicitation test and in the overall corpus of Kilivila speech. This twofold presentation should help readers maintain their orientation in spite of the large amount of data given and it should make it easier for the critical reader to evaluate the results in section 3.3.

### 3.2.1 Interpretation of the Data by Age Group

This section presents the CP data according to the age group of the consultants. First, the data that were elicited with the questionnaire are considered; then, the CP data documented in the overall corpus are presented.

Using the questionnaire, I elicited 87 CP types and 10,583 CP tokens. In Table 3.2.0, these tokens are classified according to the consultants' gender and the three word classes.

#### 3.2.1.1 Age Group I

Table 3.2.1 gives the number of responses (CP tokens) to the eliciting stimuli presented for demonstrative pronouns, numerals, and adjectives and the number of CP types produced by each consultant in age group I (age range: 4–7 years).

The number of responses elicited from the consultants ranged from 4 (consultants 2, 3, and 9) to 164 (consultant 10). Table 3.2.1 confirms that children start to acquire and to produce CPs at approximately the age of 4 (see consultants 2, 3, 9, and 7). The frequency of CPs produced rises rather dramatically at about 6 years of age; however, consultant 1 seems to be an exception to this observation; the only explanation I can offer for her very few responses to the stimuli presented is that Igiobibila is a rather shy little girl indeed. If we compare consultant 5, Kwelubituma, who is almost 6 years old, with consultant 8, Yabilosi, who just passed his fifth birthday, we can conclude that 5 is the critical age with respect to the developing CP acquisition process.

Table 3.2.1 also shows that in this age group CPs are most often produced with adjectives, then with numerals, and then with demonstrative pronouns. The frequencies can be interpreted as indices for the order of acquisition of the respective word classes; thus, I tentatively conclude that adjectives are acquired before numerals, and numerals are acquired before demonstrative

**Table 3.2.0.** CP tokens elicited from 60 consultants using the questionnaire

|       | CP/demonstrative | CP/numeral | CP/adjective | Total  |
|-------|------------------|------------|--------------|--------|
| Men   | 1,775            | 1,807      | 1,818        | 5,400  |
| Women | 1,666            | 1,734      | 1,783        | 5,183  |
| Total | 3,441            | 3,541      | 3,601        | 10,583 |

**Table 3.2.1.** Responses in age group I

| Consultant no. (age) | Demonstrative pronoun | Numeral | Adjective | No. of types |
|---|---|---|---|---|
| Girls | | | | |
| 1 (6 y) | 4 | 6 | 6 | 8 |
| 2 (4 y) | 2 | 1 | 1 | 2 |
| 3 (4 y) | 2 | 1 | 1 | 2 |
| 4 (7 y) | 26 | 42 | 45 | 18 |
| 5 (5 y) | 18 | 42 | 50 | 12 |
| 6 (6 y) | 20 | 40 | 58 | 16 |
| Total | 72 | 132 | 161 | |
| Boys | | | | |
| 7 (4 y) | 5 | 6 | 5 | 6 |
| 8 (5 y) | 4 | 4 | 5 | 5 |
| 9 (4 y) | 1 | 1 | 2 | 2 |
| 10 (6 y) | 53 | 52 | 59 | 29 |
| 11 (6 y) | 25 | 54 | 58 | 19 |
| 12 (7 y) | 53 | 54 | 54 | 20 |
| Total | 141 | 171 | 183 | |
| Total, age group I | 213 | 303 | 344 | |

pronouns. The consultants of this age group produced only 6.2% of all demonstratives, but 8.6% of all numerals and 9.6% of all adjectives elicited from the 60 consultants in the study. Consultants 4, 5, 6, and 11 produced far fewer demonstrative pronouns than numerals and adjectives, suggesting that demonstratives are more difficult to acquire and to produce than numerals and adjectives. However, these four consultants' decrease in CP production in connection with demonstratives is so dramatic that I cannot completely exclude the interpretation that it may reflect signs of diminishing attention, although this conflicts with the impression I had when I was working with these children.

Table 3.2.1 also documents a difference in the CP production of boys and girls. Adding up the production frequencies of all three word classes for girls $(72 + 132 + 161 = 365)$ versus boys $(141 + 171 + 183 = 495)$, we find that girls in age group I produced 44.1% of all their responses in connection with adjectives, 36.2% in connection with numerals, and 19.7% in connection with demonstratives, whereas boys in age group I produced 37% of all their responses in connection with adjectives, 34.5% in connection with numerals, and 28.5% in connection with demonstratives. On the basis of these findings, I conclude that the order of acquisition and production of the three word classes is even more marked in girls than in boys.

The children of age group I also showed differences with respect to the number of CP types they produced: For girls, the number of types produced ranged from 2 (consultants 2 and 3) to 18 (consultant 4). For the six girls of group I, an average of 7.7 CP types were produced. For boys, the number of types produced ranged from 2 (consultant 9) to 29 (consultant 10). For the six boys of group I, an average of 13.5 CP types were produced. Thus, the boys of this age group not only produced more responses, but they also produced a broader variety of CP types than the girls. This difference may be a result of the Trobrianders' education system, which offers boys a much broader range of possibilities for experiencing their surrounding environment than it offers to girls (see B. Senft 1985). However, the fact that the girls are responding to an adult, foreign, white, male researcher should also be kept in mind.

Before proceeding, I want to clarify my use of the term "CP type". At this stage of the data presentation, I assign provisionally to all the CPs listed in the following tables the status "CP type". The subsequent analyses will show which of these CPs are proper CP types and which are merely variants.

Table 3.2.2 lists the 37 CP types that were produced by the consultants in age group I, along with a basic gloss (for the meanings of the individual CPs, see Tables 3.1.2 in section 3.1 and 3.3.1 in section 3.3.1).

As shown in Table 3.2.2, the CPs *to/te* and *nal* were produced by all consultants; obviously, they are the first CPs that are acquired. The CPs *ke* and *kwe* were produced by 4 girls and 5 boys; thus, it can be assumed that these two CPs are acquired next. The CP *kumla* was produced by 4 girls and 3 boys; *pwanina/pona* was produced by 3 girls and 4 boys; *kova, na2, ta*, and *ya* were produced by 3 girls and 3 boys; *ka'i* was produced by 3 girls and 2 boys; and *sisi* was produced by 2 girls and 3 boys. Thus, I infer that these CPs are acquired after *to/te, nal, ke*, and *kwe*.

Only girls produced the CPs *kwoya, kaduyo, lilo, va*, and *yuma*. On the other hand, 4 boys, but only 1 girl produced the CP *gudi*; moreover, only boys produced the CPs *bubwa, buda, bukwa, duli, kai, kapwa, kweya, kwoila, luba, luva, notu, pila*, and *sa*. Again, this seems to reflect the broader range of experiences for boys compared with their female peers.

With all other CPs produced by the consultants in age group I, there were no striking asymmetries. However, the list documents the rather dramatic rise in CP production at about 6 years of age.

Table 3.2.3 shows the CP types ordered according to the number of tokens produced by the 12 consultants. It confirms the interpretations given for the data in Table 3.2.2; with the exception of *kada*, all the CP types that I propose are acquired in the first three stages of the CP acquisition process were produced most frequently (i.e., had the largest number of tokens). Consultants 6 and 12 produced the CP *kada* as a response to the stimuli presented to elicit the CPs *kada, duya*, and *kaduyo*; this explains the relatively high number of tokens (17) for this CP type. Thus, to understand the rather high number of tokens for some CP types, we must consider which CPs were expected compared with which CPs were actually produced by the consultants. Table 3.2.4 presents the result of this comparison.

A full discussion of the data presented in Table 3.2.4 will be given in section

**Table 3.2.2.** CP types/tokens produced by age group I

| CP type | No. of girls/boys producing CP type | Tokens produced by girls/boys |
|---|---|---|
| *bubwa* 'part cut off' | 0/1 | 0/1 |
| *buda* 'group' | 0/2 | 0/8 |
| *bukwa* 'fruit cluster' | 0/1 | 0/3 |
| *bwa* 'tree, wood' | 1/1 | 9/1 |
| *duli* 'cluster' | 0/1 | 0/3 |
| *gudi* 'child' | 1/4 | 1/6 |
| *iga* 'name' | 2/2 | 4/6 |
| *kada* 'road' | 1/2 | 5/2 |
| *kaduyo* 'entrance' | 1/0 | 1/0 |
| *kai* 'stone blade' | 0/1 | 0/3 |
| *ka'i* 'tooth' | 3/2 | 8/5 |
| *kapwa* 'parcel' | 0/2 | 0/5 |
| *kasa* 'row' | 1/3 | 3/8 |
| *ke* 'wood' | 4/5 | 85/119 |
| *kova* 'fire' | 3/3 | 9/8 |
| *kumla* 'earth oven' | 4/3 | 10/9 |
| *kwe* 'thing' | 4/5 | 134/171 |
| *kweya* 'limb' | 0/1 | 0/3 |
| *kwoila* 'clay pot' | 0/2 | 0/5 |
| *kwoya* 'mountain' | 1/0 | 1/0 |
| *lilo* 'walk' | 1/0 | 1/0 |
| *luba* 'bundle' | 0/1 | 0/1 |
| *luva* 'wooden dishes' | 0/1 | 0/1 |
| *na1* 'female person' | 6/6 | 15/18 |
| *na2* 'animals' | 3/3 | 22/18 |
| *notu* 'kneaded, dot' | 0/2 | 0/3 |
| *pila* 'part, piece' | 0/3 | 0/11 |
| *pwanina, pona* 'hole' | 3/4 | 7/10 |
| *sa* 'nut bunch' | 0/1 | 0/4 |
| *si* 'small bit' | 1/2 | 1/4 |
| *sisi* 'bough' | 2/3 | 4/8 |
| *ta* 'basket' | 3/3 | 10/9 |
| *to/te* 'male person' | 6/6 | 19/19 |
| *utu* 'scrap' | 2/2 | 4/4 |
| *va* 'door, window' | 1/0 | 1/0 |
| *va* 'flexible, thin' | 3/3 | 10/12 |
| *yuma* 'hand' | 1/0 | 1/0 |

**Table 3.2.3.** Number of tokens produced for each CP type—age group I

| Type | Tokens | Type | Tokens |
|------|--------|------|--------|
| *kwe* 'thing' | 305 | *ke* 'wood' | 204 |
| *na2* 'animals' | 39 | *tolte* 'male' | 38 |
| *na1* 'female' | 34 | *ya* 'flexible' | 22 |
| *kumla* 'earth oven' | 19 | *ta* 'basket' | 19 |
| *kada* 'road' | 17 | *kova* 'fire' | 17 |
| *pwaninalpona* 'hole' | 17 | *ka'i* 'tooth' | 13 |
| *sisi* 'bough' | 12 | *kasa* 'row' | 11 |
| *pila* 'part' | 11 | *bwa* 'tree' | 10 |
| *iga* 'name' | 10 | *buda* 'group' | 8 |
| *utu* 'scrap' | 8 | *gudi* 'child' | 7 |
| *kapwa* 'parcel' | 5 | *kwoila* 'pot' | 5 |
| *si* 'bit' | 5 | *bukwa* 'cluster' | 3 |
| *duli* 'cluster' | 3 | *kai* 'blade' | 3 |
| *kweya* 'limb' | 3 | *notu* 'kneaded' | 3 |
| *bubwa* 'cut off' | 1 | *kaduyo* 'entrance' | 1 |
| *kwoya* 'mountain' | 1 | *lilo* 'walk' | 1 |
| *luba* 'bundle' | 1 | *luva* 'dishes' | 1 |
| *sa* 'nut bunch' | 1 | *va* 'door' | 1 |
| *yuma* 'hand' | 1 | | |

Types total: 37; tokens total: 860

**Table 3.2.4.** CPs produced versus CPs expected—age group I

| Produced | Expected |
|----------|----------|
| *bubwa* 'cut off' | *utu* 'scrap' |
| *buda* 'group' | *buda* 'group', *yuva* 'shoal' |
| *bukwa* 'cluster' | *bukwa* 'cluster' |
| *bwa* 'tree' | *bwa* 'tree', *bubwa* 'cut off', *kabisi* 'compartment/foodhouse', *ke* 'wood', *utu* 'scrap' |
| *duli* 'cluster' | *duli* 'cluster' |
| *gudi* 'child' | *gudi* 'child' |
| *iga* 'name' | *iga* 'name' |
| *kada* 'road' | *kada* 'road', *duya* 'door', *kaduyo* 'entrance' |
| *kai* 'stone blade' | *kai* 'stone blade' |
| *ka'i* 'tooth' | *kudu2* 'tooth' |
| *kapwa* 'parcel' | *kapwa* 'parcel' |
| *kasa* 'row' | *kasa* 'row', *iga* 'name' |

**Table 3.2.4.** *(continued)*

| Produced | Expected |
|---|---|
| *ke* 'wood' | *ke* 'wood', *bubu* 'block cut off', *bubwa* 'cut off', *bukwa* 'cluster' *bwa* 'tree', *duya* 'door', *giwi* 'cut' *kabisi* 'compartment/foodhouse', *kabulo* 'point', *kabulu* 'village sector', *kasa* 'row', *kila* 'hands of bananas', *lila* 'bough', *lilo* 'walk', *luva* 'dish', *mmwa* 'bundle', *oyla* 'string', *pila* 'part', *sa* 'nut bunch', *si* 'bit', *sipu* 'sheaf', *utu* 'scrap', *uva* 'span', *vili* 'untwisted', *ya* 'thin', *yulai* 'bundle of four things', *yuva* 'shoal' |
| *kova* 'fire' | *kova* 'fire', *yuma* 'hand' |
| *kumla* 'earth oven' | *kumla* 'earth oven' |
| *kwe* 'thing' | *kwe* 'thing', *bogi* 'night', *buda* 'group', *deli* 'group', *duli* 'cluster', *gula* 'heap', *gum* 'bit', *iga* 'name', *kabisi* 'compartment/ foodhouse', *kala* 'day', *kapwa* 'parcel', *kila* 'hands of bananas', *kubila* 'land plot', *kudul* 'fibers', *kwoila* 'clay pot', *kwoya* 'mountain', *liku* 'compartments/foodhouse', *lilo* 'walk', *meila* 'song part', *nina* 'song part', *notu* 'kneaded', *nunu* 'corner/ garden', *po'ula* 'grove', *pwanina* 'hole', *sa* 'nut bunch', *sipu* 'sheaf', *siva* 'time', *siwa* 'sea portion', *uva* 'span', *vilo* 'place', *yam* 'day', *yulai* 'bundle of four things', *yuma* 'hand', *yuva* 'shoal', 0 'basketful of yams' |
| *kweya* 'limb' | *kweya* 'limb' |
| *kwoila* 'clay pot' | *kwoila* 'clay pot' |
| *kwoya* 'mountain' | *kwoya* 'mountain' |
| *lilo* 'walk' | *lilo* 'walk' |
| *luba* 'bundle' | *kapwa* 'parcel' |
| *luva* 'dish' | *luva* 'wooden dishes' |
| *na1* 'female' | *na1* 'female persons', *bubu* 'cut across', *deli* 'group', *kweya* 'limb', *uva* 'span' |
| *na2* 'animals' | *na2* 'animals', *gum* 'bit', *wela* 'batch of fish' |
| *notu* 'kneaded' | *notu* 'kneaded, dot' |
| *pila* 'part' | *pila* 'part', *kabisi* 'compartment/foodhouse', *kubila* 'land plot', *meila* 'song/part' |
| *pwanina/pona* 'hole' | *pwanina* 'hole' |
| *sa* 'nut bunch' | *sa* 'nut bunch' |
| *si* 'small bit' | *si* 'small bit', *ya* 'flexible, thin' |
| *sisi* 'bough' | *sisi* 'bough', *ya* 'flexible, thin' |
| *ta* 'basket' | *ta* 'basket', *giwi* 'cut' |
| *to/te* 'male' | *to/te* 'male persons', *deli* 'group', *yuma* 'hand' |
| *utu* 'scrap' | *utu* 'scrap', *si* 'small bit', *vili* 'untwisted' |
| *va* 'door' | *kaduyo* 'entrance' |
| *ya* 'flexible' | *ya* 'flexible, thin', *bubu* 'block cut off', *gili* 'row', *pila* 'part', *sisi* 'bough' |
| *yuma* 'hand' | *yuma* 'hand' |

3.3. However, at this point, the following can be noted:

1. *kasa* 'row/line' was produced as a response to the stimulus for the expected CP *iga* 'name'. This is not acceptable in adult Kilivila; the CP *kasa* does not agree with the noun *yegila* 'name'.

2. *Kova* 'fire' was produced as a response to the stimulus for the expected CP *yuma* 'hand'. This is not acceptable; *kova* does not agree with the noun *yamala* 'her/his hand'.

3. *na1* 'female persons' was produced as a response to the stimuli for the expected CPs *bubu* 'block cut off', *kweya* 'limb', and *uva* 'span'. This is not acceptable; *na1* does not agree with the nouns *bobu* 'log, round timber', *kuvi* 'type of long yams', and *imitabogu* 'my finger' (here the reference is unequivocal: the consultant producing this CP and the person eliciting this CP were both male).

4. *Na2* 'animals' was produced as a response to the stimulus for the expected CP *gum* 'bit'. This is not acceptable; *na2* does not agree with the noun *gum* 'bit, small piece'; however, *gum* is also the name for a snail-like ornament on a canoe board. If consultant 5 knew this rather special meaning, then *na2* would agree with the noun, presuming that the consultant wanted to refer to the snail in the ornament. However, this explanation is rather unlikely.

5. *Ta* 'basket' was produced as a response to the stimulus for the expected CP *giwi* 'cut'. The consultant may have confused the stimulus *giwi* 'cut' with *givi*. *Givi* translates as 'serving of fish', which is often presented on a small, woven, fiber mat. The consultant may have thought of this mat when she produced this (then acceptable) response.

If we correlate these observations with the individual consultants, we note that one dubious case of CP production occurred with consultants 4 and 11; with consultant 5, there were 7 dubious cases of CP production. Therefore, Table 3.2.4 demonstrates that speakers do make mistakes in the production of CPs and that they show linguistic insecurity with respect to the appropriate usage of some CPs. This becomes more evident if we look at the cases where individual consultants produced more than one CP type as a response to a given stimulus. Table 3.2.5 presents the responses documenting such multiple classification. It will be discussed in greater detail in section 3.3.

I will now present the CPs documented in the overall corpus of Kilivila speech data that were produced by children of the same age as the consultants in age group I. Table 3.2.6 lists the consultants (see appendix A) and the number of CP types and tokens for demonstrative pronouns, numerals, and adjectives.

Table 3.2.6 presents a somewhat different picture from that in Table 3.2.1. However, Table 3.2.6 does not provide any counterevidence for the interpretation of the data in Table 3.2.1 with respect to the order of acquisition of CPs with the three word classes. As documented in appendix B, the

**Table 3.2.5.** Responses documenting multiple classification in age group I

| Consultant no. | Cases of multiple classification | Percent[†] |
|---|---|---|
| Girls | | |
| 1 | 0 | 0 |
| 2 | 0 | 0 |
| 3 | 0 | 0 |
| 4 | 5 | 28 |
| 5 | 3 | 25 |
| 6 | 5 | 31 |
| | | (Average: 14) |
| Boys | | |
| 7 | 0 | 0 |
| 8 | 0 | 0 |
| 9 | 0 | 0 |
| 10 | 6 | 21 |
| 11 | 4 | 21 |
| 12 | 1 | 5 |
| | | (Average: 8) |

[†]No. of cases of multiple classification in relation to all CP types produced by the consultant.

**Table 3.2.6.** Consultants and CP types and tokens—overall corpus of Kilivila speech data

| Consultant no. (age) | Demonstrative pronoun | Numeral | Adjective | No. of types |
|---|---|---|---|---|
| Boys | | | | |
| I1/8  (5 y) | 0 | 1 | 0 | 1 |
| I2/10 (6 y) | 64 | 15 | 15 | 10 |
| I3    (7 y) | 68 | 7 | 8 | 7 |
| Total | 132 | 23 | 23 | |

relatively high frequency of CP tokens produced with demonstratives depends on the text category in which the CPs are produced: 125 of the 132 CP tokens with demonstrative pronouns were produced in the text category "fairly tale". This offers the interesting possibility that fairy tales are told not only to entertain children and to transmit cultural ideas and values, but also as a means to foster the language acquisition process (see also Erbaugh 1986:412).

The number of CP types that the three boys in the overall corpus produced ranges from 1 to 10. Table 3.2.7 presents the types and the tokens produced by consultants I1/8, I2/10, and I3. It supports, at least in part, the interpretation of Tables 3.2.2 and 3.2.3. The CPs *na1*, *to/te*, *na2*, *ke*, *kwe*, and

**Table 3.2.7.** CP types and tokens produced by the three consultants in the overall corpus of Kilivila speech data

| Type | Demonstrative pronoun | Numeral | Adjective | Total |
|---|---|---|---|---|
| *bukwa* 'cluster' | 4 | 0 | 2 | 6 |
| *dumia* 'swamp' | 0 | 0 | 1 | 1 |
| *kada* 'road' | 5 | 0 | 0 | 5 |
| *kai* 'blade' | 0 | 1 | 0 | 1 |
| *ke* 'wood' | 17 | 4 | 3 | 24 |
| *kova* 'fire' | 2 | 0 | 0 | 2 |
| *kwe* 'thing' | 9 | 4 | 6 | 19 |
| *na1* 'female' | 38 | 1 | 4 | 43 |
| *na2* 'animals' | 19 | 7 | 2 | 28 |
| *pila* 'part' | 0 | 2 | 0 | 2 |
| *pwanina* 'hole' | 1 | 0 | 0 | 1 |
| *to/te* 'male' | 27 | 3 | 5 | 35 |
| *ya* 'thin' | 10 | 1 | 0 | 11 |
| Total | 132 | 23 | 23 | 178 |

*ya* are acquired in the first stages of the CP acquisition process. The CP *dumia* 'swamplike' was produced by consultant I2/10 as part of the adjective *dumiaveaka*, but without a noun to complete the noun phrase; the noun phrase using this adjective translates as 'big swamplike ground'. There was no peculiar usage of any of these CPs with respect to the noun they referred to and agreed with. However, the following facts should be noted:

1. Consultant I2/10 produced the CP *bukwa* 'fruit cluster' with an adjective and a demonstrative pronoun to refer to the noun *bwaibwai* 'green coconut', which he introduced three and seven sentences before the respective references.

2. Consultant I3 not only played with the contextually adequate usage of the CPs *to/te* 'male persons' and *na1*, but also showed two cases of self-correction; he started the following phrase twice with a CP that did not agree with the noun: *makadana ... mmna ... manakwa koya* 'this-(*)road-this ... hm ... this-thing-this mountain'.

In summary, the following observations can be made about the acquisition and production of CPs in consultants ranging in age from 4 to 7 years:

1. Children start to acquire and produce CPs at the age of 4; 5 is the critical age with respect to CP acquisition. At about 6 years, there is an explosion in children's production of CPs.

2. If the use of specific CPs in certain text categories is ignored, the general tendency for this age group seems to be that CPs are most often produced with adjectives, then with numerals, and then with demonstrative pronouns. These frequencies are interpreted as indices for the order of the acquisition and production of the respective word classes. This order is more marked in girls than it is in boys.

3. Boys produced more CP types and tokens than girls.

4. The first CPs that are acquired are *to/te* and *na1*; *ke* and *kwe* come second; and *kumla, ka'i, kova, na2, ta, ya, pwanina/pona, sisi*, and (at least for boys) *gudi* come third.

5. Some of the CPs produced in this age group did not agree with the nouns or noun phrases they referred to. In addition to these cases of dubious or not acceptable CP usage, the production of quite a few of the CPs showed linguistic insecurity in some of the consultants (i.e., they used a CP to refer to a given nominal donatatum inappropriately).

### 3.2.1.2 Age Group II

Table 3.2.8 gives the number of responses (CP tokens) to the eliciting stimuli presented for demonstrative pronouns, numerals, and adjectives and the number of CP types produced by each consultant in age group II (8–14 years).

The number of responses elicited from the consultants ranged from 126 (consultant 14) to 210 (consultants 13, 18, and 20). However, it should be

**Table 3.2.8.** Responses in age group II

| Consultant no. (age) | Demonstrative pronoun | Numeral | Adjective | No. of types |
|---|---|---|---|---|
| Girls | | | | |
| 13 (11 y) | 70 | 70 | 70 | 22 |
| 14 (8 y) | 31 | 38 | 57 | 16 |
| 15 (11 y) | 63 | 63 | 64 | 33 |
| 16 (11 y) | 63 | 63 | 63 | 21 |
| 17 (12 y) | 69 | 69 | 69 | 32 |
| 18 (14 y) | 70 | 70 | 70 | 24 |
| Total | 366 | 373 | 393 | |
| Boys | | | | |
| 19 (13 y) | 66 | 67 | 66 | 34 |
| 20 (9 y) | 70 | 70 | 70 | 29 |
| 21 (12 y) | 68 | 68 | 68 | 35 |
| 22 (14 y) | 69 | 69 | 69 | 29 |
| 23 (10 y) | 64 | 65 | 65 | 21 |
| 24 (8 y) | 65 | 65 | 65 | 31 |
| Total | 402 | 404 | 403 | |
| Total, age group II | 768 | 777 | 796 | |

noted that consultant 14, Olopola, just passed her eighth birthday. If we compare the number of her responses with those produced by consultant 24, Luluwasikweguyau, who is almost 9 years old, and with the number produced by consultants of age group I (Table 3.2.1), the following interpretation seems plausible: The number of responses Olopola produced may indicate that 9 is another critical age with respect to the CP acquisition process. The production rate of CPs obviously increases at about 9 years of age. Thus, we can modify our first comment on Table 3.2.8 in the following way: Leaving aside consultant 14, the number of responses elicited in the other 11 consultants of age group II ranges from 189 (consultant 16) to 210 (consultants 13, 18, and 20).

There are no apparent differences with respect to the order of production of CPs with the three word classes, again excluding consultant 14. Thus, I infer that 9 is indeed not only a critical age with respect to the CP acquisition process from the point of view of CP production frequency, but also from the point of view of the balanced use of CPs with adjectives, numerals, and demonstrative pronouns.

The consultants of this age group produced 22.3% of all demonstatives, 21.4% of all numerals, and 22.1% of all adjectives elicited from the 60 consultants in the study.

Boys in age group II produced only a few more CPs than girls, and this difference becomes negligible if consultant 14 is excluded from the interpretation of Table 3.2.8 and if the average frequency of CP tokens produced is calculated for the remaining five girls (demonstratives = 67 CP tokens; numerals = 67 CP tokens, adjectives = 67.2 CP tokens) and for the boys (demonstratives = 67 CP tokens, numerals = 67.3 CP tokens, adjectives = 67.2 CP tokens).

With respect to the number of CP types produced by boys and girls the data show the following: The number of CP types produced by the girls of age group II (again, excluding consultant 14) ranged from 21 (consultant 16) to 33 (consultant 15). For the six girls of age group II, an average of 24.7 CP types were produced; if we exclude Olopola once more, the average is 26.4 CP types produced. With the boys, the number of CP types produced ranged from 21 (consultant 23) to 35 (consultant 21). For the six boys of this age group, there were an average of 29.8 CP types produced.

Thus, the boys of this age group produced only a few more CP tokens than the girls as responses to the stimuli presented; however, it should be noted that the boys still produced a broader variety of CP types than the girls did. Again, this difference may be due to differences in the Trobrianders' education system, which offers boys a much broader range of possibilities to experience their surrounding environment.

Table 3.2.9 presents the 57 CP types that were produced by the consultants of age group II. The CPs iga, kada/keda, ke, kova, kumla, kwe, na1, na2, sisi, ta, and to/te were produced by all consultants. The CP utu was produced by 6 girls and 5 boys; ya was produced by 5 girls and 6 boys; and gudi was produced by 5 girls and 5 boys. Thus, I infer that the process of acquiring

**Table 3.2.9.** CP types/tokens produced by age group II

| CP type | No. of girls/boys producing CP type | Tokens produced by girls/boys |
|---|---|---|
| *bogi* 'night' | 0/1 | 0/2 |
| *bubu* 'cut across' | 1/2 | 3/4 |
| *buda* 'team' | 5/4 | 12/8 |
| *bwa* 'tree' | 3/3 | 14/12 |
| *deli* 'group' | 1/1 | 1/3 |
| *duli* 'cluster' | 1/4 | 3/12 |
| *giwi* 'cut' | 2/5 | 4/13 |
| *gudi* 'child' | 5/5 | 15/15 |
| *gula* 'heap' | 1/1 | 5/3 |
| *gum* 'bit' | 2/4 | 3/6 |
| *iga* 'name' | 6/6 | 16/18 |
| (*) *iki* '???'† | 1/0 | 1/0 |
| *kabisi* 'compartment' | 2/2 | 4/6 |
| *kabulu* 'sector' | 0/1 | 0/2 |
| *kada/keda* 'road' | 6/6 | 32/49 |
| *kaduyo* 'entrance' | 1/0 | 1/0 |
| *kai* 'blade' | 4/6 | 10/17 |
| *ka'i* 'tooth' | 3/6 | 9/21 |
| *kapwa* 'parcel' | 3/3 | 9/9 |
| *kasa* 'row' | 3/5 | 9/23 |
| *ke* 'wood' | 6/6 | 232/267 |
| *kila* 'cluster' | 1/0 | 2/0 |
| *kova* 'fire' | 6/6 | 18/18 |
| *kubila* 'land plot' | 1/3 | 3/9 |
| *kudu* 'tooth' | 1/0 | 3/0 |
| *kumla* 'earth oven' | 6/6 | 18/18 |
| *kwe* 'thing' | 6/6 | 438/366 |
| *kweya* 'limb' | 3/5 | 9/11 |
| *kwoila* 'clay pot' | 5/4 | 15/11 |
| *kwoya* 'mountain' | 1/1 | 1/3 |
| *liku* 'compartment' | 2/3 | 2/9 |
| *luba* 'bundle' | 1/2 | 3/6 |
| *luva* 'wooden dish' | 1/0 | 3/0 |
| *megwa* 'magic' | 0/1 | 0/1 |
| *mmwa* 'bundle' | 0/1 | 0/2 |
| *na1* 'female' | 6/6 | 21/18 |
| *na2* 'animals' | 6/6 | 28/39 |

†In tables, (*) indicates that, according to my other consultants, there is no such CP in Kilivila.

**Table 3.2.9.** *(continued)*

| CP type | No. of girls/boys producing CP type | Tokens produced by girls/boys |
|---------|-------------------------------------|-------------------------------|
| *notu* 'kneaded/dot' | 1/5 | 3/9 |
| *nunu* 'corner' | 1/0 | 1/0 |
| *pila* 'part' | 3/4 | 17/22 |
| *po'ula* 'grove' | 0/1 | 0/3 |
| *pwanina* 'hole' | 4/6 | 8/16 |
| *sa* 'nut bunch' | 0/2 | 0/3 |
| *si* 'small bit' | 2/0 | 5/0 |
| *sipu* 'sheaf' | 1/4 | 1/10 |
| *sisi* 'bough' | 6/6 | 30/32 |
| *suya* 'batch/fish' | 2/0 | 6/0 |
| *ta* 'basket' | 6/6 | 16/18 |
| *tam* 'sprouting' | 0/3 | 0/10 |
| *to/te* 'male' | 6/6 | 24/22 |
| *utu* 'scrap' | 6/5 | 21/11 |
| *va* 'door' | 2/0 | 7/0 |
| *vili* 'untwisted' | 0/1 | 0/1 |
| *wela* 'batch/fish' | 1/0 | 3/0 |
| *ya* 'thin' | 5/6 | 43/45 |
| *yam* 'day' | 0/2 | 0/4 |
| *yuma* 'hand' | 0/1 | 0/2 |

these CPs has been almost completed in this age group. Six boys but only 4 girls produced the CPs *kai* and *pwanina*; 6 boys but only 3 girls produced the CP *ka'i*. Thus, I infer that the boys have acquired these CPs, while the girls are still in the process of acquiring them. Five girls and 4 boys produced the CPs *kwoila* and *buda*; 5 boys and 3 girls produced the CPs *kasa* and *kweya*. I infer that the process of acquiring these CPs has been almost completed. Five boys but only 2 girls produced the CP *giwi*, and 5 boys but only 1 girl produced the CP *notu*. Thus, I infer that boys acquire these two CPs earlier than girls. This seems to hold for the CPs *duli*, *sipu*, and *gum*, too: 4 boys but only 1 girl produced *duli* and *sipu*, and 4 boys but only 2 girls produced *gum*. The CP *pila* was produced by 4 boys and 3 girls; *bwa* and *kapwa* were produced by 3 boys and 3 girls. Boys seem to acquire the CPs *kubila*, *liku*, and *tam* earlier than girls: 3 boys produced these CPs, whereas only 1 girl produced the CP *kubila*, two girls produced the CP *liku*, and no girls produced the CP *tam*.

Consultant 15 produced the CP (\*)*iki*; however, my other consultants told me that there is no such CP in Kilivila.

Table 3.2.10 presents the CP types ordered according to the number of

**Table 3.2.10.** Number of tokens produced for each CP type—age group II

| Type | Tokens | Type | Tokens |
|---|---|---|---|
| *kwe* 'thing' | 804 | *ke* 'wood' | 499 |
| *ya* 'thin' | 88 | *kada/keda* 'road' | 81 |
| *na2* 'animals' | 67 | *sisi* 'bough' | 62 |
| *to/te* 'male' | 46 | *na1* 'female' | 39 |
| *pila* 'part' | 39 | *kumla* 'earth oven' | 36 |
| *kova* 'fire' | 36 | *iga* 'name' | 34 |
| *ta* 'basket' | 34 | *kasa* 'row' | 32 |
| *utu* 'scrap' | 32 | *gudi* 'child' | 30 |
| *ka'i* 'tooth' | 30 | *kai* 'blade' | 27 |
| *bwa* 'tree' | 26 | *kwoila* 'clay pot' | 26 |
| *pwanina* 'hole' | 24 | *buda* 'group' | 20 |
| *kweya* 'limb' | 20 | *kapwa* 'parcel' | 18 |
| *giwi* 'cut' | 17 | *duli* 'cluster' | 15 |
| *kubila* 'land plot' | 12 | *notu* 'kneaded, dot' | 12 |
| *liku* 'compartment' | 11 | *sipu* 'sheaf' | 11 |
| *kabisi* 'compartment' | 10 | *tam* 'sprouting' | 10 |
| *gum* 'bit' | 9 | *luba* 'bundle | 9 |
| *gula* 'heap' | 8 | *bubu* 'cut across' | 7 |
| *va* 'door' | 7 | *suya* 'batch/fish' | 6 |
| *si* 'small bit' | 5 | *deli* 'group' | 4 |
| *kwoya* 'mountain' | 4 | *yam* 'day' | 4 |
| *kudu* 'tooth' | 3 | *luva* 'wooden dish' | 3 |
| *po'ula* 'grove' | 3 | *sa* 'nut bunch' | 3 |
| *wela* 'batch/fish' | 3 | *bogi* 'night' | 2 |
| *kabulu* 'sector' | 2 | *kila* 'cluster' | 2 |
| *mmwa* 'bundle' | 2 | *yuma* 'hand' | 2 |
| (*) *iki* '???' | 1 | *kaduyo* 'entrance' | 1 |
| *megwa* 'magic' | 1 | *nunu* 'corner/garden' | 1 |
| *vili* 'untiwsted' | 1 | | |

Types total: 56 (57); tokens total: 2,340 (2,341)

tokens realized by all 12 consultants. Table 3.2.11 lists the CPs produced versus those expected in response to the stimuli presented. These data will be discussed in detail in section 3.3. However, the following should be noted here:

1. *Buda* 'group' was produced as a response to the stimulus presented to elicit the expected CPs *bubu* 'block cut across/cut off' and *gum* 'bit, small piece'. This is not acceptable; *buda* does not agree with the nouns *bobu* 'log, round timber' and *gum* 'bit, small piece'.

**Table 3.2.11.** CPs produced versus CPs expected—age group II

| Produced | Expected |
|---|---|
| *bogi* 'night' | *bogi* 'night' |
| *bubu* 'cut across' | *bubu* 'block cut across/cut off' |
| *buda* 'group, team' | *buda* 'group', *bubu* 'cut across', *gum* 'bit', *yuva* 'shoal' |
| *bwa* 'tree' | *bwa* 'tree, wood', *bubwa* 'parts cut off', *kabisi* 'compartment/ foodhouse', *kabulo* 'village sector', *ke* 'wooden things', *si* 'small bit', *utu* 'scrap', *vili* 'untwisted' |
| *deli* 'group' | *deli* 'group' |
| *duli* 'cluster' | *duli* 'cluster, bundle' |
| *giwi* 'cut' | *giwi* 'cut' |
| *gudi* 'child' | *gudi* 'child' |
| *gula* 'heap' | *gula* 'heap, group', *bubu* 'cut across' |
| *gum* 'bit' | *gum* 'bit' |
| *iga* 'name' | *iga* 'name' |
| (\*) *iki* '???' | *nina* 'parts/song' |
| *kabisi* 'compartment' | *kabisi* 'compartment/foodhouse' |
| *kabulu* 'sector' | *kabulu* 'village sector' |
| *kada/keda* 'road' | *kada* 'road, track', *duya* 'door, entrance', *kaduyo* 'door, entrance', *lilo* 'walk', *vilo* 'place, village' |
| *kaduyo* 'door' | *kaduyo* 'door, entrance' |
| *kai* 'stone blade' | *kai* 'stone blade' |
| *ka'i* 'tooth' | *kudu* 'tooth', *oyla* 'string' |
| *kapwa* 'parcel' | *kapwa* 'parcel, bundle' |
| *kasa* 'row' | *kasa* 'row', *gili* 'row', *giwi* 'cut', *gum* 'bit', *yuva* 'shoal' |
| *ke* 'wooden things' | *ke* 'wooden things, tree', *bubwa* 'cut across', *bukwa* 'fruit cluster', *bwa* 'tree, wood', *duli* 'cluster, bundle', *giwi* 'cut', *kabisi* 'compartment/foodhouse', *kabulo* 'point', *kabulu* 'village sector', *kaduyo* 'door, entrance', *kavi* 'tool', *kila* 'cluster/bananas', *kudu* 'tooth', *kweya* 'limb', *kwoila* 'clay pot', *liku* 'compartment/ foodhouse', *lila* 'bough', *luva* 'wooden dishes', *meila* 'song/part', *mmwa* 'conical bundle', *oyla* 'string', *pila* 'part', *sa* 'nut bunch', *si* 'small bit', *sisi* 'bough', *utu* 'scrap', *uva* 'span', *vili* 'untwisted', *ya* 'thin', *yulai* 'bundle of four things' |
| *kila* 'cluster' | *kila* 'cluster/bananas' |
| *kova* 'fire' | *kova* 'fire' |
| *kubila* 'land plot' | *kubila* 'land plot' |
| *kudu* 'tooth' | *kudu* 'tooth' |
| *kumla* 'earth oven' | *kumla* 'earth oven' |
| *kwe* 'thing' | *kwe* 'thing', *bogi* 'night', *bubu* 'cut across', *buda* 'group', *bukwa* 'cluster', *deli* 'group', *duli* 'cluster', *duya* 'entrance', *gili* 'row', *giwi* 'cut', *gula* 'heap', *gum* 'bit', *kabisi* 'compartment/ foodhouse', *kabulu* 'village sector', *kaduyo* 'door', *kai* 'stone blade', *kala* 'day', *kapwa* 'parcel', *kasa* 'row', *kavi* 'tool', *kila* 'cluster/bananas', *kubila* 'land plot', *kudu* 'band of fibers', *kudu* |

**Table 3.2.11.** (continued)

| Produced | Expected |
|---|---|
| | 'tooth', *kweya* 'limb', *kwoila* 'clay pot', *kwoya* 'mountain', *liku* 'compartment/foodhouse', *lilo* 'walk', *luva* 'wooden dishes', *meila* 'song/part', *mmwa* 'conical bundle', *nina* 'song/part', *notu* 'kneaded, dot', *nunu* 'corner/garden', *oyla* 'string', *po'ula* 'grove', *pwanina* 'hole', *sa* 'nut bunch', *si* 'small bit', *sipu* 'sheaf', *siva* 'time', *siwa* 'sea portion', *uva* 'span', *vili* 'untwisted', *vilo* 'place', *yam* 'day', *yulai* 'bundle of four things', *yuma* 'hand', *yuva* 'shoal', 0 'basketful of yams' |
| *kweya* 'limb' | *kweya* 'limb' |
| *kwoila* 'clay pot' | *kwoila* 'clay pot' |
| *kwoya* 'mountain' | *kwoya* 'mountain' |
| *liku* 'compartment' | *liku* 'compartment/foodhouse' |
| *luba* 'bundle' | *kapwa* 'parcel, bundle' |
| *luva* 'wooden dishes' | *giwi* 'cut' |
| *megwa* 'magic' | *nina* 'song/part' |
| *mmwa* 'conical bundle' | *mmwa* 'conical bundle' |
| *na1* 'female' | *na1* 'female persons', *kai* 'stone blade' *kweya* 'limb' |
| *na2* 'animals' | *na2* 'animals', *giwi* 'cut', *oyla* 'string', *wela* 'batch of fish' |
| *notu* 'kneaded, dot' | *notu* 'kneaded, dot' |
| *nunu* 'corner/garden' | *kabisi* 'compartment/foodhouse' |
| *pila* 'part' | *pila* 'part', *kavi* 'tool', *meila* 'song/part', *nina* 'song/part', *ya* 'thin' |
| *po'ula* 'grove' | *po'ula* 'grove' |
| *pwanina* 'hole' | *pwanina* 'hole' |
| *sa* 'nut bunch' | *sa* 'nut bunch' |
| *sipu* 'sheaf' | *sipu* 'sheaf' |
| *si* 'bit' | *ya* 'thin' |
| *sisi* 'bough' | *sisi* 'bough', *kai* 'stone blade', *ya* 'thin' |
| *suya* 'batch of fish' | *wela* 'batch of fish' |
| *ta* 'basket' | *ta* 'basket' |
| *tam* 'sprouting yams' | *gula* 'heap', 0 'basketful of yams' |
| *tolte* 'male' | *tolte* 'male', *deli* 'group' |
| *utu* 'scrap' | *utu* 'scrap', *gili* 'row', *gum* 'bit', *kabisi* 'compartment/foodhouse', *kabulo* 'point', *kabulu* 'village sector', *kavi* 'tool', *vili* 'untwisted', *si* 'small bit' |
| *va* 'door' | *kaduyo* 'entrance' |
| *vili* 'untwisted' | *vili* 'untwisted' |
| *wela* 'batch of fish' | *wela* 'batch of fish' |
| *ya* 'thin' | *ya* 'flexible, thin', *bubu* 'cut across', *bukwa* 'fruit cluster', *duya* 'door', *gili* 'row', *gum* 'bit', *kaduyo* 'entrance', *lilo* 'walk', *pila* 'part', *sipu* 'sheaf' |
| *yam* 'day' | *yam* 'day' |
| *yuma* 'hand' | *yuma* 'hand' |

2. *Gula* 'heap, group' was produced as a response to the stimulus for the expected *bubu* 'block cut across/cut off'. This is not acceptable; *gula* does not agree with the noun *bobu* 'log, round timber'.

3. Consultant 15 produced *iki* as a response to the stimulus for the expected *nina* 'parts of a song'; all my other consultants told me that there is no CP *iki* in Kilivila.

4. *Kada/keda* 'road, track' was produced as a response to the stimuli for the expected CPs *lilo* 'road, journey' and *vilo* 'place, village'. The stimulus *lola* 'journey, trip' may also elicit the CP *kada/keda*, although this understanding of the stimulus is somewhat idiosyncratic. The CP *kada/keda*, however, does not agree with the eliciting noun *valu* 'village' for the CP *vilo*; thus, this response is not acceptable.

5. *Ka'i* 'tooth' was produced as a response to the stimulus for the expected CP *oyla* 'string'. This is not acceptable; the CP *ka'i* does not agree with the stimulus *wela* presented to elicit the CP *oyla*.

6. *Kasa* 'row, line' was produced as a response to the stimuli for the expected CPs *giwi* 'cut', *gum* 'bit', and *yuva* 'shoal'. Though this reaction is rather dubious, the use of *kasa* as a response to the eliciting words can be explained: if we concede that the consultants may have thought of something cut in rows, of bits or pieces presented in a row, or of a group or shoal of fish swimming in a row, we can accept this response as appropriate.

7. *Luva* 'wooden dishes' was produced as a response to the stimulus *giwi* 'cut' for the expected CP *giwi* 'cut'; this is not acceptable.

8. *Na1* 'female persons' was realized as a response to the stimuli for the expected CPs *kai* 'stone blade' and *kweya* 'limb'. This is not acceptable; the CP *na1* agrees with neither the noun *beku* 'stone axe blade' nor the noun phrase *imitabogu* 'my finger'.

9. *Na2* 'animals' was produced as a response to the stimulus presented for the expected CP *giwi* 'cut'. This is not acceptable. However, it may be that the consultant misunderstood the stimulus *giwi* 'cut' as *givi* 'a serving of fish'; this misunderstanding would explain the production of the CP *na2*.

10. *Nunu* 'corner of a garden' was produced as a response to the stimulus for the expected CP *kabisi* 'compartment of a foodhouse, of a canoe'. This is not acceptable.

11. *Pila* 'part, piece' was realized as a response to the stimulus for the CP *kavi* 'tool'. This is rather dubious, if not unacceptable.

12. *Sisi* 'bough' was produced as a response to the stimulus for the expected CP *kai* 'stone blade'. This is not acceptable; *sisi* does not agree with the noun *beku* 'stone axe blade'.

13. *Utu* 'scrap, parts cut off' was produced as a response to the stimuli for the expected CPs *gili* 'row', *kavi* 'tool', and *vili* 'untwisted'. Although

the use of *utu* as a response to the phrase given to elicit the CP *vili* can be explained, the use of *utu* as a response to the stimuli presented to elicit the CPs *gili* and *kavi* is not acceptable; *utu* does not agree with the nouns *vakala* 'belt of spondylus shell discs' and *kavi* 'tool'.

If we relate these observations to the individual consultants, we find the following: With consultants 15 and 22, there were 2 dubious cases of CP production. With consultant 14, there were 4 dubious cases of CP production. Consultants 13 and 17 each produced 5 cases of dubious CP production, and consultant 23 produced 12 dubious cases.

Thus, Table 3.2.11 demonstrates that some consultants of age group II do make mistakes in the production of the acquired CPs and that they show linguistic insecurity with respect to the appropriate use of some CPs. This linguistic insecurity becomes more evident if we look at the cases where individual consultants produced more than one CP type as a response to the stimulus given. Table 3.2.12 presents the responses documenting such multiple classification; it will be discussed in more detail in section 3.3.

Table 3.2.13 lists the number of CP types and tokens for demonstrative pronouns, numerals, adjectives, and interrogative pronouns in the overall corpus of Kilivila speech data that were produced by children and adolescents of the same age as the consultants in age group II in the elicitation test (see also appendix A). The data in this table depend heavily on the text category in which the CPs were produced (see appendix B). Consultant II1/19 produced

**Table 3.2.12.** Responses documenting multiple classification in age group II

| Consultant no. | Cases of multiple classification | Percent[†] |
|---|---|---|
| Girls | | |
| 13 | 11 | 50 |
| 14 | 6 | 38 |
| 15 | 9 | 27 |
| 16 | 6 | 29 |
| 17 | 7 | 22 |
| 18 | 6 | 25 |
| | | (Average: 32) |
| Boys | | |
| 19 | 10 | 29 |
| 20 | 11 | 38 |
| 21 | 9 | 26 |
| 22 | 6 | 21 |
| 23 | 9 | 43 |
| 24 | 4 | 13 |
| | | (Average: 28) |

[†]No. of cases of multiple classification in relation to all CP types produced by the consultant.

**Table 3.2.13.** Consultants and CP types and tokens—overall corpus of Kilivila speech data

| Consultant no. (age) | Demonstrative pronoun | Numeral | Adjective | Interrogative pronoun | No. of types |
|---|---|---|---|---|---|
| Boys | | | | | |
| II1/19 (13 y) | 1 | 2 | 4 | 0 | 4 |
| II2/20 (9 y) | 7 | 2 | 0 | 2 | 4 |
| II3 (9 y) | 41 | 17 | 10 | 0 | 6 |
| II4 (12 y) | 7 | 1 | 1 | 0 | 1 |
| Total | 56 | 22 | 15 | 2 | |

his CP tokens in the process of giving a route description (see G. Senft 1986:132, 145–153); consultant II2/20 produced his CP tokens in telling fairy tales; consultant II3 produced his CP tokens during an interview about a ritualized children's fight and in connection with fairy tales. His rather abundant use of demonstrative pronouns is due to the references necessary to secure text coherence in Kilivila fairy tales (this observation supports the interpretation of Table 3.2.6); consultant II4 also produced his CP tokens during the interview about a ritualized children's fight.

The number of CP types produced by the four boys in this corpus ranges from 1 (II4) to 6 (II3). Table 3.2.14 presents the types and the tokens produced by consultants II1/19, II2/20, II3, and II4. This table supports, at least in part, the interpretation of Tables 3.2.9 and 3.2.10 (see also Table 3.2.7). There was no peculiar usage of any of these CPs with respect to the nouns they referred to and agreed with. However, the following facts should be noted: Consultant II3 produced three English numerals (see G. Senft 1987b:342, ftn. 5), two of them with a demonstrative (e.g., *mtosina seven dokonikani* 'these

**Table 3.2.14.** CP types and tokens produced by the consultants in the overall corpus of Kilivila speech data

| Type | Demonstrative pronoun | Numeral | Adjective | Interrogative pronoun | Total |
|---|---|---|---|---|---|
| *kabulo* 'sector' | 0 | 3 | 0 | 0 | 3 |
| *ke* 'wood' | 7 | 5 | 1 | 0 | 13 |
| *kwe* 'thing' | 4 | 3 | 4 | 0 | 11 |
| *na1* 'female' | 4 | 2 | 3 | 1 | 10 |
| *na2* 'animals' | 4 | 1 | 1 | 0 | 6 |
| *pila* 'part' | 0 | 1 | 0 | 0 | 1 |
| *to/te* 'male' | 37 | 7 | 4 | 1 | 49 |
| *ya* 'thin' | 0 | 0 | 1 | 0 | 1 |
| Total | 56 | 22 | 14 | 2 | 94 |

seven monsters'); however, he used the appropriate CP *ke* to refer with a numeral to the loanword *selinboti* 'sailing boat' in the phrase *ketala selinboti* 'one sailing boat' and the adequate CP *kwe* to refer with a numeral to the English word *store* in the phrase *kwetala store* 'one store'. Moreover, this consultant produced a phrase with a double classification of the loanword *poseni* 'poison', namely, *manakwa sitana keta poseni* '(thing)-this bit of (wooden material)-one poison'. It should be clear that these observations in connection with the overall corpus of Kilivila speech data are anecdotal because of the rather small database of this sample.

In summary, the following observations apply to the consultants in age group II with respect to their acquisition and production of CPs:

1. I tentatively infer from the data that 9 years old is another critical age with respect to the CP acquisition process; the frequency of CPs produced increases rather dramatically at age 9.

2. Age 9 is also a critical age with respect to the CP acquisition from the point of view of a balanced number of CP tokens produced with adjectives, numerals, and demonstrative pronouns, with the exception of the use of specific CPs in certain text categories.

3. Boys produced only a few more tokens of CPs as responses to the stimuli presented than girls; however, boys produced a broader variety of CP types than girls.

4. Comparing the CPs produced in age group II with those produced in age group I shows that consultants of age group II did not produce the CPs *bubwa* 'parts cut off', *bukwa* 'fruit cluster', *dumia* 'swamplike', and *lilo* 'walk', which were produced by the consultants of age group I. However, with the consultants of age group II we find the following newly acquired CPs: *bogi, bobu/bubu, deli, giwi, gula, gum, kabisi, kabulo, kila, kubila, kudu* 'tooth', *liku, megwa, mmwa, nunu, po'ula, sipu, suya, tam, wela, vili,* and *yam.*

5. The CPs *iga, kada/keda, ke, kova, kumla, kwe, na1, na2, sisi, ta,* and *to/te* were produced by all consultants in age group II. The CPs *uta, ya,* and *gudi* were produced by almost all consultants. The CPs *kai, ka'i,* and *pwanina* were produced by all the male consultants, whereas the female consultants were still in the process of acquiring these formatives. The acquisition process of the CPs *buda* and *kwoila* had almost been completed in both girls and boys in this age group. Boys acquire the CPs *kasa, kweya, giwi, notu, duli, sipu, gum, pila, kubila, liku,* and *tam* earlier or slightly earlier than girls. The acquisition of all the other CPs produced is still in progress.

6. Some of the CPs produced did not agree with the nouns or noun phrases they referred to, according to adult linguistic usage. In addition to these cases of dubious or not acceptable CP usage, there were also quite a few CPs used in ways that showed linguistic insecurity in the consultants with respect to using the CP to refer to a given nominal denotatum appropriately.

### 3.2.1.3 Age Group III

Table 3.2.15 gives the number of responses (CP tokens) to the eliciting stimuli presented for demonstrative pronouns, numerals, and adjectives as well as the number of CP types produced by each consultant in age group III (15–20 years). The number of responses elicited from the consultants ranged from 191 (consultant 32) to 207 (consultants 27, 28, 31, and 33–36). Table 3.2.15 records a balanced usage of CPs with adjectives, numerals, and demonstrative pronouns. The consultants of this age group produced 23.7% of all demonstrative pronouns, 23% of all numerals, and 22.7% of all adjectives elicited from the 60 consultants in the study. The male consultants produced only two more CP tokens than the female consultants; however, it should be noted that consultant 32 (male) produced only 191 CP tokens, compared with consultant 25 (female), who produced 198 CP tokens (the lowest number for the six female consultants of this age group). Thus, I conclude from Table 3.2.15 that there are no differences between male and female consultants with respect to the production of CP tokens. The average frequency of CP tokens produced by the female consultants (demonstrative pronouns = 68; numerals = 68; adjectives = 68) differs insignificantly from the average frequency of CP tokens produced by the male consultants (demonstrative pronouns = 68.2; numerals = 68; adjectives = 68.2).

The number of types produced by the female consultants ranged from 31 (consultant 25) to 48 (consultant 27); an average of 37.7 CP types were

**Table 3.2.15.** Responses in age group III

| Consultant no. (age) | Demonstrative pronoun | Numeral | Adjective | No. of types |
|---|---|---|---|---|
| Females | | | | |
| 25 (16y) | 66 | 66 | 66 | 31 |
| 26 (17y) | 68 | 68 | 68 | 42 |
| 27 (20y) | 69 | 69 | 69 | 48 |
| 28 (18y) | 69 | 69 | 69 | 40 |
| 29 (16y) | 68 | 68 | 68 | 30 |
| 30 (19y) | 68 | 68 | 68 | 35 |
| Total | 408 | 408 | 408 | |
| Males | | | | |
| 31 (19y) | 69 | 69 | 69 | 47 |
| 32 (20y) | 64 | 63 | 64 | 35 |
| 33 (16y) | 69 | 69 | 69 | 37 |
| 34 (15y) | 69 | 69 | 69 | 43 |
| 35 (16y) | 69 | 69 | 69 | 46 |
| 36 (15y) | 69 | 69 | 69 | 35 |
| Total | 409 | 408 | 409 | |
| Total, age group III | 817 | 816 | 817 | |

produced. For the male consultants, the number of CP types produced ranged from 35 (consultants 32 and 36) to 47 (consultant 31); an average of 40.5 CP types were produced. Thus, the male consultants produced a slightly broader variety of CP types than the female consultants.

Table 3.2.16 lists the CP types that were produced by the consultants of age group III. The CPs *gudi, kada, kai, kasa, ke, kova, kumla, kwe, kewya, na1, na2, pwanina, sisi, ta, to/te,* and *utu* were produced by all consultants.

**Table 3.2.16.** CP types and tokens produced in age group III

| Type | No. of girls/boys producing CP type | Tokens produced by girls/boys |
|---|---|---|
| *beku* 'stone blade' | 1/0 | 1/0 |
| *bogi* 'night' | 2/2 | 4/4 |
| (*) *boma* '???' | 1/0 | 1/0 |
| *bubu* 'cut across' | 3/5 | 9/14 |
| *bubwa* 'part cut off' | 1/2 | 2/6 |
| *buda* 'group' | 6/5 | 25/27 |
| *bwa* 'tree' | 4/2 | 7/5 |
| *bwalita* 'sea' | 1/1 | 1/1 |
| *deli* 'group' | 6/5 | 16/14 |
| *duli* 'cluster' | 6/5 | 18/15 |
| *duya* 'door' | 0/1 | 0/3 |
| *gili* 'row' | 0/1 | 0/3 |
| *giwi* 'cut' | 5/6 | 15/18 |
| *gudi* 'child' | 6/6 | 18/18 |
| *gula* 'heap' | 1/4 | 3/12 |
| *gum* 'bit' | 4/6 | 12/18 |
| *iga* 'name' | 5/6 | 14/15 |
| *kabisi* 'compartment' | 5/4 | 12/11 |
| *kabulu* 'sector' | 3/2 | 7/3 |
| *kada* 'road' | 6/6 | 44/49 |
| *kaduyo* 'entrance' | 1/1 | 6/2 |
| *kai* 'stone blade' | 6/6 | 17/18 |
| *ka'i* 'tooth' | 5/5 | 14/14 |
| *kapwa* 'parcel' | 3/0 | 6/0 |
| *kasa* 'row' | 6/6 | 28/18 |
| *ke* 'wood' | 6/6 | 202/178 |
| *kova* 'fire' | 6/6 | 18/18 |
| *kubila* 'land plot' | 4/6 | 9/17 |
| *kudu* 'tooth' | 2/2 | 4/4 |
| *kumla* 'earth oven' | 6/6 | 18/18 |
| *kwe* 'thing' | 6/6 | 292/261 |

**Table 3.2.16.** *(continued)*

| Type | No. of girls/boys producing CP type | Tokens produced by girls/boys |
|---|---|---|
| *kweya* 'limb' | 6/6 | 24/36 |
| *kwoila* 'clay pot' | 1/4 | 3/11 |
| *kwoya/koya* 'mountain' | 2/4 | 4/7 |
| *liku* 'compartment' | 4/4 | 10/12 |
| *luba* 'bundle' | 3/5 | 6/15 |
| *lola* 'walk' | 1/0 | 3/0 |
| *mmwa* 'bundle' | 0/3 | 0/8 |
| *megwa* 'magic' | 2/1 | 2/3 |
| *na1* 'female' | 6/6 | 21/18 |
| *na2* 'animals' | 6/6 | 30/24 |
| *notu/nutu* 'kneaded, dot' | 5/6 | 15/18 |
| *nunu* 'corner/garden' | 2/1 | 3/3 |
| *peta* 'basket' | 1/1 | 2/1 |
| *pila* 'part' | 5/6 | 24/40 |
| *po'ula* 'grove' | 3/3 | 9/9 |
| *pwanina/pona* 'hole' | 6/6 | 18/18 |
| *sa* 'nut bunch' | 0/1 | 0/3 |
| *si* 'small bit' | 2/1 | 4/1 |
| *sipu* 'sheaf' | 4/5 | 10/15 |
| *sisi* 'bough' | 6/6 | 25/32 |
| *suya* 'batch of fish' | 3/5 | 9/15 |
| *ta* 'basket' | 6/6 | 16/17 |
| *tam* 'sprouting' | 2/2 | 9/8 |
| *tuta* 'time' | 1/1 | 3/1 |
| *to/te* 'male' | 6/6 | 18/18 |
| *utu* 'scrap' | 6/6 | 66/48 |
| *uva* 'span' | 0/3 | 0/9 |
| *vakala* 'belt' | 1/0 | 1/0 |
| *vaya* 'door' | 0/1 | 0/1 |
| *vili* 'untwisted' | 4/5 | 11/15 |
| *vosi* 'song' | 2/2 | 2/4 |
| *wela* 'batch of fish' | 2/2 | 5/9 |
| *ya* 'thin' | 6/4 | 33/10 |
| *yam* 'day' | 2/1 | 8/3 |
| *yegila* 'name' | 2/2 | 4/3 |
| *yulai* 'bundle of four things' | 0/2 | 0/6 |
| *yuva* 'shoal' | 1/0 | 3/0 |
| *0* 'basketful of yams' | 0/1 | 0/1 |

*Giwi, notu, iga*, and *pila* were produced by 5 female and all male consultants; *buda, deli*, and *duli* were produced by all female and 5 male consultants; 5 female and 5 male consultants produced the CP *ka'i*. All male consultants and 4 female consultants produced the CPs *gum* and *kubila*; all female consultants and 4 male consultants produced the CP *ya*; 5 female consultants and 4 male consultants produced the CP *kabisi*; 4 females and 5 males produced the CPs *sipu* and *vili*. The CP *liku* was produced by 4 female and 4 male consultants; the CP *po'ula* was realized by 3 female and 3 male consultants. Five male consultants and 3 female consultants produced the CPs *bubu, luba*, and *suya*; 4 male consultants and 2 female consultants produced *kwoya/koya*, and 4 males and 1 female produced *gula* and *kwoila*; 3 female and 2 male consultants produced *kabulu*.

It is feasible to interpret some of these findings in the light of female and male preferences in producing certain CPs. This interpretation may be partly supported by the fact that we find the production of *beku, kapwa, lola, vakala*, and *yuva* only by female consultants, and *duya, gili, mmwa, sa, uva, vaya, yulai*, and 0 (zero classifier) only by male consultants. These findings obviously reflect the slightly broader variety of CP types noted earlier in male consultants compared with female consultants.

Table 3.2.17 presents the CP types ordered according to the number of tokens produced by all 12 consultants. Table 3.2.18 lists the expected CPs

**Table 3.2.17.** Number of tokens produced for each CP type—age group III

| Type | Tokens | Type | Tokens |
|---|---|---|---|
| *kwe* 'thing' | 553 | *ke* 'wood' | 380 |
| *utu* 'scrap' | 114 | *kada* 'road' | 93 |
| *pila* 'part' | 64 | *kweya* 'limb' | 60 |
| *sisi* 'bough' | 57 | *na2* 'animals' | 54 |
| *buda* 'group' | 52 | *kasa* 'row' | 46 |
| *va* 'thin' | 43 | *na1* 'female' | 39 |
| *gudi* 'child' | 36 | *kova* 'fire' | 36 |
| *kumla* 'earth oven' | 36 | *pwanina/pona* 'hole' | 36 |
| *tolte* 'male' | 36 | *kai* 'stone blade' | 35 |
| *duli* 'cluster' | 33 | *giwi* 'cut' | 33 |
| *notu/nutu* 'kneaded' | 33 | *ta* 'basket' | 33 |
| *deli* 'group' | 30 | *gum* 'bit' | 30 |
| *iga* 'name' | 26 | *vili* 'untwisted' | 26 |
| *kubila* 'land plot' | 26 | *vili* 'untwisted' | 26 |
| *sipu* 'sheaf' | 25 | *suya* 'batch/fish' | 24 |
| *bubu* 'cut across' | 23 | *kabisi* 'compartment' | 23 |
| *liku* 'compartment' | 22 | *luba* 'bundle' | 21 |
| *po'ula* 'grove' | 18 | *tam* 'sprouting' | 17 |

**Table 3.2.17.** (continued)

| Type | Tokens | Type | Tokens |
|---|---|---|---|
| gula 'heap' | 15 | kwoila 'clay pot' | 14 |
| wela 'batch/fish' | 14 | bwa 'tree' | 12 |
| kwoya/koya 'hill' | 11 | yam 'day' | 11 |
| kabulu 'sector' | 10 | uva 'span' | 9 |
| bogi 'night' | 8 | bubwa 'cut off' | 8 |
| kaduyo 'entrance' | 8 | kudu 'tooth' | 8 |
| mmwa 'bundle' | 8 | yegila 'name' | 7 |
| kapwa 'parcel' | 6 | nunu 'corner/garden' | 6 |
| vosi 'song' | 6 | yulai 'bundle of four' | 6 |
| megwa 'magic' | 5 | si 'bit' | 5 |
| tuta 'time' | 4 | duya 'door' | 3 |
| gili 'row' | 3 | lola 'walk' | 3 |
| peta 'basket' | 3 | sa 'nut bunch' | 3 |
| yuva 'shoal' | 3 | bwalita 'sea' | 2 |
| beku 'stone blade' | 1 | (*) boma '???' | 1 |
| vakala 'belt' | 1 | vaya 'door' | 1 |
| 0 'basketful of yams' | 1 | | |

Types total: 68 (69); tokens total: 2,449 (2,450)

**Table 3.2.18.** CPs produced versus CPs expected—age group III

| Produced | Expected |
|---|---|
| beku 'stone blade' | kai 'stone blade' |
| bogi 'night' | bogi 'night' |
| (*) boma '???' | utu 'scrap' |
| bubu 'cut across' | bubu 'cut across' |
| bubwa 'cut off' | bubwa 'cut off', kabulo 'point', utu 'scrap' |
| buda/boda 'group' | buda 'group', bubu 'cut across', yuva 'shoal' |
| bwa 'tree, wood' | bubwa 'cut off', kabulo 'point', utu 'scrap' |
| bwalita 'sea' | siwa 'sea portions' |
| deli 'group' | deli 'group' |
| duli 'cluster' | duli 'cluster' |
| duya 'door' | duya 'door' |
| gili 'row' | gili 'row' |
| giwi 'cut' | giwi 'cut' |
| gudi 'child' | gudi 'child' |
| gula 'heap' | gula 'heap', bubu 'cut across', po'ula 'grove' |
| gum 'bit' | gum 'bit' |

**Table 3.2.18.** *(continued)*

| Produced | Expected |
|---|---|
| *iga* 'name' | *iga* 'name' |
| *kabisi* 'compartment' | *kabisi* 'compartment/foodhouse' |
| *kabulu* 'sector' | *kabulu* 'village sector' |
| *kada* 'road' | *kada* 'road', *duya* 'door', *kabulu* 'village sector', kaduyo 'entrance' |
| *kaduyo* 'entrance' | *kaduyo* 'entrance', *duya* 'door' |
| *kai* 'stone blade' | *kai* 'stone blade' |
| *ka'i* 'tooth' | *kudu* 'tooth' |
| *kapwa* 'parcel' | *kapwa* 'parcel' |
| *kasa* 'row' | *kasa* 'row', *gili* 'row', *meila* 'song/part', *nina* 'song/part', *deli* 'group' |
| *ke* 'wood' | *ke* 'wood', *bubu* 'cut across', *bubwa* 'cut off', *bukwa* 'fruit cluster', *bwa* 'tree', *giwi* 'cut', *kabisi* 'compartment of a foodhouse', *kabulo* 'sector', *kabulo* 'point, protuberances' *kila* 'hands of bananas', *kwoila* 'clay pot', *liku* 'compartment of a foodhouse', *lila* 'bough', *luva* 'wooden dishes', *mmwa* 'conical bundle', *oyla* 'string', *sa* 'nut bunch', *utu* 'scrap', *uva* 'span', *ya* 'flexible, thin' |
| *kova* 'fire' | *kova* 'fire' |
| *koya/kwoya* 'hill' | *kwoya* 'mountain, hill' |
| *kubila* 'land plot' | *kubila* 'land plot' |
| *kudu* 'tooth' | *kudu* 'tooth' |
| *kumla* 'earth oven' | *kumla* 'earth oven' |
| *kwe* 'thing' | *kwe* 'thing', *bogi* 'night', *bubu* 'cut across', *buda* 'group', *bukwa* 'cluster', *deli* 'group', *duya* 'door', *gili* 'row', *gula* 'heap', *kabisi* 'compartment of a foodhouse', *kabulu* 'village sector', *kala* 'day', *kapwa* 'parcel', *kubila* 'land plot', *kudu* 'band of fibers', *kwoila* 'clay pot', *kwoya* 'mountain', *liku* 'compartment of a foodhouse', *lilo* 'walk', *nina* 'song/part', *nunu* 'corner of a garden', *oyla* 'string', *po'ula* 'grove', *sipu* 'sheaf', *siva* 'time', *siwa* 'sea portions', *vilo* 'place', *yam* 'day', *yulai* 'bundle of four things', *yuma* 'hand', *yuva* 'shoal', 0 'basketful of yams' |
| *kweya* 'limb' | *kweya* 'limb', *yuma* 'hand' |
| *kwoila* 'clay pot' | *kwoila* 'clay pot' |
| *liku* 'compartment' | *liku* 'compartment of a foodhouse' |
| *luba* 'bundle' | *kapwa* 'parcel, bundle' |
| *lola* 'walk' | *lilo* 'walk' |
| *megwa* 'magic' | *nina* 'song/part' |
| *mmwa* 'bundle' | *mmwa* 'conical bundle' |
| *na1* 'female' | *na1* 'female persons', *duya* 'door' |
| *na2* 'animals' | *na2* 'animals', *oyla* 'string', *wela* 'batch of fish' |
| *notu/nutu* 'kneaded' | *notu/nutu* 'kneaded, dot' |

**Table 3.2.18.** *(continued)*

| Produced | Expected |
|---|---|
| *nunu* 'corner' | *nunu* 'corner of a garden' |
| *peta* 'basket' | *ta* 'basket' |
| *pila* 'part' | *pila* 'part', *meila* 'song/part', *nina* 'song/part', *oyla* 'string' |
| *po'ula* 'grove' | *po'ula* 'grove' |
| *pwanina/pona* 'hole' | *pwanina/pona* 'hole' |
| *sa* 'nut bunch' | *sa* 'nut bunch' |
| *si* 'bit' | *ya* 'thin' |
| *sipu* 'sheaf' | *sipu* 'sheaf' |
| *sisi* 'bough' | *sisi* 'bough', *ya* 'flexible, thin' |
| *suya* 'batch of fish' | *wela* 'batch of fish' |
| *ta* 'basket' | *ta* 'basket' |
| *tam* 'sprouting (yams)' | *gula* 'heap', 0 'basketful of yams' |
| *tuta* 'time' | *siva* 'time' |
| *to/te* 'male' | *to/te* 'male persons' |
| *utu* 'scrap' | *utu* 'scrap', *kabisi* 'compartment/foodhouse', *kabulo* 'point', *kubila* 'land plot', *meila* 'song/part', *mmwa* 'conical bundle', *nina* 'song/part', *nunu* 'corner of a garden', *si* 'bit', *siwa* 'sea portions', *vili* 'untwisted' |
| *uva* 'span' | *uva* 'span' |
| *vakala* 'belt' | *gili* 'row' |
| *vaya* 'door' | *duya* 'door' |
| *vili* 'untwisted' | *vili* 'untwisted', *si* 'bit' |
| *vosi* 'song' | *meila* 'song/part' |
| *wela* 'batch of fish' | *wela* 'batch of fish', *oyla* 'string' |
| *ya* 'thin, flexible' | *ya* 'flexible, thin', *gili* 'row', *lilo* 'walk', *pila* 'part', *sisi* 'bough' |
| *yam* 'day' | *yam* 'day', *kala* 'day' |
| *yegila* 'name' | *iga* 'name' |
| *yulai* 'bundle' | *yulai* 'bundle of four things' |
| *yuva* 'shoal' | *yuva* 'shoal' |
| 0 'basketful of yams' | 0 'basketful of yams' |

versus the CPs actually produced by the consultants. The data in this table will be discussed in detail in section 3.3. However, at this stage, the following comments are pertinent.

1. My other consultants told me that there is no CP *'boma'* in Kilivila. I have no idea why consultant 25 produced this particle as part of the elicited adjective.

2. *Bubwa* 'parts cut off' was produced as a response to the stimulus presented to elicit the expected CP *kabulo* 'protuberances'. The CP

produced hardly agrees with the stimulus presented; however, if we assume that the consultant thought of a protruding piece of wood that is cut off, we may explain the rather idiosyncratic usage of this CP.

3. *Buda/boda* 'group, team, crowd' was produced as a response to the stimulus *bobu* 'log, round timber' presented to elicit the expected CP *bubu* 'block cut off'. This is not acceptable; the CP *buda* does not agree with the noun *bobu*.

4. *Gula* 'heap, group' was produced as a response to the stimulus *bobu* 'log, round timber' presented to elicit the expected CP *bubu* 'block cut off/cut across'. The CP hardly agrees with the stimulus presented; only by assuming that the consultant thought of a heap of blocks cut off can we explain the rather idiosyncratic usage of this CP.

5. *Kada* 'road, track' was produced as a response to the stimulus *kabuluyuvela* 'village sector' presented to elicit the expected CP *kabulu* 'village sector'. This is not acceptable; *kada* does not agree with the stimulus *kabuluyuvela*.

6. *Nal* 'female persons' was produced as a response to the stimulus presented to elicit the expected CP *duya* 'door, entrance'. This is not acceptable; *nal* does not agree with the eliciting noun *duyava* 'door, entrance, window'. However, it may be that the informant tried to play a trick on me by using this CP to give the eliciting noun an obscene meaning. Nevertheless, all my other consultants agreed that this response is not acceptable.

7. *Pila* 'part, piece' was produced as a response to the stimulus *wela* 'string of fish' presented to elicit the expected CP *oyla* 'string'; this is only acceptable if we assume that the consultant thought of a part or a piece of a batch of fish on strings.

8. *Utu* 'scrap, parts cut off' was produced as a response to the stimuli presented to elicit the expected CPs *kubila* 'land plot', *mmwa* 'conical bundle', and *siwa* 'sea portions'. This is not acceptable; *utu* does not agree with the nouns and phrases presented to elicit the expected CPs. We might justify the use of *utu* instead of *siwa* if we assume that the consultant wanted to refer to a part of the sea; nevertheless, the use of *utu* in this context is very idiosyncratic.

Relating these observations to the individual consultants produces the following picture: 5 dubious cases of CP production occurred with consultant 25; consultants 27 and 31 each produced only 1 dubious case of CP production; consultant 30 produced 9 dubious cases; and consultant 32 produced 3 dubious cases. These findings confirm the interpretation of Table 3.2.15 with respect to the balanced usage of CPs with the three word classes elicited in the test.

It is also clear that some consultants in age group III made mistakes in the production of CPs and showed linguistic insecurity with respect to the appropriate use of some CPs. This linguistic insecurity becomes even more evident if we look at the cases where individual consultants produced more than one CP type as a response to a single stimulus. Table 3.2.19 presents the responses documenting such multiple classification. This table will be discussed in section 3.3.

Table 3.2.20 lists the consultant (see appendix A) and the number of CP types and tokens for demonstrative pronouns, numerals, adjectives, and interrogative pronouns produced in the overall corpus of Kilivila speech data by a speaker of the same age as the consultants in age group III in the elicitation test. Consultant III1 produced these CP tokens during an interview about features of his village and in the context of a public speech he delivered. Table 3.2.21 lists the types and the tokens he produced. The database in this case is obviously too small to provide an analysis. However, I note only that the consultant used the CP *kwe* to refer to the foreign words *Papua New Guinea* and *kwestin* 'question', and that he used the CP *pa/pila* to refer to the loanword *paspoti* 'passport'.

In summary, the following can be observed with respect to the production of CPs by the consultants in age group III:

1.  The data gathered in the CP elicitation test showed a balanced usage of CP tokens with adjectives, numerals, and demonstrative pronouns. There were no differences between male and female consultants with respect to the production of CP tokens; however, the male consultants

**Table 3.2.19.** Responses documenting multiple classification in age group III

| Consultant no. | Cases of multiple classification | Percent[†] |
|---|:---:|:---:|
| Females | | |
| 25 | 3 | 10 |
| 26 | 18 | 43 |
| 27 | 9 | 19 |
| 28 | 8 | 20 |
| 29 | 2 | 7 |
| 30 | 9 | 26 |
| | | (Average: 21) |
| Males | | |
| 31 | 10 | 21 |
| 32 | 1 | 3 |
| 33 | 5 | 14 |
| 34 | 8 | 19 |
| 35 | 5 | 11 |
| 36 | 2 | 6 |
| | | (Average: 12) |

[†]No. of cases of multiple classification in relation to all CP types produced by the consultant.

**Table 3.2.20.** Consultant and CP types and tokens—overall corpus of Kilivila speech data

| Consultant no. (age) | Demonstrative pronoun | Numeral | Adjective | Interrogative pronoun | No. of types |
|---|---|---|---|---|---|
| III1 (20 y) | 31 | 21 | 7 | 1 | 5 |

**Table 3.2.21.** CP types and tokens produced by the consultant in the overall corpus of Kilivila speech data

| Type | Demonstrative pronoun | Numeral | Adjective | Interrogative pronoun | Total |
|---|---|---|---|---|---|
| *ke* 'wood' | 1 | 0 | 0 | 0 | 1 |
| *kwe* 'thing' | 16 | 9 | 4 | 1 | 30 |
| *pila/pa* 'part' | 2 | 0 | 0 | 0 | 2 |
| *na2* 'animals' | 0 | 3 | 0 | 0 | 3 |
| *to/te* 'male' | 12 | 9 | 3 | 0 | 24 |
| Total | 31 | 21 | 7 | 1 | 60 |

produced a slightly broader variety of CP types than the female consultants did.

2. Consultant 25 produced *boma* as a response to the stimulus presented to elicit the expected CP *utu*; however, my other consultants told me that there is no CP *boma* in Kilivila. The consultants of this age group did not produce the CPs *kila* 'hands of bananas', *luva* 'wooden dishes', *va* 'door', and *yuma* 'hand', which were produced by the consultants in age group II (see Table 3.2.10). However, the consultants in age group III produced the following CPs, which were not produced by the consultants in age group II: *beku*, *bubwa* (this CP was also produced by 1 consultant in age group I, see Table 3.2.2), *bwalita*, *duya*, *gili*, *yegila*, *koya*, *lola*, *peta*, *tuta*, *uva*, *vakala*, *vaya*, *vosi*, *yulai*, *yuva*, and 0.

3. The CPs *gudi*, *kada*, *kai*, *kasa*, *ke*, *kova*, *kumla*, *kwe*, *kweya*, *na1*, *na2*, *pwanina*, *sisi*, *ta*, *to/te*, and *utu* were produced by all consultants; 11 of the 12 consultants produced *buda*, *giwi*, *iga*, *notu*, *pila*, *deli* and *duli*; 10 consultants produced *ka'i*, *gum*, *kubila* and *ya*; 9 consultants produced *kabisi*, *sipu*, and *vili*; 8 consultants produced *luba*, *liku*, *bubu*, and *suya*. With some CPs, we notice gender-specific preferences in this age group.

4. Some of the CPs produced did not agree with the nouns or noun phrases they referred to. In addition to these cases of dubious or not acceptable CP usage, there were also quite a few CPs used in ways that showed linguistic insecurity in the consultants with respect to using the CP to refer to a given nominal denotatum appropriately.

I did not use the CPs produced by the consultants of age group III to draw conclusions about language acquisition. Wolfgang Klein formulated the following rule of thumb, which is generally accepted in psycholinguistic research on language acquisition: "Nach der Pubertät entwickelt sich die Sprachbeherrschung nur mehr wenig, obwohl der Lernprozeß in manchen Bereichen—z.B. im Wortschatz—nie endet' (Klein 1984:15), and 'Im allgemeinen kann man davon ausgehen, daß sich nach der Pubertät nur noch wenig ändert" (Klein 1984:21; see also pp. 16–16, 21–22, 27, 177 notes 2 and 3; ("Beyond puberty, our command of language shows little progress, though in some areas—the vocabulary, for instance—learning continues throughout our life span" [Klein 1986:3] ... "In general it is reasonable to assume that little progress is made after the age of puberty" [Klein 1986:9; see also pp. 3–4, 8–10, 14–15]); see also Lenneberg 1977:177, 186, 196–197, 202, 208, 220–221, 459, 473; for an extreme counterview, see Schmidt 1975:110).

Although this is a cautious approach, I believe it justifies the methods used in the data analyses I will present later in this chapter. To answer questions about acquisition of CPs in Kilivila native speakers, I will use the data produced by the consultants of age group III as one of my primary points of reference (see sections 3.3.2.1–3.3.2.4).

### 3.2.1.4 Age Group IV

Table 3.2.22 gives the number of responses (CP tokens) to the eliciting stimuli presented for demonstrative pronouns, numerals, and adjectives and the number of CP types produced by each consultant in age group IV (21–35 years). The number of responses elicited from the consultants ranged from 204 (consultant 37) to 207 (all other consultants). There was a balanced usage of CPs with adjectives, numerals, and demonstrative pronouns. The consultants of this age group produced 24% of all demonstrative pronouns, 23.4% of all numerals, and 23% of all adjectives elicited from the 60 consultants in the study.

With the exception of consultant 37 who produced 3 tokens less than each of the other 11 consultants of this age group, there was a balanced response from all consultants to the stimuli presented with respect to the CP tokens produced. Thus, I infer from the data in Table 3.2.22 that there are no differences between male and female consultants in this age group with respect to the production of CP tokens. The average frequency of CP tokens produced for the female consultants (demonstrative pronouns = 68.8; numerals = 68.8; adjectives = 68.8) differs insignificantly from the average frequency of CP tokens produced for the male consultants (demonstrative pronouns = 69; numerals = 69; adjectives = 69).

The number of CP types produced by the female consultants ranged from 18 (consultant 37) to 47 (consultant 41), with an average of 37.2. For male consultants, the number of CP types produced ranged from 31 (consultant 47) to 56 (consultant 45), with an average of 37.5. The difference between

**Table 3.2.22.** Responses in age group IV

| Consultant no. (age) | Demonstrative pronoun | Numeral | Adjective | No. of types |
|---|---|---|---|---|
| Females | | | | |
| 37 (26 y) | 68 | 68 | 68 | 18 |
| 38 (27 y) | 69 | 69 | 69 | 43 |
| 39 (29 y) | 69 | 69 | 69 | 33 |
| 40 (28 y) | 69 | 69 | 69 | 44 |
| 41 (32 y) | 69 | 69 | 69 | 47 |
| 42 (28 y) | 69 | 69 | 69 | 38 |
| Total | 413 | 413 | 413 | |
| Males | | | | |
| 43 (30 y) | 69 | 69 | 69 | 35 |
| 44 (35 y) | 69 | 69 | 69 | 32 |
| 45 (30 y) | 69 | 69 | 69 | 56 |
| 46 (26 y) | 69 | 69 | 69 | 37 |
| 47 (25 y) | 69 | 69 | 69 | 31 |
| 48 (27 y) | 69 | 69 | 69 | 34 |
| Total | 414 | 414 | 414 | |
| Total, age group IV | 827 | 827 | 827 | |

female and male consultants with respect to the production of CP types is insignificant.

Table 3.2.23 presents the CP types that were produced by the consultants of age group IV. The CPs *kada, kai, ke, kova, kumla, kwe, kweya, na1, na2, sisi, ta, to/te,* and *utu* were produced by all consultants. *Giwi, gudi, iga, kasa, pila, pwanina/pona,* and *suya* were produced by 5 female and all male consultants; *kubila/kwabila* was produced by all female and 5 male consultants; 5 female and 5 male consultants produced the CPs *gum, ka'i, kwoila,* and *ya;* 4 female and 5 male consultants produced the CPs *duli* and *vili;* 5 female and 4 male consultants produced the CPs *kabisi* and *luba;* 4 female and 4 male consultants produced the CPs *deli* and *nutu;* 4 female and 3 male consultants produced the CPs *liku* and *sipu;* 3 female and 4 male consultants produced the CP *gula;* 3 female and 3 male consultants produced the CPs *buda/boda, tam,* and *wela;* 3 female and 2 male consultants produced the CPs *bubu, bubwa,* and *kudu* (tooth); 3 female consultants but only 1 male consultant produced the CP *vosi;* 3 male consultants but only 1 female consultant produced the CPs *bwa* and *po'ula.*

Some of these findings can be interpreted as reflecting female and male preferences in producing certain CPs. This interpretation can be at least partly supported by the fact that the CPs *kaduyo, kila, kudu* 'fibers', *mmwa, nunu, va,* and *yama* were produced only by female consultants, whereas the CPs *beku, doba, gili, kabulu, lola, peta, sa, tetu, vakala,* and *vaya* were produced only by male consultants.

**Table 3.2.23.** CP types and tokens produced in age group IV

| Type | No. of women/men producing CP type | Tokens produced by women/men |
|---|---|---|
| *beku* 'stone blade' | 0/1 | 0/1 |
| *bogi* 'night' | 1/1 | 1/1 |
| *bubu* 'cut across' | 3/2 | 7/6 |
| *bubwa* 'cut off' | 3/2 | 6/4 |
| *buda/boda* 'group' | 3/3 | 16/16 |
| *bwa* 'tree' | 1/3 | 1/6 |
| *bwalita* 'sea' | 1/1 | 3/1 |
| *deli* 'group' | 4/4 | 12/11 |
| *doba* 'skirt' | 0/1 | 0/1 |
| *duli* 'cluster' | 4/5 | 12/15 |
| *gili* 'row' | 0/1 | 0/1 |
| *giwi* 'cut' | 5/6 | 13/18 |
| *gudi* 'child' | 5/6 | 15/18 |
| *gula* 'heap' | 3/4 | 9/11 |
| *gum* 'bit' | 5/5 | 15/13 |
| *iga* 'name' | 5/6 | 15/18 |
| *kabisi* 'compartment' | 5/4 | 15/8 |
| *kabulu* 'sector' | 0/2 | 0/2 |
| *kada* 'road' | 6/6 | 37/41 |
| *kaduyo* 'entrance' | 1/0 | 1/0 |
| *kai* 'stone blade' | 6/6 | 18/17 |
| *ka'i* 'tooth' | 5/5 | 12/14 |
| *kapwa* 'parcel' | 1/1 | 3/3 |
| *kasa* 'row' | 5/6 | 16/21 |
| *ke* 'wood' | 6/6 | 205/207 |
| *kila* 'hands/bananas' | 2/0 | 4/0 |
| *kova* 'fire' | 6/6 | 17/18 |
| *kubila* 'land plot' | 6/5 | 16/13 |
| *kudu* 'fibers' | 1/0 | 3/0 |
| *kudu* 'tooth' | 3/2 | 5/4 |
| *kumla* 'earth oven' | 6/6 | 18/18 |
| *kwe* 'thing' | 6/6 | 322/321 |
| *kweya* 'limb' | 6/6 | 33/36 |
| *kwoila* 'clay pot' | 5/5 | 13/13 |
| *kwoya* 'hill' | 2/1 | 6/1 |
| *liku* 'compartment' | 4/3 | 12/7 |
| *lola* 'walk' | 0/1 | 0/1 |
| *luba* 'bundle' | 5/4 | 13/12 |
| *luva* 'wooden dishes' | 1/2 | 4/4 |

**Table 3.2.23.** *(continued)*

| Type | No. of women/men producing CP type | Tokens produced by women/men |
|------|-----------------------------------|------------------------------|
| *mmwa* 'conical bundle' | 1/0 | 1/0 |
| *megwa* 'magic' | 2/1 | 5/1 |
| *na1* 'female' | 6/6 | 18/18 |
| *na2* 'animals' | 6/6 | 24/27 |
| *nunu* 'corner/garden' | 2/0 | 9/0 |
| *nutu* 'kneaded, dot' | 4/4 | 12/12 |
| *peta* 'basket' | 0/1 | 0/1 |
| *pila* 'part' | 5/6 | 33/34 |
| *po'ula* 'grove' | 1/3 | 3/8 |
| *pwanina/pona* 'hole' | 5/6 | 13/18 |
| *sa* 'nut bunch' | 0/1 | 0/3 |
| *sipu* 'sheaf' | 4/3 | 12/9 |
| *sisi* 'bough' | 6/6 | 31/33 |
| *suya* 'batch of fish' | 5/6 | 15/18 |
| *ta* 'basket' | 6/6 | 17/17 |
| *tam* 'sprouting' | 3/3 | 14/11 |
| *tetu* 'yams' | 0/1 | 0/1 |
| *to/te* 'male' | 6/6 | 18/18 |
| *tuta* 'time' | 1/1 | 1/2 |
| *utu* 'scrap' | 6/6 | 45/51 |
| *uva* 'span' | 2/2 | 2/4 |
| *va* 'door' | 2/0 | 6/0 |
| *vakala* 'belt' | 0/1 | 0/1 |
| *vaya/vayo* 'door' | 0/1 | 0/2 |
| *vili* 'untwisted' | 4/5 | 14/11 |
| *vosi* 'song' | 3/1 | 7/3 |
| *wela* 'batch of fish' | 3/3 | 9/9 |
| *ya* 'thin' | 5/5 | 29/25 |
| *yam* 'day' | 1/1 | 1/3 |
| *yama* 'hand' | 1/0 | 2/0 |

Table 3.2.24 presents the CP types ordered according to the number of tokens produced by all 12 consultants. Table 3.2.25 lists the CPs produced versus those expected in response to the stimuli presented. The data in this table will be discussed in detail in section 3.3. However, the following should be noted here:

**1.** The CP *bubwa* 'block cut across/cut off' was produced as a response to the stimulus presented to elicit the expected CP *vili* 'untwisted'. This

**Table 3.2.24.** Number of tokens produced for each CP type—age group IV

| Type | Tokens | Type | Tokens |
|------|--------|------|--------|
| *kwe* 'thing' | 643 | *ke* 'wood' | 412 |
| *utu* 'scrap' | 96 | *kada* 'road' | 78 |
| *kweya* 'limb' | 69 | *pila* 'part' | 67 |
| *sisi* 'bough' | 64 | *ya* 'flexible' | 54 |
| *na2* 'animals' | 51 | *kasa* 'row' | 37 |
| *kumla* 'earth oven' | 36 | *na1* 'female' | 36 |
| *to/te* 'male' | 36 | *kai* 'stone blade' | 35 |
| *kova* 'fire' | 35 | *ta* 'basket' | 34 |
| *gudi* 'child' | 33 | *iga* 'name' | 33 |
| *suya* 'batch/fish' | 33 | *buda/boda* 'group' | 32 |
| *giwi* 'cut' | 31 | *pwanina/pona* 'hole' | 31 |
| *kubila* 'land plot' | 29 | *gum* 'bit' | 28 |
| *duli* 'cluster' | 27 | *ka'i* 'tooth' | 26 |
| *kwoila* 'clay pot' | 26 | *luba* 'bundle' | 25 |
| *tam* 'sprouting' | 25 | *vili* 'untwisted' | 25 |
| *nutu* 'kneaded' | 24 | *deli* 'group' | 23 |
| *kabisi* 'compartment' | 23 | *sipu* 'sheaf' | 21 |
| *gula* 'heap' | 20 | *liku* 'compartment' | 19 |
| *wela* 'batch/fish' | 18 | *bubu* 'cut across' | 13 |
| *po'ula* 'grove' | 11 | *bubwa* 'cut off' | 10 |
| *vosi* 'song' | 10 | *kudu* 'tooth' | 9 |
| *nunu* 'corner/garden' | 9 | *luva* 'wooden dishes' | 8 |
| *bwa* 'tree' | 7 | *kwoya* 'hill' | 7 |
| *kapwa* 'parcel' | 6 | *megwa* 'magic' | 6 |
| *uva* 'span' | 6 | *va* 'door' | 6 |
| *bwalita* 'sea' | 4 | *kila* 'hands/bananas' | 4 |
| *yam* 'day' | 4 | *kudu* 'fibers' | 3 |
| *sa* 'nut bunch' | 3 | *tuta* 'time' | 3 |
| *bogi* 'night' | 2 | *kabulu* 'sector' | 2 |
| *vaya/vayo* 'door' | 2 | *yama* 'hand' | 2 |
| *beku* 'stone blade' | 1 | *doba* 'skirt' | 1 |
| *gili* 'row' | 1 | *kaduyo* 'entrance' | 1 |
| *lola* 'walk' | 1 | *mmwa* 'bundle' | 1 |
| *peta* 'basket' | 1 | *tetu* 'yams' | 1 |
| *vakala* 'belt' | 1 | | |

Types total: 69; tokens total: 2,481

**Table 3.2.25.** CPs produced versus CPs expected—age group IV

| Produced | Expected |
|---|---|
| *beku* 'stone blade' | *kai* 'stone blade' |
| *bogi* 'night' | *bogi* 'night' |
| *bubu* 'cut across' | *bubu* 'block cut across' |
| *bubwa* 'cut off' | *bubwa* 'parts cut off', *utu* 'scrap', *bubu* 'cut across', *vili* 'untwisted' |
| *buda/boda* 'group' | *buda/boda* 'group', *gula* 'heap', *mmwa* 'conical bundle', *yuva* 'shoal' |
| *bwa* 'tree, wood' | *bubu* 'cut across', *bubwa* 'cut off', *utu* 'scrap' |
| *bwalita* 'sea' | *siwa* 'sea portions' |
| *deli* 'group' | *deli* 'group' |
| *doba* 'skirt' | *kudu* 'band of fibers' |
| *duli* 'cluster' | *duli* 'cluster' |
| *gili* 'row' | *gili* 'row' |
| *giwi* 'cut' | *giwi* 'cut' |
| *gudi* 'child' | *gudi* 'child' |
| *gula* 'heap' | *gula* 'heap' |
| *gum* 'bit' | *gum* 'bit' |
| *iga* 'name' | *iga* 'name' |
| *kabisi* 'compartment' | *kabisi* 'compartment of a foodhouse' |
| *kabulu* 'sector' | *kabulu* 'village sector' |
| *kada* 'road' | *kada* 'road', *duya* 'door', *kaduyo* 'entrance' |
| *kaduyo* 'entrance' | *kaduyo* 'entrance' |
| *kai* 'stone blade' | *kai* 'stone blade' |
| *ka'i* 'tooth' | *kudu* 'tooth' |
| *kapwa* 'parcel' | *kapwa* 'parcel' |
| *kasa* 'row' | *kasa* 'row', *meila* 'song/part' |
| *ke* 'wood' | *ke* 'wood', *bubu* 'cut across', *bubwa* 'cut off', *bukwa* 'cluster', *bwa* 'tree', *duya* 'door', *giwi* 'cut', *gum* 'bit', *kabulo* 'point', *kabulu* 'village sector', *kabisi* 'compartment of a foodhouse', *kila* 'hands of bananas', *kova* 'fire', *kubila* 'land plot', *liku* 'compartment of a foodhouse', *lila* 'bough', *luva* 'wooden dishes', *mmwa* 'conical bundle', *sa* 'nut bunch', *si* 'bit', *sisi* 'bough', *utu* 'scrap', *uva* 'span', *vili* 'untwisted', *ya* 'flexible, thin' |
| *kila* 'hands/bananas' | *kila* 'hands of bananas' |
| *kova* 'fire' | *kova* 'fire' |
| *kubila* 'land plot' | *kubila* 'land plot' |
| *kudu* 'fiber' | *kudu* 'band of fibers' |
| *kudu* 'tooth' | *kudu* 'tooth' |

**Table 3.2.25.** *(continued)*

| Produced | Expected |
|---|---|
| *kumla* 'earth oven' | *kumla* 'earth oven' |
| *kwe* 'thing' | *kwe* 'thing', *bogi* 'night', *bubu* 'cut across', *bubwa* 'cut off', *buda* 'group', *deli* 'group', *duli* 'cluster', *duya* 'door', *gili* 'row', *giwi* 'cut', *gula* 'heap', *gum* 'bit', *iga* name', *kabisi* 'compartments of a foodhouse', *kabulu* 'sector', *kala* 'day', *kapwa* 'parcel', *kasa* 'row', *kila* 'hands of bananas', *kubila* 'land plot', *kudu* 'band/fibers', *kudu* 'tooth', *kwoila* 'clay pot', *kwoya* 'mountain', *lilo* 'walk', *meila* 'song/part', *nina* 'song/part', *notu* 'kneaded, dot', *nunu* 'corner of a garden', *oyla* 'string', *po'ula* 'grove', *pwanina* 'hole', *sa* 'nut bunch', *sipu* 'sheaf', *siva* 'time', *siwa* 'sea portions', *ta* 'basket', *vili* 'untwisted', *vilo* 'place', *yam* 'day', *yulai* 'bundle of four things', *yuva* 'shoal', 0 'basketful of yams' |
| *kweya* 'limb' | *kweya* 'limb', *yuma* 'hand' |
| *kwoila* 'clay pot' | *kwoila* 'clay pot' |
| *kwoya* 'hill' | *kwoya/koya* 'mountain, hill' |
| *liku* 'compartment' | *liku* 'compartment of a foodhouse' |
| *lola* 'walk' | *lilo* 'walk' |
| *luba* 'bundle' | *kapwa* 'parcel, bundle' |
| *luva* 'wooden dishes' | *bukwa* 'fruit cluster', *mmwa* 'conical bundle', *sa* 'nut bunch' |
| *mmwa* 'bundle' | *mmwa* 'conical bundle' |
| *megwa* 'magic' | *nina* 'part of a song' |
| *na1* 'female' | *na1* 'female persons' |
| *na2* 'animals' | *na2* 'animals', *oyla* 'string', *wela* 'batch of fish' |
| *nunu* 'corner/garden' | *nunu* 'corners of a garden' |
| *nutu/notu* 'kneaded' | *nutu/notu* 'kneaded, dot' |
| *peta* 'basket' | *ta* 'basket' |
| *pila* 'part' | *pila* 'part', *meila* 'song/part', *siva* 'time', *ya* 'flexible, thin', *nina* 'song/part' |
| *po'ula* 'grove' | *po'ula* 'grove', *sa* 'nut bunch' |
| *pwanina/pona* 'hole' | *pwanina/pona* 'hole' |
| *sa* 'nut bunch' | *bukwa* 'fruit cluster' |
| *sipu* 'sheaf' | *sipu* 'sheaf' |
| *sisi* 'bough' | *sisi* 'bough', *ya* 'flexible' |
| *suya* 'batch of fish' | *wela* 'batch of fish' |
| *ta* 'basket' | *ta* 'basket' |
| *tam* 'sprouting (yams)' | *gula* 'heap', *uva* 'span', 0 'basketful of yams' |
| *tetu* 'yams' | 0 'basketful of yams' |
| *to/te* 'male' | *to/te* 'male persons' |
| *tuta* 'time' | *kala* 'day', *siva* 'time' |
| *utu* 'scrap' | *utu* 'scrap', *bubwa* 'cut off', *kabulo* 'point', *mmwa* 'conical bundle', *pila* 'part', *si* 'bit', *siva* 'time', *vili* 'untwisted' |

**Table 3.2.25.** *(continued)*

| Produced | Expected |
|---|---|
| *uva* 'span' | *uva* 'span' |
| *va* 'door' | *duya* 'door' |
| *vakala* 'belt' | *gili* 'row' |
| *vaya/vayo* 'door' | *duya* 'door', *kaduyo* 'entrance' |
| *vili* 'untwisted' | *vili* 'untwisted', *gili* 'row', *pila* 'part', *si* 'bit' |
| *vosi* 'song' | *meila* 'part of a song' |
| *wela* 'batch of fish' | *oyla* 'string' |
| *ya* 'thin' | *ya* 'flexible, thin', *bukwa* 'fruit cluster', *duya* 'door', *gili* 'row', *kaduyo* 'entrance', *pila* 'part', *sipu* 'sheaf', *yuma* 'hand' |
| *yam* 'day' | *yam* 'day', *kala* 'day' |
| *yama* 'hand' | *yama* 'hand' |

can be explained by assuming that the consultant interpreted the eliciting phrase and gesture in such a way that she emphasized the concept expressed by *buwa* in her response.

2. *Luva* 'wooden dishes, tied bundle' was produced as a response to the stimuli presented to elicit the CPs *bukwa* 'fruit cluster', *sa* 'nut bunch', and *mmwa* 'conical bundle'. This can be explained by assuming that the consultants wanted to emphasize the concept 'bunch, bundle' in their responses.

3. *Utu* 'scrap, parts cut off, fragments' was produced as a response to the stimulus presented to elicit the expected CP *mmwa* 'conical bundle'. This is not acceptable; *utu* does not agree with the stimulus *budubadu uli* 'much taro' presented to elicit the CP *mmwa*.

4. *Vili* 'untwisted' was produced as a response to the stimulus presented to elicit the CP *gili* 'row'. This can be explained by assuming that the consultant wanted to emphasize the concept expressed by *vili* in connection with the eliciting noun *vakala* 'belt of spondylus shell discs'; these belts are indeed in safe keeping; they should not be twisted.

5. *Ya* 'flexible, thin things' was produced as a response to the stimulus presented to elicit the expected CP *yam/yama/yuma* 'hand'. This may be explained by assuming that the consultant wanted to emphasize the flexibility of the hand; however, this is a rather idiosyncratic usage.

If we relate these observations to the individual consultants, we find the following: With consultants 40 and 48, there was 1 dubious case of CP production; with consultants 42 and 44, there were 3 dubious cases of CP production; and with consultant 41, there were 6 dubious cases of CP production. Thus, some of the consultants showed linguistic insecurity with respect to the approrpiate usage of some CPs. This linguistic insecurity becomes more evident when we look at the cases where individual consultants produced more than one CP type as a response to the stimulus given. Table 3.2.26 presents the responses documenting such multiple classification; it will be discussed in more detail in section 3.3.

Table 3.2.27 lists the number of CP types and tokens for demonstrative pronouns, numerals, adjectives, and interrogative pronouns in the overall corpus of Kilivila speech data that were produced by adults of the same age as the consultants in age group IV in the elicitation test (see also appendix A). The data in this table depend heavily on the text category in which the CPs are produced (see appendix B). Consultant IV1/43 produced his CPs in

**Table 3.2.26.** Responses documenting multiple classification in age group IV

| Consultant no. | Cases of multiple classification | Percent[†] |
|---|---|---|
| Females | | |
| 37 | 14 | 78 |
| 38 | 7 | 16 |
| 39 | 7 | 21 |
| 40 | 4 | 9 |
| 41 | 9 | 19 |
| 42 | 3 | 8 |
| | | (Average: 25) |
| Males | | |
| 43 | 3 | 9 |
| 44 | 3 | 9 |
| 45 | 22 | 39 |
| 46 | 6 | 16 |
| 47 | 7 | 23 |
| 48 | 3 | 9 |
| | | (Average: 18) |

[†]No. of cases of multiple classification in relation to all CP types produced by the consultant.

**Table 3.2.27.** Consultants and CP types and tokens—overall corpus of Kilivila speech data

| Consultant no. (age) | Demonstrative pronoun | Numeral | Adjective | Interrogative pronoun | No. of types |
|---|---|---|---|---|---|
| IV1/43 (30 y) | 76 | 24 | 9 | 0 | 10 |
| IV2/45 (30 y) | 5 | 8 | 6 | 0 | 4 |
| IV3    (30 y) | 10 | 23 | 4 | 3 | 10 |
| IV4    (28 y) | 2 | 0 | 0 | 0 | 2 |
| IV5    (28 y) | 1 | 0 | 0 | 0 | 1 |
| Total | 94 | 55 | 19 | 3 | |

connection with fairy tales, myths, magic, songs, nursery rhymes, and a description of how to carve a *tataba*-board (which is a sign of honor for chiefs belonging to the Tabulu-subclan); it was in the fairy tales and myths that he produced 37 of the 76 CPs produced with demonstratives. Consultant IV2/45 produced his CPs in connection with a description of how to build a canoe. Consultant IV3 produced his CP tokens in connection with nursery rhymes and descriptions of how to weave a basket and a fishtrap, which accounts for his rather frequent use of numerals. Consultant IV4 produced his CPs in connection with a description of how to make a lime pot, and consultant IV5 produced his CPs in connection with a brief contribution to a public speech.

The number of CP types that these 5 men produced ranged from 1 to 10. Table 3.2.28 presents the types and the tokens realized by all 5 consultants. There was no peculiar usage of any of these CP types with respect to the noun they referred to and agreed with. However, the following should be noted:

1. Consultant IV1/43 produced the CP type variant *yule* 'bundle of four things'; he also produced two tokens of the CP type *kwe* in its meaning 'clams and shells' to refer to a white cowrie shell (*buna*).

**Table 3.2.28.** CP types and tokens produced by the consultants in the overall corpus of Kilivila speech data

| Type | Demonstrative pronoun | Numeral | Adjective | Interrogative pronoun | Total |
|---|---|---|---|---|---|
| *gula* 'heap' | 1 | 0 | 0 | 0 | 1 |
| *kai* 'blade' | 0 | 1 | 1 | 0 | 2 |
| *kasa* 'row' | 0 | 6 | 0 | 0 | 6 |
| *kauya* 'creel' | 0 | 4 | 0 | 0 | 4 |
| *ke* 'wood' | 37 | 8 | 12 | 1 | 58 |
| *kwe* 'thing' | 11 | 5 | 2 | 0 | 18 |
| *liku* 'compartment' | 0 | 4 | 0 | 0 | 4 |
| *lipu* 'compartment' | 0 | 5 | 0 | 0 | 5 |
| *na2* 'animals' | 20 | 0 | 0 | 0 | 20 |
| *pila/pa* 'part' | 9 | 4 | 1 | 0 | 14 |
| *ta* 'basket' | 1 | 2 | 3 | 0 | 6 |
| *tam* 'sprouting' | 1 | 0 | 0 | 0 | 1 |
| *to/te* 'male' | 13 | 5 | 0 | 0 | 18 |
| *uva* 'span' | 0 | 2 | 0 | 0 | 2 |
| *ya* 'thin' | 1 | 7 | 0 | 2 | 10 |
| *yule* 'bundle' | 0 | 1 | 0 | 0 | 1 |
| *yuma* 'measure' | 0 | 1 | 0 | 0 | 1 |
| Total | 94 | 55 | 19 | 3 | 171 |

2. Consultant IV3 produced the CPs *kauya* 'fish trap', *lipu* 'compartment of a creel, tier', and *yuma* 'measure of length, from the fingertips of one hand to the wrist of the other hand'. These CPs were not produced by the consultants in the CP elicitation test.

3. Consultant IV1/43 produced a phrase with double classification:

*yuletalaga makwena dabunaga*

| *yule-tala-ga* | *ma-kwe-na* |
|---|---|
| bundle of four-one-Emphasis | this-shell-this |

*da-buna-ga*
Dual incl.-cowrie-Emphasis
'indeed one bundle of four of these cowrie shells (belonging to) the two of us'

He also used a phrase where he repaired his CP choice: *makena ... e ... makwena kukwanebu* 'this (wooden) ... eh ... this (thing) story'.

4. Consultant IV2/45 produced the CP *ke* to refer with a demonstrative to the loanword *riga* 'outrigger'.

5. Consultant IV3 produced a phrase where he repaired his CP choice twice: *...yavila ... kevila kivaya ... e ... yavila ...*' (flexible) how many ... (wooden) how many fish traps ... eh (flexible) how many ...'.

To summarize, the following facts can be noted with respect to the production of CPs in age group IV:

1. The data gathered by the CP elicitation test show a balanced usage of CP tokens with adjectives, numerals, and demonstrative pronouns.

2. On average, the differences between male and female consultants with respect to the production of CP tokens and the variety of CP types produced are marginal and insignificant.

3. The consultants in this age group did not produce the CPs *duya* 'door', *yegila* 'name', *koya* 'mountain' (however, they did produce the variant *kwoya!*), *si* 'bit', *yuva* 'shoal', and 0 'basketful of yams' that were produced by the consultants of age group III (see Table 3.2.17). However, the consultants in age group IV produced the following CPs, which were not produced by the consultants in age group III: *doba, kauya, kila, kudu* 'band of fibers', *lipu, luva, tetu, va, yama,* and *yuma.*

4. The CPs *kada, kai, ke, kova, kumla, kwe, kweya, na1, na2, sisi, ta, to/te,* and *utu* were produced by all consultants; 11 of the 12 consultants produced the CPs *giwi, gudi, iga, kasa, pila, pwanina/pona, suya,* and *kubila/kwabila*; 10 consultants produced the CPs *gum, ka'i, kwoila,* and *ya*; 9 consultants produced the CPs *duli, kabisi, luba,* and *vili*; 8 consultants produced the CPs *deli* and *nutu*; 7 consultants produced the CPs *liku, sipu,* and *gula.* With some CPs, gender-specific production preference can be found in the consultants in age group IV.

5. There was only one case where the CP produced did not agree with the phrase it referred to; however, with all consultants during the elicitation test we found cases of multiple classification that may document linguistic insecurity.

### 3.2.1.5 Age Group V

Table 3.2.29 gives the number of responses (CP tokens) to the eliciting stimuli presented for demonstrative pronouns, numerals, and adjectives and the number of CP types produced by each consultant in age group V (36–75 years). The number of responses elicited from the consultants ranged from 192 (consultant 52) to 210 (consultant 59). There was a balanced use of CPs with adjectives, numerals, and demonstrative pronouns. The consultants of this age group produced 23.7% of all demonstrative pronouns, 23.1% of all numerals, and 22.7% of all adjectives elicited from the 60 consultants in the study.

The male consultants produced only 5 more CP tokens than the female consultants. The average frequency of CP tokens produced by the female consultants (demonstrative pronouns = 67.8; numerals = 68; adjectives = 68) differs insignificantly from the average frequency of CP tokens produced by the male consultants (demonstrative pronouns = 68.2; numerals = 68.3; adjectives = 68.2). Thus, I conclude that there is no significant difference between male and female consultants with respect to the production of CP tokens in this age group.

**Table 3.2.29.** Responses in age group V

| Consultant no. (age) | Demonstrative pronoun | Numeral | Adjective | No. of types |
|---|---|---|---|---|
| Females | | | | |
| 49 (56 y) | 69 | 69 | 69 | 41 |
| 50 (44 y) | 68 | 68 | 68 | 32 |
| 51 (48 y) | 69 | 69 | 69 | 41 |
| 52 (74 y) | 64 | 64 | 64 | 27 |
| 53 (58 y) | 68 | 69 | 69 | 36 |
| 54 (39 y) | 69 | 69 | 69 | 37 |
| Total | 407 | 408 | 408 | |
| Males | | | | |
| 55 (62 y) | 64 | 65 | 64 | 44 |
| 56 (37 y) | 69 | 69 | 69 | 37 |
| 57 (45 y) | 69 | 69 | 69 | 38 |
| 58 (58 y) | 68 | 68 | 68 | 41 |
| 59 (75 y) | 70 | 70 | 70 | 37 |
| 60 (48 y) | 69 | 69 | 69 | 42 |
| Total | 409 | 410 | 409 | |
| Total, age group V | 816 | 818 | 817 | |

The number of CP types produced by the female consultants ranged from 27 (consultant 52) to 41 (consultants 49 and 51), with an average of 35.7. The number of CP types produced by the male consultants ranged from 37 (consultants 56 and 59) to 44 (consultant 55), with an average of 39.8.

Table 3.2.30 presents the 72 CP types that were produced by the consultants of age group V. The CPs *deli*, *gudi*, *iga*, *kada*, *kai*, *kasa*, *ke*, *kova*, *kumla*, *kwe*, *kweya*, *na1*, *na2*, *ta*, *to/te*, and *utu* were produced by all consultants. *Notu*,

**Table 3.2.30.** CP types and tokens produced by women/men in age group V

| Type | No. of women/men producing CP type | Tokens produced by women/men |
|---|---|---|
| *bubu* 'cut across' | 4/5 | 11/14 |
| *bubwa* 'cut off' | 3/2 | 6/4 |
| *buda/boda* 'group' | 5/5 | 21/23 |
| *bwa* 'tree' | 1/2 | 2/4 |
| *deli* 'group' | 6/6 | 18/18 |
| *duli* 'cluster' | 5/5 | 15/15 |
| *duya* 'door' | 0/1 | 0/1 |
| *gili* 'row' | 2/1 | 5/3 |
| *giwi* 'cut' | 4/5 | 10/15 |
| *guba* 'bundle/taro' | 1/0 | 3/0 |
| *gudi* 'child' | 6/6 | 18/18 |
| *gula* 'heap' | 2/3 | 6/7 |
| *gum* 'bit' | 3/4 | 9/12 |
| *iga* 'name' | 6/6 | 18/18 |
| *kabisi* 'compartment' | 2/6 | 6/16 |
| *kabulo* 'point' | 1/0 | 3/0 |
| *kabulu* 'sector' | 2/1 | 4/3 |
| *kada* 'road' | 6/6 | 36/36 |
| *kaduyo* 'entrance' | 1/1 | 1/3 |
| *kai* 'stone blade' | 6/6 | 18/18 |
| *ka'i* 'tooth' | 5/5 | 15/15 |
| *kala* 'day' | 0/1 | 0/3 |
| *kapwa* 'parcel' | 3/2 | 7/4 |
| *kasa* 'row' | 6/6 | 18/21 |
| (*)*kava* '???' | 0/1 | 0/1 |
| *kavi* 'tool' | 0/1 | 0/3 |
| *ke* 'wood' | 6/6 | 219/205 |
| *kila* 'hands/bananas' | 1/0 | 1/0 |
| *kova* 'fire' | 6/6 | 17/18 |
| *kubila* 'land plot' | 3/6 | 9/18 |
| *kudu* 'fibers' | 0/2 | 0/6 |
| *kudu* 'tooth' | 1/1 | 3/3 |

**Table 3.2.30.** (continued)

| Type | No. of women/men producing CP type | Tokens produced by women/men |
|------|-----------------------------------|------------------------------|
| kumla 'earth oven' | 6/6 | 18/17 |
| kwe 'thing' | 6/6 | 310/262 |
| kweya 'limb' | 6/6 | 30/33 |
| kwoila/kwela 'clay pot' | 3/6 | 9/6 |
| kwoya 'mountain' | 1/0 | 3/0 |
| liku 'compartment' | 2/5 | 6/13 |
| lilo/lola 'walk' | 0/1 | 0/2 |
| luva 'wooden dishes' | 1/1 | 3/3 |
| luba 'bundle' | 4/4 | 11/10 |
| meila 'song/part' | 0/1 | 0/3 |
| mmwa 'conical bundle' | 2/3 | 4/8 |
| na1 'female' | 6/6 | 18/18 |
| na2 'animals' | 6/6 | 32/36 |
| nigwa 'hole' | 0/1 | 0/1 |
| nina 'song/part' | 0/1 | 0/3 |
| notu 'kneaded, dot' | 5/6 | 13/18 |
| nunu 'corner/garden' | 0/2 | 0/6 |
| peta 'basket' | 1/2 | 1/2 |
| pila 'part' | 5/5 | 35/33 |
| po'ula 'grove' | 4/3 | 12/9 |
| pwanina/pona 'hole' | 5/6 | 15/17 |
| sa 'nut bunch' | 2/0 | 6/0 |
| sipu 'sheaf' | 5/6 | 13/18 |
| sisi 'bough' | 5/6 | 26/30 |
| siva 'time' | 0/1 | 0/3 |
| suya 'batch/fish' | 5/4 | 15/12 |
| ta 'basket' | 6/6 | 17/15 |
| tam 'sprouting' | 2/1 | 14/4 |
| to/te 'male' | 6/6 | 18/20 |
| tuta 'time' | 1/0 | 1/0 |
| utu 'scrap' | 6/6 | 30/28 |
| uva 'span' | 4/3 | 10/6 |
| vili 'untwisted' | 5/4 | 13/11 |
| vosi 'song' | 1/0 | 2/0 |
| wela 'batch/fish' | 1/2 | 1/6 |
| ya 'thin, flexible' | 3/6 | 31/35 |
| yulai 'bundle of four things' | 0/1 | 0/3 |
| yuma 'hand' | 2/1 | 6/1 |
| yuva 'shoal' | 0/1 | 0/1 |
| 0 'basketful of yams' | 1/0 | 1/0 |

*pwanina/pona, sipu,* and *sisi* were produced by 5 female and all male consultants; 5 female and 5 male consultants produced the CPs *buda/boda, duli, ka'i,* and *pila;* 4 female and 5 male consultants produced the CPs *bubu* and *giwi;* 5 female and 4 male consultants produced the CPs *suya* and *vili.* All male consultants, but only 3 female consultants produced the CPs *kubila, kwoila,* and *ya.* The CP *kabisi* was produced by all male, but only 2 female consultants; 5 male and 2 female consultants produced the CP *liku;* 4 female and 4 male consultants produced the CP *luba;* 4 female and 3 male consultants produced the CPs *uva* and *po'ula;* 3 female and 4 male consultants produced the CP *gum;* 2 female and 3 male consultants produced the CPs *gula* and *mmwa;* 3 female and 2 male consultants produced the CPs *kapwa* and *bubwa.*

Some of these findings seem to reflect female and male preferences in producing certain CPs. This interpretation may be at least partly supported by the fact that only female consultants produced the CPs *sa, guba, kabulo, kila, kwoya, tuta, vosi,* and 0, and that only male consultants produced the CPs *kudu* 'band of fibers', *nunu, duya, kala,* (*)*kava, kavi, lilo/lola, meila, nigwa, nina, siva, yulai, yuma,* and *yuva.* It should be noted that my other consultants told me that there is no CP *kava* in Kilivila.

Table 3.2.31 presents the CP types ordered according to the number of tokens produced by all 12 consultants.

Table 3.2.32 presents the results of comparing the expected responses to the stimuli presented with the actual responses produced by the consultants. The data presented in this table will be discussed in detail in section 3.3. However, the following comments can be noted here:

1. *Kabulo* 'village sector' was produced as a response to the stimulus presented to elicit the expected CP *nunu* 'corners of a garden'. This response can only be explained by assuming that the speaker extended the meaning of *kabulo* from 'village sector' to 'sector (in general)' and then used the CP in this extended meaning to respond to the stimulus phrase *nunula bagula* 'corner of a garden'.

2. Consultant 58 produced the formative (*)*kava* as a response to the noun presented to elicit the expected CP *kwoila* 'clay pot'; however, all my other consultants told me that there is no CP *kava* in Kilivila.

3. *Kudu* 'band of fibers' was produced as a response to the stimuli presented to elicit the expected CPs *bubu* 'block cut across/cut off' and *yuva* 'shoal'. The CP *kudu* does not agree with the stimuli presented to elicit these two CPs; thus, these responses are not acceptable.

4. *Luva* 'wooden dishes, tied bundle' was produced as a response to the stimulus presented to elicit the expected CP *utu* 'scrap, parts (cut off)'. *Luva* does not agree with the phrase presented to elicit the expected CP *utu;* thus, this response is not acceptable.

5. *pila* 'part, piece' was produced as a response to the stimulus presented to elicit the expected CP *oyla* 'string'. This response is rather idiosyncratic.

**Table 3.2.31.** Number of tokens produced for each CP type—age group V

| Type | Tokens | Type | Tokens |
|---|---|---|---|
| *kwe* 'thing' | 572 | *ke* 'wood' | 424 |
| *kada* 'road' | 72 | *na2* 'animals' | 68 |
| *pila* 'part' | 68 | *ya* 'flexible' | 66 |
| *kweya* 'limb' | 63 | *utu* 'scrap' | 58 |
| *sisi* 'bough' | 56 | *buda* 'group' | 44 |
| *kasa* 'row' | 39 | *tolte* 'male' | 38 |
| *deli* 'group' | 36 | *gudi* 'child' | 36 |
| *iga* 'name' | 36 | *kai* 'tooth' | 36 |
| *na1* 'female' | 36 | *kova* 'fire' | 35 |
| *kumla* 'earth oven' | 35 | *ta* 'basket' | 32 |
| *pwanina/pona* 'hole' | 32 | *notu* 'kneaded' | 31 |
| *sipu* 'sheaf' | 31 | *duli* 'cluster' | 30 |
| *ka'i* 'tooth' | 30 | *kubila* 'land plot' | 27 |
| *suya* 'batch/fish' | 27 | *bubu* 'cut across' | 25 |
| *giwi* 'cut' | 25 | *kwoila* 'clay pot' | 25 |
| *vili* 'untwisted' | 24 | *kabisi* 'compartment' | 22 |
| *gum* 'bit' | 21 | *luba* 'bundle' | 21 |
| *po'ula* 'grove' | 21 | *liku* 'compartment' | 19 |
| *tam* 'sprouting' | 18 | *uva* 'span' | 16 |
| *gula* 'heap' | 13 | *mmwa* 'bundle' | 12 |
| *kapwa* 'parcel' | 11 | *bubwa* 'cut off' | 10 |
| *gili* 'row' | 8 | *kabulu* 'sector' | 7 |
| *wela* 'batch/fish' | 7 | *yama* 'hand' | 7 |
| *bwa* 'tree' | 6 | *kudu* 'fibers' | 6 |
| *kudu* 'tooth' | 6 | *luva* 'wooden dishes' | 6 |
| *nunu* 'corner/garden' | 6 | *sa* 'nut bunch' | 6 |
| *kaduyo* 'entrance' | 4 | *guba* 'bundle/taro' | 3 |
| *kabulo* 'point' | 3 | *kavi* 'tool' | 3 |
| *kala* 'day' | 3 | *kwoya* 'mountain' | 3 |
| *meila* 'song/part' | 3 | *nina* 'song/part' | 3 |
| *peta* 'basket' | 3 | *siva* 'time' | 3 |
| *yulai* 'bundle of four things' | 3 | *lilo* 'walk' | 2 |
| *vosi* 'song' | 2 | *duya* 'door' | 2 |
| (*)*kava* '???' | 1 | *kila* 'hands/bananas' | 1 |
| *nigwa* 'hole' | 1 | *tuta* 'time' | 1 |
| *yuva* 'shoal' | 1 | 0 'basketful/yams' | 1 |

Types total: 72 (71); tokens total: 2,451 (2,450)

**Table 3.2.32.** CPs produced versus CPs expected—age group V

| Produced | Expected |
|---|---|
| *bubu* 'cut across' | *bubu* 'block cut across/cut off' |
| *bubwa* 'cut off' | *bubwa* 'parts cut off', *utu* 'scrap' |
| *buda/boda* 'group' | *buda/boda* 'group', *yuva* 'shoal' |
| *bwa* 'tree' | *bwa* 'tree', *utu* 'scrap', *vili* 'untwisted' |
| *deli* 'group' | *deli* 'group' |
| *duli* 'cluster' | *duli* 'cluster' |
| *duya* 'door' | *duya* 'door' |
| *gili* 'row' | *gili* 'row' |
| *giwi* 'cut' | *giwi* 'cut' |
| *guba* 'bundle/taro' | *mmwa* 'conical bundle' |
| *gudi* 'child' | *gudi* 'child' |
| *gula* 'heap' | *gula* 'heap' |
| *gum* 'bit' | *gum* 'bit' |
| *iga* 'name' | *iga* 'name' |
| *kabisi* 'compartment' | *kabisi* 'compartment of a foodhouse' |
| *kabulo* 'point' | *nunu* 'corner of a garden' |
| *kabulu* 'sector' | *kabulu* 'village sector' |
| *kada* 'road' | *kada* 'road', *duya* 'door', *kaduyo* 'entrance' |
| *kaduyo* 'entrance' | *kaduyo* 'entrance', *duya* 'door' |
| *kai* 'stone blade' | *kai* 'stone blade' |
| *ka'i* 'tooth' | *kudu* 'tooth' |
| *kala* 'day' | *kala* 'day' |
| *kapwa* 'parcel' | *kapwa* 'parcel' |
| *kasa* 'row' | *kasa* 'row', *meila* 'song/part' |
| (*)*kava* '???' | *kwoila* 'clay pot' |
| *kavi* 'tool' | *kavi* 'tool' |
| *ke* 'wood' | *ke* 'wood', *bubu* 'cut across', *bubwa* 'cut off', *bukwa* 'fruit cluster', *bwa* 'tree', *giwi* 'cut', *gum* 'bit', *kabisi* 'compartment /foodhouse', *kabulo* 'point', *kabulu* 'village sector', *kila* 'hands of bananas', *liku* 'compartment of a foodhouse', *lila* 'bough', *luva* 'wooden dishes', *meila* 'part of a song', *mmwa* 'conical bundle', *oyla* 'string', *sa* 'nut bunch', *si* 'bit', *sisi* 'bough', *utu* 'scrap', *uva* 'span', *vili* 'untwisted', *ya* 'flexible, thin' |
| *kila* 'hands/bananas' | *kila* 'hands of bananas' |
| *kova* 'fire' | *kova* 'fire' |
| *kubila* 'land plot' | *kubila* 'land plot' |
| *kudu* 'fibers' | *kudu* 'bands of fibers', *bubu* 'cut across', *yuva* 'shoal' |
| *kudu* 'tooth' | *kudu* 'tooth' |
| *kumla* 'earth oven' | *kumla* 'earth oven' |
| *kwe* 'thing' | *kwe* 'thing', *bogi* 'night', *bubu* 'cut across', *buda* 'group', *duya* 'door', *gili* 'row', *giwi* 'cut', *gula* 'heap', *gum* 'bit', *kabulu* |

**Table 3.2.32.** *(continued)*

| Produced | Expected |
|---|---|
| | 'village sector', *kaduyo* 'entrance', *kala* 'day', *kapwa* 'parcel', *kova* 'fire', *kubila* 'land plot', *kudu* 'band of fibres', *kumla* 'earth oven', *kwoila* 'clay pot', *kwoya* 'mountain', *liku* 'compartment of a foodhouse', *lilo* 'walk', *mmwa* 'conical bundle', *nina* 'part of a song', *notu* 'kneaded, dot', *nunu* 'corners of a garden', *pila* 'part', *po'ula* 'grove', *pwanina* 'hole', *sa* 'nut bunch', *sipu* 'sheaf', *siva* 'time', *siwa* 'sea portions', *vili* 'untwisted', *vilo* 'place', *yam* 'day', *yulai* 'bundle of four things', *yuva* 'shoal', 0 'basketful of yams' |
| *kweya* 'limb' | *kweya* 'limb', *yuma* 'hand' |
| *kwoila* 'clay pot' | *kwoila* 'clay pot' |
| *kwoya* 'mountain' | *kwoya* 'mountain' |
| *liku* 'compartment' | *liku* 'compartment of a foodhouse' |
| *lilo/lola* 'walk' | *lilo/lola* 'walk' |
| *luba* 'bundle' | *kapwa* 'parcel, bundle' |
| *luva* 'wooden dishes' | *luva* 'wooden dishes', *utu* 'scrap' |
| *meila* 'song/part' | *meila* 'part of a song' |
| *mmwa* 'bundle' | *mmwa* 'conical bundle' |
| *na1* 'female' | *na1* 'female persons' |
| *na2* 'animals' | *na2* 'animals', *oyla* 'string', *wela* 'batch of fish' |
| *nigwa* 'hole' | *pwanina* 'hole' |
| *nina* 'song/part' | *nina* 'part of a song' |
| *notu* 'kneaded, dot' | *notu* 'kneaded, dot' |
| *nunu* 'corner/garden' | *nunu* 'corners of a garden' |
| *peta* 'basket' | *ta* 'basket' |
| *pila* 'part' | *pila* 'part', *meila* 'part of a song', *oyla* 'string', *nina* 'part of a song' |
| *po'ula* 'grove' | *po'ula* 'grove', *bukwa* 'fruit cluster', *sa* 'nut bunch' |
| *pwanina/pona* 'hole' | *pwanina/pona* 'hole' |
| *sa* 'nut bunch' | *sa* 'nut bunch' |
| *sipu* 'sheaf' | *sipu* 'sheaf' |
| *sisi* 'bough' | *sisi* 'bough', *ya* 'flexible, thin' |
| *siva* 'time' | *siva* 'time' |
| *suya* 'batch/fish' | *wela* 'batch of fish' |
| *ta* 'basket' | *ta* 'basket' |
| *tam* 'sprouting (yams)' | *gula* 'heap', *uva* 'span', 0 'basketful of yams' |
| *to/te* 'male' | *to/te* 'male persons', *yuma* 'hand' |
| *tuta* 'time' | *siva* 'time' |
| *utu* 'scrap' | *utu* 'scrap', *kabulo* 'village sector', *si* 'bit', *siva* 'time', *vili* 'untwisted' |
| *uva* 'span' | *uva* 'span' |
| *vili* 'untwisted' | *vili* 'untwisted', *si* 'bit' |

**Table 3.2.32.** *(continued)*

| Produced | Expected |
|---|---|
| *vosi* 'song' | *meila* 'part of a song' |
| *wela* 'batch/fish' | *wela* 'batch of fish', *oyla* 'string' |
| *ya* 'flexible, thin' | *ya* 'flexible, thin', *bukwa* 'fruit cluster', *duya* 'door', *gili* 'row', *kaduyo* 'entrance', *lilo* 'walk', *pila* 'part' |
| *yama/yuma* 'hand' | *yuma* 'hand' |
| *yulai* 'bundle of four things' | *yulai* 'bundle of four things' |
| *yuva* 'shoal' | *yuva* 'shoal' |
| 0 'basketful of yams' | 0 'basketful of yams' |

Relating these observations to the individual consultants, we find the following: Consultant 49 produced 3 dubious cases of CP production; consultant 50 produced 1 dubious case; consultant 58 produced 4 dubious cases; and consultant 59 produced 3 dubious cases.

Thus, the degree of linguistic insecurity with respect to the appropriate use of CPs is slightly higher in men than in women in this age group. This finding becomes even more striking, if we look at the cases where individual consultants produced more than one CP type as a response to a given stimulus. Table 3.2.33 presents the responses documenting such multiple classification. This table will be discussed in detail in section 3.3.

Table 3.2.34 lists the consultants (see appendix A) and the number of CP types and tokens for demonstrative pronouns, numerals, adjectives, and interrogative pronouns in the overall corpus of Kilivila speech data that were produced by adults of the same age as the consultants in age group V in the elicitation test. The data in this table depend heavily on the text category in which the CPs were produced:

1. Consultants V1/49 and V2/50 produced their CPs in connection with descriptions of how to make a grass skirt; consultant V3/51 produced her CPs in connection with a public speech and a description of how to make a grass-skirt.

2. Consultant V4/53 produced her CPs during an interview about a ghost woman; 10 of the 16 numerals referred to the number of the ghost woman's relatives.

3. Consultant V5/55 produced his CPs during a public speech and in connection with magic formulae; he produced all the adjectives during the recitation of these formulae (see G. Senft 1985c); consultant V6/56 produced his CPs during a description of how to build a house.

4. Consultant V7/60 produced his CPs during an interview about a canoe trip to Nabwageta Island where he bought clay pots. His frequent use of numerals is accounted for by the fact that he referred to the

**Table 3.2.33.** Responses documenting multiple classification in age group V

| Consultant no. | Cases of multiple classification | Percent[†] |
|---|---|---|
| Females | | |
| 49 | 8 | 20 |
| 50 | 13 | 41 |
| 51 | 3 | 7 |
| 52 | 0 | 0 |
| 53 | 1 | 3 |
| 54 | 1 | 3 |
| | | (Average: 12) |
| Males | | |
| 55 | 10 | 23 |
| 56 | 3 | 8 |
| 57 | 3 | 8 |
| 58 | 16 | 39 |
| 59 | 3 | 8 |
| 60 | 4 | 10 |
| | | (Average: 16) |

[†]No. of cases in relation to all CP types produced by the consultant.

**Table 3.2.34.** Consultants and CP types and tokens—overall corpus of speech data

| Consultant no. (age) | Demonstrative pronoun | Numeral | Adjective | Interrogative pronoun | No. of types |
|---|---|---|---|---|---|
| Females | | | | | |
| V1/49 (56 y) | 1 | 0 | 1 | 0 | 2 |
| V2/50 (44 y) | 2 | 2 | 1 | 0 | 4 |
| V3/51 (48 y) | 3 | 1 | 5 | 0 | 4 |
| V4/53 (58 y) | 35 | 16 | 6 | 0 | 7 |
| V8 (60 y) | 2 | 1 | 0 | 0 | 2 |
| Males | | | | | |
| V5/55 (62 y) | 5 | 0 | 14 | 0 | 3 |
| V6/56 (37 y) | 1 | 5 | 3 | 0 | 2 |
| V7/60 (48 y) | 9 | 20 | 6 | 0 | 6 |
| V9 (57 y) | 1 | 0 | 0 | 0 | 1 |
| V10 (39 y) | 5 | 4 | 3 | 0 | 4 |
| V11 (63 y) | 165 | 59 | 68 | 3 | 12 |
| V12 (45 y) | 4 | 2 | 0 | 0 | 1 |
| V13 (43 y) | 27 | 13 | 3 | 0 | 5 |
| V14 (60 y) | 45 | 13 | 18 | 0 | 9 |
| V15 (56 y) | 72 | 37 | 5 | 0 | 8 |
| V16 (39 y) | 79 | 27 | 13 | 2 | 9 |
| V17 (41 y) | 68 | 40 | 9 | 0 | 15 |
| V18 (65 y) | 17 | 6 | 3 | 0 | 3 |
| Total | 541 | 246 | 158 | 5 | |

number of pots he bought and how many pots he intended to give to his relatives and friends.

5. Consultant V8 produced her CPs in connection with songs, consultant V9 produced his CPs during a public ('admonishing') speech (see G. Senft 1991d), and consultant V10 produced his CPs in connection with an admonishing speech, a mythical story, and a prayer.

6. Consultant V11 produced his CPs in connection with a public speech (see G. Senft 1987d), an admonishing speech (see G. Senft 1991d), a mythical story, a joke (see G. Senft 1985e), some magical formulae, and a description of how to build a canoe and carve a canoe prow. Narrating the myth, he produced 71 demonstrative pronouns to refer unequivocally to the protagonists and important objects; describing the canoe prow, he was also forced to refer in an unequivocal way; this explains why he produced so many CPs with demonstrative pronouns.

7. Consultant V12 produced his CPs during an admonishing speech (see G. Senft 1991d). Consultant V13 also produced his CPs during an admonishing speech, and during a description of how to make a sail; both text categories forced him to refer in an unequivocal way, explaining why he produced so many CPs with demonstrative pronouns.

8. Consultant 14 produced his CPs during the narration of an important Trobriand myth; again, the text category required unequivocal references, explaining the rather frequent production of CPs with demonstrative pronouns.

9. Consultant V15 produced his CPs during an interview about a ghost woman (see consultant V4/53) and during a description of how to weave a fish trap and a basket. He produced 28 of the numerals and 64 of the demonstrative pronouns during the interview, where he had to refer to the number of the ghost woman's relatives and where his references to persons and objects had to be unequivocal.

10. Consultant V16 produced his CPs during public speeches and during a description of how to build a house. In the public speeches, he had to refer to a number of persons and objects and was forced to refer in an unequivocal way, explaining the rather frequent production of numerals and demonstrative pronouns.

11. Consultant V17 produced his CPs during a description of how to build a canoe and how to burn chalk; consultant V18 produced his CPs in connection with a public speech and during an admonishing speech (see G. Senft 1991d).

The number of CP types produced by the 18 consultants in this corpus ranged from 1 (consultants V9 and V12) to 15 (consultant V17). Table 3.2.35 presents the types and tokens produced by these consultants. There was no peculiar use of any of these CP types with respect to the nouns they referred

**Table 3.2.35.** CP types/tokens produced by the consultants in the overall corpus of Kilivila speech

| Type | Demonstrative pronoun | Numeral | Adjective | Interrogative pronoun | Total |
|------|------|------|------|------|------|
| *bililo* 'trip' | 0 | 4 | 0 | 0 | 4 |
| *bubwa* 'cut off' | 1 | 3 | 0 | 0 | 4 |
| *buda* 'group' | 4 | 7 | 5 | 0 | 16 |
| *bwa* 'tree' | 0 | 2 | 0 | 0 | 2 |
| *gudi* 'child' | 1 | 2 | 1 | 0 | 4 |
| *gula* 'heap' | 3 | 0 | 0 | 0 | 3 |
| *kabulo* 'sector' | 0 | 2 | 0 | 0 | 2 |
| *kadalkeda* 'road' | 3 | 1 | 1 | 0 | 5 |
| *kai* 'stone blade' | 6 | 0 | 0 | 0 | 6 |
| *kali* 'paddle strike' | 0 | 1 | 0 | 0 | 1 |
| *kasa* 'row' | 0 | 1 | 0 | 0 | 1 |
| *kauya* 'fish trap' | 2 | 2 | 0 | 0 | 4 |
| *ke* 'wood' | 75 | 25 | 29 | 1 | 130 |
| *kova* 'fire' | 4 | 0 | 0 | 0 | 4 |
| *kubila* 'land plot' | 1 | 0 | 0 | 0 | 1 |
| *kudu* 'fibers' | 1 | 2 | 0 | 0 | 3 |
| *kwe* 'thing' | 119 | 82 | 57 | 0 | 258 |
| *kwela* 'clay pot' | 3 | 1 | 4 | 0 | 8 |
| *kweya* 'limb' | 1 | 1 | 0 | 0 | 2 |
| *liku* 'compartment | 2 | 0 | 0 | 0 | 2 |
| *na1* 'female' | 91 | 2 | 16 | 0 | 109 |
| *na2* 'animals' | 25 | 1 | 0 | 0 | 26 |
| *na3* 'moon' | 1 | 3 | 0 | 0 | 4 |
| *na4* 'carving/human' | 3 | 0 | 0 | 0 | 3 |
| *pila* 'part' | 13 | 0 | 3 | 0 | 16 |
| *sisi* 'bough' | 1 | 0 | 0 | 0 | 1 |
| *ta* 'basket' | 0 | 2 | 0 | 0 | 2 |
| *tolte* 'male' | 160 | 82 | 37 | 4 | 283 |
| *utu* 'scrap' | 0 | 2 | 0 | 0 | 2 |
| *uva* 'span' | 0 | 5 | 0 | 0 | 5 |
| *ya* 'thin' | 21 | 12 | 5 | 0 | 38 |
| *yeni* 'handful' | 0 | 1 | 0 | 0 | 1 |
| Total | 541 | 246 | 158 | 5 | 950 |

to. However, the following facts should be noted:

1. Consultant V6/56 produced a phrase where he repaired his CP choice: *...ketala...kwetala youdila kwetala...* '...(wooden)-one... (thing)-one tool (thing)-one... (= one tool)'.

2. Consultant V7/60 produced a phrase with double classification: *...magulana kwelima kwetala...* [infer: *kwena*]... '...(heap)-this (thing)-five (thing)-one... [infer: clay pot]...(= this heap of six clay pots)'.

3. Consultant V11 produced the following two phrases with double classification: *...budakekita tevasi wala...* '(group)-small (persons)-four only...(= a small group of four persons only)'; *...tetala vivila e namanabweta minana...* '(person)-one girl yes (female)-beautiful (female)-this...(= one girl, she was really beautiful)'. He also produced the CP *kwe* 'thing' to refer with a demonstrative pronoun and an adjective to the foreign word *education*, to refer with an adjective to the loanword *lekodi* 'record', to refer with a numeral to the loanword *mani* 'money', to refer with a demonstrative pronoun to the loan-word *laita* 'light', and to refer with an adjective to the loanword *mitini* 'meeting'. Moreover, this consultant produced two tokens of the CP type *kwe* in its rarely realized meaning 'clams and shells', referring to a triton (*tauya*). He also produced two phrases where he repaired his CP choice: *...manikwena...mna... mayana vatunu...* '(thing)-this...eh...(flexible)-this rope'; *...kweta... budata boda mabudana...* '(thing)-one...(group)-one group (group)-this... (= this one group)'. Finally, consultant V11 also produced the CP *na* in its meanings 'moon, stars, planets' (= *na3*) and 'carvings in human likeness' (= *na4*); here it should be emphasized that Kilagola produced the noun phrase *minana tabuya*, thus extending the meaning 'carving of human likeness' from the *tokwalu*-figure on the upper rim of a canoe board (*lagim*) to the canoe prow (*tabuya*) (see also Scoditti 1985).

4. Consultant V13 produced the CP *ke* to refer with a demonstrative pronoun to the foreign word *dingi* 'dinghy'. Consultant V14 produced the CP *kali* 'paddle strike'; this CP was not produced by any other consultant. This consultant also produced 15 tokens of the CP type *kwe* in its meaning 'clams and shells' to refer to the melo aethiopicus shell *kweduya*. Consultant V15 produced the CP *kwe* to refer with a demonstrative and with numerals to the loanword *tepi* 'tape' and the foreign word *hour*. Consultant 16 produced the CP *kwe* to refer with demonstratives, numerals, and adjectives to the loanwords *ensini* 'engine', *wiki* 'week', *namba* 'number', *simenti* 'cement', and *mani* 'money'; the CP *ke* to refer with a demonstrative to the foreign word *dingi* 'dinghy', the CP *pila/pa* to refer to the loanword *paspoti* 'passport', and the CP *kwela* 'claypot' to refer with a numeral to the loanword *kerosina* 'kerosine'. Moreover, he produced the following phrase where he repaired his CP choice: *...mtona Nina ... minana Nina mtona Gunter...*'

(person)-this Nina ... (female)-this Nina (male)-this Gunter ... (this Nina and this Gunter).

5. Informant V17 produced the CP *yeni* 'a handful of (something)'. This CP, as well as the CPs *kali* 'paddle strike', *kauya* 'fish trap', and *bililo* 'trip', were not produced during the CP elicitation test.

Although many of these observations have only anecdotal status, the database seems to be sufficient to confirm the fact that in actual language production the choice of CPs is highly dependent on context, especially on text category.

In summary, the following observations apply to the consultants in age group V with respect to their production of CPs:

1. The data gathered by the CP elicitation test showed a balanced usage of CP tokens with adjectives, numerals, and demonstrative pronouns.

2. The differences between male and female consultants with respect to the production of CP tokens are marginal and insignificant; however, on average, the male consultants produced a broader variety of CP types than the female consultants did.

3. The CP *sam* 'ginger' in phrases like *samtala neya* 'one piece of ginger' was also produced in actual discourse; however, it was impossible for me to trace the production of this CP to an individual consultant.

4. The consultants of this age group did not produce the CPs *beku* 'stone blade', *bogi* 'night', *bwalita* 'sea', *doba* 'skirt', *lipu* 'compartment of a creel', *megwa* 'magic', *tetu* 'yams', *va* 'door', *vakala* 'belt', *vaya/vayo* 'door', and *yam* 'day', which were produced by the consultants of age group IV (see Tables 3.2.23 and 3.2.28). However, the consultants of age group V produced the following CPs, which were not produced by the consultants of age group IV: *bililo, duya, guba, kabulo, kala, kali, kavi, meila, na3, na4, nigwa, nina, siva, yeni, yuva,* and 0

5. The CPs *deli, gudi, iga, kada, kai, kasa, ke, kova, kumla, kwe, kweya, na1, na2, ta, to/te,* and *utu* were produced by all consultants; 11 of the 12 consultants produced the CPs *notu, pwanina/pona, sipu,* and *sisi;* 10 consultants produced the CPs *buda/boda, duli, ka'i,* and *pila;* 9 consultants produced the CPs *bubu, giwi, suya, kubila, kwoila, vili,* and *ya;* 8 consultants produced the CPs *kabisi* and *luba;* 7 consultants produced the CPs *liku, uva, gum,* and *po'ula.* With some CP types, there were gender-specific production preferences in the consultants of this age group.

6. Some of the CPs produced did not agree with the nouns or noun phrases they referrred to. In addition to these cases of dubious or not acceptable CP usage, quite a few CPs were used in a way that showed linguistic insecurity in some of the consultants.

**Table 3.2.36.** CP types and tokens produced but not assignable to individuals

| Type | Demonstrative pronoun | Numeral | Adjective | Total |
|------|-----------------------|---------|-----------|-------|
| *bubwa* 'cut off' | 0 | 1 | 0 | 1 |
| *buda* 'group' | 2 | 0 | 0 | 2 |
| *kai* 'stone blade' | 0 | 0 | 13 | 13 |
| *kasa* 'row' | 0 | 2 | 0 | 2 |
| *ke* 'wood' | 1 | 7 | 2 | 10 |
| *kwe* 'thing' | 8 | 11 | 6 | 25 |
| *na1* 'female' | 3 | 1 | 8 | 12 |
| *na2* 'animals' | 1 | 1 | 0 | 2 |
| *pila* 'part' | 0 | 1 | 0 | 1 |
| *sam* 'ginger' | 0 | 7 | 0 | 7 |
| *to/te* 'male' | 3 | 4 | 21 | 28 |
| *ya* 'flexible' | 2 | 3 | 1 | 6 |
| 0 'basketful of yams' | 0 | 2 | 0 | 2 |
| Total | 20 | 40 | 51 | 111 |

7. The database provided by the overall corpus of Kilivila speech data seems to be sufficient to infer that the choice of CPs in actual language production is highly context dependent

Table 3.2.36 lists the CP types and tokens that were produced in actual discourse, but that could not be assigned to individual speakers. These CPs were produced in the following text categories: interview (background), nursery rhymes, verses accompanying games, songs, public speeches, and prayers. The following observations should be noted: The CP *sam* 'ginger' was not produced during the CP elicitation test. We find the CP *to/te* produced to refer to a 'corpse', the CP *kasa* '(a) row (of)' to refer to 'men' and 'girls', and the CP *to* to refer to the loanword *referi* 'referee'.

## 3.2.2 Complete Lists of Data Used in the Analyses

So far, I have separately presented and commented on the data produced by the consultants for each of the five age groups. In this section, I list the CP types and the tokens produced by *all* consultants during the elicitation test; I indicate which consultant produced how many tokens of each CP type. The CP types are listed in alphabetical order. I then present the CP types produced by all consultants during the elicitation test, allocating the tokens of the respective CP type produced to the CP type or types expected. Finally, for the sake of completeness, I list the CP types and tokens documented in my overall corpus of Kilivila speech data.

The twofold data presentation given in sections 3.2.1 and 3.2.2, along with the first interpretations and analyses, serves as an empirically sound and checkable basis for the later analyses, which will attempt to answer the questions raised in section 3.1.

### 3.2.2.1 CP Types/Tokens Produced by All Consultants During the Elicitation Test

Tables 3.2.37 to 3.2.123 present the CP types and tokens produced by all consultants during the elicitation test. They indicate which consultant produced how many tokens of each CP type. In the tables, the following abbreviations are used: I–V = age groups; con = consultant no.; f = female; m = male; tok = tokens.

**Table 3.2.37.** *Beku* 'stone blade' (2 tokens)

|  | I con/tok | II con/tok | III con/tok | IV con/tok | V con/tok |
|---|---|---|---|---|---|
|  | 1/0 | 13/0 | 25/0 | 37/0 | 49/0 |
|  | 2/0 | 14/0 | 26/1 | 38/0 | 50/0 |
|  | 3/0 | 15/0 | 27/0 | 39/0 | 51/0 |
|  | 4/0 | 16/0 | 28/0 | 40/0 | 52/0 |
|  | 5/0 | 17/0 | 29/0 | 41/0 | 53/0 |
|  | 6/0 | 18/0 | 30/0 | 42/0 | 54/0 |
| Total f |  |  | 1 |  |  |
|  | 7/0 | 19/0 | 31/0 | 43/0 | 55/0 |
|  | 8/0 | 20/0 | 32/0 | 44/0 | 56/0 |
|  | 9/0 | 21/0 | 33/0 | 45/1 | 57/0 |
|  | 10/0 | 22/0 | 34/0 | 46/0 | 58/0 |
|  | 11/0 | 23/0 | 35/0 | 47/0 | 59/0 |
|  | 12/0 | 24/0 | 36/0 | 48/0 | 60/0 |
| Total m |  |  |  | 1 |  |
| Total all |  |  | 1 | 1 |  |

con/tok = consultant/token; f = female; m = male.

**Table 3.2.38.** *Bogi* 'night' (12 tokens)

| | I<br>con/tok | II<br>con/tok | III<br>con/tok | IV<br>con/tok | V<br>con/tok |
|---|---|---|---|---|---|
| | 1/0 | 13/0 | 25/0 | 37/0 | 49/0 |
| | 2/0 | 14/0 | 26/1 | 38/1 | 50/0 |
| | 3/0 | 15/0 | 27/3 | 39/0 | 51/0 |
| | 4/0 | 16/0 | 28/0 | 40/0 | 52/0 |
| | 5/0 | 17/0 | 29/0 | 41/0 | 53/0 |
| | 6/0 | 18/0 | 30/0 | 42/0 | 54/0 |
| Total f | | | 4 | 1 | |
| | 7/0 | 19/0 | 31/1 | 43/0 | 55/0 |
| | 8/0 | 20/0 | 32/0 | 44/0 | 56/0 |
| | 9/0 | 21/2 | 33/0 | 45/1 | 57/0 |
| | 10/0 | 22/0 | 34/3 | 46/0 | 58/0 |
| | 11/0 | 23/0 | 35/0 | 47/0 | 59/0 |
| | 12/0 | 24/0 | 36/0 | 48/0 | 60/0 |
| Total m | | 2 | 4 | 1 | |
| Total all | | 2 | 8 | 2 | |

con/tok = consultant/token; f = female; m = male.

**Table 3.2.39.** *Boma* '???' (1 token)

| | I<br>con/tok | II<br>con/tok | III<br>con/tok | IV<br>con/tok | V<br>con/tok |
|---|---|---|---|---|---|
| | 1/0 | 13/0 | 25/1 | 37/0 | 49/0 |
| | 2/0 | 14/0 | 26/0 | 38/0 | 50/0 |
| | 3/0 | 15/0 | 27/0 | 39/0 | 51/0 |
| | 4/0 | 16/0 | 28/0 | 40/0 | 52/0 |
| | 5/0 | 17/0 | 29/0 | 41/0 | 53/0 |
| | 6/0 | 18/0 | 30/0 | 42/0 | 54/0 |
| Total f | | | 1 | | |
| | 7/0 | 19/0 | 31/0 | 43/0 | 55/0 |
| | 8/0 | 20/0 | 32/0 | 44/0 | 56/0 |
| | 9/0 | 21/0 | 33/0 | 45/0 | 57/0 |
| | 10/0 | 22/0 | 34/0 | 46/0 | 58/0 |
| | 11/0 | 23/0 | 35/0 | 47/0 | 59/0 |
| | 12/0 | 24/0 | 36/0 | 48/0 | 60/0 |
| Total m | | | | | |
| Total all | | | 1 | | |

con/tok = consultant/token; f = female; m = male.

**Table 3.2.40.** *Bubu/bobu* 'block cut off/cut across' (68 tokens)

|  | I con/tok | II con/tok | III con/tok | IV con/tok | V con/tok |
|---|---|---|---|---|---|
|  | 1/0 | 13/0 | 25/0 | 37/0 | 49/0 |
|  | 2/0 | 14/0 | 26/3 | 38/3 | 50/2 |
|  | 3/0 | 15/3 | 27/3 | 39/0 | 51/3 |
|  | 4/0 | 16/0 | 28/3 | 40/1 | 52/0 |
|  | 5/0 | 17/0 | 29/0 | 41/3 | 53/3 |
|  | 6/0 | 18/0 | 30/0 | 42/0 | 54/3 |
| Total f |  | 3 | 9 | 7 | 11 |
|  | 7/0 | 19/0 | 31/2 | 43/0 | 55/0 |
|  | 8/0 | 20/0 | 32/3 | 44/0 | 56/3 |
|  | 9/0 | 21/0 | 33/0 | 45/3 | 57/3 |
|  | 10/0 | 22/1 | 34/3 | 46/3 | 58/2 |
|  | 11/0 | 23/0 | 35/3 | 47/0 | 59/3 |
|  | 12/0 | 24/3 | 36/3 | 48/0 | 60/3 |
| Total m |  | 4 | 14 | 6 | 14 |
| Total all |  | 7 | 23 | 13 | 25 |

con/tok = consultant/token; f = female; m = male.

**Table 3.2.41.** *Bubwa* 'parts cut off' (29 tokens)

|  | I con/tok | II con/tok | III con/tok | IV con/tok | V con/tok |
|---|---|---|---|---|---|
|  | 1/0 | 13/0 | 25/2 | 37/0 | 49/2 |
|  | 2/0 | 14/0 | 26/0 | 38/2 | 50/1 |
|  | 3/0 | 15/0 | 27/0 | 39/0 | 51/0 |
|  | 4/0 | 16/0 | 28/0 | 40/2 | 52/0 |
|  | 5/0 | 17/0 | 29/0 | 41/2 | 53/0 |
|  | 6/0 | 18/0 | 30/0 | 42/0 | 54/3 |
| Total f |  | 2 | 6 | 6 |  |
|  | 7/0 | 19/0 | 31/3 | 43/3 | 55/0 |
|  | 8/0 | 20/0 | 32/0 | 44/0 | 56/3 |
|  | 9/0 | 21/0 | 33/3 | 45/0 | 57/0 |
|  | 10/0 | 22/0 | 34/0 | 46/0 | 58/0 |
|  | 11/0 | 23/0 | 35/0 | 47/1 | 59/0 |
|  | 12/1 | 24/0 | 36/0 | 48/0 | 60/1 |
| Total m | 1 |  | 6 | 4 | 4 |
| Total all | 1 |  | 8 | 10 | 10 |

con/tok = consultant/token; f = female; m = male.

**Table 3.2.42.** *Buda/boda/budu* 'group, team, crowd' (156 tokens)

|          | I<br>con/tok | II<br>con/tok | III<br>con/tok | IV<br>con/tok | V<br>con/tok |
|----------|---------|---------|---------|---------|---------|
|          | 1/0     | 13/0    | 25/1    | 37/0    | 49/3    |
|          | 2/0     | 14/1    | 26/2    | 38/4    | 50/6    |
|          | 3/0     | 15/6    | 27/6    | 39/0    | 51/6    |
|          | 4/0     | 16/1    | 28/4    | 40/6    | 52/0    |
|          | 5/0     | 17/3    | 29/6    | 41/6    | 53/3    |
|          | 6/0     | 18/1    | 30/6    | 42/0    | 54/3    |
| Total f  |         | 12      | 25      | 16      | 21      |
|          | 7/0     | 19/0    | 31/6    | 43/6    | 55/2    |
|          | 8/0     | 20/0    | 32/6    | 44/0    | 56/6    |
|          | 9/0     | 21/2    | 33/0    | 45/7    | 57/6    |
|          | 10/6    | 22/2    | 34/6    | 46/3    | 58/0    |
|          | 11/2    | 23/1    | 35/6    | 47/0    | 59/3    |
|          | 12/0    | 24/3    | 36/3    | 48/0    | 60/6    |
| Total m  | 8       | 8       | 27      | 16      | 23      |
| Total all| 8       | 20      | 52      | 32      | 44      |

con/tok = consultant/token; f = female; m = male.

**Table 3.2.43.** *Bukwa* 'fruit cluster' (3 tokens)

|          | I<br>con/tok | II<br>con/tok | III<br>con/tok | IV<br>con/tok | V<br>con/tok |
|----------|---------|---------|---------|---------|---------|
|          | 1/0     | 13/0    | 25/0    | 37/0    | 49/0    |
|          | 2/0     | 14/0    | 26/0    | 38/0    | 50/0    |
|          | 3/0     | 15/0    | 27/0    | 39/0    | 51/0    |
|          | 4/0     | 16/0    | 28/0    | 40/0    | 52/0    |
|          | 5/0     | 17/0    | 29/0    | 41/0    | 53/0    |
|          | 6/0     | 18/0    | 30/0    | 42/0    | 54/0    |
| Total f  |         |         |         |         |         |
|          | 7/0     | 19/0    | 31/0    | 43/0    | 55/0    |
|          | 8/0     | 20/0    | 32/0    | 44/0    | 56/0    |
|          | 9/0     | 21/0    | 33/0    | 45/0    | 57/0    |
|          | 10/3    | 22/0    | 34/0    | 46/0    | 58/0    |
|          | 11/0    | 23/0    | 35/0    | 47/0    | 59/0    |
|          | 12/0    | 24/0    | 36/0    | 48/0    | 60/0    |
| Total m  | 3       |         |         |         |         |
| Total all| 3       |         |         |         |         |

con/tok = consultant/token; f = female; m = male.

**Table 3.2.44.** *Bwa* 'tree, wood' (61 tokens)

|  | I<br>con/tok | II<br>con/tok | III<br>con/tok | IV<br>con/tok | V<br>con/tok |
|---|---|---|---|---|---|
|  | 1/0 | 13/5 | 25/2 | 37/0 | 49/2 |
|  | 2/0 | 14/0 | 26/2 | 38/0 | 50/0 |
|  | 3/0 | 15/5 | 27/2 | 39/1 | 51/0 |
|  | 4/9 | 16/0 | 28/1 | 40/0 | 52/0 |
|  | 5/0 | 17/4 | 29/0 | 41/0 | 53/0 |
|  | 6/0 | 18/0 | 30/0 | 42/0 | 54/0 |
| Total f | 9 | 14 | 7 | 1 | 2 |
|  | 7/0 | 19/6 | 31/0 | 43/0 | 55/0 |
|  | 8/0 | 20/5 | 32/0 | 44/3 | 56/0 |
|  | 9/0 | 21/0 | 33/0 | 45/0 | 57/0 |
|  | 10/1 | 22/1 | 34/3 | 46/1 | 58/3 |
|  | 11/0 | 23/0 | 35/2 | 47/2 | 59/0 |
|  | 12/0 | 24/0 | 36/0 | 48/0 | 60/1 |
| Total m | 1 | 12 | 5 | 6 | 4 |
| Total all | 10 | 26 | 12 | 7 | 6 |

con/tok = consultant/token; f = female; m = male.

**Table 3.2.45.** *Bwalita* 'sea' (6 tokens)

|  | I<br>con/tok | II<br>con/tok | III<br>con/tok | IV<br>con/tok | V<br>con/tok |
|---|---|---|---|---|---|
|  | 1/0 | 13/0 | 25/0 | 37/0 | 49/0 |
|  | 2/0 | 14/0 | 26/0 | 38/3 | 50/0 |
|  | 3/0 | 15/0 | 27/1 | 39/0 | 51/0 |
|  | 4/0 | 16/0 | 28/0 | 40/0 | 52/0 |
|  | 5/0 | 17/0 | 29"0 | 41/0 | 53/0 |
|  | 6/0 | 18/0 | 30/0 | 42/0 | 54/0 |
| Total f |  |  | 1 | 3 |  |
|  | 7/0 | 19/0 | 31/0 | 43/0 | 55/0 |
|  | 8/0 | 20/0 | 32/0 | 44/0 | 56/0 |
|  | 9/0 | 21/0 | 33/1 | 45/1 | 57/0 |
|  | 10/0 | 22/0 | 34/0 | 46/0 | 58/0 |
|  | 11/0 | 23/0 | 35/0 | 47/0 | 59/0 |
|  | 12/0 | 24/0 | 36/0 | 48/0 | 60/0 |
| Total m |  |  | 1 | 1 |  |
| Total all |  |  | 2 | 4 |  |

con/tok = consultant/token; f = female; m = male.

**Table 3.2.46.** *Deli* 'group on the move' (93 tokens)

|  | I con/tok | II con/tok | III con/tok | IV con/tok | V con/tok |
|---|---|---|---|---|---|
|  | 1/0 | 13/0 | 25/3 | 37/0 | 49/3 |
|  | 2/0 | 14/0 | 26/3 | 38/3 | 50/3 |
|  | 3/0 | 15/0 | 27/3 | 39/0 | 51/3 |
|  | 4/0 | 16/0 | 28/1 | 40/3 | 52/3 |
|  | 5/0 | 17/0 | 29/3 | 41/3 | 53/3 |
|  | 6/0 | 18/1 | 30/3 | 42/3 | 54/3 |
| Total f |  | 1 | 16 | 12 | 18 |
|  | 7/0 | 19/0 | 31/3 | 43/3 | 55/3 |
|  | 8/0 | 20/0 | 32/3 | 44/0 | 56/3 |
|  | 9/0 | 21/0 | 33/2 | 45/3 | 57/3 |
|  | 10/0 | 22/0 | 34/3 | 46/3 | 58/3 |
|  | 11/0 | 23/0 | 35/3 | 47/2 | 59/3 |
|  | 12/0 | 24/3 | 36/0 | 48/0 | 60/3 |
| Total m |  | 3 | 14 | 11 | 18 |
| Total all |  | 4 | 30 | 23 | 36 |

con/tok = consultant/token; f = female; m = male.

**Table 3.2.47.** *Doba* '(grass) skirt' (1 token)

|  | I con/tok | II con/tok | III con/tok | IV con/tok | V con/tok |
|---|---|---|---|---|---|
|  | 1/0 | 13/0 | 25/0 | 37/0 | 49/0 |
|  | 2/0 | 14/0 | 26/0 | 38/0 | 50/0 |
|  | 3/0 | 15/0 | 27/0 | 39/0 | 51/0 |
|  | 4/0 | 16/0 | 28/0 | 40/0 | 52/0 |
|  | 5/0 | 17/0 | 29/0 | 41/0 | 53/0 |
|  | 6/0 | 18/0 | 30/0 | 42/0 | 54/0 |
| Total f |  |  |  |  |  |
|  | 7/0 | 19/0 | 31/0 | 43/0 | 55/0 |
|  | 8/0 | 20/0 | 32/0 | 44/0 | 56/0 |
|  | 9/0 | 21/0 | 33/0 | 45/1 | 57/0 |
|  | 10/0 | 22/0 | 34/0 | 46/0 | 58/0 |
|  | 11/0 | 23/0 | 35/0 | 47/0 | 59/0 |
|  | 12/0 | 24/0 | 36/0 | 48/0 | 60/0 |
| Total m |  |  |  | 1 |  |
| Total all |  |  |  | 1 |  |

con/tok = consultant/token; f = female; m = male.

**Table 3.2.48.** *Duli* `cluster, bundle' (108 tokens)

|  | I<br>con/tok | II<br>con/tok | III<br>con/tok | IV<br>con/tok | V<br>con/tok |
|---|---|---|---|---|---|
|  | 1/0 | 13/0 | 25/3 | 37/0 | 49/3 |
|  | 2/0 | 14/0 | 26/3 | 38/3 | 50/3 |
|  | 3/0 | 15/3 | 27/3 | 39/0 | 51/3 |
|  | 4/0 | 16/0 | 28/3 | 40/3 | 52/0 |
|  | 5/0 | 17/0 | 29/3 | 41/3 | 53/3 |
|  | 6/0 | 18/0 | 30/3 | 42/3 | 54/3 |
| Total f |  | 3 | 18 | 12 | 15 |
|  | 7/0 | 19/3 | 31/3 | 43/3 | 55/0 |
|  | 8/0 | 20/3 | 32/0 | 44/0 | 56/3 |
|  | 9/0 | 21/0 | 33/3 | 45/3 | 57/3 |
|  | 10/3 | 22/3 | 34/3 | 46/3 | 58/3 |
|  | 11/0 | 23/0 | 35/3 | 47/3 | 59/3 |
|  | 12/0 | 24/3 | 36/3 | 48/3 | 60/3 |
| Total m | 3 | 12 | 15 | 15 | 15 |
| Total all | 3 | 15 | 33 | 27 | 30 |

con/tok = consultant/token; f = female; m = male.

**Table 3.2.49.** *Duya* `door, entrance' (4 tokens)

|  | I<br>con/tok | II<br>con/tok | III<br>con/tok | IV<br>con/tok | V<br>con/tok |
|---|---|---|---|---|---|
|  | 1/0 | 13/0 | 25/0 | 37/0 | 49/0 |
|  | 2/0 | 14/0 | 26/0 | 38/0 | 50/0 |
|  | 3/0 | 15/0 | 27/0 | 39/0 | 51/0 |
|  | 4/0 | 16/0 | 28/0 | 40/0 | 52/0 |
|  | 5/0 | 17/0 | 29/0 | 41/0 | 53/0 |
|  | 6/0 | 18/0 | 30/0 | 42/0 | 54/0 |
| Total f |  |  |  |  |  |
|  | 7/0 | 19/0 | 31/3 | 43/0 | 55/1 |
|  | 8/0 | 20/0 | 32/0 | 44/0 | 56/0 |
|  | 9/0 | 21/0 | 33/0 | 45/0 | 57/0 |
|  | 10/0 | 22/0 | 34/0 | 46/0 | 58/0 |
|  | 11/0 | 23/0 | 35/0 | 47/0 | 59/0 |
|  | 12/0 | 24/0 | 36/0 | 48/0 | 60/0 |
| Total m |  |  | 3 |  | 1 |
| Total all |  |  | 3 |  | 1 |

con/tok = consultant/token; f = female; m = male.

**Table 3.2.50.** *Gili* 'row' (12 tokens)

| | I con/tok | II con/tok | III con/tok | IV con/tok | V con/tok |
|---|---|---|---|---|---|
| | 1/0 | 13/0 | 25/0 | 37/0 | 49/0 |
| | 2/0 | 14/0 | 26/0 | 38/0 | 50/2 |
| | 3/0 | 15/0 | 27/0 | 39/0 | 51/0 |
| | 4/0 | 16/0 | 28/0 | 40/0 | 52/3 |
| | 5/0 | 17/0 | 29/0 | 41/0 | 53/0 |
| | 6/0 | 18/0 | 30/0 | 42/0 | 54/0 |
| Total f | | | | | 5 |
| | 7/0 | 19/0 | 31/3 | 43/0 | 55/3 |
| | 8/0 | 20/0 | 32/0 | 44/0 | 56/0 |
| | 9/0 | 21/0 | 33/0 | 45/1 | 57/0 |
| | 10/0 | 22/0 | 34/0 | 46/0 | 58/0 |
| | 11/0 | 23/0 | 35/0 | 47/0 | 59/0 |
| | 12/0 | 24/0 | 36/0 | 48/0 | 60/0 |
| Total m | | | 3 | 1 | 3 |
| Total all | | | 3 | 1 | 8 |

con/tok = consultant/token; f = female; m = male.

**Table 3.2.51.** *Giwi* 'cut' (106 tokens)

| | I con/tok | II con/tok | III con/tok | IV con/tok | V con/tok |
|---|---|---|---|---|---|
| | 1/0 | 13/0 | 25/0 | 37/0 | 49/0 |
| | 2/0 | 14/1 | 26/3 | 38/3 | 50/1 |
| | 3/0 | 15/3 | 27/3 | 39/1 | 51/3 |
| | 4/0 | 16/0 | 28/3 | 40/3 | 52/0 |
| | 5/0 | 17/0 | 29/3 | 41/3 | 53/3 |
| | 6/0 | 18/0 | 30/3 | 42/3 | 54/3 |
| Total f | | 4 | 15 | 13 | 10 |
| | 7/0 | 19/3 | 31/3 | 43/3 | 55/0 |
| | 8/0 | 20/3 | 32/3 | 44/3 | 56/3 |
| | 9/0 | 21/1 | 33/3 | 45/3 | 57/3 |
| | 10/0 | 22/3 | 34/3 | 46/3 | 58/3 |
| | 11/0 | 23/0 | 35/3 | 47/3 | 59/3 |
| | 12/0 | 24/3 | 36/3 | 48/3 | 60/3 |
| Total m | | 13 | 18 | 18 | 15 |
| Total all | | 17 | 33 | 31 | 25 |

con/tok = consultant/token; f = female; m = male.

**Table 3.2.52.** *Guba* 'bundle of taro' (3 tokens)

|  | I con/tok | II con/tok | III con/tok | IV con/tok | V con/tok |
|---|---|---|---|---|---|
|  | 1/0 | 13/0 | 25/0 | 37/0 | 49/0 |
|  | 2/0 | 14/0 | 26/0 | 38/0 | 50/0 |
|  | 3/0 | 15/0 | 27/0 | 39/0 | 51/0 |
|  | 4/0 | 16/0 | 28/0 | 40/0 | 52/3 |
|  | 5/0 | 17/0 | 29/0 | 41/0 | 53/0 |
|  | 6/0 | 18/0 | 30/0 | 42/0 | 54/0 |
| Total f |  |  |  |  | 3 |
|  | 7/0 | 19/0 | 31/0 | 43/0 | 55/0 |
|  | 8/0 | 20/0 | 32/0 | 44/0 | 56/0 |
|  | 9/0 | 21/0 | 33/0 | 45/0 | 57/0 |
|  | 10/0 | 22/0 | 34/0 | 46/0 | 58/0 |
|  | 11/0 | 23/0 | 35/0 | 47/0 | 59/0 |
|  | 12/0 | 24/0 | 36/0 | 48/0 | 60/0 |
| Total m |  |  |  |  |  |
| Total all |  |  |  |  | 3 |

con/tok = consultant/token; f = female; m = male.

**Table 3.2.53.** *Gudi* 'child' (142 tokens)

|  | I con/tok | II con/tok | III con/tok | IV con/tok | V con/tok |
|---|---|---|---|---|---|
|  | 1/0 | 13/3 | 25/3 | 37/0 | 49/3 |
|  | 2/0 | 14/0 | 26/3 | 38/3 | 50/3 |
|  | 3/0 | 15/3 | 27/3 | 39/3 | 51/3 |
|  | 4/0 | 16/3 | 28/3 | 40/3 | 52/3 |
|  | 5/1 | 17/3 | 29/3 | 41/3 | 53/3 |
|  | 6/0 | 18/3 | 30/3 | 42/3 | 54/3 |
| Total f | 1 | 15 | 18 | 15 | 18 |
|  | 7/1 | 19/3 | 31/3 | 43/3 | 55/3 |
|  | 8/0 | 20/3 | 32/3 | 44/3 | 56/3 |
|  | 9/0 | 21/3 | 33/3 | 45/3 | 57/3 |
|  | 10/3 | 22/3 | 34/3 | 46/3 | 58/3 |
|  | 11/1 | 23/0 | 35/3 | 47/3 | 59/3 |
|  | 12/1 | 24/3 | 36/3 | 48/3 | 60/3 |
| Total m | 6 | 15 | 18 | 18 | 18 |
| Total all | 7 | 30 | 36 | 33 | 36 |

con/tok = consultant/token; f = female; m = male.

**Table 3.2.54.** *Gula* 'heap, group' (56 tokens)

|  | I<br>con/tok | II<br>con/tok | III<br>con/tok | IV<br>con/tok | V<br>con/tok |
|---|---|---|---|---|---|
|  | 1/0 | 13/0 | 25/0 | 37/0 | 49/0 |
|  | 2/0 | 14/0 | 26/0 | 38/0 | 50/0 |
|  | 3/0 | 15/0 | 27/0 | 39/3 | 51/0 |
|  | 4/0 | 16/0 | 28/0 | 40/3 | 52/3 |
|  | 5/0 | 17/5 | 29/3 | 41/3 | 53/3 |
|  | 6/0 | 18/0 | 30/0 | 42/0 | 54/0 |
| Total f |  | 5 | 3 | 9 | 6 |
|  | 7/0 | 19/3 | 31/7 | 43/3 | 55/1 |
|  | 8/0 | 20/0 | 32/0 | 44/3 | 56/0 |
|  | 9/0 | 21/0 | 33/1 | 45/0 | 57/0 |
|  | 10/0 | 22/0 | 34/1 | 46/3 | 58/3 |
|  | 11/0 | 23/0 | 35/3 | 47/2 | 59/3 |
|  | 12/0 | 24/0 | 36/0 | 48/0 | 60/0 |
| Total m |  | 3 | 12 | 11 | 7 |
| Total all |  | 8 | 15 | 20 | 13 |

con/tok = consultant/token; f = female; m = male.

**Table 3.2.55.** *Gum* 'bit, small piece' (88 tokens)

|  | I<br>con/tok | II<br>con/tok | III<br>con/tok | IV<br>con/tok | V<br>con/tok |
|---|---|---|---|---|---|
|  | 1/0 | 13/0 | 25/0 | 37/0 | 49/0 |
|  | 2/0 | 14/0 | 26/3 | 38/3 | 50/0 |
|  | 3/0 | 15/0 | 27/3 | 39/3 | 51/3 |
|  | 4/0 | 16/1 | 28/3 | 40/3 | 52/0 |
|  | 5/0 | 17/2 | 29/0 | 41/3 | 53/3 |
|  | 6/0 | 18/0 | 30/3 | 42/3 | 54/3 |
| Total f |  | 3 | 12 | 15 | 9 |
|  | 7/0 | 19/1 | 31/3 | 43/3 | 55/0 |
|  | 8/0 | 20/1 | 32/3 | 44/3 | 56/3 |
|  | 9/0 | 21/0 | 33/3 | 45/3 | 57/3 |
|  | 10/0 | 22/1 | 34/3 | 46/3 | 58/0 |
|  | 11/0 | 23/0 | 35/3 | 47/1 | 59/3 |
|  | 12/0 | 24/3 | 36/3 | 48/0 | 60/3 |
| Total m |  | 6 | 18 | 13 | 12 |
| Total all |  | 9 | 30 | 28 | 21 |

con/tok = consultant/token; f = female; m = male.

**Table 3.2.56.** *Iga* 'name' (142 tokens)

|  | I con/tok | II con/tok | III con/tok | IV con/tok | V con/tok |
|---|---|---|---|---|---|
|  | 1/0 | 13/3 | 25/3 | 37/0 | 49/3 |
|  | 2/0 | 14/1 | 26/2 | 38/3 | 50/3 |
|  | 3/0 | 15/3 | 27/0 | 39/3 | 51/3 |
|  | 4/3 | 16/3 | 28/3 | 40/3 | 52/3 |
|  | 5/0 | 17/3 | 29/3 | 41/3 | 53/3 |
|  | 6/1 | 18/3 | 30/3 | 42/3 | 54/3 |
| Total f | 4 | 16 | 14 | 15 | 18 |
|  | 7/0 | 19/3 | 31/3 | 43/3 | 55/3 |
|  | 8/0 | 20/3 | 32/3 | 44/3 | 56/3 |
|  | 9/0 | 21/3 | 33/3 | 45/3 | 57/3 |
|  | 10/3 | 22/3 | 34/3 | 46/3 | 58/3 |
|  | 11/3 | 23/3 | 35/1 | 47/3 | 59/3 |
|  | 12/0 | 24/3 | 36/2 | 48/3 | 60/3 |
| Total m | 6 | 18 | 15 | 18 | 18 |
| Total all | 10 | 34 | 29 | 33 | 36 |

con/tok = consultant/token; f = female; m = male.

**Table 3.2.57.** *Iki* '???' (1 token)

|  | I con/tok | II con/tok | III con/tok | IV con/tok | V con/tok |
|---|---|---|---|---|---|
|  | 1/0 | 13/0 | 25/0 | 37/0 | 49/0 |
|  | 2/0 | 14/0 | 26/0 | 38/0 | 50/0 |
|  | 3/0 | 15/1 | 27/0 | 39/0 | 51/0 |
|  | 4/0 | 16/0 | 28/0 | 40/0 | 52/0 |
|  | 5/0 | 17/0 | 29/0 | 41/0 | 53/0 |
|  | 6/0 | 18/0 | 30/0 | 42/0 | 54/0 |
| Total f |  | 1 |  |  |  |
|  | 7/0 | 19/0 | 31/0 | 43/0 | 55/0 |
|  | 8/0 | 20/0 | 32/0 | 44/0 | 56/0 |
|  | 9/0 | 21/0 | 33/0 | 45/0 | 57/0 |
|  | 10/0 | 22/0 | 34/0 | 46/0 | 58/0 |
|  | 11/0 | 23/0 | 35/0 | 47/0 | 59/0 |
|  | 12/0 | 24/0 | 36/0 | 48/0 | 60/0 |
| Total m |  |  |  |  |  |
| Total all |  | 1 |  |  |  |

con/tok = consultant/token; f = female; m = male.

**Table 3.2.58.** *Kabisi* 'compartment of a foodhouse' (78 tokens)

|  | I<br>con/tok | II<br>con/tok | III<br>con/tok | IV<br>con/tok | V<br>con/tok |
|---|---|---|---|---|---|
|  | 1/0 | 13/3 | 25/3 | 37/0 | 49/3 |
|  | 2/0 | 14/0 | 26/1 | 38/3 | 50/0 |
|  | 3/0 | 15/0 | 27/3 | 39/3 | 51/3 |
|  | 4/0 | 16/0 | 28/0 | 40/3 | 52/0 |
|  | 5/0 | 17/1 | 29/3 | 41/3 | 53/0 |
|  | 6/0 | 18/0 | 30/2 | 42/3 | 54/0 |
| Total f |  | 4 | 12 | 15 | 6 |
|  | 7/0 | 19/3 | 31/2 | 43/0 | 55/3 |
|  | 8/0 | 20/0 | 32/0 | 44/1 | 56/3 |
|  | 9/0 | 21/3 | 33/3 | 45/1 | 57/3 |
|  | 10/0 | 22/0 | 34/3 | 46/3 | 58/3 |
|  | 11/0 | 23/0 | 35/3 | 47/0 | 59/3 |
|  | 12/0 | 24/0 | 36/0 | 48/3 | 60/1 |
| Total m |  | 6 | 11 | 8 | 16 |
| Total all |  | 10 | 23 | 23 | 22 |

con/tok = consultant/token; f = female; m = male.

**Table 3.2.59.** *Kabulo1* 'protuberances, point' (3 tokens)

|  | I<br>con/tok | II<br>con/tok | III<br>con/tok | IV<br>con/tok | V<br>con/tok |
|---|---|---|---|---|---|
|  | 1/0 | 13/0 | 25/0 | 37/0 | 49/3 |
|  | 2/0 | 14/0 | 26/0 | 38/0 | 50/0 |
|  | 3/0 | 15/0 | 27/0 | 39/0 | 51/0 |
|  | 4/0 | 16/0 | 28/0 | 40/0 | 52/0 |
|  | 5/0 | 17/0 | 29/0 | 41/0 | 53/0 |
|  | 6/0 | 18/0 | 30/0 | 42/0 | 54/0 |
| Total f |  |  |  |  | 3 |
|  | 7/0 | 19/0 | 31/0 | 43/0 | 55/0 |
|  | 8/0 | 20/0 | 32/0 | 44/0 | 56/0 |
|  | 9/0 | 21/0 | 33/0 | 45/0 | 57/0 |
|  | 10/0 | 22/0 | 34/0 | 46/0 | 58/0 |
|  | 11/0 | 23/0 | 35/0 | 47/0 | 59/0 |
|  | 12/0 | 24/0 | 36/0 | 48/0 | 60/0 |
| Total m |  |  |  |  |  |
| Total all |  |  |  |  | 3 |

con/tok = consultant/token; f = female; m = male.

**Table 3.2.60.** *Kabulo2/kabulu* 'village sector' (21 tokens)

|  | I<br>con/tok | II<br>con/tok | III<br>con/tok | IV<br>con/tok | V<br>con/tok |
|---|---|---|---|---|---|
|  | 1/0 | 13/0 | 25/0 | 37/0 | 49/1 |
|  | 2/0 | 14/0 | 26/1 | 38/0 | 50/0 |
|  | 3/0 | 15/0 | 27/3 | 39/0 | 51/0 |
|  | 4/0 | 16/0 | 28/3 | 40/0 | 52/0 |
|  | 5/0 | 17/0 | 29/0 | 41/0 | 53/3 |
|  | 6/0 | 18/0 | 30/0 | 42/0 | 54/0 |
| Total f |  |  | 7 |  | 4 |
|  | 7/0 | 19/0 | 31/2 | 43/0 | 55/0 |
|  | 8/0 | 20/0 | 32/0 | 44/0 | 56/0 |
|  | 9/0 | 21/0 | 33/0 | 45/1 | 57/0 |
|  | 10/0 | 22/0 | 34/1 | 46/1 | 58/0 |
|  | 11/0 | 23/0 | 35/0 | 47/0 | 59/0 |
|  | 12/0 | 24/2 | 36/0 | 48/0 | 60/3 |
| Total m |  | 2 | 3 | 2 | 3 |
| Total all |  | 2 | 10 | 2 | 7 |

con/tok = consultant/token; f = female; m = male.

**Table 3.2.61.** *Kada/keda* 'road, track' (341 tokens)

|  | I<br>con/tok | II<br>con/tok | III<br>con/tok | IV<br>con/tok | V<br>con/tok |
|---|---|---|---|---|---|
|  | 1/0 | 13/5 | 25/6 | 37/8 | 49/3 |
|  | 2/0 | 14/8 | 26/8 | 38/3 | 50/6 |
|  | 3/0 | 15/6 | 27/3 | 39/6 | 51/6 |
|  | 4/0 | 16/3 | 28/9 | 40/9 | 52/6 |
|  | 5/0 | 17/3 | 29/9 | 41/5 | 53/6 |
|  | 6/5 | 18/7 | 30/9 | 42/6 | 54/9 |
| Total f | 5 | 32 | 44 | 37 | 36 |
|  | 7/0 | 19/9 | 31/6 | 43/9 | 55/7 |
|  | 8/0 | 20/3 | 32/12 | 44/9 | 56/3 |
|  | 9/0 | 21/9 | 33/7 | 45/5 | 57/6 |
|  | 10/3 | 22/9 | 34/6 | 46/9 | 58/8 |
|  | 11/0 | 23/10 | 35/9 | 47/3 | 59/3 |
|  | 12/9 | 24/9 | 36/9 | 48/6 | 60/9 |
| Total m | 12 | 49 | 49 | 41 | 36 |
| Total all | 17 | 81 | 93 | 78 | 72 |

con/tok = consultant/token; f = female; m = male.

**Table 3.2.62.** *Kaduyo/kaduya* `door, entrance' (15 tokens)

|           | I con/tok | II con/tok | III con/tok | IV con/tok | V con/tok |
|-----------|-----------|------------|-------------|------------|-----------|
|           | 1/0       | 13/1       | 25/0        | 37/0       | 49/0      |
|           | 2/0       | 14/0       | 26/0        | 38/0       | 50/1      |
|           | 3/0       | 15/0       | 27/6        | 39/0       | 51/0      |
|           | 4/1       | 16/0       | 28/0        | 40/0       | 52/0      |
|           | 5/0       | 17/0       | 29/0        | 41/1       | 53/0      |
|           | 6/0       | 18/0       | 30/0        | 42/0       | 54/0      |
| Total f   | 1         | 1          | 6           | 1          | 1         |
|           | 7/0       | 19/0       | 31/0        | 43/0       | 55/0      |
|           | 8/0       | 20/0       | 32/0        | 44/0       | 56/0      |
|           | 9/0       | 21/0       | 33/2        | 45/0       | 57/3      |
|           | 10/0      | 22/0       | 34/0        | 46/0       | 58/0      |
|           | 11/0      | 23/0       | 35/0        | 47/0       | 59/0      |
|           | 12/0      | 24/0       | 36/0        | 48/0       | 60/0      |
| Total m   |           |            | 2           |            | 3         |
| Total all | 1         | 1          | 8           | 1          | 4         |

con/tok = consultant/token; f = female; m = male.

**Table 3.2.63.** *Kai* `stone blade' (136 tokens)

|           | I con/tok | II con/tok | III con/tok | IV con/tok | V con/tok |
|-----------|-----------|------------|-------------|------------|-----------|
|           | 1/0       | 13/0       | 25/3        | 37/3       | 49/3      |
|           | 2/0       | 14/1       | 26/2        | 38/3       | 50/3      |
|           | 3/0       | 15/3       | 27/3        | 39/3       | 51/3      |
|           | 4/0       | 16/0       | 28/3        | 40/3       | 52/3      |
|           | 5/0       | 17/3       | 29/3        | 41/3       | 53/3      |
|           | 6/0       | 18/3       | 30/3        | 42/3       | 54/3      |
| Total f   |           | 10         | 17          | 18         | 18        |
|           | 7/0       | 19/3       | 31/3        | 43/3       | 55/3      |
|           | 8/0       | 20/3       | 32/3        | 44/3       | 56/3      |
|           | 9/0       | 21/3       | 33/3        | 45/2       | 57/3      |
|           | 10/3      | 22/3       | 34/3        | 46/3       | 58/3      |
|           | 11/0      | 23/2       | 35/3        | 47/3       | 59/3      |
|           | 12/0      | 24/3       | 36/3        | 48/3       | 60/3      |
| Total m   | 3         | 17         | 18          | 17         | 18        |
| Total all | 3         | 27         | 35          | 35         | 36        |

con/tok = consultant/token; f = female; m = male.

**Table 3.2.64.** *Ka'i* 'tooth' (127 tokens)

|  | I con/tok | II con/tok | III con/tok | IV con/tok | V con/tok |
|---|---|---|---|---|---|
|  | 1/0 | 13/0 | 25/3 | 37/2 | 49/3 |
|  | 2/0 | 14/0 | 26/3 | 38/2 | 50/3 |
|  | 3/0 | 15/0 | 27/3 | 39/3 | 51/3 |
|  | 4/2 | 16/3 | 28/3 | 40/0 | 52/0 |
|  | 5/3 | 17/3 | 29/0 | 41/2 | 53/3 |
|  | 6/3 | 18/3 | 30/2 | 42/3 | 54/3 |
| Total f | 8 | 9 | 14 | 12 | 15 |
|  | 7/0 | 19/3 | 31/3 | 43/3 | 55/3 |
|  | 8/0 | 20/3 | 32/3 | 44/0 | 56/3 |
|  | 9/0 | 21/3 | 33/3 | 45/3 | 57/3 |
|  | 10/3 | 22/3 | 34/2 | 46/3 | 58/3 |
|  | 11/2 | 23/6 | 35/3 | 47/3 | 59/0 |
|  | 12/0 | 24/3 | 36/0 | 48/2 | 60/3 |
| Total m | 5 | 21 | 14 | 14 | 15 |
| Total all | 13 | 30 | 28 | 26 | 30 |

con/tok = consultant/token; f = female; m = male.

**Table 3.2.65.** *Kala* 'day' (3 tokens)

|  | I con/tok | II con/tok | III con/tok | IV con/tok | V con/tok |
|---|---|---|---|---|---|
|  | 1/0 | 13/0 | 25/0 | 37/0 | 49/0 |
|  | 2/0 | 14/0 | 26/0 | 38/0 | 50/0 |
|  | 3/0 | 15/0 | 27/0 | 39/0 | 51/0 |
|  | 4/0 | 16/0 | 28/0 | 40/0 | 52/0 |
|  | 5/0 | 17/0 | 29/0 | 41/0 | 53/0 |
|  | 6/0 | 18/0 | 30/0 | 42/0 | 54/0 |
| Total f |  |  |  |  |  |
|  | 7/0 | 19/0 | 31/0 | 43/0 | 55/3 |
|  | 8/0 | 20/0 | 32/0 | 44/0 | 56/0 |
|  | 9/0 | 21/0 | 33/0 | 45/0 | 57/0 |
|  | 10/0 | 22/0 | 34/0 | 46/0 | 58/0 |
|  | 11/0 | 23/0 | 35/0 | 47/0 | 59/0 |
|  | 12/0 | 24/0 | 36/0 | 48/0 | 60/0 |
| Total m |  |  |  |  | 3 |
| Total all |  |  |  |  | 3 |

con/tok = consultant/token; f = female; m = male.

**Table 3.2.66.** *Kapwa/kapo* 'bundle/parcel wrapped up' (46 tokens)

|           | I con/tok | II con/tok | III con/tok | IV con/tok | V con/tok |
|-----------|-----------|------------|-------------|------------|-----------|
|           | 1/0       | 13/3       | 25/3        | 37/0       | 49/1      |
|           | 2/0       | 14/0       | 26/0        | 38/0       | 50/3      |
|           | 3/0       | 15/3       | 27/0        | 39/0       | 51/0      |
|           | 4/0       | 16/0       | 28/1        | 40/0       | 52/0      |
|           | 5/0       | 17/0       | 29/0        | 41/0       | 53/0      |
|           | 6/0       | 18/3       | 30/2        | 42/3       | 54/3      |
| Total f   |           | 9          | 6           | 3          | 7         |
|           | 7/0       | 19/3       | 31/0        | 43/0       | 55/3      |
|           | 8/0       | 20/3       | 32/0        | 44/0       | 56/0      |
|           | 9/0       | 21/0       | 33/0        | 45/0       | 57/0      |
|           | 10/2      | 22/3       | 34/0        | 46/0       | 58/1      |
|           | 11/3      | 23/0       | 35/0        | 47/3       | 59/0      |
|           | 12/0      | 24/0       | 36/0        | 48/0       | 60/0      |
| Total m   | 5         | 9          |             | 3          | 4         |
| Total all | 5         | 18         | 6           | 6          | 11        |

con/tok = consultant/token; f = female; m = male.

**Table 3.2.67.** *Kasa* 'row, line' (165 tokens)

|           | I con/tok | II con/tok | III con/tok | IV con/tok | V con/tok |
|-----------|-----------|------------|-------------|------------|-----------|
|           | 1/0       | 13/0       | 25/3        | 37/0       | 49/3      |
|           | 2/0       | 14/0       | 26/3        | 38/3       | 50/3      |
|           | 3/0       | 15/3       | 27/4        | 39/4       | 51/3      |
|           | 4/0       | 16/0       | 28/5        | 40/3       | 52/3      |
|           | 5/0       | 17/3       | 29/10       | 41/3       | 53/3      |
|           | 6/3       | 18/3       | 30/3        | 42/3       | 54/3      |
| Total f   | 3         | 9          | 28          | 16         | 18        |
|           | 7/0       | 19/4       | 31/3        | 43/3       | 55/3      |
|           | 8/0       | 20/3       | 32/3        | 44/3       | 56/3      |
|           | 9/0       | 21/3       | 33/3        | 45/3       | 57/3      |
|           | 10/2      | 22/3       | 34/3        | 46/6       | 58/3      |
|           | 11/3      | 23/10      | 35/3        | 47/3       | 59/6      |
|           | 12/3      | 24/0       | 36/3        | 48/3       | 60/2      |
| Total m   | 8         | 23         | 18          | 21         | 21        |
| Total all | 11        | 32         | 46          | 37         | 39        |

con/tok = consultant/token; f = female; m = male.

**Table 3.2.68.** *Kava* '???' (1 token)

|  | I<br>con/tok | II<br>con/tok | III<br>con/tok | IV<br>con/tok | V<br>con/tok |
|---|---|---|---|---|---|
|  | 1/0 | 13/0 | 25/0 | 37/0 | 49/0 |
|  | 2/0 | 14/0 | 26/0 | 38/0 | 50/0 |
|  | 3/0 | 15/0 | 27/0 | 39/0 | 51/0 |
|  | 4/0 | 16/0 | 28/0 | 40/0 | 52/0 |
|  | 5/0 | 17/0 | 29/0 | 41/0 | 53/0 |
|  | 6/0 | 18/0 | 30/0 | 42/0 | 54/0 |
| Total f |  |  |  |  |  |
|  | 7/0 | 19/0 | 31/0 | 43/0 | 55/0 |
|  | 8/0 | 20/0 | 32/0 | 44/0 | 56/0 |
|  | 9/0 | 21/0 | 33/0 | 45/0 | 57/0 |
|  | 10/0 | 22/0 | 34/0 | 46/0 | 58/1 |
|  | 11/0 | 23/0 | 35/0 | 47/0 | 59/0 |
|  | 12/0 | 24/0 | 36/0 | 48/0 | 60/0 |
| Total m |  |  |  |  | 1 |
| Total all |  |  |  |  | 1 |

con/tok = consultant/token; f = female; m = male.

**Table 3.2.69.** *Kavi* 'tool' (3 tokens)

|  | I<br>con/tok | II<br>con/tok | III<br>con/tok | IV<br>con/tok | V<br>con/tok |
|---|---|---|---|---|---|
|  | 1/0 | 13/0 | 25/0 | 37/0 | 49/0 |
|  | 2/0 | 14/0 | 26/0 | 38/0 | 50/0 |
|  | 3/0 | 15/0 | 27/0 | 39/0 | 51/0 |
|  | 4/0 | 16/0 | 28/0 | 40/0 | 52/0 |
|  | 5/0 | 17/0 | 29/0 | 41/0 | 53/0 |
|  | 6/0 | 18/0 | 30/0 | 42/0 | 54/0 |
| Total f |  |  |  |  |  |
|  | 7/0 | 19/0 | 31/0 | 43/0 | 55/0 |
|  | 8/0 | 20/0 | 32/0 | 44/0 | 56/0 |
|  | 9/0 | 21/0 | 33/0 | 45/0 | 57/0 |
|  | 10/0 | 22/0 | 34/0 | 46/0 | 58/0 |
|  | 11/0 | 23/0 | 35/0 | 47/0 | 59/3 |
|  | 12/0 | 24/0 | 36/0 | 48/0 | 60/0 |
| Total m |  |  |  |  | 3 |
| Total all |  |  |  |  | 3 |

con/tok = consultant/token; f = female; m = male.

**Table 3.2.70.** *Ke* 'wood' ('long objects, inanimates, fire') (1,919 tokens)

|  | I<br>con/tok | II<br>con/tok | III<br>con/tok | IV<br>con/tok | V<br>con/tok |
|---|---|---|---|---|---|
|  | 1/3 | 13/34 | 25/36 | 37/47 | 49/33 |
|  | 2/0 | 14/31 | 26/28 | 38/27 | 50/40 |
|  | 3/0 | 15/35 | 27/28 | 39/28 | 51/29 |
|  | 4/23 | 16/44 | 28/35 | 40/30 | 52/48 |
|  | 5/26 | 17/38 | 29/43 | 41/32 | 53/39 |
|  | 6/33 | 18/50 | 30/32 | 42/41 | 54/30 |
| Total f | 85 | 232 | 202 | 205 | 219 |
|  | 7/3 | 19/37 | 31/22 | 43/33 | 55/37 |
|  | 8/3 | 20/40 | 32/39 | 44/35 | 56/33 |
|  | 9/0 | 21/49 | 33/33 | 45/33 | 57/35 |
|  | 10/31 | 22/39 | 34/25 | 46/36 | 58/34 |
|  | 11/36 | 23/54 | 35/22 | 47/38 | 59/36 |
|  | 12/46 | 24/48 | 36/37 | 48/32 | 60/30 |
| Total m | 119 | 267 | 178 | 207 | 205 |
| Total all | 204 | 499 | 380 | 412 | 424 |

con/tok = consultant/token; f = female; m = male.

**Table 3.2.71.** *Kila* 'clusters/hands of bananas' (7 tokens)

|  | I<br>con/tok | II<br>con/tok | III<br>con/tok | IV<br>con/tok | V<br>con/tok |
|---|---|---|---|---|---|
|  | 1/0 | 13/0 | 25/0 | 37/0 | 49/1 |
|  | 2/0 | 14/0 | 26/0 | 38/0 | 50/0 |
|  | 3/0 | 15/2 | 27/0 | 39/3 | 51/0 |
|  | 4/0 | 16/0 | 28/0 | 40/0 | 52/0 |
|  | 5/0 | 17/0 | 29/0 | 41/1 | 53/0 |
|  | 6/0 | 18/0 | 30/0 | 42/0 | 54/0 |
| Total f |  | 2 |  | 4 | 1 |
|  | 7/0 | 19/0 | 31/0 | 43/0 | 55/0 |
|  | 8/0 | 20/0 | 32/0 | 44/0 | 56/0 |
|  | 9/0 | 21/0 | 33/0 | 45/0 | 57/0 |
|  | 10/0 | 22/0 | 34/0 | 46/0 | 58/0 |
|  | 11/0 | 23/0 | 35/0 | 47/0 | 59/0 |
|  | 12/0 | 24/0 | 36/0 | 48/0 | 60/0 |
| Total m |  |  |  |  |  |
| Total all |  | 2 |  | 4 | 1 |

con/tok = consultant/token; f = female; m = male.

**Table 3.2.72.** *Kova* 'fire' (159 tokens)

|  | I con/tok | II con/tok | III con/tok | IV con/tok | V con/tok |
|---|---|---|---|---|---|
|  | 1/0 | 13/3 | 25/3 | 37/2 | 49/3 |
|  | 2/0 | 14/3 | 26/3 | 38/3 | 50/2 |
|  | 3/0 | 15/3 | 27/3 | 39/3 | 51/3 |
|  | 4/3 | 16/3 | 28/3 | 40/3 | 52/3 |
|  | 5/3 | 17/3 | 29/3 | 41/3 | 53/3 |
|  | 6/3 | 18/3 | 30/3 | 42/3 | 54/3 |
| Total f | 9 | 18 | 18 | 17 | 17 |
|  | 7/0 | 19/3 | 31/3 | 43/3 | 55/3 |
|  | 8/0 | 20/3 | 32/3 | 44/3 | 56/3 |
|  | 9/0 | 21/3 | 33/3 | 45/3 | 57/3 |
|  | 10/3 | 22/3 | 34/3 | 46/3 | 58/3 |
|  | 11/2 | 23/3 | 35/3 | 47/3 | 59/3 |
|  | 12/3 | 24/3 | 36/3 | 48/3 | 60/3 |
| Total m | 8 | 18 | 18 | 18 | 18 |
| Total all | 17 | 36 | 36 | 35 | 35 |

con/tok = consultant/token; f = female; m = male.

**Table 3.2.73.** *Kubila/kwabila* 'land plot' (94 tokens)

|  | I con/tok | II con/tok | III con/tok | IV con/tok | V con/tok |
|---|---|---|---|---|---|
|  | 1/0 | 13/0 | 25/3 | 37/1 | 49/3 |
|  | 2/0 | 14/0 | 26/2 | 38/3 | 50/0 |
|  | 3/0 | 15/0 | 27/3 | 39/3 | 51/3 |
|  | 4/0 | 16/0 | 28/0 | 40/3 | 52/3 |
|  | 5/0 | 17/3 | 29/0 | 41/3 | 53/0 |
|  | 6/0 | 18/0 | 30/1 | 42/3 | 54/0 |
| Total f |  | 3 | 9 | 16 | 9 |
|  | 7/0 | 19/3 | 31/2 | 43/3 | 55/3 |
|  | 8/0 | 20/0 | 32/3 | 44/3 | 56/3 |
|  | 9/0 | 21/3 | 33/3 | 45/2 | 57/3 |
|  | 10/0 | 22/0 | 34/3 | 46/2 | 58/3 |
|  | 11/0 | 23/0 | 35/3 | 47/0 | 59/3 |
|  | 12/0 | 24/3 | 36/3 | 48/3 | 60/3 |
| Total m |  | 9 | 17 | 13 | 18 |
| Total all |  | 12 | 26 | 29 | 27 |

con/tok = consultant/token; f = female; m = male.

**Table 3.2.74.** *Kudu1* 'band of fibres' (9 tokens)

| | I con/tok | II con/tok | III con/tok | IV con/tok | V con/tok |
|---|---|---|---|---|---|
| | 1/0 | 13/0 | 25/0 | 37/0 | 49/0 |
| | 2/0 | 14/0 | 26/0 | 38/0 | 50/0 |
| | 3/0 | 15/0 | 27/0 | 39/0 | 51/0 |
| | 4/0 | 16/0 | 28/0 | 40/0 | 52/0 |
| | 5/0 | 17/0 | 29/0 | 41/0 | 53/0 |
| | 6/0 | 18/0 | 30/0 | 42/3 | 54/0 |
| Total f | | | | 3 | |
| | 7/0 | 19/0 | 31/0 | 43/0 | 55/3 |
| | 8/0 | 20/0 | 32/0 | 44/0 | 56/0 |
| | 9/0 | 21/0 | 33/0 | 45/0 | 57/0 |
| | 10/0 | 22/0 | 34/0 | 46/0 | 58/3 |
| | 11/0 | 23/0 | 35/0 | 47/0 | 59/0 |
| | 12/0 | 24/0 | 36/0 | 48/0 | 60/0 |
| Total m | | | | | 6 |
| Total all | | | | 3 | 6 |

con/tok = consultant/token; f = female; m = male.

**Table 3.2.75.** *Kudu2* 'tooth' (26 tokens)

| | I con/tok | II con/tok | III con/tok | IV con/tok | V con/tok |
|---|---|---|---|---|---|
| | 1/0 | 13/0 | 25/0 | 37/0 | 49/0 |
| | 2/0 | 14/0 | 26/0 | 38/1 | 50/0 |
| | 3/0 | 15/3 | 27/0 | 39/0 | 51/0 |
| | 4/0 | 16/0 | 28/0 | 40/3 | 52/3 |
| | 5/0 | 17/0 | 29/3 | 41/1 | 53/0 |
| | 6/0 | 18/0 | 30/1 | 42/0 | 54/0 |
| Total f | | 3 | 4 | 5 | 3 |
| | 7/0 | 19/0 | 31/0 | 43/0 | 55/0 |
| | 8/0 | 20/0 | 32/0 | 44/3 | 56/0 |
| | 9/0 | 21/0 | 33/0 | 45/0 | 57/0 |
| | 10/0 | 22/0 | 34/1 | 46/0 | 58/0 |
| | 11/0 | 23/0 | 35/0 | 47/0 | 59/3 |
| | 12/0 | 24/0 | 36/3 | 48/1 | 60/0 |
| Total m | | | 4 | 4 | 3 |
| Total all | | 3 | 8 | 9 | 6 |

con/tok = consultant/token; f = female; m = male.

**Table 3.2.76.** *Kumla* 'earth oven' (162 tokens)

|         | I<br>con/tok | II<br>con/tok | III<br>con/tok | IV<br>con/tok | V<br>con/tok |
|---------|--------------|---------------|----------------|---------------|--------------|
|         | 1/1          | 13/3          | 25/3           | 37/3          | 49/3         |
|         | 2/0          | 14/3          | 26/3           | 38/3          | 50/3         |
|         | 3/0          | 15/3          | 27/3           | 39/3          | 51/3         |
|         | 4/3          | 16/3          | 28/3           | 40/3          | 52/3         |
|         | 5/3          | 17/3          | 29/3           | 41/3          | 53/3         |
|         | 6/3          | 18/3          | 30/3           | 42/3          | 54/3         |
| Total f | 10           | 18            | 18             | 18            | 18           |
|         | 7/0          | 19/3          | 31/3           | 43/3          | 55/2         |
|         | 8/0          | 20/3          | 32/3           | 44/3          | 56/3         |
|         | 9/0          | 21/3          | 33/3           | 45/3          | 57/3         |
|         | 10/3         | 22/3          | 34/3           | 46/3          | 58/3         |
|         | 11/3         | 23/3          | 35/3           | 47/3          | 59/3         |
|         | 12/3         | 24/3          | 36/3           | 48/3          | 60/3         |
| Total m | 9            | 18            | 18             | 18            | 17           |
| Total all | 19         | 36            | 36             | 36            | 35           |

con/tok = consultant/token; f = female; m = male.

**Table 3.2.77.** *Kwe* 'thing, inanimates' (2,877 tokens)

|         | I<br>con/tok | II<br>con/tok | III<br>con/tok | IV<br>con/tok | V<br>con/tok |
|---------|--------------|---------------|----------------|---------------|--------------|
|         | 1/1          | 13/107        | 25/65          | 37/101        | 49/44        |
|         | 2/0          | 14/52         | 26/58          | 38/34         | 50/71        |
|         | 3/0          | 15/48         | 27/27          | 39/69         | 51/35        |
|         | 4/39         | 16/80         | 28/41          | 40/40         | 52/54        |
|         | 5/51         | 17/62         | 29/55          | 41/39         | 53/55        |
|         | 6/43         | 18/89         | 30/46          | 42/39         | 54/51        |
| Total f | 134          | 438           | 292            | 322           | 310          |
|         | 7/3          | 19/59         | 31/36          | 43/42         | 55/33        |
|         | 8/3          | 20/74         | 32/27          | 44/57         | 56/40        |
|         | 9/0          | 21/49         | 33/62          | 45/30         | 57/45        |
|         | 10/51        | 22/74         | 34/46          | 46/54         | 58/47        |
|         | 11/55        | 23/64         | 35/34          | 47/72         | 59/55        |
|         | 12/59        | 24/46         | 36/56          | 48/66         | 60/42        |
| Total m | 171          | 366           | 261            | 321           | 262          |
| Total all | 305        | 804           | 553            | 643           | 572          |

con/tok = consultant/token; f = female; m = male.

Classificatory Particles in Kilivila

**Table 3.2.78.** *Kweya/kwaya/keya* '(severed) limb' (215 tokens)

|         | I con/tok | II con/tok | III con/tok | IV con/tok | V con/tok |
|---------|-----------|------------|-------------|------------|-----------|
|         | 1/0       | 13/0       | 25/3        | 37/6       | 49/6      |
|         | 2/0       | 14/0       | 26/3        | 38/6       | 50/6      |
|         | 3/0       | 15/0       | 27/6        | 39/6       | 51/3      |
|         | 4/0       | 16/3       | 28/6        | 40/3       | 52/6      |
|         | 5/0       | 17/3       | 29/3        | 41/6       | 53/3      |
|         | 6/0       | 18/3       | 30/3        | 42/6       | 54/6      |
| Total f |           | 9          | 24          | 33         | 30        |
|         | 7/0       | 19/1       | 31/6        | 43/6       | 55/3      |
|         | 8/0       | 20/3       | 32/6        | 44/6       | 56/6      |
|         | 9/0       | 21/3       | 33/6        | 45/6       | 57/6      |
|         | 10/3      | 22/3       | 34/6        | 46/6       | 58/6      |
|         | 11/0      | 23/1       | 35/6        | 47/6       | 59/6      |
|         | 12/0      | 24/0       | 36/6        | 48/6       | 60/6      |
| Total m | 3         | 11         | 36          | 36         | 33        |
| Total all | 3       | 20         | 60          | 69         | 63        |

con/tok = consultant/token; f = female; m = male.

**Table 3.2.79.** *Kwoila/kwela* 'clay pot' (96 tokens)

|         | I con/tok | II con/tok | III con/tok | IV con/tok | V con/tok |
|---------|-----------|------------|-------------|------------|-----------|
|         | 1/0       | 13/3       | 25/0        | 37/3       | 49/3      |
|         | 2/0       | 14/0       | 26/0        | 38/0       | 50/3      |
|         | 3/0       | 15/3       | 27/0        | 39/1       | 51/0      |
|         | 4/0       | 16/3       | 28/3        | 40/3       | 52/0      |
|         | 5/0       | 17/3       | 29/0        | 41/3       | 53/0      |
|         | 6/0       | 18/3       | 30/0        | 42/3       | 54/3      |
| Total f |           | 15         | 3           | 13         | 9         |
|         | 7/0       | 19/3       | 31/2        | 43/3       | 55/3      |
|         | 8/0       | 20/2       | 32/3        | 44/3       | 56/3      |
|         | 9/0       | 21/3       | 33/0        | 45/3       | 57/3      |
|         | 10/2      | 22/3       | 34/0        | 46/0       | 58/2      |
|         | 11/0      | 23/0       | 35/3        | 47/1       | 59/2      |
|         | 12/3      | 24/0       | 36/3        | 48/3       | 60/3      |
| Total m | 5         | 11         | 11          | 13         | 16        |
| Total all | 5       | 26         | 14          | 26         | 25        |

con/tok = consultant/token; f = female; m = male.

**Table 3.2.80.** *Kwoya/koya* 'mountain, hill' (26 tokens)

|           | I con/tok | II con/tok | III con/tok | IV con/tok | V con/tok |
|-----------|-----------|------------|-------------|------------|-----------|
|           | 1/1       | 13/0       | 25/0        | 37/0       | 49/0      |
|           | 2/0       | 14/0       | 26/0        | 38/0       | 50/0      |
|           | 3/0       | 15/1       | 27/3        | 39/0       | 51/0      |
|           | 4/0       | 16/0       | 28/1        | 40/0       | 52/0      |
|           | 5/0       | 17/0       | 29/0        | 41/3       | 53/3      |
|           | 6/0       | 18/0       | 30/0        | 42/3       | 54/0      |
| Total f   | 1         | 1          | 4           | 6          | 3         |
|           | 7/0       | 19/0       | 31/2        | 43/0       | 55/0      |
|           | 8/0       | 20/0       | 32/2        | 44/0       | 56/0      |
|           | 9/0       | 21/3       | 33/0        | 45/1       | 57/0      |
|           | 10/0      | 22/0       | 34/2        | 46/0       | 58/0      |
|           | 11/0      | 23/0       | 35/1        | 47/0       | 59/0      |
|           | 12/0      | 24/0       | 36/0        | 48/0       | 60/0      |
| Total m   |           | 3          | 7           | 1          |           |
| Total all | 1         | 4          | 11          | 7          | 3         |

con/tok = consultant/token; f = female; m = male.

**Table 3.2.81.** *Liku* 'compartment of a foodhouse' (71 tokens)

|           | I con/tok | II con/tok | III con/tok | IV con/tok | V con/tok |
|-----------|-----------|------------|-------------|------------|-----------|
|           | 1/0       | 13/0       | 25/0        | 37/0       | 49/3      |
|           | 2/0       | 14/0       | 26/1        | 38/3       | 50/0      |
|           | 3/0       | 15/1       | 27/3        | 39/3       | 51/3      |
|           | 4/0       | 16/0       | 28/3        | 40/3       | 52/0      |
|           | 5/0       | 17/1       | 29/0        | 41/0       | 53/0      |
|           | 6/0       | 18/0       | 30/3        | 42/3       | 54/0      |
| Total f   |           | 2          | 10          | 12         | 6         |
|           | 7/0       | 19/3       | 31/0        | 43/3       | 55/3      |
|           | 8/0       | 20/0       | 32/3        | 44/0       | 56/3      |
|           | 9/0       | 21/3       | 33/3        | 45/1       | 57/0      |
|           | 10/0      | 22/0       | 34/3        | 46/0       | 58/2      |
|           | 11/0      | 23/0       | 35/3        | 47/0       | 59/3      |
|           | 12/0      | 24/3       | 36/0        | 48/3       | 60/2      |
| Total m   |           | 9          | 12          | 7          | 13        |
| Total all |           | 11         | 22          | 19         | 19        |

con/tok = consultant/token; f = female; m = male.

**Table 3.2.82.** *Lilo/lola* 'walk, journey' (7 tokens)

|  | I con/tok | II con/tok | III con/tok | IV con/tok | V con/tok |
|---|---|---|---|---|---|
|  | 1/1 | 13/0 | 25/0 | 37/0 | 49/0 |
|  | 2/0 | 14/0 | 26/0 | 38/0 | 50/0 |
|  | 3/0 | 15/0 | 27/3 | 39/0 | 51/0 |
|  | 4/0 | 16/0 | 28/0 | 40/0 | 52/0 |
|  | 5/0 | 17/0 | 29/0 | 41/0 | 53/0 |
|  | 6/0 | 18/0 | 30/0 | 42/0 | 54/0 |
| Total f | 1 |  | 3 |  |  |
|  | 7/0 | 19/0 | 31/0 | 43/0 | 55/2 |
|  | 8/0 | 20/0 | 32/0 | 44/0 | 56/0 |
|  | 9/0 | 21/0 | 33/0 | 45/1 | 57/0 |
|  | 10/0 | 22/0 | 34/0 | 46/0 | 58/0 |
|  | 11/0 | 23/0 | 35/0 | 47/0 | 59/0 |
|  | 12/0 | 24/0 | 36/0 | 48/0 | 60/0 |
| Total m |  |  |  | 1 | 2 |
| Total all | 1 |  | 3 | 1 | 2 |

con/tok = consultant/token; f = female; m = male.

**Table 3.2.83.** *Luba* 'bundle' (77 tokens)

|  | I con/tok | II con/tok | III con/tok | IV con/tok | V con/tok |
|---|---|---|---|---|---|
|  | 1/0 | 13/0 | 25/0 | 37/1 | 49/2 |
|  | 2/0 | 14/0 | 26/0 | 38/3 | 50/0 |
|  | 3/0 | 15/0 | 27/3 | 39/3 | 51/3 |
|  | 4/0 | 16/0 | 28/2 | 40/3 | 52/3 |
|  | 5/0 | 17/3 | 29/0 | 41/3 | 53/3 |
|  | 6/0 | 18/0 | 30/1 | 42/0 | 54/0 |
| Total f |  | 3 | 6 | 13 | 11 |
|  | 7/0 | 19/0 | 31/3 | 43/0 | 55/0 |
|  | 8/0 | 20/0 | 32/3 | 44/3 | 56/2 |
|  | 9/0 | 21/3 | 33/3 | 45/3 | 57/3 |
|  | 10/1 | 22/0 | 34/3 | 46/3 | 58/2 |
|  | 11/0 | 23/0 | 35/3 | 47/0 | 59/0 |
|  | 12/0 | 24/3 | 36/0 | 48/3 | 60/3 |
| Total m | 1 | 6 | 15 | 12 | 10 |
| Total all | 1 | 9 | 21 | 25 | 21 |

con/tok = consultant/token; f = female; m = male.

**Table 3.2.84.** *Luva* 'wooden dishes' (18 tokens)

|  | I<br>con/tok | II<br>con/tok | III<br>con/tok | IV<br>con/tok | V<br>con/tok |
|---|---|---|---|---|---|
|  | 1/0 | 13/0 | 25/0 | 37/0 | 49/0 |
|  | 2/0 | 14/0 | 26/0 | 38/0 | 50/0 |
|  | 3/0 | 15/0 | 27/0 | 39/0 | 51/0 |
|  | 4/0 | 16/0 | 28/0 | 40/0 | 52/0 |
|  | 5/0 | 17/3 | 29/0 | 41/4 | 53/0 |
|  | 6/0 | 18/0 | 30/0 | 42/0 | 54/3 |
| Total f |  | 3 |  | 4 | 3 |
|  | 7/0 | 19/0 | 31/0 | 43/0 | 55/0 |
|  | 8/1 | 20/0 | 32/0 | 44/3 | 56/0 |
|  | 9/0 | 21/0 | 33/0 | 45/0 | 57/0 |
|  | 10/0 | 22/0 | 34/0 | 46/0 | 58/0 |
|  | 11/0 | 23/0 | 35/0 | 47/0 | 59/3 |
|  | 12/0 | 24/0 | 36/0 | 48/1 | 60/0 |
| Total m | 1 |  |  | 4 | 3 |
| Total all | 1 | 3 |  | 8 | 6 |

con/tok = consultant/token; f = female; m = male.

**Table 3.2.85.** *Megwa* 'magic' (12 tokens)

|  | I<br>con/tok | II<br>con/tok | III<br>con/tok | IV<br>con/tok | V<br>con/tok |
|---|---|---|---|---|---|
|  | 1/0 | 13/0 | 25/0 | 37/0 | 49/0 |
|  | 2/0 | 14/0 | 26/0 | 38/3 | 50/0 |
|  | 3/0 | 15/0 | 27/1 | 39/0 | 51/0 |
|  | 4/0 | 16/0 | 28/1 | 40/2 | 52/0 |
|  | 5/0 | 17/0 | 29/0 | 41/0 | 53/0 |
|  | 6/0 | 18/0 | 30/0 | 42/0 | 54/0 |
| Total f |  |  | 2 | 5 |  |
|  | 7/0 | 19/0 | 31/0 | 43/0 | 55/0 |
|  | 8/0 | 20/0 | 32/0 | 44/0 | 56/0 |
|  | 9/0 | 21/0 | 33/3 | 45/1 | 57/0 |
|  | 10/0 | 22/0 | 34/0 | 46/0 | 58/0 |
|  | 11/0 | 23/0 | 35/0 | 47/0 | 59/0 |
|  | 12/0 | 24/1 | 36/0 | 48/0 | 60/0 |
| Total m |  | 1 | 3 | 1 |  |
| Total all |  | 1 | 5 | 6 |  |

con/tok = consultant/token; f = female; m = male.

**Table 3.2.86.** *Meila* `part of a song' (3 tokens)

|         | I con/tok | II con/tok | III con/tok | IV con/tok | V con/tok |
|---------|-----------|------------|-------------|------------|-----------|
|         | 1/0       | 13/0       | 25/0        | 37/0       | 49/0      |
|         | 2/0       | 14/0       | 26/0        | 38/0       | 50/0      |
|         | 3/0       | 15/0       | 27/0        | 39/0       | 51/0      |
|         | 4/0       | 16/0       | 28/0        | 40/0       | 52/0      |
|         | 5/0       | 17/0       | 29/0        | 41/0       | 43/0      |
|         | 6/0       | 18/0       | 30/0        | 42/0       | 54/0      |
| Total f |           |            |             |            |           |
|         | 7/0       | 19/0       | 31/0        | 43/0       | 55/3      |
|         | 8/0       | 20/0       | 32/0        | 44/0       | 56/0      |
|         | 9/0       | 21/0       | 33/0        | 45/0       | 57/0      |
|         | 10/0      | 22/0       | 34/0        | 46/0       | 58/0      |
|         | 11/0      | 23/0       | 35/0        | 47/0       | 59/0      |
|         | 12/0      | 24/0       | 36/0        | 48/0       | 60/0      |
| Total m |           |            |             |            | 3         |
| Total all |         |            |             |            | 3         |

con/tok = consultant/token; f = female; m = male.

**Table 3.2.87.** *Mmwa* `conical bundle' (23 tokens)

|         | I con/tok | II con/tok | III con/tok | IV con/tok | V con/tok |
|---------|-----------|------------|-------------|------------|-----------|
|         | 1/0       | 13/0       | 25/0        | 37/0       | 49/3      |
|         | 2/0       | 14/0       | 26/0        | 38/0       | 50/0      |
|         | 3/0       | 15/0       | 27/0        | 39/0       | 51/1      |
|         | 4/0       | 16/0       | 28/0        | 40/0       | 52/0      |
|         | 5/0       | 17/0       | 29/0        | 41/1       | 53/0      |
|         | 6/0       | 18/0       | 30/0        | 42/0       | 54/0      |
| Total f |           |            |             | 1          | 4         |
|         | 7/0       | 19/2       | 31/3        | 43/0       | 55/3      |
|         | 8/0       | 20/0       | 32/0        | 44/0       | 56/0      |
|         | 9/0       | 21/0       | 33/0        | 45/0       | 57/3      |
|         | 10/0      | 22/0       | 34/2        | 46/0       | 58/2      |
|         | 11/0      | 23/0       | 35/3        | 47/0       | 59/0      |
|         | 12/0      | 24/0       | 36/0        | 48/0       | 60/0      |
| Total m |           | 2          | 8           |            | 8         |
| Total all |         | 2          | 8           | 1          | 12        |

con/tok = consultant/token; f = female; m = male.

**Table 3.2.88.** *Na1* 'persons of female gender' (184 tokens)

|  | I<br>con/tok | II<br>con/tok | III<br>con/tok | IV<br>con/tok | V<br>con/tok |
|---|---|---|---|---|---|
|  | 1/3 | 13/6 | 25/6 | 37/3 | 49/3 |
|  | 2/1 | 14/3 | 26/3 | 38/3 | 50/3 |
|  | 3/1 | 15/3 | 27/3 | 39/3 | 51/3 |
|  | 4/4 | 16/3 | 28/3 | 40/3 | 52/3 |
|  | 5/4 | 17/3 | 29/3 | 41/3 | 53/3 |
|  | 6/3 | 18/3 | 30/3 | 42/3 | 54/3 |
| Total f | 16 | 21 | 21 | 18 | 18 |
|  | 7/3 | 19/3 | 31/3 | 43/3 | 55/3 |
|  | 8/3 | 20/3 | 32/3 | 44/3 | 56/3 |
|  | 9/1 | 21/3 | 33/3 | 45/3 | 57/3 |
|  | 10/3 | 22/3 | 34/3 | 46/3 | 58/3 |
|  | 11/5 | 23/3 | 35/3 | 47/3 | 59/3 |
|  | 12/3 | 24/3 | 36/3 | 48/3 | 60/3 |
| Total m | 18 | 18 | 18 | 18 | 18 |
| Total all | 34 | 39 | 39 | 36 | 36 |

con/tok = consultant/token; f = female; m = male.

**Table 3.2.89.** *Na2* 'animals' (279 tokens)

|  | I<br>con/tok | II<br>con/tok | III<br>con/tok | IV<br>con/tok | V<br>con/tok |
|---|---|---|---|---|---|
|  | 1/0 | 13/4 | 25/3 | 37/6 | 49/4 |
|  | 2/0 | 14/6 | 26/6 | 38/3 | 50/7 |
|  | 3/0 | 15/6 | 27/3 | 39/3 | 51/6 |
|  | 4/6 | 16/6 | 28/9 | 40/3 | 52/3 |
|  | 5/9 | 17/3 | 29/3 | 41/3 | 53/6 |
|  | 6/6 | 18/3 | 30/6 | 42/6 | 54/6 |
| Total f | 21 | 28 | 30 | 24 | 32 |
|  | 7/0 | 19/6 | 31/3 | 43/6 | 55/6 |
|  | 8/0 | 20/6 | 32/3 | 44/6 | 56/6 |
|  | 9/0 | 21/6 | 33/3 | 45/3 | 57/6 |
|  | 10/6 | 22/9 | 34/6 | 46/3 | 58/6 |
|  | 11/6 | 23/6 | 35/6 | 47/6 | 59/9 |
|  | 12/6 | 24/6 | 36/3 | 48/3 | 60/3 |
| Total m | 18 | 39 | 24 | 27 | 36 |
| Total all | 39 | 67 | 54 | 51 | 68 |

con/tok = consultant/token; f = female; m = male.

Classificatory Particles in Kilivila

**Table 3.2.90.** *Nigwa* `hole' (1 token)

|  | I con/tok | II con/tok | III con/tok | IV con/tok | V con/tok |
|---|---|---|---|---|---|
|  | 1/0 | 13/0 | 25/0 | 37/0 | 49/0 |
|  | 2/0 | 14/0 | 26/0 | 38/0 | 50/0 |
|  | 3/0 | 15/0 | 27/0 | 39/0 | 51/0 |
|  | 4/0 | 16/0 | 28/0 | 40/0 | 52/0 |
|  | 5/0 | 17/0 | 29/0 | 41/0 | 53/0 |
|  | 6/0 | 18/0 | 30/0 | 42/0 | 54/0 |
| Total f |  |  |  |  |  |
|  | 7/0 | 19/0 | 31/0 | 43/0 | 55/1 |
|  | 8/0 | 20/0 | 32/0 | 44/0 | 56/0 |
|  | 9/0 | 21/0 | 33/0 | 45/0 | 57/0 |
|  | 10/0 | 22/0 | 34/0 | 46/0 | 58/0 |
|  | 11/0 | 23/0 | 35/0 | 47/0 | 59/0 |
|  | 12/0 | 24/0 | 36/0 | 48/0 | 60/0 |
| Total m |  |  |  |  | 1 |
| Total all |  |  |  |  | 1 |

con/tok = consultant/token; f = female; m = male.

**Table 3.2.91.** *Nina* `part of a song' (3 tokens)

|  | I con/tok | II con/tok | III con/tok | IV con/tok | V con/tok |
|---|---|---|---|---|---|
|  | 1/0 | 13/0 | 25/0 | 37/0 | 49/0 |
|  | 2/0 | 14/0 | 26/0 | 38/0 | 50/0 |
|  | 3/0 | 15/0 | 27/0 | 39/0 | 51/0 |
|  | 4/0 | 16/0 | 28/0 | 40/0 | 52/0 |
|  | 5/0 | 17/0 | 29/0 | 41/0 | 53/0 |
|  | 6/0 | 18/0 | 30/0 | 42/0 | 54/0 |
| Total f |  |  |  |  |  |
|  | 7/0 | 19/0 | 31/0 | 43/0 | 55/3 |
|  | 8/0 | 20/0 | 32/0 | 44/0 | 56/0 |
|  | 9/0 | 21/0 | 33/0 | 45/0 | 57/0 |
|  | 10/0 | 22/0 | 34/0 | 46/0 | 58/0 |
|  | 11/0 | 23/0 | 35/0 | 47/0 | 59/0 |
|  | 12/0 | 24/0 | 36/0 | 48/0 | 60/0 |
| Total m |  |  |  |  | 3 |
| Total all |  |  |  |  | 3 |

con/tok = consultant/token; f = female; m = male.

**Table 3.2.92.** *Notu/nutu* `kneaded, dot, drop' (103 tokens)

|  | I<br>con/tok | II<br>con/tok | III<br>con/tok | IV<br>con/tok | V<br>con/tok |
|---|---|---|---|---|---|
|  | 1/0 | 13/0 | 25/0 | 37/0 | 49/3 |
|  | 2/0 | 14/0 | 26/3 | 38/3 | 50/1 |
|  | 3/0 | 15/0 | 27/3 | 39/0 | 51/3 |
|  | 4/0 | 16/0 | 28/3 | 40/3 | 52/0 |
|  | 5/0 | 17/3 | 29/3 | 41/3 | 53/3 |
|  | 6/0 | 18/0 | 30/3 | 42/3 | 54/3 |
| Total f |  | 3 | 15 | 12 | 13 |
|  | 7/0 | 19/1 | 31/3 | 43/3 | 55/3 |
|  | 8/0 | 20/1 | 32/3 | 44/3 | 56/3 |
|  | 9/0 | 21/3 | 33/3 | 45/3 | 57/3 |
|  | 10/0 | 22/1 | 34/3 | 46/3 | 58/3 |
|  | 11/1 | 23/0 | 35/3 | 47/0 | 59/3 |
|  | 12/2 | 24/3 | 36/3 | 48/0 | 60/3 |
| Total m | 3 | 9 | 18 | 12 | 18 |
| Total all | 3 | 12 | 33 | 24 | 31 |

con/tok = consultant/token; f = female; m = male.

**Table 3.2.93.** *Nunu* `corner of a garden' (22 tokens)

|  | I<br>con/tok | II<br>con/tok | III<br>con/tok | IV<br>con/tok | V<br>con/tok |
|---|---|---|---|---|---|
|  | 1/0 | 13/0 | 25/0 | 37/0 | 49/0 |
|  | 2/0 | 14/0 | 26/2 | 38/3 | 50/0 |
|  | 3/0 | 15/1 | 27/0 | 39/0 | 51/0 |
|  | 4/0 | 16/0 | 28/1 | 40/0 | 52/0 |
|  | 5/0 | 17/0 | 29/0 | 41/0 | 53/0 |
|  | 6/0 | 18/0 | 30/0 | 42/3 | 54/0 |
| Total f |  | 1 | 3 | 9 |  |
|  | 7/0 | 19/0 | 31/0 | 43/0 | 55/3 |
|  | 8/0 | 20/0 | 32/0 | 44/0 | 56/3 |
|  | 9/0 | 21/0 | 33/0 | 45/0 | 57/0 |
|  | 10/0 | 22/0 | 34/0 | 46/0 | 58/0 |
|  | 11/0 | 23/0 | 35/3 | 47/0 | 59/0 |
|  | 12/0 | 24/0 | 36/0 | 48/0 | 60/0 |
| Total m |  |  | 3 |  | 6 |
| Total all |  | 1 | 6 | 9 | 6 |

con/tok = consultant/token; f = female; m = male.

**Table 3.2.94.** *Peta* 'basket' (7 tokens)

| | I<br>con/tok | II<br>con/tok | III<br>con/tok | IV<br>con/tok | V<br>con/tok |
|---|---|---|---|---|---|
| | 1/0 | 13/0 | 25/0 | 37/0 | 49/0 |
| | 2/0 | 14/0 | 26/0 | 38/0 | 50/1 |
| | 3/0 | 15/0 | 27/2 | 39/0 | 51/0 |
| | 4/0 | 16/0 | 28/0 | 40/0 | 52/0 |
| | 5/0 | 17/0 | 29/0 | 41/0 | 53/0 |
| | 6/0 | 18/0 | 30/0 | 42/0 | 54/0 |
| Total f | | | 2 | | 1 |
| | 7/0 | 19/0 | 31/0 | 43/0 | 55/0 |
| | 8/0 | 20/0 | 32/0 | 44/0 | 56/0 |
| | 9/0 | 21/0 | 33/0 | 45/1 | 57/1 |
| | 10/0 | 22/0 | 34/0 | 46/0 | 58/0 |
| | 11/0 | 23/0 | 35/0 | 47/0 | 59/0 |
| | 12/0 | 24/0 | 36/1 | 48/0 | 60/1 |
| Total m | | | 1 | 1 | 2 |
| Total all | | | 3 | 1 | 3 |

con/tok = consultant/token; f = female; m = male.

**Table 3.2.95.** *Pila/pa* 'part, piece' (249 tokens)

| | I<br>con/tok | II<br>con/tok | III<br>con/tok | IV<br>con/tok | V<br>con/tok |
|---|---|---|---|---|---|
| | 1/0 | 13/3 | 25/6 | 37/4 | 49/6 |
| | 2/0 | 14/0 | 26/5 | 38/0 | 50/7 |
| | 3/0 | 15/8 | 27/7 | 39/8 | 51/7 |
| | 4/0 | 16/0 | 28/3 | 40/3 | 52/9 |
| | 5/0 | 17/6 | 29/0 | 41/8 | 53/0 |
| | 6/0 | 18/0 | 30/3 | 42/10 | 54/6 |
| Total f | | 17 | 24 | 33 | 35 |
| | 7/0 | 19/6 | 31/8 | 43/7 | 55/0 |
| | 8/0 | 20/3 | 32/9 | 44/10 | 56/4 |
| | 9/0 | 21/4 | 33/1 | 45/2 | 57/6 |
| | 10/7 | 22/9 | 34/8 | 46/3 | 58/9 |
| | 11/1 | 23/0 | 35/8 | 47/3 | 59/5 |
| | 12/3 | 24/0 | 36/6 | 48/9 | 60/9 |
| Total m | 11 | 22 | 40 | 34 | 33 |
| Total all | 11 | 39 | 64 | 67 | 68 |

con/tok = consultant/token; f = female; m = male.

**Table 3.2.96.** *Po'ula* 'plantation, grove' (53 tokens)

| | I<br>con/tok | II<br>con/tok | III<br>con/tok | IV<br>con/tok | V<br>con/tok |
|---|---|---|---|---|---|
| | 1/0 | 13/0 | 25/0 | 37/0 | 49/3 |
| | 2/0 | 14/0 | 26/0 | 38/0 | 50/0 |
| | 3/0 | 15/0 | 27/3 | 39/0 | 51/3 |
| | 4/0 | 16/0 | 28/3 | 40/3 | 52/0 |
| | 5/0 | 17/0 | 29/3 | 41/0 | 53/3 |
| | 6/0 | 18/0 | 30/0 | 42/0 | 54/3 |
| Total f | | | 9 | 3 | 12 |
| | 7/0 | 19/0 | 31/0 | 43/0 | 55/0 |
| | 8/0 | 20/0 | 32/3 | 44/0 | 56/0 |
| | 9/0 | 21/3 | 33/0 | 45/3 | 57/3 |
| | 10/0 | 22/0 | 34/0 | 46/3 | 58/3 |
| | 11/0 | 23/0 | 35/3 | 47/0 | 59/0 |
| | 12/0 | 24/0 | 36/3 | 48/2 | 60/3 |
| Total m | | 3 | 9 | 8 | 9 |
| Total all | | 3 | 18 | 11 | 21 |

con/tok = consultant/token; f = female; m = male.

**Table 3.2.97.** *Pwanina/pona* 'punctured, hole' (140 tokens)*

| | I<br>con/tok | II<br>con/tok | III<br>con/tok | IV<br>con/tok | V<br>con/tok |
|---|---|---|---|---|---|
| | 1/(3) | 13/0 | 25/(3) | 37/0 | 49/3 |
| | 2/0 | 14/0 | 26/3 | 38/2(1) | 50/0 |
| | 3/0 | 15/1 | 27/1(2) | 39/(1) | 51/(3) |
| | 4/3 | 16/1 | 28/3 | 40/(3) | 52/3 |
| | 5/0 | 17/3 | 29/2(1) | 41/2(1) | 53/(3) |
| | 6/1 | 18/3 | 30/1(2) | 42/(3) | 54/3 |
| Total f | 7 | 8 | 18 | 13 | 15 |
| | 7/(3) | 19/1 | 31/1(2) | 43/(3) | 55/2 |
| | 8/0 | 20/3 | 32/(3) | 44/3 | 56/3 |
| | 9/0 | 21/3 | 33/2(1) | 45/2(1) | 57/3 |
| | 10/3 | 22/3 | 34/3 | 46/3 | 58/3 |
| | 11/1 | 23/3 | 35/(3) | 47/3 | 59/3 |
| | 12/3 | 24/3 | 36/(3) | 48/3 | 60/3 |
| Total m | 10 | 16 | 18 | 18 | 17 |
| Total all | 17 | 24 | 36 | 31 | 32 |

con/tok = consultant/token; f = female; m = male.
*The number of tokens for the variant *pona* is given in parentheses.

**Table 3.2.98.** *Sa* 'nut bunch' (16 tokens)

|  | I<br>con/tok | II<br>con/tok | III<br>con/tok | IV<br>con/tok | V<br>con/tok |
|---|---|---|---|---|---|
|  | 1/0 | 13/0 | 25/0 | 37/0 | 49/3 |
|  | 2/0 | 14/0 | 26/0 | 38/0 | 50/0 |
|  | 3/0 | 15/0 | 27/0 | 39/0 | 51/3 |
|  | 4/0 | 16/0 | 28/0 | 40/0 | 52/0 |
|  | 5/0 | 17/0 | 29/0 | 41/0 | 53/0 |
|  | 6/0 | 18/0 | 30/0 | 42/0 | 54/0 |
| Total f |  |  |  |  | 6 |
|  | 7/0 | 19/0 | 31/3 | 43/0 | 55/0 |
|  | 8/0 | 20/1 | 32/0 | 44/0 | 56/0 |
|  | 9/0 | 21/0 | 33/0 | 45/3 | 57/0 |
|  | 10/1 | 22/0 | 34/0 | 46/0 | 58/0 |
|  | 11/0 | 23/2 | 35/0 | 47/0 | 59/0 |
|  | 12/0 | 24/0 | 36/0 | 48/0 | 60/0 |
| Total m | 1 | 3 | 3 | 3 |  |
| Total all | 1 | 3 | 3 | 3 | 6 |

con/tok = consultant/token; f = female; m = male.

**Table 3.2.99.** *Si* 'small bit' (15 tokens)

|  | I<br>con/tok | II<br>con/tok | III<br>con/tok | IV<br>con/tok | V<br>con/tok |
|---|---|---|---|---|---|
|  | 1/0 | 13/2 | 25/3 | 37/0 | 49/0 |
|  | 2/0 | 14/3 | 26/1 | 38/0 | 50/0 |
|  | 3/0 | 15/0 | 27/0 | 39/0 | 51/0 |
|  | 4/1 | 16/0 | 28/0 | 40/0 | 52/0 |
|  | 5/0 | 17/0 | 29/0 | 41/0 | 53/0 |
|  | 6/0 | 18/0 | 30/0 | 42/0 | 54/0 |
| Total f | 1 | 5 | 4 |  |  |
|  | 7/0 | 19/0 | 31/1 | 43/0 | 55/0 |
|  | 8/0 | 20/0 | 32/0 | 44/0 | 56/0 |
|  | 9/0 | 21/0 | 33/0 | 45/0 | 57/0 |
|  | 10/1 | 22/0 | 34/0 | 46/0 | 58/0 |
|  | 11/0 | 23/0 | 35/0 | 47/0 | 59/0 |
|  | 12/3 | 24/0 | 36/0 | 48/0 | 60/0 |
| Total m | 4 |  | 1 |  |  |
| Total all | 5 | 5 | 5 |  |  |

con/tok = consultant/token; f = female; m = male.

**Table 3.2.100.** *Sipu* 'sheaf' (88 tokens)

|           | I con/tok | II con/tok | III con/tok | IV con/tok | V con/tok |
|-----------|-----------|------------|-------------|------------|-----------|
|           | 1/0       | 13/0       | 25/0        | 37/0       | 49/3      |
|           | 2/0       | 14/0       | 26/1        | 38/3       | 50/1      |
|           | 3/0       | 15/1       | 27/3        | 39/0       | 51/3      |
|           | 4/0       | 16/0       | 28/3        | 40/3       | 52/0      |
|           | 5/0       | 17/0       | 9/3         | 41/3       | 53/3      |
|           | 6/0       | 18/0       | 30/0        | 42/3       | 54/3      |
| Total f   |           | 1          | 10          | 12         | 13        |
|           | 7/0       | 19/1       | 31/3        | 43/3       | 55/3      |
|           | 8/0       | 20/0       | 32/3        | 44/0       | 56/3      |
|           | 9/0       | 21/3       | 33/0        | 45/3       | 57/3      |
|           | 10/0      | 22/0       | 34/3        | 46/3       | 58/3      |
|           | 11/0      | 23/3       | 35/3        | 47/0       | 59/3      |
|           | 12/0      | 24/3       | 36/3        | 48/0       | 60/3      |
| Total m   |           | 10         | 15          | 9          | 18        |
| Total all |           | 11         | 25          | 21         | 31        |

con/tok = consultant/token; f = female; m = male.

**Table 3.2.101.** *Sisi* 'bough' (251 tokens)

|           | I con/tok | II con/tok | III con/tok | IV con/tok | V con/tok |
|-----------|-----------|------------|-------------|------------|-----------|
|           | 1/0       | 13/2       | 25/3        | 37/5       | 49/5      |
|           | 2/0       | 14/5       | 26/3        | 38/6       | 50/6      |
|           | 3/0       | 15/6       | 27/6        | 39/6       | 51/6      |
|           | 4/1       | 16/5       | 28/6        | 40/6       | 52/0      |
|           | 5/0       | 17/6       | 29/6        | 41/5       | 53/6      |
|           | 6/3       | 18/6       | 30/1        | 42/3       | 54/3      |
| Total f   | 4         | 30         | 25          | 31         | 26        |
|           | 7/0       | 19/6       | 31/5        | 43/6       | 55/6      |
|           | 8/0       | 20/6       | 32/6        | 44/6       | 56/6      |
|           | 9/0       | 21/6       | 33/6        | 45/6       | 57/5      |
|           | 10/3      | 22/3       | 34/6        | 46/3       | 58/4      |
|           | 11/2      | 23/6       | 35/6        | 47/6       | 59/3      |
|           | 12/3      | 24/5       | 36/3        | 48/6       | 60/6      |
| Total m   | 8         | 32         | 32          | 33         | 30        |
| Total all | 12        | 62         | 57          | 64         | 56        |

con/tok = consultant/token; f = female; m = male.

**Table 3.2.102.** *Siva* 'time' (3 tokens)

| | I con/tok | II con/tok | III con/tok | IV con/tok | V con/tok |
|---|---|---|---|---|---|
| | 1/0 | 13/0 | 25/0 | 37/0 | 49/0 |
| | 2/0 | 14/0 | 26/0 | 38/0 | 50/0 |
| | 3/0 | 15/0 | 27/0 | 39/0 | 51/0 |
| | 4/0 | 16/0 | 28/0 | 40/0 | 52/0 |
| | 5/0 | 17/0 | 29/0 | 41/0 | 53/0 |
| | 6/0 | 18/0 | 30/0 | 42/0 | 54/0 |
| Total f | | | | | |
| | 7/0 | 19/0 | 31/0 | 43/0 | 55/3 |
| | 8/0 | 20/0 | 32/0 | 44/0 | 56/0 |
| | 9/0 | 21/0 | 33/0 | 45/0 | 57/0 |
| | 10/0 | 22/0 | 34/0 | 46/0 | 58/0 |
| | 11/0 | 23/0 | 35/0 | 47/0 | 59/0 |
| | 12/0 | 24/0 | 36/0 | 48/0 | 60/0 |
| Total m | | | | | 3 |
| Total all | | | | | 3 |

con/tok = consultant/token; f = female; m = male.

**Table 3.2.103.** *Suya* 'batch of fish' (90 tokens)

| | I con/tok | II con/tok | III con/tok | IV con/tok | V con/tok |
|---|---|---|---|---|---|
| | 1/0 | 13/0 | 25/0 | 37/0 | 49/3 |
| | 2/0 | 14/0 | 26/0 | 38/3 | 50/0 |
| | 3/0 | 15/0 | 27/3 | 39/3 | 51/3 |
| | 4/0 | 16/0 | 28/0 | 40/3 | 52/3 |
| | 5/0 | 17/3 | 29/3 | 41/3 | 53/3 |
| | 6/0 | 18/3 | 30/3 | 42/3 | 54/3 |
| Total f | | 6 | 9 | 15 | 15 |
| | 7/0 | 19/0 | 31/0 | 43/3 | 55/0 |
| | 8/0 | 20/0 | 32/3 | 44/3 | 56/3 |
| | 9/0 | 21/0 | 33/3 | 45/3 | 57/3 |
| | 10/0 | 22/0 | 34/3 | 46/3 | 58/3 |
| | 11/0 | 23/0 | 35/3 | 47/3 | 59/0 |
| | 12/0 | 24/0 | 36/3 | 48/3 | 60/3 |
| Total m | | | 15 | 18 | 12 |
| Total all | | 6 | 24 | 33 | 27 |

con/tok = consultant/token; f = female; m = male.

**Table 3.2.104.** *Ta* 'basket' (152 tokens)

|           | I con/tok | II con/tok | III con/tok | IV con/tok | V con/tok |
|-----------|-----------|------------|-------------|------------|-----------|
|           | 1/0       | 13/3       | 25/3        | 37/2       | 49/3      |
|           | 2/0       | 14/1       | 26/3        | 38/3       | 50/2      |
|           | 3/0       | 15/3       | 27/1        | 39/3       | 51/3      |
|           | 4/3       | 16/3       | 28/3        | 40/3       | 52/3      |
|           | 5/4       | 17/3       | 29/3        | 41/3       | 53/3      |
|           | 6/3       | 18/3       | 30/3        | 42/3       | 54/3      |
| Total f   | 10        | 16         | 16          | 17         | 17        |
|           | 7/0       | 19/3       | 31/3        | 43/3       | 55/3      |
|           | 8/0       | 20/3       | 32/3        | 44/3       | 56/2      |
|           | 9/0       | 21/3       | 33/3        | 45/2       | 57/2      |
|           | 10/3      | 22/3       | 34/3        | 46/3       | 58/3      |
|           | 11/3      | 23/3       | 35/3        | 47/3       | 59/3      |
|           | 12/3      | 24/3       | 36/2        | 48/3       | 60/2      |
| Total m   | 9         | 18         | 17          | 17         | 15        |
| Total all | 19        | 34         | 33          | 34         | 32        |

con/tok = consultant/token; f = female; m = male.

**Table 3.2.105.** *Tam* 'sprouting (yams etc)' (70 tokens)

|           | I con/tok | II con/tok | III con/tok | IV con/tok | V con/tok |
|-----------|-----------|------------|-------------|------------|-----------|
|           | 1/0       | 13/0       | 25/0        | 37/0       | 49/0      |
|           | 2/0       | 14/0       | 26/3        | 38/8       | 50/0      |
|           | 3/0       | 15/0       | 27/0        | 39/0       | 51/6      |
|           | 4/0       | 16/0       | 28/6        | 40/3       | 52/0      |
|           | 5/0       | 17/0       | 29/0        | 41/0       | 53/0      |
|           | 6/0       | 18/0       | 30/0        | 42/3       | 54/8      |
| Total f   |           |            | 9           | 14         | 14        |
|           | 7/0       | 19/0       | 31/0        | 43/6       | 55/0      |
|           | 8/0       | 20/6       | 32/0        | 44/3       | 56/0      |
|           | 9/0       | 21/1       | 33/0        | 45/2       | 57/0      |
|           | 10/0      | 22/0       | 34/2        | 46/0       | 58/0      |
|           | 11/0      | 23/3       | 35/0        | 47/0       | 59/4      |
|           | 12/0      | 24/0       | 36/6        | 48/0       | 60/0      |
| Total m   |           | 10         | 8           | 11         | 4         |
| Total all |           | 10         | 17          | 25         | 18        |

con/tok = consultant/token; f = female; m = male.

**Table 3.2.106.** *Tetu* 'yams' (1 token)

|         | I<br>con/tok | II<br>con/tok | III<br>con/tok | IV<br>con/tok | V<br>con/tok |
|---------|--------------|---------------|----------------|---------------|--------------|
|         | 1/0 | 13/0 | 25/0 | 37/0 | 49/0 |
|         | 2/0 | 14/0 | 26/0 | 38/0 | 50/0 |
|         | 3/0 | 15/0 | 27/0 | 39/0 | 51/0 |
|         | 4/0 | 16/0 | 28/0 | 40/0 | 52/0 |
|         | 5/0 | 17/0 | 29/0 | 41/0 | 53/0 |
|         | 6/0 | 18/0 | 30/0 | 42/0 | 54/0 |
| Total f |     |      |      |      |      |
|         | 7/0 | 19/0 | 31/0 | 43/0 | 55/0 |
|         | 8/0 | 20/0 | 32/0 | 44/0 | 56/0 |
|         | 9/0 | 21/0 | 33/0 | 45/1 | 57/0 |
|         | 10/0 | 22/0 | 34/0 | 46/0 | 58/0 |
|         | 11/0 | 23/0 | 35/0 | 47/0 | 59/0 |
|         | 12/0 | 24/0 | 36/0 | 48/0 | 60/0 |
| Total m |     |      |      | 1    |      |
| Total all |   |      |      | 1    |      |

con/tok = consultant/token; f = female; m = male.

**Table 3.2.107.** *To/te* 'persons of male gender, human beings' (194 tokens)

|         | I<br>con/tok | II<br>con/tok | III<br>con/tok | IV<br>con/tok | V<br>con/tok |
|---------|--------------|---------------|----------------|---------------|--------------|
|         | 1/3 | 13/3 | 25/3 | 37/3 | 49/3 |
|         | 2/3 | 14/3 | 26/3 | 38/3 | 50/3 |
|         | 3/3 | 15/6 | 27/3 | 39/3 | 51/3 |
|         | 4/3 | 16/6 | 28/3 | 40/3 | 52/3 |
|         | 5/3 | 16/3 | 29/3 | 41/3 | 53/3 |
|         | 6/4 | 18/3 | 30/3 | 42/3 | 54/3 |
| Total f | 19 | 24 | 18 | 18 | 18 |
|         | 7/3 | 19/6 | 31/3 | 43/3 | 55/5 |
|         | 8/3 | 20/4 | 32/3 | 44/3 | 56/3 |
|         | 9/3 | 21/3 | 33/3 | 45/3 | 57/3 |
|         | 10/3 | 22/3 | 34/3 | 46/3 | 58/3 |
|         | 11/4 | 23/3 | 35/3 | 47/3 | 59/3 |
|         | 12/3 | 24/3 | 36/3 | 48/3 | 60/3 |
| Total m | 19 | 22 | 18 | 18 | 20 |
| Total all | 38 | 46 | 36 | 36 | 38 |

con/tok = consultant/token; f = female; m = male.

**Table 3.2.108.** *Tuta* 'time' (8 tokens)

|  | I con/tok | II con/tok | III con/tok | IV con/tok | V con/tok |
|---|---|---|---|---|---|
|  | 1/0 | 13/0 | 25/0 | 37/0 | 49/0 |
|  | 2/0 | 14/0 | 26/0 | 38/0 | 50/0 |
|  | 3/0 | 15/0 | 27/3 | 39/0 | 51/1 |
|  | 4/0 | 16/0 | 28/0 | 40/1 | 52/0 |
|  | 5/0 | 17/0 | 29/0 | 41/0 | 53/0 |
|  | 6/0 | 18/0 | 30/0 | 42/0 | 54/0 |
| Total f |  |  | 3 | 1 | 1 |
|  | 7/0 | 19/0 | 31/0 | 43/0 | 55/0 |
|  | 8/0 | 20/0 | 32/0 | 44/0 | 56/0 |
|  | 9/0 | 21/0 | 33/0 | 45/2 | 57/0 |
|  | 10/0 | 22/0 | 34/0 | 46/0 | 58/0 |
|  | 11/0 | 23/0 | 35/1 | 47/0 | 59/0 |
|  | 12/0 | 24/0 | 36/0 | 48/0 | 60/0 |
| Total m |  |  | 1 | 2 |  |
| Total all |  |  | 4 | 3 | 1 |

con/tok = consultant/token; f = female; m = male.

**Table 3.2.109.** *Utu* 'scrap, parts cut off' (308 tokens)

|  | I con/tok | II con/tok | III con/tok | IV con/tok | V con/tok |
|---|---|---|---|---|---|
|  | 1/0 | 13/4 | 25/7 | 37/4 | 49/5 |
|  | 2/0 | 14/4 | 26/9 | 38/16 | 50/4 |
|  | 3/0 | 15/2 | 27/13 | 39/5 | 51/6 |
|  | 4/2 | 16/2 | 28/7 | 40/8 | 52/6 |
|  | 5/0 | 17/7 | 29/6 | 41/6 | 53/6 |
|  | 6/2 | 18/2 | 30/24 | 42/6 | 54/3 |
| Total f | 4 | 21 | 66 | 45 | 30 |
|  | 7/0 | 19/1 | 31/6 | 43/13 | 55/1 |
|  | 8/0 | 20/1 | 32/6 | 44/9 | 56/9 |
|  | 9/0 | 21/2 | 33/9 | 45/6 | 57/6 |
|  | 10/3 | 22/1 | 34/9 | 46/8 | 58/2 |
|  | 11/0 | 23/0 | 35/9 | 47/9 | 59/3 |
|  | 12/1 | 24/6 | 36/9 | 48/6 | 60/7 |
| Total m | 4 | 11 | 48 | 51 | 28 |
| Total all | 8 | 32 | 114 | 96 | 58 |

con/tok = consultant/token; f = female; m = male.

**Table 3.2.110.** *Uva* 'span' (31 tokens)

| | I con/tok | II con/tok | III con/tok | IV con/tok | V con/tok |
|---|---|---|---|---|---|
| | 1/0 | 13/0 | 25/0 | 37/0 | 49/3 |
| | 2/0 | 14/0 | 26/0 | 38/1 | 50/0 |
| | 3/0 | 15/0 | 27/0 | 39/0 | 51/0 |
| | 4/0 | 16/0 | 28/0 | 40/0 | 52/3 |
| | 5/0 | 17/0 | 29/0 | 41/1 | 53/3 |
| | 6/0 | 18/0 | 30/0 | 42/0 | 54/1 |
| Total f | | | | 2 | 10 |
| | 7/0 | 19/0 | 31/3 | 43/0 | 55/0 |
| | 8/0 | 20/0 | 32/3 | 44/0 | 56/0 |
| | 9/0 | 21/0 | 33/0 | 45/3 | 57/0 |
| | 10/0 | 22/0 | 34/0 | 46/0 | 58/1 |
| | 11/0 | 23/0 | 35/3 | 47/0 | 59/2 |
| | 12/0 | 24/0 | 36/0 | 48/1 | 60/3 |
| Total m | | | 9 | 4 | 6 |
| Total all | | | 9 | 6 | 16 |

con/tok = consultant/token; f = female; m = male.

**Table 3.2.111.** *Va* 'door' (14 tokens)

| | I con/tok | II con/tok | III con/tok | IV con/tok | V con/tok |
|---|---|---|---|---|---|
| | 1/0 | 13/0 | 25/0 | 37/0 | 49/0 |
| | 2/0 | 14/0 | 26/0 | 38/0 | 50/0 |
| | 3/0 | 15/1 | 27/0 | 39/0 | 51/0 |
| | 4/1 | 16/6 | 28/0 | 40/0 | 52/0 |
| | 5/0 | 17/0 | 29/0 | 41/3 | 53/0 |
| | 6/0 | 18/0 | 30/0 | 42/3 | 54/0 |
| Total f | 1 | 7 | | 6 | |
| | 7/0 | 19/0 | 31/0 | 43/0 | 55/0 |
| | 8/0 | 20/0 | 32/0 | 44/0 | 56/0 |
| | 9/0 | 21/0 | 33/0 | 45/0 | 57/0 |
| | 10/0 | 22/0 | 34/0 | 46/0 | 58/0 |
| | 11/0 | 23/0 | 35/0 | 47/0 | 59/0 |
| | 12/0 | 24/0 | 36/0 | 48/0 | 60/0 |
| Total m | | | | | |
| Total all | 1 | 7 | | 6 | |

con/tok = consultant/token; f = female; m = male.

**Table 3.2.112.** *Vakala* 'belt' (2 tokens)

| | I<br>con/tok | II<br>con/tok | III<br>con/tok | IV<br>con/tok | V<br>con/tok |
|---|---|---|---|---|---|
| | 1/0 | 13/0 | 25/0 | 37/0 | 49/0 |
| | 2/0 | 14/0 | 26/0 | 38/0 | 50/0 |
| | 3/0 | 15/0 | 27/1 | 39/0 | 51/0 |
| | 4/0 | 16/0 | 28/0 | 40/0 | 52/0 |
| | 5/0 | 17/0 | 29/0 | 41/0 | 53/0 |
| | 6/0 | 18/0 | 30/0 | 42/0 | 54/0 |
| Total f | | | 1 | | |
| | 7/0 | 19/0 | 31/0 | 43/0 | 55/0 |
| | 8/0 | 20/0 | 32/0 | 44/0 | 56/0 |
| | 9/0 | 21/0 | 33/0 | 45/1 | 57/0 |
| | 10/0 | 22/0 | 34/0 | 46/0 | 58/0 |
| | 11/0 | 23/0 | 35/0 | 47/0 | 59/0 |
| | 12/0 | 24/0 | 36/0 | 48/0 | 60/0 |
| Total m | | | | 1 | |
| Total all | | | 1 | 1 | |

con/tok = consultant/token; f = female; m = male.

**Table 3.2.113.** *Vaya/vayo* 'door' (3 tokens)

| | I<br>con/tok | II<br>con/tok | III<br>con/tok | IV<br>con/tok | V<br>con/tok |
|---|---|---|---|---|---|
| | 1/0 | 13/0 | 25/0 | 37/0 | 49/0 |
| | 2/0 | 14/0 | 26/0 | 38/0 | 50/0 |
| | 3/0 | 15/0 | 27/0 | 39/0 | 51/0 |
| | 4/0 | 16/0 | 28/0 | 40/0 | 52/0 |
| | 5/0 | 17/0 | 29/0 | 41/0 | 53/0 |
| | 6/0 | 18/0 | 30/0 | 42/0 | 54/0 |
| Total f | | | | | |
| | 7/0 | 19/0 | 31/0 | 43/0 | 55/0 |
| | 8/0 | 20/0 | 32/0 | 44/0 | 56/0 |
| | 9/0 | 21/0 | 33/0 | 45/2 | 57/0 |
| | 10/0 | 22/0 | 34/1 | 46/0 | 58/0 |
| | 11/0 | 23/0 | 35/0 | 47/0 | 59/0 |
| | 12/0 | 24/0 | 36/0 | 48/0 | 60/0 |
| Total m | | | 1 | 2 | |
| Total all | | | 1 | 2 | |

con/tok = consultant/token; f = female; m = male.

**Table 3.2.114.** *Vili* `untwisted' (76 tokens)

|  | I<br>con/tok | II<br>con/tok | III<br>con/tok | IV<br>con/tok | V<br>con/tok |
|---|---|---|---|---|---|
|  | 1/0 | 13/0 | 25/0 | 37/0 | 49/1 |
|  | 2/0 | 14/0 | 26/3 | 38/0 | 50/0 |
|  | 3/0 | 15/0 | 27/0 | 39/5 | 51/3 |
|  | 4/0 | 16/0 | 28/2 | 40/3 | 52/3 |
|  | 5/0 | 17/0 | 29/3 | 41/1 | 53/3 |
|  | 6/0 | 18/0 | 30/3 | 42/5 | 54/3 |
| Total f |  | 11 | 14 | 13 |  |
|  | 7/0 | 19/1 | 31/3 | 43/1 | 55/0 |
|  | 8/0 | 20/0 | 32/0 | 44/0 | 56/3 |
|  | 9/0 | 21/0 | 33/3 | 45/3 | 57/2 |
|  | 10/0 | 22/0 | 34/3 | 46/3 | 58/3 |
|  | 11/0 | 23/0 | 35/3 | 47/1 | 59/0 |
|  | 12/0 | 24/0 | 36/3 | 48/3 | 60/3 |
| Total m | 1 | 15 | 11 | 11 |  |
| Total all | 1 | 26 | 25 | 24 |  |

con/tok = consultant/token; f = female; m = male.

**Table 3.2.115.** *Vosi* `song' (18 tokens)

|  | I<br>con/tok | II<br>con/tok | III<br>con/tok | IV<br>con/tok | V<br>con/tok |
|---|---|---|---|---|---|
|  | 1/0 | 13/0 | 25/0 | 37/0 | 49/0 |
|  | 2/0 | 14/0 | 26/1 | 38/3 | 50/0 |
|  | 3/0 | 15/0 | 27/1 | 39/0 | 51/2 |
|  | 4/0 | 16/0 | 28/0 | 40/3 | 52/0 |
|  | 5/0 | 17/0 | 29/0 | 41/1 | 53/0 |
|  | 6/0 | 18/0 | 30/0 | 42/0 | 54/0 |
| Total f |  |  | 2 | 7 | 2 |
|  | 7/0 | 19/0 | 31/0 | 43/0 | 55/0 |
|  | 8/0 | 20/0 | 32/0 | 44/0 | 56/0 |
|  | 9/0 | 21/0 | 33/3 | 45/3 | 57/0 |
|  | 10/0 | 22/0 | 34/0 | 46/0 | 58/0 |
|  | 11/0 | 23/0 | 35/1 | 47/0 | 59/0 |
|  | 12/0 | 24/0 | 36/0 | 48/0 | 60/0 |
| Total m |  |  | 4 | 3 |  |
| Total all |  |  | 6 | 10 | 2 |

con/tok = consultant/token; f = female; m = male.

**Table 3.2.116.** *Wela* 'batch of fish' (42 tokens)

| | I con/tok | II con/tok | III con/tok | IV con/tok | V con/tok |
|---|---|---|---|---|---|
| | 1/0 | 13/3 | 25/3 | 37/0 | 49/0 |
| | 2/0 | 14/0 | 26/0 | 38/3 | 50/1 |
| | 3/0 | 15/0 | 27/2 | 39/0 | 51/0 |
| | 4/0 | 16/0 | 28/0 | 40/3 | 52/0 |
| | 5/0 | 17/0 | 29/0 | 41/3 | 53/0 |
| | 6/0 | 18/0 | 30/0 | 42/0 | 54/0 |
| Total f | | 3 | 5 | 9 | 1 |
| | 7/0 | 19/0 | 31/6 | 43/0 | 55/3 |
| | 8/0 | 20/0 | 32/0 | 44/0 | 56/0 |
| | 9/0 | 21/0 | 33/0 | 45/3 | 57/0 |
| | 10/0 | 22/0 | 34/0 | 46/3 | 58/0 |
| | 11/0 | 23/0 | 35/0 | 47/0 | 59/0 |
| | 12/0 | 24/0 | 36/3 | 48/3 | 60/3 |
| Total m | | | 9 | 9 | 6 |
| Total all | | 3 | 14 | 18 | 7 |

con/tok = consultant/token; f = female; m = male.

**Table 3.2.117.** *Ya* 'flexible, thin' (273 tokens)

| | I con/tok | II con/tok | III con/tok | IV con/tok | V con/tok |
|---|---|---|---|---|---|
| | 1/0 | 13/7 | 25/6 | 37/0 | 49/13 |
| | 2/0 | 14/0 | 26/9 | 38/11 | 50/0 |
| | 3/0 | 15/11 | 27/1 | 39/9 | 51/12 |
| | 4/6 | 16/7 | 28/6 | 40/4 | 52/0 |
| | 5/2 | 17/12 | 29/3 | 41/4 | 53/0 |
| | 6/2 | 18/6 | 30/8 | 42/1 | 54/6 |
| Total f | 10 | 43 | 33 | 29 | 31 |
| | 7/0 | 19/3 | 31/0 | 43/3 | 55/4 |
| | 8/0 | 20/15 | 32/3 | 44/2 | 56/15 |
| | 9/0 | 21/7 | 33/2 | 45/5 | 57/6 |
| | 10/5 | 22/9 | 34/2 | 46/0 | 58/3 |
| | 11/4 | 23/5 | 35/3 | 47/9 | 59/4 |
| | 12/3 | 24/6 | 36/0 | 48/6 | 60/3 |
| Total m | 12 | 45 | 10 | 25 | 35 |
| Total all | 22 | 88 | 43 | 54 | 66 |

con/tok = consultant/token; f = female; m = male.

**Table 3.2.118.** *Yam1* 'day' (19 tokens)

|           | I con/tok | II con/tok | III con/tok | IV con/tok | V con/tok |
|-----------|-----------|------------|-------------|------------|-----------|
|           | 1/0       | 13/0       | 25/0        | 37/0       | 49/0      |
|           | 2/0       | 14/0       | 26/3        | 38/1       | 50/0      |
|           | 3/0       | 15/0       | 27/5        | 39/0       | 51/0      |
|           | 4/0       | 16/0       | 28/0        | 40/0       | 52/0      |
|           | 5/0       | 17/0       | 29/0        | 41/0       | 53/0      |
|           | 6/0       | 18/0       | 30/0        | 42/0       | 54/0      |
| Total f   |           |            | 8           | 1          |           |
|           | 7/0       | 19/0       | 31/3        | 43/0       | 55/0      |
|           | 8/0       | 20/0       | 32/0        | 44/0       | 56/0      |
|           | 9/0       | 21/1       | 33/0        | 45/3       | 57/0      |
|           | 10/0      | 22/0       | 34/0        | 46/0       | 58/0      |
|           | 11/0      | 23/0       | 35/0        | 47/0       | 59/0      |
|           | 12/0      | 24/3       | 36/0        | 48/0       | 60/0      |
| Total m   |           | 4          | 3           | 3          |           |
| Total all |           | 4          | 11          | 4          |           |

con/tok = consultant/token; f = female; m = male.

**Table 3.2.119.** *Yam2/yama/yuma* 'hand' (12 tokens)

|           | I con/tok | II con/tok | III con/tok | IV con/tok | V con/tok |
|-----------|-----------|------------|-------------|------------|-----------|
|           | 1/0       | 13/0       | 25/0        | 37/0       | 49/0      |
|           | 2/0       | 14/0       | 26/0        | 38/0       | 50/0      |
|           | 3/0       | 15/0       | 27/0        | 39/0       | 51/3      |
|           | 4/0       | 16/0       | 28/0        | 40/2       | 52/0      |
|           | 5/1       | 17/0       | 29/0        | 41/0       | 53/3      |
|           | 6/0       | 18/0       | 30/0        | 42/0       | 54/0      |
| Total f   | 1         |            |             | 2          | 6         |
|           | 7/0       | 19/0       | 31/0        | 43/0       | 55/1      |
|           | 8/0       | 20/0       | 32/0        | 44/0       | 56/0      |
|           | 9/0       | 21/2       | 33/0        | 45/0       | 57/0      |
|           | 10/0      | 22/0       | 34/0        | 46/0       | 58/0      |
|           | 11/0      | 23/0       | 35/0        | 47/0       | 59/0      |
|           | 12/0      | 24/0       | 36/0        | 48/0       | 60/0      |
| Total m   |           | 2          |             |            | 1         |
| Total all | 1         | 2          |             | 2          | 7         |

con/tok = consultant/token; f = female; m = male.

**Table 3.2.120.** *Yegila* 'name' (7 tokens)

| | I<br>con/tok | II<br>con/tok | III<br>con/tok | IV<br>con/tok | V<br>con/tok |
|---|---|---|---|---|---|
| | 1/0 | 13/0 | 25/0 | 37/0 | 49/0 |
| | 2/0 | 14/0 | 26/1 | 38/0 | 50/0 |
| | 3/0 | 15/0 | 27/3 | 39/0 | 51/0 |
| | 4/0 | 16/0 | 28/0 | 40/0 | 52/0 |
| | 5/0 | 17/0 | 29/0 | 41/0 | 53/0 |
| | 6/0 | 18/0 | 30/0 | 42/0 | 54/0 |
| Total f | | | 4 | | |
| | 7/0 | 19/0 | 31/0 | 43/0 | 55/0 |
| | 8/0 | 20/0 | 32/0 | 44/0 | 56/0 |
| | 9/0 | 21/0 | 33/0 | 45/0 | 57/0 |
| | 10/0 | 22/0 | 34/0 | 46/0 | 58/0 |
| | 11/0 | 23/0 | 35/2 | 47/0 | 59/0 |
| | 12/0 | 24/0 | 36/1 | 48/0 | 60/0 |
| Total m | | | 3 | | |
| Total all | | | 7 | | |

con/tok = consultant/token; f = female; m = male.

**Table 3.2.121.** *Yulai/yule* 'bundle of 4 things' (9 tokens)

| | I<br>con/tok | II<br>con/tok | III<br>con/tok | IV<br>con/tok | V<br>con/tok |
|---|---|---|---|---|---|
| | 1/0 | 13/0 | 25/0 | 37/0 | 49/0 |
| | 2/0 | 14/0 | 26/0 | 38/0 | 50/0 |
| | 3/0 | 15/0 | 27/0 | 39/0 | 51/0 |
| | 4/0 | 16/0 | 28/0 | 40/0 | 52/0 |
| | 5/0 | 17/0 | 29/0 | 41/0 | 53/0 |
| | 6/0 | 18/0 | 30/0 | 42/0 | 54/0 |
| Total f | | | | | |
| | 7/0 | 19/0 | 31/3 | 43/0 | 55/3 |
| | 8/0 | 20/0 | 32/0 | 44/0 | 56/0 |
| | 9/0 | 21/0 | 33/0 | 45/0 | 57/0 |
| | 10/0 | 22/0 | 34/0 | 46/0 | 58/0 |
| | 11/0 | 23/0 | 35/3 | 47/0 | 59/0 |
| | 12/0 | 24/0 | 36/0 | 48/0 | 60/0 |
| Total m | | | 6 | | 3 |
| Total all | | | 6 | | 3 |

con/tok = consultant/token; f = female; m = male.

**Table 3.2.122.** *Yuva* 'shoal' (4 tokens)

|  | I con/tok | II con/tok | III con/tok | IV con/tok | V con/tok |
|---|---|---|---|---|---|
|  | 1/0 | 13/0 | 25/0 | 37/0 | 49/0 |
|  | 2/0 | 14/0 | 26/0 | 38/0 | 50/0 |
|  | 3/0 | 15/0 | 27/0 | 39/0 | 51/0 |
|  | 4/0 | 16/0 | 28/0 | 40/0 | 52/0 |
|  | 5/0 | 17/0 | 29/0 | 41/0 | 53/0 |
|  | 6/0 | 18/0 | 30/3 | 42/0 | 54/0 |
| Total f |  |  | 3 |  |  |
|  | 7/0 | 19/0 | 31/0 | 43/0 | 55/1 |
|  | 8/0 | 20/0 | 32/0 | 44/0 | 56/0 |
|  | 9/0 | 21/0 | 33/0 | 45/0 | 57/0 |
|  | 10/0 | 22/0 | 34/0 | 46/0 | 58/0 |
|  | 11/0 | 23/0 | 35/0 | 47/0 | 59/0 |
|  | 12/0 | 24/0 | 36/0 | 48/0 | 60/0 |
| Total m |  |  |  |  | 1 |
| Total all |  |  | 3 |  | 1 |

con/tok = consultant/token; f = female; m = male.

**Table 3.2.123.** 0 'basketful of yams' (2 tokens)

|  | I con/tok | II con/tok | III con/tok | IV con/tok | V con/tok |
|---|---|---|---|---|---|
|  | 1/0 | 13/0 | 25/0 | 37/0 | 49/0 |
|  | 2/0 | 14/0 | 26/0 | 38/0 | 50/0 |
|  | 3/0 | 15/0 | 27/0 | 39/0 | 51/0 |
|  | 4/0 | 16/0 | 28/0 | 40/0 | 52/0 |
|  | 5/0 | 17/0 | 29/0 | 41/0 | 53/1 |
|  | 6/0 | 18/0 | 30/0 | 42/0 | 54/0 |
| Total f |  |  |  |  | 1 |
|  | 7/0 | 19/0 | 31/1 | 43/0 | 55/0 |
|  | 8/0 | 20/0 | 32/0 | 44/0 | 56/0 |
|  | 9/0 | 21/0 | 33/0 | 45/0 | 57/0 |
|  | 10/0 | 22/0 | 34/0 | 46/0 | 58/0 |
|  | 11/0 | 23/0 | 35/0 | 47/0 | 59/0 |
|  | 12/0 | 24/0 | 36/0 | 48/0 | 60/0 |
| Total m |  |  | 1 |  |  |
| Total all |  |  | 1 |  | 1 |

con/tok = consultant/token; f = female; m = male.

At this stage of the data presentation, I have assigned—provisionally—to all classifiers listed in the table headings the status "CP type." In the analyses that follow the data presentation, I will define the concept "CP type" and decide which of these classifiers are CP types proper and which are variants of CP types.

Table 3.2.124 presents the number of the provisionally defined types produced by each of the 60 informants; it also presents the average resulting from the subtraction of the average for the types produced by the female informants from the average for the types produced by the male informants (see also section 3.2.1).

What strikes even the casual reader of Tables 3.2.37 to 3.2.123 is the wide spectrum of tokens produced, ranging from 1 to 2,877. Table 3.2.125 lists the 87 CP types elicited, ordering them according to the number of tokens produced for each CP type. The table also presents percentages based on the calculus that (with the exception of the CP 0) 180 tokens of each CP type produced by 60 consultants with three word classes equals 100% of elicitation success. With the 87 types, the consultants produced 10,583 tokens altogether in the elicitation test.

**Table 3.2.124.** Consultants and number of CP types produced

|  | I con/ types | II con/ types | III con/ types | IV con/ types | V con/ types |
|---|---|---|---|---|---|
|  | 1/8 | 13/22 | 25/31 | 37/18 | 49/41 |
|  | 2/2 | 14/16 | 26/42 | 38/43 | 50/32 |
|  | 3/2 | 15/33 | 27/48 | 39/33 | 51/41 |
|  | 4/18 | 16/21 | 28/40 | 40/44 | 52/27 |
|  | 5/12 | 17/32 | 29/30 | 41/47 | 53/36 |
|  | 6/16 | 18/24 | 30/35 | 42/38 | 54/37 |
| Average f | 9.7 | 24.7 | 37.7 | 37.2 | 35.7 |
|  | 7/6 | 19/34 | 31/47 | 43/35 | 55/44 |
|  | 8/5 | 20/29 | 32/35 | 44/32 | 56/37 |
|  | 9/2 | 21/35 | 33/37 | 45/56 | 57/38 |
|  | 10/29 | 22/29 | 34/43 | 46/37 | 58/41 |
|  | 11/19 | 23/21 | 35/46 | 47/31 | 59/37 |
|  | 12/20 | 24/31 | 36/35 | 48/34 | 60/42 |
| Average m | 13.5 | 29.8 | 40.5 | 37.5 | 39.8 |
| Average all | 11.6 | 27.3 | 39.1 | 37.3 | 37.8 |
| Average m − Average f | 3.8 | 5.1 | 2.8 | 0.3 | 4.1 |

con/types = consultant/CP types; f = female; m = male.

**Table 3.2.125.** CP types and tokens—all consultants (elicitation test)

| CP Type | Tokens | Percent (180 tokens + = 100%) |
|---|---|---|
| *kwe* 'thing' | 2,877 | 1,598 |
| *ke* 'wood' | 1,919 | 1,066 |
| *kada* 'road' | 341 | 189 |
| *utu* 'scrap' | 308 | 171 |
| *na2* 'animals' | 279 | 155 |
| *ya* 'flexible' | 273 | 152 |
| *sisi* 'bough' | 251 | 139 |
| *pila* 'part' | 249 | 138 |
| *kweya* 'limb' | 215 | 119 |
| *to/te* 'male' | 194 | 108 |
| *na1* 'female' | 184 | 102 |
| *kasa* 'row' | 165 | 92 |
| *kumla* 'earth oven' | 162 | 90 |
| *kova* 'fire' | 159 | 88 |
| *buda/boda* 'group' | 156 | 87 |
| *ta* 'basket' | 152 | 84 |
| *gudi* 'child' | 142 | 79 |
| *iga* 'name' | 142 | 79 |
| *pwanina/pona* 'hole' | 140 | 78 |
| *kai* 'stone blade' | 136 | 76 |
| *ka'i* 'tooth' | 127 | 71 |
| *duli* 'cluster' | 108 | 60 |
| *giwi* 'cut' | 106 | 59 |
| *notu/nutu* 'kneaded, dot' | 103 | 57 |
| *kwoila* 'clay pot' | 96 | 53 |
| *kubila* 'land plot' | 94 | 52 |
| *deli* 'group' | 93 | 52 |
| *suya* 'batch of fish' | 90 | 50 |
| *gum* 'bit' | 88 | 49 |
| *sipu* 'sheaf' | 88 | 49 |
| *kabisi* 'compartment' | 78 | 43 |
| *luba* 'bundle' | 77 | 43 |
| *vili* 'untwisted' | 76 | 42 |
| *liku* 'compartment' | 71 | 39 |
| *tam* 'sprouting' | 70 | 39 |
| *bubu/bobu* 'cut across' | 68 | 38 |
| *bwa* 'tree' | 61 | 34 |
| *gula* 'heap' | 56 | 31 |
| *po'ula* 'grove' | 53 | 29 |

**Table 3.2.125.** *(continued)*

| CP Type | Tokens | Percent (180 tokens + = 100%) |
|---|---|---|
| *kapwa/kapo* 'parcel' | 46 | 26 |
| *wela* 'batch of fish' | 42 | 23 |
| *uva* 'span' | 31 | 17 |
| *bubwa* 'cut off' | 29 | 16 |
| *kudu* 'tooth' | 26 | 14 |
| *kwoya* 'mountain' | 26 | 14 |
| *mmwa* 'bundle' | 23 | 13 |
| *nunu* 'corner/garden' | 22 | 12 |
| *kabulo* 'sector' | 21 | 12 |
| *yam* 'day' | 19 | 11 |
| *vosi* 'song' | 18 | 10 |
| *luva* 'wooden dishes' | 18 | 10 |
| *sa* 'nut bunch' | 16 | 9 |
| *kaduyo* 'entrance' | 15 | 8 |
| *si* 'small bit' | 15 | 8 |
| *va* 'door' | 14 | 8 |
| *bogi* 'night' | 12 | 7 |
| *gili* 'row' | 12 | 7 |
| *megwa* 'magic' | 12 | 7 |
| *yama/yuma* 'hand' | 12 | 7 |
| *kudu* 'band of fibers' | 9 | 5 |
| *yulai* 'bundle of four things' | 9 | 5 |
| *tuta* 'time' | 8 | 4 |
| *kila* 'hands of bananas' | 7 | 4 |
| *lilo/lola* 'walk' | 7 | 4 |
| *peta* 'basket' | 7 | 4 |
| *yegila* 'name' | 7 | 4 |
| *bwalita* 'sea' | 6 | 3 |
| 0 'basketful of yams' | 2 | 3[†] |
| *duya* 'door' | 4 | 2 |
| *yuva* 'shoal' | 4 | 2 |
| *bukwa* 'fruit cluster' | 3 | 2 |
| *guba* 'bundle/taro' | 3 | 2 |
| *kabulo* 'point' | 3 | 2 |
| *kala* 'day' | 3 | 2 |
| *kavi* 'tool' | 3 | 2 |
| *meila* 'song/part' | 3 | 2 |
| *nina* 'song/part' | 3 | 2 |
| *siva* 'time' | 3 | 2 |

**Table 3.2.125.** *(continued)*

| CP Type | Tokens | Percent (180 tokens + = 100%) |
|---|---|---|
| *vaya/vayo* 'door' | 3 | 2 |
| *beku* 'stone blade' | 2 | 1 |
| *vakala* 'belt' | 2 | 1 |
| (*)*boma* '???' | 1 | 0.6 |
| *doba* 'skirt' | 1 | 0.6 |
| (*)*iki* '???' | 1 | 0.6 |
| (*)*kava* '???' | 1 | 0.6 |
| *nigwa* 'hole' | 1 | 0.6 |
| *tetu* 'yams' | 1 | 0.6 |

[†]The CP 0 is only produced with numerals to count baskets of yams; thus, in connection with this CP, 60 tokens produced by 60 consultants during the test would total 100% of elicitation success.

### 3.2.2.2 CP Types/Tokens Produced Versus CP Types Expected During the Elicitation Test

The tables presented so far show that a number of CPs were produced by the consultants as a response to stimuli that should have elicited other CPs. Tables 3.2.126 to 3.2.212 present all the CP types produced by the consultants of the five age groups during the elicitation test allocating the tokens of each CP type produced to the CP type or types actually expected. When necessary, table footnotes provide the following information: first, which other CP(s) were produced when the CP under consideration was expected and second brief comments on the CP produced and/or on those reactions of the consultants that were idiosyncratic, dubious, or difficult to understand.

If we compare the data in these tables with the expectations that were the basis for compiling the questionnaire, we note the following:

1. Four types of expected CPs were not realized by the consultants during the elicitation test:
   a. *Lila* 'bough, branch, leaf'. The CP *ke* 'wood, long objects' (I–V; 125 tokens) was produced instead.
   b. *Oyla* 'string/fish.' The CPs *ke* 'wood, inanimates' (I–III, V; 34 tokens), *ka'i** 'stone blade' (II; 3 tokens), *kwe* 'thing' (II–IV; 14 tokens), *na2* 'animals' (II–V; 53 tokens), *pila** 'part' (II, V; 2 tokens), and *wela* 'batch of fish' (II–V; 30 tokens) were produced instead.
   c. *Siwa* 'sea portions.' The CPs *bwalita* 'sea' (III, IV; 6 tokens), *kwe* 'thing' (I–V; 137 tokens), and *utu** 'scrap' (III; 3 tokens) were produced instead.
   d. *Vilo* 'place, village.' The CPs *kada** 'road' (II; 2 tokens) and *kwe* 'thing' (I–V; 153 tokens) were produced instead.
2. A number of CPs that were produced were not expected; Table 3.2.213 lists these CPs. Moreover, it should be noted that consultants of age

group IV produced the CP *luva* in its meaning 'tied bundle' instead of the expected CPs *bukwa* (2 tokens), *mmwa* (3 tokens), and *sa* (3 tokens). The production of the CP *luva* in its meaning 'tied bundle' was not expected, either.

3. The data documenting dubious cases of CP production are presented in Table 3.2.214. These cases of dubious (including not acceptable) CP production are distributed across the sexes as shown in Table 3.2.215.

**Table 3.2.126.** *Beku* 'stone blade'

| | Tokens of CP *beku* produced by age group | | | | | |
|---|---|---|---|---|---|---|
| CP expected | I | II | III | IV | V | Tokens total |
| *kai* 'stone blade' | | | 1 | 1 | | 2 |

*Beku* is a repeater; the production of this CP was not expected.

**Table 3.2.127.** *Bogi* 'night'

| | Tokens of CP *bogi* produced by age group | | | | | |
|---|---|---|---|---|---|---|
| CP expected | I | II | III | IV | V | Tokens total |
| bogi 'night' | | 2 | 8 | 2 | | 12 |

1. CP produced, *bogi* expected: *kwe* (I–V; 138 tokens).
2. *Bogi* is a repeater.

**Table 3.2.128.** *Boma* '???'

| | Tokens of CP (*) *boma* produced by age group | | | | | |
|---|---|---|---|---|---|---|
| CP expected | I | II | III | IV | V | Tokens total |
| utu 'scrap' | | | 1 | | | 1 |

There is no CP *boma* in Kilivila.

**Table 3.2.129.** *Bubu/bobu* 'block cut off/cut across'

| | Tokens of CP *bubu/bobu* produced by age group | | | | | |
|---|---|---|---|---|---|---|
| CP expected | I | II | III | IV | V | Tokens total |
| *bubu/bobu* 'cut across' | | 7 | 23 | 13 | 25 | 68 |

CPs produced, *bubu/bobu* expected: *bubwa* (IV; 2 tokens), *buda** (II, III; 4 tokens), *bwa* (IV; 3 tokens), *gula** (II,III; 3 tokens), *ke* (I, III–V; 18 tokens), *kudu1** (V; 1 token), *kwe* (II–V; 28 tokens), *na1** (I; 1 token), *ya* (I, II; 4 tokens).

**Table 3.2.130.** *Bubwa* 'parts cut off'

| CP expected | Tokens of CP *bubwa* produced by age group | | | | | Tokens total |
|---|---|---|---|---|---|---|
| | I | II | III | IV | V | |
| *bubwa* 'cut off' | | | 6 | 5 | 5 | 16 |
| *utu* 'scrap' | 1 | | 1 | 1 | 5 | 8 |
| *kabulol* 'point' | | | 1 | | | (1*) |
| *bubu* 'cut across' | | | | 2 | | 2 |
| *vili* 'untwisted' | | | | 2 | | (2*) |
| Total | 1 | | 8 | 10 | 10 | |

1. CPs produced, *bubwa* expected: *bwa* (I–V; 16 tokens), *ke* (I–V; 130 tokens), *kwe* (IV; 1 token), *utu* (IV; 2 tokens).
2. I can justify the production of the CP *bubwa* as a response to the stimulus presented to elicit the CP *kabulol*, assuming that the consultant thought of a 'protruding piece of wood that is cut off'.

**Table 3.2.131.** *Buda/boda/budu* 'group, team'

| CP expected | Tokens of CP *buda/boda/budu* produced by age group | | | | | Tokens total |
|---|---|---|---|---|---|---|
| | I | II | III | IV | V | |
| *buda/boda/budu* 'group' | 3 | 7 | 24 | 12 | 17 | 63 |
| *yuva* 'shoal' | 5 | 11 | 25 | 18 | 27 | 86 |
| *bubu* 'cut across' | | 1 | 3 | | | (4*) |
| *gum* 'bit' | | 1 | | | | (1*) |
| *gula* 'heap, group' | | | | 1 | | 1 |
| *mmwa* 'conical bundle' | | | | 1 | | 1 |
| Total | 8 | 20 | 52 | 32 | 44 | |

1. CP produced, *buda* expected: *kwe* (I–V; 85 tokens).
2. See table 3.2.166 below; see the comments on dubious (*) CP usage (see section 3.2.1).

**Table 3.2.132.** *Bukwa* 'fruit cluster'

| CP expected | Tokens of CP *bukwa* produced by age group | | | | | Tokens total |
|---|---|---|---|---|---|---|
| | I | II | III | IV | V | |
| *bukwa* 'fruit cluster' | 3 | | | | | 3 |

CPs produced, *bukwa* expected: *ke* (I–V; 122 tokens), *kwe* (II, III; 4 tokens), *luva** (IV; 2 tokens), *po'ula* (V; 1 token), *sa* (IV; 3 tokens), *ya* (II, IV, V; 14 tokens).

**Table 3.2.133.** *Bwa* 'tree, wood'

| CP expected | Tokens of CP *bwa* produced by age group | | | | | Tokens total |
| --- | --- | --- | --- | --- | --- | --- |
| | I | II | III | IV | V | |
| *utu* 'scrap' | 3 | 11 | 1 | 1 | 4 | 20 |
| *bubwa* 'cut off' | 1 | 2 | 10 | 3 | | 16 |
| *bwa* 'tree, wood' | 2 | 2 | | | 1 | 5 |
| *kabisi* 'compartment' | 3 | 1 | | | | 4 |
| *kabulo1* 'point' | | 2 | 1 | | | 3 |
| *ke* 'wood' | 1 | 1 | | | | 2 |
| *vili* 'untwisted' | | 1 | | | 1 | 2 |
| *si* 'small bit' | | 6 | | | | 6 |
| *bubu* 'cut across' | | | | 3 | | 3 |
| Total | 10 | 26 | 12 | 7 | 6 | |

1. CP produced, *bwa* expected: *ke* (I–V; 155 tokens).
2. In some cases, this CP was produced because some consultants referred only to the noun and not to its modification within the noun phrases presented as stimuli.

**Table 3.2.134.** *Bwalita* 'sea'

| CP expected | Tokens of CP *bwalita* produced by age group | | | | | Tokens total |
| --- | --- | --- | --- | --- | --- | --- |
| | I | II | III | IV | V | |
| *siwa* 'sea portions' | | | 2 | 4 | | 6 |

The CP *bwalita* is a repeater; the production of this CP was not expected.

**Table 3.2.135.** *Deli* 'group on the move'

| CP expected | Tokens of CP *deli* produced by age group | | | | | Tokens total |
| --- | --- | --- | --- | --- | --- | --- |
| | I | II | III | IV | V | |
| *deli* 'group' | | 4 | 30 | 23 | 36 | 93 |

1. CPs produced, *deli* expected: *kasa* (III; 2 tokens), *kwe* (I–IV; 37 tokens), *na1* (I; 1 token), *tolte* (I, II; 11 tokens).
2. See also Tables 3.2.156 (*kasa*) and 3.2.166 (*kwe*).

**Table 3.2.136.** *Doba* '(grass) skirt'

| CP expected | Tokens of CP *doba* produced by age group | | | | | Tokens total |
|---|---|---|---|---|---|---|
| | I | II | III | IV | V | |
| *kudu* 'band of fibres' | | | | 1 | | 1 |

The CP *doba* is a repeater; the production of this CP was not expected.

**Table 3.2.137.** *Duli* 'cluster, bundle'

| CP expected | Tokens of CP *duli* produced by age group | | | | | Tokens total |
|---|---|---|---|---|---|---|
| | I | II | III | IV | V | |
| *duli* 'cluster' | 3 | 15 | 33 | 27 | 30 | 108 |

CPs produced, *duli* expected: *ke* (II; 6 tokens), *kwe* (I, II, IV; 29 tokens).

**Table 3.2.138.** *Duya* 'door, entrance'

| CP expected | Tokens of CP *duya* produced by age group | | | | | Tokens total |
|---|---|---|---|---|---|---|
| | I | II | III | IV | V | |
| *duya* 'door, entrance' | | | 3 | | 1 | 4 |

CPs produced, *duya* expected: *kada* (I–V; 70 tokens), *ke* (II; 5 tokens), *kwe* (II, V; 21 tokens), *ya* (II, IV, V; 28 tokens), *na1** (III; 3 tokens), *va* (II, IV; 10 tokens), *vaya/vayo* (III, IV; 2 tokens), *kaduyo* (III, V; 8 tokens).

**Table 3.2.139.** *Gili* 'row'

| CP expected | Tokens of CP *gili* produced by age group | | | | | Tokens total |
|---|---|---|---|---|---|---|
| | I | II | III | IV | V | |
| *gili* 'row' | | | 3 | 1 | 8 | 12 |

CPs produced, *gili* expected: *kasa* (II, III; 3 tokens), *kwe* (II–V; 29 tokens), *utu** (II; 1 token), *vili** (IV; 3 tokens), *ya* (I–V; 101 tokens), *vakala* (III, IV; 2 tokens).

**Table 3.2.140.** *Giwi* 'cut'

| CP expected | Tokens of CP *giwi* produced by age group | | | | | Tokens total |
|---|---|---|---|---|---|---|
| | I | II | III | IV | V | |
| *giwi* 'cut' | | 17 | 33 | 31 | 25 | 106 |

CPs produced, *giwi* expected: *kasa*\* (I; 3 tokens), *ke* (I–V; 16 tokens), *kwe* (II, IV, V; 11 tokens), *luva*\* (II; 3 tokens), *na2*\* (II; 1 token), *ta*\* (I; 1 token).

**Table 3.2.141.** *Guba* 'bundle of taro'

| CP expected | Tokens of CP *guba* produced by age group | | | | | Tokens total |
|---|---|---|---|---|---|---|
| | I | II | III | IV | V | |
| *mmwa* 'conical bundle' | | | | | 3 | 3 |

The production of the CP *guba* was not expected.

**Table 3.2.142.** *Gudi* 'child'

| CP expected | Tokens of CP *gudi* produced by age group | | | | | Tokens total |
|---|---|---|---|---|---|---|
| | I | II | III | IV | V | |
| *gudi* 'child' | 7 | 30 | 36 | 33 | 36 | 142 |

**Table 3.2.143.** *Gula* 'heap, group'

| CP expected | Tokens of CP *gula* produced by age group | | | | | Tokens total |
|---|---|---|---|---|---|---|
| | I | II | III | IV | V | |
| *gula* 'heap, group' | | 6 | 11 | 20 | 13 | 50 |
| *bubu* 'cut across' | | 2 | 1 | | | (3\*) |
| *po'ula* 'grove' | | | 3 | | | 3 |
| Total | | 8 | 15 | 20 | 13 | |

1. CPs produced, *gula* expected: *buda* (IV; 1 token), *kwe* (I–V; 82 tokens), *tam* (II–V; 28 tokens).
2. See the comments on dubious (\*) CP usage (see section 3.2.1).

**Table 3.2.144.** *Gum* 'bit, small piece'

| CP expected | Tokens of CP *gum* produced by age group | | | | | Tokens total |
|---|---|---|---|---|---|---|
| | I | II | III | IV | V | |
| *gum* 'bit, small piece' | | 9 | 30 | 28 | 21 | 88 |

CPs produced, *gum* expected: *buda*\* (II; 1 token), *kasa*\* (II; 3 tokens), *ke* (IV, V; 6 tokens), *kwe* (I, II, IV, V; 22 tokens), *na2*\* (I; 3 tokens), *utu* (II; 1 token), *ya* (II; 6 tokens).

**Table 3.2.145.** *Iga* 'name'

| CP expected | Tokens of CP *iga* produced by age group | | | | | Tokens total |
|---|---|---|---|---|---|---|
| | I | II | III | IV | V | |
| *iga* 'name' | 10 | 34 | 29 | 33 | 36 | 142 |

CPs produced, *iga* expected: *kasa*\* (I; 1 token), *kwe* (I, IV; 6 tokens), *yegila* (III; 7 tokens).

**Table 3.2.146.** *Iki* '???'

| CP expected | Tokens of CP *\*iki* produced by age group | | | | | Tokens total |
|---|---|---|---|---|---|---|
| | I | II | III | IV | V | |
| *nina* 'part of a song' | | 1 | | | | 1 |

There is no CP *iki* in Kilivila; it may be that the consultant wanted to produce the CP *igi* 'wind': if we assume that the consultant wanted to refer to wind or rain magic as a reaction to the stimulus *megwa* 'magic', we may understand this reaction, although it is highly idiosyncratic (see also G. Senft 1985c).

**Table 3.2.147.** *Kabisi* 'compartment of a foodhouse'

| CP expected | Tokens of CP *kabisi* produced by age group | | | | | Tokens total |
|---|---|---|---|---|---|---|
| | I | II | III | IV | V | |
| *kabisi* 'compartment' | | 10 | 23 | 23 | 22 | 78 |

CPs produced, *kabisi* expected: *bwa* (I, II; 4 tokens), *ke* (I–V; 53 tokens), *kwe* (I–IV; 10 tokens), *nunu*\* (II; 1 token), *pila* (I; 1 token), *utu* (II, III; 4 tokens).

**Table 3.2.148.** *Kabulo1* 'protuberances, point'

| CP expected | Tokens of CP *kabulo1* produced by age group | | | | | Tokens total |
|---|---|---|---|---|---|---|
| | I | II | III | IV | V | |
| *nunu* 'corner of a garden' | | | | | 3 | (*3) |

1. CPs produced, *kabulo1* expected: *bubwa** (III; 1 token), *bwa* (II, III; 3 tokens), *ke* (I–V; 107 tokens), *utu* (II–V; 38 tokens).

2. The CP *kabulo* was produced as a response to the stimulus presented to elicit the expected CP *nunu*; this can be explained by assuming that the speaker either (1) mixed up the CPs *kabulo1* and *kabulu/kabulo2*, extending the meaning of *kabulo2* from 'village sector' to 'sector in general' and then responding to the stimulus presented to elicit the CP *nunu* with the CP *kabulo2* in its extended meaning, or (2) wanted to use the meaning 'point' of this CP to refer to a 'corner of a graden'.

**Table 3.2.149.** *Kabulu/kabulo2* 'village sector'

| CP expected | Tokens of CP *kabulu/kabulo2* produced by age group | | | | | Tokens total |
|---|---|---|---|---|---|---|
| | I | II | III | IV | V | |
| *kabulu* 'village sector' | | 2 | 10 | 2 | 7 | 21 |

CPs produced, *kabulu* expected: *kada** (III; 3 tokens), *ke* (I–V; 92 tokens), *kwe* (II–V; 40 tokens), *utu* (II; 1 token).

**Table 3.2.150.** *Kada/keda* 'road, track'

| CP expected | Tokens of CP *kada/keda* produced by age group | | | | | Tokens total |
|---|---|---|---|---|---|---|
| | I | II | III | IV | V | |
| *kada* 'road, track' | 8 | 36 | 36 | 36 | 36 | 152 |
| *duya* 'door, entrance' | 5 | 20 | 21 | 14 | 10 | 70 |
| *kaduyo* 'entrance, door' | 4 | 22 | 33 | 28 | 26 | 113 |
| *lilo* 'walk, journey' | | 1 | | | | (1*) |
| *vilo* 'place, village' | | 2 | | | | (2*) |
| *kabulu* 'village sector' | | | 3 | | | (3*) |
| Total | 17 | 81 | 93 | 78 | 72 | |

See the comments on dubious (*) CP usage (see section 3.2.1).

**Table 3.2.151.** *Kaduyo/kaduya* 'entrance, door'

| CP expected | Tokens of CP *kaduyo* produced by age group | | | | | Tokens total |
|---|---|---|---|---|---|---|
| | I | II | III | IV | V | |
| *kaduyo* 'door, entrance' | 1 | 1 | 3 | 1 | 1 | 7 |
| *duya* 'door, entrance' | | | 5 | | 3 | 8 |
| Total | 1 | 1 | 8 | 1 | 4 | |

CPs produced, *kaduyo* expected: *kada* (I–V; 113 tokens), *ke* (II; 4 tokens), *kwe* (II, V; 4 tokens), *ya* (II, IV, V; 17 tokens), *va* (I, II; 4 tokens), *vaya/vayo* (IV; 1 token).

**Table 3.2.152.** *Kai* 'stone blade'

| CP expected | Tokens of CP *kai* produced by age group | | | | | Tokens total |
|---|---|---|---|---|---|---|
| | I | II | III | IV | V | |
| *kai* 'stone blade' | 3 | 27 | 35 | 35 | 36 | 136 |

CPs produced, *kai* expected: *kwe* (II; 2 tokens), *na1** (II; 1 token), *sisi** (II; 2 tokens), *beku* (III, IV; 2 tokens).

**Table 3.2.153.** *Ka'i* 'tooth'

| CP expected | Tokens of CP *ka'i* produced by age group | | | | | Tokens total |
|---|---|---|---|---|---|---|
| | I | II | III | IV | V | |
| *kudu2* 'tooth' | 13 | 27 | 28 | 26 | 30 | 124 |
| *oyla* 'string' | | 3 | | | | 3* |
| Total | 13 | 30 | 28 | 26 | 30 | |

The production of the CP *ka'i* was not expected, see the comments on dubious (*) CP usage (see section 3.2.1).

**Table 3.2.154.** *Kala* 'day'

| CP expected | Tokens of CP *kala* produced by age group | | | | | Tokens total |
|---|---|---|---|---|---|---|
| | I | II | III | IV | V | |
| *kala* 'day' | | | | | 3 | 3 |

CPs produced, *kala* expected: *kwe* (I–V; 144 tokens), *tuta* (IV; 1 token), *yam* (III, IV; 5 tokens).

**Table 3.2.155.** *Kapwa* 'bundle/parcel wrapped up'

| | Tokens of CP *kapwa* produced by age group | | | | | |
|---|---|---|---|---|---|---|
| CP expected | I | II | III | IV | V | Tokens total |
| *kapwa* 'parcel' | 5 | 18 | 6 | 6 | 11 | 46 |

CPs produced, *kapwa* expected: *kwe* (I–V; 30 tokens), *luba* (I–V; 77 tokens).

**Table 3.2.156.** *Kasa* 'row, line'

| | Tokens of CP *kasa* produced by age group | | | | | |
|---|---|---|---|---|---|---|
| CP expected | I | II | III | IV | V | Tokens total |
| *kasa* 'row, line' | 10 | 24 | 36 | 33 | 36 | 139 |
| *meila* 'song/part' | | | 3 | 4 | 3 | 10 |
| *gili* 'row' | | 1 | 2 | | | 3 |
| *iga* 'name' | 1 | | | | | (1*) |
| *giwi* 'cut' | | 3 | | | | (3*) |
| *gum* 'bit' | | 3 | | | | (3*) |
| *yuva* 'shoal' | | 1 | | | | (1*) |
| *nina* 'song/part' | | | 3 | | | 3 |
| *deli* 'group' | | | 2 | | | 2 |
| Total | 11 | 32 | 46 | 37 | 39 | |

1. CPs produced, *kasa* expected: *ke* (I; 2 tokens), *kwe* (II, IV; 9 tokens).
2. See the comments on dubious (*) CP usage (see section 3.2.1); the CP *kasa* was produced as a response to the stimuli presented to elicit the expected CPs *meila*, *nina*, and *deli*; assuming that the consultants thought of 'a line as part of a song' and of 'a group on the move, walking one behind the other in a row', we can justify the production of this CP.

**Table 3.2.157.** *Kava* '???'

| | Tokens of CP *\*kava* produced by age group | | | | | |
|---|---|---|---|---|---|---|
| CP expected | I | II | III | IV | V | Tokens total |
| *kwoila* 'clay pot' | | | | | 1 | 1 |

There is no CP *kava* in Kilivila.

**Table 3.2.158.** *Kavi* 'tool'

| | Tokens of CP *kavi* produced by age group | | | | | |
|---|---|---|---|---|---|---|
| CP expected | I | II | III | IV | V | Tokens total |
| *kavi* 'tool' | | | | | 3 | 3 |

CPs produced, *kavi* expected: *ke* (II; 7 tokens), *kwe* (II; 6 tokens), *pila*\* (I; 1 token), *utu*\* (II; 1 token).

**Table 3.2.159.** *Ke1-4* 'wood (1), long objects (2), inanimate (3), fire' (4)

| | Tokens of CP *ke* produced by age group | | | | | |
|---|---|---|---|---|---|---|
| CP expected | I | II | III | IV | V | Tokens total |
| *ke* 'wood' | 23 | 35 | 36 | 36 | 36 | 166 |
| *bubwa* 'cut off' | 12 | 36 | 20 | 31 | 31 | 130 |
| *bukwa* 'fruit cluster' | 9 | 24 | 33 | 25 | 31 | 122 |
| *bwa* 'tree' | 14 | 34 | 36 | 36 | 35 | 155 |
| *giwi* 'cut' | 4 | 2 | 3 | 1 | 6 | 16 |
| *kabulo* 'point' | 8 | 32 | 12 | 26 | 29 | 107 |
| *kabulu* 'sector' | 15 | 21 | 12 | 26 | 18 | 92 |
| *kila* 'hands/bananas' | 9 | 33 | 36 | 29 | 35 | 142 |
| *lila* 'bough' | 8 | 36 | 36 | 36 | 36 | 152 |
| *luva* 'wooden dishes' | 10 | 34 | 36 | 36 | 33 | 149 |
| *mmwa* 'conical bundle' | 15 | 33 | 27 | 28 | 18 | 121 |
| *sa* 'nut bunch' | 8 | 22 | 33 | 25 | 26 | 114 |
| *utu* 'scrap' | 5 | 18 | 3 | 4 | 6 | 36 |
| *uva* 'span' | 7 | 34 | 27 | 25 | 17 | 110 |
| *ya* 'flexible, thin' | 3 | 1 | 3 | 3 | 8 | 18 |
| *kabisi* 'compartment' | 6 | 12 | 9 | 12 | 14 | 53 |
| *liku* 'compartment' | | 3 | 2 | 17 | 10 | 32 |
| *vili* 'untwisted' | 12 | 28 | | 1 | 8 | 49 |
| *si* 'small bit' | 9 | 11 | | 2 | 6 | 28 |
| *bubu* 'cut across' | 3 | | 6 | 3 | 6 | 18 |
| *oyla* 'string' | 13 | 10 | 9 | | 2 | 34 |
| *sisi* 'bough' | | 2 | | 2 | 4 | 8 |
| *meila* 'song/part' | | 6 | | | 6 | 12 |
| *gum* 'bit' | | | | 3 | 3 | 6 |
| *duya* 'door' | 2 | | | 3 | | 5 |
| *kova* 'fire' | | | | 1 | | 1 |
| *kubila* 'land plot' | | | | 1 | | 1 |
| *kwoila* 'clay pot' | | 4 | 1 | | | 5 |

**Table 3.2.159.** *(continued)*

| CP expected | Tokens of CP *ke* produced by age group | | | | | Tokens total |
|---|---|---|---|---|---|---|
| | I | II | III | IV | V | |
| *pila* 'part, piece' | 2 | 3 | | | | 5 |
| *yulai* 'bundle of four things' | 1 | 1 | | | | 2 |
| *kweya* 'limb' | | 5 | | | | 5 |
| *kudu* 'tooth' | | 2 | | | | 2 |
| *kavi* 'tool' | | 7 | | | | 7 |
| *kaduyo* 'entrance' | | 4 | | | | 4 |
| *duli* 'cluster' | | 6 | | | | 6 |
| *yuva* 'shoal' | 1 | | | | | 1 |
| *sipu* 'sheaf' | 2 | | | | | 2 |
| *lilo* 'walk' | 1 | | | | | 1 |
| *kasa* 'row' | 2 | | | | | 2 |
| Total | 204 | 499 | 380 | 412 | 424 | |

1. CP produced, *ke* expected: *bwa* (I, II; 2 tokens).
2. The CP *yuva*, which was replaced by *ke*, normally implies animation of the objects referred to.

**Table 3.2.160.** *Kila* 'clusters/hands of bananas'

| CP expected | Tokens of CP *kila* produced by age group | | | | | Tokens total |
|---|---|---|---|---|---|---|
| | I | II | III | IV | V | |
| *kila* 'hands of bananas' | 2 | | | 4 | 1 | 7 |

CPs produced, *kila* expected: *ke* (I–V; 142 tokens), *kwe* (I, II, IV; 8 tokens).

**Table 3.2.161.** *Kova* 'fire'

| CP expected | Tokens of CP *kova* produced by age group | | | | | Tokens total |
|---|---|---|---|---|---|---|
| | I | II | III | IV | V | |
| *kova* 'fire' | 16 | 36 | 36 | 35 | 35 | 158 |
| *yuma* 'hand' | 1 | | | | | (1*) |
| Total | 17 | 36 | 36 | 35 | 35 | |

1. CPs produced, *kova* expected: *ke* (IV; 1 token), *kwe* (V; 1 token).
2. See the comments on dubious (*) CP usage (see section 3.2.1).

**Table 3.2.162.** *Kubila* 'large land plot'

| CP expected | Tokens of CP *kubila* produced by age group | | | | | Tokens total |
|---|---|---|---|---|---|---|
| | I | II | III | IV | V | |
| *kubila* 'land plot' | | 12 | 26 | 29 | 27 | 94 |

CPs produced, *kubila* expected: *ke* (IV; 1 token), *kwe* (I–V; 53 tokens), *pila* (I; 1 token), *utu\** (III; 2 tokens).

**Table 3.2.163.** *Kudu1* 'band of fibers'

| CP expected | Tokens of CP *kudu1* produced by age group | | | | | Tokens total |
|---|---|---|---|---|---|---|
| | I | II | III | IV | V | |
| *kudu* 'fibers' | | | | 3 | 3 | 6 |
| *bubu* 'cut across' | | | | | 1 | (1\*) |
| *yuva* 'shoal' | | | | | 2 | (2\*) |

1. CPs produced, *kudu1* expected: *kwe* (I–V; 145 tokens), *doba* (IV; 1 token).
2. See the comments on dubious (\*) CP usage (see section 3.2.1).

**Table 3.2.164.** *Kudu2* 'tooth'

| CP expected | Tokens of CP *kudu2* produced by age group | | | | | Tokens total |
|---|---|---|---|---|---|---|
| | I | II | III | IV | V | |
| *kudu* 'tooth' | | 3 | 8 | 9 | 6 | 26 |

CPs produced, *kudu2* expected: *ke* (II; 2 tokens), *kwe* (II, IV; 2 tokens), *ka'i* (I–V; 127 tokens).

**Table 3.2.165.** *Kumla* 'earth oven'

| CP expected | Tokens of CP *kumla* produced by age group | | | | | Tokens total |
|---|---|---|---|---|---|---|
| | I | II | III | IV | V | |
| *kumla* 'earth oven' | 19 | 36 | 36 | 36 | 35 | 162 |

CP produced, *kumla* expected: *kwe* (V; 1 token).

**Table 3.2.166.** *Kwe* 'thing, unmarked form for inanimates'

| | Tokens of CP *kwe* produced by age group | | | | | |
|---|---|---|---|---|---|---|
| CP expected | I | II | III | IV | V | Tokens total |
| *kwe* 'thing' | 20 | 36 | 36 | 36 | 36 | 164 |
| *bogi* 'night' | 15 | 28 | 25 | 34 | 36 | 138 |
| *buda* 'group' | 6 | 26 | 13 | 24 | 16 | 85 |
| *gula* 'heap' | 17 | 27 | 14 | 7 | 17 | 82 |
| *kala* 'day' | 13 | 35 | 30 | 33 | 33 | 144 |
| *kapwa* 'parcel' | 5 | 7 | 9 | 5 | 4 | 30 |
| *kubila* 'land plot' | 10 | 20 | 8 | 6 | 9 | 53 |
| *kudu* 'fibers' | 10 | 34 | 36 | 32 | 33 | 145 |
| *kwoila* 'clay pot' | 2 | 6 | 21 | 10 | 10 | 49 |
| *kwoya* 'mountain' | 14 | 31 | 25 | 29 | 33 | 132 |
| *lilo* 'walk' | 12 | 29 | 27 | 35 | 28 | 131 |
| *nina* 'song/part' | 7 | 25 | 10 | 10 | 9 | 61 |
| *nunu* 'corner/garden' | 10 | 32 | 28 | 27 | 27 | 124 |
| *po'ula* 'grove' | 12 | 28 | 12 | 27 | 14 | 93 |
| *sipu* 'sheaf' | 5 | 17 | 10 | 12 | 5 | 49 |
| *siva* 'time' | 10 | 36 | 29 | 28 | 31 | 134 |
| *siwa* 'sea portions' | 13 | 28 | 28 | 32 | 36 | 137 |
| *vilo* 'place' | 12 | 33 | 36 | 36 | 36 | 153 |
| *yam* 'day' | 18 | 26 | 27 | 34 | 36 | 141 |
| *yulai* 'bundle of four things' | 14 | 35 | 30 | 36 | 33 | 148 |
| *yuva* 'shoal' | 4 | 20 | 7 | 18 | 3 | 52 |
| 0 'basketful of yams' | 15 | 27 | 29 | 23 | 23 | 117 |
| *bubu* 'cut across' | | 12 | 3 | 12 | 1 | 28 |
| *duya* 'door' | | 4 | 3 | 1 | 13 | 21 |
| *gili* 'row' | | 4 | 9 | 12 | 4 | 29 |
| *kabulu* 'sector' | | 10 | 11 | 8 | 11 | 40 |
| *gum* 'bit' | 2 | 12 | | 5 | 3 | 22 |
| *liku* 'compartment' | 14 | 22 | 12 | | 7 | 55 |
| *notu* 'kneaded, dot' | 1 | 15 | | 12 | 5 | 33 |
| *pwanina* 'hole' | 3 | 12 | | 5 | 3 | 23 |
| *sa* 'nut bunch' | 2 | 9 | | 6 | 3 | 20 |
| *giwi* 'cut' | | 5 | | 4 | 2 | 11 |
| *vili* 'untwisted' | | 2 | | 1 | 1 | 4 |
| *kaduyo* 'entrance' | | 1 | | | 3 | 4 |
| *mmwa* 'conical bundle' | | 1 | | | 3 | 4 |
| *kova* 'fire' | | | | | 1 | 1 |

**Table 3.2.166.** (continued)

| | Tokens of CP *kwe* produced by age group | | | | | |
|---|---|---|---|---|---|---|
| CP expected | I | II | III | IV | V | Tokens total |
| *kumla* 'earth oven' | | | | | 1 | 1 |
| *pila* 'part, piece' | | | | | 3 | 3 |
| *deli* 'group' | 1 | 19 | 4 | 13 | | 37 |
| *kabisi* 'compartment' | 1 | 5 | 3 | 1 | | 10 |
| *duli* 'cluster' | 11 | 9 | | 9 | | 29 |
| *kila* 'hands/bananas' | 4 | 1 | | 3 | | 8 |
| *meila* 'song/part' | 2 | 5 | | 2 | | 9 |
| *oyla* 'string' | | 5 | 3 | 6 | | 14 |
| *iga* 'name' | 3 | | | 3 | | 6 |
| *kasa* 'row' | | 6 | | 3 | | 9 |
| *kudu* 'tooth' | | 1 | | 1 | | 2 |
| *bubwa* 'cut off' | | | | 1 | | 1 |
| *ta* 'basket' | | | | 1 | | 1 |
| *yuma* 'hand' | 11 | 33 | 12 | | | 56 |
| *bukwa* 'fruit cluster' | | 1 | 3 | | | 4 |
| *uva* 'span' | 6 | 2 | | | | 8 |
| *kai* 'stone blade' | | 2 | | | | 2 |
| *kavi* 'tool' | | 6 | | | | 6 |
| *kweya* 'limb' | | 9 | | | | 9 |
| *luva* 'wooden dishes' | | 2 | | | | 2 |
| *si* 'small bit' | | 3 | | | | 3 |
| Total | 305 | 804 | 553 | 643 | 572 | |

The CPs *buda, deli,* and *yuva,* which were replaced by the CP *kwe,* normally imply animation of the subjects referred to.

**Table 3.2.167.** *Kweya/kwaya/keya* 'limb'

| | Tokens of CP *kweya* produced by age group | | | | | |
|---|---|---|---|---|---|---|
| CP expected | I | II | III | IV | V | Tokens total |
| *kweya* 'limb' | 3 | 20 | 36 | 36 | 36 | 131 |
| *yuma* 'hand' | | | 24 | 33 | 27 | 84 |
| Total | 3 | 20 | 60 | 69 | 63 | |

CPs produced, *kweya* expected: *ke* (II; 5 tokens), *kwe* (II; 9 tokens), *nal\** (I, II; 4 tokens).

**Table 3.2.168.** *Kwoila/kwela* 'clay pot'

| CP expected | Tokens of CP *kwoila* produced by age group | | | | | Tokens total |
|---|---|---|---|---|---|---|
| | I | II | III | IV | V | |
| *kwoila* 'clay pot' | 5 | 26 | 14 | 26 | 25 | 96 |

CPs produced, *kwoila* expected: *ke* (II, III; 5 tokens), *kwe* (I–V; 49 tokens), *kava** (V; 1 token).

**Table 3.2.169.** *Kwoya/koya* 'mountain, hill'

| CP expected | Tokens of CP *kwoya* produced by age group | | | | | Tokens total |
|---|---|---|---|---|---|---|
| | I | II | III | IV | V | |
| *kwoya* 'mountain' | 1 | 4 | 11 | 7 | 3 | 26 |

CPs produced, *kwoya* expected: *kwe* (I–V; 132 tokens).

**Table 3.2.170.** *Liku* 'compartment of a foodhouse'

| CP expected | Tokens of CP *liku* produced by age group | | | | | Tokens total |
|---|---|---|---|---|---|---|
| | I | II | III | IV | V | |
| *liku* 'compartment' | | 11 | 22 | 19 | 19 | 71 |

CPs produced, *liku* expected: *ke* (II–V; 32 tokens), *kwe* (I–III, V; 55 tokens).

**Table 3.2.171.** *Lilo/lola* 'walk, journey'

| CP expected | Tokens of CP *lilo/lola* produced by age group | | | | | Tokens total |
|---|---|---|---|---|---|---|
| | I | II | III | IV | V | |
| *lilo* 'walk, journey' | 1 | | 3 | 1 | 2 | 7 |

CPs produced, *lilo* expected: *kada** (I; 1 token), *ke* (I; 1 token), *kwe* (I–V; 131 tokens), *ya* (II, III, V; 16 tokens).

**Table 3.2.172.** *Luba* 'bundle'

| CP expected | Tokens of CP *luba* produced by age group | | | | | Tokens total |
|---|---|---|---|---|---|---|
| | I | II | III | IV | V | |
| *kapwa* 'bundle, parcel' | 1 | 9 | 21 | 25 | 21 | 77 |

This CP was not expected; the CP *luba* is a repeater.

**Table 3.2.173.** *Luva1* + 2 'wooden dishes, tied bundle'

| CP expected | Tokens of CP *luva* produced by age group | | | | | Tokens total |
|---|---|---|---|---|---|---|
| | I | II | III | IV | V | |
| *luva1* 'wooden dishes' | 1 | | | | 3 | 4 |
| *giwi* 'cut' | | 3 | | | | (3*) |
| *bukwa* 'fruit cluster' | | | | 2 | | (2*) |
| *mmwa* 'conical bundle' | | | | 3 | | (3*) |
| *sa* 'nut-bunch' | | | | 3 | | (3*) |
| *utu* 'scrap' | | | | | 3 | (3*) |
| Total | 1 | 3 | | 8 | 6 | |

1. CPs produced, *luva* expected: *ke* (I–V; 149 tokens), *kwe* (II; 2 tokens).
2. See the comments on dubious (*) CP usage (see section 3.2.1).

**Table 3.2.174.** *Megwa* 'magic'

| CP expected | Tokens of CP *megwa* produced by age group | | | | | Tokens total |
|---|---|---|---|---|---|---|
| | I | II | III | IV | V | |
| *nina* 'part of a song' | | 1 | 5 | 6 | | 12 |

This CP was not expected; the CP *megwa* is a repeater.

**Table 3.2.175.** *Meila* 'part of a song'

| CP expected | Tokens of CP *meila* produced by age group | | | | | Tokens total |
|---|---|---|---|---|---|---|
| | I | II | III | IV | V | |
| *meila* 'part of a song' | | | | | 3 | 3 |

CPs produced, *meila* expected: *kasa* (III–V; 10 tokens), *ke* (II, V; 12 tokens), *kwe* (I, II, IV; 9 tokens), *pila* (I–V; 91 tokens), *utu* (III; 4 tokens), *vosi* (III–V; 18 tokens).

**Table 3.2.176.** *Mmwa* 'conical bundle'

| CP expected | Tokens of CP *mmwa* produced by age group | | | | | Tokens total |
|---|---|---|---|---|---|---|
| | I | II | III | IV | V | |
| *mmwa* 'conical bundle' | | 2 | 8 | 1 | 12 | 23 |

CPs produced, *mmwa* expected: *buda* (IV; 1 token), *ke* (I–V; 121 tokens), *kwe* (II, V; 4 tokens), *luva** (IV; 3 tokens), *utu** (III, IV; 4 tokens), *guba* (V; 3 tokens).

**Table 3.2.177.** *Na1* 'persons of female gender'

| | Tokens of CP *na1* produced by age group | | | | | |
|---|---|---|---|---|---|---|
| CP expected | I | II | III | IV | V | Tokens total |
| *na1* 'female persons' | 30 | 35 | 36 | 36 | 36 | 173 |
| *kweya* 'limb' | 1 | 3 | | | | (4*) |
| *bubu* 'cut across' | 1 | | | | | (1*) |
| *deli* 'group' | 1 | | | | | 1 |
| *uva* 'span' | 1 | | | | | (1*) |
| *kai* 'stone blade' | | 1 | | | | (1*) |
| *duya* 'door' | | | 3 | | | (3*) |
| Total | 34 | 39 | 39 | 36 | 36 | |

See the comments on dubious (*) CP usage (see section 3.2.1).

**Table 3.2.178.** *Na2* 'animals'

| | Tokens of CP *na2* produced by age group | | | | | |
|---|---|---|---|---|---|---|
| CP expected | I | II | III | IV | V | Tokens total |
| *na2* 'animals' | 18 | 36 | 36 | 36 | 36 | 162 |
| *oyla* 'string (of fish)' | | 3 | 12 | 12 | 26 | 53 |
| *wela* 'batch of fish' | 18 | 27 | 6 | 3 | 6 | 60 |
| *gum* 'bit, small piece' | 3 | | | | | (3*) |
| *giwi* 'cut' | | 1 | | | | (1*) |
| Total | 39 | 67 | 54 | 51 | 68 | |

See the comments on dubious (*) CP usage (see section 3.2.1).

**Table 3.2.179.** *Nigwa* 'hole, nest'

| | Tokens of CP *nigwa* produced by age group | | | | | |
|---|---|---|---|---|---|---|
| CP expected | I | II | III | IV | V | Tokens total |
| *pwanina/pona* 'hole' | | | | | 1 | 1 |

This CP was not expected.

**Table 3.2.180.** *Nina* 'part of a song'

| CP expected | Tokens of CP *nina* produced by age group | | | | | Tokens total |
|---|---|---|---|---|---|---|
| | I | II | III | IV | V | |
| *nina* 'part of a song' | | | | | 3 | 3 |

CPs produced, *nina* expected: *\*iki* (II; 1 token), *kasa* (III; 3 tokens), *kwe* (I–V; 61 tokens), *pila* (II–V; 67 tokens), *utu* (III; 3 tokens), *megwa* (II–IV; 12 tokens).

**Table 3.2.181.** *Nutu/notu* 'kneaded, dot, drop'

| CP expected | Tokens of CP *nutu/notu* produced by age group | | | | | Tokens total |
|---|---|---|---|---|---|---|
| | I | II | III | IV | V | |
| *notu* 'kneaded, dot' | 3 | 12 | 33 | 24 | 31 | 103 |

CP produced, *nutu/notu* expected: *kwe* (I, II, IV, V; 33 tokens).

**Table 3.2.182.** *Nunu* 'corner of a garden'

| CP expected | Tokens of CP *nunu* produced by age group | | | | | Tokens total |
|---|---|---|---|---|---|---|
| | I | II | III | IV | V | |
| *nunu* 'corner/garden' | | | 6 | 9 | 6 | 21 |
| *kabisi* 'compartment' | | 1 | | | | (1\*) |
| Total | | 1 | 6 | 9 | 6 | |

1. CPs produced, *nunu* expected: *kabulo1\** (V; 3 tokens), *kwe* (I–V; 124 tokens), *utu* (III; 2 tokens).
2. See the comments on dubious (\*) CP usage (see section 3.2.1).

**Table 3.2.183.** *Peta* 'basket'

| CP expected | Tokens of CP *peta* produced by age group | | | | | Tokens total |
|---|---|---|---|---|---|---|
| | I | II | III | IV | V | |
| *ta* 'basket' | | | 3 | 1 | 3 | 7 |

This CP was not expected; the CP *peta* is a repeater.

**Table 3.2.184.** *Pila* 'part, piece'

| CP expected | Tokens of CP *pila* produced by age group | | | | | Tokens total |
|---|---|---|---|---|---|---|
| | I | II | III | IV | V | |
| *pila* 'part, piece' | 3 | 7 | 25 | 25 | 21 | 81 |
| *meila* 'part/song' | 6 | 20 | 23 | 20 | 22 | 91 |
| *nina* 'part/song' | | 8 | 15 | 20 | 24 | 67 |
| *ya* 'flexible, thin' | | 3 | | 1 | | 4 |
| *oyla* 'string' | | | 1 | | 1 | (2*) |
| *siva* 'time' | | | | 1 | | 1 |
| *kavi* 'tool' | | 1 | | | | (1*) |
| *kabisi* 'compartment' | 1 | | | | | 1 |
| *kubila* 'land plot' | 1 | | | | | 1 |
| Total | 11 | 39 | 64 | 67 | 68 | |

1. CPs produced, *pila* expected: *ke* (I, II; 5 tokens), *kwe* (V; 3 tokens), *utu* (IV; 1 token), *vili* (IV; 1 token), *ya* (I–V; 60 tokens).
2. See the comments on dubious (*) CP usage (see section 3.2.1).

**Table 3.2.185.** *Po'ula* 'plantation, grove'

| CP expected | Tokens of CP *po'ula* produced by age group | | | | | Tokens total |
|---|---|---|---|---|---|---|
| | I | II | III | IV | V | |
| *po'ula* 'grove' | | 3 | 18 | 9 | 19 | 49 |
| *sa* 'nut bunch' | | | | 2 | 1 | 3 |
| *bukwa* 'fruit cluster' | | | | | 1 | 1 |
| Total | | 3 | 18 | 11 | 21 | |

CPs produced, *po'ula* expected: *gula* (III; 3 tokens), *kwe* (I–V; 93 tokens).

**Table 3.2.186.** *Pwanina/pona* 'hole, punctured'

| CP expected | Tokens of CP *pwanina/pona* produced by age group | | | | | Tokens total |
|---|---|---|---|---|---|---|
| | I | II | III | IV | V | |
| *pwanina/pona* 'hole' | 17 | 24 | 36 | 31 | 32 | 140 |

CPs produced, *pwanina/pona* expected: *kwe* (I, II, IV, V; 23 tokens), *nigwa* (V; 1 token).

**Table 3.2.187.** *Sa* 'nut bunch'

| CP expected | Tokens of CP *sa* produced by age group | | | | | Tokens total |
|---|---|---|---|---|---|---|
| | I | II | III | IV | V | |
| *sa* 'nut bunch' | 1 | 3 | 3 | | 6 | 13 |
| *bukwa* 'fruit cluster' | | | | 3 | | 3 |
| Total | 1 | 3 | 3 | 3 | 6 | |

CPs produced, *sa* expected: *ke* (I–V; 114 tokens), *kwe* (I, II, IV, V; 20 tokens), *luva*\* (IV; 3 tokens), *po'ula* (IV, V; 3 tokens).

**Table 3.2.188.** *Si* 'small bit'

| CP expected | Tokens of CP *si* produced by age group | | | | | Tokens total |
|---|---|---|---|---|---|---|
| | I | II | III | IV | V | |
| *si* 'small bit' | 1 | | | | | 1 |
| *ya* 'flexible, thin' | 4 | 5 | 5 | | | 14 |
| Total | 5 | 5 | 5 | | | |

1. CPs produced, *si* expected: *bwa* (II; 6 tokens), *ke* (I, II, IV, V; 28 tokens), *kwe* (II; 3 tokens), *utu* (I–V; 118 tokens), *vili* (III–V; 4 tokens).
2. The CP *si* was produced as a response to the stimulus *yoyu* 'palm branch' presented to elicit the CP *ya*; this can be explained by assuming that the consultants thought of 'a small bit of a flexible, thin palm branch'.

**Table 3.2.189.** *Sipu* 'sheaf'

| CP expected | Tokens of CP *sipu* produced by age group | | | | | Tokens total |
|---|---|---|---|---|---|---|
| | I | II | III | IV | V | |
| *sipu* 'sheaf' | | 11 | 25 | 21 | 31 | 88 |

CPs produced, *sipu* expected: *ke* (I; 2 tokens), *kwe* (I–V; 49 tokens), *ya* (II–IV; 7 tokens).

**Table 3.2.190.** *Sisi* 'bough'

| CP expected | Tokens of CP *sisi* produced by age group | | | | | Tokens total |
|---|---|---|---|---|---|---|
| | I | II | III | IV | V | |
| *sisi* 'bough' | 7 | 34 | 33 | 34 | 32 | 140 |
| *ya* 'flexible, thin' | 5 | 26 | 24 | 30 | 24 | 109 |
| *kai* 'stone blade' | | 2 | | | | (2\*) |
| Total | 12 | 62 | 57 | 64 | 56 | |

1. CPs produced, *sisi* expected: *ke* (II, IV, V; 8 tokens), *ya* (I, III; 6 tokens).
2. See the comments on dubious (\*) CP usage (see section 3.2.1).

**Table 3.2.191.** *Siva* 'time'

| CP expected | Tokens of CP *siva* produced by age group | | | | | Tokens total |
|---|---|---|---|---|---|---|
| | I | II | III | IV | V | |
| *siva* 'time' | | | | | 3 | 3 |

CPs produced, *siva* expected: *kwe* (I–V; 134 tokens), *pila* (IV; 1 token), *utu* (IV, V; 6 tokens), *tuta* (III–V; 7 tokens).

**Table 3.2.192.** *Suya* 'batch of fish'

| CP expected | Tokens of CP *suya* produced by age group | | | | | Tokens total |
|---|---|---|---|---|---|---|
| | I | II | III | IV | V | |
| *wela* 'batch of fish' | | 6 | 24 | 33 | 27 | 90 |

This CP was not expected.

**Table 3.2.193.** *Ta* 'basket'

| CP expected | Tokens of CP *ta* produced by age group | | | | | Tokens total |
|---|---|---|---|---|---|---|
| | I | II | III | IV | V | |
| *ta* 'basket' | 18 | 34 | 33 | 34 | 32 | 151 |
| *giwi* 'cut' | 1 | | | | | (1*) |
| Total | 19 | 34 | 33 | 34 | 32 | |

1. CPs produced, *ta* expected: *peta* (III–V; 7 tokens), *kwe* (IV; 1 token), *ya* (V; 1 token).

2. See the comments on dubious (*) CP usage (see section 3.2.1).

**Table 3.2.194.** *Tam* 'sprouting'

| CP expected | Tokens of CP *tam* produced by age group | | | | | Tokens total |
|---|---|---|---|---|---|---|
| | I | II | III | IV | V | |
| *gula* 'heap' | | 3 | 11 | 8 | 6 | 28 |
| 0 'basketful of yams' | | 7 | 6 | 12 | 9 | 34 |
| *uva* 'span' | | | | 5 | 3 | 8 |
| Total | | 10 | 17 | 25 | 18 | |

This CP was not expected.

**Table 3.2.195.** *Tetu* 'yams'

| | Tokens of CP *tetu* produced by age group | | | | | |
|---|---|---|---|---|---|---|
| CP expected | I | II | III | IV | V | Tokens total |
| 0 'basketful of yams' | | | | 1 | | 1 |

This CP was not expected; the CP *tetu* is a repeater.

**Table 3.2.196.** *To/te* 'persons of male gender, human beings'

| | Tokens of CP *to/te* produced by age group | | | | | |
|---|---|---|---|---|---|---|
| CP expected | I | II | III | IV | V | Tokens total |
| *to/te* 'male persons' | 36 | 36 | 36 | 36 | 36 | 180 |
| *deli* 'group' | 1 | 10 | | | | 11 |
| *yuma* 'hand' | 1 | | | | 2 | 3 |
| Total | 38 | 46 | 36 | 36 | 38 | |

Consultants 6 and 55 produced the CP *to/te* as a response to the stimulus presented to elicit the CP *yuma*; these two consultants took the stimulus *yamala* 'his/her hand' obviously as a *pars pro toto* and then referred to 'human beings' in general.

**Table 3.2.197.** *Tuta* 'time'

| | Tokens of CP *tuta* produced by age group | | | | | |
|---|---|---|---|---|---|---|
| CP expected | I | II | III | IV | V | Tokens total |
| *siva* 'time' | | | 4 | 2 | 1 | 7 |
| *kala* 'day' | | | | 1 | | 1 |
| Total | | | 4 | 3 | 1 | |

This CP was not expected; the CP *tuta* is a repeater.

**Table 3.2.198.** *Utu* 'scrap, parts cut off'

| CP expected | Tokens of CP *utu* produced by age group | | | | | Tokens total |
|---|---|---|---|---|---|---|
| | I | II | III | IV | V | |
| *utu* 'scrap' | 2 | 6 | 30 | 30 | 19 | 87 |
| *si* 'small bit' | 5 | 16 | 35 | 34 | 28 | 118 |
| *vili* 'untwisted' | 1 | 2 | 11 | 13 | 3 | 30 |
| *kabulo* 'point' | | 1 | 22 | 8 | 7 | 38 |
| *kabisi* 'compartment' | | 3 | 1 | | | 4 |
| *mmwa* 'conical bundle' | | | 1 | 3 | | (4*) |
| *siva* 'time' | | | | 5 | 1 | 6 |
| *gili* 'row' | | 1 | | | | (1*) |
| *gum* 'small piece' | | 1 | | | | 1 |
| *kabulu* 'sector' | | 1 | | | | 1 |
| *kavi* 'tool' | | 1 | | | | (1*) |
| *kubila* 'land plot' | | | 2 | | | (2*) |
| *meila* 'song/part' | | | 4 | | | 4 |
| *nina* 'song/part' | | | 3 | | | 3 |
| *nunu* 'corner/garden' | | | 2 | | | 2 |
| *siwa* 'sea portions' | | | 3 | | | (3*) |
| *bubwa* 'cut off' | | | | 2 | | 2 |
| *pila* 'part, piece' | | | | 1 | | 1 |
| Total | 8 | 32 | 114 | 96 | 58 | |

1. CPs produced, *utu* expected: *boma (III; 1 token), bubwa (I, III–V; 8 tokens), bwa (I–V; 20 tokens), ke (I–V; 36 tokens), *luva (V; 3 tokens).

2. See the comments on dubious (*) CP usage (see section 3.2.1). The consultants produced the CP *utu* as a response to the stimuli presented to elicit the expected CPs *kabulo* and *siva*; if we assume that the consultants wanted to emphasize the aspect of 'division' and 'part' that may be an inherent characteristic of 'village sectors' and 'time' in their idiolect we can accept these responses.

**Table 3.2.199.** *Uva* 'span'

| CP expected | Tokens of CP *uva* produced by age group | | | | | Tokens total |
|---|---|---|---|---|---|---|
| | I | II | III | IV | V | |
| *uva* 'span' | | | 9 | 6 | 16 | 31 |

CPs produced, *uva* expected: *ke* (I–V; 110 tokens), *kwe* (I, II; 8 tokens), *naI** (I; 1 token), *tam* (IV, V; 8 tokens).

**Table 3.2.200.** *Va* 'door, window'

| CP expected | Tokens of CP *va* produced by age group | | | | | Tokens total |
|---|---|---|---|---|---|---|
| | I | II | III | IV | V | |
| *kaduyo* 'entrance' | 1 | 3 | | | | 4 |
| *duya* 'door' | | 4 | | 6 | | 10 |
| Total | 1 | 7 | | 6 | | |

This CP was not expected.

**Table 3.2.201.** *Vakala* 'belt'

| CP expected | Tokens of CP *vakala* produced by age group | | | | | Tokens total |
|---|---|---|---|---|---|---|
| | I | II | III | IV | V | |
| *gili* 'row' | | | 1 | 1 | | 2 |

This CP was not expected; the CP *vakala* is a repeater.

**Table 3.2.202.** *Vaya/vayo* 'door, window'

| CP expected | Tokens of CP *vaya/vayo* produced by age group | | | | | Tokens total |
|---|---|---|---|---|---|---|
| | I | II | III | IV | V | |
| *duya* 'door' | | | 1 | 1 | | 2 |
| *kaduyo* 'entrance' | | | 1 | | | 1 |
| Total | | | 2 | 1 | | |

This CP was not expected.

**Table 3.2.203.** *Vili* 'untwisted'

| CP expected | Tokens of CP *vili* produced by age group | | | | | Tokens total |
|---|---|---|---|---|---|---|
| | I | II | III | IV | V | |
| *vili* 'untwisted' | | 1 | 25 | 19 | 23 | 68 |
| *si* 'small bit' | | | 1 | 2 | 1 | 4 |
| *gili* 'row' | | | | 3 | | (3*) |
| *pila* 'part, piece' | | | | 1 | | 1 |
| Total | | 1 | 26 | 25 | 24 | |

1. CPs produced, *vili* expected: *bubwa** (IV; 2 tokens), *bwa* (II, V; 2 tokens), *ke* (I, II, IV, V; 49 tokens), *kwe* (II, IV, V; 4 tokens), *utu* (I–V; 30 tokens).
2. See the comments on dubious (*) CP usage (see section 3.2.1).

**Table 3.2.204.** *Vosi* 'song'

| | Tokens of CP *vosi* produced by age group | | | | | |
|---|---|---|---|---|---|---|
| **CP expected** | **I** | **II** | **III** | **IV** | **V** | **Tokens total** |
| *meila* 'part of a song' | | | 6 | 10 | 2 | 18 |

This CP was not expected; the CP *vosi* is a repeater.

**Table 3.2.205.** *Wela* 'batch of fish'

| | Tokens of CP *wela* produced by age group | | | | | |
|---|---|---|---|---|---|---|
| **CP expected** | **I** | **II** | **III** | **IV** | **V** | **Tokens total** |
| *wela* 'batch of fish' | | 3 | 6 | | 3 | 12 |
| *oyla* 'string of fish' | | | 8 | 18 | 4 | 30 |
| Total | | 3 | 14 | 18 | 7 | |

CPs produced, *wela* expected: *na2* (I–V; 60 tokens), *suya* (II–V; 90 tokens).

**Table 3.2.206.** *Ya* 'flexible, thin'

| | Tokens of CP *ya* produced by age group | | | | | |
|---|---|---|---|---|---|---|
| **CP expected** | **I** | **II** | **III** | **IV** | **V** | **Tokens total** |
| *ya* 'flexible, thin' | 1 | 1 | 4 | 2 | 4 | 12 |
| *gili* 'row' | 12 | 28 | 18 | 19 | 24 | 101 |
| *pila* 'part, piece' | 5 | 23 | 11 | 9 | 12 | 60 |
| *bukwa* 'fruit cluster' | | 7 | | 3 | 4 | 14 |
| *duya* 'door' | | 8 | | 11 | 9 | 28 |
| *kaduyo* 'entrance' | | 5 | | 6 | 6 | 17 |
| *lilo* 'walk, journey' | | 4 | 6 | | 6 | 16 |
| *sipu* 'sheaf' | | 3 | 1 | 3 | | 7 |
| *sisi* 'bough' | 3 | | 3 | | | 6 |
| *bubu* 'cut across' | 1 | 3 | | | | 4 |
| *gum* 'bit, small piece' | | 6 | | | | 6 |
| *yuma* 'hand' | | | | 1 | | (1*) |
| *ta* 'basket' | | | | | 1 | 1 |
| Total | 22 | 88 | 43 | 54 | 66 | |

1. CPs produced, *ya* expected: *ke* (I–V; 18 tokens), *pila* (II, IV; 4 tokens), *si* (I–III; 14 tokens), *sisi* (I–V; 109 tokens).

2. See the comments on dubious (*) CP usage (see section 3.2.1). The CP *ya* was also produced as a response to the stimulus presented to elicit the CP *lilo*; the production of the CP in this context can be justified by assuming that the consultants thought of the rather small paths that connect the villages on the islands.

**Table 3.2.207.** *Yam* 'day'

| CP expected | Tokens of CP *yam* produced by age group | | | | | Tokens total |
|---|---|---|---|---|---|---|
| | I | II | III | IV | V | |
| *yam* 'day' | | 4 | 8 | 2 | | 14 |
| *kala* 'day' | | | 3 | 2 | | 5 |
| Total | | 4 | 11 | 4 | | |

CP produced, *yam* expected: *kwe* (I–V; 141 tokens).

**Table 3.2.208.** *Yam/yama/yuma* 'hand'

| CP expected | Tokens of CP *yam/yama/yuma* produced by age group | | | | | Tokens total |
|---|---|---|---|---|---|---|
| | I | II | III | IV | V | |
| *yuma* 'hand' | 1 | 2 | | 2 | 7 | 12 |

CPs produced, *yuma* expected: *kova*\* (I; 1 token), *kwe* (I–III; 56 tokens), *kweya* (III–V; 84 tokens), *tolte* (I, V; 3 tokens), *ya*\* (IV; 1 token).

**Table 3.2.209.** *Yegila* 'name'

| CP expected | Tokens of CP *yegila* produced by age group | | | | | Tokens total |
|---|---|---|---|---|---|---|
| | I | II | III | IV | V | |
| *iga* 'name' | | | 7 | | | 7 |

This CP was not expected; the CP *yegila* is a repeater.

**Table 3.2.210.** *Yulai/yule* 'bundle of four things'

| CP expected | Tokens of CP *yulai/yule* produced by age group | | | | | Tokens total |
|---|---|---|---|---|---|---|
| | I | II | III | IV | V | |
| *yulai* 'bundle of four things' | | | 6 | | 3 | 9 |

CPs produced, *yulai* expected: *ke* (I, II; 2 tokens), *kwe* (I–V; 148 tokens).

**Table 3.2.211.** *Yuva* 'shoal'

| CP expected | Tokens of CP *yuva* produced by age group | | | | | Tokens total |
|---|---|---|---|---|---|---|
| | I | II | III | IV | V | |
| *yuva* 'shoal' | | | 3 | | 1 | 4 |

CPs produced, *yuva* expected: *buda* (I–V; 86 tokens), *kasa*\* (II; 1 token), *ke* (I; 1 token), *kudul*\* (V; 2 tokens), *kwe* (I–V; 52 tokens).

**Table 3.2.212.** O 'basketful of yams'

| CP expected | Tokens of CP O produced by age group | | | | | Tokens total |
|---|---|---|---|---|---|---|
| | I | II | III | IV | V | |
| 0 'basketful of yams' | | | 1 | | 1 | 2 |

CPs produced, 0 expected: *kwe* (I–V; 117 tokens), *tetu* (IV; 1 token), *tam* (II–V; 34 tokens).

### 3.2.2.3 CP Types and Tokens Documented in the Corpus of Transcribed Kilivila Speech

Up to this point, we have been dealing primarily with data elicited by the questionnaire. In this section, I present the CP types and tokens together with the nouns and word classes with which they were used in my overall corpus of Kilivila speech data. This sample encompasses 34,955 transcribed words. Tables 3.2.216 and 3.2.217 present the relevant CP data; the CPs are listed alphabetically.

These 41 types can be ordered according to the number of tokens produced for each type. Table 3.2.218 presents the CPs in this order and gives the percentage of tokens produced for each type in relation to the number of tokens produced for all types (1,564 tokens).

With this second set of data, the following CPs were not produced during the elicitation test:

| | |
|---|---|
| *bililo* 'trip' | 4 tokens (consultant V17) |
| *dumia* 'swamplike' | 1 token (consultant I2/10) |
| *kali* 'paddle strike' | 1 token (consultant V14) |
| *kauya* 'creel' | 4 tokens (consultant IV3/33) |
| | 4 tokens (consultant V15) |
| *lipu* 'compartment/creel' | 5 tokens (consultant IV3/33) |
| *na3* 'moon, stars' | 4 tokens (consultant V11) |
| *na4* 'carving in human likeness' | 3 tokens (consultant V11) |
| *sam* 'ginger' | 7 tokens (not assignable to individual speakers) |
| *yeni* 'handful' | 1 token (consultant V17) |

We will now turn to the questions raised in section 3.1.

Table 3.2.213. CPs produced although not expected

| CP produced | Tokens | CP expected | Tokens in each age group | | | | |
|---|---|---|---|---|---|---|---|
| | | | I | II | III | IV | V |
| *beku* 'stone blade' | 2 | *kai* 'stone blade' | | | 1 | 1 | |
| (*)*boma* '???' | 1 | *utu* 'scrap' | | | 1 | | |
| *bwalita* 'sea' | 6 | *siwa* 'sea portions' | | | | 2 | 4 |
| *doba* 'skirt' | 1 | *kudu1* 'band of fibres' | | | | 1 | |
| *guba* 'bundle/taro' | 3 | *mmwa* 'conical bundle' | | | | | 3 |
| **iki* '???' | 1 | *nina* 'part of a song' | 1 | | | | |
| *ka'i* 'tooth' | 124 | *kudu2* 'tooth' | 13 | 27 | 28 | 26 | 30 |
| (*)*ka'i* 'tooth' | 3 | *oyla* 'string' | | 3 | | | |
| (*) *kava* '???' | 1 | *kwoila* 'clay pot' | | | | | 1 |
| *luba* 'bundle' | 77 | *kapwa* 'bundle' | 1 | 9 | 21 | 25 | 21 |
| *megwa* 'magic' | 12 | *nina* 'part of a song' | | 1 | 5 | 6 | |
| *nigwa* 'hole' | 1 | *pwanina* 'hole' | | | | | 1 |

162

| | n | | | | | | |
|---|---|---|---|---|---|---|---|
| peta 'basket' | 7 | ta 'basket' | | 3 | 1 | 3 | |
| suya 'batch/fish' | 90 | wela 'batch of fish' | | 6 | 24 | 33 | 27 |
| tam 'sprouting' | 28 | gula 'heap' | 3 | 11 | 8 | 6 | |
| tam 'sprouting' | 8 | uva 'span' | | | | 5 | 3 |
| tam 'sprouting' | 34 | 0 'basketful of yams' | | 7 | 6 | 12 | 9 |
| tetu 'yams' | 1 | 0 'basketful of yams' | | | | 1 | |
| tuta 'time' | 7 | siva 'time' | | | 4 | 2 | 1 |
| tuta 'time' | 1 | kala 'day' | | | 1 | | |
| va 'door' | 10 | duya 'door' | | 4 | | 6 | |
| va 'door' | 4 | kaduyo 'entrance' | 1 | 3 | | | |
| vakala 'belt' | 2 | gili 'row' | | | 1 | 1 | |
| vaya/vayo 'door' | 2 | duya 'door' | | | 1 | 1 | |
| vaya/vayo 'door' | 1 | kaduyo 'entrance' | | | | 1 | |
| vosi 'song' | 18 | meila 'part of a song' | | | 6 | 10 | 2 |
| yegila 'name' | 7 | iga 'name' | | | 7 | | |
| Total | | | 15 | 67 | 119 | 147 | 104 |

# Table 3.2.214. Dubious cases of CP production

| CP expected | CP produced (dubious usage) | Tokens by age group | | | | |
|---|---|---|---|---|---|---|
| | | I | II | III | IV | V |
| *bubu* | *buda* | | 1 | 3 | | |
| | *gula* | | 2 | 1 | | |
| | *kudu1* | | | | | 1 |
| | *na1* | 1 | | | | |
| *bukwa* | *luva* | | | | 2 | |
| *duya* | *na1* | | | 3 | | |
| *gili* | *utu* | | 1 | | | |
| | *vili* | | | | 3 | |
| *giwi* | *kasa* | | 3 | | | |
| | *na2* | | 1 | | | |
| | *ta* | 1 | | | | |
| | *luva* | | 3 | | | |
| *gum* | *buda* | | 1 | | | |
| | *kasa* | | 3 | | | |
| | *na2* | 3 | | | | |
| *iga* | *kasa* | 1 | | | | |
| *kabisi* | *nunu* | | 1 | | | |
| *kabulo1* | *bubwa* | | | 1 | | |
| *kabulu2* | *kada* | | | 3 | | |
| *kai* | *na1* | | 1 | | | |
| | *sisi* | | 2 | | | |
| *kavi* | *pila* | | 1 | | | |

|  |  |  |  |  |  |  |
|---|---|---|---|---|---|---|
| *kubila* | *utu* |  | 1 |  |  |  |
| *kweya* | *utu* |  |  | 2 |  |  |
| *kwoila* | *nal* |  | 3 |  |  | 1 |
| *lilo* | *kava* |  | 1 |  |  |  |
|  | *kada* |  |  |  |  |  |
| *mmwa* | *luva* |  |  |  | 3 |  |
|  | *utu* |  |  | 1 | 3 |  |
| *nina* | *iki* |  | 1 |  |  |  |
| *numu* | *kabulo2* |  |  |  |  | 3 |
| *oyla* | *ka'i* |  | 3 | 1 |  |  |
|  | *pila* |  |  |  |  | 1 |
| *sa* | *luva* |  |  | 3 | 3 |  |
| *siwa* | *utu* |  |  |  |  |  |
| *utu* | *luva* |  |  | 1 |  | 3 |
|  | *boma* |  |  |  |  |  |
| *uva* | *nal* | 1 |  |  |  |  |
| *vili* | *bubwa* |  |  |  | 2 |  |
| *vilo* | *kada* |  | 2 |  |  |  |
| *yamalyuma* | *kova* | 1 |  |  | 1 |  |
|  | *ya* |  |  |  |  |  |
| *yuva* | *kasa* |  | 1 |  |  | 2 |
|  | *kudu1* |  |  |  |  |  |
| Total |  | 9 | 32 | 19 | 17 | 11 |
| Total not acceptable |  | 8 | 22 | 14 | 3 | 7 |
| Total dubious/acceptable |  | 1 | 10 | 5 | 14 | 4 |

165

**Table 3.2.215.** Dubious cases of CP production by gender of consultants

| Age group | Females | Males | All |
|---|---|---|---|
| I | 8 | 1 | 9 |
| II | 16 | 16 | 32 |
| III | 15 | 4 | 19 |
| IV | 10 | 7 | 17 |
| V | 4 | 7 | 11 |
| Total | 53 | 35 | 88 |
|  | (= 60%) | (= 40%) | (= 100%) |

**Table 3.2.216.** CP types and tokens in the corpus of Kilivila speech data

| Tokens/CP type | Noun(s) CP refers to |
|---|---|
| 4/*bililo* 'trip' | — |
| 5/*bubwa* 'cut' | *kova* 'fire', *kebudaka* 'beam', *kelagim* 'beam', *tou* 'sugar cane' |
| 18/*buda* 'group' | —, *kukumatua* 'bachelor', *boda* 'group', *gugwadi* 'children', *vivila* 'girl' |
| 6/*bukwa* 'cluster' | *nuya* 'coconut', *bwebwai* 'green coconut' |
| 2/*bwa* 'tree' | *kebasi* 'kind of wood' |
| 1/*dumia* 'swamp' | — |
| 4/*gudi* 'child' | *vivila* 'girl', *gwadi* 'child' |
| 4/*gula* 'heap' | *mani* 'money', *kena* 'spatula' |
| 5/*kabulu* 'sector' | *valu* 'village', *kabulu* 'village sector' |
| 10/*kada* 'road' | *koya* 'mountain' (but: repaired),[†] *vaya* 'river', *keda* 'road' |
| 22/*kai* 'blade' | *regisa* 'axe', *kema* 'axe', *ligogu* 'adze' (+ kinship term produced in several mourning formulae) |
| 1/*kali* 'paddle' | — |
| 9/*kasa* 'row' | *buna* 'cowrie shell', *kai* 'tree', *tauwau* 'men', *vivila* 'girl' |
| 8/*kauya* 'creel' | — |
| 236/*ke* 'wood' | *kai* 'tree, tree and fruit names', *poseni* 'poison', *keyala* 'spear', *gebaku* 'bow', *kaimili* 'mortar', *kaboma* 'plate', *yaguma* 'lime pot', *kenuya* 'dish', *sinata* 'comb', *waga* 'canoe', *selinboti* 'sailing boat', *dingi* 'dinghy', *kemolu* 'canoe', *riga* 'outrigger', *lamina* 'outrigger', *lagim* 'canoe board', *sukusaku* 'top on a canoe prow', *kivaya* 'fish trap', *vadola* 'opening of a basket', *vilivili* 'body of a basket', *medisini* 'medicine', *peni* 'pen', *youdila* 'tool', *kevalapu* 'rafter', *kavala* 'perlin', *kivi* 'rafter', *dagala* 'stick used as support', *budaka* 'plank', *liku* 'foodhouse', *kaitukwa* 'walking stick', *tataba* 'carved board', *boi* 'symbol in a canoe prow', *koni* 'sign of honor', *kabululu* 'point', *salibu* 'mirror', *kuvi* 'type of yams', *pwaka* 'lime', *tobaki* 'tobacco', *ka'eki* 'shell', *dakuna* 'stone', *bweta* 'wreath of flowers', *kova* 'fire', *kenuba* 'firewood', *bela* 'drum', *paledi* 'plate', *kukwanebu* 'story' (but: repaired!), *serota* 'platform', *lubakatakela* 'rainbow', *keyoyova* 'plane', *tuta kevau* 'time for launching' |

**Table 3.2.216.** *(continued)*

| Tokens/CP type | Noun(s) CP refers to |
|---|---|
| 6/*kova* 'fire' | *kova* 'fire' |
| 3/*kudu* 'fibers' | *doba* 'skirt', *vana* 'decoration, herbs' |
| 1/*kubila* 'land' | — |
| 361/*kwe* 'thing' | *vavagi* 'thing', *gugua* 'goods', *valu* 'village', *PNG* 'Papua New Guinea', *simla* 'island', *koya* 'mountain', *yam* 'day', *wiki* 'week', *tetu* 'year', *manakapu* 'reef', *bwala* 'house', *kebila* 'veranda', *kwadeva* 'beach', *pwepwaya* 'ground', *bagula* 'garden', *bugulela* 'plants in the garden', *kuvi* 'yams', *tetu* 'yams', *salutu* 'yams', *kaula* 'yams', *kuku* 'tobacco', *vadila* 'pandanus', *kauveluva* 'food, not yams', *kwetutum* 'your knee', *kunula* 'her/his hair', *pwaneta* 'skull', *puvala* 'his testicles', *matala* 'her/his eyes', *bulaga* 'shadow', *boda* 'group', *biga* 'word', *bigatona* 'speech', *kwestin* 'question', *liliu* 'myth', *livala* 'talk', *livalela* 'news' *nanam'sa* 'idea', *kukwanebu* 'story', *katupoi* 'question', *megwa* 'magic', *bomala* 'tabu', *sula* 'mistake', *mokita* 'truth', *kabitam* 'skill', *mitin* 'meeting', *mwasawa* 'fun', *kovesa* 'competition', *pilasi* 'help', *paisewa* 'work', *agutoki* 'thanks', *bubunela* 'custom', *kato'ula* 'illness', *tauya* 'triton', *buna* 'cowrie shell', *kweduya* 'shell', *poseni* 'poison', *dakuna* 'stone', *youdila* 'tool', *kebudaka* 'beam', *vatila* 'construction to transport something', *vatunu* 'rope', *nabala* 'bottom of a basket', *kena* 'spatula', *kwena* 'pot', *moi* 'mat', *doba* 'skirt', *tarapwapwa* 'carved symbol', *katukwaka* 'cave', *sopi* 'water', *ginigini* 'writing', *stoa* 'store', *kwestin* 'question', *edyukesen* 'education', *bela* 'bell', *lekodi* 'record', *mani* 'money', *laita* 'light', *tepi* 'tape', *proyecta* 'projector', *ensini* 'engine', *hour* 'hour', *namba* 'number', *simenti* 'cement', *mamwa* 'hour', *niva'ila* 'calm sea', *mokolu* 'tree' |
| 8/*kwela* 'pot' | *kwena* 'clay pot', *kerosina* 'drum full of kerosine' |
| 2/*kweya* 'limb' | *kaikela* 'her/his leg' |
| 6/*liku* 'compartment' | *kemolu* 'small canoe', *liu* 'beams connecting the outrigger with the canoe', *vatota* 'stick connecting outrigger and outrigger platform' |
| 5/*lipu* 'compartment of a creel' | — |
| 174/*na1* 'female' | — (names of several women), *vivila* 'girl', *numwaya* 'old woman', *sinebada* 'lady', *kwava* 'wife', *gwadi* 'child', 'kinship terms', *bwagau* 'sorceress', *tokwam* 'cannibal', *dokonikani* 'man-eating monster', *beila* 'monster' |
| 85/*na2* 'animals' | —, *mauna* 'animal, name of specific animals', *yena* 'fish', *tabuya* 'canoe prow' |
| 4/*na3* 'moon' | *tubukona* 'moon' |
| 3/*na4* 'carving' | *tokwalu* 'carved figure on a canoe board' |
| 36/*pila* 'part' | —, *kukwanebu* 'story', *vinavina* 'verses', *sopa* 'joke', *wosi* 'song', *megwa* 'magic', *tegala* 'her/his ear', *kekwabula* 'drawing', *pasporti* 'passport' |

**Table 3.2.216.** *(continued)*

| Tokens/CP type | Noun(s) CP refers to |
|---|---|
| 1/*pwana* 'hole' | *moropu* 'hole' |
| 7/*sam* 'ginger' | *neya* 'ginger' |
| 1/*sisi* 'bough' | *revaya* 'name of a tree' |
| 8/*ta* 'basket' | *peta* 'basket', *taboda* 'door' |
| 1/*tam* 'sprouting' | *kuvi* 'type of yams' |
| 437/*to/te* 'human, male' | — (names of several men), *tau* 'man', *tauwau* 'men', *tomwaya* 'old man', *vivila* 'girl', *nunumwaya* 'old woman', *gwadi* 'child', *gugwadi* 'children', *tommota* 'people' (corpse, kinship terms, forms of address), *pikisila* 'picture', *gumanuma* 'Europeans', *dimdim* 'Europeans', *doketa* 'doctor', *toliwaga* 'owner of a canoe', *referi* 'referee', *kini* 'king', *dokonikani* 'man-eating monster', *tobiu* 'referee' |
| 2/*utu* 'scrap' | —, *unasu* 'small yams' |
| 7/*uva* 'span' | —, *peta* 'basket', *kivaya* 'fish trap', *nuya* 'coconut' |
| 66/*ya* 'flexible' | *bologu* 'tree leaves', *sasova* 'banana leaves', *yakvesi* 'banana leaves', *kum* 'bread fruit', *keibwibwi* 'pandanus', *bisila* 'pandanus streamer', *veyugwa* 'tree leaves', *kwega* 'tree leaves', *yagavana* 'tree leaves', *peta* 'basket', *kivaya* 'fish trap', *kauya* 'shoulder bag', *vatunu* 'rope', *yuvaiyo'ula* 'rope, name of several knots', *naya* 'sail', *pwepu* 'paper', *leta* 'letter', *tau* 'man' (metaphor!) |
| 1/*yeni* 'handful' | *pwaka* 'lime' |
| 1/*yule* 'bundle' | — |
| 1/*yuma* 'length' | *pepe'u* 'small basket' |
| 2/0 'basketful of yams' | — |

Total: 41 types; 1,564 tokens

---

† The note "(but: repaired)" refers to the fact that a speaker first produced this CP with the noun but then repaired the inadequate or ungrammatical phrase, replacing the inappropriate CP with a grammatically correct CP.

**Table 3.2.217.** CP type and tokens—word classes (corpus of transcribed Kilivila speech)

| CP type | Demonstrative pronoun | Numeral | Adjective | Interrogative pronoun | Total |
|---|---|---|---|---|---|
| *bililo* 'trip' | | 4 | | | 4 |
| *bubwa* 'cut off' | 1 | 4 | | | 5 |
| *buda* 'group' | 6 | 7 | 5 | | 18 |
| *bukwa* 'cluster' | 4 | | 2 | | 6 |

**Table 3.2.217.** *(continued)*

| CP type | Demonstrative pronoun | Numeral | Adjective | Interrogative pronoun | Total |
|---|---|---|---|---|---|
| *bwa* 'tree' | | 2 | | | 2 |
| *dumia* 'swamp' | | | 1 | | 1 |
| *gudi* 'child' | 1 | 2 | 1 | | 4 |
| *gula* 'heap' | 4 | | | | 4 |
| *kabulu* 'sector' | | 5 | | | 5 |
| *kada/keda* 'road' | 8 | 1 | 1 | | 10 |
| *kai* 'stone blade' | 6 | 2 | 14 | | 22 |
| *kali* 'paddle' | | 1 | | | 1 |
| *kasa* 'row' | | 9 | | | 9 |
| *kauya* 'creel' | 2 | 6 | | | 8 |
| *ke* 'wood' | 138 | 49 | 47 | 2 | 236 |
| *kova* 'fire' | 6 | | | | 6 |
| *kudu* 'fibers' | 1 | 2 | | | 3 |
| *kwabila* 'land' | 1 | | | | 1 |
| *kwe* 'thing' | 167 | 114 | 79 | 1 | 361 |
| *kwela* 'pot' | 3 | 1 | 4 | | 8 |
| *kweya* 'limb' | 1 | 1 | | | 2 |
| *liku* 'compartment' | 2 | 4 | | | 6 |
| *lipu* 'compartment' | | 5 | | | 5 |
| *na1* 'female' | 136 | 6 | 31 | 1 | 174 |
| *na2* 'animals' | 69 | 13 | 3 | | 85 |
| *na3* 'moon' | 1 | 3 | | | 4 |
| *na4* 'carving' | 3 | | | | 3 |
| *pila* 'part' | 24 | 8 | 4 | | 36 |
| *pwanina* 'hole' | 1 | | | | 1 |
| *sam* 'ginger' | | 7 | | | 7 |
| *sisi* 'bough' | 1 | | | | 1 |
| *ta* 'basket' | 1 | 4 | 3 | | 8 |
| *tam* 'sprouting' | 1 | | | | 1 |
| *to/te* 'male' | 252 | 110 | 70 | 5 | 437 |
| *utu* 'scrap' | | 2 | | | 2 |
| *uva* 'span' | | 7 | | | 7 |
| *ya* 'flexible' | 34 | 23 | 7 | 2 | 66 |
| *yeni* 'handful' | | 1 | | | 1 |
| *yule* 'bundle' | | 1 | | | 1 |
| *yuma* 'length' | | 1 | | | 1 |
| 0 'basketful of yams' | | 2 | | | 2 |
| Total | 874 | 407 | 272 | 11 | 1,564 |

**Table 3.2.218.** Percentage of tokens for each CP type in corpus of Kilivila speech

| CP type | Tokens | Percent (100% = 1,564 tokens) |
|---|---|---|
| *tolte* 'male, human' | 437 | 28 |
| *kwe* 'thing' | 361 | 23 |
| *ke* 'wood' | 236 | 15 |
| *na1* 'female' | 174 | 11 |
| *na2* 'animal' | 85 | 5 |
| *ya* 'flexible' | 66 | 4 |
| *pila* 'part' | 36 | 2 |
| *kai* 'stone blade' | 22 | 1 |
| *buda* 'group' | 18 | 1 |
| *kada* 'road' | 10 | 0.6 |
| *kasa* 'row' | 9 | 0.6 |
| *kauya* 'creel' | 8 | 0.5 |
| *kwela* 'pot' | 8 | 0.5 |
| *ta* 'basket' | 8 | 0.5 |
| *sam* 'ginger' | 7 | 0.4 |
| *uva* 'span' | 7 | 0.4 |
| *bukwa* 'cluster' | 6 | 0.4 |
| *kova* 'fire' | 6 | 0.4 |
| *liku* 'compartment' | 6 | 0.4 |
| *bubwa* 'cut off' | 5 | 0.3 |
| *kabulu* 'sector' | 5 | 0.3 |
| *lipu* 'compartment' | 5 | 0.3 |
| *bililo* 'trip' | 4 | 0.3 |
| *gudi* 'child' | 4 | 0.3 |
| *gula* 'heap' | 4 | 0.3 |
| *na3* 'moon' | 4 | 0.3 |
| *kudu* 'fibers' | 3 | 0.2 |
| *na4* 'carving' | 3 | 0.2 |
| *bwa* 'tree' | 2 | 0.1 |
| *kweya* 'limb' | 2 | 0.1 |
| *utu* 'scrap' | 2 | 0.1 |
| 0 'basketful of yams' | 2 | 0.1 |
| *dumia* 'swamp' | 1 | 0.06 |
| *kali* 'paddle strike' | 1 | 0.06 |
| *kwabila* 'land plot' | 1 | 0.06 |
| *pwanina* 'hole' | 1 | 0.06 |
| *sisi* 'bough' | 1 | 0.06 |
| *tam* 'sprouting' | 1 | 0.06 |
| *yeni* 'handful' | 1 | 0.06 |
| *yule* 'bundle' | 1 | 0.06 |
| *yuma* 'length' | 1 | 0.06 |

## 3.3 RESULTS

In this section, I try to answer the questions raised in section 3.1. The headings within this section repeat the questions as they were stated in section 3.1.

### 3.3.1 Which Formulatives Constitute the Kilivila CP System and What is the Actual Occurrence of CPs in Recorded Tests?

Before I can start listing the formatives that constitute the Kilivila CP system, I first have to classify the CPs given in section 3.2. From the beginning, I have emphasized that I only provisionally assigned the status "CP type" to all the CPs listed. Now, with all the data presented, I will further refine this rather broad and preliminary concept. The reasons that force me to do this are obvious. The attentive reader of the tables presented in section 3.2 will notice that the label "CP type" was assigned not only to CPs like *kai*, *bogi*, and *kova*, but also to CPs like *buda*, *kada*, *kweya*, and *kwoila*, which were listed with variants (*boda*, *budu*; *keda*; *kwaya*, *keya*; and *kwela*, respectively). To arrive at a consistent description and nomenclature, the label "CP type (proper)" should subsume all variants of a CP type.

On the basis of this consideration, the following modifications in the definition of CP type are necessary:

1. The formatives *iga* 'name' and *yegila* 'name' are to be regarded as two variants of one CP type (see Tables 3.2.18, 3.2.56, 3.2.120, 3.2.145, and 3.2.209).

2. The formatives *duya* 'door, entrance' and *kaduya*, *kaduyo* 'entrance, door' are to be regarded as three variants of one CP type (see Tables 3.2.11, 3.2.18, 3.2.49, 3.2.62, 3.2.138, and 3.2.151).

3. The formatives *peta* 'basket' and *ta* 'basket' are to be regarded as two variants of one CP type (see Tables 3.2.18, 3.2.25, 3.2.32, 3.2.49, 3.2.104, 3.2.183, and 3.2.193).

4. The CPs *va* 'door' and *vaya*, *vayo* 'door' are to be regarded as three variants of one CP type (see Tables 3.2.111, 3.2.113, 3.2.200, and 3.2.202).

The reasons for these redefinitions are obvious in the cases of *iga/yegila* and *peta/ta*. *Yegila* is a repeater, and *iga* is a classifier, probably the shortened form of the repeater. The same holds true for *peta* and *ta*. Here, *peta* is the repeater and *ta* is the classifier (again, a shortened form of the repeater).

Similarly, I can justify handling the CP variants *duya/kaduya/kaduyo* and *va/vaya/vayo* in this way. Although only the formative *vaya* is a repeater (at least to a certain degree), *duya* can be regarded as a shortened form of *kaduya* and *va* as a shortened form of *vaya*. As stated elsewhere (G. Senft 1986:242, 219, 400, 407), the Trobrianders do not differentiate between the formatives *duya* and *kaduyo* and *va* and *vaya* lexically and semantically. The meaning of *va* includes the meaning of *duya*. Thus, we might also regard the formatives *va*, *vaya*, *vayo*, *duya*, *kaduya*, *kaduyo* as variants of only one

CP type (see also Tables 3.2.4, 3.2.11, 3.2.18, 3.2.25, 3.2.138, 3.2.151, 3.2.200, 3.2.202). However, this proceeding also implies a chain of development that leads from the formatives *kaduya/duya* and *vaya/vaya* to the classifier *va*. Although this argument is plausible, it is highly speculative. Therefore, having hinted at such a possible interpretation of the data, I will continue to differentiate between the CP type *va/vaya/vayo*, on the one hand, and the CP type *duya/kaduya/kaduyo*, on the other hand.

In the Tables of section 3.2, I generally listed polysemous CPs like *kwe* and *ke* without any differentiation of their various meanings. However, I differentiated between the meanings of some CP types like *na* (*na1–na4*). Again, for the sake of a consistent description and nomenclature, the following modifications with respect to the definition of the concept CP type are necessary:

1. *Kabulo/kabulu* is to be regarded as one polysemous CP.
2. *Kudu* is to be regarded as one polysemous CP.
3. *Na* is to be regarded as one polysemous CP.

According to my consultants, the formatives \**boma*, \**iki*, and \**kava* cannot be accepted as belonging to the system of Kilivila CPs.

If I take all these considerations into account, I can now list the CP types that constitute the elicited, observed, and documented system of CPs in Kilivila. Table 3.3.1 presents these CP types together with their meanings. Some of these meanings are not documented in my corpus of transcribed Kilivila speech data, but are the result of my lexicographic work.

I should mention here that during my restudy on the Trobiand Islands in 1989, my consultants produced three additional CPs, namely, *num* 'magic, magical formula' (consultant: Vadomna); *tili* 'bits of lime clinging to a lime spatula' (consultant Vadomna); *sebulu* 'grass skirt for little girls' (consultants: Ilakelava and Kadawaya). However, these CPs seem to be either very rarely used or almost obsolete, and they are mentioned here only for the sake of completeness.

I want to emphasize that it is the 88 classifiers presented in Table 3.3.1 that are the focus of attention of the analyses presented here. As stated in section 3.1, a complete description of the CPs should include the formulation of the rules speakers use in their production of a certain CP. This description is given in section 3.3.4.2. For the purposes of the present section, the mere list of CPs that constitute the elicited, observed, and documented (sub)system of CPs in Kilivila should suffice.

For the sake of completeness, a list of the CPs and their glosses that are mentioned in Lawton (1980:213–256), but were not produced by my consultants, are presented in Table 3.3.2.

Capell (1969:60–62) lists three formatives that have not been mentioned so far: *gubwa*, *ilu*, and *ukdu*. My consultants rejected Capell's gloss 'square' for *gubwa*, replacing it with 'group of four'; however, they emphasized that

**Table 3.3.1.** Kilivila CP types

| CP type | Gloss(es) and comments |
| --- | --- |
| 1/*beku* | 'stone blade' |
| 2/*bililo* | 'trip'[†] |
| 3/*bogi* | 'night' |
| 4/*bubu/bobu/bobo* | 'cut across, cut transversely, (block) cut off' |
| 5/*bubwa* | 'cut across, part(s) cut off' |
| 6/*buda/boda/budu* | 'group, team, crowd' |
| 7/*bukwa/buko* | a. 'fruit cluster' |
|  | b. 'cowries tied into a specific cluster'[‡] |
| 8/*bwa* | 'trees, wooden things' |
| 9/*bwalita* | 'sea' |
| 10/*deli* | 'company, group on the move' |
| 11/*doba* | 'skirt made of banana leaves, grass skirt' |
| 12/*duli* | 'cluster, bundle' |
| 13/*dumia* | 'swamp, swamplike'[†] |
| 14/*duya/duyo/kaduya/kaduyo* | 'door, entrance' |
| 15/*gili* | 'row' |
| 16/*giwi* | 'cut' |
| 17/*guba* | 'bundles of taro' |
| 18/*gudi* | a. 'child'; |
|  | b. 'immature human'[†] |
| 19/*gula/guli/gulo/guno* | 'heap, group' |
| 20/*gum* | 'bit, small piece' |
| 21/*iga/yegila* | 'name' |
| 22/*kabisi* | 'compartment of a foodhouse, section/division in a foodhouse' |
| 23/*kabulo/kabulu* | a. 'protuberances' |
|  | b. 'village sectors; areas of authority'[†] |
|  | c. 'cape, point, peninsula'[‡] |
|  | d. 'half of something'[‡] |
| 24/*kada/keda* | a. 'road, track' |
|  | b. 'way in which something is done'[‡] |
| 25/*kai* | 'stone blade' |
| 26/*ka'i* | 'tooth' |
| 27/*kala* | 'day' |
| 28/*kali* | 'paddle strike'[†] |
| 29/*kapwa/kapo* | a. 'bundles (wrapped up), parcel' |
|  | b. 'nest of birds'[‡] |
| 30/*kasa* | 'row, line' |

[†]This meaning of the CP type was not elicited in the test.

[‡]This (these) meaning(s) of the CP type are the result of my lexicographic research.

**Table 3.3.1.** *(continued)*

| CP type | Gloss(es) and comments |
|---|---|
| 31/*kauya* | 'fish trap, creel'[†] |
| 32/*kavi* | 'tool' |
| 33/*ke* | a. 'wooden things' |
| | b. 'rigid, long objects' |
| | c. 'unmarked form for inanimates' (general classifier) |
| | d. 'fire' |
| 34/*kila* | 'clusters/hands of bananas' |
| 35/*kova* | 'fire, fireplace' |
| 36/*kubila/kwabila* | 'large land plot' |
| 37/*kudu* | a. 'band of fibers' (especially the band of fibers at the waistband of a grass skirt) |
| | b. 'tooth' |
| | c. 'bundles of lashing creeper'[†] |
| 38/*kumla* | 'earth oven' |
| 39/*kwe* | a. 'thing, anything indefinite or unknown, unmarked form for inanimates' (general classifier) |
| | b. 'shells and clams' |
| 40/*kweya/kwaya/keya* | a. 'limb, severed limb' |
| | b. 'yard (land adjacent to a house)'[‡] |
| 41/*kwoila/kwela/kway/kwaila/ kweikwa/kwena* | 'clay pot, potlike' |
| 42/*kwoya/koya* | 'mountain, hill' |
| 43/*liku* | a. 'compartments of a foodhouse, compartments of a canoe' |
| | b. 'area of authority'[‡] |
| 44/*lila* | 'bough, branch, leaf' |
| 45/*lilo/lola/lilo'u* | a. 'walk, journey' |
| | b. 'number of times going somewhere'[‡] |
| | c. 'number of times doing something'[‡] |
| 46/*lipu* | 'compartment of a creel, tier'[†] |
| 47/*luba* | 'bundle (of rolls), parcels (of taro pudding)' |
| 48/*luva* | a. 'wooden dishes' (*kaboma*-type, full of one's share of food during a food-distribution ceremony/ritual) |
| | b. 'tied bundle' |
| 49/*megwa* | 'magic, magical formula' |
| 50/*meila/mavila* | a. 'part of a song, part of a magical formula' |
| | b. 'part of a (Bible) chapter'[‡] |
| | c. 'part of a day'[‡] |
| 51/*mmwa/mmo* | 'conical bundle (of taro)' |
| 52/*na* | a. 'persons of female gender' |
| | b. 'animals' |
| | c. 'stars, planets, moon'[†] |
| | d. 'carvings in human likeness'[†] |
| | e. 'corpses'[‡] |
| | f. 'spirits, dwarfs'[‡] |

**Table 3.3.1.** (continued)

| CP type | Gloss(es) and comments |
|---|---|
| 53/nigwa/nigo | a. 'hole'<br>b. 'nest'[‡] |
| 54/nina | a. 'parts of a song'<br>b. 'idea, thought'[‡] |
| 55/nutu/notu | 'kneaded things, dot, drop' |
| 56/nunu | 'corner(s) of a garden' |
| 57/oyla | a. 'string'<br>b. 'fish on strings' |
| 58/peta/ta | a. 'basket'<br>b. 'contents of a basket' (but not baskets of yams!)[‡] |
| 59/pila/pa | 'part, piece' |
| 60/po'ula | a. 'plantation, grove'<br>b. 'heap, group'[‡] |
| 61/pwanina/pona/ponina/ponu/polu/pwana | 'punctured, something with a hole in it, hole' |
| 62/sa | 'nut bunch' |
| 63/sam | 'ginger' (in play accompanying verses)[†] |
| 64/si | 'small bit' |
| 65/sipu | 'sheaf' (Lawton (1980) gives the additional meanings 'tangle, tangled line, rope, net, string') |
| 66/sisi | a. 'bough'<br>b. 'cut off part of a tree'[†]<br>c. 'division of a magical formula'[‡] |
| 67/siva | a. 'time'<br>b. 'number of times doing something'[‡] |
| 68/siwa | 'sea portions, ownership division with reference to fishing rights' |
| 69/suya/suye | 'batch of fish on strings' |
| 70/tam | 'sprouting, sprouting yams' |
| 71/tetu | 'yams' |
| 72/to/te | a. 'persons of male sex'<br>b. 'human beings' |
| 73/tuta/tuto | 'time, occasion' |
| 74/utu | 'scrap, parts (cut off), small particles, fragments' |
| 75/uva | a. 'span, measure (the span of two extended arms, from tip to tip)'<br>b. 'items measured in spans'[‡] |
| 76/val/vaya/vayo/vala | a. 'door, window'<br>b. 'river, creek, sea passage'[‡] |
| 77/vakala | 'belt of spondylus shell discs' |
| 78/vili | 'untwisted' |
| 79/vilo | 'place, area, village' |
| 80/vosi/wosi | 'song, parts of a song' |

**Table 3.3.1.** *(continued)*

| CP type | Gloss(es) and comments |
|---|---|
| 81/*wela* | 'batch of fish, string of fish' |
| 82/*ya* | 'flexible things, thin things' |
| 83/*yam* | a. 'day'<br>b. 'number of days'[‡] |
| 84/*yuma*/*yam*/*yuma*/*yama* | a. 'hand'<br>b. 'length, measure (the span of two extended arms, from the fingertips of one hand to the wrist of the other hand)'[†]<br>c. 'yard' (measurement)[‡] |
| 85/*yeni* | 'a handful of something'[†] |
| 86/*yulai*/*yule* | 'bundle of four things' |
| 87/*yuva*/*yuwo* | 'shoal' |
| 88/0 | 'a basketful of yams' (this zero classifier is only used when baskets of yams are counted) |

**Table 3.3.2.** CP types from Lawton 1980 that were not listed in Table 3.3.1

| CP type | Gloss |
|---|---|
| L1/*biga* | 'word, statement, message, public speech' |
| L2/*biko* | 'coconut bunch' |
| L3/*bili* | 'roll, anything rolled up' |
| L4/*bo* | 'cut across' |
| L5/*bubulo* | 'anything manufactured or created' |
| L6/*buko*/*buku* | 'buried' |
| L7/*buliga* | 'floor or story'; 'drawers or shelves in series'; 'horizontal divisions in a foodhouse' |
| L8/*bulu* | 'half-submerged (boat)' |
| L9/*buluwo* | 'ten-group (animals)' |
| L10/*dala*/*dila* | 'family line within the clan group' |
| L11/*dodiga* | 'load, contents' |
| L12/*gabu*/*gubu* | 'fireplace; place where fire or sparks have burned body; batch of roasted food' |
| L13/*gibu* | 'sufficient' |
| L14/*gini* | 'mouthful of food' |
| L15/*givi* | 'serve of fish' |
| L16/*gubo*/*gubu* | 'garden division' |
| L17/*gugulo* | 'heap; meeting, gathering' |
| L18/*gulo* | 'group; heap; bundle of fibres laid side by side' |

**Table 3.3.2.** *(continued)*

| CP type | Gloss |
|---------|-------|
| L19/*igi* | 'wind' |
| L20/*ika* | 'tens of things' |
| L21/*iwo* | 'group' |
| L22/*kabila* | 'large cut/serving of meat, fish, etc.' |
| L23/*kabilikova* | 'fireplace' |
| L24/*kadida* | 'very small garden division; division of a task between several workers' |
| L25/*kaiga/kaigi* | 'sound of a voice' |
| L26/*kailiku* | 'suburb, part of a village' |
| L27/*kaiyuvai/yuvai* | 'layers, rows of things' |
| L28/*kalipo* | 'site, part selected for some purpose' |
| L29/*kalivisi/kaluvisi* | 'large garden division' |
| L30/*kalo* | 'two-bundle crustacean' |
| L31/*kaluwo* | 'ten days; ten groups of *kai, ke* items' |
| L32/*kapu* | 'mouthful of drink' |
| L33/*kapuli* | 'group of parcels, cargo of goods, load of people' |
| L34/*kapupu* | 'grove tuft of hair left on head after head shaved' |
| L35/*kasila* | 'ten group (wealth)' |
| L36/*katukuni* | 'reel, one turn in a roll of anything' |
| L37/*katuluwo* | 'large group' |
| L38/*katupo* | 'section, quarter' |
| L39/*kaulo* | 'ten group (strings of fish)' |
| L40/*kaya* | 'half (piece of food)' |
| L41/*kevala* | 'batch drying' |
| L42/*kipu* | 'cut of meat, mouthful of flesh' |
| L43/*kumila* | 'clan' |
| L44/*kuno/kuna* | 'rain' |
| L45/*kununu* | 'serving of greens, number of fibres laid together' |
| L46/*kupa* | 'line rolled in loose bundles; serving of greens (uncooked)' |
| L47/*kupo* | 'two-string (fish, marine creatures)' |
| L48/*kuwo* | 'crumb' |
| L49/*kwailuwo* | 'tens of things' |
| L50/*lada* | 'small fishing spot' |
| L51/*lapou* | 'a third of' |
| L52/*ligila* | 'group action, group of acts completed' |
| L53/*lilivi* | 'forked stick' |
| L54/*livisi* | 'shelf, divisions in a foodhouse, contents of one division' |
| L55/*lukuva* | 'growing bundle' |
| L56/*lupo* | 'very small garden division' |
| L57/*miga* | 'appearance, face' |

**Table 3.3.2.** (continued)

| CP type | Gloss |
|---------|-------|
| L58/*moya* | 'limb; position in family line' |
| L59/*mweli* | 'practices; bundle of leaves' |
| L60/*nakwa* | 'thing' |
| L61/*no* | 'blow' |
| L62/*puli* | 'bunch' |
| L63/*pulu* | 'garden mound' |
| L64/*pupai* | 'layer of filth' |
| L65/*pwa* | 'excrement' |
| L66/*pwasa* | 'rotten' |
| L67/*sega* | 'branching' |
| L68/*seluva* | 'bundle being tied' |
| L69/*seuyo* | 'lagoon' |
| L70/*sisili* | 'cut of meat' |
| L71/*siyo*/*suyo* | 'things strung through hole' |
| L72/*sobulo* | 'growing (shoot)' |
| L73/*soulo* | 'fishing spot' |
| L74/*tabili* | 'roll' |
| L75/*tabudo* | 'room' |
| L76/*tavi* | 'loose coil' |
| L77/*teni* | 'tight coil' |
| L78/*tubo* | 'generation' |
| L79/*tupila* | 'fleet' |
| L80/*udi*/*udila* | 'land tract' |
| L81/*umila* | 'grove' |
| L82/*uwo* | 'two bundle' |
| L83/*vala* | 'small garden division' |
| L84/*wouyo* | 'newness' |
| L85/*yivi* | 'serving of food pieces' |

this CP is hardly ever used. My consultants did not recognize the CPs *ilu* and *ukdu*; it should be mentioned here that Capell's formative *ukdu* does not agree with Kilivila syllable patterns (G. Senft 1986:20–122).

Thus, if we add to the 88 CPs in Table 3.3.1 the three newly found CPs *num*, *sebulu*, and *tili*, as well as the 85 CPs mentioned by Lawton (1980) and the CP *gubwa* quoted by Capell (and confirmed by my consultants), we arrive at an overall CP inventory of 177 formatives.[2] However, I want to emphasize

[2] The discrepancy between the number of CPs given here and in G. Senft (1986:69–75) is due to considerations similar to those presented in the introductory paragraphs of this section.

**Table 3.3.3.** Percent of CP tokens in relation to all transcribed words in overall corpus of Kilivila speech data

| Word class | No. of CP tokens | Percent[†] |
|---|---|---|
| Demonstrative pronouns | 874 | 2.5% |
| Numerals | 407 | 1.2% |
| Adjectives | 272 | 0.8% |
| Interrogative pronouns/adverbs | 11 | 0.03% |
| Total | 1,564 | 4.53% |

[†]34,955 words = 100%.

once more that only the 88 CPs presented in Table 3.1.1 are used in the research presented in this book.

I will now address the issue of the actual occurrence of CPs in recorded texts. To do this, I must refer to the data in appendix B, to the discussion of the CP types and tokens produced in my overall corpus of Kilivila language given in section 3.2.1, and especially to Tables 3.2.216 and 3.2.217.

As I mentioned in section 3.2.1, the production of CPs in actual communication is highly dependent on the text category. The text category influences not only the number of CP tokens found with demonstrative pronouns, numerals, adjectives, or interrogative pronouns/adverbs, but also the number of different CP types produced by the consultants. With the different text categories produced by the consultants in the second data set, I cannot justify any inferences from CP production to characteristics of the individual consultants' speech behavior. Thus, it remains an open question whether the text category or the individual consultant's characteristics of speech behavior, or both, are responsible for the CP production observed in this data set.

As stated in section 3.2.1, I only dare to assign to the observations and interpretations presented there the status of anecdotal findings. Nevertheless, as far as I know, Tables 3.2.216 and 3.2.217 present for the first time in the published literature a detailed summation of classifier types and tokens from actual speech (and, in the Kilivila case, with all four word classes that use CPs as a means of their word formation). On the basis of the data presented in these tables, I can answer the question about the actual occurrence of CPs in recorded texts, keeping in mind the precautions mentioned previously.

My corpus of transcribed Kilivila speech data consists of 34,955 words,[3] including 1,564 CP tokens representing 41 different CP types. If I relate the number of CP tokens to the total number of words, I find that words using CPs in their word formation represent 4.5% of all words documented in the recorded and transcribed texts. Table 3.3.3 gives the exact percentages of the actual occurrence of CPs for all four word classes.

[3]The definition of "word" is based on G. Senft (1986:28–102); however, affixes are not counted separately here.

Although we lack similar data from other classifier languages, these data may serve as a guideline for future discussions about the actual occurrence of CPs in recorded texts. Whether these numbers should be interpreted as being relatively low is a question that remains open.

### 3.3.2 How Is the CP System Acquired by Trobriand Children?

As stated in section 3.1, this question comprises a number of different aspects. I will try to answer these separate subquestions in the same order that they were raised in section 3.1.

#### 3.3.2.1 What Is the General Temporal Progress of the CP Acquisition Process?

In section 3.1, I mentioned that the informal pretests I carried out revealed that children start to acquire the CP system at the age of approximately 4 ($\pm 6$ months). This result of the informal pretests is confirmed by the data presented in section 3.2. As the first analyses and interpretations of the data presented in sections 3.2.1.1–3.2.1.3 show, I can record the following results with respect to the temporal progress of the childrens' CP acquisition documented in their CP production.

1. Children start to acquire and to produce CPs at the age of 4 ($\pm 6$ months).
2. Five years is the critical age with respect to the CP acquisition process.
3. At about 6 years of age, there is a kind of "explosion" in the production of CPs (see Tables 3.2.1 and 3.2.2).
4. Nine years is another critical age with respect to the CP acquisition process: the frequency of CPs produced (in the elicitation test) increases rather dramatically at this age (see Tables 3.2.8–3.2.10).

The 'rule of thumb' generally accepted in psycholinguistic acquisition research, quoted in section 3.2.1.3 in Klein's formulation (Klein 1984:21) is confirmed by our data. If we compare the data produced by the consultants in age group III with that produced by the consultants in age groups I and II, on the one hand, and with the data produced by the consultants of the age groups IV and V, on the other hand, it is clear that, on the whole, the CP acquisition process ends during or after puberty. The 12 consultants in age group III produced 109 CP tokens more than the consultants in age group II; however, they only produced 1 token less than the consultants in age group V and 31 CP tokens less than the consultants in the age group IV (see Tables 3.2.15, 3.2.8, 3.2.22, and 3.2.29). Moreover, the consultants in age group III showed the highest mean value of different CP types produced of all five age groups (see Table 3.2.124). Although this value exceeds the respective means for age groups IV and V by 2 and 1 points only, it surpasses the value for age group II by 12 points.

### 3.3.2.2 Are There Any Differences in the CP Acquisition Process With Respect to the Production of Demonstrative Pronouns, Adjectives, and Numerals That Use CPs as Morphemes in Their Word Formation?

I can answer this question by summarizing the first analyses and interpretations of the data presented in sections 3.2.1.1–3.2.1.5. The results are based on the data presented in Tables 3.2.1, 3.2.8, 3.2.15, 3.2.22, and 3.2.29. If we compare the data presented there, we note the following:

1. Children who range in age from 4 to 7 years produce CPs most often with adjectives, then with numerals, and then with demonstrative pronouns. I assume that the different CP production frequencies documented in Table 3.2.1 can be interpreted as indices for the sequential order of the acquisition (and production) of the respective word classes. This results mirrors the general tendency documented in the elicited CP data. It neglects the specific use of CPs with the three word classes that depends on certain documented text categories in my overall corpus of Kilivila speech data (see section 3.2.1.1 and the comments on Table 3.2.6).

2. Nine years is not only a critical age with respect to the rather dramatic increase of CPs produced, it is also a critical age with respect to a balanced usage of CPs with adjectives, numerals, and demonstrative pronouns. This result again neglects the specific use of CPs in certain (documented) text categories (see section 3.2.1.2 and the comments on Table 3.2.13). The data gathered during the CP elicitation test show a balanced use of CPs with the three word classes elicited for all consultants in age groups III, IV, and V.

For the sake of completeness, it should be noted that the data documented in the overall corpus of Kilivila speech show that the actual occurrence in recorded texts of the interrogative pronoun/adverb that uses CPs in its word formation is rather low indeed (see Tables 3.2.14, 3.2.21, 3.2.28, 3.2.35, and 3.3.3).

Finally, I want to mention here once more the rather interesting interpretation provoked by the first analyses of the data presented in Table 3.2.6 (see also Table 3.2.13). These data show a rather high proportion of demonstrative pronouns in recorded texts produced by children from 4 to 7 years old. Because these pronouns were produced within the text category "fairy tale," I arrived at the following interpretation: It may be that fairy tales are told not only to enterain children and transmit cultural ideas and values, but also as a means to foster the acquisition process with respect to certain grammatical features—here demonstrative pronouns—that are obviously difficult to acquire by children of this age.

### 3.3.2.3 Are There Any Gender-Specific Differences in the CP Acquisition Process?

I can answer this question by summarizing and elaborating on the first interpretations and analyses presented in section 3.2, especially in section 3.2.1. Thus, I note the following: Children ranging from 4 to 7 years old show rather distinct gender-specific differences in the CP acquisition process (see Table 3.2.1). Boys produce more CP types (4 on the average) and more CP tokens (130) than girls. Moreover, the order of acquisition and production of CPs with first adjectives, then numerals, and then demonstrative prounouns is more marked in girls than in boys.

These results obviously hold for children who are 8 years old, too, as the data produced by consultant 14 in age group II (see Table 3.2.8) indicate. However, these gender-specific differences become less marked if we look at the speech behavior of children ranging from 9 to 14 years of age. I emphasized before that 9 years is another critical age in the CP acquisition process. Thus, I had to exclude consultant 14, Olopola, who had just passed her eighth birthday, from my first interpretation of the data presented in Table 3.2.8 in section 3.2.1.2 (see the arguments given there). With this modification of Table 3.2.8, I note the following:

If we calculate the average frequency of CP tokens produced for the 5 girls ranging in age from 9 to 14 years (201.2 tokens) and if we do the same for the 6 boys of the same age group (201.5 tokens), the difference in the production of CP tokens becomes a *quantité négligeable*, that is, insignificant. Consultants who are about 9 years of age and older show a balanced use of CP tokens with the three word classes elicited in the test. However, if we calculate the average number of CP types produced by the 5 girls and the 6 boys in age group II (9–14 years, note that consultant 24 is almost 9 years old), we find the following results (see Tables 3.2.8 and 3.2.124): For girls, the average number of CP types produced is 26.4; for boys, it is 29.8. Thus, boys in age group II produced more CP types than girls of the same age. As mentioned in sections 3.2.1.3–3.2.1.5 and as documented in Table 3.2.124, this gender difference holds for 4 of the 5 age groups tested. It is only with the consultants of age group IV that the average number of CP types produced by men does not surpass that for women.

The gender-specific difference in the acquisition (and production) of CP types may be a result of the Trobrianders' education practices, which offer boys a much broader range of possibilities to experience their surrounding environment than they offer girls (see B. Senft 1985). Moreover, as my data show (see, e.g., G. Senft 1987d), men participate in public speeches much more often than women, although the women's social status in the Trobriand matrilineal society is rather high (see, e.g., Weiner 1976, 1988). Thus, it may be that parents and relatives especially promote their sons' or their young male relatives' rhetorical abilities and qualities. Here, we have to keep in mind that male adolescents usually develop a rather close relationship with their fathers and their male relatives. What should also be emphasized is that the Trobriand society, strictly stratified according to clan hierarchies, offers social prestige to men who are born in lower-ranking clans if they prove to be good gardeners and/or good rhetoricians (see Malinowski 1935; Senft 1985e, 1987c, 1987d, 1991b; Weiner 1976, 1982, 1983, 1988). These social, extralinguistic facts may explain the gender differences we find in the acquisition and production of CP types—not only in children, but also in adolescents during and after puberty and in adults older than 36 years. Why we do not find this difference in the production of CP types in men and women in age group IV (21–35 years) is a question that will be discussed in section 3.3.3.3 below.

Gender differences in the CP acquisition process that find their expression in preferences for the production of certain CP types will be discussed in the following section.

It should be noted that the data documented in the overall corpus of Kilivila speech data confirm, at least in part, the results just presented, which were based on the analyses of the data elicited by the questionnaire (see sections 3.2.1.1–3.2.1.3; also 3.2.1.4 and 3.2.1.5).

### 3.3.2.4 What Is the Order in Which the Individual CPs Are Acquired?

To answer this question, I will first present a table listing the CP types and their respective tokens produced by the consultants of the five age groups during the elicitation test. The table also lists the CP types that were not produced by the consultants in the elicitation test and the CP types and tokens produced in the overall corpus of Kilivila speech data that were not documented in the elicitation test data.

I will now examine the individual CP types, following the order given in Tables 3.2.2, 3.2.9, and 3.2.16. In addition to these tables and Table 3.3.4, the tables presented in section 3.2.2 are relevant to the discussion of the order in which the individual CP types are acquired.

The CP types *to/te* 'persons of male gender, human beings' and *na* (in its meaning 'persons of female gender' ( = *na1*) were produced by all consultants in age group I. As the tables show, only a few consultants produced more (or less) than the three expected tokens of these two CPs (these will be discussed in sections 3.3.3 and 3.3.4). On the basis of these data, I conclude that *to/te* and *na1* are the first CPs that are acquired by Trobriand children.

The CP *kwe* 'thing' was produced by 4 girls and 5 boys in age group I. Six of these 9 children show a rather high number of CP tokens produced during the elicitation test. Thus I conclude that children acquire this CP type with its broad range of accepted uses. The number of *kwe* tokens produced in the elicitation test rises quite dramatically with the consultants of age group II; however, it decreases again with the consultants of age group III (these phenomena are discussed in sections 3.3.3 and 3.3.4).

The CP *ke* 'wood, long objects, inanimates' was also produced by 4 girls and 5 boys in age group I. With this CP type, we observe phenomena that

**Table 3.3.4.** CP types and tokens produced by all consultants

| CP type | No. of tokens produced by age group | | | | |
|---|---|---|---|---|---|
| | I | II | III | IV | V |
| *beku* 'stone blade' | | | 1 | 1 | |
| *bogi* 'night' | | 2 | 8 | 2 | |
| *bubu/bobu* 'cut across' | | 7 | 23 | 13 | 25 |
| *bubwa* 'cut off' | 1 | | 8 | 10 | 10 |
| *buda/boda/budu* 'group' | 8 | 20 | 52 | 32 | 44 |
| *bukwa* 'fruit cluster' | 3 | | | | |
| *bwa* 'tree' | 10 | 26 | 12 | 7 | 6 |
| *bwalita* 'sea' | | | 2 | 4 | |
| *deli* 'group' | | 4 | 30 | 23 | 36 |
| *doba* 'grass skirt' | | | | 1 | |
| *duli* 'cluster' | 3 | 15 | 33 | 27 | 30 |
| *duya/kaduya/kaduyo* 'door' | 1 | 1 | 11 | 1 | 5 |
| *gili* 'row' | | | 3 | 1 | 8 |
| *giwi* 'cut' | | 17 | 33 | 31 | 25 |
| *guba* 'bundle of taro' | | | | | 3 |
| *gudi* 'child' | 7 | 30 | 36 | 33 | 36 |
| *gula* 'heap' | | 8 | 15 | 20 | 13 |
| *gum* 'bit' | | 9 | 30 | 28 | 21 |
| *iga/yegila* 'name' | 10 | 34 | 36 | 33 | 36 |
| *kabisi* 'compartment' | | 10 | 23 | 23 | 22 |
| *kabulo1* 'point' | | | | | 3 |
| *kabulo2/kabulu* 'sector' | | 2 | 10 | 2 | 7 |
| *kada/keda* 'road' | 17 | 81 | 93 | 78 | 72 |
| *kai* 'stone blade' | 3 | 27 | 35 | 35 | 36 |
| *ka'i* 'tooth' | 13 | 30 | 28 | 26 | 30 |
| *kala* 'day' | | | | | 3 |
| *kapwa/kapo* 'parcel' | 5 | 18 | 6 | 6 | 11 |
| *kasa* 'row' | 11 | 32 | 46 | 37 | 39 |
| *kavi* 'tool' | | | | | 3 |
| *ke* 'tree, inanimates' | 204 | 499 | 380 | 412 | 424 |
| *kila* 'hands of bananas' | | 2 | 4 | 1 | |
| *kova* 'fire' | 17 | 36 | 36 | 35 | 35 |
| *kubila/kwabila* 'land plot' | | 12 | 26 | 29 | 27 |
| *kudu1* 'band of fibres' | | | | 3 | 6 |
| *kudu2* 'tooth' | | 3 | 8 | 9 | 6 |
| *kumla* 'earth oven' | 19 | 36 | 36 | 36 | 35 |
| *kwe* 'thing' | 305 | 804 | 553 | 643 | 527 |
| *kweya/kwaya/keya* 'limb' | 3 | 20 | 60 | 69 | 63 |

**Table 3.3.4.** (continued)

| CP type | No. of tokens produced by age group | | | | |
|---|---|---|---|---|---|
| | I | II | III | IV | V |
| kwoila/kwela 'clay pot' | 5 | 26 | 14 | 26 | 25 |
| kwoya/koya 'mountain' | 1 | 4 | 11 | 7 | 3 |
| liku 'compartment' | | 11 | 22 | 19 | 19 |
| lilo/lola 'walk' | 1 | | 3 | 1 | 2 |
| luba 'bundle' | 1 | 9 | 21 | 25 | 21 |
| luva 'wooden dishes' | 1 | 3 | | 8 | 6 |
| megwa 'magic' | | 1 | 5 | 6 | |
| meila 'part of a song' | | | | | 3 |
| mmwa 'conical bundle' | | 2 | 8 | 1 | 12 |
| na1 'female person' | 34 | 39 | 39 | 36 | 36 |
| na2 'animals' | 39 | 67 | 54 | 51 | 68 |
| nigwa 'hole' | | | | | 1 |
| nina 'part of a song' | | | | | 3 |
| notu/nutu 'kneaded, dot' | 3 | 12 | 33 | 24 | 31 |
| nunu 'corner of a garden' | | 1 | 6 | 9 | 6 |
| peta/ta 'basket' | 19 | 34 | 36 | 35 | 35 |
| pila 'part' | 11 | 39 | 64 | 67 | 68 |
| po'ula 'grove' | | 3 | 18 | 11 | 21 |
| pwanina/pona 'hole' | 17 | 24 | 36 | 31 | 32 |
| sa 'nut bunch' | 1 | 3 | 3 | 3 | 6 |
| si 'small bit' | 5 | 5 | 5 | | |
| sipu 'sheaf' | | 11 | 25 | 21 | 31 |
| sisi 'bough' | 12 | 62 | 57 | 64 | 56 |
| siva 'time' | | | | | 3 |
| suya 'batch of fish' | | 6 | 24 | 33 | 27 |
| tam 'sprouting' | | 10 | 17 | 25 | 18 |
| tetu 'yams' | | | | 1 | |
| to/te 'male, human' | 38 | 46 | 36 | 36 | 38 |
| tuta 'time' | | | 4 | 3 | 1 |
| utu 'scrap' | 8 | 32 | 114 | 96 | 58 |
| uva 'span' | | | 9 | 6 | 16 |
| va/vaya/vayo 'door' | 1 | 7 | 1 | 8 | |
| vakala 'belt' | | | 1 | 1 | |
| vili 'untwisted' | | 1 | 26 | 25 | 24 |
| vosi 'song' | | | 6 | 10 | 2 |
| wela 'batch of fish' | | 3 | 14 | 18 | 7 |
| ya 'flexible, thin' | 22 | 88 | 43 | 54 | 66 |
| yam 'day' | | 4 | 11 | 4 | |

**Table 3.3.4.** *(continued)*

| CP type | No. of tokens produced by age group | | | | |
|---|---|---|---|---|---|
| | I | II | III | IV | V |
| *yamalyuma* 'hand' | 1 | 2 | | 2 | 7 |
| *yulailyule* 'bundle of four things' | | | 6 | 3 | |
| *yuvalyuwo* 'shoal' | | | 3 | 1 | |
| 0 'basketful of yams' | | | 1 | 1 | |
| CPs from the overall corpus of Kilivila speech data: | | | | | |
| *bililo* 'trip' | | | | 4 | |
| *dumia* 'swamp' | 1 | | | | |
| *kali* 'paddle strike' | | | | 1 | |
| *kauya* 'creel' | | | 4 | 4 | |
| *lipu* 'compartment/creel' | | | 5 | | |
| *na3* 'stars, moon, planets' | | | | 4 | |
| *na4* 'carvings' | | | | 3 | |
| *yeni* 'handful' | | | | 1 | |
| CP produced but not assignable to individual consultants: | | | | | |
| *sam* 'ginger' | | | | | |
| CPs not produced in the elicitation test: | | | | | |
| *lila* 'bough', *oyla* 'string', *siwa* 'sea portions', *vilo* 'place' | | | | | |

are very similar to those mentioned for *kwe*. On the basis of these data, I conclude that the CPs *kwe* and *ke* come second in the CP acquisition process.

The CPs *kova* 'fire', *na* in its meaning 'animals ( = *na2*), *ta* 'basket', and *ya* 'flexible, thin' were produced by 3 girls and 3 boys in age group I. Although 1 consultant of age group II and 2 consultants in age group III did not produce the CP *ya*, the data justify the conclusion that 9-year-old children have acquired these CP types. Only with *na2* and *ya* do we observe more tokens than expected in the elicitation test. For *ya*, it is again the consultants in age group II who show a rather dramatic rise in the number of tokens produced during the elicitation test.

The CPs *kumla* 'earth oven' and *pwanina/pona* 'punctured, hole' were produced by 7 consultants in age group I. The data document that children in age group II have acquired the CP *kumla*. Five of the 6 boys in this age group have also acquired the CP *pwanina/pona*.

Five consultants in age group I produced the CPs *ka'i* 'tooth', *gudi* 'child', and *sisi* 'bough'. The acquisition of the CP *ka'i* is completed in boys in age group II. All children in age group II have acquired the CP *sisi*. With this CP, we also observe that the consultants in age groups II–V produced more tokens than expected in the elicitation test.

On the basis of these data, I conclude that the CPs *kova, na2, ta, ya, kumla, pwanina/pona, ka'i, gudi*, and *sisi* come third in the CP acquisition process. The acquisition of *gudi*, however, is earlier in boys than in girls.

Two boys and 2 girls in age group I produced the CPs *utu* 'scrap' and *iga* 'name'. The acquisition of these two types is completed in children in age group II. With the CP *utu*, we observe again that more tokens than expected were produced by the consultants in age groups III–V.

One boy and 1 girl in age group I produced tokens of the CP *bwa* 'tree'. Although we find 26 tokens of this CP produced by 6 consultants of age group II, it seems to play a secondary role in everyday speech, if we accept the token frequency as the *tertium comparationis* for such a judgment (this argument is explicitly described in section 3.3.3.1).

Two boys and 1 girl produced tokens of the CP *kada* 'road' and *si* 'bit'. The CP *si* documented by only 5 tokens each produced by the consultants in the first three age groups; thus, it does not seem to play a large role in everyday speech. This is not the case with the CP *kada*, however, The acquisition of this CP is already completed in children in age group II. With this CP, we also observe that the consultants produced more tokens than expected.

Three boys but only 1 girl produced tokens of the CP *kasa* 'row'. With this CP, we again observe that some consultants in age groups II–V produced more tokens than expected.

The gender differences in the production of certain CPs is even more marked in the following cases: *Buda* 'group', *duli* 'cluster', *kai* 'stone blade', *kweya* 'limb', *pila* 'part, piece', and *notu* 'kneaded, dot' are produced only by boys in age group I. Boys in age group II are still ahead of girls in their acquisition of 4 of these 6 CPs, the exceptions being *pila* and *buda*. With the CPs *pila, buda*, and *kweya*, we again observe that more tokens than expected were produced by the consultants in age groups III–V.

The CPs *bubwa* 'cut off', *bukwa* 'fruit cluster', *kapwa* 'parcel', *kwoila* 'clay pot', *luba* 'bundle', *luva* 'wooden dishes', and *sa* 'nut bunch' were produced by boys in age group I. Consultant 10 produced the only 3 tokens of the CP type *bukwa* that occurred during the elicitation test. In the overall corpus of Kilivila speech data, we find only 6 more tokens of this type, which were produced by the same consultant, 6-year-old Towesei. The CP *bubwa* does not seem to play a role in everyday speech, either. It was produced only once by consultant 12 in age group I. With age group III, we find 8 tokens of this type produced by only 3 consultants. As for the CP *kapwa*, we find 5 tokens produced by 2 boys in age group I. Three girls and 3 boys in age group II produced 18 tokens of this CP type. Only 3 girls in age group III produced 6 tokens of *kapwa*. Thus, this CP seems to play a secondary role in everyday speech. The same is true for the CP *luva*. We find only 18 tokens produced by the consultants. The CP *sa* was also documented by only 16 tokens. The CP *luba* was only produced once, by consultant 10. With the consultants in age group II, we find 9 tokens, and the consultants in age group III produced 21 tokens of this CP. For the CP *kwoila/kwela*, we find a few more tokens. Consultants 10 and 12 in age group I produced 5 tokens. Nine consultants in age group II produced 26 tokens of this CP. However, with the consultants in age group III, we find only 14 tokens.

The CPs *kaduyo* 'door', *kwoya/koya* 'mountain', *lilo/lola* 'trip', *va* 'door', and *yuma* 'hand' were produced only by girls in age group I. However, as Table 3.3.4 shows, these CP types play a secondary role in everyday speech.

For the sake of completeness, it should be noted that 6-year-old Towesei produced one token of the CP *dumia* 'swamp' in the overall corpus of Kilivila speech data.

We can now summarize the results for CP acquisition in children ranging in age from 4 to 7 years, as follows. These children produced 37 CP types. The data show that the first CPs acquired are *to/te* 'male persons, human beings' and *na1* 'female persons'; the CPs *kwe* 'thing' and *ke* 'wood, long objects, inanimates' come second, and the CPs *kova* 'fire', *na2* 'animals', *ta* 'basket', *ya* 'flexible things', *kumla* 'earth oven', *pwanina/pona* 'punctured, hole' *ka'i* 'tooth', *gudi* 'child', and *sisi* 'bough' come third in these children's language acquisition process. In a fourth phase of this process, the CPs *utu* 'scrap', *iga* 'name', *bwa* 'tree', *kada* 'road', *si* 'bit', and *kasa* 'row' are acquired. With the other CPs acquired in this phase, we note marked gender differences. The data for the CPs *gudi*, *kada*, *si*, and *kasa* already pointed in this direction. In addition, we note that the CPs *buda* 'group', *duli* 'cluster', *dumia* 'swamp', *kai* 'stone blade', *kweya* 'limb', *pila* 'part', *notu* 'kneaded, dot,' *bubwa* 'cut off', *bukwa* 'fruit cluster', *kapwa* 'parcel', *kwoila* 'clay pot', *luba* 'bundle', *luva* 'wooden dishes', and *sa* 'nut bunch' are produced only by boys in this age group, whereas the CPs *kaduyo* 'door', *kwoya/koya* 'mountain', *lilo/lola* 'walk', *va* 'door', and *yuma* 'hand' are produced only by girls of this age group.

As Table 3.2.214 shows, we find only 1 dubious and 8 unacceptable cases with these children's CP production. If we relate these 9 dubious or unacceptable responses to certain stimuli to the total number of tokens produced by the 12 children in this age group (860 tokens), we note that these dubious and unacceptable cases account for only 1.2%. Thus, we note that the children in age group I produced almost all their CPs in correct and acceptable contexts. Nevertheless, as shown in Table 3.2.5, the mean values with respect to cases of multiple classification were 14% for girls and 8% for boys in age group I; thus, linguistic insecurity exists in children of this age with respect to adequate and unequivocal CP production.

With children ranging in age from 8 to 14 years, we find the following CP types first realized in the elicitation test: The CP *giwi* 'cut' was produced by 2 girls and 5 boys. Two girls and 4 boys produced tokens of the CP *gum* 'bit'. Two girls and 3 boys produced the CP *liku* 'compartment of a foodhouse'. The CP *sipu* 'sheaf' was produced by 1 girl, but by 4 boys. The CPs *bogi* 'night' and *kabisi* 'compartment of a foodhouse' were produced by 2 girls and 2 boys. As Table 3.3.4 shows, the CP *boti* seems to play a secondary role in everyday speech production. Three boys, but only 1 girl, produced the CP *kubila* 'land plot'. The CP *bubu* 'cut across' was produced by 2 boys and 1 girl. The CPs *deli* 'group' and *gula* 'heap, group' are produced by 1 boy and by 1 girl.

Only boys produce the CPs *tam* 'sprouting', *yam* 'day', *kabulo2* 'sector', *megwa* 'magic', *mmwa* 'conical bundle', *po'ula* 'grove', and *vili* 'untwisted'. With these CPs, it should be noted that 3 boys produced the CP *tam* and that 2 boys produced the CP *yam*. All other CPs were produced by 1 male consultant only. Moreover, Table 3.3.4 indicates that the CPs *yam*, *kabulo2*, *megwa*, *mmwa*, and *po'ula* play a rather small role in everyday speech production.

Only girls in age group II produced the CPs *suya* 'batch of fish', *ilia* 'hands of bananas', *kudu2* 'tooth', *nunu* 'corner of a garden', and *wela* 'batch of fish'. The CP *suya* was produced by 2 girls. All other CPs are produced by 1 female consultant only. Moreover, as Table 3.3.4 indicates, these CPs, with the exception perhaps of *suya* seem to play a secondary role in everyday speech production. It should be noted that the CP *kudu2* is synonymous with the CP *ka'i*; the acquisition of this CP is completed in boys in age group II.

In addition to these CP types, the consultants in age group II produced all the CP types produced by the children in age group I except the CP types *bubwa* 'cut off', *bukwa* 'fruit cluster', *dumia* 'swamp', and *lilo* 'walk', which seem to play a secondary role in everyday speech production.

Summarizing the results for CP acquisition in children ranging in age from 8 to 14 years, we note that these children produced 55 CP types; they acquired 22 new CP types.

The production of these CP types shows rather pronounced gender differences in these children's CP acquisition process. Boys produced 17 of the 22 newly acquired CPs; they acquired 13 of them earlier and faster than girls in this age group. This result is especially marked for the CPs *giwi* 'cut', *gum* 'bit', *sipu* 'sheaf', *liku* 'compartment of a foodhouse', *kubila* 'land plot', and *tam* 'sprouting'. Girls produced 15 of the 22 newly acquired CP types. However, as we can infer from the data presented, they were just starting to acquire these CP types.

As Table 3.2.214 shows, there were 10 dubious and 22 unacceptable cases of CP production in this age group. If we relate these 32 cases to the overall number of CP tokens produced by the 12 consultants in this age group (2,341 tokens) we note that these dubious and unacceptable cases account for only 1.4% of the CPs produced. Thus, we note that the children in age group II produced almost all acquired CPs in correct and acceptable contexts. Nevertheless, Table 3.2.12 shows that mean values with respect to cases of multiple classification were 32% for girls and 28% for boys in age group II; thus, linguistic insecurity exists in children of this age with respect to adequate and unequivocal CP production.

With the adolescents ranging in age from 15 to 20 years, we note the following results: The consultants in age group III produced 64 CP types. Three CP type variants and 10 CP types proper were produced in the elicitation test for the first time by the consultants of this age group: The variant *duya* of the CP *duya/kaduya/kaduyo* 'door, entrance' and the variant *vaya* of the CP *va/vaya/vayo* 'door' were produced by 1 male consultant in each case. Two female and 2 male consultants produced the variant *yegila* of the CP *iga/yegila* 'name'. The other variants of these 3 CP types, however, can already be found in the language production of the consultants in age group I.

The CPs *bwalita* 'sea' and *tuta* 'time' were each produced by 1 male and 1 female consultant. Two female and 2 male consultants produced the CP *vosi* 'song'.

The CPs *uva* 'span', *yulai* 'bundle of four things', *gili* 'row', and 0 'baskets of yams' were only produced by male consultants.

Only 1 female consultant in each case produced the CPs *beku* 'stone blade', *vakala* 'belt', and *yuva* 'shoal'.

Thus, we still find gender-differences in this age group in the production and acquisition of CP types. However, as Table 3.3.4 shows, all these CP types and CP type variants seem to play a secondary role in everyday speech production.

As Table 3.2.214 shows, there were 5 dubious and 14 unacceptable cases of these consultants' CP production. If we relate these 19 cases to the overall number of CP tokens produced by the 12 consultants in this age group (2,450 tokens), we note that these dubious or unacceptable cases account for only 0.8% of all CPs produced. Thus, the adolescents in age group III produced almost all their CPs in correct and acceptable contexts. Nevertheless, Table 3.2.19 shows that mean values with respect to cases of multiple classification were 21% for female and 12% for male consultants in age group III; thus, linguistic insecurity exists in consultants of this age with respect to adequate and unequivocal CP production.

For the sake of completeness, I want to note that the CPs *kudu1* 'band of fibers', *kauya* 'creel', *doba* 'grass skirt', *lipu* 'compartment of a creel', and *tetu* 'yams' were only found in the language production of the consultants in age group IV. Moreover, the CPs *kabulo1* 'protuberances', *na3* 'moon', and *na4* 'carvings in human likeness', *kavi* 'tool', *kala* 'day', *meila* 'part of a song', *nigwa* 'hole', *nina* 'part of a song', *siva* 'time', *bililo* 'trip', *kali* 'paddle strike', and *yeni* 'a handful of something' were only found in the language production of consultants in age group V. It should be noted here, however, that the CP *kudu1* 'band of fibers' was produced by 1 woman in age group IV but by 2 men in age group V. The CP *kabulo1* 'protuberances' was produced only by 1 woman. All the other CP types just mentioned were produced by only 1 man in age groups IV and V. Thus, we again find marked gender-differences in the CP production of these consultants. However, as Table 3.3.4 documents, all these CPs seem to play a secondary role in everyday speech production. I will discuss these phenomena, together with the problem of dubious and unacceptable cases of CP production, in section 3.3.3.

I can now summarize the answer to the question concerning the order in which the individual CPs are acquired by listing the CPs in Table 3.3.5 according to this order, expressed in six phases.

Although I elicited the production of the CPs *lila* 'bough, branch, leaf', *oyla* 'string', *siwa* 'sea portions', and *vilo* 'place' in the informal pretests, these CPs were not produced during the elicitation test proper; moreover, these

**Table 3.3.5.** The order of CP type acquisition

| Age group/phase | CP type 'gloss(es)' ⟨comment⟩ |
|---|---|
| I/1 | *to/te* 'male persons, human beings'<br>*na1* 'female persons' |
| I/2 | *ke* 'wood, long objects, inanimates'<br>*kwe* 'thing' |
| I/3 | *kova* 'fire'<br>*na2* 'animals'<br>*ta* 'basket' ⟨see: III/6⟩<br>*ya* 'flexible, thin'<br>*kumla* 'earth oven'<br>*pwanina/pona* 'punctured, hole'<br>*ka'i* 'tooth'<br>*gudi* 'child' ⟨acquired earlier by boys⟩<br>*sisi* 'bough' |
| I/4 | *utu* 'scrap'<br>*iga* 'name' ⟨see: III/6⟩<br>*bwa* 'tree'<br>*kada* 'road' ⟨acquired earlier by boys⟩<br>*si* 'bit' ⟨acquired earlier by boys⟩<br>*kasa* 'row' ⟨acquired earlier by boys⟩<br>*buda* 'group' ⟨acquired by boys only⟩<br>*duli* 'cluster' ⟨produced by 1 boy only⟩<br>*dumia* 'swamp' ⟨produced by 1 boy only⟩<br>*kai* 'stone blade' ⟨produced by 1 boy only⟩<br>*kweya* 'limb' ⟨produced by 1 boy only⟩<br>*pila* 'part' ⟨acquired by boys only⟩<br>*notu* 'kneaded' ⟨acquired by boys only⟩<br>*bubwa* 'cut off' ⟨produced by 1 boy only⟩<br>*bukwa* 'cluster' ⟨produced by 1 boy only⟩<br>*kapwa* 'parcel' ⟨acquired by boys only⟩<br>*kwoila* 'clay pot' ⟨acquired by boys only⟩<br>*luba* 'bundle' ⟨produced by 1 boy only⟩<br>*luva* 'dishes' ⟨produced by 1 boy only⟩<br>*sa* 'nut bunch' ⟨produced by 1 boy only⟩<br>*kaduyo* 'door' ⟨see III/6; produced by 1 girl only⟩<br>*kwoya/koya* 'mountain' ⟨produced by 1 girl only⟩<br>*lilo/lola* 'walk' ⟨produced by 1 girl only⟩<br>*va* 'door' ⟨see III/6; produced by 1 girl only⟩<br>*yuma* 'hand' ⟨produced by 1 girl only⟩ |
| II/5 | *giwi* 'cut' ⟨acquired earlier by boys⟩<br>*gum* 'bit' ⟨acquired earlier by boys⟩<br>*sipu* 'sheaf' ⟨acquired earlier by boys⟩<br>*liku* 'compartment' ⟨acquired earlier by boys⟩<br>*kubila* 'land plot' ⟨acquired earlier by boys⟩<br>*bubu* 'cut across' ⟨acquired earlier by boys⟩<br>*bogi* 'night'<br>*kabisi* 'compartment of a foodhouse' |

**Table 3.3.5.** *(continued)*

| Age group/phase | CP type 'gloss(es)' ⟨comment⟩ |
|---|---|
| | *deli* 'group' |
| | *gula* 'heap' |
| | *tam* 'sprouting' ⟨acquired by boys only⟩ |
| | *yam* 'day' ⟨acquired by boys only⟩ |
| | *kabulo2* 'sector' ⟨produced by 1 boy only⟩ |
| | *megwa* 'magic' ⟨produced by 1 boy only⟩ |
| | *mmwa* 'bundle' ⟨produced by 1 boy only⟩ |
| | *po'ula* 'grove' ⟨produced by 1 boy only⟩ |
| | *vili* 'untwisted' ⟨produced by 1 boy only⟩ |
| | *suya* 'batch/fish' ⟨acquired by girls only⟩ |
| | *kila* 'hands of bananas' ⟨produced by 1 girl only⟩ |
| | *kudu2* 'tooth' ⟨produced by 1 girl only⟩ |
| | *nunu* 'corner of a garden' ⟨produced by 1 girl only⟩ |
| | *wela* 'batch/fish' ⟨produced by 1 girl only⟩ |
| III/6 | *duya* 'door' ⟨see I/4; produced by 1 man only⟩ |
| | *vaya* 'door' ⟨see I/4; produced by 1 man only⟩ |
| | *yegila* 'name' ⟨see I/4⟩ |
| | *peta* 'basket' ⟨see I/3⟩ |
| | *bwalita* 'sea' |
| | *tuta* 'time' |
| | *vosi* 'song' |
| | *uva* 'span' ⟨acquired by men only⟩ |
| | *yulai* 'bundle of four things' ⟨acquired by men only⟩ |
| | *gili* 'row' ⟨produced by 1 man only⟩ |
| | 0 'basketful of yams' ⟨produced by 1 man only⟩ |
| | *beku* 'stone blade' ⟨produced by 1 woman only⟩ |
| | *vakala* 'belt' ⟨produced by 1 woman only⟩ |
| | *yuva* 'shoal' ⟨produced by 1 woman only⟩ |

Additional CP types produced by consultants in age groups IV and V:

| | |
|---|---|
| IV | *kudu1* 'band of fibres' ⟨in IV produced by 1 woman; in V produced by 1 woman and 2 men⟩ |
| | *doba* 'skirt' ⟨produced by 1 woman only⟩ |
| | *kauya* 'creel' ⟨in IV and in V produced by 1 man only⟩ |
| | *lipu* 'compartment of a creel' ⟨produced by 1 man only⟩ |
| | *tetu* 'yams' ⟨produced by 1 man only⟩ |
| V | *guba* 'bundle/taro' ⟨produced by 1 woman only⟩ |
| | *kabulo1* 'protuberances' ⟨produced by 1 woman only⟩ |
| | *na3* 'moon' ⟨produced by 1 man only⟩ |
| | *na4* 'carvings in human likeness' ⟨produced by 1 man only⟩ |
| | *kavi* 'tool' ⟨produced by 1 man only⟩ |
| | *kala* 'day' ⟨produced by 1 man only⟩ |
| | *meila* 'part/song' ⟨produced by 1 man only⟩ |
| | *nigwa* 'hole' ⟨produced by 1 man only⟩ |
| | *nina* 'part/song' ⟨produced by 1 man only⟩ |
| | *siva* 'time' ⟨produced by 1 man only⟩ |
| | *bililo* 'trip' ⟨produced by 1 man only⟩ |
| | *kali* 'paddle strike' ⟨produced by 1 man only⟩ |
| | *yeni* 'handful of something' ⟨produced by 1 man only⟩ |

CPs were not produced in my overall corpus of Kilivila speech data. Thus, I cannot provide any information with respect to the acquisition of these CP types.

The CP *sam* 'ginger' is documented in Senft and Senft (1986:142) in data on Trobriand string figures and the verses that accompany these figures. In the present study, the CP *sam* was produced by a 6-year-old boy and a girl of the same age. It is not possible to draw any inferences about the order in which the CP types are acquired from this small sample for the CP *sam*.

In summary, the following main trends can be noted regarding the order in which CPs are acquired:

1. CPs that distinguish sex in human beings are acquired first.

2. CPs that take over the function of unmarked forms for inanimates are acquired next. The overgeneralization of these CPs is documented in our data.

3. The CPs that are acquired next denote concrete, specific objects and certain features of objects.

4. The fourth phase of CP acquisition adds CPs that are characteristic of the third phase, as well as CPs that denote parts, groups, clusters, and specific features of certain objects.

5. The characteristics of the fourth phase of CP acquisition become even more marked in the fifth phase. In addition, we find CPs that denote abstract concepts.

6. The final phase of CP acquisition increases the inventory of CPs characteristic of the fourth and fifth phases.

7. Boys not only acquire more CP types than girls, but also acquire these types earlier than girls (see section 3.3.2.3).

8. The majority of CPs that are produced by adults who have finished their first language acquisition can be characterized as technical terms of different terminologies. We may regard all these CPs as evidence for the continuing acquisition process with respect to the vocabulary of a language.

At this stage of the analysis, I must postpone any attempt to answer the question of why the CPs are acquired in the order just presented. I will try to answer this question after having defined the semantic domains that are established and covered by the individual CP types (see section 3.3.4.3).

### 3.3.2.5 Are There Any Parallels Between Kilivila CP Acquisition and CP Acquisition Data for Other Classifier Languages?

As mentioned in section 3.1, there are very few studies that deal with this question in other classifier languages (if we leave aside literature on sign languages such as American Sign Language). Nevertheless, if we compare the results presented by Gandour et al. (1984), Erbaugh (1986), Carpenter

(1991), Matsumoto (1985), Sanches (1977), Chin (1989), Luke and Harrison (1986), and all the remarks on this topic in Allan (1977:295) quoting Burling (1965:261) and Haas (1942:201) with the answers to the questions raised in the previous sections, some interesting parallels emerge.

Burling's observation of an overgeneralizing use of the Burmese classifier *khu* in children "in situations in which an adult would probably use a more precise classifier" (Burling 1965:261) parallels my observation of a rather dramatic rise of tokens for a number of CP types, but especially for the CPs *kwe* 'thing, unmarked form for inanimates' and *ke* 'wood, long objects, unmarked form for inanimates') in the language production of children in age groups II and III. From these data, I infer the Trobriand children produce at least these two CPs in situations in which an adult, or even an adolescent, would use a more precise classifier. Moreover, the observed "tendency to use the general classifier instead of the specific classifier" (Gandour et al. 1984:465, 468), the overgeneralization and "semantic overextension" (Carpenter 1991:105) of certain CPs in Thai and Japanese children (Carpenter 1991; Matsumoto 1985; Sanches 1977:58–59), and the "tendency for overgeneralization" of certain noun classes documented in Bantu language acquisition data (Demuth et al. 1986:463–465), as well as the fact that Chinese children "overwhelmingly preferred the general *ge* classifier" (Erbaugh 1986:413), are in agreement with my observations, especially with respect to the Trobriand children's production of the two CP types mentioned above, namely *kwe* and *ke*. However, with the acquisition of noun classes in Sesotho, a Bantu language, there are no cases of such overgeneralization (see Demuth 1988:310, 316; 1992:591, 594, 596–597).

In connection with Chinese (Mandarin) noun classifiers, Erbaugh (1986:412) emphasizes "overheard adult narratives are a more important source of classifier input than speech directed to the child," and that the "majority of classifiers appeared in formal storytelling and songs" in adult-child conversations. Moreover, she notes that "children used special classifiers in exactly the same discourse settings as the adults" (1986:425) and points to "discourse sensitivity" (1986:426) in the Chinese children's use of classifiers. Erbaugh's observations are similar to my observations with respect to the specific use of CPs with demonstrative pronouns, adjectives, and numerals in Trobriand children ranging in age from 4 to 14 years. In section 3.3.2.2, I especially emphasized the role of the text category "fairy tale" for the acquisition process of different CP types used in the word formation of demonstrative pronouns. I also mentioned that the CP *sam* 'ginger', for example, was only used in connection with a string figure accompanying verse.

This discourse or text category sensitivity observed with the CP production of Trobriand and Chinese children may also support the strategy mentioned by Haas (1942:201) in connection with classifiers in Thai: "...it is desirable to memorize the classifier to be used with a noun at the same time that one hears the noun...". The rather frequent use of certain CPs in fairy tales, songs, and verses, where the word classes that use CPs in their word formation are immediately followed by the noun the CP refers to, may indicate that Trobriand adults as well as the children citing these verses, singing these songs, or telling these fairy tales apply just the strategy described by Haas to foster the acquisition process of CPs, especially with demonstrative pronouns. Moreover, the Trobianders seem to use this strategy to foster the acquisition of more special or specific CP types.

As to these more special classifiers, Erbaugh (1986:415) records that with Chinese children "special classifiers developed slowly and stayed rare between the ages of 1.10 and 3.10." She notes more specifically (1986:417) that the Chinese children investigated "almost never used special classifiers before the age of 2.6." If I compare my observations with Erbaugh's results, I have to note that in Trobriand children these special classifiers develop even more slowly than in Chinese children (cf. also Carpenter 1991:103, Matsumoto 1985). However, the observations of Gandour et al. that in Thai children "...the rate of acquisition of ... classifiers was slow. ...10-year-old Thai children have still not mastered the classifier system" (Gandour et al. 1984:460) and Chin's (1989:92) findings on the acquisition of classifiers in Hokkien agree with my results. My data show that we can with good reason assume that the core of the Kilivila CP system is acquired at the end of puberty. The fact that "repeaters and general classifiers are ... easier ... to learn" (Gandour et al. 1984:463) and that "animate classifiers ... are acquired earlier than classifiers in other categories" (Gandour et al. 1984:459) also holds for Thai and Hokkien (Chin 1989:123), Mandarin, and Cantonese (Luke and Harrison 1986) children, as well as for Trobriand children.

With these few observations, I must conclude the discussion of results reported in other studies, which agree at least in part with my findings on the Kilivila CP acquisition process.

### 3.3.2.6 Excursus: Are There Parallels Between the Kilivila Data and Acquisition Data With Respect to Demonstrative Pronouns, Adjectives, and Numerals for such Indo-European Languages as English and German?

I want to conclude section 3.3.2 with a few general and rather anecdotal remarks on the question of whether we can find any parallels between the results reported so far and acquisition data with respect to demonstrative pronouns, adjectives, and numerals for Indo-European languages like English and German. This question is so complex that this excursus cannot claim to provide anything more than rather cursory information on the topic. The literature cited in the following paragraphs was chosen more or less at random, just to indicate the course the argument will take. Thus, I want to emphasize that I am completely aware that my proceeding here does not adhere to the usual psycholinguistic standards. Nevertheless, I hope that the following anecdotal remarks may serve as an incentive to linguists to overcome the disproportion between research on Indo-European languages, on the one hand, and other so-called exotic languages, on the other hand.

In their classic monograph, Stern and Stern (1928:280) emphasize the following: "Die Zahlwörter treten dem äußeren Anschein nach relativ früh auf; doch verbindet sich erst spät mit ihnen wirklicher Zahlensinn.... So 'zählte' unsere Eva 2;0 ziemlich richtig bis zwölf, natürlich ohne jeden Zahlensinn". As to the acquisition of adjectives, they state: "Ferner aber zeigen die Listen von SCUPIN, NICE und DESCOEUDRES völlig übereinstimmend, daß die *Adjektiva* in der gleichen Zeit noch nicht Stabilität gewonnen haben, sondern um 3;9 herum und noch jahrelang später einen prozentualen *Aufstieg* zeigen, der ihren relativen Anteil um die Hälfte gegenüber dem Stande um 2;0 erhöht" (Stern and Stern 1928:245).

With the exception of personal pronouns, Stern and Stern (1928:279) remark: "Die übrigen Pronomina scheinen uns keine Entwicklungsphänomene von allgemeinerem psychologischen Interesse zu bieten." Thus, with respect to demonstrative pronouns, we find only anecdotal remaks about their usage in the researchers' own children at the ages of 2 years 4 months (1928:100), 2 years 6 months (1928:54), and 3 years 2 months (1928:66).

However, Böhme, who studied children between 4 and 5 years 6 months of age, emphasizes the "relatively late acquisition" of pronouns that are "variable in their referential function" (Böhme 1983:191).

If we compare these statements with our Kilivila data, we can note that in Indo-European languages like German, numerals and adjectives are also acquired before demonstrative pronouns. Having noted this parallel between German and Kilivila acquisition data, we must emphasize that the process of the acquisition of the three word classes starts later and develops more slowly in Kilivila than in German.

If we compare the Kilivila data with the results on the order in which number and countability distinctions are acquired by English-speaking children reported by Mufwene (1984:207–208), we again find certain parallels; albeit with the same time shift in Kilivila as emphasized previously.

Tversky (1986:72), on the basis of acquisition data from studies on English-speaking children, states:

> The perceptual features children use as a basis for categorization in preference to the functional features characterizing superordinates are also the features common in many classifiers. . . . It has been proposed . . . that children prefer to group different basic level objects by perceptual features than by functional features because unlike functional features, perceptual features are readily observable; they are also the features successfully used in basic level categorization. According to this argument, children shift to functionally-based groupings because the latter are more informative than perceptually-based groupings.

My Kilivila data support this proposition to a certain degree. I will use it as a starting point for trying to answer the question of why the individual CPs are acquired in the order described in section 3.3.2.4 (see section 3.3.4.3).

Finally, I would like to emphasize that the Kilivila data also support, at least to a certain degree, the developmental sequence proposed by the "common assumption in philosophy ... and psychology" that Tyler (1969:19) quotes with so much reservation and suspicion. With respect to Kilivila CP acquisition, it seems to be the case that the "child first acquires concepts for concrete objects and gradually expands its semantic domain by extension and generalization to include more abstract conceptions" (Tyler 1969:19). However, we will discuss this problem once more in section 3.3.4.3.

### 3.3.3 What Is the Realization of the Individual CP Types in Actual Speech?

To answer this complex question, I will first look at the rate of frequency with which the individual CP types were produced by the consultants during the elicitation test and in my recorded texts. This analysis will result in a tripartite classification of the CP types, the classes being characterized as follows:

1. CPs that form the core of the Kilivila classifiers produced in actual speech.
2. CPs that play a secondary role in actual speech.
3. CPs that play a secondary role in everyday speech because they belong to a special technical language variety or because they are extremely rare or even "almost obsolete" (Malinowski 1920:44).

I will then look at the individual CP types and check Tables 3.2.126–3.2.212 with respect to the question of which CP type or types were actually produced versus which were expected during the elicitation test. This analysis is a first step leading to a definition of the semantic domains established by the system of Kilivila CPs. Thus, this analysis is a prerequisite to the analyses that will be presented in section 3.3.4. However, this analysis will also enable us to answer the question of whether we can observe any language change in progress that affects this complex CP system. Attempts to answer this question involve discussion of the following problems:

1. Which CP types are affected by such a language change?
2. Why are they affected?
3. What about the use of certain CP types that are produced as stylistic variables or variants?
4. Is the usage of certain CP types determined by the age and/or status and/or gender of the speaker?

The section ends with some speculations about the consequences any observed changes might have for Kilivila grammar as a whole.

### 3.3.3.1 Can a Classification of the CP System Be Devised?

One of the most obvious and straightforward observations that can be made about the data presented is the enormous differences between the number of tokens produced for the individual CP types. In section 3.3.2, I argued that, on the basis of token frequency, some CP types or CP type variants seem to play a secondary role in everyday speech production.

In the elicitation test, I asked 60 consultants to produce one token of each type with three different word classes. Thus, the maximum of tokens to be elicited for one CP type was, at least in theory, 180 tokens per type ( = 60 consultants × 1 token each for 3 word classes). If I elicited more than 180 tokens per type in all consultants, it would mean that one or more consultant(s) produced one or more token(s) of the respective CP type as a response to one or more stimulus/stimuli presented to elicit a different CP type. If I cannot exclude these CP usages on the basis of Table 3.2.214 as dubious or unacceptable cases of CP production, I infer that such CP usage documents the semantic scope of the CP type. If the number of tokens elicited surpasses the number 180 to a high degree, I infer that this CP type is a kind of "general" classifier, a classifier used in an overgeneralized way, or a classifier with a rather broad (though not general) semantic scope.

If the number of tokens elicited fell well below 180, I inferred that this CP type does not play an important role in everyday speech production. If the number of tokens elicited fell below 180 to an extreme degree, I inferred that this CP type plays a secondary role in actual speech because it belongs to a special technical language variety, is only very rarely used, or is almost obsolete.

I want to emphasize once again that I have not used statistical analyses because the data show only a nominal scale standard. Thus, in interpreting the data I am confronted with problems of the following kind: In Table 3.2.125, for example, I count 42 tokens for the CP *wela*; for the CP *uva* I count 31 tokens. Is the difference of 11 tokens large enough to justify a different classification of these two CP types? This raises the classic procedural question: "What can we go by?" The arguments that follow are based on the evidence of the data presented in the tables. Thus, I must leave it to the critical reader's discretion whether or not he or she agrees with my interpretations. I have demonstrated elsewhere (G. Senft 1982) that this pragmatic proceeding leads to presentable results.

Keeping these considerations in mind, we can now start to answer the question raised at the beginning of this section.

Table 3.2.125 lists 84 CP types or CP type variants, ordering them according to the number of tokens produced for each. For the sake of a more complete description, this table also presents percentages based on the actual number of tokens produced. I interpret these data in the following way:

1. The exceptional status of the two CPs *kwe* 'thing, inanimates' and *ke* 'wood, long objects, inanimates' is obvious. With their function as

unmarked forms for inanimates, their semantic scope seems to be that of so-called general classifiers.

2. The CPs *kada* 'road', *utu* 'scrap', *na1* 'female person', *na2* 'animals' *ya* 'flexible', *sisi* 'bough', *pila* 'part', *kweya* 'limb', and *to/te* 'male persons, human beings' play an important role in the consultants' actual speech.

3. If we compare the tokens and percentages noted for the CP types/variants *na1* 'female persons' and *kasa* 'row', on the one hand, and *ka'i* 'tooth' and *duli* 'c'uster', on the other hand, in Table 3.2.125, we note that the CP types/variants *kasa* 'row', *kumla* 'earth oven', *kova* 'fire, *buda/boda* 'group', *ta* 'basket', *gudi* 'child', *iga* 'name', *pwanina/pona* 'hole', *kai* 'stone blade', and *ka'i* 'tooth' are an essential part of the CP inventory of actual speech.

4. If we compare the tokens and percentages noted for the CP types *gum* 'bit' and *sipu* 'sheaf', on the one hand, and *kabisi* 'compartment', on the other hand, in Table 3.2.125, and if we concede that CPs whose expected production totals almost 50% in actual speech can be incorporated into the group of CP types that form the core of the Kilivila CP system, we have to mention the CP types *duli* 'cluster', *giwi* 'cut', *notu, nutu* 'kneaded, dot', *kwoila/kwela* 'clay pot', *kubila* 'land plot', *deli* 'group', *suya* 'batch of fish', *gum* 'bit', and *sipu* 'sheaf' here, too.

Thus, on the basis of the data presented in Table 3.2.125, we can argue that the following 29 CP types/variants constitute the core of the Kilivila CP system realized in actual speech: *kwe, ke, na1 + 2, kada, utu, ya, sisi, pila, kweya, to/te, kasa, kumla, kova, buda/boda, ta, gudi, iga, pwanina/pona, kai, ka'i, duli, giwi, notu/nutu, kwoila/kwela, kubila, deli, suya, gum,* and *sipu.*

Although the CP types *kabisi* 'compartment', *luba* 'bundle/taro', *vili* 'untwisted', *liku* 'compartment', *tam* 'sprouting', *bubu/bobu* 'cut across', *bwa* 'tree', *gula* 'heap', *po'ula* 'grove', *kapwa/kapo* 'parcel', and *wela* 'batch of fish' are realized more frequently than the CP types/variants *uva* 'span', *bubwa* 'cut off', *kudu2* 'tooth', *kwoya/koya* 'mountain', *mmwa* 'conical bundle', *nunu* 'corner/garden', *kabulo2* 'sector', *yam* 'day', *vosi* 'song', and *luva* 'wooden dishes', I think it is justifiable to group these 21 CP types/variants together and to note that they seem to play a secondary role in actual speech. If we keep in mind that *duya* and *kaduyo* 'door, entrance' are variants of one CP type, we can include this CP type in this second group, too. Thus, this group contains 22 CP types.

Although the line I will draw between these 22 CP types/variants and the secondary CP types/variants may seem to be unclear, I think it is justifiable to group together those CPs with a realization of less than 10%. Thus, I conclude that the following CP types/variants play a secondary role in everyday speech because they belong either to a special technical language variety (e.g., *gili* 'row', *megwa* 'magic', *kudu1* 'band of fibers', *meila* 'part/song', *nina* 'part/song' *beku* 'stone blade', *vakala* 'belt', *vakala* 'belt', and 0 'basketful of yams') or because they are extremely rare or almost obsolete (e.g., *sa* 'nut bunch', *si* 'bit', *va/vaya/vayo* 'door', *bogi* 'night', *yama/yuma* 'hand', *yulai/yule* 'bundle of four things', *tuta* 'time', *kila* 'hands of bananas', *lilo/lola* 'walk', *peta* 'basket', *yegila* 'name', *bwalita* 'sea', *yuva* 'shoal', *bukwa* 'fruit cluster', *guba* 'bundle/taro', *kabulo1* 'point', *kala* 'time', *kavi* 'tool', *siva* 'time', *doba* 'grass skirt', *nigwa* 'hole', and *tetu* 'yams').

Considering the CP that occur in my recorded and transcribed texts (presented in Table 3.2.218), I can incorporate the CP types/variants *kauya* 'creel', *lipu* 'compartment/creel', *bililo* 'trip', *dumia* 'swamp', *kali* 'paddle strike', *na3* 'moon', *na4* 'carvings in human likeness', *sam* 'ginger', and *yeni* 'a handful of something' into the last group. Moreover, the CP types *lila* 'bough', *oyla* 'string', *siwa* 'sea portions', and *vilo* 'place' that were not produced during the elicitation test and were not documented in the recorded texts also belong to this third group.

Table 3.3.6 summarizes the results of this section.

In his article "Classificatory Particles in the Language of Kiriwina," Malinowski classified the formatives he presented according to their "degree of obsoleteness" (Malinowski 1920:55–57). I will conclude this section by comparing Malinowski's results and remarks with my findings.

First, it is evident to anyone familiar with Malinowski's article that my spelling of some of the CPs is different from his. These differences document phonological changes within the last 65 years or so, although I do not exclude the possibility that some of these differences may be a result of language varieties.

Looking at some individual CP types, I note the following: My data on the CP *sisi* 'bough' imply, contrary to Malinowski, that this CP is capable of semantic extension. Table 3.2.190 shows that *sisi* was quite often produced when the CP *ya* 'thin, flexible' was expected. The CP *lila* 'bough, branch, leaf' is replaced now by the CP *ke* 'wood, inanimates, long objects', as Malinowski assumed it would be (see Table 3.2.159); however, my pretests showed that my consultants still know this CP.

The CP *siwa* 'sea portions' is also no longer produced by my consultants, as Malinowski predicted; it has been replaced by *kwe* 'thing'. The CP *siva*, as well as the CP *kala*, however, are no longer "perfectly vital" (Malinowski 1920:56), as Malinowski reported. This observation also holds for the CPs *sa* 'nut bunch', *si* 'bit', and 0 'basketful of yams' (but see the discussion of this CP type in 3.3.4.2). Thus, I note the following differences between Malinowski's and my observations on the Kilivila CP system, leaving aside the phonological changes mentioned:

1. Some formatives Malinowski mentioned are rarely or never used by my consultants.

2. With some formatives, I found differences between Malinowski's definition of the CP and my consultants' actual production of them.

However, it should be emphasized that with the majority of the CP types Malinowski mentioned, my findings agree more or less with his results,

**Table 3.3.6.** Classification of the CP system in Kilivila

| The core of CP types/variants[†] | CP types/variants that play a secondary role in actual speech | CP types/variants that belong to a technical language variety or are extremely rare or almost obsolete | |
|---|---|---|---|
| kwe | kabisi | sa | si |
| ke | luba | va/vaya/vayo | bogi |
| *na1 + 2 | vili | gili | megwa |
| kada | liku | yama/yuma | *kudu1 |
| utu | tam | yulai/yule | tuta |
| ya | bubu/bobu | kila | lilo/llola |
| sisi | bwa | *peta | *yegila |
| pila | gula | bwalita | yuva |
| kweya | po'ula | bukwa | guba |
| to/te | kapwa/kapo | *kabulo1 | kala |
| kasa | wela | kavi | meila |
| kumla | uva | nina | siva |
| kova | bubwa | beku | vakala |
| buda/boda | *kudu2 | 0 | doba |
| *ta | kwoya/koya | nigwa | tetu |
| gudi | mmwa | kauya | lipu |
| *iga | nunu | bililo | dumia |
| pwanina/pona | *kabulo2 | kali | *na3 + 4 |
| kai | yam | sam | yeni |
| ka'i | vosi | lila | oyla |
| duli | luva | siwa | vilo |
| giwi | kaduya/duya | | |
| nutu/notu | | | |
| kwoila/kwela | | | |
| kubila | | | |
| deli | | | |
| suya | | | |
| gum | | | |
| sipu | | | |
| 29 CP types/variants | 22/CP types/variants | 42 CP types/variants | |

[†]Variants are marked with an asterisk.

remarks, and predictions, at least with respect to their "degree of obsoleteness". This observation once more highlights this great scholar's exceptional scientific qualities.

### 3.3.3.2 How Do the Consultants Realize the Individual CP Types and Can We Observe Any Processes of Language Change in Progress?

To answer these questions, I will first look at the individual CP types presented in Tables 3.2.37–3.2.123 and especially in Tables 3.2.126–3.2.212 and check which types were actually produced when I expected certain CPs during the elicitation test. This procedure will serve as the basis for a discussion of the observable processes of language change in progress, namely:

1. Which CP types are affected by such a language change?
2. Why are they affected?
3. What about the use of certain CP types that are produced as stylistic variables or variants?
4. Is the usage of certain CP types determined by the age, and/or status, and/or gender of the speaker?

To provide answers to all these questions, of course, I must take into account all the relevant tables presented in section 3.2. In the following paragraphs, I will discuss these questions for the individual CP types.

Table 3.2.126 showed that only 2 tokens of the CP type *beku* 'stone blade' were produced by 2 consultants instead of the expected CP *kai* 'stone blade'. If we consider Tables 3.2.37 and 3.2.124 and appendix A, we realize that the number of types the 2 consultants Itakeda (consultant 27) and Bwetadou (consultant 45) produced is clearly above average compared with the speech behavior of other consultants in that age group. Itakeda is a member of the highest-ranking clan, Malasi; Bwetadou is heir to his father's (!) weather magic, and thus also has a relatively high social status, although he is a member of the lowest-ranking clan. Thus, on the basis of these considerations, we may tentatively assume that the use of this CP may serve the speakers as a means to mark their societal status. They produce an uncommon "repeater", which is extremely rare, as a stylistic variant together with the respective tokens of the actually expected and elicited CP type *kai* (see Table 3.2.63).

The CP type *bililo* 'trip' was produced 4 times by 41-year-old Tosulala describing the construction of a canoe (see Tables 3.2.216, 3.2.217, and appendix B). Tosulala is a member of the highest-ranking clan. I assume that the CP *bililo* is almost obsolete and that consultant V17 produced it in his thorough and careful description as a stylistic variant.

As Tables 3.2.38 and 3.2.127 show, only 12 tokens of the CP type *bogi* 'night' were realized by 7 consultants, 4 of them in age group III. The consultants 26, 31, 34, and 38 are members of the highest-ranking clan. Consultant 45 is heir to the weather magician of Tauwema village, and consultant 21 is the chief's grandson. Only consultant 27 does not have any special status within the village (see appendix A). Thus, I infer that this CP is produced by villagers of status as a sociolinguistic variable, as it is defined by Labov (1972b:237).[4] The repeater is obviously replaced by the CP type *kwe* 'thing' (see Table 3.2.166). The frame of reference of the CP *bogi* is distinct, of course.

Tables 3.2.40 and 3.2.129 confirm our finding that the CP *bubu/bobu* 'block cut across/cut off' plays a secondary role in actual speech production. As the comments to Table 3.2.129 indicate, this CP type seems to have become a bit problematic with respect to a clearcut and adequate usage in connection with nominal references. We find 4 unacceptable reactions of the consultants to the stimulus presented to elicit this CP type; moreover, the consultants produced the CP types *kwe* 'thing', *ke* 'wood, long objects, inanimates', *ya* 'flexible', *bwa* 'tree', and *bubwa* '(parts) cut off' when *bubu/bobu* was expected. It seems that the CP *kwe*, but also the CP *ke*, have started to supersede this CP type. As Table 3.2.166 shows, the use of *kwe* instead of *bubu/bobu* can be observed rather markedly in consultants in age groups II and IV.

As Tables 3.2.41 and 3.2.130 document, the CP *bubwa* 'parts cut off' plays a secondary role in actual speech. Table 3.2.130 shows that the frame of reference of this CP type is not definite, but rather is quite fuzzy. My consultants produced the CP *bubwa* when I expected the CPs *utu* 'scrap', *bubu* 'cut across', *kabulo1* 'point', and *vili* 'untwisted', although these last two cases of *bubwa* are rather dubious, if not unacceptable (see Table 3.2.214). The CP type *ke* 'wood, long objects, inanimates' seems to have superseded the CP *bubwa*. If we compare Table 3.2.41 with the data in appendix A, we find the following: 8 of the 14 consultants producing the CP *bubwa* belong to the highest-ranking Malasi clan (consultants 25, 31, 38, 41, 47, 49, 56, and 60); Toybokwatauya (consultant 43) and Sogeya (consultant 50) are chief Kilagola's children. Thus, I note that 10 of the 14 consultants that produced the CP *bubwa* are of high status in Tauwema society. Although we find the dubious cases of *bubwa* production with two of these consultants (consultants 25 and 41), I nevertheless infer that the CP *bubwa* is produced by villagers of status as a sociolinguistic variable. This finding is confirmed by Tables 3.2.216, 3.2.217, and appendix B.

The Tables 3.2.42 and 3.2.131 show that the CP type *buda/boda/budu* 'group, team' not only belongs to the core group of Kilivila CP types (see also Tables 3.2.216, 3.2.217, and 3.3.6), but also seems to take over the referential function of the CP *yuva* 'shoal'. However, this finding was expected

---

[4]Labov (1972:237) states, "We may define a *sociolinguistic variable* as one which is correlated with some nonlinguistic variable of the social context: of the speaker, the addressee, the audience, the setting, etc. Some linguistic features (which we will call *indicators*) show a regular distribution over socioeconomic, ethnic, or age groups, but are used by each individual in more or less the same way in any context. If the social contexts concerned can be ordered in some kind of hierarchy (like socioeconomic or age groups), these indicators can be said to be *stratified*. More highly developed sogiolinguistic variables (which we will call *markers*) not only show social distribution, but also stylistic differentiation." See also Labov (1972b:237–240). In connection with the concept "sociolinguistic variable", I will also refer to the concepts "role" and "status"; for a discussion of these concepts see especially Goodenough (1969); for the importance of sociolinguistics for the study of classifier languages, see Barz and Diller (1985) and Diller (1985:56, 64–66).

at the beginning of my research. My consultants gave me the "prototypical" noun *buda* 'group' as the stimulus to elicit these two CP types. In discussing the CP type *yuva*, I will return to this observation. As Table 3.2.131 also documents, this CP was produced when I expected the CPs *gula* 'heap, group' and *mmwa* 'conical bundle' (consultant 45 produced 1 token of the CP *buda/boda* in each of these cases). The CP type *buda/boda/budu* normally implies animation of the subjects it refers to; thus, the use of this CP as a response to the stimuli presented to elicit the CPs *gula* and *mmwa* is at least somewhat problematic. The CP *buda/boda/budu* was also produced when I expected *bubu* 'cut across' and *gum* 'bit'. These two cases of *buda* production as a response to the stimuli presented are not acceptable (see also Table 3.2.214). As noted in connection with Table 3.2.131, the CP *kwe* 'thing' is rather frequently produced by consultants of all five age groups, but especially by consultants of age group IV, instead of the expected CP *buda*.

Table 3.2.43 documents that 3 tokens of the CP type *bukwa* 'fruit cluster' were produced by 6-year-old Towesei (consultant 10) only. It should be mentioned that Towesei's father Mwasei is highly respected and quite an influential man in Tauwema village. Mwasei, a Malasi, is rather conservative with respect to Trobriand tradition and cultural heritage. As indicated in connection with Table 3.2.132, the CP *ke* 'wood, long objects, inanimates' obviously supersedes the almost obsolete CP type *bukwa*.

The Tables 3.2.44 and 3.2.133 confirm that the CP type *bwa* 'tree, wood' plays a secondary role in actual speech (see also Table 3.3.6). It should be noted that the consultants in age group II produce markedly more tokens of this CP type than the consultants in the four other age groups. However, they produce tokens of the CP *bwa* when I expected *utu* 'scrap', *bubwa* 'cut off', *kabisi* 'compartment/foodhouse', *kabulol* 'point', *ke* 'wood', *vili* 'untwisted', and *si* 'bit'. Thus, their definition of the referential frame of this CP is rather broad. Table 3.2.133 shows that we find the production of the CP *bwa* instead of the expected CPs just mentioned with consultants belonging to other age groups, too. For the sake of completeness, I must mention that the consultants in age group IV produced 3 tokens of the CP *bwa* instead of the expected CP *bubu* 'cut across'. It is rather striking that most tokens of the CP *bwa* were produced when I expected the CPs *utu* 'scrap' and *bubwa* 'parts cut off'. I elicited only 5 tokens of *bwa* with the "prototypical" nominal stimulus *kai* 'tree'. As could have been expected, this stimulus elicited the CP *ke* 'wood': my consultants gave me the prototypical noun *kai* as the stimulus to elicit these two CP types. Obviously, *ke* is the more common of these two CPs. That this is indeed the case becomes even more evident when we compare Table 3.2.44 and the data in appendix A. Twelve of the 21 consultants who produced the CP *bwa* are members of the Malasi clan (consultants 4, 15, 17, 20, 25, 26, 34, 39, 44, 47, 49, and 60), two consultants are the chief's children (consultants 28 and 22) and two are his grandchildren (consultants 13 and 19). Moreover, Towesei (consultant 10), whom I already mentioned in connection with the production of the almost obsolete CP *bukwa*, is also one of the consultants who produced the CP *bwa*.

Thus, 17 of the 21 consultants are of high status in Tauwema. On the basis of these observations, I infer that the CP *bwa* is a sociolinguistic variable. This finding is confirmed by Tables 3.2.216, 3.2.217, and appendix B. However, the consultants in age group II who produced this CP focused with their responses on the general quality "wooden" of the eliciting noun and not on the eliciting noun phrases, which required more specific classifications. Moreover, the production of the CP *bwa* instead of the expected *vili* 'untwisted' seems to indicate that some consultants also mixed up the concept 'rigid long objects', which the CP *ke* refers to, with the CP *bwa*, thus extending the frame of reference of *bwa*. The data I elicited in consultants in age group III indicate that this "overgeneralized" use of a sociolinguistic variable should be restricted again. If this does not happen, the consultants in age group II may change the status of the CP *bwa* from a sociolinguistic variable to a CP type playing a secondary role in actual speech. Finally it should be noted that this CP type, together with the variant of the CP type *ke* in its meaning 'wood, wooden things', contradicts Carpenter's (1992:133) remark with respect to "consistent cross-linguistic omission of material".

Tables 3.2.45 and 3.2.134 show that the repeater *bwalita* 'sea' was produced by 4 consultants as a response to the stimulus presented to elicit the CP *siwa* 'sea portions'. Two of these 4 consultants are of high status in Tauwema: Yebwaku (consultant 38) is a Malasi and Bwetadou (consultant 45) is the weather magician heir. On the basis of this observation, I tentatively infer that although this CP type is becoming obsolete, a few consultants produce it as a sociolinguistic variable.

Tables 3.2.46 and 3.2.135 show that although the acquisition of the CP type *deli* 'group' is somewhat late, this CP nevertheless belongs to the core of the Kilivila CP system. Although the CPs *kwe* 'thing', *kasa* 'row', *to/te* 'male persons, humans' and *nal* 'female persons' were also produced when I expected the CP *deli*, the frame of reference of this CP seems to be rather distinct (see Table 3.2.135). However, it must be emphasized that the CP *deli* generally implies animation of the subject it refers to. Thus, I must note that the CP *kwe*, the unmarked form for inanimates, here enters the domain of animate subjects. If we look at Table 3.2.166, we realize that the consultants in age groups II and IV are the protagonists of this remarkable development (see also sections 3.2.1.2 and 3.2.1.4) that may eventually cause a loss of distinctness of this CP's frame of reference.

Tables 3.2.47 and 3.2.136 document that Bwetadou (consultant 45), the weather magician heir, produced 1 token of the repeater *doba* 'grass skirt' instead of the expected CP *kudul* 'band of fibers'. Table 3.2.124 shows that Bwetadou produces strikingly more CP types than all the other consultants in age group IV. Again, it seems that an almost obsolete CP type is used by this consultant to mark his special status within the village society.

Tables 3.2.48 and 3.2.137 confirm that the CP type *duli* 'cluster, bundle' belongs to the core group of Kilivila CPs. Its frame of reference is rather distinct; nevertheless, we note once more that consultants in age groups I,

II, and IV produce the CP *kwe* 'thing', and that consultants in age group II also produce a few tokens of the CP *ke* 'inanimates' instead of the expected CP *duli*. Thus, I note again that the consultants in age groups II and IV foster the frequent use of the CP *kwe*.

As mentioned in section 3.2.1.1, consultant I2/10, Towesei, produced 1 token of the repeater *dumia* 'swamp' (see Table 3.2.7) in connection with a play accompanying verse transcribed in my overall corpus of Kilivila speech data. Although this CP type seems to be almost obsolete, we should note that it is again Towesei who produces a token of an obviously extremely rare CP (see the previous discussion of the CPs *bukwa* and *bwa*).

Tables 3.2.49, 3.2.62, 3.2.138, and 3.2.151 document the production of the CP type *duya/kaduya/kaduyo* 'door, entrance' in its three variants. The variant *duya* is becoming obsolete. Most consultants produced the CPs *kada* 'road, track' and *ya* 'flexible, thin' instead of the expected CP variant *duya*. However, we also observe the production of a few tokens of the CP types *va/vaya/vayo* 'door', *ke* 'wood, long objects, inanimates', and *kwe* 'thing' instead of the expected CP variant *duya*. Moreover, some consultants produced the variant *kaduyo*, and we find 3 tokens of the CP *nal* 'female persons', an unacceptable response to the stimulus presented to elicit the variant *duya* (if we exclude the possibility that the informant tried to play a trick on me, using this CP to give the eliciting noun an obscene meaning). The CP variants *kaduyo* and *kaduya* are produced more often than the variant *duya*. However, most consultants produced the CP type *kada* 'road, track' as a reaction to the stimulus presented to elicit these two variants. Let us set out here on the uncertain terrain of speculation, for a moment, at least. It may be that the variant *duya*, almost a repeater of the eliciting noun *duyava* 'door, entrance, window', was superseded by the variants *kaduyo* and *kaduya*. The fact that the CP type *kada* was realized rather frequently instead of the variants *kaduyo* and *kaduya* may represent a somewhat similar process. On the basis of this line of speculation, we may assume that *kada* here is a shortened version of *kaduya* that is either accidentally homophonous with the CP variant *kada* of the CP type *kada/keda* or represents another meaning of the CP type *kada/keda*. Be that as it may, we also observe the production of the CP types *ya* 'flexible, thin', *ke* 'wood, inanimates', *kwe* 'thing', and *va/vaya/vayo* 'door' instead of the CP variants *kaduya/kaduyo*. On the whole, we can record that the CP type *duya/kaduya/kaduyo* plays a secondary role in actual speech. If we compare Tables 3.2.49 and 3.2.62 with the data in appendix A, the following interesting picture emerges: The tokens of the variant *duya* were produced by 2 consultants belonging to the highest-ranking Malasi clan (consultants 31 and 55). Three Malasi (consultants 4, 41, and 57), and the chief's daughter (consultant 50) and granddaughter (consultant 13) are 5 of 7 consultants who produced tokens of the variants *kaduya/kaduyo*. Thus, we can infer that this CP type, variants of which are produced, with two exceptions, only by consultants of high status, serves the function of a relatively rarely realized sociolinguistic variable.

Tables 3.2.50 and 3.2.139 show that the CP *gili* 'row' is very rarely produced.

Most consultants produce the CP *ya* 'flexible, thin' instead of the expected *gili*. Moreover, we also observe tokens of the CP types *kwe* 'thing', *kasa* 'row', and *vili* 'untwisted' produced as reactions to the noun that should elicit the CP *gili*. We also notice 1 token of the CP *utu* 'scrap' that was produced instead of the CP *gili*; however, this reaction to the stimulus is not acceptable. Again, if we compare Table 3.2.50 with the data in appendix A, we realize that 3 of the 5 consultants producing the CP *gili* are members of the Malasi clan. The other two consultants are the chief's daughter (consultant 50) and the weather magician heir (consultant 45). Thus, only persons of high status produce a token of this CP type, which obviously also serves the function of a sociolinguistic variable.

Tables 3.2.51 and 3.2.140 document that the CP type *giwi* 'cut' belongs to the core of the Kilivila CP system. Although some tokens of the CPs *ke* 'wood, inanimates', *kwe* 'thing', and *luva* 'wooden dishes' were also produced instead of the expected CP *giwi*, and although the stimulus presented to elicit this CP elicited also the rather dubious CPs *kasa* 'row', *ta* 'basket', and *na2* 'animals' (see sections 3.2.1.1 and 3.2.1.2), we note that the frame of reference of this CP type is rather distinct. This is quite obvious if we look at the male consultants (see Table 3.2.51). The female consultants not only acquire this CP type later than male consultants, but this CP type also seems to play a somewhat secondary role in their actual language production, especially if we compare their reactions to those of the male consultants in age groups III–V.

Tables 3.2.52 and 3.2.141 document that 74-year-old Sedaka (consultant 52, see appendix A) produced 3 tokens of the CP type *guba* 'bundle of taro'. The production of this CP was not expected. It should be noted that it was, once again, a consultant belonging to the Malasi clan who produced tokens of an extremely rare and almost obsolete CP type.

The Tables 3.2.53 and 3.2.142 show that the CP type *gudi* 'child' belongs definitely to the core of the Kilivila system. Moreover, it is evident that the frame of reference of this CP type is distinct and unequivocal (see also Tables 3.2.216 and 3.2.217).

Tables 3.2.54 and 3.2.143 document that the CP type *gula* 'heap, group' plays a secondary role in actual speech (see also Tables 3.2.216 and 3.2.217). Consultants 17 and 31 also produced a few tokens of the CP *gula* as a response to the stimulus presented to elicit the CP *bubu* 'cut across'; however, the use of the *gula* is not acceptable in this context (see sections 3.2.1.2 and 3.2.1.3). The CP type *gula* was also produced by consultant 31 as a reaction to the stimulus presented to elicit the CP type *po'ula* 'grove'. Although this usage is rather idiosyncratic, it is acceptable. Morevoer, Table 3.2.143 shows that tokens of the CP types *kwe* 'thing', *tam* 'sprouting', and *buda* 'group' were also produced as reactions to the stimulus presented to elicit the CP *gula*. As the data document, the CP *kwe* has almost superseded the CP *gula*.

Tables 3.2.55 and 3.2.144 show that the CP *gum* 'bit, small piece' must still be classified as belonging to the core of the Kilivila CP system. However, as Table 3.2.144 shows, a few tokens of the CP types *kwe* 'thing', *ke* 'inanimates', *ya* 'thin', and *utu* 'scrap' were also produced in response to the stimulus presented to elicit the CP type *gum*. Moreover, a few tokens of the CPs *na2* 'animals', *buda* 'group', and *kasa* 'row' were realized when the CP *gum* was expected. As explained in sections 3.2.1.1 and 3.2.1.2, the CPs *na2* and *buda* are not acceptable in this context, and *kasa* is quite dubious. On the basis of these findings, we may conclude that the frame of reference of the CP *gum* is starting to lose its distinctness and this CP is thus probably losing its status as one of the core types of the Kilivila CP system.

Tables 3.2.56, 3.2.120, 3.2.145, and 3.2.209 document the production of the CP type *iga/yegila* 'name' in its two variants. The variant *yegila* seems to be almost obsolete; it is produced by only 4 consultants in age group III. The tables confirm that this CP belongs to the core of the Kilivila CP system. Although we find a few tokens of the CP *kwe* 'thing' produced by 2 consultants as a reaction to the stimulus presented to elicit this CP, and although we note that 1 token of the CP *kasa* 'row' was produced when the variant *iga* was expected (a response that is not acceptable; see section 3.2.1.1), we note that the frame of reference of this CP type is distinct.

Tables 3.2.58 and 3.2.147 confirm that the CP type *kabisi* 'compartment of a foodhouse' plays a secondary role in actual speech. As Table 3.2.147 shows, tokens of the CP types *ke* 'wood, inanimates', *kwe* 'thing', *bwa* 'tree, wood', *utu* 'scrap, parts cut off', and *pila* 'part' were also produced when *kabisi* was expected. It should be noted that the "general" CP type *ke* is starting to supersede the more specific CP *kabisi*. For the sake of completeness, I also should mention that 1 token of the CP *nunu* 'corner of a garden' was produced by 1 consultant in age group II when the CP *kabisi* was expected; this usage, however, is not acceptable (see section 3.2.1.2).

Tables 3.2.148, 3.2.149, 3.2.59, and 3.2.60 document the production of the CP type *kabulo/kabulu*. With two different noun phrases I wanted to elicit two (of four) meanings of this CP type, namely: (1) protuberances, points (see Tables 3.2.59 and 3.2.148 ( = *kabulo1*) and (2) village sectors, areas of authority (see Tables 3.2.60 and 3.2.149 ( = *kabulo2*)). As these tables show, I could not elicit any token of the CP type *kabulo/kabulu* in its first meaning with the "prototypical" phrase my consultants mentioned in the test preparatory phase. However, 3 tokens of the CP variant *kabulo1* were produced by consultant 49 as a response to the stimulus presented to elicit the CP type *nunu* 'corner of a garden'. I explained this usage in connection with Table 3.2.148, which shows that tokens of the CPs *ke* 'wood, long objects, inanimates', *utu* 'scrap', *bwa* 'tree, wood', and *bubwa* 'cut off' were realized instead of tokens of the variant to be elicited. The production of all these CPs is acceptable, and this is obviously due to the consultants understanding of the eliciting phrase, which does not seem to be as "prototypical" as the consultants in the test preparatory phase claimed.

As to the second variant of *kabulo/kabulu*, Tables 3.2.149 and 3.2.60 show that *kabulo2* plays a secondary role in actual speech (see also Tables 3.2.216 and 3.2.217). However, if we compare Table 3.2.60 and appendix A, we note that 6 of the 11 consultants producing this CP type variant are members of the highest-ranking Malasi clan (consultants 24, 26, 31, 34, 49, and 60), that consultants 28 and 53 are the chief's daughter and wife, that consultant 45 is the weather magician heir, and that consultant 46 is one of the most respected navigators in Tauwema. Thus, 10 of 11 consultants producing this CP are of high status in the Tauwema village community. Therefore, I infer that the CP type *kabulo/kabulu*, at least in its second meaning (= *kabulo2*), is a sociolinguistic variable. This is also confirmed by Tables 3.2.216 and 3.2.217 and appendix B.

Table 3.2.149 also shows that the CP type *ke* 'wood, long objects, inanimates' and, though to a lesser degree, the CP type *kwe* 'thing, inanimates' have superseded the CP variant *kabulo2*. We also find 1 token of the CP *utu* 'scrap' produced when *kabulo2* was expected. Moreover, 3 tokens of the CP *kada* 'road' were also produced instead of the expected CP variant; however, *kada* in this context is not acceptable (see section 3.2.1.3).

We conclude that the CP type *kabulo/kabulu* plays a secondary role in actual speech and is superseded by the general CP types *ke* and *kwe*. If this CP is produced, however, at least in its second meaning (*kabulo2*), it serves the function of a sociolinguistic variable.

Tables 3.2.61 and 3.2.150 document the production of the CP *kada/keda* 'road, track', which obviously belongs to the core of the Kilivila CP system (see also Tables 3.2.216 and 3.2.217). Its frame of reference encompasses not only the expected frame but also, to a rather large degree, the frame of reference of the CP type *duya/kaduya/kaduyo* 'door, entrance' (see the previous discussion of this CP type). A few tokens of the CP type *kada/keda* were also produced when the CP types *lilo* 'walk', *vilo* 'place', and *kabulu/kabulo* 'village sector' (= *kabulo2*) were expected. However, the use of the CP type in these contexts is either dubious or not acceptable (see sections 3.2.1.2 and 3.2.1.3).

Tables 3.2.63 and 3.2.152 document the production of the CP type *kai* 'stone blade', one of the core types of the Kilivila CP system (see also Tables 3.2.216 and 3.2.217). The tables show that the frame of reference of this CP type is distinct. We only find 2 tokens each of the synonymous repeater *beku* 'stone blade' and of the general CP type *kwe* 'thing' produced instead of the expected CP *kai*. The production of 1 token of the CP variant *na1* 'female persons' and of 2 tokens of the CP type *sisi* 'bough' produced instead of the expected CP *kai* is not acceptable in this context (see section 3.2.1.2).

Tables 3.2.64 and 3.2.153 document the production of the CP type *ka'i* 'tooth', which was not expected. Nevertheless, it belongs to the core of the Kilivila CP system. As Table 3.2.153 shows, the CP *ka'i* was produced when the synonymous CP variant *kudu2* 'tooth' was expected. Obviously, the CP *ka'i* has superseded the CP variant *kudu2* (see also the later discussion of the CP type *kudu*). We note 3 tokens of the CP *ka'i* produced as a response to the stimulus presented to elicit the CP *oyla* 'string'. However, as stated in section 3.2.1.2, the use of the CP *ka'i* in this context is not acceptable. Thus, we conclude that the CP *ka'i* has superseded the synonymous CP variant *kudu2* and that the frame of reference of this CP is distinct.

Tables 3.2.65 and 3.2.145 and appendix A show that only Weyei (consultant 55), the 62-year-old weather magician and the chief's brother, produced 3 tokens of the CP *kala* 'day'. The general CP type *kwe* 'thing' has obviously superseded this almost obsolete CP type. For the sake of completeness, I mention that the consultants produced 1 token of the repeater *tuta* 'time' and 5 tokens of the repeater *yam* 'day' when the CP *kala* was expected. Again, I have to note that a consultant of status (Weyei is also a member of the highest-ranking Malasi clan) produced an extremely rare and almost obsolete classifier.

In my recorded and transcribed texts, there is 1 token of the CP type *kali* 'paddle strike" realized by 60-year-old Mokopei (consultant V14) telling a Trobriand mythical story (see Tables 3.2.216 and 3.2.217 and appendix B). Discussing this CP with my consultants, I found that this CP type is almost obsolete and only preserved in important texts of oral tradition.

Tables 3.2.66 and 3.2.155 document the production of the CP *kapwa/kapo* 'parcel, bundles (wrapped up)'. This CP type plays a secondary role in actual speech. It is superseded by the CP *luba* 'bundle'. Moreover, 30 tokens of the general CP *kwe* 'thing' were produced by consultants of all five age groups when the CP *kapwa/kapo* was expected. If we compare Table 3.2.66 with the data in appendix A, we note the following: 8 of the 18 consultants who produced tokens of the CP *kapwa/kapo* are members of the highest-ranking Malasi clan (consultants 11, 15, 20, 25, 30, 47, 49, and 55). Five of the other 10 consultants are either the chief's children (consultants 22, 28, and 50) or his grandchildren (consultants 13 and 19). Towesei (consultant 10), whom we already mentioned in connection with the CP types *bukwa* and *bwa*, is among the five remaining consultants. Thus, we record that 13, or, if we include Towesei, 14 of the 18 consultants that produced the CP *kapwa/kapo* are of high status within the Tauwema community. We may infer from this observation that the CP *kapwa/kapo* also functions as a sociolinguistic variable.

Tables 3.2.67 and 3.2.156 document the production of the CP *kasa* 'row, line' which belongs to the core of the Kilivila CP system (see also Tables 3.2.216 and 3.2.217). We also note that a few tokens of this CP were produced when the CP types *meila* 'part of a song', *gili* 'row', *nina* 'part of a song', and *deli* 'group on the move' were expected. With one consultant (consultant 23), we find 3 cases of dubious realization of the CP *kasa* instead of the expected CPs *giwi* 'cut', *gum* 'bit', and *yuva* 'shoal' (see section 3.2.1.2). Moreover, consultant 6 produced 1 token of the CP *kasa* instead of the expected CP *iga* 'name'; the use of *kasa* is not acceptable in this context (see section 3.2.2.1). As Table 3.2.156 indicates, we only find a few tokens of the general CP types *ke* 'inanimates' and *kwe* 'thing', which were produced when *kasa* was expected. Thus, we note that the frame of reference of this CP is distinct.

In my recorded and transcribed texts, I find 8 tokens of the CP type *kauya* 'fish trap, creel' produced by Kalavatu (consultant IV3) and Tokunupei (consultant V15) in their description of their special skills as the basket makers in Tauwema. Thus, we note that this repeater belongs to the technical language variety of Trobriand wicker workers.

Tables 3.2.69 and 3.2.158 and appendix A document that 75-year-old Vaka'ila, a member of the highest-ranking Malasi clan, is the only consultant who produces 3 tokens of the CP type *kavi* 'tool'. Table 3.2.158 also documents that the noun presented to elicit this repeater only elicited the production of a few tokens of the general CPs *ke* 'inaminates' and *kwe* 'thing' and the dubious and unacceptable production of 1 token each of the CPs *pila* 'part' and *utu* 'scrap'. What is striking here is that only consultants in age group II produced these responses to the eliciting noun. We may interpret this as an indication of the children's high motivation to acquire the Kilivila CP system. In any case, we can assume that the CP type *kavi* is becoming obsolete.

Tables 3.2.70 and 3.2.159 document the production of the CP *ke* 'wood, long objects, inanimates, fire'. The exceptional status of this CP type is obvious (see also Tables 3.2.216 and 3.2.217). It is not only one of the first CP types acquired, but its frame of reference with respect to the meaning 'rigid, long objects' and its function as one of the two "unmarked forms for inanimates" is very broad. However, its frame of reference with respect to the meanings 'wooden things' and 'fire' is distinct. Only 2 tokens of the CP type *bwa* 'tree, wood' were produced instead of the expected CP *ke*. Moreover, Table 3.2.159 documents that the CP *ke* has superseded the CP *bwa*. However, this is also true for the CP types *lila* 'bough, branch, leaf' and *luva* 'wooden dishes'. The CP *ke* has almost superseded the CP types *bubwa* '(parts) cut off', *bukwa* 'fruit cluster', *kabulo/kabulu* 'point, sector', *kila* 'hands of bananas', *mmwa* 'conical bundle', and *sa* 'nut bunch'. The fact that so many tokens of the CP type *ke* were produced instead of the expected CP *uva* 'span', however, is obviously a result of the consultants' focussing on the 'yams' mentioned in the eliciting noun phrase instead of referring to the concept expressed by the eliciting noun phrase as a whole. We also find tokens of the CP type *ke* produced by consultants of all five age groups instead of the expected CPs *utu* 'scrap', *kabisi* 'compartment of a foodhouse', *giwi* 'cut', and *ya* 'flexible, thin'. However, as the data document, the CP *ke* plays a secondary role as an acceptable substitute for these CP types. This is also true for the production of the CP *ke* instead of the expected CPs *liku* 'compartment of a foodhouse', *vili* 'untwisted', *si* 'bit', *bubu* 'cut across', *oyla* 'string', *sisi* 'bough', *meila* 'part of a song', *gum* 'bit' *duya/kaduya* 'door, entrance', *kubila* 'land plot', *kwoila* 'clay pot', *pila* 'part', *yulai* 'bundle of four things', *kweya* 'limb', *kudu2* 'tooth', *kavi* 'tool', *duli* 'cluster', *yuva* 'shoal', *sipu* 'sheaf', *lilo* 'walk', and *kasa* 'row'. We also find only 1 token of the CP *ke* in its meaning 'fire' (= *ke4*) produced instead of the expected, synonymous repeater *kova* 'fire'.

As mentioned in connection with Table 3.2.159, it should be emphasized that consultant 12 produced 1 token of the CP *ke* instead of the expected CP *yuva* 'shoal', which normally implies animation of the subjects it refers to. However, whether this can be regarded as a first indication that the CP type *ke* is starting to invade the semantic domains characterized by the feature 'animation' must remain an open question here (see section 3.3.4).

Tables 3.2.70 and 3.2.159 also show that the consultants in age group II produced by far the most tokens of this CP type. If we list the number of cases where *ke* was produced instead of the expected CP type, we find the following: The consultants in age group II produced tokens of the CP *ke* for 29 different expected CP types, 3 more than we find with the consultants in age group I. However, the older consultants in age groups IV and V also produced tokens of the CP *ke* for 24 and 23 different expected CP types, respectively. The consultants in age group III produced tokens of the CP *ke* for 19 different expected CP types. These data suggest the following interpretation: Consultants in age group II produced the CP *ke* in its broadest frame of possible reference. On the other hand, the consultants in age group III seem to be more selective in, and aware of, their choice of more specific CPs within the Kilivila CP system (see also Table 3.2.124). It goes without saying that we must regard this interpretation with all necessary caution.

What we can conclude, however, is that, on the one hand, the frame of reference of the CP type *ke* in its meanings 'wooden things' and 'fire' is distinct, and, on the other hand, the frame of reference of this CP in its meaning 'rigid long objects', and especially in its function as one of the unmarked forms for inanimates, is so broad that we can assign it the status of a so-called general classifier, especially the last mentioned CP variant (cf. Adams 1989:182).

Tables 3.2.71 and 3.2.160 document the production of the CP type *kila* 'clusters/hands of bananas', We note 7 tokens of this CP type realized by 4 women only. Table 3.2.71 and the data in appendix A document that these women are all members of the highest-ranking Malasi clan. As mentioned previously in connection with the CP type *ke*, Table 3.2.160 shows that *ke* has superseded the CP type *kila*. We also find a few tokens of the CP type *kwe* 'thing' produced instead of the expected CP *kila*. Thus, we can conclude that the CP *kila* is becoming obsolete; however, it seems to function as a sociolinguistic variable for high-ranking Trobriand women who still use the distinct frame of reference of this CP as a special mass term.

Tables 3.2.72 and 3.2.161 document the production of the CP type *kova* 'fire', which belongs to the core of the Kilivila CP system. Although we notice that consultant 5 produced 1 token of the CP *kova* instead of the expected CP *yuma* 'hand' (a use of *kova* that is not acceptable; see section 3.2.1.1), and although 1 token of the CP *kwe* 'thing' was produced instead of the expected CP *kova*, we can state that the frame of reference of this repeater is distinct (see also Tables 3.2.216 and 3.2.217). It should also be noted that Table 3.2.161 documents 1 token of the CP type *ke* in its meaning 'fire', produced instead of the synonymous repeater *kova* (see the previous discussion of the CP *ke*).

Tables 3.2.73 and 3.2.162 document the production of the CP type *kubila/kwabila* 'large land plot', which also belongs to the core of the Kilivila CP system. It seems that this CP is somewhat more important in the language of men than in that of women, thus reflecting the division of labor in Trobriand society (see, e.g., Malinowski 1929, 1935; Hutchins 1980). Table 3.2.162 also shows that only 2 tokens of the CP type *utu* 'scrap' were produced instead of the expected CP *kubila/kwabila*; this use of the CP *utu*, however, is not acceptable. We also note that the consultants produced 1 token each of the CP types *ke* 'inanimates' and '*pila* 'part' instead of the expected CP *kubila/ kwabila*. What is striking, however, is that this CP type with its distinct frame of reference seems to also be in danger of being superseded by the CP type *kwe* 'thing': there were 53 tokens of the CP *kwe* produced by consultants of all five age groups instead of the expected specific CP. The fact that in my recorded and transcribed texts only 1 token of the CP *kubila/kwabila* was produced may be a result of the text categories recorded and transcribed (see Tables 3.2.216 and 3.2.217 and appendix B).

Tables 3.2.74, 3.2.75, 3.2.163 and 3.2.164 document the production of the CP type *kudu* in its meanings 'band of fibers' (*kudu1*) and 'tooth' (*kudu2*). As Tables 3.2.74 and 3.2.163 show, the variant *kudu1* 'band of fibers' is becoming obsolete (see also Tables 3.2.216 and 3.2.217). Moreover, consultant 58 produced tokens of this CP variant when the CP types *bubu* 'cut across' and *yuva* 'shoal' were expected; all my other consultants agreed that the use of the variant *kudu1* is not acceptable in either context (see section 3.2.1.5). Table 3.2.163 also shows that this CP variant has been superseded by the CP *kwe* 'thing'. We also notice the production of the repeater *doba* 'grass skirt' as a reaction to the stimulus presented to elicit the variant *kudu1* (see the previous discussion of the repeater *doba*).

Tables 3.2.75 and 3.2.164 document that the CP variant *kudu2* 'tooth' plays only a secondary role in actual speech. However, if we compare Table 3.2.75 and the data in appendix A, we realize that 9 of the 12 consultants producing this CP variant belong to the highest-ranking Malasi clan. Thus, we may infer that the variant *kudu2* functions as a sociolinguistic variable.

In the previous discussion of the CP *ka'i* I mentioned that this CP type has almost superseded the variant *kudu2*. For the sake of completeness, I should also mention that the consultants produced 2 tokens each of the CP types *ke* 'long objects, inanimates' and *kwe* 'thing' instead of the expected CP variant *kudu2*.

Tables 3.2.76 and 3.2.165 document the production of the CP type *kumla* 'earth oven', one of the core types of the Kilivila CP system. It is quite obvious that the frame of reference of this CP is distinct. Only 1 token of the CP *kwe* 'thing' was produced instead of the expected CP *kumla*.

Tables 3.2.77 and 3.2.166 document the production of the CP type *kwe* 'thing', unmarked form for inanimates, clams, and shells'. Again, the exceptional status of this CP is obvious (see also Tables 3.2.216 and 3.2.217). The broad range of meaning that is covered by this CP type is clearly documented in Table 3.2.166. The CP *kwe* has superseded the CPs *bogi* 'night', *kala* 'day', *kudu1* 'band of fibers', *kwoya/koya* 'mountain', *lilo* 'walk', *siva* 'time', *siwa* 'sea portions', *vilo* place', *yam* 'day', and *yulai* 'bundle of four things'. It has almost superseded the CP types *gula* 'heap', *nunu* 'corner of a garden', *po'ula* 'grove', and 0 'basketful of yams'. The fact that all consultants produced tokens of the CP *kwe* instead of the actually expected CPs *buda* 'group', *kapwa* 'parcel', *kubila* 'land plot', *kwoila* 'clay pot', *nina* 'part of a song', *sipu* 'sheaf', *yuva* 'shoal', and *duya/kaduyo* 'door, entrance' may indicate that these CPs are also in danger of being superseded by this classifier. The same seems to hold for the CPs *bubu* 'cut across', *gili* 'row', *kabulo2* 'sector', *deli* 'group', *kabisi* 'compartment of a foodhouse', *gum* 'bit', *liku* 'compartment of a foodhouse', *notu* 'kneaded, dot', '*pwanina/pona* 'hole', *sa* 'nut bunch', and *yuma* 'hand'.

The fact that we find the CPs *buda*, *deli*, and *yuva* among this group is worthy of note. These CPs normally imply animation of the subjects they refer to. On the basis of the data presented, we can infer that the CP *kwe* has started to invade the semantic domains characterized by the feature 'animate' (for a similar situation in Hokkien, see Chin 1989:37–39).

The fact that we find tokens of the CP *kwe* produced instead of the expected CPs *giwi* 'cut', *vili* 'untwisted', *duli* 'cluster', *kila* 'hands of bananas', *meila* 'part of a song', *oyla* 'string', *mmwa* 'conical bundle', *iga/yegila* 'name', *kasa* 'row', *kudu2* 'tooth', *bukwa* 'fruit cluster', *uva* 'span', *kova* 'fire', *kumla* 'earth oven', *pila* 'part', *bubwa* 'cut off', *ta/peta* 'basket', *kai* 'stone blade', *kavi* 'tool', *kweya* 'limb', *luva* 'wooden dishes', and *si* 'bit' documents the enormous possibilities of an acceptable usage of this CP type. We can attribute to the CP *kwe* the status of a so-called general classifier.

A closer look at Table 3.2.77 reveals that the consultants in age groups II and IV especially seem to foster the development of the CP *kwe* from the 'unmarked form for inanimates' to a general classifier. This observation is at least in part confirmed if we look at the data presented in Table 3.2.166, which document the production of the CP *kwe* instead of the expected CPs *buda*, *yuva*, and *deli*. Here, too, we observe that it is the consultants in age groups II and IV that foster the invasion of the CP *kwe* into the semantic domains characterized by the feature 'animate'.

In connection with this observation, we should emphasize, too, that *kwe* is also the adequate CP to refer to 'shells and clams' (see Tables 3.2.216 and 3.2.217). In my recorded and transcribed texts, Toybokwatauya (consultant IV1/43) and Kilagola (consultant V11) produce 2 tokens each of the CP type *kwe* in this meaning. Mokopei (consultant V14) produced 15 tokens of the CP *kwe* in its meaning 'shells and clams'. The corpus on Trobriand myths offers an interesting, though highly speculative, possibility to explain this meaning of the CP *kwe*, which implies also an exception in the frame of reference of the CP *na* in its meaning 'animals (but not shells and clams)'. One of the most important mythical folktales is the story of Imdeduya and Yolina (see, e.g., J. W. Leach 1981; Kasaipwalova 1980). I recorded and transcribed three different versions of this folktale, the longest and most elaborate version of which was told to me by Mokopei from Kaduwaga village. I assume that Imdeduya and Yolina are the personifications of the moon and sun. Yolina had to paddle a long distance in his canoe before he came to the place where Imdeduya lived. Mokopei mentioned that the canoe of Yolina was a *kweduya*; this is the archaic name for a shell that is now called *duya* (i.e., Melo aethiopicus [Linnaeus] of the family Volutidae). It may be that the CP *kwe* in its meaning 'clams and shells' is a mythical relic, a honorific and revertential reminiscence of Yolina's excellent ocean-going canoe. I want to emphasize again that this attempt to explain this meaning of the CP *kwe*, is of course, highly speculative; however, on the basis of my Trobriand experience, it is quite plausible.[5]

Tables 3.2.78 and 3.2.167 document the production of the CP *kweya/kwaya/keya* '(severed) limb', one of the core types of the Kilivila CP system. The frame of reference of this CP type is distinct (see also Tables 3.2.216 and 3.2.217). As the more general CP type, it seems to supersede the CP type *yuma* 'hand', as Table 3.2.167 shows. We find only a few tokens of the general CPs *ke* 'inanimates' and *kwe* 'thing' produced instead of the expected CP *kweya*. Table 3.2.167 also shows 4 tokens of the CP variant *nal* 'female persons' that were produced instead of the expected CP *kweya*; however, the use of this CP variant in the given context was not acceptable (see sections 3.2.1.1 and 3.2.1.2).

Tables 3.2.79 and 3.2.168 document the production of the CP *kwoila/kwela* 'clay pot', which belongs to the core of the Kilivila CP system. The frame of reference of this CP type is distinct (see also Tables 3.2.216 and 3.2.217). However, as Table 3.2.168 shows, the CP *kwe* is starting to supersede this CP. We also note the production of a few tokens of the CP *ke* 'inanimates' instead of the expected CP *kwoila/kwela*. Consultant 58, Kasilasila, also produced one token of *\*kava* in this context; however, according to all my other consultants, such a CP does not exist in Kilivila (see Tables 3.2.68 and 3.2.157); I can only assume that *\*kava* was an error of speech production.

Tables 3.2.80 and 3.2.169 document the production of the CP *kwoya/koya* 'mountain, hill', which plays a secondary role in actual speech. The frame of reference of this CP is distinct; however, the CP *kwe* 'thing' has superseded it. If we compare Table 3.2.80 and the data in appendix A, we find the following: 5 of the 13 consultants who produced the CP *kwoya/koya* are members of the highest-ranking Malasi clan (consultants 1, 15, 31, 34, and 41); 4 of the other consultants belong to the chief's family (consultants 21, 32, 28, 53), and consultant 45 is the weather magician heir. Thus, 10 of the 13 consultants producing tokens of this CP type are of high status in Tauwema. Hence, we may infer that the CP *kwoya/koya* functions as a sociolinguistic variable.

Tables 3.2.81 and 3.2.170 document the production of the CP *liku* 'compartments of a foodhouse/of a canoe', which plays a secondary role in actual speech. Its frame of reference is distinct (see also Tables 3.2.216 and 3.2.217); however, it is in danger of being superseded by the CP *kwe* 'thing' and also by the CP *ke* 'wood, inanimates'. If we compare Table 3.2.81 and the data in appendix A, we find the following: 27 consultants produced tokens of the CP *liku*; 14 of these consultants are members of the highest-ranking

---

[5] In connection with this speculation, Bousfield (1979:217) stated, "Any theoretical account must first deal with the complicated, untidy logics actually found". See also Chin (1989:33–34); Dixon (1972:302–304).

Malasi clan (consultants 15, 17, 24, 26, 30, 34, 38, 39, 49, 51, 55, 56, 59, and 60); 6 consultants belong to the chief's family (consultants 19, 21, 32, 28, 43, and 48), and 1 consultant is the weather magician heir (consultant 45). Thus, 21 of the 27 consultants who produced tokens of the CP *liku* are of high status, and we may assume that the CP *liku* functions as a sociolinguistic variable (see also Tables 3.2.216 and 3.2.217 and appendix B).

As mentioned in section 3.2.2.2, the CP type *lila* 'bough, branch, leaf' was not produced by my consultants during the elicitation test; nor was it produced in the recorded and transcribed speech data (see Tables 3.2.216 and 3.2.217). Instead of the expected CP *lila*, consultants of all five age groups produced 125 tokens of the CP *ke* 'wood, long objects, inanimates' in the elicitation test. Thus, although the consultants claimed during the informal pretests in the test preparatory phase that this CP type is well known and used in their speech community, it seems that the CP *lila* is either obsolete or extremely rare and that the CP *ke* has superseded it.

Tables 3.2.82 and 3.2.171 document the production of the CP *lilo/lola* 'walk, journey'. This extremely rare and almost obsolete CP type has been superseded by the CP *kwe* 'thing'. We also note some tokens of the CP *ya* 'flexible, thin' produced instead of the expected *lilo/lola*. My consultants also produced 1 token each of the CPs *ke* 'inanimates' and *kada* 'road' instead of the expected *lilo/lola*; the use of the CP *kada* in this context, however, is somewhat dubious (see section 3.2.1.2). If we compare Table 3.2.82 and the data in appendix A, we see that 2 of the 4 consultants producing the CP *lilo/lola* are members of the Malasi clan and that the weather magician heir also produced 1 token of this CP type. However, the database is too small to decide whether we can regard the CP *lilo/lola* as a sociolinguistic variable.

As documented in Tables 3.2.216 and 3.2.217 and appendix B, Kalavatu (consultant IV3) produced tokens of the CP type *lipu* 'compartment of a creel'. As mentioned in connection with the previous discussion of the CP *kauya* 'creel', Kalavatu is one of the basket makers of Tauwema village. Thus, we can infer that this extremely rare CP type belongs to the technical language variety used by Trobriand wicker workers.

Tables 3.2.83 and 3.2.172 document the production of the CP *luba* 'bundle'. This repeater, which was not expected, plays a secondary role in actual speech. However, it has superseded the CP *kapwa* 'parcel, bundle'.

Tables 3.2.84 and 3.2.173 document the production of the CP *luva* 'wooden dishes, tied bundle', which plays a secondary role in actual speech production. As Table 3.2.173 indicates, only 4 tokens of the variant *luva1* 'wooden dishes' were produced by consultants belonging to age groups I and V. We note 3 tokens each of the CP variant *luva2* 'tied bundle' produced by consultants belonging to age group IV, instead of the expected CPs *mmwa* 'conical bundle' and *sa* 'nut bunch', and 2 tokens of this CP variant produced by a speaker of the same age group instead of the expected CP *bukwa* 'fruit cluster'. The production of the variant *luva2* was not elicited. As noted in Table 3.2.173, the production of the CP *luva* instead of the expected CPs *utu* 'scrap' and *giwi* 'cut' is not acceptable. The CP *ke* 'wood, inanimates' has superseded the CP *luva*. We also find 2 tokens of the CP *kwe* 'thing' produced instead of the expected CP *luva*. It seems that the CP *luva* is becoming obsolete.

Tables 3.2.85 and 3.2.174 document the production of the CP *megwa* 'magic, magical formula'. The production of this extremely rare repeater was not expected. Only 7 consultants produced tokens of this CP instead of the expected CP *nina* 'part of a song'. Although a comparison of Table 3.2.85 and the data in appendix A shows that 1 of the 7 consultants is a member of the highest-ranking Malasi clan (consultant 38), that 2 other consultants belong to the chief's family (consultants 24 and 38), and that 1 consultant is the weather magician heir (consultant 45), it is not possible to determine whether this CP type functions as a sociolinguistic variable or belongs to the technical language variety of Trobriand magicians.

Tables 3.2.86 and 3.2.175 document that only Weyei (consultant 55) produced 3 tokens of the extremely rare and almost obsolete CP *meila* 'part of a song/a magic formula'. The CP *pila* 'part' has obviously superseded the CP *meila*. We also note the production of some tokens of the CPs *vosi* 'song', *ke* 'inanimates', *kasa* 'row', *kwe* 'thing', and *utu* 'scrap, parts' as responses to the stimulus presented to elicit the CP *meila*.

Tables 3.2.87 and 3.2.176 document the production of the CP *mmwa* 'conical bundle (most often of taro)', which plays a secondary role in actual speech. The CP *ke* 'inanimates' has almost superseded it. We also note the production of a few tokens of the CPs *kwe* 'thing', *guba* 'bundle of taro', *buda* 'group' and *luva2* 'tied bundle', and *utu* 'scrap, part' instead of the expected CP *mmwa*. The production of the CP *luva2* in this context is a bit dubious, and the production of the CP *utu* in this context is not acceptable (see sections 3.2.1.3 and 3.2.1.4). If we compare Table 3.2.87 and the data in appendix A, we find the following: 7 of the 10 consultants who produced tokens of the CP *mmwa* are members of the highest-ranking Malasi clan (consultants 31, 34, 41, 49, 51, 55 and 57) and 1 consultant is the chief's grandson (consultant 19). Thus, 8 of these 10 consultants are of high status. Only 3 of these 8 consultants are women. We may tentatively conclude that the CP *mmwa* functions as a sociolinguistic variable and that this function seems to be important especially for Trobriand men.

Tables 3.2.88, 3.2.89, 3.2.177, 3.2.178, 3.2.216, and 3.2.217 document the production of the CP type *na* in 4 of its 6 meanings. With its meanings 'persons of female gender' (*na1*) and 'animals, but not shells and clams' (*na2*), this CP type belongs to the core of the Kilivila CP system. As Tables 3.2.216 and 3.2.217 indicate, the CP *na* is not often produced in its meanings 'stars, planets, moon' (*na3*) and 'carvings in human likeness' (*na4*).

Tables 3.2.88 and 3.2.177 show that the variant *na1* 'female persons' is acquired very early; its frame of reference is distinct. With consultants of the first two age groups we also note the production of a few tokens of this CP variant instead of the CPs *kweya* 'limb', *bubu* 'cut across', *uva* 'span', *kai* 'stone blade', and *deli* 'group'. With the exception of *deli*, the production of the variant *na1* as a substitute for these CPs mentioned is not acceptable in the respective elicitation contexts (see sections 3.2.1.1 and 3.2.1.2). One consultant of age group III, Namnabai (consultant 25), produced 3 tokens of the variant *na1* as a response to the stimulus presented to elicit the CP *duya* 'door, entrance'. If we exclude a possibly metaphorical, though rather obscene, extension of the meaning 'person of female gender' of the variant *na1*, we have to record that the use of *na1* instead of the expected CP *duya* is not acceptable (see also section 3.2.1.3).

Tables 3.2.89 and 3.2.178 show that the frame of reference of the CP variant *na2* 'animals, but not shells and clams' (see the previous discussion of the CP *kwe*) is also distinct. Table 3.2.178 shows that the variant *na2* was also produced when the CPs *oyla* 'string, fish on strings' and *wela* 'batch of fish' were expected; these CPs refer specifically to caught fish. A few tokens of the CP variant *na2* were also produced instead of the expected CPs *gum* 'bit' and *giwi* 'cut'; these were not acceptable. However, it may be that the consultant mistook the stimulus *giwi* 'cut' for the CP type *givi*, which refers to 'a serving of fish' (see section 3.3.1, Table 3.3.2, L15); such a misunderstanding would explain the production of the CP variant *na2*, which would then be acceptable.

For the sake of completeness, I should mention that my consultants also gave the meanings 'corpses' (*na5*) and 'spirits, dwarfs' (*na6*) for the CP type *na*; however, these variants are not documented in my corpus of recorded and transcribed speech data. Moreover, I would like to mention here that in the Mayan language Mixtec there is also a classifier that refers not only to animals, but also to the rainbow, the moon, and the stars (see de León 1988:146).

Tables 3.2.90 and 3.2.179 and appendix A document that 62-year-old Weyei (consultant 55) produced only 1 token of the CP type *nigwa* 'hole' instead of the expected CP type *pwanina/pona* 'punctured, hole'. The production of this almost obsolete CP was not expected.

Tables 3.2.91 and 3.2.180 and appendix A document that the same consultant produced only 3 tokens of the CP type *nina* 'part of a song', which is almost obsolete. It has been superseded by the CP types *pila* 'part' and *kwe* 'thing'. As Table 3.2.179 also shows, we find a few tokens of the CP types *megwa* 'magic', *utu* 'scrap, part', and *kasa* 'row' instead of the expected CP *nina*. We also note 1 token of a formative *\*iki* produced instead of the expected CP *nina*. All my other consultants told me that such a CP type does not exist in Kilivila (see Tables 3.2.146 and 3.2.57). However, as noted in connection with Table 3.2.146, it may be that the consultant wanted to produce the CP type *igi* 'wind' (see Table 3.3.2, L19), a rather idiosyncratic, although understandable response to the stimulus presented to elicit the CP *nina*.

Tables 3.2.92 and 3.2.181 document the production of the CP *nutu/notu* 'kneaded, dot, drop', which belongs to the core of the Kilivila CP system. The frame of reference of this CP type is distinct. Table 3.2.181 also shows that consultants in four of the five age groups produced 33 tokens of the general CP *kwe* 'thing' instead of the expected CP *nutu/notu*. Thus, we may infer that the CP *nutu/notu* is also in danger of being superseded by the CP *kwe*.

Tables 3.2.93 and 3.2.182 document the production of the CP *nunu* 'corner of a garden', which plays a secondary role in actual speech. As mentioned in connection with Table 3.2.182, the CP *kwe* 'thing' has almost superseded *nunu*. We also note a few tokens of the CPs *utu* 'scrap, part' and *kabulo2* 'sector' produced instead of the expected CP *nunu*. The production of 1 token of the CP *kabisi* 'compartment of a foodhouse' as a reaction to the stimulus presented to elicit the CP *nunu* is not acceptable (see section 3.2.1.2). If we compare Table 3.2.93 and the data in appendix A, we find the following: 6 of the 9 consultants who produced tokens of the CP type *nunu* are members of the highest-ranking Malasi clan (consultants 15, 26, 38, 39, 55 and 56) and consultant 28 is the chief's daughter. Thus, 7 of the 9 consultants who produced this CP type are of high status in Tauwema. We may tentatively conclude therefore that the CP type *nunu* may also function as a sociolinguistic variable. In addition, it should be noted that the frame of reference of this CP type is distinct.

As mentioned at the end of section 3.2.2.2, the CP type *oyla* 'string, fish on strings' was neither produced by my consultants during the elicitation test nor found in the recorded and transcribed texts (see Tables 3.2.216 and 3.3.217). Instead of the expected CP type *oyla*, the consultants produced tokens of the CPs *na2* 'animals', *ke* 'long objects, inanimates', *wela* 'batch of fish', and *kwe* 'thing'. We also find a few tokens of the CPs *ka'i* 'tooth' and *pila* 'part' produced instead of the expected CP *oyla*. However, the two last mentioned responses to the stimuli presented to elicit *oyla* are not acceptable or are rather dubious. Thus, although my consultants claimed during the informal pretests that this CP type is well known and used in their speech community, it seems that *oyla* is either obsolete or extremely rare and that the CPs *na2* 'animals', *ke* 'long objects, inanimates', and *wela* 'batch of fish' have superseded it.

Tables 3.2.94, 3.2.104, 3.2.183, and 3.2.193 document the production of the two variants of the CP type *peta/ta* 'basket'. The variant *ta* obviously belongs to the core of the Kilivila CP system, whereas the repeater *peta* is extremely rare or almost obsolete. If we compare Tables 3.2.94 and 3.2.104, we note that the 6 consultants who produced the variant *peta* produced it together with the variant *ta*. It may be that the repeater functions as a sociolinguistic variable: 3 of the 6 consultants producing the variant *peta* are members of the highest-ranking Malasi clan (consultants 27, 57, and 60), consultant 50 is the chief's daughter, and consultant 45 is the weather magician heir (see appendix A); however, the database is rather small for such a hypothesis. We only note one dubious use of the CP *ta*: 1 token of the variant was produced instead of the expected CP *giwi* 'cut' (see section 3.2.1.1). Moreover, we only observe the production of 1 token of the CP type *kwe* 'thing' instead of the expected variant *ta*. Thus, we conclude that the frame of reference of the CP type *peta/ta* is distinct (see also Tables 3.2.216 and 3.2.217). Moreover, Table 3.2.104 confirms the observation that this CP type is acquired rather early.

Tables 3.2.95 and 3.2.184 document the production of the CP *pila* 'part', which belongs to the core of the Kilivila CP system. Table 3.2.184 records the rather broad frame of reference of this CP type (see also Tables 3.2.216 and 3.2.217). The CP *pila* has started to supersede or has almost superseded the CPs *nina* 'part of a song' and *meila* 'part of a song'. Moreover, we also find a few tokens of the CP *pila* that were produced instead of the CPs *ya* 'flexible, thin', *siva* 'time', *kabisi* 'compartment of a foodhouse', and *kubila* 'land plot'. The few tokens of the CP *pila* that were produced instead of the expected CPs *oyla* 'string' and *kavi* 'tool', however, document dubious uses of this CP type (see the previous discussion of the CP *oyla*). We also note that consultants of all five age groups produced 60 tokens of the CP *ya* 'flexible, thin' instead of the expected CP *pila*; the CP *ya* seems to cover a rather important part of the obviously broad frame of reference defined for the CP *pila*. A few tokens of the CPs *ke* 'wood, inanimates', *kwe* 'thing', *utu* 'scrap', and *vili* 'untwisted' were also produced instead of the expected CP *pila*.

Tables 3.2.96 and 3.2.185 record the production of the CP *po'ula* 'plantation, grove', which plays a secondary role in actual speech. Although Table 3.2.185 documents that a few tokens of this CP were also produced instead of the expected CP types *sa* 'nut bunch' and *bukwa* 'fruit cluster' (a completely acceptable response to the stimuli presented to elicit these two types), it should be noted that the frame of reference of the CP *po'ula* is distinct. However, as mentioned previously, the CP *po'ula* has been almost superseded by the CP *kwe*. The fact that we find 3 tokens of the CP *gula* 'heap, group' produced instead of the CP *po'ula* is not significant; it is mentioned here only for the sake of completeness.

Tables 3.2.97 and 3.2.186 document the production of the two variants of the CP type *pwanina/pona* 'punctured, hole', which belongs to the core of the Kilivila CP system. As noted in Table 3.2.97, the ratio of production for the two variants *pwanina* and *pona* is 94:45. Thus, with this CP type, the repeater variant is still preferred by my consultants. Table 3.2.186 documents that the frame of reference of this CP type is distinct (see also Tables 3.2.216 and 3.2.217). We only note 23 tokens of the CP *kwe* 'thing' and 1 token of the CP *nigwa* 'hole' produced instead of the expected CP *pwanina/pona*.

Tables 3.2.98 and 3.2.187 record the production of the CP *sa* 'nut bunch', which is obviously extremely rare or almost obsolete. Although 3 tokens of the CP *sa* were produced instead of the expected CP *bukwa* 'fruit cluster', the frame of reference of the CP *sa* is distinct. As also documented in Table 3.2.187, the CP type *ke* 'wood, inanimates' has almost superseded *sa*. Moreover, we also find a number of tokens of the CP *kwe* 'thing' and a few tokens of the CPs *po'ula* 'grove' and *luva2* 'tied bundle' instead of the CP *sa*. The production of the CP *luva2* instead of the CP *sa* is somewhat dubious, however (see section 3.2.1.4). If we compare Table 3.2.98 and the data in appendix A, we find the following: 5 of the 7 consultants who produced the CP *sa* are members of the highest-ranking Malasi clan (consultants 20, 23, 31, 49, and 51). Consultant 45 is the weather magician heir, and consultant 10 is little Towesei, who was previously mentioned in the discussion of the CPs *bukwa* and *bwa*. Thus, all 7 consultants who produced the CP *sa* are of high status in Tauwema. We may tentatively conclude that the CP *sa* functions as a sociolinguistic variable.

As Table 3.2.215 documents, there were 7 tokens of the CP type *sam* 'ginger' produced in connection with play accompanying verses. My data do not specify which consultants produced these CP tokens. Thus, I can only note that this CP type is extremely rare in actual speech and that its frame of reference is very distinct: the CP *sam* is only used to refer to 'ginger' (*neya*) in play accompanying verses. In other contexts, the CP *tam* 'sprouting' is used to refer to ginger.

Tables 3.2.99 and 3.2.188 document the production of the CP *si* 'small bit', which is extremely rare. As Table 3.2.188 documents, 14 of the 15 tokens of this CP type were produced instead of the expected CP *ya* 'flexible, thin'. Although I explained this use in my comments on Table 3.2.188, it should be noted that the frame of reference of this CP type is not distinct at all. The CP *si* has obviously been superseded by the CP *utu* 'scrap'. Moreover, the CPs *ke* 'wood, inanimates', *bwa* 'tree, wood', *vili* 'untwisted', and *kwe* 'thing' were produced instead of the expected CP *si*. What is rather astounding is that all 7 consultants who produced this CP type belong to the first three age groups, and that 6 of these consultants are of high status in Tauwema (see appendix A; consultants 4, 25, 26, 31, 10, and 13). However, the database is too small to justify any speculation about the sociolinguistic status of the CP *si*.

Tables 3.2.100 and 3.2.189 document the production of the CP *sipu* 'sheaf', which belongs to the core of the Kilivila CP system. The frame of reference of this CP is distinct. As Table 3.2.189 shows, the CP *sipu* is in danger of being superseded by the CP *kwe* 'thing'. A few tokens of the CPs *ya* 'flexible, thin' and *ke* 'inanimates' were produced instead of the expected CP *sipu*.

Tables 3.2.101 and 3.2.190 document the production of the CP *sisi* 'bough', which belongs to the core of the Kilivila CP system. As Table 3.2.190 documents, the CP *sisi* has almost superseded the CP type *ya* 'flexible, thin', at least in its prototypical meaning (see the later discussion of the CP *ya*). Only 2 tokens of the CP *sisi* were produced as a response to the stimulus presented to elicit the CP *kai* 'stone blade'; this use of the CP *sisi* is not acceptable (see section 3.2.1.2). A few tokens of the CPs *ke* 'wood, inanimates' and *ya* 'flexible, thin' were also produced instead of the expected CP *sisi*. The frame of reference of this CP type is distinct (see also Tables 3.2.216 and 3.2.217).

Tables 3.2.102 and 3.2.191 and appendix A document that 62-year-old Weyei produced only 3 tokens of the CP type *siva* 'time'. This CP type is obviously almost obsolete. It has been superseded by the CP *kwe* 'thing'. As Table 3.2.191 also records, we find a few tokens of the CPs *tuta* 'time', *utu* 'scrap, part', and *pila* 'part' produced instead of the expected CP *siva*.

As mentioned at the end of section 3.2.2.2, the CP type *siwa* 'sea portions' was neither produced by my consultants during the elicitation test nor found in the recorded and transcribed texts (see Tables 3.2.216 and 3.2.217). This type has obviously been superseded by the CP *kwe* 'thing', although my consultants claimed during the informal pretests that this CP is well known and used in their speech community. A few tokens of the repeater *bwalita* 'sea' and the CP *utu* 'scrap' were produced instead of the expected CP *siwa*; however, the use of the CP *utu* in this context is rather dubious (see section 3.2.1.3).

Tables 3.2.103 and 3.2.192 document the production of the CP type *suya* 'batch of fish'. Although I did not expect this CP, it belongs to the core of the Kilivila CP system. As Table 3.2.192 records, the CP *suya* has almost superseded the synonymous CP *wela* 'batch of fish', which was expected as a response to the eliciting stimulus presented. The frame of reference of the CP *suya* is distinct.

Tables 3.2.105 and 3.2.194 document the production of the CP *tam* 'sprouting (yams)'. The production of this CP, which plays a secondary role in actual speech, was not expected. Its production instead of the expected CP types *gula* 'heap' and *uva* 'span' probably resulted from the consultants focusing on the nouns mentioned in the two eliciting noun phrases and not on the general concept expressed by the noun phrases. The production of the CP *tam* instead of the expected CP 0 can be explained as follows: the consultants chose to select a more specifying CP type as a more sophisticated response to the stimulus presented to elicit the CP type 0, and a number of them decided to use the CP *tam*. Keeping this interpretation in mind, it should be noted that the frame of reference of this CP is distinct (see also Tables 3.2.216 and 3.2.217).

Tables 3.2.106 and 3.2.195 and appendix A document that 30-year-old Bwetadou (consultant 45), the weather magician heir produced 1 token of the CP type *tetu* 'yams'. The production of this repeater as a response to the stimulus presented to elicit the CP 0 was not expected. Its frame of reference is distinct, of course. However, we must note that this CP type is extremely rare and almost obsolete.

Tables 3.2.107 and 3.2.196 document the production of the CP *to/te* 'male persons, human beings', one of the core types of the Kilivila CP system. The variant *to* is used in the word formation of adjectives and demonstratives, and the varient *te* is used in the word formation of numerals and the interrogative pronoun/adverb. The frame of reference of this CP is distinct (see also Tables 3.2.216 and 3.2.217). A few tokens of the CP *to/te* were also produced instead of the expected CPs *deli* 'group' and *yuma* 'hand'. The use of the CP *to/te* as a response to the stimulus presented to elicit the CP *yuma* is somewhat strange; however, as noted in connection with Table 3.2.196, if we assume that the consultants took the presented stimulus *yamala* 'her/his hand' as a *pars pro toto* to refer to human beings, this use of the CP *to/te* can be justified.

Tables 3.2.108 and 3.2.197 document the production of the CP *tuta* 'time'. This extremely rare repeater was not expected. Five of my consultants produced a few tokens of this CP instead of the expected CPs *siva* 'time' and *kala* 'day'. The frame of reference of this repeater is distinct, of course.

Tables 3.2.109 and 3.2.198 document the production of the CP *utu* 'scrap, parts cut off', which belongs to the core of the Kilivila CP system. Both tables record the broad scope of the frame of reference of this CP type, which has superseded the CP *si* 'bit' and may have started to supersede the CPs *vili* 'untwisted' and *kabulo1* 'point' (see also Tables 3.2.216 and 3.2.217). Table 3.2.198 also records a few tokens of this CP produced by the consultants instead of the expected CPs *kabisi* 'compartment of a foodhouse', *siva* 'time', *gum* 'bit', *kabulo2* 'sector', *meila* 'part of a song', *nina* 'part of a song', *nunu* 'corner of a garden' *bubwa* 'parts cut off', and *pila* 'part'. Moreover, a few tokens of the CP *utu* were also produced by a few consultants instead of the expected CPs *mmwa* 'conical bundle', *gili* 'row', *kavi* 'tool', *kubila* 'land plot', and *siwa* 'sea portions'. The use of the CP *utu* in these contexts, however, is either not acceptable or rather dubious (see sections 3.2.1.2, 3.2.1.3, and 3.2.1.4). In connection with Table 3.2.198, it should also be noted that the consultants produced some tokens of the CP types *ke* 'wood, inanimates' and *bwa* 'tree, wood', as well as a few tokens of the CPs *bubwa* 'parts cut off', *luva* 'wooden dishes, tied bundle', and the formative *\*boma* instead of the expected CP *utu*. As noted in Table 3.2.128, all my other consultants told me that there is no CP *\*boma* in Kilivila. The production of the CP *luva* as a response to the stimulus presented to elicit the CP *utu* is not acceptable (see section 3.2.1.5).

Tables 3.2.110 and 3.2.199 document the production of the CP *uva* 'span', which plays a secondary role in actual speech. The frame of reference of this CP is distinct (see also Tables 3.2.216 and 3.2.217). As already mentioned in connection with the CP *ke* 'long objects, inanimates', the number of tokens of *ke* that were produced instead of the expected CP *uva* was obviously a result of the consultants' selective perception of the eliciting noun phrase. This also holds for the production of a few tokens of the CP *tam* 'sprouting (yams)' instead of *uva*. Moreover, a few tokens of the CP *kwe* 'thing' were produced instead of the expected CP *uva*. The 1 token of the CP *na1* documents an unacceptable use of this CP as a response to the stimulus presented to elicit the CP *uva*. If we compare Table 3.2.110 and the data in appendix A, we find the following: 7 of the 14 consultants producing tokens of this CP are members of the highest-ranking Malasi clan (consultants 31, 38, 41, 49, 52, 59, and 60); 3 consultants belong to the chief's family (consultants 32, 48, and 53), and consultant 45 is the weather magician heir. Thus, 11 of the 14 consultants producing the CP type *uva* are of high status in Tauwema. We may infer from this observation that the CP *uva* functions as a sociolinguistic variable.

Tables 3.2.111, 3.2.113, 3.2.200, and 3.2.202 document the production of the CP *va/vaya/vayo* 'door'. The production of this CP, which is extremely rare, was not expected. Five female consultants produced 14 tokens of the variant *va* and 2 male consultants produced 3 tokens of the variants *vaya/vayo* instead of the expected CP *duya/kaduyo* 'door, entrance'. If we compare Tables 3.2.111 and 3.2.113 and appendix A, we find the following: 4 of the 5 female consultants producing this CP are members of the highest-ranking Malasi clan (consultants 4, 15, 16, and 41), 1 of the 2 male consultants who produced this CP is a member of this clan, too (consultant 34), and the other consultant (45) is the weather magician heir. Thus, 6 of the 7 consultants who produced the CP *va/vaya/vayo* are of high status. Although the database is rather small, we may tentatively assume that this CP functions as a sociolinguistic variable (especially for women of rank).

Tables 3.2.112 and 3.2.201 and appendix A document that the consultants Kapatu (consultant 27) and Bwetadou (consultant 45) produced 1 token each of the obviously extremely rare or almost obsolete CP *vakala* 'belt' instead of the expected CP *gili* 'row'. The production of this repeater was not expected.

Tables 3.2.114 and 3.2.203 document the production of the CP *vili* 'untwisted', which plays a secondary role in actual speech. Although a few tokens of the CP *vili* were produced instead of the expected CPs *si* 'bit', *pila* 'part', and *gili* 'row' (a rather idiosyncratic if not dubious use of the CP *vili*, indeed; see section 3.2.1.4), the frame of reference of this CP is distinct. In connection with Table 3.2.203, we also note that the consultants produced a number of tokens of the CPs *ke* 'inanimates' and *utu* 'scrap', as well as a few tokens of the CPs *kwe* 'thing', *bwa* 'tree, wood', and *bubwa* 'parts cut off', instead of the expected CP *vili*. The production of the CP *bubwa* as a response to the stimulus presented to elicit the CP *vili* is a somewhat dubious use of this CP, however (see section 3.2.1.4).

As mentioned at the end of section 3.2.2.2, the CP type *vilo* was not produced by my consultants during the elicitation test and did not appear in the recorded and transcribed texts (see Tables 3.2.216 and 3.2.217). This CP type is obviously superseded by the CP *kwe* 'thing'. Two tokens of the CP *kada* 'road' were produced instead of the expected CP *vilo*; however, the production of the CP *kada* as a response to the stimulus presented to elicit the CP *vilo* is not acceptable. Thus, although my consultants claimed during the informal pretests that the CP *vilo* is well known and used in their speech community, it seems that this CP type is actually extremely rare or almost obsolete.

Tables 3.2.115 and 3.2.204 document the production of the CP *vosi* 'song'. This repeater, the production of which was not expected, plays a secondary role in actual speech. It was produced by 9 consultants instead of the expected CP *meila* 'part of a song'. If we compare Table 3.2.115 and the data in appendix A, we find the following: 4 of the 6 female consultants who produced the repeater *vosi* are members of the highest-ranking Malasi clan (consultants 26, 51, 38, and 41); 1 of the 3 male consultants who produced this CP is the weather magician heir (consultant 45). Thus, 5 of the 9 consultants who produced this CP are of high status in Tauwema. Although the database is rather small, we may tentatively assume that this repeater functions as a sociolinguistic variable (especially for women of status).

Tables 3.2.116 and 3.2.205 document the production of the CP *wela* 'batch of fish', which plays a secondary role in actual speech. As shown in Table 3.2.205, the CP *wela* also takes over the referential function of the CP type *oyla* 'string, fish on strings' (see the previous discussion of this CP). However, this finding was expected at the beginning of my research on the CP system: my consultants supplied the noun *wela* 'batch of fish' as the 'prototypical' noun to elicit the CP *oyla*. Thus, a number of consultants produced some tokens of the CP *wela*, as a repeater in this case, as a response to the nominal stimulus presented. As mentioned in connection with Table 3.2.205, the CPs *suya* 'batch of fish' and *na2* 'animal' have started to supersede the CP *wela*. However, if we compare Table 3.2.116 and the data in appendix A, we find the following: 6 of the 14 consultants who produced this CP belong to the highest-ranking Malasi clan (consultants 25, 31, 38, 41, 55, and 60), 3 consultants belong to the chief's family (consultants 13, 48, and 50), and consultants 45 is the weather magician heir. Thus, 10 of 14 consultants who produced the CP *wela* are of high status in Tauwema. On the basis of this observation we may infer that the CP *wela* functions as a sociolinguistic variable.

Tables 3.2.117 and 3.2.206 document the production of the CP *ya* 'flexible, thin', which belongs to the core of the Kilivila CP system. Both tables show that the frame of reference of this CP is rather broad. Although the consultants produced 109 tokens of the CP *sisi* 'bough' and a few tokens of the CPs *ke* 'long objects, inanimates', *si* 'bit', and *pila* 'part' as a response to the stimulus presented to elicit the CP *ya*, the CP *ya* seems itself to have started to supersede the CP *gili* 'row' and *pila* 'part', especially in the speech of the consultants in age group II. The CP *ya* is also rather frequently produced instead of the expected CP *duya/kaduyo* 'door, entrance'. Moreover, we also find tokens of the CP *ya* produced instead of the expected CPs *bukwa* 'fruit cluster', *lilo* 'walk' (see comments on Table 3.2.206), *sipu* 'sheaf', *sisi* 'bough', *bubu* 'cut across', *gum* 'bit', and *ta* 'basket'. One token of the CP *ya* was also produced instead of the expected CP *yuma* 'hand'; however, this use of *ya* is somewhat dubious (see section 3.2.1.4). Thus, we should emphasize that the frame of reference of this CP is not only broad, but also rather indefinite (see also Tables 3.2.216 and 3.2.217).

Tables 3.2.118 and 3.2.207 document the production of the CP *yam* 'day'; this repeater plays a secondary role in actual speech. The CP *kwe* 'thing' has obviously superseded the CP *yam*, some tokens of which were also produced by the consultants when the synonymous CP type *kala* 'day' was expected. If we compare Table 3.2.118 and the data in appendix A, we find the following: 4 of the 7 consultants who produced this CP are members of the highest-ranking Malasi clan (consultants 24, 26, 31 and 38), consultant 21 is the chief's grandson, and consultant 45 is the weather magician heir. Thus, we record that 6 of the 7 consultants who produced the CP *yam* are of high status. Although the database is rather small, I tentatively assume that the CP *yam* functions as a sociolinguistic variable.

Tables 3.2.119 and 3.2.208 document the production of the CP *yam/yama/yuma* 'hand, measure, yard'. This CP is extremely rare or almost obsolete (see also Tables 3.2.216 and 3.2.217). It has almost been superseded by the CPs *kweya* 'limb' and *kwe* 'thing'. In connection with Table 3.2.208, we also note the production of a few tokens of the CPs *to/te* 'human beings', *ya* 'flexible', and *kova* 'fire' instead of the expected CP *yam/yama/yuma*; however, the production of these CPs as a response to the stimulus presented to elicit the CP *yam/yama/yuma* is a bit strange (see the discussion of the

CP *to/te* above), or dubious (see section 3.2.1.5), or not acceptable (see section 3.2.1.1). However, if we compare Table 3.2.119 and the data in appendix A, we find the following: 3 of the 6 consultants who produced the CP *yam/yama/yuma* are members of the highest-ranking Malasi clan (consultants 5, 51, and 55), the other 2 consultants are the chief's grandson (consultant 21) and the chief's wife (consultant 53). Moreover, Kalavatu (consultant IV3) also produced 1 token of this CP in the recorded and transcribed texts (see Tables 3.2.216 and 3.2.217 and appendix B). He is one of the *misinari*, that is, the local village priests. Although the database is very small, these data indicate that the CP *yam/yama/yuma* may function as a sociolinguistic variable (especially for women of status).

In his description of how to make lime that is eaten together with betel nuts, 41-year-old Tosulala (consultant V17; see appendix B) produced 1 token of the CP type *yeni* 'a handful of something' as part of a numeral (for body-centered measures, see de Léon 1988:82; Vater 1991:43). This CP type is obviously extremely rare, and I assume that it belongs to the technical language variety of Trobriand lime burners and lime sellers.

Tables 3.2.121 and 3.2.210 document the production of the CP *yulai/yule* 'bundle of four things'. This CP was only produced by 3 male consultants in the elicitation test. In the recorded and transcribed texts (see Table 3.2.216 and 3.2.217 and appendix B), we find 1 token of this CP, also produced by a man (consultant IV1/43). Obviously, this CP is either extremely rare or almost obsolete. Two of the 4 men who produced this CP are members of the highest-ranking Malasi clan (consultants 31 and 55), and consultant IV1/43 is the chief's son. However, the database is too small to speculate about whether this CP is a sociolinguistic variable, especially for men of rank and high status. As mentioned in connection with Table 3.2.210, the CP *kwe* 'thing' has obviously superseded the CP *yulai/yule*. For the sake of completeness I should mention that 2 tokens of the CP *ke* 'wood, inanimates' were also produced instead of the expected CP *yulai/yule*, the frame of reference of which, however, is distinct.

Tables 3.2.122 and 3.2.211 document the production of the CP *yuva* 'shoal'. Only 2 consultants, members of the highest-ranking Malasi clan (consultants 30 and 55; see appendix A), produced 4 tokens of this extremely rare and almost obsolete CP. The CP *buda/boda* 'group, team' seems to have taken over the referential function of the CP *yuva*. The fact that the CP *yuva* is almost obsolete is confirmed by the observation that the consultants gave me the "prototypical" noun *buda* to elicit the CPs *yuva* and *buda* (see also the previous discussion of the CP *buda/boda*). However, the CP *kwe* 'thing' also is starting to supersede the CP *yuva*. Moreover, a few tokens of the CPs *ke* 'inanimates' (general CP), *kasa* 'row', and *kudul* 'band of fibers' were produced instead of the expected CP *yuva*; however, the use of *kasa* in this context is rather dubious (see section 3.2.1.2), and the use of *kudul* in this context is not acceptable (see section 3.2.1.5).

Tables 3.2.123 and 3.2.212 document that only 2 consultants, both of high status in Tauwema (see appendix A), produced 1 token each of the CP type

0 'basketful of yams', the "zero classifier". In my recorded and transcribed texts, only 2 tokens of this CP type were produced. Although we record 34 tokens of the CP *tam* 'sprouting (yams)' and 1 token of the repeater *tetu* 'yams', the 117 tokens of the CP *kwe* 'thing' that were produced instead of the expected CP 0 indicate that *kwe* has almost superseded the CP 0, at least in everyday speech; the CP 0 is only realized during the *dadodiga*, the festive filling of the yam houses, when baskets of yams are counted. Thus, it has clearly defined context restrictions.

### 3.3.3.3 Why Are the CP Types Affected by Processes of Language Change, and Who Opposes and Who Fosters Language Change?

So far, I have described how the consultants use the various CP types. This description included observations about processes of language change in progress that affect individual CP types. I also inferred from my data the direction of the language change with respect to the CP types.

The discussion of the individual CP types illustrated the important role that the frame of reference plays in the production of individual CP types. If we examine these frames of reference now in a summarizing survey, we find the following:

1. If the frame of reference of a certain type loses its distinctness and becomes "fuzzy", and if the meaning of this CP type is not broadened at the same time, then this CP type will be affected by further processes of linguistic change, which may result in this CP type being superseded by another CP type. This observation holds for the CP types *bubu/bobu*, *bubwa*, *luva*, *si*, and also, to a certain degree at least, for the CP types *bwa* and *gum* (see section 3.3.3.2).

2. If the frame of reference of a certain CP type loses its distinctness and even becomes fuzzy, and if the meaning of this CP type is broadened at the same time, then this CP type will affect and may finally even supersede a number of other CP types and their frames of reference. This observation holds for the CP types *ke* and *kwe*, of course, but also for the CP types *pila*, *utu*, *ya*, and, to a certain extent, for the CP type *sisi* and maybe even for the CP types *kada*, *buda/boda/budu*, *kweya/kwaya/keya*, *luba*, and *suya* (see section 3.3.3.2).

3. CP types with a rather special, specific, and even distinct, frame of reference may be in danger of being superseded by CP types with broader and more general frames of reference. This observation holds for the CPs *bubu/bobu*, *bubwa*, *gula*, *kabisi*, *kabulo/kabulu*, *kila*, *kudu1*, *lila*, *lilo/lola*, *luva*, *mmwa*, *nunu*, *oyla*, *po'ula*, *sa*, *vilo*, *yam/yama/yuma*, *yulai/yule*, *yuva*, 0 and also to a certain extent for the CPs *bwa*,[6] *kubila/kwabila*, *kwoila/kwela*, *liku*, *nutu/notu*, and *sipu* (see section 3.3.3.2).

[6] The CP *ke* 'wood' (=*ke1*) is more common than the CP *bwa* 'tree, wood', but *bwa* itself is more general than other CP types in this semantic domain.

In addition to the frame of reference, another characteristic of CP types seems to play an important role with respect to processes of language change. A closer look at the CPs *bogi, bwalita, yegila, kudu2, tuta, vakala, wela, yam, duya,* and *megwa* (see section 3.3.3.2) shows that CP types that are repeaters seem to be superseded by CP types that are not repeaters. However, this observation does not hold for the CP *luba* (which superseded the CP *kapwa*) and the CP variant *pwanina* (which is still preferred to the variant *pona* of the CP type *pwanina/pona*).

A third observation that is relevant in attempting to answer the question of who opposes language change is the following: A number of CP types that are affected by the process of language change are not and will probably never be superseded by other CP types (or at least not easily), because they are produced by a certain group of speakers who use these CP types to mark their societal status. These CP types function as sociolinguistic variables.

In section 3.3.3.2, we recorded the following CPs that serve this function: *bogi, bubwa, bwa, bwalita, duya/kaduya/kaduyo, gili, kabulo/kabulu2, kudu2, kwoya/koya, liku, nunu, uva, wela,* and *yam* and probably *beku, kapwa/kapo, lilo/lola, negwa, peta, sa,* and *si* as well. The CP types *kila, va/vaya/vayo,* and *vosi* and probably also *yam/yama/yuma* are sociolinguistic variables that are especially produced by women of high status. The CP type *mmwa* and probably also the CP type *yulai/yule* function as sociolinguistic variables that are especially produced by men of high status. Thus, Trobriand Islanders of high status prevent the processes of linguistic change that would lead to a dramatic decrease of CP types in the Kilivila CP inventory.

Some individuals that belong to this group of Trobriand Islanders of high status are also the only consultants who produced a few tokens of CP types that are either extremely rare or almost obsolete; thus, they are keeping these CP types "alive" in the speech community's lexicon. For example, consultants 26, 30, 31, 52, 55, and 59 produced tokens of the almost obsolete CPs *beku, yuva, 0, guba, kala, meila, nigwa, nina, siva, yule,* and *kavi.* All these consultants are members of the highest-ranking Malasi clan (see appendix A). Towesei (consultant 10), whose father is also a Malasi and who is very conservative with respect to Trobriand cultural heritage, is the only consultant who produced tokens of the CPs *bukwa* and *dumia.* Bwetadou (consultant 45), the weather magician heir, produced tokens of the CPs *doba, tetu, vakala,* and *beku.* Sibwesa (consultant 53), the chief's wife, produced one token of the CP 0. Here, I should emphasize that the previous discussion of the individual CP types revealed that members of the chief's family use a rather broad variety of CP types, especially CPs that function as sociolinguistic variables. We may infer from this that Kilagola, the chief of Tauwema, is very much aware of this function of CPs and supports and promotes the use of these CP types within his family (although he is not related to his children and grandchildren in the Trobriand matrilineal society). It should also be mentioned that experts such as the storyteller Mokopei (consultant V14), the wicker workers Kalavatu (consultant V3) and Tokunupei (consultant V15), and the lime burner and lime seller Tosulala (consultant V17) will pass on the CP types *kali, kauya, lipu,* and *yeni* as part of their technical language variety, together with their expert knowledge, to their respective heirs or successors.

Finally, it is clear that consultants whose production of CP types during the elicitation test surpassed the average number of different CP types produced by consultants in the same age group also prevent a too dramatic decrease of CP types in the Kilivila CP inventory. If we compare appendix A and Table 3.2.124, we find the following:

1. Payaya (consultant 4), a member of the Malasi clan, and Towesei (consultant 10), who was mentioned previously, produced the highest number of different CP types within their age group (18 and 29 types, respectively).

2. Within age group II, consultants 15 and 17 produced 33 and 32 different CP types, respectively; both girls are members of the highest-ranking Malasi clan. Consultants 19 and 21 produced 34 and 35 different CP types, respectively; both boys are the chief's grandsons.

3. As for age group III, Kapatu (consultant 27) produced 48 different CP types; Gayoboda (consultant 31), a Malasi, produced 47 different CP types; and Kwelava (consultant 35) produced 46 different CP types. Although Kapatu and Kwelava are members of the third-ranking Lukwasisiga clan, a closer look at my ethnographic data reveals that Kapatu's father, Sakau, and Kwelava's father, Yoya, are members of the highest-ranking Malasi clan. It may well be that Sakau and Yoya also promote and support the elaborate use of the CP type inventory in their children's speech.

4. Within age group IV, consultant 41, who produced 47 different CP types, is a member of the highest-ranking Malasi clan, and consultant 45, who produced 56 different CP types, is the weather magician heir of Tauwema.

5. The two female consultants of age group V, Vadomna (consultant 49) and Kadawaya (consultant 51), produced 41 different CP types each. Weyei (consultant 55) produced 44 different CP types. These three consultants are members of the highest-ranking Malasi clan.

*Thus, the members of the highest-ranking clan, as well as other consultants of societal status and experts like storytellers, wicker workers, and lime burners, oppose the processes of language change that would result in a decrease of the CP type inventory in Kilivila.*

Who fosters these processes of language change, then? To answer this question we must check four different sources of information:

1. Table 3.2.124 includes consultants whose production of CP types is clearly below average.

2. Tables 3.2.214 and 3.2.215 and the corresponding discussion in section 3.2.1 describe the number of dubious or unacceptable cases of CP production and the consultants who produced them.

3. Tables 3.2.5, 3.2.12, 3.2.19, 3.2.26, and 3.2.33 document the cases of multiple classification, that is, those cases where the consultants produced two or three different CP types as a response to the stimulus that was presented to elicit a particular CP type with an adjective, a numeral, and a demonstrative pronoun.

4. The discussion of the individual CP types given in section 3.3.3.2 includes some useful information about the relationship between the age of the consultants and processes of language change.

In addition, we can use information about individual consultants and the general structure of the Trobriand society, if necessary.

If we now check Table 3.2.124 and appendix A with respect to the question raised, we find surprisingly that in addition to the consultants of age group I, who produced fewer CP types than average because of their age, consultants 23 (age group II), 25 and 29 (age group III), 44 and 47 (age group IV), 52, 56, 57, and 59 (age group V), who all produced fewer CP types than the average in their respective age group, are all members of the highest-ranking Malasi clan. Consultant 32 (age group III), whose production of different CP types is also below average, is the chief's grandson. Thus, only consultants 14 (age group II; see also section 3.2.1.2), 36 (age group III), and 37 (age group IV), whose production of different CP types is also below average, have low status in Tauwema.

This observation seems to contradict our previous conclusion about who opposes the processes of language change. However, this finding shows that processes of language change are so strong that they also affect individuals belonging to groups that in general oppose language change. It should be mentioned here that consultants 52 and 59, who produced less CP types than average, are nevertheless among those consultants who produced tokens of almost obsolete CP types, thus keeping these CP types alive in the speech community.

If we compare Table 3.2.214 with the discussion in section 3.2.1 about dubious and unacceptable CP use by individual consultants, and if we check these consultants in appendix A, a similarly puzzling picture emerges:

1. All consultants in age group I, who produced 1 dubious and 8 unacceptable cases of CP production, are members of the highest-ranking Malasi clan.

2. Of the consultants in age group II who produced the 10 dubious and 22 unacceptable cases of CP production, Olopola (consultant 14) is the only one of low status. Consultants 15, 17, 20, and 23 are members of the Malasi clan, and consultants 13 and 22 are the chief's grandchildren.

3. Of the consultants in age group II who produced the 5 dubious and 14 unacceptable cases of CP production, Kapatu (consultant 27) is the only one of low status; however, as mentioned previously, Kapatu's father is a Malasi. Consultants 25, 30, and 31 are also members of this highest-ranking clan, and consultant 32 is the chief's grandson.

4. Of the consultants in age group IV who produced the 14 dubious and 3 unacceptable cases of CP production, 2 (consultants 41 and 44) are members of the Malasi clan, and 2 (consultants 43 and 48) are the chief's sons. Dakevau (consultant 40) and Igogosa (consultant 42) are the only consultants of low status.

5. Of the consultants in age group V who produced the 4 dubious and 7 unacceptable cases of CP production, 2 are members of the Malasi clan (consultants 49 and 59), and 1 (consultant 50) is the chief's daughter. Kasilasila (consultant 58) is the only consultant who does not belong to a group of status.

Again, these findings confirm that the processes of language change are so strong that they also affect individuals belonging to groups that in general oppose such processes of language change.

Table 3.2.215 lists the cases of dubious and unacceptable CP type production for all five age groups and differentiates them according to the gender of the speaker. The following picture emerges:

1. The female consultants in age groups I and III produced more dubious and unacceptable cases of CP production than the male consultants within these groups.

2. The female and male consultants in age group II show no differences with respect to the number of cases of dubious and unacceptable CP production.

3. The female consultants in age group IV produced only 3 more cases of dubious and unacceptable CP use than their male peers.

4. The male consultants of age group V produced only 3 more cases of dubious and unacceptable CP use than their female peers.

All in all, Table 3.2.215 records that female consultants produced more cases of dubious and unacceptable CP use than male consultants; however, it should also be noted that the consultants of age group II produced most cases of dubious and unacceptable CP use.

I interpret these findings as follows:

1. The consultants who belong to groups that oppose linguistic change must be aware of these linguistic processes to some degree. They must also be aware that these processes of language change affect their own speech. Thus, the clash between their "linguistic awareness' (see Sinclair

et al. 1978; Böhme 1983:47–70), which opposes these changes, on the one hand, and their own involvement in these processes of language change, on the other hand, may result in "linguistic insecurity" that gives rise to the dubious and even unacceptable cases of CP production recorded in just these consultants' speech.

2. That the girls in age group I are more affected by linguistic insecurity than the boys is easy to understand if we remember that girls in general seem to have more difficulties in acquiring the CP system than boys.

3. That boys and girls of age group II are most seriously affected by linguistic insecurity is also evident: This age group covers the developmental phase that is critical for CP acquisition. In section 3.3.2.1 we noted a kind of explosion in the children's production of CP types, which stops with the consultants in age group III. Thus, this critical phase of the acquisition process documents a strong motivation in these children to use the CP system in an adequate way. This motivation implies a rather high degree of linguistic awareness not only in boys, but also in girls, especially if they are of high status. With the consultants in this age group, we must keep in mind, too, that the 32 cases of dubious and unacceptable CP production are due not only to the clash between their linguistic awareness and the processes of language change in which they themselves are involved, but also to these consultants' readiness and maybe even disposition for a playful exploration of the possibilities such a complex system as the Kilivila CP paradigm offers them.

4. That the male adolescents of age group III clearly show fewer cases of dubious and unacceptable CP production than their female contemporaries, whose behavior is similar to that of the consultants in age group II, is probably due to societal constraints on male adolescents: They must bring their language behavior into line with their claims for societal status. The female adolescents must also obey these societal constraints, convincingly described and analyzed by Weiner (1988), but only after having become adults, that is, generally when they have married, have become mothers, and are thus completely integrated members of the Trobiand adult society (see also Weiner 1976).

With respect to the question of who fosters language change, however, we have not yet gathered enough information to offer a convincing answer. Therefore, we will now consider Tables 3.2.5, 3.2.12, 3.2.19, 3.2.26, and 3.2.33 which document the cases of multiple classification. These tables present the number of cases where the stimuli presented to elicit a certain CP type actually elicited two or three different CP types (with the three word classes adjective, numeral, and demonstrative pronoun). I will focus my attention here on the percentages given in the tables; these percentages express the relationship between the number of cases of multiple classification with different elicited CP types and the total number of different CP types

**Table 3.3.7.** The averages of the multiple classification percentages

| Consultants, female/male | Average m.c. of female consultants, % | Average m.c. of male consultants, % | Average m.c. of all consultants, % |
|---|---|---|---|
| Age group I 3/3 | 14 | 8 | 12 |
| Age group II 6/6 | 32 | 28 | 30 |
| Age group III 6/6 | 21 | 12 | 17 |
| Age group IV 6/6 | 25 | 18 | 21 |
| Age group V 5/6 | 12 | 16 | 14 |

m.c. = multiple classification.

produced by all the consultants. Table 3.3.7 summarizes the averages of these multiple classification percentages for the 12 consultants of all five age groups as well as for the female consultants versus the male consultants; it also notes the number of female and male consultants producing each case of multiple classification.

Before interpreting this table, I should exlplain why I consider these cases of multiple classification to be relevant to the question raised here. I assume that multiple classification is an indication of at least the following two production strategies that a speaker may pursue: (1) speakers may use multiple classification to display their competence in exploiting the possibilities that the complex CP system offers skillful rhetoricians; (2) speakers may use multiple classification because they are insecure about producing the appropriate CP in a given context. Thus, multiple classification may indicate either skillful language use or linguistic insecurity.

Table 3.3.7 shows that with only one exception all consultants in age groups II–V produced cases of multiple classification. The mean or average values presented in the table include, of course, the individual opponents to the observed language changes. We noted previously, however, that the processes of language change are so strong that they affect consultants who belong to groups that oppose these processes of change. Thus, I think it is justifiable to interpret the cases of multiple classification primarily as indications of linguistic insecurity.

With this in mind, I will now consider Table 3.3.7 in more detail. The mean values of the consultants in age group II clearly surpass the values for the consultants of the other age groups. The means for the girls of age group II (32%) are slightly higher than for the boys of this age group (28%). The second highest mean values were in age group IV. The consultants in age groups I and V showed only slightly different values if we compare the means for all 12 consultants (12% versus 14%). The consultants in age groups III and V also showed only slightly different values if we compare the means for all 12 consultants (17% versus 14%). If we compare the means for the male and the female consultants, we notice that with the exception of the women of age group V, the values of all other female consultants surpass the values of their male peers.

The values for the consultants in age group II and age group IV are of special interest and relevance. Keeping in mind that boys and girls of high status in age group II are most seriously affected by the form of linguistic insecurity that results in the clash between linguistic awareness to oppose changes and involvement in the process of this language change, and keeping in mind the discussion of the CP types *bubu/bobu*, *bwa*, *deli*, *kavi*, *ke*, *kwe*, and *ya*[7] in section 3.3.3.2, which emphasized the role the consultants in age groups II and IV play in the process of language change, especially involving CPs, we can interpret the data presented in Table 3.3.7 in as follows. The data suggest that the language behavior of children in age group II (8–14 years) is not only most seriously affected by the processes of language change within the Kilivila CP system, but also these children could be the agents of change, perhaps because of their previously mentioned readiness and their disposition for playful exploration of the possibilities that the complex CP system offers them. That the children in this age group show much linguistic flexibility and attention, which makes them agents of processes of language change affecting other paradigms in Kilivila, has been documented in connection with Kilivila color terms (G. Senft 1987b). In my research on these color terms, I emphasized that most of my consultants between 8 and 14 years of age were schoolchildren starting to acquire English as a second language (G. Senft 1987b:338). Six of the schoolchildren who were consultants in my study on color terms also took part in the study on the Kilivila CP system (G. Senft 1987b:321 and appendix A in the present volume). In the sample used in my study of CPs, 8 of the 12 children in age group II attended school regularly; only consultant 16 did not go to school at all. Thus, I propose here, too, that confrontation with a foreign language at school may increase linguistic awareness as well as playful linguistic exploration in these children and perhaps cause them to become agents of processes of language change.

The schoolchildren in age group II are joined in their role as agents of the language change by the consultants of age group IV, especially by the women of this age group. I can explain this finding only by relying on my knowledge of the structure of Trobriand society. The consultants in age group IV have acquired the status of adulthood. However, this does not imply that they have also reached the social status that they may strive for within their village community, on the basis of their own personal qualities and possibilities. One way to acquire status in Trobriand society is through linguistic competence, versatility, and elegance (see G. Senft 1985e; 1987d; Weiner 1976; 1983; 1988). To become a skillful and respected speaker.

[7]Compare also the tables documenting the production of the CPs *na2*, *sisi*, *to/te*, and *utu*.

Trobrianders of this age are forced to explore the sophisticated and subtle possibilities of their mother tongue. This does not contradict the result presented in section 3.3.2.1, where I stated that the process of acquisition of the CP system can be considered terminated during or after puberty. It is only after the acquisition of this complex system of CPs that speakers can start to use its full semantic power. This kind of revelation and exploration requires readiness and willingness to experiment (see also, e.g., B. Senft and G. Senft 1986:200–221). If speakers realize that a certain level of linguistic competence is reserved to a limited number of persons of high status only, then they may attempt to reach this level of competence if they are of high status themselves, or they may try to reduce these status-making linguistic qualities so that they match their own, more modest, linguistic possibilities. The two groups, being peers, surely influence each other with respect to speech behavior. On the basis of these considerations, it is plausible that consultants in this age group foster (and perhaps are forced to foster) the processes of language change observed within the Kilivila CP system. It is remarkable that this situation is much more evident in the data for female consultants than for male consultants in age group IV (see Table 3.3.7). I can only offer the interpretation that in a matrilineal society women may be more aware that linguistic competence is one expression of the social stratification based on kinship and clan membership. This may also be the key for explaining why we do not note any serious differences in the production of different CP types between men and women in age group IV (see Table 3.2.124 and section 3.3.2.3). On average, women in age group IV, having realized the social importance of the CP system, produce as many different CP types as their male contemporaries; however, as Table 3.3.7 shows, their production of these CP types reveals a higher degree of linguistic insecurity.

I can now summarize the findings and interpretations presented in this section with respect to the question of who fosters language change in the CP system:

1. *The consultants in age group II foster, and probably also initiate, the processes of language change because of their readiness for a playful exploration of the possibilities the CP system offers and because of their increased linguistic awareness, which may result from their strong motivation to use this system adequately and their confrontation with English as a second language at school.*

2. *Language change is also fostered and supported by consultants in age group IV, probably because some consultants with low status want to overcome language barriers that mark intrasocietal status, whereas other speakers with high status want to maintain these language barriers. It seems that female consultants in this age group foster language change even more than their male peers, probably because they are more aware of the social stratification of linguistic competence based on kinship and clan membership in their matrilinear society.*

### 3.3.3.4 What Are the Possible Consequences of Language Change for the Grammar of Kilivila?

As stated at the beginning of the previous section, the frames of reference of the CPs and the characteristics of certain CPs being repeaters or functioning as sociolinguistic variables are crucial qualities for the dynamics of processes of language change that affect the Kilivila CP system. In this section, I will speculate about the direction these processes of language change may take and about the possible consequences of these changes for the grammar of Kilivila.

The processes of language change that have been described may result in a rather reduced inventory of core CP types or variants. Although some CP types that function as sociolinguistic variables may be maintained in the lexicon of certain speakers of high status, the use of these CP types may be constrained and constricted to ever more specific contexts. This may, in turn, result in a decrease in the semantic content and power of the CPs. Such a loss must be compensated for in one way or another. As described in chapter 2, the CPs fulfill among other things an important function in constituting Kilivila noun phrases (NPs). Thus, the direction of the changes could lead to a loss of semantic content and information that was previously carried by the CPs in relatively simple NP constructions. The compensation for such a loss may then lead to a more complex expansion of Kilivila NP construction. Thus, more complex attributes or even attributive clauses may take over the functions formerly fulfilled by the complex and highly differentiated CP system. That such a development would also affect the means of securing discourse cohesion, modes of reference, concord, and probably even word formation can be inferred from the description of the functions the CPs fulfill (see chapter 2). In the extreme case, processes of language change affecting the CP system might eventually lead to a complete restructuring of Kilivila grammar.

### 3.3.4 What Semantic Domains Are Constituted by the Kilivila CP Systems?

Now that I have discussed the inventory, the acquisition, and the production of the documented Kilivila CP (sub)system and the processes of language change affecting it, I can proceed to try determine the semantic domains constituted by this system.[8]

In the first part of this section, I will discuss the semantic domains constituted by the Kilivila CP system described to this point. The second part of this section is an attempt to answer questions about the possible

---

[8] I am aware that the CPs discussed so far represent only a subset of all Kilivila classifiers. I mentioned in section 3.3.1 that Lawton (1980) lists 85 additional CPs, which he collected during his research on Kilivila. However, I do not have references to these CPs in my recorded and transcribed speech data. Thus, I agree with Wittgenstein's maxim: "*Wovon man nicht sprechen kann, darüber muß man schweigen*" (Wittgenstein 1971:115).

dynamics of these semantic domains; I will try to determine the rules speakers may adhere to in their production of certain CPs. In the final part of this section, I return to the acquisition problems speakers have with the CP system and propose an answer to the question of why the CPs are acquired in the order described in section 3.3.2.4.

### 3.3.4.1 What Semantic Domains Are Constituted by the Described Subset of the Kilivila CP System?

If we examine the English glosses for the CPs given in Table 3.3.1 in section 3.3.1, we can group the 88 CP types into 20 semantic domains that cover the following concepts:

1. **a.** Persons
   **b.** Body parts
2. Animals
3. Quantities
   **a.** Living beings in general
   **b.** Things in general
4. General CPs (unmarked forms for inanimates)
5. Measures
6. Time
7. Place
8. Qualities
9. Shape
10. Trees, wood, wooden things
11. Utensils
12. Yams
13. Part of a foodhouse, a canoe, a creel
14. Door, entrance, window
15. Fire, oven
16. Road, journey
17. Texts
18. Ritual items
19. Dress, adornment
20. Names

The order in which these domains are given here is completely arbitrary. Before I discuss these 20 semantic domains in detail, I want to emphasize that these groupings are primarily based on common sense considerations that, among other things, take into account ethnographic information and knowledge of and about the speech community. One may call such a procedure arbitrary; however, to my mind it is an acceptable and pragmatic (and perhaps the only) starting point and may even be a means for developing a model of the cognitive system that is used to order human perception and is thus the basis for all communication about perceived phenomena.

The groupings are based on the fact that all the CPs that constitute a certain semantic domain share certain important features; however, some CPs have inherent features that allow them to be assigned to more than one semantic domain. Such multiple assignment raises questions about the dynamics within such a classificatory system of classifiers. However, before I can discuss such questions, I will present the individual domains and the CPs that constitute them in detail, assuming (or, better, pretending) at this stage of the study that semantic domains can be described as static and more or less closed systems:

*Domain 1: Persons and body parts*
The first semantic domain covers the concepts 'person' and 'body part'. I differentiate between these concepts and subdivide the domain into Domain 1a and Domain 1b.

*Domain 1a: Persons*
The following CP types constitute this subdomain:

| | |
|---|---|
| *to/te* | persons of male gender, human beings' (see Table 3.3.1) |
| *na* | 'persons of female gender' (=*na1*) (for the meaning 'animals', see Domain 2; for the meaning 'carvings in human likeness', see Domain 10; for the meaning 'stars, moon, planets', see Domain 7; for the meanings 'corpses' and 'spirits, dwarfs', see Table 3.3.1) |
| *gudi* | 'child' (see Table 3.3.1) |

*Domain 1b: Body parts*
The following CP types constitute this subdomain:

| | |
|---|---|
| *kweya/kwaya/keya* | 'limb, severed limb' (see Table 3.3.1) |
| *yam/yuma/yama* | 'hand' (for the meaning 'length', see Domain 5) |
| *ka'i* | 'tooth' |
| *kudu* | 'tooth' (=*kudu2*) (for the connotation 'band of fibers', see Domain 19). |

*Domain 2: Animals*
The following CP types constitute this domain:

| | |
|---|---|
| *na* | 'animals' (but not shells and clams) (=*na2*); see also Domain 1 |
| *kwe* | 'shells and clams' (=*kwe2*); see also Domain 4 and Table 3.3.1 |

*Domain 3: Quantities*
Here I differentiate between quantities that generally refer to animate referents (Domain 3a) and quantities that generally refer to inanimate referents (Domain 3b).

*Domain 3a: Quantities* (*living beings in general*)
The following CP types constitute this subdomain:

| | |
|---|---|
| *buda/boda/budu* | 'group, team, crowd' |
| *deli* | 'company, group on the move' |
| *yuva* | 'shoal' |
| *wela* | 'batch of fish, string of fish' |
| *suya* | 'batch of fish on strings' |
| *oyla* | 'fish on strings' (the meaning of this CP has changed from 'string' [see Domain 11] to 'fish on strings'). |

*Domain 3b: Quantities* (*things in general*)
The following CP types constitute this subdomain:

| | |
|---|---|
| *gula* | 'heap, group' |
| *po'ula* | 'plantation, grove' (see Table 3.3.1) |
| *bukwa* | 'fruit cluster' (see Table 3.3.1) |
| *duli* | 'cluster, bundle' |
| *guba* | 'bundles of taro' |
| *kapwa/kapo* | 'bundle (wrapped up), parcel' (see Table 3.3.1) |
| *luba* | 'bundle (of rolls), parcels (of taro pudding)' |
| *si* | 'small bit' |
| *gum* | 'bit, small piece' |
| *pila* | 'part, piece' |
| *utu* | 'scrap, parts (cut off), small particles, fragments' |
| *kila* | 'clusters of bananas, hands of bananas' |
| *luva* | 'wooden dishes (full of one's share of food during a food distribution ceremony), tied bundle' |
| *mmwa* | 'conical bundle' |
| *sa* | 'nut bunch' |
| *sipu* | 'sheaf' (see Table 3.3.1) |
| *yulai/yule* | 'bundle of four things' |
| *yeni* | 'a handful of something' (see Table 3.3.1) |

*Domain 4: General CPs*
The fourth semantic domain covers the "unmarked" forms of inanimates in general. The following CP types constitute this domain:

| | |
|---|---|
| *kwe* | 'thing, anything indefinite or unknown' (unmarked form for inanimates in general) (=*kwe1*) (see Domain 2) |
| *ke* | unmarked form for inanimates in general (=*ke3*); this meaning of *ke* was not elicited in the test; however, as discussed in section 3.3.3.2, the results of the CP elicitation test show that *ke* has the status of a general CP, too; for the meaning 'rigid long objects' (=*ke2*), see Domain 9; for the meaning 'fire' (=*ke4*), see Domain 15; for the meaning 'tree, wooden things' (=*ke1*), see Domain 10) |

*Domain 5: Measures*
The following CP types constitute this domain:

| | |
|---|---|
| *uva* | 'span, measure' (the span of two extended arms from tip to tip; see Table 3.3.1) |
| *yuma* | 'length, measure' (the span of two extended arms from the fingertips of one hand to the wrist of the other hand; see Table 3.3.1) |

*Domain 6: Time*
The following CP types constitute this domain:

| | |
|---|---|
| *bogi* | 'night' |
| *kala* | 'day' |
| *siva* | 'time' (see Table 3.3.1) |
| *tuta* | 'time, occasion' |
| *yam* | 'day' (see Table 3.3.1) |

*Domain 7: Place*
The following CP types constitute this domain:

| | |
|---|---|
| *kabulo/kabulu* | 'village sectors, areas of authority' (= *kabulo2/kabulu*; see Table 3.3.1; see also Domain 14) |
| *vilo* | 'place, area, village' |
| *bwalita* | 'sea' |
| *siwa* | 'sea portions, ownership divisions with reference to fishing rights' |
| *kubila/kwabila* | 'large land plot' |
| *nunu* | 'corner(s) of a garden' |
| *koya/kwoya* | 'mountain, hill' |
| *dumia* | 'swamp' (see Table 3.3.1) |
| *na* | 'stars, planets, moon' (= *na3*; see also Domains 1a, 2, and 10 and Table 3.3.1) |

*Domain 8: Qualities*
The following CP types constitute this domain:

| | |
|---|---|
| *bubu/bobu/bobo* | 'cut across, cut transversely, (block) cut off' |
| *bubwa* | 'cut across, (parts) cut off' |
| *giwi* | 'cut' |
| *pwanina/pona/ponina* | 'punctured, something with a hole in it, hole' |
| *nigwa* | 'hole' (see Table 3.3.1) |
| *ya* | 'flexible things, thin things' |
| *vili* | 'untwisted' |

*Domain 9: Shape*
The following CP types constitute this domain:

| | |
|---|---|
| *ke* | 'rigid, long objects' (= *ke2*; see also Domains 4, 10, and 15) |
| *kabulo* | 'protuberances' (= *kabulo1*; see also Domain 7) |

*kasa*　　　　'row, line'
*gili*　　　　'row'
*nutu/notu*　　'kneaded things, dot, drop'

*Domain 10: Trees, wood, wooden things*
The following CP types constitute this domain:

*ke*　　'wooden thing' (=*ke1* ; see also Domains 4, 9, and 15)
*bwa*　　'tree, wooden thing'
*sisi*　　'bough, cut off part of a tree' (see Table 3.3.1)
*lila*　　'bough, branch' (see Table 3.3.1)
*na*　　'carvings in human likeness' (=*na4*; see also Domains 1a, 2, and 7; Table 3.3.1)

*Domain 11: Utensils*
The following CP types constitute this domain:

*kavi*　　　　　　　'tool'
*oyla*　　　　　　　'string' (see also Domain 3a)
*peta/ta*　　　　　'basket' (see Table 3.3.1)
*kauya*　　　　　　'fish trap, creel' (see Table 3.3.1)
*kwoila/kwela/kwai*　'clay pot' (see Table 3.3.1)

*Domain 12: Yams*
The following CP types constitute this domain:

*tam*　　'sprouting, sprouting yams'
0　　　'a basketful of yams'
*tetu*　　'yams'

*Domain 13: Part of a foodhouse/a canoe/a creel*
The following CP types constitute this domain:

*lipu*　　'compartment of a creel, tier' (see Table 3.3.1)
*kabisi*　　'compartment of a foodhouse, section/division in a foodhouse'
*liku*　　'compartment of a foodhouse, compartment of a canoe' (see Table 3.3.1)

*Domain 14: Door, entrance, window*
The following CP types constitute this domain:

*duya/kaduyo*　　'door, entrance'
*va/vaya/vayo*　　'door, window' (see Table 3.3.1)

*Domain 15: Fire, oven*
The following CP types constitute this domain:

*kova*　　'fire, fireplace'
*ke*　　'fire' (=*ke4*; see also Domains 4, 9, and 10)
*kumla*　　'earth oven'

*Domain 16: Road, journey*
The following CP types constitute this domain:

| | |
|---|---|
| *kada/keda* | 'road, track' (see Table 3.1.1) |
| *bililo* | 'trip' (see Table 3.3.1) |
| *lilo* | 'walk, journey' (see Table 3.3.1) |
| *kali* | 'paddle strike' (see Table 3.3.1) |

*Domain 17: Texts*
The following CP types constitute this domain:

| | |
|---|---|
| *megwa* | 'magic, magical formula' |
| *nina* | 'part(s) of a song' (see Table 3.3.1) |
| *meila* | 'part(s) of a song, part(s) of a magical formula' (see Table 3.3.1) |
| *vosi* | 'song, part(s) of a song' |

*Domain 18: Ritual items*
The following CP types constitute this domain:

| | |
|---|---|
| *beku* | 'stone blade' (see Malinowski 1922:358; Weiner 1976:179–183) |
| *kai* | 'stone blade' |
| *sam* | 'ginger' (in play accompanying verses); (see G. Senft 1985c:70; B. Senft, G. Senft 1986:142; this CP type was not elicited in the elicitation test; see Table 3.3.1) |

*Domain 19: Dress, adornment*
The following CP types constitute this domain:

| | |
|---|---|
| *doba* | 'skirt made of banana leaves, "grass" skirt' |
| *kudu* | 'band of fibers' (especially the band of fibers at the waistband of a grass skirt (= *kudu1*; see also Domain 1b, see Table 3.3.1) |
| *vakala* | 'belt, belt of spondylus shell discs' |

*Domain 20: Names*
The following CP type constitutes this domain:

| | |
|---|---|
| *iga/yegila* | 'name' |

### 3.3.4.2 What Are the Dynamics of the Semantic Domains Constituted by the CPs and What Rules Do Speakers Use in Their Production of a Certain CP?

The semantic domains presented in the preceding section are based on the assumption, or rather the pretense, that such domains can be described as static or closed systems. However, some of the cross references given for certain CPs, as well as the actual production of the individual CP types described in section 3.3.3.2, make it obvious that this is an idealization. Such an idealization is necessary to establish the basis for discussing the problem of the dynamics of semantic domains, of course, but it has nothing to do with the actual use of CP types in speech.

To tackle the task of describing the semantic domains and the dynamics of their constitution by the CP types in actual speech production more adequately, I propose the following proceeding:

First, I use the data presented in Tables 3.2.37–3.2.123 and Tables 3.2.126–3.2.218 and the discussion of the production of the individual CPs in actual speech presented in section 3.3.3.2. On the basis of these data and analyses, I assign to the CP types that constitute the semantic domains described in section 3.3.4.1 the tokens that occurred in elicited and observed speech production. I then note any possible "intradomain substitution" of an expected CP type by tokens of one or more unexpected CP type(s). The CP types involved constitute one and the same semantic domain; hence, I call these observed, but unexpected uses of CP types "intradomain substitution."

The notation

$$\begin{array}{c} | \\ | \\ |\cdot| \end{array}$$

indicates

| tokens of CP | $X$ |
| are produced | $|$ |
| instead of the | $|$ |
| expected | $|\cdot|$ |
| tokens of CP | $Y$ within one domain. |

Next, I note how many tokens of CP types assigned in section 3.3.4.1 to other semantic domains are produced by the consultants instead of tokens of the expected CP type(s) constituting the respective domain examined. Because these CP types and their tokens come from other semantic domains into the respective domain examined, I call these observed, acceptable, but unexpected uses *in-domain substitution*. In-domain substitution is indicated by the notation + + +.

Moreover, I also note how many tokens of CP types that constitute the domain examined are used instead of tokens of other CP types constituting one or more different semantic domain(s). Because these CP types and their tokens, so to speak, "drop out" of the semantic domain examined, I call these observed, acceptable, but unexpected uses of these CP types *off-domain substitution*. Off-domain substitution is indicated by the notation —.

With both in-domain and off-domain substitution, I note the types and the tokens observed in these substitution processes as well as all the domains involved in these processes.

To provide a basis for comparison, the relative frequency (r.f.) of the tokens of all CP types is computed and presented in italics. The r.f. is computed on the basis of 180 tokens (60 consultants producing, in the ideal case, three tokens of a certain CP type; note that here the CP 0 'basketful of yams' is again an exception since it is only produced in connection with numerals and thus, for this CP, 60 tokens produced by 60 consultants total 100% of elicitation success). If 180 tokens of a certain CP type were produced in the test, the r.f. is *1.0*. If no tokens were produced of a CP type that was expected, the CP type gets the r.f. 0 (see, also, G. Senft 1982:84–86, 203–204). I want to emphasize that these relative frequencies are used for the purposes of comparison only. Naturally, these frequencies are only computed for tokens of CP types elicited in the test. Tokens of CP types that were not elicited in the test but were found in the corpus of the transcribed Kilivila speech data are presented in angle brackets ($\langle$ $\rangle$) when I describe the relevant semantic domain.

The results of this proceeding are presented in tables that attempt to reflect the dynamics involved in the constitution of all 20 semantic domains by the CP types. After the presentation of these 20 tables, all tokens of the CP types that actually constitute a specific semantic domain (and this includes all tokens of CP types that are noted as in-domain substitution cases) are counted and ordered according to the frequency of their production.[9] These figures are then totaled. On the basis of this sum, the r.f. for all tokens in each domain, are computed to give a comparative figure for evaluating the intradomain weighting of each CP type. The r.f.s for all CP types constituting a domain add up to 1.0.[10]

On the basis of these data, I then propose rules that speakers may use in their production of a certain CP of the semantic domain discussed. I regard these rules as the expression of the transformation of a given semantic concept into an appropriate classifier. The rules must cope with both domain-inherent and domain-affecting dynamics. Thus, most, if not all, of the rules proposed and formulated are actually *variable rules* (for a discussion and further references, see Romaine 1985; G. Senft 1982, 6–8, as well as sections 4.3.3 and 4.5.3 in the present volume). I dispense with a formal notation of these rules in favor of a comprehensive formulation that I hope will be easier to understand. In my opinion, these rules are the only way to meet the expectation discussed in section 3.1, namely, to predict which CPs a speaker will produce to refer to certain nominal concepts. I believe that variable rules can most appropriately describe and record such dynamic processes.

We can now examine the semantic domains in detail. Tables 3.4.1.1a and b attempt to present the dynamics of Domain 1a and provide an evaluation of the CP types that constitute this domain.

Table 3.4.1.1a documents that within Domain 1a there were 3 cases of off-domain substitution, affecting Domain 1b (body part) and Domain 3a

---

[9] It should be clear that we must ignore the off-domain substitution cases here. Off-domain substitution cases observed with one domain are in-domain substitution cases in other domains!

[10] If the r.f.s add up to 1.01 or .99, it is not a computing deficiency; it is the result of rounding off the individual values.

**Table 3.4.1.1a.** Domain 1a: Persons

|  |  |  | Off-domain substitution |  |  |  |  |
|---|---|---|---|---|---|---|---|
| *<to1>* |  |  |  |  |  |  |  |
| *te/to2* | 180 | *1.00* | —— | 3 | *.02* | *yam/yuma/yama* | (Domain 1b) |
|  |  |  | —— | 11 | *.06* | *deli* | (Domain 3a) |
| *na1* | 173 | *.96* | —— | 1 | *.01* | *deli* | (Domain 3a) |
| *gudi* | 142 | *.79* |  |  |  |  |  |
| *<na5>* |  |  |  |  |  |  |  |

**Table 3.4.1.1b.** Domain 1a: Relative frequencies interpreted as figures for the evaluation of CP types (in-domain and intradomain)

| 1. | *te/to2* 'male' | 180 | = | 180 | r.f. | *.36* |
|---|---|---|---|---|---|---|
| 2. | *na1* 'female' | 173 | = | 173 | r.f. | *.35* |
| 3. | *gudi* 'child' | 142 | = | 142 | r.f. | *.29* |
|  |  |  |  | 495 |  | *1.00* |
| 4. | *te/to1* 'human beings' | -/- (= not elicited in the test) |  |  |  |  |
| 5. | *na5* 'corpses' | -/- |  |  |  |  |
| 6. | *na6* 'spirits, dwarfs' | -/- |  |  |  |  |

(quantities). Table 3.4.1.1b presents all the CPs that constitute Domain 1a and gives the r.f.s for the production of the individual CP types within the entire domain.

On the basis of these two tables, I have formulated the following variable rules that speakers use in their production of a certain CP type of Domain 1a:

*If speakers want to refer to the concept 'persons of male or female sex' or to the concept 'children', their choice of the CP types te/to2, na1, and gudi is unequivocal (r.f.s 1.0; .96; .79).*

*If speakers want to refer to the concept 'human being', this semantic domain offers the CP to1; if speakers want to refer to the concept 'spirits, dwarfs' or to the concept 'corpses', this semantic domain offers the CP type na in its variants na5 and na6.* However, the references to these concepts were not elicited in the test, and thus there are no comparative values to describe their position within this semantic domain.

Table 3.4.1.1b documents that the three CPs *te/to2, na1,* and *gudi* are of almost equal rank with respect to their importance for the constitution of Domain 1a, if we base this on language production data similar to those elicited in the test.

Tables 3.4.1.2a and b attempt to present the dynamics of Domain 1b and provide an evaluation of the CP types that constitute this domain.

Classificatory Particles in Kilivila

**Table 3.4.1.2a.** Domain 1b: Body part

In-domain substitution

| | | | | | |
|---|---|---|---|---|---|
| (Domain 4) | kwe | 9 | +++ | kweya/kwaya/keya | 131 |
| | | 0.5 | | | .73 |
| (Domain 4) | ke | 5 | +++ | | |
| | | 0.3 | | | |
| (Domain 1a) | to2 | 3 | +++ | yam2/yuma1/yama1 | 12 ——— 84 |
| | | 0.2 | | | .07 ——— .47 |
| (Domain 4) | kwe | 56 | +++ | | |
| | | .31 | | | |
| (Domain 8) | ya | 1 | +++ | | |
| | | .01 | | | |
| | | | | ka'i | |
| (Domain 4) | ke | 2 | +++ | kudu2 | 26 ——— 124 |
| | | .01 | | | .14 ——— .69 |
| (Domain 4) | kwe | 2 | +++ | | |
| | | .01 | | | |

**Table 3.4.1.2b.** Domain 1b: Relative frequencies interpreted as figures for the evaluation of CP types (in-domain and intradomain)

| | | | | | |
|---|---|---|---|---|---|
| 1. | kweya 'limb' | 131 + 84 | = 215 | r.f. | .47 |
| 2. | ka'i 'tooth' | 124 | = 124 | r.f. | .27 |
| 3. | kwe 'thing' | 9 + 56 + 2 | = 67 | r.f. | .15 |
| 4. | kudu2 'tooth' | 26 | = 26 | r.f. | .06 |
| 5. | yam/yuma 'hand' | 12 | = 12 | r.f. | .03 |
| 6. | ke 'inanimate' | 5 + 2 | = 7 | r.f. | .02 |
| 7. | te/to2 'male' | 3 | = 3 | r.f. | .01 |
| 8. | ya 'flexible' | 1 | = 1 | r.f. | .002 |
| | | | 455 | | 1.012 |

Table 3.4.1.2a documents that within Domain 1b there were 2 cases of intradomain substitution and 7 cases of in-domain substitution, affecting CPs that constitute the Domains 1a (persons), 4 (general CPs), and 8 (qualities).

Table 3.4.1.2b presents all the CPs that constitute Domain 1b and gives the r.f.s for the production of the individual CPs within the entire domain.

On the basis of these two tables I have formulted the following variable rules that speakers use in their production of a certain CP type of Domain 1b:

*If speakers want to refer to the concept 'limb (severed or not)', they will generally use the CP kweya/kwaya/keya (r.f. .73); however, it is also possible, although rather rarely observed, to produce one of the two general classifiers (ke (r.f. .03), kwe (r.f. .05)).*

*If speakers want to refer to the concept 'hand', they will only rarely use the special and most appropriate CP type yam/yuma/yama (r.f. .07). As stated in section 3.3.3.2, this CP type functions as a sociolinguistic variable. Instead of this CP type, the CP kweya/kwaya/keya (r.f. .47) will be produced. The production of the general CP kwe is another alternative here (r.f. .31). Moreover, it is also possible, although rather rarely observed, to produce either the CP te/to (r.f. .02) or the CP ya (r.f. .01).*

*If speakers want to refer to the concept 'tooth', they will generally produce the CP ka'i (r.f. .69). Another alternative is the production of the CP kudu2 (r.f. .14); however, this CP variant functions as a sociolinguistic variable (see section 3.3.3.2) and is thus only used by persons of high status. It is also possible, although rather rarely observed, to use one of the general CPs ke, (r.f. .01) or kwe (r.f. .01).*

As for the cases of in-domain substitution, we may note the following: Table 3.4.1.2b documents that the CPs *ya*, *te/to*, *ke*, *yam/yuma/yama*, and *kudu2* play a secondary role only; the CPs *kweya/kwaya/keya*, *ka'i*, and *kwe* are the most important CPs in Domain 1b, if we base this constitution on language production data similar to those elicited in the test. What should be emphasized here is the rather high value of *.15* for the general CP *kwe* in Table 3.4.1.2b. Obviously, *kwe* has already invaded a semantic domain the main feature of which is 'animacy'. Thus, the frame of reference of the CP *kwe* seems to be in the process of broadening from an unmarked form for inanimates to an unmarked form in general.

Tables 3.4.2a and b attempt to present the dynamics of Domain 2 and provide an evaluation of the CP types that constitute this domain.

**Table 3.4.2a.** Domain 2: Animals

|  |  |  | Off-domain substitution |  |  |  |
|---|---|---|---|---|---|---|
| *na2* | 162 | .90 | —— | 60 | .33 | *wela* (Domain 3) |
|  |  |  | —— | 53 | .29 | *oyla* (Domain 3 (11)) |
| *kwe2* | <19> |  |  |  |  |  |

**Table 3.4.2b.** Domain 2: Relative frequencies interpreted as figures for the evaluation of CP types (in-domain and intradomain)

| 1. | *na2* 'animals' | 162 | = 162 | r.f. | *1.0* |
|---|---|---|---|---|---|
| 2. | *kwe2* 'clams, shells' | -/- (= not elicited in the test) |  |  |  |

Table 3.4.2a shows that within Domain 2 there were 2 cases of off-domain substitution, affecting Domain 3 (quantities); see Domain 11 (utensils).

Table 3.4.2b presents all the CPs that constitute Domain 2 and gives the r.f.s for the production of the individual CP types within the entire domain.

On the basis of these two tables, I have formulated the following variable rules that speakers use in their production of a certain CP type of Domain 2:

*If speakers want to refer to the concept 'animals' (but not 'shells and clams'), they will only use the CP type na (=na2 (r.f. .90)).*

*If speakers want to refer to the concept 'shells and clams', this semantic domain offers the CP type kwe (=kwe2).* However, the references to these concepts were not elicited in the test, and thus I have no comparative values to describe the position of this CP type within Domain 2 (see also section 3.3.3.2).

There were no cases of in-domain substitution and only 2 cases of off-domain substitution; thus, we conclude that Domain 2 is an almost closed

**Table 3.4.3.1a** Domain 3a: Quantities (living beings in general)

| In-domain substitution | | | | | Off-domain substitution | | | |
|---|---|---|---|---|---|---|---|---|
| (Domain 4) | *kwe* | 85 .47 | +++ | *buda/boda/budu* | 63 .35 | —— | 1 .01 | *mmwa;* (Domain 3b) |
| | | | | 86 .48 | | —— | 1 .01 | *gula;* (Domain 3b) |
| (Domain 9) | *kasa* | 1 .01 | +++ | *yuva* | 4 .02 | | | |
| (Domain 4) | *ke* | 1 .01 | +++ | | | | | |
| (Domain 4) | *kwe* | 52 .29 | +++ | | | | | |
| (Domain 4) | *kwe* | 37 .21 | +++ | *deli* | 93 .52 | | | |
| (Domain 1) | *to* | 11 .06 | +++ | | | | | |
| (Domain 1) | *na1* | 1 .01 | +++ | | | | | |
| (Domain 9) | *kasa* | 2 .01 | +++ | | | | | |
| | | | | *suya* | 90 .50 | | | |
| (Domain 2) | *na2* | 60 .33 | +++ | *wela* | 12 .07 | | | |
| | | | | 30 .17 | | | | |
| (Domain 2) | *na2* | 53 .29 | +++ | *oyla* | | | | |

**Table 3.4.3.1b.** Domain 3a: Relative frequencies interpreted as figures for the evaluation of CP types (in-domain and intradomain)

| | | | | | | |
|---|---|---|---|---|---|---|
| 1. | *kwe* 'thing' | 85 + 37 + 52 | = | 174 | r.f. | .26 |
| 2. | *buda* 'group' | 63 + 86 | = | 149 | r.f. | .22 |
| 3. | *na2* 'animals' | 60 + 53 | = | 113 | r.f. | .17 |
| 4. | *deli* 'group' | 93 | = | 93 | r.f. | .14 |
| 5. | *suya* 'batch/fish' | 90 | = | 90 | r.f. | .13 |
| 6. | *wela* 'batch/fish' | 12 + 30 | = | 42 | r.f. | .06 |
| 7. | *te/to* 'male' | 11 | = | 11 | r.f. | .02 |
| 8. | *yuva* 'shoal' | 4 | = | 4 | r.f. | .01 |
| 9. | *na1* 'female' | 1 | = | 1 | r.f. | .001 |
| 10. | *kasa* 'row' | 1 + 2 | = | 3 | r.f. | .001 |
| 11. | *ke* 'inanimates' | 1 | = | 1 | r.f. | .001 |
| | | | | 681 | | 1.013 |
| | | | | | | |
| 12. | *oyla* 'string'/('fish') | 0 (= not realized) | | | | |

semantic domain; the frames of reference of its CP types are very distinct indeed.

Tables 3.4.3.1a and b attempt to present the dynanics of Domain 3a and provide an evaluation of the CP types that constitute this domain.

Table 3.4.3.1a documents that within Domain 3a there were 3 cases of intradomain substitution, affecting CPs that constitute Domains 1 (persons, body parts), 2 (animals), 4 (general CPs), and 9 (shapes). There were also 2 cases of off-domain substitution, affecting Domain 3b.

Table 3.4.3.1b presents all the CPs that constitute Domain 3a and gives the r.f.s for the production of the individual CP types within the entire domain.

On the basis of these two tables, I have formulated the following variable rules that speakers use in their production of a certain CP type of Domain 3a:

*If speakers want to refer to the concept 'group, team, crowd', they use either the general CP kwe (r.f. .47) or the special and more appropriate CP buda/boda/budu (r.f. .35). The general CP is observed more often than the special classifier; nevertheless, buda/boda/budu belongs to the core of Kilivila CP types (see Table 3.3.6).*

*If speakers want to refer to the concept 'company, group on the move', they most often use the CP deli (r.f. .52); another alternative to refer to this concept is the general CP kwe (r.f. .21). Moreover, it is also possible, although rather rarely observed, to use the CP to/te (r.f. .06) or the CPs na1 (r.f. .01) and kasa (r.f. .01) (see Table 3.2.156).*

*If speakers want to refer to the concept 'shoal', they generally produce the CP buda/boda/budu (r.f. .48), thus broadening the frame of reference of this CP from 'group, team, crowd' in such a way that it includes the concept 'shoal'. Another alternative is the general CP kwe (r.f. .29). Moreover, it is also possible, although rarely observed, to refer to this concept either with the special and more appropriate CP yuva (r.f. .02) or the other general CP ke (r.f. .01). To produce the CP kasa in this context seems to be possible; however, it is rather idiosyncratic.*

*If speakers want to refer to the concept 'batch of fish, string of fish', they most often use the CP suya (r.f. .50). Another alternative to refer to this concept is the CP na in its meaning 'animals' (r.f. .33); however, the CP suya is clearly preferred. Only speakers of high status will (rather rarely) produce the special and more appropriate CP wela (r.f. .07) to refer to this concept. As stated in section 3.3.3.2, the CP wela functions as a sociolinguistic variable.*

*If speakers want to refer to the concept 'fish on strings' they use either the CP na in its meaning 'animals' (r.f. .29) or—if they are speakers of high status—the CP wela (r.f. .17). The CP oyla, the special and more appropriate CP to refer to this concept, was not produced in the test and did not occur in my corpus of transcribed Kilivila speech data.*

As for the cases of in-domain substitution, we may note that the general CP *kwe* plays the most important role within this domain. Here, the general CP has already invaded a semantic domain that includes 'quantities that generally refer to animate (!) referents'. Although the other general CP (*ke*) plays only a secondary role within this domain, we can take this finding as another sign for the broadening of the frame of reference of at least the CP *kwe* to an unmarked form in general. According to Table 3.4.3.1b, the other CPs that play a role within Domain 3a are *buda, na2, deli, suya,* and—with the restrictions discussed—*wela*, if we base the constitution of this domain on language production data similar to those elicited in the test.

Tables 3.4.3.2a and b attempt to present the dynamics of Domain 3b and provide an evaluation of the CP types that constitute this domain.

Table 3.4.3.2a documents that within Domain 3b there were 12 cases of intradomain substitution and 37 cases of in-domain substitution, affecting CPs in Domains 3a (quantities, living beings in general), 4 (general CPs), 8 (qualities), 9 (shape), 10 (trees, wood, wooden things), and 12 (yams). There were also 19 cases of off-domain substitution, affecting Domains 6 (time), 7 (place), 8 (qualities), 9 (shape), 11 (utensils), 13 (part of a foodhouse/a canoe/a creel), and 17 (texts).

Table 3.4.3.2b presents all the CPs that constitute Domain 3b and gives the r.f.s for the production of the individual CP types within the entire domain.

On the basis of these two tables, I have formulated the following variable rules that speakers use in their production of a certain CP type in Domain 3b.

*If speakers want to refer to the concept 'heap, group '(inanimate)' they use the general CP kwe (r.f. .46) more often than the special and more appropriate CP gula (r.f. .28). It is also possible to use the CP tam (r.f. .16), if the speaker intends to refer especially to a 'heap or group of sprouting yams'. Use of the CP buda (r.f. .01) in this context seems to be possible; however, the use of this CP, which generally refers to animate groups, is rather idiosyncratic here.*

*If speakers want to refer to the concept 'plantation, grove', they use the general CP kwe (r.f. .52) more often than the special and more appropriate*

**Table 3.4.3.2a.** Domain 3b: Quantities (things in general)

| In-domain substitution | | | | | Off-domain substitution |
|---|---|---|---|---|---|
| (Domain 3a) | *buda* | 1 .01 | +++ | *gula* | 50 .28 |
| (Domain 12) | *tam* | 28 .16 | +++ | | |
| (Domain 4) | *kwe* | 82 .46 | +++ | | |

3
.02
||

| (Domain 4) | *kwe* | 93 .52 | +++ | *po'ula* | 49 .27 |

1
.01
||

sa
below
||

| (Domain 10) | *ke* | 122 .68 | +++ | *bukwa* | 3 .02 |
| (Domain 4) | *kwe* | 4 .02 | +++ | | |
| (Domain 8) | *ya* | 14 .08 | +++ | | |

*luva2*    *sa*
below     below
2          3
.01        .02

| (Domain 4) | *kwe* | 29 .16 | +++ | *duli* | 108 .60 |
| (Domain 4) | *ke* | 6 .03 | +++ | | |
| (Domain 4) | *kwe* | 30 .17 | +++ | *kapwa* | 46 .26 |

77
.43
|
*luba*

| (Domain 4) | *ke* | 28 .16 | +++ | *si* | 1 .01 — 14 .08 *ya;* (Domain 8) |
| (Domain 4) | *kwe* | 3 .02 | +++ | | |
| (Domain 10) | *bwa* | 6 .03 | +++ | | |
| (Domain 8) | *vili* | 4 .02 | +++ | | *utu* below 118 .66 |

**Table 3.4.3.2a.** *(continued)*

| In-domain substitution | | | | | Off-domain substitution | | | |
|---|---|---|---|---|---|---|---|---|
| (Domain 4) | *kwe* | 22 .12 | +++ | *gum* | 88 .49 | | | |
| (Domain 4) | *ke* | 6 .03 | +++ | | | | | |
| (Domain 8) | *ya* | 6 .03 | +++ | | *utu* below | | | |
| (Domain 9) | *kasa* | 3 .02 | +++ | | 1 .01 | | | |
| (Domain 4) | *ke* | 5 .03 | +++ | *pila* | 81 .45 | —— | 91 .51 | *meila;* (Domain 17) |
| (Domain 4) | *kwe* | 3 .02 | +++ | | | —— | 67 .37 | *nina;* (Domain 17) |
| (Domain 8) | *ya* | 60 .33 | +++ | | | —— | 4 .02 | *ya;* (Domain 8) |
| (Domain 8) | *vili* | 1 .01 | +++ | | | —— | 2 .01 | *oyla;* (Domain 11) |
| | | | | | | —— | 1 .01 | *kavi;* (Domain 11) |
| | | | | | | —— | 1 .01 | *siva;* (Domain 6) |
| | | | | | | —— | 1 .01 | *kabisi;* (Domain 13) |
| | | | | | | —— | 1 .01 | *kubila;* (Domain 7) |

see *gum* above

see *si* above

see *pila* above
1
.01

| (Domain 10) | *ke* | 36 .20 | +++ | *utu* | 87 .48 | —— | 30 .17 | *vili;* (Domain 8) |
| (Domain 10) | *bwa* | 20 .11 | +++ | | | —— | 38 .21 | *kabulo1;* (Domain 9) |
| (Domain 8) | *bubwa* | 8 .04 | +++ | | | —— | 4 .02 | *kabisi;* (Domain 13) |
| | | | | | | —— | 6 .03 | *siva;* (Domain 6) |
| | | | | | | —— | 1 .01 | *kabulo2;* (Domain 7) |
| | | | | | | —— | 4 .02 | *meila;* (Domain 17) |
| | | | | | | —— | 3 .02 | *nina;* (Domain 17) |
| | | | | | | —— | 2 .01 | *nunu;* (Domain 7) |

**Table 3.4.3.2a.** *(continued)*

| In-domain substitution | | | | | Off-domain substitution |

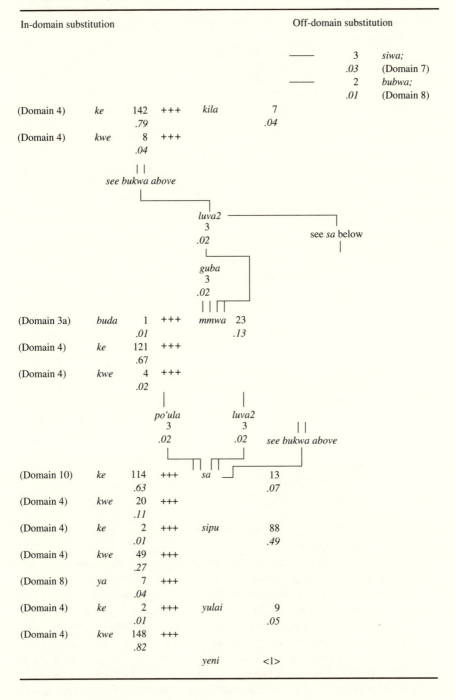

In-domain substitution      Off-domain substitution

|  |  |  |  |  |  |
|---|---|---|---|---|---|
|  |  |  |  | —— 3 | *siwa;* |
|  |  |  |  | .03 | (Domain 7) |
|  |  |  |  | —— 2 | *bubwa;* |
|  |  |  |  | .01 | (Domain 8) |
| (Domain 4) | *ke* | 142 +++ | *kila* | 7 | |
|  |  | .79 |  | .04 | |
| (Domain 4) | *kwe* | 8 +++ |  |  | |
|  |  | .04 |  |  | |

| |
see *bukwa* above

*luva2*
3
.02      see *sa* below

*guba*
3
.02

| (Domain 3a) | *buda* | 1 +++ | *mmwa* 23 |
|---|---|---|---|
|  |  | .01 | .13 |
| (Domain 4) | *ke* | 121 +++ | |
|  |  | .67 | |
| (Domain 4) | *kwe* | 4 +++ | |
|  |  | .02 | |

*po'ula*      *luva2*
3      3
.02      .02    see *bukwa* above

| (Domain 10) | *ke* | 114 +++ | *sa* | 13 |
|---|---|---|---|---|
|  |  | .63 |  | .07 |
| (Domain 4) | *kwe* | 20 +++ | | |
|  |  | .11 | | |
| (Domain 4) | *ke* | 2 +++ | *sipu* | 88 |
|  |  | .01 |  | .49 |
| (Domain 4) | *kwe* | 49 +++ | | |
|  |  | .27 | | |
| (Domain 8) | *ya* | 7 +++ | | |
|  |  | .04 | | |
| (Domain 4) | *ke* | 2 +++ | *yulai* | 9 |
|  |  | .01 |  | .05 |
| (Domain 4) | *kwe* | 148 +++ | | |
|  |  | .82 | | |
|  |  |  | *yeni* | <1> |

**Table 3.4.3.2b.** Domain 3b: Relative frequencies interpreted as figures for the evaluation of CP types (in-domain and intradomain)

| | | | | | | |
|---|---|---|---|---|---|---|
| 1. | *kel* 'wood' | 122 +36 + 114 | = | 272 | (r.f. | *.13*) |
| | *ke3* 'inanimates' | 6 + 28 + 6 + 5 + 142 + | | | | |
| | | 121 + 2 + 2 | = | 312 | (r.f. | *.15*) |
| | *kel+3* | | = | 584 | r.f. | *.28* |
| 2. | *kwe* 'inanimates' | 82 + 93 + 4 + 29 + 30 + | | | | |
| | | 3 + 22 + 3 + 8 + 4 + 20 + | | | | |
| | | 49 + 148 | = | 495 | r.f. | *.24* |
| 3. | *utu* 'scrap' | 118 + 1 + 1 + 87 | = | 207 | r.f. | *.10* |
| 4. | *duli* 'cluster' | 108 | = | 108 | r.f. | *.05* |
| 5. | *gum* 'bit' | 88 | = | 88 | r.f. | *.04* |
| 6. | *sipu* 'sheaf' | 88 | = | 88 | r.f. | *.04* |
| 7. | *ya* 'flexible' | 14 + 6 + 60 + 7 | = | 87 | r.f. | *.04* |
| 8. | *pila* 'part' | 81 | = | 81 | r.f. | *.04* |
| 9. | *luba* 'bundle' | 77 | = | 77 | r.f. | *.04* |
| 10. | *gula* 'heap' | 50 + 3 | = | 53 | r.f. | *.03* |
| 11. | *po'ula* 'grove' | 49 + 1 + 3 | = | 53 | r.f. | *.03* |
| 12. | *kapwa* 'parcel' | 46 | = | 46 | r.f. | *.02* |
| 13. | *tam* 'sprouting' | 28 | = | 28 | r.f. | *.01* |
| 14. | *bwa* 'tree' | 6 + 20 | = | 26 | r.f. | *.01* |
| 15. | *mmwa* 'bundle' | 23 | = | 23 | r.f. | *.01* |
| 16. | *sa* 'nut-bunch' | 3 + 13 | = | 16 | r.f. | *.01* |
| 17. | *yulai* '4/bundle' | 9 | = | 9 | r.f. | *.004* |
| 18. | *luva2* 'bundle' | 2 + 3 + 3 | = | 8 | r.f. | *.004* |
| 19. | *bubwa* 'cut off' | 8 | = | 8 | r.f. | *.004* |
| 20. | *kila* 'cluster/bananas' | 7 | = | 7 | r.f. | *.003* |
| 21. | *vili* 'untwisted' | 5 | = | 5 | r.f. | *.002* |
| 22. | *bukwa* 'cluster' | 3 | = | 3 | r.f: | *.001* |
| 23. | *kasa* 'row' | 3 | = | 3 | r.f. | *.001* |
| 24. | *guba* 'bundle/taro' | 3 | = | 3 | r.f. | *.001* |
| 25. | *buda* 'group' | 1 + 1 | = | 2 | r.f. | *.001* |
| 26. | *si* 'bit' | 1 | = | 1 | r.f. | *.001* |
| | | | | 2,109 | | *1.012* |

27.      *yeni* 'a handful' -/- (= not elicited in the test)

*CP po'ula (r.f. .27). It is also possible, although rather rarely observed, to use the CP gula (r.f. .02) in this context.*

*If speakers want to refer to the concept 'fruit cluster', they most often use the CP ke in its meaning 'wooden things' (r.f. .68), obviously referring to clusters of fruit with wooden shells, skins, or husks like the omnipresent coconuts or the very popular betel nuts. It is also possible to use the CP ya (r.f. .08) in this context, thus emphasizing the flexible quality of fruit clusters. Use of the special and more appropriate CP bukwa (r.f. .02) is as rarely observed as the production of the general CP kwe (r.f. .02) and the CPs sa (r.f. .02), luva (r.f. .01; 'tied bundle of fruit'), and po'ula (r.f. .01; here the speaker may intend to refer to the fruit clusters found on plantations and in groves).*

*If speakers want to refer to the concept 'cluster, bundle', they generally use the special and more appropriate CP duli (r.f. .60). Another alternative is the general CP kwe (r.f. .16). It is also possible to use the general CP ke; however, this is rather rarely observed (r.f. .03).*

*If speakers want to refer to the concept 'bundle (wrapped up)', they most often use the CP luba (r.f. .43; 'bundle of rolls'); obviously, this CP type has broadened its frame of reference. Only speakers of high status produce the sociolinguistic variable kapwa/kapo, the special and most appropriate CP in this context (r.f. .26). It is also possible to use the general CP kwe (r.f. .17) here.*

*If speakers want to refer to the concept 'small bit', they most often use the CP utu (r.f. .66). The special and more appropriate CP si is as rarely produced (r.f. .01) as the CPs vili (r.f. .02; here the speaker may intend to refer to a 'small untwisted bit'), kwe (r.f. .02), and bwa (r.f. .03; here the speaker may intend to refer to a 'small bit of wood'). A more often produced alternative is the general CP ke (r.f. .16).*

*If speakers want to refer to the concept 'bit, small piece', they most often use the special and more appropriate CP gum (r.f. .49). They may also use the general CP kwe (r.f. .12); moreover, it is also possible, although rather rarely observed, to produce the CPs ke (r.f. .03), ya (r.f. .03; here the speaker may intend to emphasize the 'flexibility' or 'thinness' of a 'small piece' of something)', kasa (r.f. .02; here the speaker may intend, somewhat idiosyncratically, to refer to the concept 'bits in a row'), and utu (r.f. .01).*

*If speakers want to refer to the concept 'part, piece', they either use the special and more appropriate CP pila (r.f. .45) or, although less frequently, the CP 'ya' (r.f. .33; here the speaker intend to emphasize the 'thinness' of a 'part' or 'piece' of something). It is also possible, although rather rarely observed, to produce the two general CPs ke (r.f. .03) and kwe (r.f. .02), and the CPs vili (r.f. .01) and utu (r.f. .01).*

*If speakers want to refer to the concept 'scrap, parts (cut off), small particles, fragments', they most often use the special and more appropriate CP utu (r.f. .48). Another alternative is to produce either the CP ke (r.f. .20) or bwa (r.f. .11) to emphasize that 'cut off parts' on the Trobriands are in general 'wooden things'. It is also possible, although rather rarely observed, to use the CP bubwa (r.f. .04) to emphasize the 'cut off' aspect of the concept 'parts cut off'; however, only speakers of high status use this CP, which functions as a sociolinguistic variable (see section 3.3.3.2).*

*If speakers want to refer to the concept 'clusters/hands of bananas', they most often use the general CP ke (r.f. .79). Only women of high status use the special and more appropriate CP kila (r.f. .04); however, the use of this sociolinguistic variable is rather rarely observed. It is also possible, although rarely observed, to use the general CP kwe (r.f. .04) in this context.*

*If speakers want to refer to the concept 'conical bundle', they produce the special and more appropriate CP mmwa only if they are persons of high status (r.f. .13); mmwa functions as a sociolinguistic variable. To refer to this concept, speakers most often use the general CP ke (r.f. .67). It is also possible, although rather rarely observed, to produce the CPs luva (r.f. .02), guba (r.f. .02), kwe (r.f. .02), and buda (r.f. .01); however, the production of the CP buda is somewhat idiosyncratic, if not dubious, in this context.*

*If speakers want to refer to the concept 'nut bunch', they use the special and appropriate CP sa only if they are persons of status (r.f. .13); sa functions as a sociolinguistic variable. To refer to this concept, speakers most often use the CP ke (r.f. .63). It is also possible, although not often observed, to use the CPs kwe (r.f. .11), luva (r.f. .02), and po'ula (r.f. .02); however, the use of po'ula in this context is rather idiosyncratic.*

*If speakers want to refer to the concept 'sheaf', they most often use the special and appropriate CP sipu (r.f. .49). It is also possible to use either the general CP kwe (r.f. .27) or the CP ya (r.f. .04) or the general CP ke (r.f. .01); however, the production of the last two CPs is rather rarely observed.*

*If speakers want to refer to the concept 'bundles of four things', they usually use the general CP 'kwe' (r.f. .82); the use of the other general CP 'ke' (r.f. .01) is possible, but rather rarely observed. The production of the special and appropriate CP 'yulai' is only rather rarely observed (r.f. .05).*

*If speakers want to refer to the concept 'a handful of something', this semantic domain offers the CP type yeni.* However, reference to this concept was not used in the test, and thus there is no comparative value to describe the position of this CP within Domain 3b (see also section 3.3.3.2).

As for the cases of in-domain substitution, we may note the following: With the exception of the CPs *kwe, ke* (=*ke1,* and *ke3*), and perhaps *ya,* all the other CPs (*buda, bwa, bubwa, kasa, tam, vili*) obviously play only a minor role. As Table 3.4.3.2b shows, Domain 3b is dominated by the CPs *kwe, ke,* and *utu,* although there are 27 CPs in this domain.

Tables 3.4.4a and b attempt to present the dynamics of Domain 4 and provide an evaluation of the CPs that constitute this domain.

Table 3.4.4a documents that within Domain 4 there were 82 cases of off-domain substitution, affecting 17 domains (Domains 3a and 3b are counted as one domain).

Table 3.4.4b presents the two CP types that constitute this domain and gives the r.f.s for the production of the CP types within the entire domain. On the basis of these two tables, I have formulated the following variable rules that speakers use in their production of the CP types of Domain 4:

*If speakers want to refer to the concept 'thing, anything unknown or indefinite', they produce the unmarked form, the general CP kwe (r.f. .91). This semantic domain also includes the CP ke in its meaning 'unmarked form (for inanimates)' (=ke3) as another general CP.* However, this CP was not elicited in the test.

Domain 4 shows cases of off-domain substitution, but no cases of in-domain substitution or intradomain substitution. Thus, we note that the CPs of Domain 4 play an important role in other semantic domains, but Domain 4 itself is rather closed; it is not affected by the dynamic processes of other domains nor by such processes internally.

Tables 3.4.5a and b attempt to present the dynamics of Domain 5 and

**Table 3.4.4a.** Domain 4: General CPs

| | | | | | | |
|---|---|---|---|---|---|---|
| *kwe* 'thing' | 164 | *.91* | —— | 56 | *.31* | *yam/yama* | (Domain 1) |
| | | | —— | 9 | *.05* | *kweya/keya* | (Domain 1) |
| | | | —— | 2 | *.01* | *kudu* | (Domain 1) |
| | | | —— | 85 | *.47* | *buda/boda* | (Domain 3a) |
| | | | —— | 37 | *.21* | *deli* | (Domain 3a) |
| | | | —— | 52 | *.29* | *yuva* | (Domain 3a) |
| | | | —— | 82 | *.46* | *gula* | (Domain 3b) |
| | | | —— | 93 | *.52* | *po'ula* | (Domain 3b) |
| | | | —— | 4 | *.02* | *bukwa* | (Domain 3b) |
| | | | —— | 29 | *.16* | *duli* | (Domain 3b) |
| | | | —— | 30 | *.17* | *kapwa/kapo* | (Domain 3b) |
| | | | —— | 3 | *.02* | *si* | (Domain 3b) |
| | | | —— | 22 | *.12* | *gum* | (Domain 3b) |
| | | | —— | 3 | *.02* | *pila* | (Domain 3b) |
| | | | —— | 8 | *.04* | *kila* | (Domain 3b) |
| | | | —— | 4 | *.02* | *mmwa* | (Domain 3b) |
| | | | —— | 20 | *.11* | *sa* | (Domain 3b) |
| | | | —— | 49 | *.27* | *sipu* | (Domain 3b) |
| | | | —— | 148 | *.82* | *yulai/yule* | (Domain 3b) |
| | | | —— | 8 | *.04* | *uva* | (Domain 5) |
| | | | —— | 138 | *.77* | *bogi* | (Domain 6) |
| | | | —— | 144 | *.80* | *kala* | (Domain 6) |
| | | | —— | 134 | *.74* | *siva* | (Domain 6) |
| | | | —— | 141 | *.78* | *yam* | (Domain 6) |
| | | | —— | 40 | *.22* | *kabulo2* | (Domain 7) |
| | | | —— | 153 | *.85* | *vilo* | (Domain 7) |
| | | | —— | 137 | *.76* | *siwa* | (Domain 7) |
| | | | —— | 53 | *.29* | *kubila* | (Domain 7) |
| | | | —— | 124 | *.69* | *nunu* | (Domain 7) |
| | | | —— | 132 | *.73* | *kwoya/koya* | (Domain 7) |
| | | | —— | 28 | *.16* | *bubu/bobu* | (Domain 8) |
| | | | —— | 1 | *.01* | *bubwa* | (Domain 8) |
| | | | —— | 11 | *.06* | *giwi* | (Domain 8) |
| | | | —— | 23 | *.13* | *pwanina* | (Domain 8) |
| | | | —— | 4 | *.02* | *vili* | (Domain 8) |
| | | | —— | 9 | *.05* | *kasa* | (Domain 9) |
| | | | —— | 29 | *.16* | *gili* | (Domain 9) |
| | | | —— | 33 | *.18* | *nutu/notu* | (Domain 9) |
| | | | —— | 2 | *.01* | *luva* | (Domain 10) |
| | | | —— | 6 | *.03* | *kavi* | (Domain 11) |
| | | | —— | 14 | *.08* | *oyla* | (Domain 11) |
| | | | —— | 1 | *.01* | *peta/ta* | (Domain 11) |
| | | | —— | 49 | *.27* | *kwoila* | (Domain 11) |
| | | | —— | 117 | *.65* | *Ø* | (Domain 12) |
| | | | —— | 10 | *.06* | *kabisi* | (Domain 13) |
| | | | —— | 55 | *.31* | *liku* | (Domain 13) |
| | | | —— | 25 | *.07* | *duya/kaduyo* | (Domain 14) |
| | | | —— | 1 | *.01* | *kova* | (Domain 15) |
| | | | —— | 1 | *.01* | *kumla* | (Domain 15) |
| | | | —— | 131 | *.73* | *lilo* | (Domain 16) |
| | | | —— | 9 | *.05* | *meila* | (Domain 17) |
| | | | —— | 61 | *.34* | *nina* | (Domain 17) |

**Table 3.4.4a.** *(continued)*

| | | | | | |
|---|---|---|---|---|---|
| | —— | 2 | *.01* | *kai* | (Domain 18) |
| | —— | 145 | *.81* | *kudu* | (Domain 19) |
| | —— | 6 | *.03* | *iga/yegila* | (Domain 20) |
| *ke (=ke3) -/-* | —— | 5 | *.03* | *kweya/keya* | (Domain 1b) |
| | —— | 2 | *.01* | *kudu* | (Domain 1b) |
| | —— | 1 | *.01* | *yuva* | (Domain 3a) |
| | —— | 6 | *.03* | *duli* | (Domain 3b) |
| | —— | 28 | *.16* | *si* | (Domain 3b) |
| | —— | 6 | *.03* | *gum* | (Domain 3b) |
| | —— | 5 | *.03* | *pila* | (Domain 3b) |
| | —— | 142 | *.79* | *kila* | (Domain 3b) |
| | —— | 149 | *.83* | *luva* | (Domain 3b) |
| | —— | 121 | *.67* | *mmwa* | (Domain 3b) |
| | —— | 2 | *.01* | *sipu* | (Domain 3b) |
| | —— | 2 | *.01* | *yulai/yule* | (Domain 3b) |
| | —— | 110 | *.61* | *uva* | (Domain 5) |
| | —— | 92 | *.51* | *kabulo2* | (Domain 7) |
| | —— | 1 | *.01* | *kubila* | (Domain 7) |
| | —— | 18 | *.10* | *bubu/bobu* | (Domain 8) |
| | —— | 130 | *.72* | *bubwa* | (Domain 8) |
| | —— | 16 | *.09* | *giwi* | (Domain 8) |
| | —— | 18 | *.10* | *ya* | (Domain 8) |
| | —— | 49 | *.27* | *vili* | (Domain 8) |
| | —— | 2 | *.01* | *kasa* | (Domain 9) |
| | —— | 7 | *.04* | *kavi* | (Domain 11) |
| | —— | 34 | *.19* | *oyla* | (Domain 11) |
| | —— | 5 | *.03* | *kwoila* | (Domain 11) |
| | —— | 9 | *.05* | *duya/kaduyo* | (Domain 14) |
| | —— | 1 | *.01* | *lilo* | (Domain 16) |
| | —— | 12 | *.07* | *meila* | (Domain 17) |

**Table 3.4.4b.** Domain 4: Relative frequencies interpreted as figures for the evaluation of CP types (in-domain and intradomain)

| | | | | | | |
|---|---|---|---|---|---|---|
| 1. | *kwe* 'thing' | 164 | | = 164 | (r.f. | *1.00)* |
| 2. | ke 'inanimate' | -/- (= not elicited in the test) | | | | |

**Table 3.4.5a.** Domain 5: Measure

| | | | | | | |
|---|---|---|---|---|---|---|
| (Domain 4) | *ke* | 110 | +++ | *uva* | 31 | |
| | | .61 | | | .17 | |
| (Domain 4) | *kwe* | 8 | +++ | | | |
| | | .04 | | | | |
| (Domain 12) | *tam* | 8 | +++ | | | |
| | | .04 | | | | |
| | | | | *yuma* | <1> | |

**Table 3.4.5b.** Domain 5: Relative frequencies interpreted as figures for the evaluation of CP types (in-domain and intradomain)

| | | | | | | |
|---|---|---|---|---|---|---|
| 1. | *ke* 'inanimates' | 110 | = | 110 | r.f. | .70 |
| 2. | *uva* 'span' | 31 | = | 31 | r.f. | .20 |
| 3. | *kwe* 'thing' | 8 | = | 8 | r.f. | .05 |
| 4. | *tam* 'sprouting' | 8 | = | 8 | r.f. | .05 |
| | | | | 157 | | *1.00* |
| 5. | yuma'length' | | -/- (=not elicited in the test) | | | |

provide an evaluation of the CP types that constitute this domain.

Table 3.4.5a documents that within Domain 5 there were 3 cases of in-domain substitution, affecting CPs that constitute Domains 4 (general CPs) and 12 (yams).

Table 3.4.5b presents all the CPs that constitute Domain 5 and gives the r.f.s for the production of the individual CP types within the entire domain.

On the basis of these two tables, I have formulated the following variable rules that speakers use in their production of CPs in Domain 5:

*If speakers want to refer to the concept 'span, measure, the span of two extended arms, from tip to tip', they use the special and appropriate CP uva only if they are persons of high status; the CP uva functions as a sociolinguistic variable (r.f. .17). Usually the general CP ke (r.f. .61) is used in this context. It is also possible, although rather rarely observed, to use the other general CP kwe (r.f. .04) or the CP tam (r.f. .04; here, the speaker intends to refer to a "kuvi"-type of long yams that are measured in such a way, thus emphasizing the item measured).*

*This domain also includes the CP yuma to refer to the concept "length, measure; the span of two extended arms from the fingertips of one hand to the wrist of the other hand'.* However, this CP type was not elicited in the test. It was used only once in my corpus of transcribed Kilivila speech data. Thus, we have no comparative value to describe the position of this CP type within Domain 5 (see also section 3.3.3.2).

Table 3.4.5b shows that the two CPs *ke* (=*ke3*) and *uva* are the most important CPs in Domain 5. I should note here that the CP 0 could also be included as one of the CP types in Domain 5. However, it could also be argued that the zero classifier actually belongs to Domain 3b. I decided to place the zero classifier in Domain 12. This CP illustrates the difficulties inherent in grouping classifiers into semantic domains (see section 3.3.4.1).

Tables 3.4.6a and b attempt to present the dynamics of Domain 6 and provide an evaluation of the CP types that constitute this domain.

Table 3.4.6a documents that within Domain 6 there were 3 cases of intradomain substitution and 6 cases of in-domain substitution affecting CPs in Domains 3b (quantities) and 4 (general CPs).

**Table 3.4.6a.** Domain 6: Time

In-domain substitution

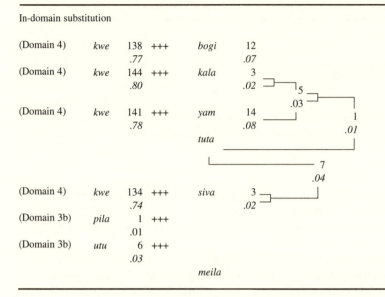

| (Domain 4) | kwe | 138 +++ | bogi | 12 |
| | | .77 | | .07 |
| (Domain 4) | kwe | 144 +++ | kala | 3 |
| | | .80 | | .02 |
| (Domain 4) | kwe | 141 +++ | yam | 14 |
| | | .78 | | .08 |
| | | | tuta | |
| (Domain 4) | kwe | 134 +++ | siva | 3 |
| | | .74 | | .02 |
| (Domain 3b) | pila | 1 +++ | | |
| | | .01 | | |
| (Domain 3b) | utu | 6 +++ | | |
| | | .03 | | |
| | | | meila | |

**Table 3.4.6b.** Domain 6: Relative frequencies interpreted as figures for the evaluation of CP types (in-domain and intradomain)

| 1. | kwe 'thing' | 138 + 144 + 134 + 141 | = | 557 | r.f. | .91 |
|----|----|----|----|----|----|----|
| 2. | yam 'day' | 14 + 5 | = | 19 | r.f. | .03 |
| 3. | bogi 'night' | 12 | = | 12 | r.f. | .02 |
| 4. | tuta 'time' | 8 | = | 8 | r.f. | .01 |
| 5. | utu 'fragment' | 6 | = | 6 | r.f. | .01 |
| 6. | kala 'day' | 3 | = | 3 | r.f. | .01 |
| 7. | siva 'time' | 3 | = | 3 | r.f. | .01 |
| 8. | pila 'part' | 1 | = | 1 | r.f. | .002 |
| | | | | 609 | | 1.002 |
| 9. | meila 'part of a day'  -/- (=not elicited in the test) | | | | | |

Table 3.4.6b presents the CP types that constitute this domain and gives the r.f.s for the production of the CP types within the entire domain.

On the basis of these two tables, I have formulated the following variable rules that speakers use in their production of CPs in Domain 6:

*If speakers want to refer to the concept 'night', they usually use the general CP kwe (r.f. .77). Only if they are persons of high status, do they use the special and most appropriate CP bogi (r.f. .07); bogi functions as a sociolinguistic variable (see section 3.3.3.2).*

*If speakers want to refer to the concept 'day', they usually use the general CP kwe (r.f. 80). The special and appropriate CP kala is only very rarely used (r.f. .02). Here, it is also possible, although rather rarely observed, to* use the CP *tuta* (*r.f. .01*), *including the more specific concept 'day' into the more general concept 'time'. Moreover, speakers of high status may also use the second special and appropriate CP yam (= yam1); however, the use of this CP is rather rarely observed (r.f. .03). This holds also for the use of this sociolinguistic variable if it is observed separately: The use of the CP yam—referring to the concept 'day'—is only rather rarely observed (r.f. .08); here, again, most speakers use the general CP kwe (r.f. .78).*

*If speakers want to refer to the concept 'time', they usually use the general CP kwe (r.f. .74). The production of the two special and appropriate CPs tuta (r.f. .04) and siva (r.f. .02) is only rather rarely observed. It is also possible, although rare, to produce the CPs utu (r.f. .03; here, the speaker may intend to refer to 'parts, fragments of time') and pila (r.f. .01; here, the speaker may intend to refer to 'parts, pieces of time') in this context. However, the use of these two CPs is somewhat idiosyncratic.*

I should note here that this semantic domain also includes the CP type *meila* to refer to the concept 'part of a day'. However, this meaning of the CP *meila* was neither elicited in the test, nor observed in my corpus of transcribed Kilivila speech data. I discovered the meaning of *meila* during my lexicographic work with consultants. Table 3.4.6b shows that the general CP *kwe* dominates Domain 6.

Tables 3.4.7a and b attempt to present the dynamics of Domain 7 and provide an evaluation of the CP types that constitute this domain.

Table 3.4.7a documents that within Domain 7 there was only 1 case of intradomain substitution and 13 cases of in-domain substitution, affecting CPs that constitute Domains 3b (quantities), 4 (general CPs), and 9 (shape).

Table 3.4.7b presents the CP types that constitute this domain and gives the r.f.s for the production of the CP types within the domain as a whole.

On the basis of these two tables, I have formulated the following variable rules that speakers use in their production of CPs in Domain 7:

*If speakers want to refer to the concept 'village sector, area of authority', they use the special and appropriate CP kabulo2/kabulu (r.f. .12) only if they are persons of high status; the CP kabulo2/kabulu functions as a sociolinguistic variable. To refer to this concept, speakers usually use either the general CP ke (r.f. .51) or, although less frequently, the general CP kwe (r.f. .22). It is also possible, although rather rarely observed, to produce the CP utu (r.f. .01).*

*If speakers want to refer to the concept 'place, area, village', they use the general CP kwe (r.f. .85). The special and appropriate CP vilo seems to have become obsolete; this CP is no longer observed in actual speech.*

*If speakers want to refer to the concept 'sea portions, ownership division with reference to fishing rights', they usually use the general CP kwe (r.f. .76). It is also possible, although rather rarely observed, to use the CP bwalita (r.f. .03), if the speaker is a person of high status, or to use the CP utu (r.f. .02), although the CP utu in this context is somewhat idiosyncratic. The special and appropriate CP siwa seems to have become obsolete; the realization of this CP is no longer observed in actual speech production.*

*If speakers want to refer to the concept 'large land plot', they usually use*

**Table 3.4.7a.** Domain 7: Place

In-domain substitution

| | | | | | |
|---|---|---|---|---|---|
| (Domain 4) | *ke* | 92 .51 | +++ | *kabulo2/kabulu* | 21 .12 |
| (Domain 4) | *kwe* | 40 .22 | +++ | | |
| (Domain 3b) | *utu* | 1 .01 | +++ | | |
| (Domain 4) | *kwe* | 153 .85 | +++ | *vilo* | — |
| | | | | *bwalita* ⎤ | |
| | | | | | 6 .03 |
| (Domain 4) | *kwe* | 137 .76 | +++ | *siwa* ⊐ ⎦ | |
| (Domain 3b) | *utu* | 3 .02 | +++ | | |
| (Domain 4) | *kwe* | 53 .29 | +++ | *kubila/kwabila* | 94 .52 |
| (Domain 4) | *ke* | 1 .01 | +++ | | |
| (Domain 3b) | *pila* | 1 .01 | +++ | | |
| (Domain 4) | *kwe* | 124 .69 | +++ | *nunu* | 21 .12 |
| (Domain 3b) | *utu* | 2 .01 | +++ | | |
| (Domain 9) | *kabulo1* | 3 .02 | +++ | | |
| (Domain 4) | *kwe* | 132 .73 | +++ | *koya/kwoya* | 26 .14 |
| | | | | *dumia* | <1> |
| | | | | *na3* | <4> |

*the special and appropriate CP kubila/kwabila (r.f. .52). The general CP kwe (r.f. .29) is also produced in this context. Moreover, it is also possible, although rather rarely observed, to produce the general CP ke (r.f. .01) or the CP pila (r.f. .01).*

*If speakers want to refer to the concept 'corner(s) of a garden', they use the special and appropriate CP nunu (r.f. .12) only if they are persons of high status. To refer to this concept, the general CP kwe (r.f. .69) is usually used. It is also possible, although rather rarely observed, to use the CP kabulo1/kabulu (r.f. .02; here the speaker may intend to refer to the way in which the corners of a garden are marked), or to use the CP utu (r.f. .01) in this context.*

**Table 3.4.7b.** Domain 7: Relative frequencies interpreted as figures for the evaluation of CP types (in-domain and intradomain)

| 1. | *kwe* 'thing' | 40 + 153 + 137 + 53 + 124 + 132 | = | 639 | r.f. | *.70* |
|----|----|----|----|----|----|----|
| 2. | *kubila* 'land plot' | 94 | = | 94 | r.f. | *.10* |
| 3. | *ke* 'inanimates' | 92 + 1 | = | 93 | r.f. | *.10* |
| 4. | *koya* 'mountain' | 26 | = | 26 | r.f. | *.03* |
| 5. | *kabulo2* 'sector' | 21 | = | 21 | r.f. | *.02* |
| 6. | *nunu* 'corner' | 21 | = | 21 | r.f. | *.02* |
| 7. | *utu* 'part' | 1 + 3 + 2 | = | 6 | r.f. | *.01* |
| 8. | *bwalita* 'sea' | 6 | = | 6 | r.f. | *.01* |
| 9. | *kabulo1* 'point' | 3 | = | 3 | r.f. | *.003* |
| 10. | *pila* 'part' | 1 | = | 1 | r.f. | *.001* |
|   |   |   |   | 910 |   | *.994* |

| 11. | *siwa* 'sea portion' | 0 (= not realized) |
|----|----|----|
| 12. | *dumia* 'swamp' | -/- (= not elicited in the test) |
| 13. | *na3* 'stars, moon' | -/- |
| 14. | *liku* 'authority area' | -/- |
| 15. | *va/vaya* 'river, creek' | -/- |

*If speakers want to refer to the concept 'mountain, hill', they only use the special and appropriate CP koya/kwoya (r.f. .14) if they are persons of high status. To refer to this concept, the general CP kwe (r.f. .73) is most often produced.*

*Domain 7 also include the CP dumia to refer to the concept 'swamp' and the CP na to refer to the concept 'stars, planets, moon' (=na3).* However, these two CPs were not elicited in the test, and thus we have no comparative values to describe the position of these CPs within Domain 7. *Moroever, I should note that Domain 7 also includes the CP liku to refer to the concept 'area of authority' and the CP va/vaya/vayo to refer to the concept 'river, creek, sea passage'.* However, the meanings of these CPs were not elicited in the test; they are the result of my lexicographic work. Table 3.4.7b shows that Domain 7 is also dominated by the general CP *kwe.*

Tables 3.4.8a and b attempt to present the dynamics of Domain 8 and provide an evaluation of the CP types that constitute this domain.

Table 3.4.8a documents that within Domain 8 there were 3 cases of intradomain substitution and 19 cases of in-domain substitution, affecting CPs in Domains 3b (quantities), 4 (general CPs), 9 (shape), and 10 (trees, wood, wooden things).

There were also 14 cases of off-domain substitution, affecting CPs in Domains 1b (body parts), 3b (quantities), 9 (shape), 10 (trees), 11 (utensils), 14 (door, window, entrance), and 16 (journey, road).

Table 3.4.8b presents the CP types that constitute Domain 8 and gives the r.f.s for the production of the individual CP types within the entire domain.

**Table 3.4.8a.** Domain 8: Qualities

| In-domain substitution | | | | | Off-domain substitution | | | |
|---|---|---|---|---|---|---|---|---|
| (Domain 4) | ke | 16 .09 | +++ | giwi | 106 .59 | | | |
| (Domain 4) | kwe | 11 .06 | +++ | | | | | |
| (Domain 9) | kasa | 3 .02 | +++ | | | | | |
| (Domain 4) | kwe | 23 .13 | +++ | pwanina/pona | 140 .78 | | 1 .01 | |
| (Domain 4) | ke | 130 .72 | +++ | nigwa bubwa | 16 .09 | | 8 .04 | utu (Domain 3b) |
| (Domain 4) | kwe | 1 .01 | +++ | | | | | |
| (Domain 10) | bwa | 16 .09 | +++ | | | | | |
| (Domain 3b) | utu | 2 .01 | +++ | | 2 .01 | | | |
| (Domain 4) | kwe | 28 .16 | +++ | bubu/bobu/bobo | 68 .38 | | | |
| (Domain 4) | ke | 18 .10 | +++ | | 4 .02 | | | |
| (Domain 10) | bwa | 3 .02 | +++ | | | | | |
| (Domain 4) | ke | 18 .10 | +++ | ya | 12 .07 | | 101 .26 | gili (Domain 9) |
| (Domain 3b) | pila | 4 .02 | +++ | | | | 60 .33 | pila (Domain 3b) |
| (Domain 3b) | si | 14 .08 | +++ | | | | 14 .08 | bukwa (Domain 3b) |
| (Domain 10) | sisi | 109 .61 | +++ | | | | 6 .03 | gum (Domain 3b) |
| | | | | | | | 7 .04 | sipu (Domain 3b) |
| | | | | | | | 1 .01 | yam/yama (Domain 1b) |
| | | | | | | | 6 .03 | sisi (Domain 10) |
| | | | | | | | 1 .01 | peta/ta (Domain 11) |
| | | | | | | | 45 .12 | duya/kaduyo (Domain 14) |
| | | | | | | | 16 .09 | lilo (Domain 16) |
| (Domain 4) | ke | 49 .27 | +++ | vili | 68 .38 | | 4 .02 | si (Domain 3b) |

**Table 3.4.8a.** *(continued)*

| In-domain substitution | | | | Off-domain substitution | | |
|---|---|---|---|---|---|---|
| (Domain 4) | *kwe* | 4 | +++ | —— | 1 | *pila* |
| | | .02 | | | .01 | (Domain 3b) |
| (Domain 3b) | *utu* | 30 | +++ | —— | 3 | *gili* |
| | | .17 | | | .02 | (Domain 9) |
| (Domain 10) | *bwa* | 2 | +++ | | | |
| | | .01 | | | | |

**Table 3.4.8b.** Domain 8: Relative frequencies interpreted as figures for the evaluation of CP types (in-domain and intradomain)

| | | | | | | |
|---|---|---|---|---|---|---|
| 1. | *ke3* 'inanimates' | 18 + 130 + 16 + 18 + 49 | = | 231 | r.f. | .26 |
| 2. | *pwanina* 'hole' | 140 | = | 140 | r.f. | .16 |
| 3. | *sisi* 'bough' | 109 | = | 109 | r.f. | .12 |
| 4. | *giwi* 'cut' | 106 | = | 106 | r.f. | .12 |
| 5. | *bubu* 'cut across' | 68 | = | 68 | r.f. | .08 |
| 6. | *vili* 'untwisted' | 68 | = | 68 | r.f. | .08 |
| 7. | *kwe* 'thing' | 28 + 1 + 11 + 23 + 4 | = | 67 | r.f. | .07 |
| 8. | *utu* 'scrap' | 2 + 30 | = | 32 | r.f. | .04 |
| 9. | *bwa* 'tree' | 3 + 16 + 2 | = | 21 | r.f. | .02 |
| 10. | *bubwa* 'cut off' | 16 + 2 | = | 18 | r.f. | .02 |
| 11. | *ya* 'flexible' | 12 + 4 | = | 16 | r.f. | .02 |
| 12. | *si* 'small bit' | 14 | = | 14 | r.f. | .02 |
| 13. | *pila* 'part' | 4 | = | 4 | r.f. | .004 |
| 14. | *kasa* 'row' | 3 | = | 3 | r.f. | .003 |
| 15. | *nigwa* 'hole' | 1 | = | 1 | r.f. | .001 |
| | | | | 898 | | 1.018 |

On the basis of these two tables, I have formulated the following variable rules that speakers use in their production of CPs in Domain 8:

*If speakers want to refer to the concept 'cut', they usually use the special and appropriate CP giwi (r.f. .59). It is also possible, although not often observed, to use the general CPs ke (r.f. .09) and kwe (r.f. .06) and the CP kasa (r.f. .02; here, the speaker may intend to refer to 'something cut in rows'); however, the production of the CP kasa in this context is somewhat idiosyncratic.*

*If speakers want to refer to the concept 'punctured, something with a hole in it, hole', they usually use the special and appropriate CP pwanina/pona (r.f. .78). It is also possible to use the general CP kwe (r.f. .13) or the almost synonymous CP nigwa (r.f. .01); however, nigwa is only rather rarely observed.*

*If speakers want to refer to the concept 'cut across, parts cut off', they use the special and appropriate CP bubwa only if they are persons of high status (r.f. .09). To refer to this concept, speakers most often use the general CP ke (r.f. .72). It is also possible, although not often observed, to use the CP bwa (r.f. .09; here, the speaker may intend to refer to 'wooden parts cut off', emphasizing the wooden quality of these parts), the CP utu (r.f. .01), and the general CP kwe (r.f. .01) in this context.*

*If speakers want to refer to the concept 'cut across, cut transversely, block cut off', they usually use the special and appropriate CP bubu/bobu/bobo (r.f. .38). The two general CPs kwe (r.f. .16) and ke (r.f. .10) are found less frequently in this context. It is also possible, although rather rarely observed, to use the CPs bwa (r.f. .02; here, the speaker may intend to refer to a 'block of wood cut off'), ya (r.f. .02; here, the speaker may intend to refer to 'flexible things that are cut'), and, if the speaker is a person of high status, the almost synonymous CP bubwa (r.f. .01).*

*If speakers want to refer to the concept 'flexible things, thin things', they only rather rarely use the special and appropriate CP ya (r.f. .07). To refer to this concept, the CP sisi (r.f. .61) is most often used; here, the speakers obviously extend the meaning of the CP sisi. Moreover, it is also possible, although not so often if not rather rarely observed, to produce the general CP ke (r.f. .10), the CP si (r.f. .08; here, the speaker may intend to refer to the concept 'a small bit of a thin, flexible thing'), and the CP pila (r.f. .02; here, the speaker may intend to refer to the concept 'a part of a thin, flexible thing') in this context.*

*If speakers want to refer to the concept 'untwisted', they use the special and appropriate CP vili (r.f. .38) more often than the general CP ke (r.f. .27) and the CP utu (r.f. .17; here the speaker may intend to refer to the concept 'untwisted particles, fragments, parts cut off', emphasing their untwisted quality). It is also possible, although rather rarely observed, to use the CPs kwe (r.f. .02) and bwa, although bwa is somewhat idiosyncratic in this context.*

Table 3.4.8b shows that the CPs *ke3, pwanina/pona, sisi*, as well as *bubu/bobu/bobo, vili,* and *kwe* are the most important CPs in Domain 8.

Tables 3.4.9a and b attempt to present the dynamics of Domain 9 and provide an evaluation of the CP types that constitute this domain.

Table 3.4.9a documents that within Domain 9 there were 2 cases of intradomain substitution and 9 cases of in-domain substitution, affecting CPs in Domains 3b (quantities), 4 (general CPs), 8 (qualities), 10 (trees, wood, wooden things), and 19 (dress, adornment).

There were also 7 cases of off-domain substitution, affecting Domains 3a and b (quantities), 7 (place), 8 (qualities), and 17 (texts).

Table 3.4.9b presents the CP types that constitute Domain 9 and gives the r.f.s for the production of the individual CPs within the entire domain.

On the basis of these two tables, I have formulated the following variable rules that speakers use in their production of CPs in Domain 9:

*If speakers want to refer to the concept 'protuberances', they do not use the special and appropriate CP kabulo1; instead, they usually use the CP ke2 (r.f. .59). The CP utu is also used in this context (r.f. .21; here, the speaker may intend to refer to a 'protuberant part'). Moreover, it is possible, although rather rarely observed, to use the CP bwa in this context (r.f. .02; here, the speaker may intend to refer to 'proturberant wooden things').*

**Table 3.4.9a.** Domain 9: Shape

| In-domain substitution | | | | | | Off-domain substitution | | |
|---|---|---|---|---|---|---|---|---|
| | | | | ke2 ⌐ .107 .59 | | | | |
| (Domain 10) | bwa | 3 .02 | +++ | kabulo1 | | — 3 .02 | nunu (Domain 7) | |
| (Domain 3b) | utu | 38 .21 | +++ | | | | | |
| (Domain 4) | ke | 2 .01 | +++ | kasa | 139 .77 | — 10 .06 | meila (Domain 17) | |
| (Domain 4) | kwe | 9 .05 | +++ | | | — 3 .02 | nina (Domain 17) | |
| | | | | | | — 3 .02 | giwi (Domain 8) | |
| | | | | | | — 3 .02 | gum (Domain 3b) | |
| | | | | | | — 1 .01 | yuva (Domain 3a) | |
| | | | | | | — 2 .01 | deli (Domain 3a) | |
| | | | | 3 .02 | | | | |
| (Domain 4) | kwe | 29 .16 | +++ | gili | 12 .07 | | | |
| (Domain 8) | vili | 3 .02 | +++ | | | | | |
| (Domain 8) | ya | 101 .56 | +++ | | | | | |
| (Domain 19) | vakala | 2 .01 | +++ | | | | | |
| (Domain 4) | kwe | 33 .18 | +++ | nutu/notu | 103 .57 | | | |

**Table 3.4.9b.** Domain 9: Relative frequencies interpreted as figures for the evaluation of CP types (in-domain and intradomain)

| | | | | | | |
|---|---|---|---|---|---|---|
| 1. | kasa 'row, line' | 139 + 3 | = | 142 | r.f. | .24 |
| 2. | ke2 'rigid, long' | 107 | (= | 107 | r.f. | .18) |
| | ke3 'inanimates' | 2 | (= | 2 | r.f. | .003) |
| | | +109 | = | 109 | r.f. | .19 |
| 3. | notu 'kneaded/dot' | 103 | = | 103 | r.f. | .18 |
| 4. | ya 'flexible/thin' | 101 | = | 101 | r.f. | .17 |
| 5. | kwe 'thing' | 9 + 29 + 33 | = | 71 | r.f. | .12 |
| 6. | utu 'scrap' | 38 | = | 38 | r.f. | .06 |
| 7. | gili 'row' | 12 | = | 12 | r.f. | .02 |
| 8. | vili 'untwisted' | 3 | = | 3 | r.f. | .005 |
| 9. | bwa 'tree' | 3 | = | 3 | r.f. | .005 |
| 10. | vakala 'belt' | 2 | = | 2 | r.f. | .003 |
| | | | | 585 | | .99 |

If speakers want to refer to the concept 'row, line', they usually use the special and appropriate CP kasa (r.f. .77). It is also possible, although rather rarely observed, to use the general CPs kwe (r.f. .05) and ke (r.f. .01) in this context.

If speakers want to refer to the concept 'row', they use the special and appropriate CP gili only if they are of high status (r.f. .07). To refer to this concept, a speaker usually uses the CP ya (r.f. .56; here the speaker may intend to emphasize the flexible quality of a row). Another possibility is to use the general CP kwe, of course (r.f. .16). Moreover, it is also possible, although rather rarely observed, to use the CP vili (r.f. .02; here the speaker may intend to refer to a 'row brought into an untwisted line'), the almost synonymous CP kasa (r.f. .02), or the CP vakala (r.f. .01); however, vakala in this context is somewhat idiosyncratic.

If speakers want to refer to the concept 'kneaded things, dot, drop', they usually use the special and appropriate CP nutu/notu (r.f. .57). It is also possible to use the general CP kwe (r.f. .18) in this context.

Table 3.4.9b shows that the CPs kasa, ke3, nutu/notu, ya, and kwe play the most important roles within Domain 9.

Tables 3.4.10a and b attempt to present the dynamics of Domain 10 and provide an evaluation of the CPs that constitute this domain.

Table 3.4.10a documents that within Domain 10 there were 5 cases of intradomain substitution and 2 cases of in-domain substitution, affecting CPs in Domains 4 (general CPs) and 8 (qualities).

There were also 13 cases of off-domain substitution, affecting Domains 3b (quantities), 8 (qualities), 9 (shape), and 13 (part of a foodhouse/a canoe).

Table 3.4.10b presents the CP types that constitute Domain 10 and gives the r.f.s for the production of the individual CP types within the entire domain.

On the basis of these two tables, I have formulated the following variable rules that speakers use in their production of CPs in Domain 10:

If speakers want to refer to the concept 'wood, wooden things', they usually use the special and appropriate CP ke1 (r.f. .92). It is also possible, although

**Table 3.4.10a.** Domain 10: Tree, Wood, Wooden Thing

| In-domain substitution | | Off-domain substitution | |
|---|---|---|---|
| ke1 | 166 | —— 114 | sa |
| | .92 | .63 | (Domain 3b) |
| 2 | | —— 122 | bukwa |
| .01 | | .68 | (Domain 3b) |
| | | —— 53 | kabisi |
| | | .30 | (Domain 13) |
| | | —— 32 | liku |
| see sisi, lila | | .18 | (Domain 13) |
| luva below | | —— 36 | utu |
| | | .20 | (Domain 3b) |

**Table 3.4.10a.** *(continued)*

| In-domain substitution | | | | | Off-domain substitution | | |
|---|---|---|---|---|---|---|---|
| | | | └─ 155 | | | | |
| | | | .86 | | | | |
| | | | ┌─── *bwa* | 5 | ── | 20 | *utu* |
| | | | | .03 | | .11 | (Domain 3b) |
| | | | | | | 6 | *si* |
| | | | | | | .03 | (Domain 3b) |
| | | | | | | 16 | *bubwa* |
| | | | | | | .09 | (Domain 8) |
| | | | | | | 2 | *vili* |
| | | | | | | .01 | (Domain 8) |
| | | | | | | 3 | *kabulo1* |
| | | | │ | | | .02 | (Domain 9) |
| | | | *ke1* | | | 4 | *kabisi* |
| | | | 8 | | | .02 | (Domain 13) |
| | | | .04 | | | 3 | *bubu/bobu* |
| | | | └── ┐ | | | .02 | (Domain 8) |
| (Domain 8) | *ya* | 6 +++ | *sisi* | 140 | ── | 109 | *ya* |
| | | .03 │ | | .78 | | .61 | (Domain 8) |
| | | *ke1* | | | | | |
| | | 152 | | | | | |
| | | .84 | | | | | |
| | | └── ┐ | | | | | |
| | | │ *lila* | | | | | |
| | | *ke1* | | | | | |
| | | 149 | | | | | |
| | | .83 | | | | | |
| | | └── ┐ | | | | | |
| (Domain 4) | *kwe* | 2 +++ | *luva1* | 4 | | | |
| | | .01 | | .02 | | | |
| | | | *na4* | <3> | | | |

---

**Table 3.4.10b.** Domain 10: Relative frequencies interpreted as figures for the evaluation of CP types (in-domain and intradomain)

| | | | | | | |
|---|---|---|---|---|---|---|
| 1. | *ke1* 'wood' | 166 + 155 + 8 + | | | | |
| | | 152 + 149 + 114 | = | 744 | r.f. | .82 |
| 2. | *sisi* 'bough' | 140 | = | 140 | r.f. | .16 |
| 3. | *bwa* 'tree' | 5 + 2 | = | 7 | r.f. | .01 |
| 4. | *ya* 'flexible' | 6 | = | 6 | r.f. | .01 |
| 5. | *luva* 'wooden dish' | 4 | = | 4 | r.f. | .004 |
| 6. | *kwe* 'thing' | 2 | = | 2 | r.f. | .002 |
| | | | | 903 | | 1.006 |
| 7. | *lila* 'bough' | 0   (= not realized) | | | | |
| 8. | *na4* 'carving' | -/-   (= not elicited in the test) | | | | |

*rather rarely observed, to use the almost synonymous CP bwa (r.f. .01) in this context. However, bwa functions as a sociolinguistic variable and is thus only used by persons of high status.*

*If speakers want to refer to the concept 'trees, wooden things', they also usually use the CP kel (r.f. .86); the special and appropriate CP bwa is rather rarely produced and only by persons of high status (r.f. .03).*

*If speakers want to refer to the concept 'bough, cut-off part of a tree', they usually use the special and appropriate CP sisi (r.f. .78). It is also possible, although rather rarely observed, to use the CP ya (r.f. .03) in this context.*

*If speakers want to refer to the concept 'bough, branch', they use the CP kel (r.f. .84). The special and appropriate CP lila was not produced in the test; moreover, it did not occur in my corpus of transcribed Kilivila speech data.*

*If speakers want to refer to the concept 'wooden dishes', they usually use the CP kel (r.f. .83). Use of the special and appropriate CP luva (r.f. .02) is only rather rarely observed. It is also possible to refer to this concept with the general CP kwe (r.f. .01); however, the use of kwe in this context is only rather rarely observed.*

*Domain 10 also includes the CP na to refer to the concept 'carvings in human likeness' (=na4).* However, this meaning was not elicited in the test, and thus we have no comparative value to describe the position of this CP within Domain 10.

Table 3.4.10b shows that Domain 10 is dominated by the CP *kel* and that the only other CP that plays an important role within this domain is *sisi*.

Tables 3.4.11a and b attempt to present the dynamics of Domain 11 and provide an evaluation of the CP types that constitute this domain.

Table 3.4.11a documents that within Domain 11 there were 10 cases of in-domain substitution, affecting CPs in Domains 3b (quantities), 4 (general CPs), and 8 (qualities).

Table 3.4.11b presents the CP types that constitute Domain 11 and gives the r.f.s for the production of the individual CP types within the entire domain.

On the basis of these two tables, I have formulated the following variable rules that speakers use in their production of CPs in Domain 11:

*If speakers want to refer to the concept 'tool', they use either the special and appropriate CP kavi (r.f. .02), the general CPs ke (r.f. .04) and kwe (r.f. .03), or the CP pila (r.f. .01). However, the production of all these CPs and thus the reference to this concept is only very rarely observed; moreover, the use of pila in this context is rather idiosyncratic.*

*If speakers want to refer to the concept 'string', they produce either the general CP ke (r.f. .19) or, although less frequently, the general CP kwe (r.f. .08). It seems to be also possible to use the CP pila (r.f. .01) in this context; however, the use of pila in this context is rather idiosyncratic. The special and appropriate CP oyla occurred neither in the test nor in my corpus of transcribed Kilivila speech data (see also Domain 3a).*

*If speakers want to refer to the concept 'basket', they usually use the special and appropriate CP peta/ta (r.f. .88). The variant peta, however, is only used*

**Table 3.4.11a.** Domain 11: Utensils

In-domain substitution

| (Domain 4) | ke | 7 .04 | +++ | kavi | 3 .02 | |
|---|---|---|---|---|---|---|
| (Domain 4) | kwe | 6 .03 | +++ | | | |
| (Domain 3b) | pila | 1 .01 | +++ | | | |
| (Domain 4) | ke | 34 .19 | +++ | oyla (see also Domain 3a) | | |
| (Domain 4) | kwe | 14 .08 | +++ | | | |
| (Domain 3b) | pila | 2 .01 | +++ | | | |
| (Domain 4) | kwe | 1 .01 | +++ | peta/ta | 158 .88 | (= .04 + .84) |
| (Domain 8) | ya | 1 .01 | +++ | | | |
| (Domain 4) | kwe | 49 .27 | +++ | kwoila | 96 .53 | |
| (Domain 4) | ke | 5 .03 | +++ | | | |
| | | | | kauya | <8> | |

**Table 3.4.11b.** Domain 11: Relative frequencies interpreted as figures for the evaluation of CP types (in-domain and intradomain)

| 1. | peta/ta 'basket' | 158 | = | 158 | r.f. | .42 |
|---|---|---|---|---|---|---|
| 2. | kwoila 'clay pot' | 96 | = | 96 | r.f. | .25 |
| 3. | kwe 'thing' | 6+14+1+49 | = | 70 | r.f. | .19 |
| 4. | ke3 'inanimate' | 7+34+5 | = | 46 | r.f. | .12 |
| 5. | kavi 'tool' | 3 | = | 3 | r.f. | .01 |
| 6. | pila 'part' | 1+2 | = | 3 | r.f. | .01 |
| 7. | ya 'thin' | 1 | = | 1 | r.f. | .003 |
| | | | | 377 | | 1.003 |
| 8. | oyla 'string' | 0 | (= not realized) | | | |
| 9. | kauya 'utensil' | -/- | (= not elicited in the test) | | | |

*by persons of high status (r.f. .04). It is also possible, although rather rarely observed, to use the general CP kwe (r.f. .01) or the CP ya (r.f. .01).*

*If speakers want to refer to the concept 'clay pot, potlike', they usually use the special and appropriate CP kweila/kwela/kwai (r.f. .53). It is also possible* to use the general CP *kwe* (*r.f.* .27), and, although rather rarely observed, to use the general CP *ke* (*r.f.* .03).

This semantic domain also offers the expert wicker worker the CP *kauya* to refer to the concept 'fish trap, creel'. However, this CP was not elicited in the test, and thus we have no comparative value to describe the position of this CP type within Domain 11.

Table 3.4.11b shows that the CPs *peta/ta*, *kweila/kwela/kwai*, *kwe*, and *ke3* play the most important roles within Domain 11.

Tables 3.4.12a and b attempt to present the dynamics of Domain 12 and provide an evaluation of the CP types that constitute this domain.

Table 3.4.12a documents that within Domain 12 there was 1 case of in-domain substitution, affecting the general CP *kwe* of Domain 4, and 2 cases of intradomain substitution.

We also observe two cases of off-domain substitution, affecting Domains 3b (quantities) and 5 (measures).

Table 3.4.12b presents the CP types that constitute Domain 12 and gives the r.f.s for the production of the individual CP types within the entire domain.

**Table 3.4.12a.** Domain 12: Yam

| In-domain substitution | | | | Off-domain substitution | |
|---|---|---|---|---|---|
| | | *tam* | | —— 8 | *uva* |
| | | | | .04 | (Domain 5) |
| | | | | —— 28 | *gula* |
| | | | | .16 | (Domain 3b) |
| | | 34 | | | |
| | | .19 | | | |
| (Domain 4) | *kwe* 117 +++ | 0 | 2 | | |
| | .65 | | .03 | | |
| | | 1 | | | |
| | | .01 | | | |
| | | *tetu* | | | |

**Table 3.4.12b.** Domain 12: Relative frequencies interpreted as figures for the evaluation of CP types (in-domain and intradomain)

| | | | | | |
|---|---|---|---|---|---|
| 1. | *kwe* 'thing' | 117 | | r.f. | .76 |
| 2. | *tam* 'sprouting' | 34 | | r.f. | .22 |
| 3. | *0* 'basketful of yams' | 2 | | r.f. | .01 |
| 4. | *tetu* 'yams' | 1 | | r.f. | .01 |
| | | 154 | | | 1.00 |

On the basis of these two tables, I have formulated the following variable rules that speakers use in their production of CPs in Domain 12:

*If speakers want to refer to the concept 'yams, a basketful of yams', they usually use the general CP kwe (r.f. .65). The CP tam is also produced (r.f. .19; here the speakers have obviously broadened the concept of this CP from 'sprouting yams' to the general concept 'yams'). The use of the special and appropriate zero classifier (r.f. .03) to refer to the concept 'basketful of yams' is almost as rarely observed as the production of the CP tetu (r.f. .01) to refer to the concept 'yams'. However, it must be noted here that the zero classifier is only used with numerals when basketfuls of yams are counted.*

Table 3.4.12b shows that Domain 12 is dominated by the general CP *kwe* and that the only other CP type that plays an important role in this domain is *tam*, with a frame of reference that seems to be broadened to also encompass the general concept 'yams'.

I should note here that it may well be that the zero classifier is so closely associated with the ritual *dadodiga* (the festive filling of the yam houses just before the ceremonious harvest festival period *milamala*) that this CP is not produced in more profane situations and thus cannot be elicited in a language production test (for a discussion of this CP type, see also the description of Domain 5 given previously).

Tables 3.4.13a and b attempt to present the dynamics of Domain 13 and provide an evaluation of the CP types that constitute this domain.

Table 3.4.13a documents that within Domain 13 there were 7 cases of in-domain substitution, affecting CPs in Domains 3b (quantities), 4 (general CPs), and 10 (trees, wood, wooden things).

Table 3.4.13b presents the CP types that constitute Domain 13 and gives the r.f.s for the production of the individual CP types within the entire domain.

**Table 3.4.13a.** Domain 13: Part of a foodhouse/a canoe/a creel

In-domain substitution

| (Domain 10) | *kel* | 53<br>.29 | +++ | *kabisi* | 78<br>.43 |
| (Domain 4) | *kwe* | 10<br>.06 | +++ | | |
| (Domain 3b) | *pila* | 1<br>.01 | +++ | | |
| (Domain 3b) | *utu* | 4<br>.02 | +++ | | |
| (Domain 10) | *bwa* | 4<br>.02 | +++ | | |
| (Domain 4) | *kwe* | 55<br>.31 | +++ | *liku* | 71<br>.39 |
| (Domain 10) | *kel* | 32<br>.18 | +++ | | |

**Table 3.4.13b.** Domain 13: Relative frequencies interpreted as figures for the evaluation of CP types (in-domain and intradomain)

| 1. | *kel* 'wood' | 53 + 32 | = | 85 | r.f. | .28 |
|----|------|---------|---|-----|------|-----|
| 2. | *kabisi* 'compartment' | 78 | = | 78 | r.f. | .25 |
| 3. | *liku* 'compartment' | 71 | = | 71 | r.f. | .23 |
| 4. | *kwe* 'thing' | 10 + 55 | = | 65 | r.f. | .21 |
| 5. | *bwa* 'tree, wood' | 4 | = | 4 | r.f. | .01 |
| 6. | *utu* 'part' | 4 | = | 4 | r.f. | .01 |
| 7. | *pila* 'part' | 1 | = | 1 | r.f. | .003 |
| | | | | 308 | | .993 |
| 8. | *lipu* 'compartment/creel' | -/- (= not elicited in the test) | | | | |

On the basis of these two tables, I have formulated the following variable rules that speakers use in their production of CPs in Domain 13:

*If speakers want to refer to the concept 'compartment of a foodhouse, section/division in a foodhouse', they usually use the special and appropriate CP type kabisi (r.f. .43). The CP kel (r.f. .29) is also used in this context, but less frequently. Moreover, it is also possible, although rather rarely observed, to refer to this concept with the CPs kwe (r.f. .06), bwa (r.f. .02), utu (r.f. .02), and pila (r.f. .02).*

*If speakers want to refer to the concepts 'compartment of a canoe, compartment of a foodhouse', they use the special and appropriate CP liku only if they are persons of status (r.f. .39). Otherwise, the general CP kwe (r.f. .31) or, although less frequently, the CP kel (r.f. .18) is used.*

*Domain 13 also offers the expert wicker worker the CP lipu to refer to the concept 'compartment of a creel'. However, this CP was not elicited in the test, and thus we have no comparative value to describe the position of lipu within Domain 13.*

Table 3.4.13b shows that the CPs *kel, kabisi, liku,* and *kwe* play the most important roles within Domain 13.

(Tables 3.4.14a and b attempt to present the dynamics of Domain 14 and provide an evaluation of the CP types that constitute this domain.

Table 3.4.14a documents that within Domain 14 there was 1 case of intradomain substitution and 4 cases of in-domain substitution, affecting CPs in Domains 4 (general CPs), 8 (qualities), and 16 (road, journey).

Table 3.4.14b presents the CPs that constitute Domain 14 and gives the r.f.s for the production of the individual types within the entire domain.

On the basis of these two tables, I have formulated the following variable rules that speakers use in their production of CPs in Domain 14:

*If speakers want to refer to the concept 'door entrance', they use the special and appropriate CP type duya/kaduyo only if they are persons of high status (r.f. .05). Only women of high status use the CP va/vaya/vayo (in its first meaning 'door') to refer to this concept (r.f. .05). Speakers usually use the CP kada/keda (r.f. .51), obviously broadening the frame of reference of this*

**Table 3.4.14a.** Domain 14: Door, entrance, window

In-domain substitution

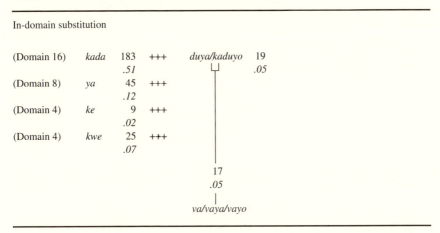

| (Domain 16) | *kada* | 183 .51 | +++ | *duya/kaduyo* | 19 .05 |
| (Domain 8) | *ya* | 45 .12 | +++ | | |
| (Domain 4) | *ke* | 9 .02 | +++ | | |
| (Domain 4) | *kwe* | 25 .07 | +++ | | |

17
.05

*va/vaya/vayo*

**Table 3.4.14b.** Domain 14: Relative frequencies interpreted as figures for the evaluation of CP types (in-domain and intradomain)

| 1. | *kada* 'road, track' | 183 | r.f. | .61 |
|----|----------------------|-----|------|-----|
| 2. | *ya* 'flexible, thin' | 45 | r.f. | .15 |
| 3. | *kwe* 'thing' | 25 | r.f. | .08 |
| 4. | *duya/kaduyo* 'door, entrance' | 19 | r.f. | .06 |
| 5. | *va/vaya/vayo* 'window, door' | 17 | r.f. | .06 |
| 6. | *ke3* 'inanimates' | 9 | r.f. | .03 |
| | | 298 | | .99 |

*CP to encompass the general concept 'passage, way, opening'. It is also possible, although not very often observed for speakers to use the CPs ya (r.f. .12; doors are generally made of palm branches; they are thin and flexible), kwe (r.f. .07), and ke (r.f. .07).*

It should be noted here that one of the results of the elicitation test was that the formative *duya* and *kaduyo/kaduya* should be regarded as variants of a single CP type. However, I elicited the formatives *duya* and *kaduya/kaduyo* separately. Thus, the r.f.s given in the variable rule above are computed on the basis of a possible 360 tokens, in the ideal case.

Table 3.4.14b shows that Domain 14 is dominated by the CP *kada/keda*; however, probably only the general CP *ke* does not play a role within this domain.

Tables 3.4.15a and b attempt to present the dynamics of Domain 15 and provide an evaluation of the CP types that constitute this domain.

Table 3.4.15a documents that within Domain 15 there was 1 case of intradomain substitution and 2 cases of in-domain substitution, affecting the general CP *kwe* of Domain 4.

**Table 3.4.15a.** Domain 15: Fire, oven

In-domain substitution

| (Domain 4) | kwe | 1 +++ | kova | 158 |
|---|---|---|---|---|
| | | .01 | ⊔ | .88 |
| | | | 1 | |
| | | | .01 | |
| | | | ke4 | |
| (Domain 4) | kwe | 1 +++ | kumla | 162 |
| | | .01 | | .90 |

**Table 3.4.15b.** Domain 15: Relative frequencies interpreted as figures for the evaluation of CP types (in-domain and intradomain)

| 1. | kumla 'earth-oven' | 162 | = | 162 | r.f. | .50 |
|---|---|---|---|---|---|---|
| 2. | kova 'fire' | 158 | = | 158 | r.f. | .49 |
| 3. | kwe 'thing' | 1 + 1 | = | 2 | r.f. | .01 |
| 4. | ke4 'fire' | 1 | = | 1 | r.f. | .003 |
| | | | | 323 | | 1.003 |

Table 3.4.15b presents the CPs that constitute Domain 15 and gives the r.f.s for the production of the individual CP types within the entire domain.

On the basis of these two tables, I have formulated the following variable rules that speakers use in their production of CPs in Domain 15:

*If speakers want to refer to the concept 'fire, fireplace', they generally use the special and appropriate CP kova (r.f. .88). It is also possible, although rather rarely observed, to use the CP ke4, in its meaning 'fire' (r.f. .01) and to use the general CP kwe (r.f. .01).*

*If speakers want to refer to the concept 'earth oven', they generally use the special and appropriate CP kumla (r.f. .90). It is also possible, although rather rarely observed, to use the general CP kwe (r.f. .01) in this context.*

Table 3.4.15b shows that this domain is dominated by the CPs *kumla* and *kova*.

Tables 3.4.16a and b attempt to present the dynamics of Domain 16 and provide an evaluation of the CP types that constitute this domain.

Table 3.4.16a documents that within Domain 16 there was 1 case of intradomain substitution and 3 cases of in-domain substitution, affecting CPs in Domains 4 (general CPs) and 8 (qualities).

There was also 1 case of off-domain substitution, affecting Domain 14 (door, entrance, window); see the previous discussion of Domain 14.

**Table 3.4.16a.** Domain 16: Road, journey

| In-domain substitution | | | | | | | | Off-domain substitution |
|---|---|---|---|---|---|---|---|---|
| | | | | kada/keda | 152 | —— | 183 | duya/kaduyo |
| | | | | │ | .84 | | .51 | (Domain 14) |
| | | | | 1 | | | | |
| | | | | .01 | | | | |
| | | | | \|\| | | | | |
| (Domain 4) | kwe | 131 | +++ | lilo/lola | 7 | | | |
| | | .73 | | | .04 | | | |
| (Domain 4) | ke | 1 | +++ | | | | | |
| | | .01 | | | | | | |
| (Domain 8) | ya | 16 | +++ | | | | | |
| | | .09 | | | | | | |
| | | | | bililo | <4> | | | |
| | | | | kali | <1> | | | |

**Table 3.4.16b.** Domain 16: Relative frequencies interpreted as figures for the evaluation of CP types (in-domain and intradomain)

| | | | | | | |
|---|---|---|---|---|---|---|
| 1. | kada 'road, track' | 152 + 1 | = | 153 | r.f. | .50 |
| 2. | kwe 'thing' | 131 | = | 131 | r.f. | .43 |
| 3. | ya 'flexible, thin' | 16 | = | 16 | r.f. | .05 |
| 4. | lilo 'walk, journey' | 7 | = | 7 | r.f. | .02 |
| 5. | ke 'inanimates' | 1 | = | 1 | r.f. | .003 |
| | | | | 308 | | 1.003 |
| 6. | kali 'paddle strike' | -/- (= not elicited in the test) | | | | |
| 7. | bililo 'trip' | -/- | | | | |

Table 3.4.16b presents the CPs that constitute Domain 16 and gives the r.f.s for the production of the individual CP type within the entire domain.

On the basis of these two tables, I have formulated the following variable rules that speakers use in their production of CPs in Domain 16:

*If speakers want to refer to the concept 'road, track', they produce the special and appropriate CP kada/keda (r.f. .84).*

*If speakers want to refer to the concept 'walk, journey', they only very rarely use the special and appropriate CP lilo/lola (r.f. .04). Instead, speakers usually use the general CP kwe (r.f. .73). It is also possible, although not very often observed, for speakers to use the CPs ya (r.f. .09; here the speaker may intend to emphasize the narrowness of most paths on the islands), kada/keda (r.f. .01; here the speaker may intend to emphasize the road one uses on the journey or the trace one follows in one's walk), and the general CP ke (r.f. .01). However, ya and kada/keda in this context seem to be at least somewhat idiosyncratic.*

*Domain 16 also includes the CP bililo to refer to the concept 'trip' and the CP kali to refer to the concept 'paddle strike'.* However, these two CPs were not elicited in the test, and thus we have no comparative value to describe their position within Domain 16.

Table 3.4.16b shows that only the CPs *kada/keda* and *kwe* play a role within Domain 16.

Tables 3.4.17a and b attempt to present the dynamics of Domain 17 and provide an evaluation of the CP types that constitute this domain.

Table 3.4.17a documents that within Domain 17 there were 2 cases of intradomain substitution and 9 cases of in-domain substitution, affecting CPs in Domains 3b (quantities), 4 (general CPs), and 9 (shape).

Table 3.4.17b presents the CP types that constitute Domain 17 and gives the r.f.s for the production of the individual CP types within the entire domain.

On the basis of these two tables, I have formulated the following variable rules that speakers use in their production of CPs in Domain 17:

**Table 3.4.17a.** Domain 17: Text

In-domain substitution

|  |  |  |  |  |  |
|---|---|---|---|---|---|
|  |  |  |  | *megwa* |  |
|  |  |  |  | │ |  |
|  |  |  |  | 12 |  |
|  |  |  |  | .07 |  |
|  |  |  |  | │ │ |  |
| (Domain 3b) | *pila* | 67 | +++ | *nina* | 3 |
|  |  | .37 |  |  | .02 |
| (Domain 3b) | *utu* | 3 | +++ |  |  |
|  |  | .02 |  |  |  |
| (Domain 4) | *kwe* | 61 | +++ |  |  |
|  |  | .34 |  |  |  |
| (Domain 9) | *kasa* | 3 | +++ |  |  |
|  |  | .02 |  |  |  |
|  |  |  |  | *vosi* |  |
|  |  |  |  | │ |  |
|  |  |  |  | 18 |  |
|  |  |  |  | .10 |  |
|  |  |  |  | │ │ |  |
| (Domain 9) | *kasa* | 10 | +++ | *meila* | 3 |
|  |  | .06 |  |  | .02 |
| (Domain 4) | *ke* | 12 | +++ |  |  |
|  |  | .07 |  |  |  |
| (Domain 4) | *kwe* | 9 | +++ |  |  |
|  |  | .05 |  |  |  |
| (Domain 3b) | *pila* | 91 | +++ |  |  |
|  |  | .51 |  |  |  |
| (Domain 3b) | *utu* | 4 | +++ |  |  |
|  |  | .02 |  |  |  |
|  |  |  |  | (see also *sisi*) |  |

**Table 3.4.17b.** Domain 17: Relative frequencies interpreted as figures for the evaluation of CP types (in-domain and intradomain)

| | | | | | | |
|---|---|---|---|---|---|---|
| 1. | *pila* 'part, piece' | 67 + 91 | = | 158 | r.f. | .53 |
| 2. | *kwe* 'thing' | 61 + 9 | = | 70 | r.f. | .24 |
| 3. | *vosi* 'song' | 18 | = | 18 | r.f. | .06 |
| 4. | *kasa* 'row, line' | 3 + 10 | = | 13 | r.f. | .04 |
| 5. | *megwa* 'magic' | 12 | = | 12 | r.f. | .04 |
| 6. | *ke* 'inanimates' | 12 | = | 12 | r.f. | .04 |
| 7. | *utu* 'part, fragment' | 3 + 4 | = | 7 | r.f. | .02 |
| 8. | *nina* 'part of a song' | 3 | = | 3 | r.f. | .01 |
| 9. | meila 'part of a song' | 3 | = | 3 | r.f. | .01 |
| | | | | 296 | | .99 |

*If speakers want to refer to the general concept 'part(s) of a song', they only very rarely use the special and appropriate CP type nina (r.f. .02). Speakers usually use either the CP pila (r.f. .37) or the general CP kwe (r.f. .34) in this context. It is also possible, although not very often observed for speakers to use the CPs megwa (r.f. .07; here it should be noted that many magical formulae are recited in a way that resembles a song), utu (r.f. .02), and kasa (r.f. .02; here the speaker may intend to refer to a 'row/line of a song').*

*If speakers want to refer to the concept 'part of a song, of a magic formula', they only very rarely use the special and appropriate CP meila (r.f. .02). Speakers usually use the CP pila (r.f. .51) in this context. It is also possible, although not often observed, for speakers to use the CP vosi, if the speaker is a woman of high status (r.f. .10), to use the general CPs ke (r.f. .07) and kwe (r.f. .05), or to use the CPs kasa (r.f. .06; here the speaker may intend to refer to a 'row/line of a song/magical formula'), and utu (r.f. .02).*

It should be noted here that Domain 17 also includes the CP *sisi* to refer to the concept 'division of a magical formula'. However, this meaning was not elicited in the test; I only discovered it during lexicographic work with consultants. Thus, we have no comparative value to describe the position of *sisi* within Domain 17.

Table 3.4.17b shows that Domain 17 is dominated by the CP *pila* and that the only other CP that plays an important role is the general CP *kwe*.

Tables 3.4.18a and b attempt to present the dynamics of Domain 18 and provide an evaluation of the CP types that constitute this domain.

Table 3.4.18a documents that within Domain 18 there was 1 case of intradomain substitution and 1 case of in-domain substitution, affecting the general CP *kwe* of Domain 4.

Table 3.4.18b presents the CP types that constitute this domain and gives the r.f.s for the production of the individual CP types within the entire domain.

On the basis of these two tables, I have formulated the following variable rules that speakers use in their production of CPs in Domain 18:

**Table 3.4.18a.** Domain 18: Ritual items

---

In-domain substitution

```
                              beku
                               |
                               2
                              .01
                              | |
(Domain 4)     kwe      2 +++    kai           136
                       .01                     .76

                              sam           <7>
```

---

**Table 3.4.18b.** Domain 18: Relative frequencies interpreted as figures for
the evaluation of CP types (in-domain and intradomain)

---

| 1. | kai 'stone blade' | 136 | r.f. | .97 |
|----|----|----|----|----|
| 2. | beku 'stone blade' | 2 | r.f. | .01 |
| 3. | kwe 'thing' | 2 | r.f. | .01 |
|  |  | 140 |  | .99 |
| 4. | sam 'ginger' | -/- (= not elicited in the test) |  |  |

---

*If speakers want to refer to the concept 'stone blade', they generally produce
the special and appropriate CP kai (r.f. .76). It is also possible, although
rather rarely observed, to use the synonymous CP beku (r.f. .01) or the general
CP kwe (r.f. .01).*

*This domain also includes the CP sam to refer to the concept 'ginger' in
play accompanying verses; ginger plays an important role in Trobriand magic*
(see section 3.3.4.1). However, this CP type was not elicited in the text, and
thus we have no comparative value to describe the position of *sam* within
Domain 18.

Table 3.4.18b shows that Domain 18 is dominated by the CP *kai*.

Tables 3.4.19a and b attempt to present the dynamics of Domain 19 and
provide an evaluation of the CP types that constitute this domain.

Table 3.4.19a documents that within Domain 19 there was 1 case of
intradomain substitution and 1 case of in-domain substitution, affecting the
general CP *kwe* of Domain 4. There was also 1 case of off-domain substitution,
affecting Domain 9 (shape).

Table 3.4.19b presents the CP types that constitute Domain 19 and gives
the r.f.s for the production of the individual CP types within the entire
domain.

**Table 3.4.19a.** Domain 19: Dress, adornment

| In-domain substitution | | | | | Off-domain substitution | | |
|---|---|---|---|---|---|---|---|

```
                                       doba
                                        |
                                        1
                                       .01
                                        ||
(Domain 4)    kwe    145  +++    kudul        6
                     .81                     .03


                                 vakala    ____   2      gili
                                                  .01    (Domain 9)
```

**Table 3.4.19b.** Domain 19: Relative frequencies interpreted as figures for the evaluation of CP types (in-domain and intradomain)

| | | | | |
|---|---|---|---|---|
| 1. | *kwe* 'thing' | 145 | r.f. | .95 |
| 2. | *kudul* 'band of fibers' | 6 | r.f. | .04 |
| 3. | *doba* 'grass-skirt' | 1 | r.f. | .01 |
| | | 152 | | 1.00 |
| 4. | vakala 'belt' | 0 (= not realized within this domain; see Domain 9 above) | | |

On the basis of these two tables, I have formulated the following variable rules that speakers use in their production of CPs in Domain 19:

*If speakers want to refer to the concept 'band of fibers' (at the waistband of a grass skirt), they usually use the general CP kwe (r.f. .81). The use of the special and appropriate CP kudul (r.f. .03) is almost as rare as the more general CP doba (r.f. .01) in this context.*

*This domain also includes the CP vakala to refer to the concept 'belt of spondylus shell discs'.* However, this CP was only used in a rather idiosyncratic way to refer to the concept 'row' in Domain 9.

Table 3.4.19b shows that the general CP *kwe* dominates Domain 19.

Tables 3.4.20a and b attempt to present the dynamics of Domain 20 and provide an evaluation of the CP types that constitute this domain.

Table 3.4.20a documents that within Domain 20 there was 1 case of in-domain substitution, affecting the general CP *kwe* of Domain 4.

Table 3.4.20b presents the CP types that constitute Domain 20 and gives the r.f.s for the production of the individual CP types within the entire domain.

On the basis of these two tables, I have formulated the following variable rules that speakers use in their production of CPs in Domain 20:

*If speakers want to refer to the concept 'name', they generally produce the*

**Table 3.4.20a** Domain 20: Names

---

In-domain substitution

| (Domain 4) | *kwe* | 6 +++ | *iga/yegila* | 149 |
|---|---|---|---|---|
| | | .03 | (142)   (7) | .83 |
| | | | (.79)  (.04) | |

---

**Table 3.4.20b.** Domain 20: Relative frequencies interpreted as figures for the evaluation of CP types (in-domain and intradomain)

---

| 1. | *iga/yegila* 'name' | 142 + 7 | = | 149 | r.f. | .96 |
|---|---|---|---|---|---|---|
| 2. | *kwe* 'thing' | 6 | = | 6 | r.f. | .04 |
| | | | | 155 | | 1.00 |

---

*special and appropriate CP iga/yegila (r.f. .83). It is also possible although rather rarely observed, to use the general CP kwe (r.f. .03) in this context.*

Table 3.4.20b shows that Domain 20 is dominated by the CP *iga/yegila*.

Now that I have presented the dynamics of all 20 semantic domains and the rules that speakers may use in their production of CPs, it is time to reflect once again on the proceeding proposed in this section and to further define the concept "dynamic semantic domain".

My goal in this section has been to present the dynamics of the 20 semantic domains and to formulate language production rules that predict a speaker's choice of a certain CP type to refer to certain nominally expressed concept(s) of referents in the extralinguistic world. To reach this goal, I first defined the semantic domains by grouping together certain CPs, based primarily on common sense considerations that took into account ethnographic and sociological information about the speech community. This procedure provided the basis for describing what actually happens if a certain CP type is produced to refer to a given semantic concept. The observation of the processes that I have called intradomain and in-domain substitution and the weighting and evaluation of these processes by computing the relative frequency with which a certain CP is used within the domain as a whole resulted, on the one hand, in the formulation of variable rules, which I interpreted as rules that speakers use in their production of a certain CP type of the semantic domain, and, on the other hand, in an insight into the evaluated distribution of the individual CP types within each semantic domain.

The logic inherent in this proceeding can be summarized as follows:

*If speakers want to transform a given semantic concept into an appropriate CP to refer to this concept, they first must assign the semantic concept to the semantic domain that encompasses this concept.*

*Next, speakers must call in and activate the variable rule or rules that they use in their production of a certain CP type of this domain that refers to the concept given.*

*If the rule allows the production of more than one CP type in this context, they must decide which of the possible CP types is most appropriate for their purposes pursued in referring to the given concept. If they are persons of high status and if the variable rule activated includes a CP type that functions as a sociolinguistic variable, they must decide whether they want to use this CP with its sociolinguistic implications.*

*All these decision processes then lead to the production of the CP that the speakers assume to be most appropriate to refer to the given semantic concept and for the means and ends they want to pursue with their verbal reference.*

Thus, my attempt to predict a speakers's choice of a certain CP to refer to a certain nominal concept (or concepts) also emphasizes that, among other things, CPs must be understood as formatives that can be used *strategically* to serve certain means and ends a speaker wants to pursue and express. Moreover, my proceeding also emphasizes that semantic domains as those constituted by the CPs are not static at all. These *semantic domains are dynamic* and interact with each other. They can be understood as "program clusters, procedures, scripts" or "functional pathways" (see Pribram 1987:7–12) that speakers employ and rely on in their speech production.[11]

Before I discuss this important point in more detail (see chapter 6), I will summarize the data from Tables 3.4.1.1b to 3.4.20b (see Table 3.4.21).

Table 3.4.21 shows that the 20 semantic domains are connected or "short-circuited" by 18 CP types (two of which are represented with two different meanings each). As might be expected, the general CP *kwe* ( = *kwe1*) plays a role in 19 different semantic domains. The only domain where *kwe* does not play a role is Domain 2; however, here *kwe* in its meaning 'shells and clams' ( = *kwe2*) is one of the domain-constituting CPs. The other general CP *ke* ( = *ke3*) plays a role in 11 different semantic domains. The CP *ya* connects 8 and the CPs *pila* and *utu* each connect 7 semantic domains. The CP *bwa* plays a role in 5 domains, and the CP *kasa* occurs in 4 domains. The CPs *kel*, *tam*, and *vili* connect 3 domains each. Finally, the CPs *bubwa*, *kada*, *meila*, *na* ( = *na1 + na2*), *oyla*, *si*, *sisi*, *to/te* ( = *to/te2*), and *vakala* play a role in 2 domains each.

---

[11] In a heuristic phase of the analysis of the dynamics of these domains, I noted the cases of in-domain, intra-domain, and off-domain substitution for all 20 domains on a rather large sheet of paper. The result was a kind of "drawing" that looked like a mycelium. Any reader whose enthusiasm about Kilivila CPs equals that of the author can easily redraw this picture by putting the semantic domains described together and then connecting them according to the notation conventions marking the cases of in-domain and off-domain substitution.

**Table 3.4.21.** CPs and their semantic domains[†]

| CP | | Domains | No. of domains | r.f. |
|---|---|---|---|---|
| *beku* | 18 | Ritual items | 1 | *.01* |
| *bililo* | 16 | Road, journey | 1 | *-/-* |
| *bogi* | 6 | Time | 1 | *.02* |
| *bubu/bobu* | 8 | Qualities | 1 | *.08* |
| *bubwa* | 3b | Quantities | | *.004* |
| | 8 | Qualities | 2 | *.02* |
| *buda* | 3a | Quantities | | *.22* |
| | 3b | Quantities | 1 | *.001* |
| *bukwa* | 3b | Quantities | 1 | *.001* |
| *bwa* | 3b | Quantities | | *.01* |
| | 8 | Qualities | | *.02* |
| | 9 | Shape | | *.005* |
| | 10 | Trees, wood, wooden things | | *.01* |
| | 13 | Part of a foodhouse/canoe/creel | 5 | *.01* |
| *bwalita* | 7 | Place | 1 | *.01* |
| *deli* | 3a | Quantities | 1 | *.14* |
| *doba* | 19 | Dress, adornment | 1 | *.01* |
| *duli* | 3b | Quantities | 1 | *.05* |
| *dumia* | 7 | Place | 1 | *-/-* |
| *duya/kaduyo* | 14 | Entrance, window | 1 | *.06* |
| *gili* | 9 | Shape | 1 | *.02* |
| *giwi* | 8 | Qualities | 1 | *.12* |
| *guba* | 3b | Quantities | 1 | *.001* |
| *gudi* | 1a | Persons | 1 | *.29* |
| *gula* | 3b | Quantities | 1 | *.03* |
| *gum* | 3b | Quantities | 1 | *.04* |
| *iga/yegila* | 20 | Names | 1 | *.96* |
| *kabisi* | 13 | Part of a foodhouse/canoe/creel | 1 | *.25* |
| *kabulo* | | | | |
| *kabulo1* | 7 | Place | 1 | *.003* |
| *kabulo2* | 7 | Place | 1 | *.02* |
| *kada/keda* | 14 | Entrance, window | | *.61* |
| | 16 | Road, journey | 2 | *.50* |
| *kai* | 18 | Ritual items | 1 | *.97* |
| *ka'i* | 1b | Body parts | 1 | *.27* |
| *kala* | 6 | Time | 1 | *.01* |
| *kali* | 16 | Road, journey | 1 | *-/-* |
| *kapwa* | 3b | Quantities | 1 | *.02* |
| *kasa* | 3a | Quantities | | *.001* |
| | 3b | Quantities | | *.001* |
| | 8 | Qualities | | *.003* |

**Table 3.4.21.** *(continued)*

| CP | | Domains | No. of domains | r.f. |
|---|---|---|---|---|
| | 9 | Shape | | .24 |
| | 17 | Texts | 4 | .04 |
| *kauya* | 11 | Utensils | 1 | -/- |
| *kavi* | 11 | Utensils | 1 | .01 |
| *ke* | | | | |
| *ke1* | 3b | Quantities | | .13 |
| | 10 | Trees, wood, wooden things | | .82 |
| | 13 | Part of a foodhouse/canoe/creel | 3 | .28 |
| *ke2* | 9 | Shape | 1 | .18 |
| *ke3* | 1b | Body parts | | .02 |
| | 3a | Quantities | | .001 |
| | 3b | Quantities | | .15 |
| | 4 | General CPs | | -/-; 0 |
| | 5 | Measures | | .70 |
| | 7 | Place | | .10 |
| | 8 | Qualities | | .26 |
| | 9 | Shape | | .003 |
| | 11 | Utensils | | .12 |
| | 14 | Entrance, window | | .03 |
| | 16 | Road, journey | | .003 |
| | 17 | Texts | 11 | .04 |
| *ke4* | 15 | Fire, oven | 1 | .003 |
| *kila* | 3b | Quantities | 1 | .003 |
| *kova* | 15 | Fire, oven | 1 | .49 |
| *koya/kwoya* | 7 | Place | 1 | .03 |
| *kubila/kwabila* | 7 | Place | 1 | .10 |
| *kudu* | | | | |
| *kudu1* | 19 | Dress, adornment | 1 | .04 |
| *kudu2* | 1b | Body parts | 1 | .06 |
| *kumla* | 15 | Fire, oven | 1 | .50 |
| *kwe* | | | | |
| *kwe1* | 1b | Body parts | | .15 |
| | 3a | Quantities | | .26 |
| | 3b | Quantities | | .24 |
| | 4 | General CPs | | 1.00 |
| | 5 | Measures | | .05 |
| | 6 | Time | | .91 |
| | 7 | Place | | .70 |
| | 8 | Qualities | | .07 |
| | 9 | Shape | | .12 |
| | 10 | Trees, wood, wooden things | | .002 |
| | 11 | Utensils | | .12 |
| | 12 | Yams | | .76 |
| | 13 | Part of a foodhouse/canoe/creel | | .21 |
| | 14 | Entrance, window | | .08 |
| | 15 | Fire, oven | | .01 |
| | 16 | Road, journey | | .43 |

**Table 3.4.21.** *(continued)*

| CP | | Domains | No. of domains | r.f. |
|---|---|---|---|---|
| | 17 | Texts | | .24 |
| | 18 | Ritual items | | .01 |
| | 19 | Dress, adornment | | .95 |
| | 20 | Names | 19 | .04 |
| *kwe2* | 2 | Animals | 1 | -/- |
| *kweya* | 1b | Body parts | 1 | .47 |
| *kwoila/kweya* | 11 | Utensils | 1 | .25 |
| *liku* | 13 | Part of a foodhouse/canoe/creel | 1 | .23 |
| *lila* | 10 | Trees, wood | 1 | 0 |
| *lilo/lola* | 16 | Road, journey | 1 | .02 |
| *lipu* | 13 | Part of a foodhouse/canoe/creel | 1 | .-/- |
| *luba* | 3b | Quantities | 1 | .04 |
| *luva* | | | | |
| *luva1* | 10 | Trees, wood, wooden things | 1 | .004 |
| *luva2* | 3b | Quantities | 1 | .004 |
| *megwa* | 17 | Texts | 1 | .04 |
| *meila* | 6 | Time | | -/- |
| | 17 | Texts | 2 | .01 |
| *mmwa* | 3b | Quantities | 1 | .01 |
| *na* | | | | |
| *na1* | 1a | Persons | | .35 |
| | 3a | Quantities | 2 | .001 |
| *na2* | 2 | Animals | | 1.00 |
| | 3a | Quantities | 2 | .17 |
| *na3* | 7 | Place | 1 | -/- |
| *na4* | 10 | Wooden things | 1 | -/- |
| *na5* | 1 | Persons | 1 | -/- |
| *na6* | 1 | Persons | 1 | -/- |
| *nigwa* | 8 | Qualities | 1 | .001 |
| *nina* | 17 | Texts | 1 | .01 |
| *notu/nutu* | 9 | Shape | 1 | .18 |
| *nunu* | 7 | Place | 1 | .02 |
| *oyla* | 3a | Quantities | | 0 |
| | 11 | Utensils | 2 | 0 |
| *pila* | 3b | Quantities | | .04 |
| | 6 | Time | | .002 |
| | 7 | Place | | .001 |
| | 8 | Qualities | | .004 |
| | 11 | Utensils | | .01 |
| | 13 | Part of a foodhouse/canoe/creel | | .003 |
| | 17 | Texts | 7 | .53 |
| *po'ula* | 3b | Quantities | 1 | .03 |
| *pwanina/pona* | 8 | Qualities | 1 | .16 |
| *sa* | 3b | Quantities | 1 | .01 |

**Table 3.4.21.** *(continued)*

| CP | | Domains | No. of domains | r.f. |
|---|---|---|---|---|
| *sam* | 18 | Ritual items | 1 | -/- |
| *si* | 3b | Quantities | | .001 |
| | 8 | Qualities | 2 | .02 |
| *sipu* | 3b | Quantities | 1 | .04 |
| *sisi* | 8 | Qualities | | .12 |
| | 10 | Trees, wood, wooden things | 2 | .16 |
| *siva* | 6 | Time | 1 | .01 |
| *siwa* | 7 | Place | 1 | 0 |
| *suya* | 3a | Quantities | 1 | .13 |
| *talpeta* | 11 | Utensils | 1 | .42 |
| *tam* | 3b | Quantities | | .01 |
| | 5 | Measures | | .05 |
| | 12 | Yams | 3 | .22 |
| *tetu* | 12 | Yams | 1 | .01 |
| *tolte* | | | | |
|    *tolte1* | 1a | Persons | 1 | -/- |
|    *tolte2* | 1a | Persons | | .36 |
| | 1b | Body parts | | .01 |
| | 3a | Quantities | 2 | .02 |
| *tuta* | 6 | Time | 1 | .01 |
| *utu* | 3b | Quantities | | .10 |
| | 6 | Time | | .01 |
| | 7 | Place | | .01 |
| | 8 | Qualities | | .04 |
| | 9 | Shape | | .06 |
| | 13 | Part of a foodhouse/canoe/creel | | .01 |
| | 17 | Texts | 7 | .02 |
| *uva* | 5 | Measures | 1 | .20 |
| *valvayalvayo* | 14 | Entrance, window | 1 | .06 |
| *vakala* | 9 | Shape | | .003 |
| | 19 | Dress, adornment | 2 | 0 |
| *vili* | 3b | Quantities | | .002 |
| | 8 | Qualities | | .08 |
| | 9 | Shape | 3 | .005 |
| *vosi* | 17 | Texts | 1 | .06 |
| *wela* | 3a | Quantities | 1 | .06 |
| *ya* | 1b | Body parts | | .002 |
| | 3b | Quantities | | .04 |
| | 8 | Qualities | | .02 |
| | 9 | Shape | | .17 |
| | 10 | Trees, wood, wooden things | | .01 |
| | 11 | Utensils | | .003 |
| | 14 | Entrance, window | | .15 |
| | 16 | Road, journey | 8 | .05 |

**Table 3.4.21.** *(continued)*

| CP | | Domains | No. of domains | r.f. |
|---|---|---|---|---|
| *yam1* | 6 | Time | 1 | *.03* |
| *yam2/yuma1/yama* | 1b | Body parts | 1 | *.03* |
| *yeni* | 3b | Quantities | 1 | *-/-* |
| *yulai/yule* | 3b | Quantities | 1 | *.004* |
| *yuma2* | 5 | Measures | 1 | *-/-* |
| *yuva* | 3a | Quantities | 1 | *.01* |
| 0 | 12 | Yams | 1 | *.01* |

[†] -/- = not elicited in the test; 0 = not produced; r.f. = relative frequency.

*Thus, we can record that roughly a fifth[12] of the 88 CPs that make up the 20 semantic domains are decisive for the domain-connecting dynamics of this linguistic phenomenon.*

Now that I have highlighted the CP types that are most important for the dynamics of the CP system, I also want to answer the question of whether there is a *hierarchical order* for the 20 semantic domains.

So far, I have presented the semantic domains in a random order in which all domains were considered to be of equal rank. However, if we again examine the semantic domains with respect to the question of a possible hierarchical order, we can hardly refrain from hypothesizing such a hierarchy. The problem with this hypothesis, however, is that we must devise a way to express the hierarchical relations between the semantic domains adequately. To solve this problem, we must set out once more on the rather uncertain path of speculation, as follows:

So far, I have been using absolute and relative frequencies to describe subsets of the Kilivila CPs. Continuing with this methodological device, I assume that the sum of all the produced tokens of the CPs that constitute a semantic domain can be taken as an indication of the importance of that domain. However, the number of CPs that constitute the 20 semantic domains varies from 1 to 34. Thus, to take this variable into consideration, I have divided the sum of the number of CP *tokens* produced within a domain by the number of CP *types* produced within that domain. The result is an index that I regard as the measure that expresses the hierarchical status of the domain within the Kilivila speech community. This admittedly rather simple and unsophisticated proceeding leads to the results presented in Table 3.4.22. This table shows the 20 semantic domains in the hierarchical order expressed by the "hierarchy index".

---

[12] We can ignore the CPs *meila, oyla,* and *vakala* here. Although they connect two domains, as Table 3.4.21 shows, they are not realized in one or both of these domains. Thus, we are left with 15 CP types (17% of the 88 CP types described) that are decisive for the domain-connecting dynamics.

**Table 3.4.22.** The 20 semantic domains of Kilivila CPs in hierarchical order

| Domain group | | | Domain no. | | Hierarchy index |
|---|---|---|---|---|---|
| I | | | | | |
| | 1. | Persons | 1a | 495: 3 = | 165.0 |
| | 2. | General CPs | 4 | 164: 1 = | 164.0 |
| | 3. | Animals | 2 | 162: 1 = | 162.0 |
| | 4. | Trees, wooden things | 10 | 903: 6 = | 150.5 |
| II | | | | | |
| | 5. | Persons, body parts | 1a and b | 950: 10 = | 95.0 |
| | 6. | Place | 7 | 910: 10 = | 91.0 |
| | 7. | Quantities | 3a and b | 2,790: 34 = | 82.1 |
| | 8. | Quantities (–animate) | 15 | 2,109: 26 = | 81.1 |
| | 9. | Fire, oven | | 323: 4 = | 80.8 |
| III | | | | | |
| | 10. | Names | 20 | 155: 2 = | 77.5 |
| | 11. | Time | 6 | 609: 8 = | 76.1 |
| | 12. | Quantities (+animate) | 3a | 681: 11 = | 61.9 |
| | 13 | Road, journey | 16 | 308: 5 = | 61.6 |
| | 14. | Qualities | 8 | 898: 15 = | 59.9 |
| IV | | | | | |
| | 15. | Shape | 9 | 585: 10 = | 58.5 |
| | 16. | Body parts | 1b | 455: 8 = | 56.9 |
| | 17. | Utensils | 11 | 377: 7 = | 53.9 |
| | 18. | Dress, adornment | 19 | 152: 3 = | 50.7 |
| | 19. | Door, entrance, window | 14 | 298: 6 = | 49.7 |
| | 20. | Ritual items | 18 | 140: 3 = | 46.7 |
| | 21. | Part of a foodhouse/a canoe/a creel | 13 | 308: 7 = | 44.0 |
| V | | | | | |
| | 22. | Measures | 5 | 157: 4 = | 39.3 |
| | 23. | Yams | 12 | 154: 4 = | 38.5 |
| | 24. | Texts | 17 | 296: 9 = | 32.9 |

The computing of the hierarchy index for the 20 semantic domains orders the domains in such a way that they can be roughly classified into five different groups (I–V).[13]

If we consider subdomain 1a as a domain, the semantic domain covering the concept "persons" is highest in the hierarchy. This domain is followed by the domains covering the concepts "general CPs", "animals", and "trees, wood, wooden things". These four domains form a group of the most important semantic domains.

The second group contains subdomain 1a and subdomain 1b, encompassing the concepts "persons and body parts", and the domains that cover the concepts "place", "quantities", and "fire, oven". If we consider the subdomain 3b as a domain, encompassing the concept "quantities, with generally inanimate referents", then it also belongs to this second group.

---

[13] These numbers indicating the five groups of semantic domains should not be confused with the Roman numerals used to indicate the five age groups of the consultants (see section 3.2).

A third group, which may be considered as occupying an intermediate position with respect to rank and importance of the semantic domains, includes the domains that cover the concepts "names", "time", "road, journey", and "qualities". Domain 3a, covering the concept "quantities with generally animate referents", also belongs to this third group of semantic domains.

The group of less important semantic domains (group IV) consists of the domains covering the concepts "shape", "utensils", "dress, adornment", "door, entrance, window", "ritual items", and "part of a foodhouse/a canoe/a creel". Considering subdomain 1b as a domain, encompassing the concept "body parts", it also belongs to this fourth group.

The fifth and last group of semantic domains is formed by the least important domains, covering the concepts "measures", "yams", and "texts".

More detailed comments on Table 3.4.22 will be given in chapter 5. However, I will state one caveat here and briefly remark on one of the semantic domains with respect to its status within this computed hierarchy.

First, the caveat: I must emphasize again that the hierarchy presented in Table 3.4.22 is based on speculation. Although I include this table in the arguments given in the next section and in chapter 5, this warning should be kept in mind.

The second remark I want to make here refers to Semantic domain 12, which covers the concept "yams". Those familiar with Trobriand ethnography may doubt that this domain holds the second lowest rank within the hierarchy, since yams are one of the most important factors in Trobriand society (see Malinowski 1935; Weiner 1976, 1988; Senft 1985d:476, 490, 1987d). However, in my previous discussion of Domain 12, I noted that at least the zero classifier may be so closely linked with ritual and ceremony that it is not produced in profane situations and, thus, cannot be elicited in a language production test. This may explain the rather low rank of Domain 12; it is probably an artifact of the computation of the hierarchy index.

I want to again state that we are on safe groud if we assume that all semantic domains are of equal rank. However, if we dare to speculate that there is a hierarchy of semantic domains, we may be rewarded by some further ideas and maybe even insights. Before I proceed with an argument along these lines, one question remains with respect to the acquisition of the CPs. This question will be discussed in the next section.

### 3.3.4.3 A Flashback: Why Are the Individual CPs Acquired in a Certain Order?

I have tried to describe the processes of language change affecting the CPs and the dynamics of the semantic domains constituted by the CPs, and I have speculated on a possible hierarchical order of these domains. I can now attempt to answer the question that was raised in section 3.3.2.4 but could not be answered at that time because of lack of information. As Chin has stated, "to adequately understand acquisition studies on numeral classifiers, one needs to understand the adult usage of the system" (Chin 1989:87; see also p. 105).

The arguments in this section refer back to Table 3.3.5 in section 3.3.2.4 and to the first interpretation of this table given there. Moreover, they rely on the results presented in sections 3.3.3 and 3.3.4.

Table 3.3.5 (see pp. 191–192) shows that CPs that distinguish gender in human beings (*to/te2, na1*) are acquired first. They come first because their frame of reference is distinct and because they constitute the highest ranking semantic domain of the domain hierarchy. To be able to refer to persons is obviously so important that the CPs needed for this are acquired first (I/1, Table 3.3.5).

General CPs (*kwe, ke3*) are acquired next because the semantic domain of these CPs occupies the second highest rank within the domain hierarchy. General CPs allow a grammatically correct, although semantically void, reference to everything, and soon probably also to everyone (I/2, Table 3.3.5; see also Adams 1989:177).

The CPs that are acquired next (*kova, na2, ta, ya, kumla, pwanina/pona, gudi*, and *sisi*) have, with the exception of *ya*, a distinct frame of reference. They all denote concrete, specific objects or features of objects; moreover, most of them are in semantic domains that are the most important within the domain hierarchy. The exceptions are *ta, ya*, and *pwanina/pona*; they occur in semantic domains that are intermediate in the domain hierarchy. However, *ta* and *pwanina/pona* refer unequivocally to concrete objects, and *ya* plays a rather important role with respect to the dynamics of the semantic domains (see Table 3.4.21). Therefore, it seems necessary for establishing the whole system of semantic domains that this CP type is acquired at a rather early stage of the acquisition process (I/3, Table 3.3.5).

The same explanation holds for the CPs that are acquired in the fourth phase of the acquisition process (I/4, Table 3.3.5) by girls and boys, regardless of whether some of them are acquired earlier by boys than by girls. The CPs *utu, bwa, kada, si*, and *kasa* play a rather important role with respect to the dynamics of the semantic domains (see Table 3.4.21). This function seems to be so important that even a CP like *si*, which is rarely produced in actual speech, is nevertheless acquired rather early. The CP *iga* has a distinct frame of reference and occurs in one of the domains that is intermediate in the domain hierarchy. As for the CPs that are acquired by boys in this stage of the acquisition process, we note once again that *pila* and *bubwa* play a rather important role with respect to the dynamics of the semantic domains (see Table 3.4.21). The CPs *duli, kai, kweya, notu/nutu*, and *kweila/kwela* all have a distinct frame of reference. The CPs *buda, dumia, bukwa, kapwa, luba, luva*, and *sa* all occur in semantic domains that are important within the domain hierarchy. Obviously at this stage of the acquisition process, it becomes necessary for boys to be able to refer to concepts that denote quantity. What is striking, however, is that among these CPs we find two that are almost obsolete (*dumia, bukwa*), two that play a secondary role in actual speech (*luba, luva*), and three that function as sociolinguistic variables (*bubwa, kapwa, sa*). This observation of the acquisition of almost obsolete

CPs and CPs that play a secondary role in actual speech production may be a coincidental result. However, the fact that the acquisition of CPs that function as sociolinguistic variables is noted at this stage of the acquisition process emphasizes the important societal role of this system of formatives. The last observation also holds for the CPs that are acquired only by girls at this stage of the acquisition process. The CP *lilo/lola* is almost obsolete, and the CPs *kaduyo*, *kwoya/koya*, *va*, and *yuma* function as sociolinguistic variables; moreover, the CPs *va* and *yuma* are found only in the speech of women of status. For a possible explanation of the gender-specific differences in the CP acquistion process, the reader is referred to section 3.3.2.3.

In the fifth phase of the acquisition process (II/5, Table 3.3.5), we note the acquistion of the following CPs by boys and girls (regardless of whether some are acquired earlier by boys than by girls): *giwi*, *sipu*, *kubila*, and *deli* all have a distinct frame of reference; *bubu*, *kabisi*, and *gula* are also acquired at this stage of the acquisition process, although they play a secondary role in actual speech. What is most striking here is that the CP *kabisi*, which occurs in a semantic domain that is less important, is acquired at this stage. This seems to be coincidental. The CPs *liku* and *bogi* are also acquired in this fifth phase. They function as sociolinguistic variables, a result that again emphasizes the societal role of Kilivila CPs. The CP *gum*, which is also acquired at this stage, ocurs in a semantic domain that is more important within the domain hierarchy. With the exception of the CP *kabisi*, all these CPs are in domains that are important or intermediate within the domain hierarchy. As for the CPs that are acquired only by boys at this stage, the following can be noted: *tam*, *po'ula*, and *vili* play a rather secondary role in actual speech; however, the frames of reference of *po'ula* and *vili* are distinct. Moreover, *tam* and *vili* play a rather important role with respect to the dynamics of the semantic domains (see Table 3.4.21). The CPs *yam*, *kabulo2*, and *mmwa* function as sociolinguistic variables, again an indication for the importance of these formatives within the highly stratified Trobriand society. That the CP *megwa*, belonging to a rather technical language variety and occurring in the domain that ranks lowest in the domain hierarchy, is acquired at this stage may be coincidental; however, the consultant producing this CP (consultant 24) will probably inherit important garden and canoe magic from his relatives; thus, this result may reflect the fact that it is with children belonging to age group II (8–14 years) where future magic-specialists are already beginning their education towards a career. As for the CPs that are acquired only by girls at this stage, the following can be noted: *suya* has a distinct frame of reference; *kila*, *kudu2*, *nunu*, and *wela* all function as sociolinguistic variables; *kila* especially marks women of high status. With the exception of *tam* and *megwa*, all CPs that are acquired either only by boys or only by girls at this stage occur in semantic domains that are important or intermediate within the domain hierarchy. For a possible explanation of gender-specific differences in the CP acquisition process, see section 3.3.2.3.

In the final phase of the acquisition process (III/6, Table 3.3.5), the variants *yegila* and *peta* of the CP types *iga/yegila* and *ta/peta* are acquired. Their frame of reference is distinct; however, their acquisition at this stage seems to be nothing more than a somewhat "belated echo" of the much earlier acquired variants *iga* (I/4) and *ta* (I/3). The CP *tuta* is rather rarely produced but has a distinct frame of reference. The CPs *bwalita* and *vosi* function as sociolinguistic variables. As for the CPs that are acquired only by boys at this stage, the following can be noted. The CP *yulai/yule* is rather rarely produced, but has a distinct frame of reference. The CPs *duya, vaya, uva,* and *gili* function as sociolinguistic variables. Finally, it is at this stage that the zero classifier 0 is acquired by boys. The CP types *beku, vakala,* and *yuva* are acquired only by girls at this stage; these CPs are rather rarely produced; thus, this result may be somewhat coincidental. In this phase of the acquisition process, we note that the consultants also start to acquire CPs that occur in semantic domains of lesser importance within the domain hierarchy.

As for the CP types that were produced by consultants who were finished their first language acquisition (IV + V, Table 3.3.5) we find that most of these CPs occur in the less important semantic domains within the domain hierarchy. For example, *kauya, lipu, nigwa,* and *yeni* mark technical language varieties; it is plausible to include the CPs *kudu1* and *doba*, as well as *nina* and *meila*, in this subset of CPs that mark technical language varieties.

To summarize, the following reasons can be given to explain the order in which Kilivila CPs are acquired: To differentiate people according to their gender and to refer to things in a grammatically correct way is obviously so necessary for children in Trobriand society that the CPs *na1, to/te2, kwe* and *ke3* are acquired first. For all other CPs, the following factors play a determinant role: (1) frame of reference, (2) role in the dynamics of the CP system, and (3) rank of the semantic domain containing the CP in the domain hierarchy.

On the basis of these results, the following general trends, crucial for the acquisition process, can be formulated:

1. The more distinct the frame of reference for a certain CP, the earlier it is acquired.

2. CPs that play an important role in the dynamics of the CP system as a whole (because they connect two or more semantic domains) are acquired earlier than CPs that are not important with respect to these dynamics.

3. The higher the semantic domain containing a CP within the domain hierarchy, the earlier this CP is acquired.

4. CPs that function as sociolinguistic variables are acquired in the phases that characterize the first language acquisition process. Thus, children belonging to clans of high status will acquire these CPs before or during

puberty (see also section 3.3.2.1). For these CPs, the first three general trends also hold true.[14]

It should be emphasized that the first three trends cannot be observed separately; they are intertwined and interact with each other.

I will now briefly reflect on some considerations about this topic by Tversky (1986) and Tyler (1969). At the end of section 3.3.2.6, I quoted Tversky (1986:72) and Tyler (1969:19), emphasizing that we can use their propositions as a starting point for our attempt to explain the order in which Kilivila CPs are acquired. Now we can understand Tyler's reservations about the common assumption that a "child first acquires concepts for concrete objects and gradually expands its semantic domain by extension and generalization to include more abstract conceptions" (Tyler 1969:19). This assumption and Tversky's statement that perceptually based groupings precede functionally based groupings in the categorization of children (see Tversky 1986:72) are insights that, considering the results of the Kilivila CP data analysis presented here, cover only one aspect of the intricate and complex acquisition process of categorizing formatives. As this section demonstrates, the order in which the categorizing Kilivila CPs are acquired depends on a number of different, interacting factors and variables.

---

[14]The results that led to the formulation of this general trend, which is crucial for the CP acquisition process, emphasize once again how persons of rank within the highly stratified Trobriand clan and subclan society use some of these formatives to mark their societal status. That children who will occupy a high-ranking social standing learn to handle this CP system may serve as a good indication for the fact that the societal function of some of these CPs is a linguistic tool that persons of status consciously use. Being aware of the function of these CPs, they pass this information on to their successors, making sure that they acquire these CPs in childhood during first language acquisition.

# Chapter

# 4

# On the Validity of Some of the Presented Results: Six Years Later—A Restudy

The results presented in section 3.3 are based on the data I gathered in 1982 and 1983. I started analyzing these data in 1988 and finished in the spring of 1989. Thus, I dealt with this complex system of CPs without having been immersed in the Kilivila speech community for almost six years. After such a long period of separation from the language and the speech community, it goes without saying, at least for the empirical linguist doing field research, that researchers may be somewhat suspicious about their findings, fearing that they may be artifacts produced in their study, far from the reality of the language and speech community that is the object of study. The only way to overcome this "suspicious feeling" is to do field work again and to test the results of one's analyses with the native speakers of the language studied, in keeping with Aristotle's statement:

> . . . truth is assessed in the light of the facts of actual life; because it is in these that the decisive factor lies. So we must bring what we have already said to the test of facts of life; and if it accords with the facts, we can accept it, but if it conflicts with them we must regard it as no more than a theory.

> ARISTOTLE, THE NICOMACHEAN ETHICS,
> Book X, 9, 1179a, 4-26

Thus, In May 1989 I revisited Papua New Guinea for four months to continue my field research on the Trobriand Islands. I conducted a restudy of the system of CPs and checked with my consultants in Tauwema village on Kaile'una Island the following four aspects of the results of my analyses:

**1.** Do new observations verify or falsify the results I noted with respect to the general temporal progress of the CP acquisition process?

2. Do Kilivila native speakers accept the semantic domains constituted by the CP types proposed in section 3.3.4.2 or do they modify these domains either by rejecting certain CP types in the domains (as proposed in my analyses) or by adding other CP types?

3. Do Kilivila native speakers accept or reject or modify the variable rules formulated in section 3.3.4.2? Or, to phrase it differently: Do Kilivila native speakers producing a certain CP type referring to a certain nominal concept actually use the variable rules formulated in section 3.3.4.2?

4. Do Kilivila native speakers accept the weighting and ordering of the semantic domains as expressed by the hierarchy index in Table 3.4.22 in section 3.3.4.2 or do they modify and change this weighting?

This chapter presents the methods of data gathering that I used and the results of this restudy. In the followong paragraphs, I first briefly comment on the methods used and the results found with respect to the first and the fourth aspect of my restudy and then present the methods used and the results found with respect to the second and third aspect of this restudy.

To gather new data on the general temporal progress of the CP acquisition process, I initially wanted to put a small bag with a tape recorder around the neck of our two- and four-year-old children to record verbal exchanges of Trobriand children with whom they played. Although our children managed to get accepted within the children's group of our village sector 'Vaseda' after three weeks, my plan to gather data failed completely: the children most often played on the reef or at the beach and the rather wild games they played there would have damaged the recorders sooner or later. However, among our equipment we had a swing with a good rope to fasten it. Our neighbors, seeing this rope, erected a wooden supporting structure for the swing just in front of our house immediately after our arrival (and after a few weeks they exchanged, with our consent, of course, the new rope for an old one, using the better material for their canoe on one of their travels to Simsim Island). The swing was frequently used during the following three months; its location allowed me to sit in our house and observe and overhear the children's conversation without disturbing or irritating them. Observations were made at random and lasted between four and thirty-eight minutes. During these sessions, I noted the names of the children and the CP types and tokens they produced. I will not present these data in detail; for my purposes here, it suffices to record that these observations verified, without any exceptions, the results presented in section 3.3.2.1 with respect to the general temporal progress of the CP acquisition process.

To answer the question of whether Kilivila native speakers accept, modify, or change the weighting and ordering of the semantic domains as expressed by the hierarchy index in Table 3.4.22, I developed the following test: I approached at random 24 consultants (12 female, 12 male) of four different age groups (see appendix C) and asked them to order a set of 24 drawings on postcards; these drawings were meant to symbolize the 24 semantic domains I found in my 1983 Kilivila CP data. The instruction given was the following: *Kulakisi pikisi makala kudoki bukulivala tutatuta kena mimilisi wala. Avaka bukulivala tutatuta bikugwa, avaka mimilisi wala alavigimkoila.* (Free translation: 'Order the pictures in the way you think you always or rather rarely talk [about the concepts presented]. What you always talk about comes first, what [you] rather rarely [talk about] comes last'). I must confess that my efforts to analyze these data were in vain; I could not find any systematic pattern in my consultants' responses to this test. This may be because they perceived the drawings presented as stimuli in very idiosyncratic ways. Moreover, I cannot control whether the consultants reacted to the topics symbolized in the drawings or whether they responded to aesthetic aspects of the drawings or whether some other factors influenced them. Thus, the question raised here must remain unanswered. With this confession of a poor, inadequate, and therefore unsuccessful test design I have to go on to the presentation of the methods pursued, data gathered, and results found with respect to checking the other two aspects of my restudy that concern the semantic domains postulated and the variable rules of CP production formulated.

My next task was to ascertain if Kilivila native speakers accept the semantic domains proposed in section 3.3.4.2 or modify these domains by rejecting certain CP types in the domains or by adding other CP types. Therefore, I approached at random 30 consultants (15 female and 15 male) in five different age groups (see appendix C) and asked them whether they would like to cooperate. All 30 responded positively. I then used the following elicitation format: *Olopola kwetala biga dabigasi esisusi sitana makala "na" pela "na-manabweta vivila", makala "to" pela "to-manabweta tau". Kidamwa magigu balivala avaka avaka bakebiga pela ....* (Free translation: 'Within certain words of our language there are bits like *na* for *na-manabweta vivila* ['female-beautiful girl'] or like *to* for *to-manabweta tau* ['male-beautiful man']. If I want to speak about something I will say referring to ....') I then finished the sentence with a noun or a noun phrase describing the 20 semantic domains; for example, *tommota kumwedona* 'all people', *vovosi tommota* 'people's body (parts)', *mauna* 'animals'.

Next, I presented all the classifiers in that domain, together with an appropriate noun or a noun phrase; for example, *Esisu 'gudi' pela gwadi kena gugwadi.* (Free translation: 'There is *gudi* for 'child' or 'children"). 

After the presentation of all CPs in the domain, I asked the following questions:

1. *Kudoki sena bwena?* (Free translation: 'Do you think this is all right?')

2. *Kudoki kunanamsa akigagi kena ayogagi kwetala kwetala kena bigatala makala kwetala biga sitana?* (Free translation: 'Do you think that I forgot something or made a mistake (somewhere) with some part, with one of these bits of words?')

If the second question was answered positively, I continued with the following questions: *Avaka akigagi? Avaka ayogagi?* (Free translation: 'What did I forget? Where did I make a mistake?') I noted the answer, and I asked again: *Kudoki mabigasina sitana kwetala biga lalivala oluvi kumwedona biga Tauwema mokita? Kena asula kidamwa alivala makala? Kidamwa asula, magigu bukulivala ambe asula.* (Free translation: 'Do you think that all these parts of our language I mentioned before [represent] correct Tauwema speech? Or do I make a mistake when I speak in this way? If I make a mistake, I want you to tell me where I make it').

All the 30 interviews with my consultants were tape recorded; moreover, I also wrote down the reactions of my consultants. I do not think it is necessary to present the complete elicitation test here; rather, this sample presentation should suffice.

My analysis of the data collected using this elicitation test showed the following results:

First, the responses of the children 4–7 years old confirmed my earlier results with respect to the CP acquisition process. The children could only respond to the CPs that they had already acquired (see section 3.3.2.4, Table 3.3.5), of course. Thus, the responses of this age group were not useful in answering the questions raised here.

With the consultants in age groups II–V, the following interesting trend was noted: the observed overgeneralization of the two general CPs *kwe* and *ke* was rejected by a number of consultants. Thus, for Domain 1b (body parts), 3 consultants rejected the CP *kwe* and 8 consultants rejected the CP *ke*. For Domain 3a (quantities ( + animate)), 9 consultants rejected the CP *kwe* and 13 consultants rejected the CP *ke*. For Domain 7, (place), 7 consultants rejected the CP *ke*. For Domain 10 (trees, wood, wooden things), 4 consultants rejected the CP *kwe*. For Domain 17 (texts), 2 consultants rejected the CP *kwe* and 5 consultants rejected the CP *ke*. And for Domain 20 (names), 4 consultants rejected the CP *kwe*. From a sociolinguistic point of view, this result is not surprising; it is a nice example of the generally observable discrepancy between "official" language norms and actual language production (see also Unterbeck 1990b:60–61). This discrepancy is observed especially when consultants are confronted with such official norm-violating utterances presented out of context.

A number of consultants also rejected some CP types as members of the semantic domains proposed. I mention here only those cases where 6 or more of the 24 consultants rejected a certain CP within a certain semantic domain: 7 consultants rejected *kudu* for Domain 1b (3 of these consultants substituted *ka'i* for *kudu*); 9 consultants rejected *yam* for Domain 1b (2 of these consultants substituted *kweya* for *yam*); for Domain 6, 6 consultants each rejected *utu*, *kala*, and *pila*, and 8 consultants rejected *meila*; for Domain 7, 6 consultants each rejected *siwa* and *va* and 11 consultants rejected *liku*. I should note here that 4 consultants offered the CP *katupo* ('section, quarter'; see section 3.3.1, Table 3.3.2) as a substitute for the CP *liku*. With the exception of this substitution, all these observations confirm the results of the evaluation of CP types within their semantic domains presented previously in section 3.3.4.2. Obviously, the rank of these CPs within their semantic domains is so low that they are no longer regarded as members of the domain by a number of native speakers.

In addition, consultant 20, Vadomna, emphasized that the CP *num* ('magic, magical formula') belongs to Domain 17 (texts). This CP, however, is very rarely used and is almost obsolete; only some of my older consultants in Tauwema recognize it. Furthermore, after the completion of this elicitation test, during one of our evening "gossip" sessions with our friends in Tauwema, the CPs *sebulu* ('grass skirt for little girls') and *tili* ('bits of lime clinging at a lime spatula') were also produced (see section 3.3.1, Table 3.3.1). Thus, just as *katupo* should be mentioned as a member of Domain 7 and *num* as a member of Domain 17, the CP *tili* should also be mentioned as a member of Domain 3b (quantities, things) and the CP *sebulu* as a member of Domain 19 (dress, adornment). However, it is obvious that these CP types play only a minor role in Kilivila.

Thus, the results of my restudy confirm my grouping of the 88 CP types into the 20 semantic domains presented in section 3.3.4. Kilivila native speakers accept the semantic domains proposed. Their modification of these domains was marginal: on the one hand, they rejected only CPs that rank very low within a domain and, on the other hand, they added only three new CP types in three different domains; these new CPs are very rarely used and are almost obsolete.

To answer the question of whether Kilivila native speakers accept, reject, or modify the variable rules formulated in section 3.3.4.2—that is, to check whether Kilivila native speakers producing a certain CP type referring to a certain nominal concept really adhere to the variable rules formulated in the section mentioned—I proceeded as follows: I designed a language evaluation test in which I, as the experimenter, presented my consultants with a number of phrases and then asked them to evaluate them. I approached at random 24 consultants (12 female and 12 male) belonging to four different age groups (see appendix C) and asked them to cooperate. Previous tests showed that it was not useful to include children between 4 and 7 years of age in such a complex test. The number of phrases presented during this test depended on the alternatives that the 87 variable rules, formulated in section 3.3.4.2, provide for speakers. Thus, the number of phrases varied from one to seven (seven phrases occurred only twice); fortunately this number of phrases is within the limits of our capacity for processing information (Miller 1956). The order in which I presented the phrases was random to exclude information processing variables such as the "last in, first out" phenomenon. Moreover, I randomly alternated the word classes that incorporated the CPs; however, checking the tape recorded interviews I realized that I used the CPs most often with demonstrative pronouns. To illustrate my method of data collection, I give the following example using the standardized questions for the variable rule of CP production to refer to the concept 'tooth' (see section 3.3.4.2, Tables 3.4.1.2a and b):

[Consultant's name], *kulivala "makena kudula" kena "makuduna kudula" kena "maka'ina kudula" kena "makwena kudula"*? (Free translation: '[Consultant's name], do you say "this (*ke*) tooth" or "this (*kudu*) tooth" or "this (*ka'i*) tooth" or "this (*kwe*) tooth?"')

If the consultant answered that he or she uses all these variants, I specified the consultant's task in the following way: *Gala, magigu yokwa kukanta'i kwetala wala bukulivala.* (Free translation: 'No, I want you to decide on one [phrase] only and you will say it.')

After the consultant decided on a phrase, I asked him or her: *Kumwedona avaka alivala biga bwena, kida*? (Free translation: 'Everything I said is correct [Kilivila], isn't it?)

If this question had been answered negatively, which never happened during the test, I would have wanted the consultant to correct the unacceptable phrase. After this checking of my test phrases, I asked the following two questions and noted the consultants reactions:

*Amakala kudoki guyau mokita bukulivala*? (Free translation: 'What do you think a real big chief would say?') *Amakala kudoki tommwaya tokunibogwa elivalisi*? (Free translation: 'What do you think the ancestors would have said?')

I asked these questions to get more information about sociolinguistic variables and the consultants' linguistic awareness with respect to these variables, on the one hand, and to elicit some archaic CPs, on the other hand. However, this plan failed; all the consultants claimed that the big chiefs as well as the ancestors would have decided on exactly the same phrases they chose.

All the noun phrases used during this language evaluation test are given in appendix C. The data gathered during this test were ordered and analyzed in two ways. First, I noted the CPs the 24 consultants chose to refer to the 87 nominal concepts that I presented. I counted the tokens of the CPs and calculated their relative frequencies (r.f.s) for all 24 consultants (if all the consultants produced the same CP type, the r.f. for this CP type is 1.00; if the r.f.s for the CPs produced with one variable rule do not add up to 1.00, this means that the consultants could not decide on one CP or did not know the particular CP type or types). I then compared these r.f.s with the r.f.s I computed for the CP production in the 1983 database (see r.f.s in Tables 3.4.1.1a to 3.4.20a in section 3.3.4.2). Second, I checked the consultant's choices and compared them with the variable rules of CP production formulated in section 3.3.4.2. These variable rules predict the consultants' CP choice when they want to refer to nominal concepts. I counted how many of my consultant's responses were the predicted first or second choice (according to the r.f.s given in the variable rules). I also counted the number of CPs that function as sociolinguistic variables (SLVs) and checked the choice of SLVs with the consultants' clan membership. I then calculated the percentage of my 24 consultants' speech behavior that was correctly predicted by the variable rules formulated in section 3.3.4.2 Table 4.1 summarizes the results of the first analysis of these data. This table reflects the following

**Table 4.1.** Relative frequencies of CPs within the 20 semantic domains in the restudy compared with those in the 1983 database

| Semantic domain | Nominal concept | CP | r.f. (restudy) | r.f. (1983 database) |
|---|---|---|---|---|
| 1a | male person | *to* | | *1.00* |
| | female person | *na* | | *.96* |
| | child | *gudi* | | *.79* |
| | all humans | *to/na/gudi* | *.83* | |
| | all humans | *to* | *.17* | |
| | corpse | *na* | *.96* | — |
| | spirit | *na* | *.96* | — |
| 1b | limb | *kweya* | *.96* | *.73* |
| | | *kwe* | *.04* | *.05* |
| | | *ke* | — | *.03* |
| | hand | *kweya* | *.92* | *.47* |
| | | *to* | *.08* | *.02* |
| | | *kwe* | — | *.31* |
| | | *yam* | — | *.07* |
| | | *ya* | — | *.01* |
| | tooth | *ka'i* | *1.00* | *.69* |
| | | *kudu* | — | *.14* |
| | | *ke* | — | *.01* |
| | | *kwe* | — | *.01* |
| 2 | animal | *na* | *1.00* | *.90* |
| | shell | *kwe* | *.96* | — |
| 3a | group/team | *buda* | *.71* | *.35* |
| | | *kwe* | *.29* | *.47* |
| | group move | *deli* | *.50* | *.52* |
| | | *kasa* | *.38* | *.01* |
| | | *to* | *.04* | *.06* |
| | | *ke* | *.04* | — |
| | | *kwe* | — | *.21* |
| | | *na* | — | *.01* |
| | shoal | *buda* | *.67* | *.48* |
| | | *kwe* | *.25* | *.29* |
| | | *kasa* | *.08* | *.01* |
| | | *yuva* | — | *.02* |
| | | *ke* | — | *.01* |
| | batch/fish | *suya* | *.46* | *.50* |
| | | *wela* | *.46* | *.07* |
| | | *na* | *.08* | *.33* |
| | fish/strings | *wela* | *.50* | *.17* |
| | | *na* | *.46* | *.29* |
| | | *oyla* | *.04* | — |
| 3b | heap | *gula* | *.50* | *.28* |
| | | *kwe* | *.29* | *.46* |
| | | *tam* | *.17* | *.16* |
| | | *buda* | *.04* | *.01* |
| | plantation | *kwe* | *.29* | *.52* |
| | | *po'ula* | *.46* | *.27* |
| | | *buda* | *.08* | — |
| | | *gula* | — | *.02* |

**Table 4.1.** *(continued)*

| Semantic domain | Nominal concept | CP | r.f. (restudy) | r.f. (1983 database) |
|---|---|---|---|---|
| | fruit cluster | *ke* | .37 | .68 |
| | | *po'ula* | .21 | .01 |
| | | *luva* | .21 | .01 |
| | | *bukwa* | .13 | .02 |
| | | *ya* | .04 | .08 |
| | | *luba* | .04 | — |
| | | *kwe* | — | .02 |
| | | *sa* | — | .02 |
| | cluster/bundle | *duli* | .83 | .60 |
| | | *kwe* | .17 | .16 |
| | | *ke* | — | .03 |
| | bundle/wrapped | *luba* | .67 | .43 |
| | | *kapwa* | .25 | .26 |
| | | *kwe* | .08 | .17 |
| | small bit | *utu* | .46 | .66 |
| | | *ke* | .29 | .16 |
| | | *si* | .13 | .01 |
| | | *bwa* | .13 | .01 |
| | | *vili* | — | .02 |
| | | *kwe* | — | .02 |
| | bit/piece | *kasa* | .37 | .02 |
| | | *gum* | .29 | .49 |
| | | *kwe* | .13 | .12 |
| | | *ke* | .13 | .03 |
| | | *utu* | .04 | .01 |
| | | *buda* | .04 | — |
| | | *ya* | — | .03 |
| | part/piece | *pila* | .50 | .45 |
| | | *utu* | .33 | .01 |
| | | *ya* | .13 | .33 |
| | | *ke* | .04 | .03 |
| | | *kwe* | — | .02 |
| | | *vili* | — | .01 |
| | scrap | *bubwa* | .37 | .04 |
| | | *utu* | .33 | .48 |
| | | *bwa* | .17 | .11 |
| | | *ke* | .13 | .20 |
| | cluster/bananas | *ke* | .54 | .79 |
| | | *kila* | .46 | .04 |
| | | *kwe* | — | .04 |
| | conical bundle | *mmwa* | .88 | .13 |
| | | *luva* | .08 | .02 |
| | | *ke* | .04 | .67 |
| | | *guba* | — | .02 |
| | | *kwe* | — | .02 |
| | | *buda* | — | .01 |
| | nut bunch | *sa* | .46 | .13 |
| | | *po'ula* | .33 | .02 |
| | | *luva* | .17 | .02 |
| | | *ke* | .04 | .63 |
| | | *kwe* | — | .11 |

**Table 4.1.** *(continued)*

| Semantic domain | Nominal concept | CP | r.f. (restudy) | r.f. (1983 database) |
|---|---|---|---|---|
| | sheaf | *sipu* | *.71* | *.49* |
| | | *kwe* | *.13* | *.27* |
| | | *ya* | *.08* | *.04* |
| | | *utu* | *.04* | — |
| | | *ke* | *.04* | *.01* |
| | bundles of four things | *kwe* | *.71* | *.82* |
| | | *yulai* | *.13* | *.05* |
| | | *ke* | *.08* | *.01* |
| | | *utu* | *.04* | — |
| | | *ka'i* | *.04* | — |
| | handful | *yeni* | *1.00* | — |
| 4 | anything | *kwe* | *1.00* | *.91* |
| | | *ke* | *1.00* | — |
| 5 | span | *ke* | *.50* | *.61* |
| | | *uva* | *.25* | *.17* |
| | | *tam* | *.21* | *.04* |
| | | *kwe* | *.04* | *.04* |
| | length | *yuma* | *.58* | — |
| | | *ta* | *.08* | — |
| 6 | night | *kwe* | *.71* | *.77* |
| | | *bogi* | *.29* | *.07* |
| | day | *kwe* | *.79* | *.80* |
| | | *tuta* | *.13* | *.01* |
| | | *yam* | *.04* | *.03* |
| | | *kala* | *.04* | *.02* |
| | time | *kwe* | *.71* | *.74* |
| | | *tuta* | *.17* | *.04* |
| | | *siva* | *.13* | *.02* |
| | | *utu* | — | *.03* |
| | | *pila* | — | *.01* |
| | day/part | *meila* | *.63* | — |
| | | *kwe* | *.08* | — |
| 7 | village sector | *kabulo* | *.75* | *.12* |
| | | *ke* | *.13* | *.51* |
| | | *utu* | *.08* | *.01* |
| | | *kwe* | *.04* | *.22* |
| | place/area | *kwe* | *.79* | *.85* |
| | | *vilo* | *.17* | — |
| | | *utu* | *.04* | — |
| | sea portion | *kwe* | *.88* | *.76* |
| | | *utu* | *.13* | *.02* |
| | | *bwalita* | — | *.03* |
| | land plot | *kubila* | *.83* | *.52* |
| | | *kwe* | *.17* | *.29* |
| | | *ke* | — | *.01* |
| | | *pila* | — | *.01* |
| | corner/garden | *kwe* | *.63* | *.69* |
| | | *nunu* | *.25* | *.12* |
| | | *kabulo* | *.08* | *.02* |
| | | *utu* | *.04* | *.01* |

**Table 4.1.** *(continued)*

| Semantic domain | Nominal concept | CP | r.f. (restudy) | r.f. (1983 database) |
|---|---|---|---|---|
| | mountain | *kwe* | .92 | .73 |
| | | *koya* | .08 | .14 |
| | swamp | *dumia* | .71 | — |
| | | *kwe* | .17 | — |
| | moon | *na* | 1.00 | — |
| | star | *na* | .96 | — |
| | | *kwe* | .04 | — |
| | area/authority | *liku* | .88 | — |
| | | *kabulo* | .04 | — |
| | river/creek | *va/vaya* | .88 | — |
| | | *kwe* | .04 | — |
| 8 | cut | *giwi* | .88 | .59 |
| | | *kwe* | .08 | .06 |
| | | *ke* | .04 | .09 |
| | | *kasa* | — | .02 |
| | punctured | *pwanina/pona* | .75 | .78 |
| | | *nigwa* | .25 | .01 |
| | | *kwe* | — | .13 |
| | cut off | *bubwa* | .50 | .09 |
| | | *ke* | .29 | .72 |
| | | *utu* | .17 | .01 |
| | | *bwa* | .04 | .09 |
| | | *kwe* | — | .01 |
| | cut across | *bubwa* | .42 | .01 |
| | | *ke* | .21 | .10 |
| | | *bubu* | .17 | .38 |
| | | *kwe* | .13 | .16 |
| | | *utu* | .04 | — |
| | | *ya* | .04 | .02 |
| | | *bwa* | — | .02 |
| | flexible/thin | *sisi* | .75 | .61 |
| | | *ya* | .13 | .07 |
| | | *ke* | .08 | .10 |
| | | *pila* | .04 | .02 |
| | | *si* | — | .08 |
| | untwisted | *ke* | .50 | .27 |
| | | *vili* | .37 | .38 |
| | | *utu* | .08 | .17 |
| | | *bwa* | .04 | .01 |
| | | *kwe* | — | .02 |
| 9 | protuberances | *ke* | .54 | .59 |
| | | *utu* | .25 | .21 |
| | | *kabulo* | .17 | — |
| | | *bwa* | .04 | .02 |
| | row/line | *kasa* | 1.00 | .77 |
| | | *kwe* | — | .05 |
| | | *ke* | — | .01 |
| | row | *gili* | .37 | .07 |
| | | *ya* | .33 | .56 |
| | | *vakala* | .08 | .01 |

**Table 4.1.** *(continued)*

| Semantic domain | Nominal concept | CP | r.f. (restudy) | r.f. (1983 database) |
|---|---|---|---|---|
| | | *kwe* | .08 | .16 |
| | | *vili* | .04 | .02 |
| | | *utu* | .04 | — |
| | | *kasa* | — | .02 |
| | kneaded/dot | *notu* | .50 | .57 |
| | | *kwe* | .50 | .18 |
| 10 | wood | *ke* | .63 | .92 |
| | | *bwa* | .37 | .01 |
| | trees | *bwa* | .54 | .03 |
| | | *ke* | .46 | .86 |
| | bough/cut off | *sisi* | .92 | .78 |
| | | *ya* | .08 | .03 |
| | bough/branch | *ke* | .83 | .84 |
| | | *lila* | .17 | — |
| | wooden dishes | *ke* | 1.00 | .83 |
| | | *luva* | — | .02 |
| | | *kwe* | — | .01 |
| | carving/human | *na* | .96 | — |
| 11 | tool | *pila* | .46 | .01 |
| | | *ke* | .29 | .04 |
| | | *kwe* | .17 | .03 |
| | | *kavi* | .08 | .02 |
| | string | *ke* | .29 | .19 |
| | | *oyla* | .29 | — |
| | | *kwe* | .21 | .08 |
| | | *wela* | .13 | — |
| | | *pila* | .08 | .01 |
| | basket | *ta* | .96 | .88 |
| | | *kwe* | .04 | .01 |
| | | *ya* | — | .01 |
| | pot/potlike | *kwoila* | .88 | .53 |
| | | *kwe* | .13 | .27 |
| | | *ke* | — | .03 |
| | fish trap | *kauya* | .96 | — |
| 12 | yams/basketful | *tam* | .79 | .19 |
| | | *kwe* | .21 | .65 |
| | | 0 | — | .03 |
| | | *tetu* | — | .01 |
| 13 | compartment/ foodhouse | *kabisi* | .54 | .43 |
| | | *ke* | .33 | .29 |
| | | *bwa* | .08 | .02 |
| | | *kwe* | .04 | .06 |
| | | *utu* | — | .02 |
| | | *pila* | — | .02 |
| | compartment/canoe/ foodhouse | *liku* | .54 | .39 |
| | | *ke* | .42 | .18 |
| | | *kwe* | .04 | .31 |
| | compartment/creel | *lipu* | .88 | — |

**Table 4.1.** *(continued)*

| Semantic domain | Nominal concept | CP | r.f. (restudy) | r.f. (1983 database) |
|---|---|---|---|---|
| 14 | door/entrance | *ke* | .29 | .07 |
|  |  | *kada* | .17 | .51 |
|  |  | *duya* | .17 | .05 |
|  |  | *kwe* | .13 | .07 |
|  |  | *ya* | .08 | .12 |
|  |  | *pila* | .08 | — |
|  |  | *va* | .04 | .05 |
|  |  | *tabuda* | .04 | — |
| 15 | fire/fireplace | *kova* | .88 | .88 |
|  |  | *ke* | .08 | .01 |
|  |  | *kwe* | .04 | .01 |
|  | earth oven | *kumla* | 1.00 | .90 |
|  |  | *kwe* | — | .01 |
| 16 | road/track | *kada* | 1.00 | .84 |
|  | walk/journey | *ya* | .46 | .09 |
|  |  | *kwe* | .33 | .73 |
|  |  | *kada* | .13 | .01 |
|  |  | *lilo* | .08 | .04 |
|  |  | *ke* | — | .01 |
|  | trip | *bililo/bili* | .88 | — |
|  |  | *vili* | .04 | — |
|  |  | *duli* | .04 | — |
|  | paddle strike | *kali/kai* | .96 | — |
| 17 | part/song | *pila* | .71 | .37 |
|  |  | *kasa* | .13 | .02 |
|  |  | *kwe* | .08 | .34 |
|  |  | *nina* | .04 | .02 |
|  |  | *meila* | .04 | — |
|  |  | *megwa* | — | .07 |
|  |  | *utu* | — | .02 |
|  | part/song/magic | *pila* | .50 | .51 |
|  |  | *meila* | .21 | .02 |
|  |  | *kasa* | .17 | .06 |
|  |  | *utu* | .13 | .02 |
|  |  | *vosi* | — | .10 |
|  |  | *ke* | — | .07 |
|  |  | *kwe* | — | .05 |
|  | division/magic | *sisi* | .79 | — |
|  |  | *megwa* | .04 | — |
|  |  | *kwe* | .04 | — |
|  |  | *utu* | .04 | — |
| 18 | stone blade | *kai* | .71 | .76 |
|  |  | *beku* | .21 | .01 |
|  |  | *kwe* | .08 | .01 |
|  | ginger | *sam* | .71 | — |
|  |  | *tam* | .17 | — |
|  |  | *luva* | .08 | — |
| 19 | band of fibers | *kwe* | .58 | .81 |
|  |  | *kudu* | .33 | .03 |

**Table 4.1.** *(continued)*

| Semantic domain | Nominal concept | CP | r.f. (restudy) | r.f. (1983 database) |
|---|---|---|---|---|
| | | *utu* | *.04* | — |
| | | *luba* | *.04* | — |
| | | *doba* | — | *.01* |
| | belt/shells | *vakala* | *.83* | — |
| | | *gili* | *.08* | — |
| | | *suya* | *.04* | — |
| | | *kwe* | *.04* | — |
| 20 | name | *iga/yegila* | *.96* | *.83* |
| | | *kwe* | *.04* | *.03* |

trends in the consultants' reactions to the language evaluation test presented. First, we notice that the presentation of CP variants with which a speaker can refer to a certain nominal concept in isolation from context (a presentation similar to that of minimal pairs) induces the consultants to choose special and more specifying CP types over the more general ones offered by the variable rule as reference variants (see, e.g., Domain 3a, 'fish/strings'; Domain 3b, 'cluster/bundle', 'cluster/bananas', 'nut bunch'; Domain 7, 'village sector'; Domain 8, 'punctured'; Domain 11, 'pot'; Domain 17, 'part/song/magic'). Moreover, with the CP variants presented in this way, the consultants obviously prefer to choose CPs that function as sociolinguistic variables, even if they are not persons of high status within their speech community (see, e.g., Domain 3a, 'batch/fish'—*wela*, 'fish/strings'—*wela*; Domain 3b, 'scrap'—*bubwa*, 'cluster/bananas'—*kila*, 'conical bundle'—*mmwa*, 'nut bunch'—*sa*; Domain 7, 'corner/garden'—*nunu*; Domain 8, 'cut across'—*bubwa*, 'cut off'—*bubwa*; Domain 9, 'row'—*gili*; Domain 10, 'wood'—*bwa*, 'tree'—*bwa*; Domain 13, 'compartment/canoe/foodhouse'—*liku*). However, this is not surprising, either, from the sociolinguistic point of view, if data like these are presented in a way that is similar to the presentation of minimal pairs.

Second, the language evaluation test provides us with interesting information about some CPs that were mentioned in connection with the variable rules within certain semantic domains but could not be evaluated with respect to their status within these domains because of lack of sufficient data (see, e.g., Domain 7, 'village'—CP *vilo*; Domain 9, 'protuberances'—CP *kabulo*; Domain 13, 'compartment/creel'—CP *lipu*; Domain 16, 'paddle strike'—CP *kali*; Domain 17, 'division/magic'—CP *sisi*).

Third, the language evaluation test provides us with some new information: Thus, consultants 22 and 24 (see appendix C) produced the CP *ta* to refer to the concept 'span' in Domain 5 instead of the CPs presented for evaluation. This usage can be explained by the fact that a palm leaf as big as the span of two extended arms is generally used to weave a basket (remember that the CP *ta* refers to the concept 'basket'). Therefore, we must consider the CP *ta*, as a member of Domain 5 (measures).

Consultants 15 and 17 used the CP *wela* 'string of fish' to refer to the concept 'string' in Domain 11 (utensils) instead of the other CPs presented for evaluation; obviously, the CP *wela* loses its more specific meaning in this case. Therefore, *wela* must be considered a member of Domain 11.

For Domain 14 consultant 8 produced the CP *tabuda* to refer to the concept 'door, entrance' instead of the other CPs presented for evaluation. *Tabuda* is obviously a variant of the CP *tabudo* (Lawton 1980; see Table 3.3.2 in section 3.3.1). I conclude that this CP also has the meaning 'room' (which Lawton mentions) and the meaning 'door entrance'. Therefore, the CP *tabuda/tabudo* must be considered a member of Domain 14.

The consultants' reactions to the phrase presented to check the use of the CP *sam* in Domain 18 (ritual items) is extremely interesting. Most of the consultants explained that the CP *sam* is only used in connection with play accompanying verses to refer to the concept 'ginger'; in all other contexts, the CPs *tam* 'sprouting' and *luva* '(tied) bundle' should be used to refer to this concept. Therefore, these two CP types must be considered members of Domain 18, too.

Finally, in connection with Domain 19 (dress, adornment), the consultants used the CPs *utu* and *luba* to refer to the concept 'band of fibers' and the CPs *gili* and *suya* to refer to the concept 'belt' instead of the other CPs presented for evaluation. Therefore, these four CPs must be considered members of Domain 19, too.

Fourth, this evaluation test modified a few of the results presented in section 3.3.4.2. Thus, the use of the CP *kasa* in Domain 3b to refer to the concept 'bit, piece' is obviously not as idiosyncratic as claimed, and the CP *pila*, used in Domain 11 to refer to the concept 'tool', is obviously much more important for this domain than was claimed on the basis of the 1983 data. Whether these modifications represent language change, however, is a question that must remain open.

Finally, this first ordering and analysis of the evaluation test data not only confirms some of the trends observed with respect to processes of language change (processes that predicted that the CP *ka'i* is going to supersede the CP *kudu* in Domain 1b and that the CP *kwe* is going to supersede the CP *koya* in Domain 7, to give just the two most striking examples), but also confirms the results presented in section 3.3.4.2 in general.

After this first data analysis, I ordered and analyzed the data so that I could check the consultants' CP choices in the evaluation test in relation to the variable rules formulated in section 3.3.4.2 As mentioned above, these variable rules predict the consultants' CP choice when they want to refer to certain nominal concepts. To test the predictive power of these variable rules, I counted my consultants responses with respect to the first and second choice to be expected according to the relative frequencies as indicators of CP type production given in these variable rules. Moreover, as mentioned, I also counted the number of CPs that function as sociolinguistic variables (SLVs) that were chosen by the consultants during the language evaluation test and recorded the clan membership of the consultants producing these SLVs. Table 4.2 presents the results of this analysis.

**Table 4.2.** The predictive power of the variable rules in 24 consultants' responses to the phrases presented in the CP language evaluation test

| Consultant no. (age, years) | Clan membership | No. of 1st choice expected in 87 rules | No. of 2nd choice expected in 87 rules | No. of SLV CPs chosen | Percent CP production correctly predicted (100% = 87 rules) |
|---|---|---|---|---|---|
| 1 (12) | Malasi | 49 | 13 | 7 | 79 |
| 2 (10) | Malasi | 43 | 13 | 6 | 71 |
| 3 (13) | Malasi | 61 | 7 | 10 | 90 |
| 4 (10) | Malasi | 50 | 7 | 8 | 75 |
| 5 (12) | Lukwasisiga | 54 | 14 | 6 | 78 (85†) |
| 6 (14) | Lukwasisiga | 63 | 10 | 2 | 84 (86†) |
| 7 (17) | Malasi | 54 | 7 | 9 | 81 |
| 8 (20) | Lukwasisiga | 58 | 6 | 5 | 74 (79†) |
| 9 (19) | Malasi | 49 | 10 | 5 | 74 |
| 10 (16) | Malasi | 58 | 6 | 7 | 82 |
| 11 (15) | Malasi | 72 | 2 | 7 | 93 |
| 12 (15) | Malasi | 64 | 7 | 11 | 94 |
| 13 (35) | Malasi | 63 | 8 | 9 | 92 |
| 14 (25) | Malasi | 51 | 8 | 7 | 76 |
| 15 (30) | Malasi | 62 | 8 | 6 | 87 |
| 16 (26) | Lukwasisiga | 61 | 6 | 7 | 77 (85†) |
| 17 (30) | Malasi | 61 | 9 | 8 | 90 |
| 18 (34) | Malasi | 54 | 10 | 10 | 85 |
| 19 (39) | Lukwasisiga | 64 | 8 | 5 | 89 |
| 20 (48) | Malasi | 55 | 7 | 9 | 82 |
| 21 (54) | Malasi | 65 | 6 | 11 | 94 |
| 22 (45) | Lukwasisiga | 61 | 10 | 6 | 82 (89†) |
| 23 (62) | Malasi | 69 | 4 | 12 | 98 |
| 24 (69) | Malasi | 63 | 9 | 7 | 91 |

(continued on next page)

**Table 4.2.** (continued)

| Consultant nos. | Mean value (%) | Consultant nos. | Mean value (%) |
| --- | --- | --- | --- |
| 1–3 | 80 | 4–6 | 79 (82†) |
| 7–9 | 76 (78†) | 10–12 | 90 |
| 13–15 | 85 | 16–18 | 84 (87†) |
| 19–21 | 88 | 22–24 | 90 (93†) |
| 1–3 | | 4–6 | |
| 7–9 | | 10–12 | |
| 13–15 | | 16–18 | |
| 19–21 | 82 (83†) | 22–24 | 86 (88†) |

†SLV = sociolinguistic variable. SLV included, although consultant is not a person of high social status with respect to clan membership.

As Table 4.2 documents, the range of correctly predicted CP types that Kilivila native speakers use to refer to certain nominal concepts varies from 71% (consultant 2) to 98% (consultant 23). If we look at the mean values, the variable rules correctly predicted 82% (83% when SLV is added) of the 12 female consultants' CP production (with a range of 71% to 94%) and 86% (88% when SLV is added) of the 12 male consultants' CP production (with a range of 75% to 98%). Although some of the consultants choosing CPs that function as SLVs do not belong to the group of persons of status defined on the basis of their clan membership, we can nevertheless consider these cases of CP production in our analysis, keeping in mind the general finding of sociolinguistics that with speech data presented in isolation most speakers chose the most prestigious variant, at least in a test situation, even if (as in the present case) they would face sanctions like ridicule, e.g., if they used these variants in their own public language production. Anyhow, with all due modesty but also with the field researcher's legitimate pride after the successful confrontation of his theoretical analyses with empirical reality I can state that the variable rules formulated in section 3.3.4.2 describing Kilivila native speakers' CP production are verified, confirmed, and proved to be accurate on the basis of this restudy in a rather impressive way.

# Chapter

# 5

# Excursus: Language, Culture, and Cognition?

> ... even if there *were* a large number of roots for different snow types in some Arctic language, this would not, objectively, be intellectually interesting; it would be a most mundane and unremarkable fact. Horse breeders have various names for breeds, sizes, and ages of horses; botanists have names for leaf shapes; interior decorators have names for shades of mauve; printers have many different names for different fonts (Caslon, Garamond, Helvetica, Times Roman, and so on), naturally enough. If these obvious truths of specialization are supposed to be interesting facts about language, thought, and culture, then I'm sorry, but include me out.
>
> GEOFFREY K. PULLUM (1991:165)

In this chapter, I will discuss possible interdependencies between language, culture, and cognition as they relate to the CP system in Kilivila. This is a venture that requires great caution. I am certainly aware that most of what will be said in this chapter is highly speculative; nevertheless, I dare to set out on the rather uncertain ground of speculation recalling Albert Szent-Györgyi's statement, quoted by Koestler (1978:154): "There is but one safe way to avoid mistakes: to do nothing ... ."

The discussion of human categorization has a long philosophical tradition. Royen (1929:1), for example, emphasizes that even the linguistic problem this volume addresses, namely, the question of nominal classification, can be traced back to the Greek sophistic philosopher Protagoras (485–414 B.C.). Obviously, the problems of "category" and "categorization" and especially the interdependencies between category, categorization, and classification, on the one hand, and naming, language, thought, perception, and culture, on the other hand, have been discussed as an important feature of human existence at least since the ancient Greek schools of philosophy. We may even quote the famous first lines of the evangelist John's gospel:

---

In principio erat verbum, et verbum erat apud Deum, et Deus erat verbum. Hoc erat in principio apud Deum. Omnia per ipsum facta sunt: et sine ipso factum est nihil, quod factum est, in ipso vita erat, wt vita erat lux hominum: et lux in tenebris lucet et tenebrae eam non comprehenderunt.

---

Thus, we may argue that this philosophical problem is an original one, indeed. The history of the discussion of this topic is fascinating (see, e.g., Foucault 1966; Rosch 1988; Vollmer 1988a and b); however, in this excursus I can only emphasize once again that in linguistics the study of the question of the interdependence between categorization, classification, language, thought, perception, mind, and culture has a long tradition as well. The work of Herder (1770), Humboldt (1836), (see also Heeschen 1972; Malmberg 1987), Schleiermacher (1838), and Whorf (1958) is familiar to most linguists, I suppose, and still provokes fervent discussions about the sense and nonsense of the so-called linguistic relativity principle or the Sapir-Whorf hypothesis, which Whorf (1958:5) summarized as follows:

---

We are thus introduced to a new principle of relativity, which holds that all observers are not led by the same physical evidence to the same picture of the universe, unless their linguistic backgrounds are similar, or can in some ways be calibrated.

---

In 1972, Gipper published an excellent monograph summarizing the discussion of this hypothesis, and, more recently, the contributors to *Noun Classes and Categorization* edited by Colette Craig (1986), especially Lakoff, have taken up this discussion again.[1] Lakoff (1987) carries on the debate using Rosch's pioneering research on the problem (see Rosch 1978; 1988; Rosch and Lloyd 1978) as his main point of departure to present extremely interesting insights. He provides some evidence against the traditional "objectivist view" and for the new "experientalist view" of human reasoning, claiming that reason is embodied and imaginative. Throughout this book it is not only emphasized but also quite evident that a discussion of the interdependencies among categorization, classification, language, thought,

---

[1] In connection with the general problem, as well as with its relevance for classifiers, see also Durkheim and Mauss (1970:vii, 9, 81; Broadfield 1946:1, 25, 27; Lenneberg 1953; Carroll and Casagrande 1958: 18–19; Bruner et al. 1962:245–255, 247, 277, 311–312; Frake 1969:30; Tyler 1969:3, 6; Cole et al. 1971; Leach 1972:43–44; Berry and Dasen 1974; Cole and Scribner 1974; Haugen 1977; Lenneberg 1977:401–11, 444–448; Denny 1979:102; Ellen 1979:3; Hallpike 1979:2, 25, 79, 92; Harweg 1987b:264; Bechert 1988:1.

perception, and culture is necessarily an interdisciplinary enterprise involving not only linguists, but also anthropologists, psychologists, and philosophers. This insight is not, strictly speaking, original; the issue was also raised in the work of Malinowski (1922:1–25), Royen (1929:iii, 37, 85, 98, 110, 192, 206, 269, 363–364, 889), Schieffelin and Ochs (1986:164–165, 168–169, 183), and Watson-Gegeo and Gegeo (1986), to name just a few; however, the present situation seems to require this emphasis, and we can only regret that insights that were taken for granted in the time of Wilhelm Wundt and Karl Bühler need special reference today. In any event, the following paragraphs discuss what kinds of interdependencies among language, perception, culture, and cognition can be detected if we look at the system of CPs in Kilivila.

As a starting point for our discussion, we should keep in mind the literature just mentioned, as well as Lakoff's statement that there "is nothing more basic than categorization to our thought, action, and speech" (Lakoff 1987:5) and Rosch's comment that when "we speak of the formation of categories we mean their formation in the culture" (Rosch 1978:28). Moreover, a speaker of any classifier language, and especially a speaker of Kilivila, must classify all nominal denotata—an infinite set probably—with CPs that may, in theory, be infinite but in everyday speech constitute a finite set of formatives; thus, the statements that "classifiers are linguistic correlates to perception" (Allan 1977:308) and "linguistic classifiers relate people to the world' (Becker 1975:118) are quite plausible and convincing (see also Unterbeck 1990b:43).

One of the main functions of classification and categorization is to organize and order the perceived world. Although human cognition is a result of biological evolution and thus is constrained by a number of biological filters, as psychologists and adherents of the philosophy of evolutionary epistemology have shown (see, e.g., Vollmer 1988a and b; Koestler 1978:201), nevertheless we need to further "cut down the diversity of objects and events" with which we as "organism(s) of limited capacities" must deal (see Bruner et al. 1962:245). Otherwise, our cognitive capacities would be stretched beyond their limits. Thus, we may interpret the semantic domains constituted by the system of Kilivila CPs as categories that native speakers have developed (and are still developing) to order their perceived world, as it is encoded and represented in the nominal denotata of their language. This interpretation assigns to the semantic domains constituted by the CPs the status of linguistic manifestations of Trobriand classification and categorization of their perceived world. The questions to be raised and answered now are the following (see G. Senft 1989:162): Do the linguistic manifestations of the Trobriand perception of the world allow any kind of inferences to Trobriand cognition? Do these categories "frame" Trobriand thought, in Goffman's (1974) sense? Do the linguistic manifestations of the Trobriand perception of the world allow any kind of inferences to Trobriand culture? Or, alternatively, Do these linguistic manifestations of Trobriand perception represent universals of human cognitive processes, completely or in part, or do they merely represent language-specific or culture-specific characteristics of Trobriand thought?

These questions make clear the speculative nature of the arguments that will be used to attempt to answer these questions. In the following paragraphs, I rely heavily on the hierarchical order of the semantic domains constituted by the CPs, as presented in Table 3.4.22 in chapter 3. Of course, this hierarchy is itself based on speculation, as stated in section 3.3.4.2. Nevertheless, I hope that we will be rewarded for this daring enterprise by some further ideas and maybe even some insights.

In chapter 3, I grouped the 88 CP types into 20 semantic domains with two domains containing subdomains. This grouping was primarily based on commonsense considerations; however, as the restudy presented in chapter 4 showed, this grouping is not at all an etic one; on the contrary, my consultants accepted the semantic domains proposed, modifying them only marginally. I will now discuss the 20 semantic domains in the hierarchical order presented in Table 3.4.22 with respect to the questions raised here.

### 1. Persons

If we consider Domain 1a as a subdomain of Domain 1, the semantic domain covering the concept 'persons' is on top of the hierarchy and thus is the most important concept for linguistic reference. This result is not extraordinary. As developmental psychologists and human ethologists have documented for many cultures, and as we all know, to refer to, and to communicate with, a fellow human is a strong and universal need for Man, the *ens sociale*. This is also reflected in the fact that CPs in Domain 1a are the first to be acquired by Trobriand children. Moreover, if we look at classifier languages in general, the semantic domain for humans seems to have a special status. For example, Adams (1989:177) points out that classes "for humans, because they represent or include the self, are unlikely candidates for oblivion" (see also Adams 1992). However, the Tzotzil dialects Mitontik and Chenalhó provide an interesting counterexample, because they no longer have a classifier for persons (de León 1988:108).

### 2. General CPs

It is not surprising that the domain containing the two general CPs comes next in the hierarchy of semantic domains. As pointed out previously, the general CPs can be used to refer to everything except human beings; they are acquired at the same time as the CPs that refer to human beings, that is, in the first phase of CP acquisition. They allow the production of grammatically correct noun phrases with numerals, demonstrative pronouns, and adjectives, and they are produced in connection with most abstract nouns and most loan words (see G. Senft 1991a: 1992a). Adams (1989:177) comments on the important role of general CPs with respect to processes of language change, a role that was discussed in detail in section 3.3.3. Adams refers to general classifiers as "cannibalising classifiers" (because they devour other classifiers in the system). She mentions the example of Khasi, a Mon-Khmer language that "has only two classifiers, one for humans and one for everything else," thus emphasizing the special status of CPs belonging to the domains 'persons' and 'general CPs'.

### 3. Animals

The semantic domain 'animals' comes third in our hierarchy of semantic domains, which is understandable because animals play a rather important role in Trobriand life. Fishing is one of the two main sources (the other is gardening) of the Trobrianders' subsistence (see Malinowski 1935; Bell-Krannhals 1987). My data document the Trobrianders' incredible abilities of taxonomic differentation with respect to fish and shells (clams and snails). With respect to gardening, the Trobrianders have to safeguard their gardens against roaming wild bush pigs, bush kangaroos, and wallabies; the knowledge of a number of insects, especially of vermin, is, of course, very important in gardening. The slaughtering and communal eating of domestic pigs is one of the main events of a number of Trobriand festivals. In addition, animals play a prominent role in Trobriand culture. Malinowski (1974:112) described how the Trobrianders' four main clans are associated with clan animals (the iguana for the Lukulabuta clan, the dog for the Lukuba clan, the pig for the Malasi clan, and the crocodile, snake, or opossum for the Lukwasisiga clan). The myth about the behavior of these animals, which are the clan representatives or totems, after their emergence from a hole close to the village of Labai on Kiriwina island lays the foundation for the ranking of the four main clans, a fact extremely important for the understanding of the Trobriand social construction of reality. In addition, the members of the socially stratified clans must obey a number of food taboos that also affect animals, especially fish (see, e.g., Malinowski 1929:26–27). Thus, there are general as well as culture-specific arguments that explain the importance of this semantic domain for the Trobrianders.

### 4. Trees, wooden things

The group of the most important semantic domains is completed by the domain 'trees, wooden things'. Until quite recently, almost everything of the Trobriand material culture—from the lime spatula to the house and the canoe—was made out of wood and/or leaves of trees or at least had a wooden component.[2] Moreover, the overall importance of the coconut palm for human life in Oceania is well known.

### 5. Persons/body parts

The fifth place in our hierarchy of semantic domains constituted by Kilivila CPs is occupied by the compound domain 'person *and* body part'. However, for the purposes pursued here, it seems to be more appropriate to split up this compound domain and to treat the two subdomains separately in our discussion.

---

[2]To give just one example: During my data collection on how to build a *masawa*-type canoe and how to make its sail, my consultants named 24 different kinds of trees and other wooden materials that are needed for the construction of this impressive boat (see also Malinowski:1922, chap IV and V).

## 6. Place

Orientation abilities are necessary for our survival as a species (Schöne 1983). In some situations, we are very much aware of this fact, whereas in other situations we seem to be completely unconscious of the working mechanisms of these orientation abilities (see Hallpike 1979:304–313). Given the general necessity of methods for deictic reference for survival, it is not surprising that the domain "place" belongs to the second group of important semantic domains constituted by Kilivila CPs.

## 7. Quantities

For our purposes, it seems appropriate to split this compound domain into the two subdomains 'quantities, with generally inanimate referents' and 'quantities, with generally animate referents' and to treat these two subdomains separately in our discussion.

## 8. Quantities, with generally inanimate referents

Reference to quantities of things is a rather basic need in human communication. The Trobrianders are highly competitive (see Malinowski 1935, vol. 1: chaps. V and VI; Powell 1957, 1960; Hutchins 1980; G. Senft 1987d:195–203; Weiner 1988), and they test the socially regulative norms of behavior in everyday ritualized communicative forms of requesting, giving, and taking, for example, tobacco or betel nuts (see G. Senft 1987c:109–111). Therefore, the domain 'quantities, with generally inanimate references' is especially important, and it is easy to understand that this subdomain is another member of the second group of important semantic domains constituted by the CPs.

## 9. Fire, oven

As in European mythology and philosophical tradition, where we have the myth of Prometheus, on the one hand, and that of Heraklit, who claimed that fire was the primary principle of the world, on the other hand (see Vollmer 1989, 202–204), fire also plays an extremely important role in Oceanic mythology. However, these mythological aspects aside, the importance of both a fire and an oven in everyday life and the need to refer to these concepts verbally is obvious. Thus, it might have been expected that this semantic domain would belong to the second group of important semantic domains constituted by the CPs.

## 10. Names

In the Trobrianders' hierarchically structured clan society, proper names are clan property.[3] Thus, anyone hearing the name of another person can

---

[3] In the Trobriands, we find a matrilineal society with patrilocal residence. Children belong to their mother's clan. This has far-reaching consequences for Trobriand society in general. Hereditary titles and land rights, as well as myths and magical formulae are obtained through the mother's side (see, e.g., Malinowski 1929; Hutchins 1980; G. Senft 1985c, 1985d; Weiner 1976, 1988).

immediately identify their clan membership. This is true for the whole Massim area. If we keep in mind that the Massim[4] are famous seafarers and cover long distances with their canoes, and that they stop at various places and are dependent on the hospitality of other islanders in the area, this principle is very important, indeed. Wherever the Massim put their canoe ashore, they are welcomed and asked their names. They are immediately identified as members of certain clans and thus can hope to rely on the hospitality of their co-clan members. Thus, the clans' possession of proper names creates a more or less binding net of kinship throughout the Massim area. Therefore, the concept 'name' is rather important for the Trobrianders, especially on journeys and trips. However, the importance of this concept also holds for other ethnic groups. The semantic domain 'name' is the first of a group of domains with intermediate importance in Kilivila.

## 11. Time

Everyone familiar with the "Melanesian way of life" and especially with the Trobrianders' everyday idea of time must be astonished to find this category so high in our hierarchy of semantic domains. However, if we keep in mind the importance of the Trobriand calendar, especially for the seasonal rhythm of gardening (Malinowski 1935, vol. 1: chap. 1; Austen 1939, 1949/50; Leach 1949/50), this result is not so surprising. This domain holds an intermediate position in the hierarchy of semantic domains constituted by Kilivila CPs.

## 12. Quantities, with generally animate referents

Because the domains covering 'persons' and 'animals' rank rather high in our hierarchy, it may seem surprising that a semantic domain covering quantity, with generally animate referents is in an intermediate position in the domain hierarchy. I do not know how to interpret this fact.

## 13. Road, journey

In discussing the domain 'time', I mentioned the seasonal calendar of the Trobrianders. This calendar is important for gardening, of course; however, as indicated by Malinowski (1935, vol. 1: chap. 1), this calendar affects all the Trobrianders' activities, including journeys and trips. The big "kula" expeditions (see Malinowski:1922) have their season, too. Therefore, the need to refer to journeys is seasonally constrained and seems to be a matter of secondary importance. Moreover, on islands that are generally easy to survey, the need to refer to roads, most of which are actually small footpaths, does not seem to be vital. It is obviously more important to refer to certain places as a means of orientation. This difference of importance is documented in the rank the domain 'place' occupies within the hierarchy of semantic domains constituted by the CPs; that is, it holds an intermediate rank within the hierarchy.

[4] The Trobrianders belong to the North Massim ethnic group. For a geographical definition of the Massim area, see Malinowski (1922:26).

## 14. Qualities

The last domain in the group of semantic domains of intermediate importance covers the concept 'qualities'. Again, the relatively low rank of this domain may be surprising. However, the importance of the domain covering 'trees, wood, wooden things' is such that reference to qualities other than 'being of wooden material' is secondary.

## 15. Shape

The first in the group of not so important semantic domains in our hierarchy covers the concept 'shape'. Considering the emphasis Friedrich (1970) puts on this concept, this is surprising. However, I have no idea how to interpret this finding.

## 16. Body parts

Compared with references to the concept 'person', references to the concept 'body parts' of the comprehensive domain 'persons, body parts' are of minor importance (but see G. Senft 1992c for body part idioms). This is not necessarily true for other ethnic groups in Oceania—for example, consider the different ways of counting that use body parts (see, e.g., Biersack 1982; Koch 1984:122; Lean 1986; Wassmann and Dasen 1994) or of sign languages that use body parts to refer to kinfolk (see, e.g., Kendon 1988: chap. 11). However, in Kilivila, the subdomain 'body parts' belongs to the group of not so important semantic domains within the hierarchy of domains constituted by CPs.

## 17. Utensils

The domain covering 'utensils', like the domain covering 'qualities' seems also to be eclipsed by the domain covering 'trees, wooden things'. Most utensils of the Trobriand material culture are completely or partly made of wooden material. Nevertheless, among the CPs in this domain are those used for referring to baskets (*peta*) and to clay pots (*kwoila*), two items that play an important role in Trobriand society (see Malinowski 1922, 1935 vol. 1; G. Senft 1985d; Weiner 1988). However, this domain is obviously of minor importance in the hierarchy of semantic domains constituted by CPs.

## 18. Dress, adornment

Although dress and adornment, especially skirts and body decorations, play an important role in Trobriand culture (see, e.g., Weiner 1976, especially appendix 1; G. Senft in press) the domain that covers this concept occupies a rather low rank within the hierarchy of semantic domains constituted by the CPs.

## 19. Door, entrance, window

Anyone looking at a Trobriand house or a picture of a house will immediately understand why this domain is rather low in the hierarchy of semantic domains constituted by CPs. Obviously, it is sometimes necessary to refer to these concepts; however, this reference is of only minor importance.

## 20. Ritual items

This domain essentially comprises CPs that are used to refer to stone blades (*beku*). These blades play an important role in Trobriand culture as tokens of wealth (see, e.g., Malinowski 1922: 358, 481; Weiner 1976:179–181, 1988:47). However, they are only very rarely shown and referred to, explaining why this domain ranks so low in the hierarchy of semantic domains.

## 21. Part of a foodhouse/a canoe/a creel

The last domain that belongs to the group of the not so important semantic domains covers the concepts 'part of a foodhouse/a canoe/a creel'. During the filling of the yam houses, on trips in a canoe, and during fishing activities, it is certainly necessary to refer to parts of a foodhouse or a canoe or a creel; however, these references seem to be of only minor importance in Trobriand everyday life.

## 22. Measures

The domain that covers the concept 'measure' is the head of the group that encompasses the least important semantic domains constituted by CPs in Kilivila. The activity of measuring becomes important on the Trobriands when the islanders make a new sail, the size of which must be coordinated with the size of the canoe, and especially after the yam harvest. First the yam tubers are cleaned and piled up in big conical heaps in the gardens. These heaps are critically inspected and measured by the gardener himself, by the fellow gardeners of his village community, and by neighbours who are invited to inspect the harvest (see, e.g., Malinowski 1935, vol 1; illustrations 48, 56, 57, 65; Eibl-Eibesfeldt 1984:401; Schiefenhövel and Bell-Krannhals 1986:29–30, especially illustrations 1 & 3; Weiner 1988:82). Then the long *kuvi*-type yams are cleaned, fastened to the *kedai* stakes with which they are transported and displayed, and are carefully measured (see Malinowski 1935, vol. 1; illustration 69; G. Senft 1986:435; Weiner 1988:90). These *kuvi* yams play an important ritual role on the Trobriand Islands in connection with the *buritila'ulo* competition (Malinowski 1935, vol 1: chap. V). It is necessary and very important for the Trobrianders to measure sails for their canoes and yams after the harvest; however, the activity of measuring is of secondary importance in their everyday life. Therefore, it is understandable that the semantic domain covering the concept 'measure' is one of the least important domains in the hierarchy of semantic domains constituted by the CPs.

## 23. Yams

As mentioned at the end of section 3.3.4.2, the low rank of the semantic domain that covers the concept 'yams' is probably an artifact of the proposed computation of the hierarchy index on which we based the hierarchical order of the semantic domains constituted by the CPs. Those familiar with Trobriand ethnography may be doubtful that this domain holds the next to the last rank within the semantic domain hierarchy. Of course, yams are one of the most constitutive factors of Trobriand society (see Malinowski 1935; Weiner 1976; 1988; G. Senft 1985d:476, 490; 1987d). However, when I discussed Domain 12 in section 3.3.4.2, I noted that the zero classifier may be too closely linked with ritual and ceremony and that it is just not produced in profane situations (and thus cannot be elicited in a language production test). This may explain the low rank of this domain within our hierarchy. I am convinced that this domain actually must belong to the first group of the most important semantic domains.

### 24. Texts

The semantic domain that covers the concept 'texts' ranks lowest in our hierarchy of semantic domains constituted by CPs. If we keep in mind that we can expect the knowledge of, and competence to produce, metalinguistic terms than refer to texts and text structure only in expert storytellers, dance masters who coordinate song and dance in festivals, and magicians (see G. Senft 1985c, 1985e), this result is not surprising at all. Four of the nine CPs that constitute this semantic domain are classified in section 3.3.3.1 (see Table 3.3.6) as either CP types that play a secondary role in actual speech production (*vosi*) or as CP types that belong to a technical language variety or that are extremely rare or almost obsolete (*megwa*, *nina*, and *meila*). I am convinced that this low rank of the domain covering the concept 'texts' also documents processes of fundamental cultural change that have taken place on the Trobriand Islands in the last sixty years or so.

Now that we have looked at each of the semantic domains separately, we can try to answer the questions raised earlier in this chapter. The discussion of the domains constituted by the CPs show that, perhaps with the exception of the two domains covering the concepts 'part of a foodhouse/a canoe/a creel' and 'yams', the concepts incorporated in these domains are quite general and seem to be universal for human speech communities. If we alter the label of Domain 23 from 'yams' into 'food' and if we change the label of Domain 21 from 'part of a foodhouse/a canoe/a creel' into 'part of objects' (changes that are quite plausible), this statement holds for all the domains discussed. However, the discussion of the semantic domains also shows that these probably universal categories are defined in a culture-specific way—a result that becomes even more evident if we look at the CPs that actually constitute these domains. This finding fits perfectly well with the general picture we obtain from looking at various classificatory systems (see section 1.3). As the Kilivila CP system shows, the hierarchical order and the culture-specific definitions or "fillings" of these probably universal semantic domains (or categories or concepts) give us much information about speakers' culture and certainly "frame," in Goffman's (1974) sense, the speakers' perception, their kind of perceptive awareness, and their preferred ways of thinking, at least to a certain extent.[5] However, this does not imply that this frame cannot be broken or changed if the speech community feels the need to do so. That this changing of frames is generally an "evolutionary" process covering a relatively long period of time is a different matter, indeed; however, it must be kept in mind if we do not want to get trapped in the behaviorists' pitfall once more.

---

[5] See also Slobin (1991:23) who concludes that "we can only talk and understand one another in terms of a particular language. The language or languages that we learn in childhood are not neutral coding systems of objective reality. Rather, each one is a subjective orientation to the world of human experience, and this orientation *affects the ways in which we think while we are speaking*".

# Chapter

# 6

# Closing Remarks: Using Network Models to Describe Classifier Systems

In this chapter, I summarize the aims of my study and then present network models for the description of complex classifier systems, based on the insights attained during the analyses of the Kilivila CP system.

One of the aims of the study presented in this volume was to list the formatives that constitute the Kilivila CP inventory. The elicitation work I did with my consultants in Tauwema village resulted in the description of the meanings of 91 different CP types; Lawton (1980) lists another 85 CP types,[1] and Capell (1969) lists one more CP type that was accepted by my consultants. Therefore, Kilivila makes use of an inventory of at least 177 CPs (see section 3.3.1). My study describes in detail 88 of these CP types. Moreover, for the first time, this study provides information about the actual occurrence of 41 different CP types realized by 1,564 tokens in a corpus of speech data encompassing 34,955 words (see section 3.3.1).

Another aim of this study was to determine how this complex morphological system is acquired by Trobriand children; this issue is addressed in sections 3.3.2 and 3.3.4.2. It became obvious that some aspects of this complex psycholinguistic problem could only be understood using information about the actual production of CPs, changes affecting the CP system, and the semantics of the system. The study describes and explains in detail the general temporal progress of the CP acquisition process, the differences in the acquisition process with respect to the production of three of the word classes that use CPs as morphemes in their word formation,

---

[1] When I checked Lawton's CP list with my informants in 1989, there were quite a few CPs that they did not know. However, they emphasized that these CPs, as well as CPs that they know but do not themselves produce, are either characteristic markers for the *biga galagoki* dialect of the people living in Kavataria village (see G. Senft 1986:6) or archaic classifiers. As mentioned in section 3.3.4, I do not have references to the CPs Lawton provides in his 1980 thesis in my data (with one exception, mentioned in chapter 4). Thus, I agree with Wittgenstein's maxim: "*Wovon man nich sprechen kann, darüber soll man schweigen*" (Wittgenstein 1971:115).

gender-specific differences in the CP acquisition process, the order in which the CPs are acquired, and the reasons that CPs are acquired in a certain order. Moreover, the question of possible parallels between the acquisition process described for Kilivila and that of other classifier languages, as well as English and German, is briefly discussed. The results of the study are too complex to summarize here; I refer the reader to the sections previously mentioned.

The third aim of this study was to answer the question of how the CP types are realized in actual speech. Again, the data analyses showed that this complex question, (which seems at first to be a psycholinguistic one) could only be answered in a satisfying way by using sociolinguistic information. The results are too complex to summarize here; they are given in section 3.3.3.

The fourth aim of this study was to describe the semantic domains constituted by the CP system in a way that would elucidate the dynamics inherent in the system. On the basis of this description, variable rules of CP production were formulated to predict a speaker's choice of CPs to refer to certain nominal concepts. This description and the variable rules are presented in sections 3.3.4.1 and 3.3.4.2.

Before I address this aspect of the study in more detail, I want to mention that chapter 5—an excursus on the general argument—discussed the question of interdependencies among language, culture, and cognition. Rather than summarize the results of this discussion here, I refer the interested reader to the last paragraph of the chapter 5. However, I want to make the following general, mostly methodological remarks.

First, the study presented in this volume not only provides the reader with all the methodological devices used to elicit the data, but also presents all the data used in the study. This large-scale presentation requires space, of course; however, it allows the critical reader to check (and countercheck) all the analyses and all the conclusions drawn from these data. Even the restudy is presented in such a way that the analyses can be reproduced. This replicability of results is one of the basic methodological requirements the studies presented here meet without any restrictions.

In addition, the fact that the results of the restudy conducted in 1989 confirmed the results of the main study, based on data gathered in 1982 and 1983, emphasizes the extremely high degree of validity of my analyses.

Finally, the methods of research presented in this book show that differentiation of linguistics into psycholinguistics, sociolinguistics, ethnolinguistics, and other hyphenated subdisciplines of linguistics is academic and rather arbitrary. Without a sound morphological, grammatical description of the CP system, without information about Trobriand ethnography, without the insights and analyses provided by psycholinguistic as well as sociolinguistic research interests, without any insight into the semantics of the Kilivila CP system and into the pragmatics of the Kilivila speech community—in effect, without the productive and fruitful interplay of all these different disciplines—it would have been impossible to answer the questions raised by this fascinating phenomenon in the Kilivila language.

Complex phenomena require comprehensive analyses. Linguists sitting at their desks developing elegant and beautiful theories on the basis of examples taken from their own language competence can avoid the inclusion of these different aspects of their discipline, they are accountable to their peer group of linguists for their own personal dialect only. Linguists doing empirical field research, however, are in a different position. They are accountable to the speech community for their analyses of its language. Their analyses must be as complete as possible, because they are finally verified or falsified by the speech community. It is an empirical fact that the speech community will not accept rearguard action and immunizing strategies with which linguists can withdraw from their analyses to a fuzzy concept such as their "dialect". In the field, the linguist's "dialect" serves only one function: it is a welcome source for their consultants and friends to ridicule them.

I now return to the discussion of the semantic system established by the Kilivila CPs. Among other things, this discussion will emphasize once again that linguists doing field research should not be denounced as "positivists" (see Adorno et al. 1969); rather, they combine their empirical linguistics with theory and even theoretical speculation. However, their theoretical speculations are empirically based.

After the presentation of the 20 semantic domains and the variable rules of CP production in section 3.3.4.2, I emphasized that my analyses proved that the semantic domains are not static, but rather must be regarded as dynamic and interacting. I pointed out that these dynamic domains can be understood as "program clusters, procedures, scripts" or "functional pathways" (see Pribram 1987:7–12) that speakers use in their speech production. I also noted that combining the individual tables, which attempt to describe the dynamic processes observed within the semantic domains, into one comprehensive table results in a strange kind of "drawing" that looks like a mycelium, or a network to use a different simile. I am aware that the term "network" has been used in the fields of semantics and psycholinguistics (see Collins and Quillian 1969; Lakoff 1987: 116; Miller and Johnson-Laird 1976:272–274; Fox 1975:112, 115–119; Koch 1986:23; Wallace 1989) and that it was also used by Hundius and Kölver (1983:192; see also Unterbeck 1990b:68). I will nevertheless use this network simile in the discussion that follows because I am convinced that it is the most appropriate term to describe the facts observed (see also G. Senft 1991c).

On the basis of the analyses presented here, I understand the semantic domains constituted by the CPs types as a network in which the CPs are realized in at least two different ways:

First, some are realized within only one semantic domain; I characterize these CPs as elements that are uniquely represented and uniquely localized within the semantic network.

Second, some CPs are realized within more than one semantic domain; I characterize these CPs as elements that are multiply represented and multiply localized within the semantic network. These multiply represented and localized CPs can be understood as the network-linking elements, that is, the network ramifications or the network switches that open up and offer the speakers new ways for creative and innovative use of the CPs.

Moreover, I assume, on the basis of the results with respect to the actual production of CPs and the processes of language change in progress, that CPs that are uniquely represented and localized elements of the network can change their status and become multiply represented and localized elements. This change of status may be temporary, for example, if a speaker uses this device to pursue certain aims, such as using a certain CP strategically to produce a new metaphor. Alternatively, this change of status may become permament if the speech community accepts the CP as a member of one or more semantic domains that are different from the domain this CP originally co-constituted. This process of status change of an element within the network may also occur in the opposite direction, that is, a multiply represented and localized CP may become a uniquely represented and localized CP if the speech community no longer accepts or uses this CP as a network-linking element. Thus, the dynamics of the network offer the speaker an excellent point of departure in the comprehensive framework of the *Sprachspiel* (Wittgenstein 1958a 1958b). These dynamics of the network explain the semantic power inherent in the CP system, and they allow consideration of the semantic network established by the CPs as an infinite system—at least in principle.

The semantic network which is itself constituted by the semantic domains that in their turn are constituted by the CPs can be described in at least three different ways. First, we could present the network in a linear order. All semantic domains are considered to have the same status and quality within this network, that is, there is no evaluation of the semantic domains that constitute the network. This idea is one-dimensional; however, it has the advantage of offering a model of description with a minimum of basic axioms: we postulate only that a number of CPs establish a number of semantic domains, which, in turn, establish a semantic network.

Second, we could present the network in a linear and one-dimensional, but hierarchical, order. Here, we assume that the semantic domains are differentiated with respect to quality or status within the network.

Third, we could present the network in a multidimensional hierarchical order. In this case, we would assume that certain semantic domains are located in different levels within the comprehensive hierarchically structured network. This idea, which I can only sketch briefly here, may result in a two-, three-, or even multidimensional model of description. Following the basic idea of the "variety grammar" developed by Klein (1974) and Klein and Dittmar (1979) (see also G. Senft 1982), the dimension of the network in this model depends on intralinguistic and extralinguistic variables (e.g., speaker's gender, age and status, the speech situation) chosen to define the "hierarchy space" the linguist wants to use. With such a multidimensional hierarchy space, the linguist also defines the degree of the netting complexity, the *Vernetzungsgrad*, to use Vollmer's expression (1988a:136; 1988b:265–267), of the network. That this model is much more complex and needs many more processes of abstraction is evident. I do not want to develop this idea further, but I want to note that such a complex network may well be a good starting point for the linguist's attempt to arrive at a description of language production processes that simulate the actual decision processes and strategies a speaker follows in producing a certain CP.

In this monograph, I have extensively developed the first of the three models just presented to describe complex CP systems; I also briefly indicated what the second model might be like. To describe the Kilivila CP system in the framework indicated by the third model would require a separate study; however, such a study would have to be based on insights such as those gained by the research presented here. Of course, these models for describing complex classifier systems can be applied not only to the Kilivila system, but in principle to all classifier languages with a complex inventory of CPs.

My work on the Kilivila CP system, especially my idea of presenting the system as a network, has led me to indulge in some general theoretical speculations, and I would like to end this book with these speculations.

I have shown that Kilivila native speakers acquire the system of CPs during their maturation process. However, not only the speaker matures; a maturation process also occurs with respect to the CP system: the more CPs speakers acquire and handle in their everyday speech production, the more processes of specification and elaboration of their use of the CP system are observed. These maturation processes seem to be organic. To carry this comparison further, we may characterize the network constituted by the system of CPs as something like an organ with a specific function. We then assume that not only classifier systems but also other systems of speech, as they are described by phonetics, phonology, morphology, syntax, semantics, and pragmatics (as well as some of the speaker's mental abilities and world knowledge), can be regarded as networks, and these networks, in turn, are like organs fulfilling different functions. These networks are interconnected and interact, in hierarchical or in parallel "wiring", as parts of a whole. In our case, this "whole" is language. That this "whole is more than the sum of its parts, and its attributes as a whole are more complex than the attributes of its parts" (Koestler 1978:25; see also Lakoff 1987:273–274) may seem trivial, but is a true insight. I am convinced that this is the reason that linguists are only able to provide descriptions that are complete for the various parts, and that they will never be able to claim that they have described a natural language as a whole. There is always something more that removes itself from the scientist's reach, and this "something more" is what happens in the interaction processes of the interconnected "parts" of the "whole". Wilhelm von Humboldt (1836:CCVII) attempts to compare these processes with the process of crystallization:

Die Sprache entsteht, wenn man sich ein Gleichnis erlauben darf, wie in der physischen Natur ein Krystall an den anderen anschießt. Die Bildung geschieht allmälig, aber nach einem Gesetz. . . . Wenn diese Krystallisation geendigt ist, steht die

Sprache gleichsam fertig da. Das Werkzeug ist vorhanden, und es fällt nun dem Geiste anheim, es zu gebrauchen und sich hineinzubauen.[2]

---

In biologically based philosophy, we find an even better expression than Humboldt's "crystallization" simile. Konrad Lorenz (1973:47–49), in his book *Die Rückseite des Spiegels*, (re)introduced the term *fulguratio* in his biologically founded epistemology:

---

Theistische Philosophen und Mystiker des Mittelalters haben für den Akt der Neuschöpfung den Ausdruck "Fulguratio", Blitzstrahl, geprägt. . . .

   Durch einen etymologischen Zufall, wenn nicht aufgrund tieferer unvermuteter Zusammenhänge, trifft dieser Terminus den Vorgang des In-Existenz-Tretens von etwas vorher nicht Dagewesenem viel besser als all die vorerwähnten Ausdrücke. Der Donnerkeil des Zeus ist für uns Naturforscher ein elektrischer Funke wie jeder andere, und wenn wir an einer unerwarteten Stelle eines Systems einen Funken aufblitzen sehen, so ist das erste, woran wir denken, ein Kurzschluß, eine neue Verbindung. Wenn z.B. zwei voneinander unabhängige Systeme zusammengeschaltet werden . . . so entstehen damit schlagartig *völlig neue Systemeigenschaften*, die vorher nicht, und zwar auch *nicht in Andeutungen*, vorhanden gewesen waren. Genau dies ist der tiefe Wahrheitsgehalt des mystisch klingenden, aber durchaus richtigen Satzes der Gestaltpsychologen: Das Ganze ist mehr als seine Teile.[3]

---

Let me summarize the train of thought presented here: I assume that language is the whole that "fulgurates" in the process of interconnecting the different and more or less distinct parts that the linguist (the sociolinguist, the ethnolinguist, the psycholinguist, the typologist from her or his point of view) describes on the levels of phonetics, phonology, morphology, syntax,

---

[2] "Language emerges, if the simile is permitted, like one crystal buds off from another in physical nature. The formation occurs gradually; however, it is governed by a rule . . . . If this crystallization process ends, the language stands there, practically ready. The tool is available, now it falls to the mind to use it and to build itself into it" (Humboldt 1836: CCVII [my translation, G.S.]).

[3] "Theistic philosophers and mystics of the Middle Ages coined the term *fulguratio*, 'flash of lightning,' to denote the act of creation . . . ." By an etymological accident or perhaps through deeper, unsuspected associations, this term is far more appropriate than those mentioned above for designating the coming into existence of something previously not there. A thunderbolt from Zeus is for the scientist an electric spark like any other, and if we see a spark at an unexpected point in a system, the first thing we think of is a short circuit, a new connection.

   "If, for example, two independent systems are coupled together . . . entirely new, unexpected system characteristics will emerge, of whose appearance there was previously not the slightest suggestion. This is the profound truth behind the Gestalt psychologists' principle, mystical in tone but absolutely correct, that the whole is more than the sum of its parts." (Lorenz 1977:29–30 [translated by Ronald Taylor].)

semantics, and pragmatics. These parts clearly constitute what can be understood as complex networks. We can achieve a more or less complete description of the network parts; however, we cannot achieve a description of the result of the interconnection of these parts—the "whole" of language—as long as we are ignorant of what happens in the process of fulguration.

I hope that I have reached my goal, namely, to describe as comprehensively as possible one part of the language I have been working with for almost seven years: the network system of classificatory particles within Kilivila—the "CP-part" of the "Kilivila-whole."

# Appendix

# Consultants in 1982/1983 Study

### Elicitation Test Consultant Data

| Consultant no. and approximate age | Name | Clan |
|---|---|---|
| | Group I | |
| Females | | |
| 1  (6 y) | Igiobibila | Malasi |
| 2  (4 y) | Vesali | Lukulabuta |
| 3  (4 y) | Omnava | Lukuba |
| 4  (7 y) | Payaya | Malasi |
| 5  (5 y) | Kwelubituma | Malasi |
| 6  (6 y) | Inukwala | Malasi |
| Males | | |
| 7  (4 y) | Topsikauya | Lukulabuta |
| 8  (5 y) | Yabilosi | Lukwasisiga |
| 9  (4 y) | Yogima | Lukwasisiga |
| 10  (6 y) | Towesei | Lukuba |
| 11  (6 y) | Milavatu | Malasi |
| 12  (7 y) | Morona | Lukulabuta |

Average age: females = 5.3 y, males = 5.3 y, All = 5.3 y.

| | Group II | |
|---|---|---|
| Females | | |
| 13 (11 y) | Bolubatau | Lukwasisiga |
| 14  (8 y) | Olopola | Lukwasisiga |
| 15 (11 y) | Imkubula | Malasi |
| 16 (11 y) | Emi-Iborogu | Malasi |
| 17 (12 y) | Namyogai | Malasi |
| 18 (14 y) | Iluboku | Lukwasisiga |
| Males | | |
| 19 (13 y) | Pulia | Lukwasisiga |
| 20  (9 y) | Tosulebu | Malasi |

**Table** (continued)

| Consultant no. and approximate age | Name | Clan |
|---|---|---|
| 21 (12 y) | Buligesi | Lukwasisiga |
| 22 (14 y) | Gumsakapu | Lukwasisiga |
| 23 (10 y) | Morona | Malasi |
| 24  (8 y) | Luluwasikweguyau | Malasi |

Average age: females = 11.2 y, males = 11.0 y, All = 11.1 y.

### Group III

Females
| | | |
|---|---|---|
| 25 (16 y) | Namnabai | Malasi |
| 26 (17 y) | Itakeda | Malasi |
| 27 (20 y) | Kapatu | Lukwasisiga |
| 28 (18 y) | Asinata | Lukwasisiga |
| 29 (16 y) | Bomsamesa | Malasi |
| 30 (19 y) | Ibonoma | Malasi |

Males
| | | |
|---|---|---|
| 31 (19 y) | Gayoboda | Malasi |
| 32 (20 y) | Moagawa | Lukwasisiga |
| 33 (16 y) | Kaluvalu | Lukwasisiga |
| 34 (15 y) | Pwaraesa | Malasi |
| 35 (16 y) | Kwelava | Lukwasisiga |
| 36 (15 y) | Moromata | Lukulabuta |

Average age: females = 17.7 y, males = 16.8 y, All = 17.3 y.

### Group IV

Females
| | | |
|---|---|---|
| 37 (26 y) | Naukwatai | Lukwasisiga |
| 38 (27 y) | Yebwaku | Malasi |
| 39 (29 y) | Bwetagava | Malasi |
| 40 (28 y) | Dakevau | Lukulabuta |
| 41 (32 y) | Bokamata | Malasi |
| 42 (28 y) | Igogosa | Lukwasisiga |

Males
| | | |
|---|---|---|
| 43 (30 y) | Toybokwatauya | Lukwasisiga |
| 44 (35 y) | Tokuyumila | Malasi |
| 45 (30 y) | Bwetadou | Lukulabuta |
| 46 (26 y) | Tokwakuva | Lukwasisiga |
| 47 (25 y) | Mogega | Malasi |
| 48 (27 y) | Moagwana | Lukwasisiga |

Average age: females = 28.3 y, males = 28.8 y, All = 28.6 y.

### Group V

Females
| | | |
|---|---|---|
| 49 (56 y) | Vadomna | Malasi |
| 50 (44 y) | Sogeya | Lukwasisiga |
| 51 (48 y) | Kadawaya | Malasi |
| 52 (74 y) | Sedaka | Malasi |
| 53 (58 y) | Sibwesa | Lukwasisiga |
| 54 (39 y) | Rita-Isadoga | Lukwasisiga |

**Table** *(continued)*

| Consultant no. and approximate age | Name | Clan |
|---|---|---|
| Males | | |
| 55  (62 y) | Weyei | Malasi |
| 56  (37 y) | John-Bomyoyewo | Malasi |
| 57  (45 y) | Nusai | Malasi |
| 58  (58 y) | Kasilasila | Lukwasisiga |
| 59  (75 y) | Vaka'ila | Malasi |
| 60  (48 y) | Vapalaguyau | Malasi |

Average age: females = 53.2 y, males = 54.2 y, All = 53.7 y.

## Overall Corpus of Kilivila Speech Data

| Sex | Age group | No./no. in elicitation test | Age | Name | Clan |
|---|---|---|---|---|---|
| M | I | 1/8 | (5 y) | Yabilosi | Lukwasisiga |
| M | I | 2/10 | (6 y) | Towesei | Lukuba |
| M | I | 3 | (7 y) | Dudauvelu | Malasi |
| M | II | 1/19 | (13 y) | Pulia | Lukwasisiga |
| M | II | 2/20 | (9 y) | Tosulebu | Malasi |
| M | II | 3 | (9 y) | Dauya | Malasi |
| M | II | 4 | (12 y) | Mosuelebu | Malasi |
| M | III | 1 | (20 y) | Stanley-Uveaka | Lukwasisiga |
| M | IV | 1/43 | (30 y) | Toybokwatauya | Lukwasisiga |
| M | IV | 2/45 | (30 y) | Bwetadou | Lukulabuta |
| M | IV | 3 | (30 y) | Kalavatu | Lukwasisiga |
| M | IV | 4 | (28 y) | Kalitaiga | Malasi |
| M | IV | 5 | (28 y) | Tolivalu | Malasi |
| F | V | 1/49 | (56 y) | Vadomna | Malasi |
| F | V | 2/50 | (44 y) | Sogeya | Lukwasisiga |
| F | V | 3/51 | (48 y) | Kadawaya | Malasi |
| F | V | 4/53 | (58 y) | Sibwesa | Lukwasisiga |
| M | V | 5/55 | (62 y) | Weyei | Malasi |
| M | V | 6/56 | (37 y) | John-Bomyoyewo | Malasi |
| M | V | 7/60 | (48 y) | Vapalaguyau | Malasi |
| F | V | 8 | (60 y) | Bomesa | Malasi |
| M | V | 9 | (57 y) | Bwema'utila | Lukulabuta |
| M | V | 10 | (39 y) | Gerubara | Lukwasisiga |
| M | V | 11 | (63 y) | Kilagola | Malasi |
| M | V | 12 | (45 y) | Katubai | Malasi |
| M | V | 13 | (43 y) | Mokeilobu | Malasi |
| M | V | 14 | (60 y) | Mokopei | Lukwasisiga |
| M | V | 15 | (56 y) | Tokonupei | Malasi |
| M | V | 16 | (39 y) | Tomalala | Lukulabuta |
| M | V | 17 | (41 y) | Tosulala | Malasi |
| M | V | 18 | (65 y) | Yaurabina | Malasi |

# Appendix

# B

## Number of CP Tokens Produced for Each CP Type by Text and Word Class for Consultants in Corpus of Kilivila Speech Data

| Age group, consultant no., name | Text category | CP type | CP tokens[†] N | D | A | IP |
|---|---|---|---|---|---|---|
| I 1/8 Yabilosi | Fairy tale | kwe | 1 | | | |
| I 2/10 Towesei | Fairy tale | bukwa | | 4 | 2 | |
| | | kai | 1 | | | |
| | | ke | | 10 | | |
| | | kwe | | 6 | 1 | |
| | | na | 3 | 20 | 4 | |
| | | pila | 1 | | | |
| | | pwanina | | 1 | | |
| | | tolte | 4 | 13 | 3 | |
| | | ya | | 3 | | |
| | Nursery rhymes | dumia | | | 1 | |
| | | ke | 2 | | 2 | |
| | | na | 3 | 2 | 2 | |
| | | pila | 1 | | | |
| | Interview | tolte | | 5 | | |
| I 3 Dudauvelu | Fairy tale | kada | | 5 | | |
| | | ke | 2 | 7 | 1 | |
| | | kova | | 2 | | |
| | | kwe | 2 | 3 | 6 | |
| | | na | 2 | 35 | | |
| | | tolte | | 9 | 1 | |
| | | ya | 1 | 7 | | |

[†]N = numeral; D = demonstrative pronoun; A = adjective; IP = interrogative pronoun.

**Table** *(continued)*

| Age group, consultant no., name | Text category | CP type | CP tokens[†] N | D | A | IP |
|---|---|---|---|---|---|---|
| II 1/19 Pulia | Description | *ke* | | 1 | 1 | |
| | | *kwe* | 1 | | 2 | |
| | | *tolte* | 1 | | | |
| | | *ya* | | | 1 | |
| II 2/20 Tosulebu | Fairy tale | *ke* | 1 | 1 | | |
| | | *kwe* | | 2 | | |
| | | *na* | | | | 1 |
| | | *tolte* | 1 | 4 | | 1 |
| II 3 Dauya | Fairy tale | *kabulu* | 3 | | | |
| | | *ke* | 4 | 5 | | |
| | | *kwe* | 1 | 1 | 2 | |
| | | *na* | 3 | 8 | 4 | |
| | | *pila* | 1 | | | |
| | | *tolte* | 4 | 22 | 4 | |
| | Interview | *kwe* | 1 | 1 | | |
| | | *tolte* | | 4 | | |
| II 4 Mosuelebu | Interview | *tolte* | 1 | 7 | | |
| III 1 Stanley-Uveaka | Public speech | *ke* | | 1 | | |
| | | *kwe* | 8 | 13 | 4 | 1 |
| | | *palpila* | | 2 | | |
| | | *tolte* | 1 | 10 | 2 | |
| | Interview | *kwe* | 1 | 3 | | |
| | | *na* | 3 | | | |
| | | *tolte* | 8 | 2 | 1 | |
| IV 1/43 Toybokwatauya | Fairy tale | *ke* | | 2 | | |
| | | *kwe* | | 3 | | |
| | | *na* | | 16 | | |
| | | *tolte* | | 6 | | |
| | Myth | *ke* | 4 | 3 | | |
| | | *kwe* | | 2 | 1 | |
| | | *palpila* | | 1 | | |
| | | *tolte* | | 3 | | |
| | | *uva* | 1 | | | |
| | | *ya* | | 1 | | |
| | Magic | *ke* | | 3 | | |
| | | *tam* | | 1 | | |
| | Nursery rhymes | *yule* | 1 | | | |
| | | *ke* | | 1 | | |
| | | *kwe* | 2 | 1 | | |
| | | *palpila* | 1 | 2 | | |
| | | *tolte* | 4 | | | |
| | Nursery rhymes | *ke* | 1 | 2 | 1 | |
| | Songs | *ke* | | | 1 | |
| | | *palpila* | 1 | 5 | | |
| | Description | *kasa* | 6 | | | |
| | | *ke* | | 15 | 6 | |
| | | *kwe* | 2 | 4 | | |

**Table** *(continued)*

| Age group, consultant no., name | Text category | CP type | CP tokens[†] | | | |
|---|---|---|---|---|---|---|
| | | | N | D | A | IP |
| | | *na* | | 4 | | |
| | | *to/te* | 1 | 1 | | |
| IV 2/45 Bwetadou | Description | *kai* | 1 | | 1 | |
| | | *ke* | 3 | 5 | 4 | |
| | | *kwe* | | | 1 | |
| | | *liku* | 4 | | | |
| IV 3 Kalavatu | Nursery rhymes | *ke* | | 1 | | |
| | | *to/te* | | 1 | | |
| | Description | *kauya* | 4 | | | |
| | | *ke* | | 2 | | 1 |
| | | *kwe* | 1 | | | |
| | | *lipu* | 5 | | | |
| | | *pa/pila* | 1 | 1 | 1 | |
| | | *to/te* | | 1 | | |
| | | *ya* | | | | 2 |
| | Description | *ke* | | 2 | | |
| | | *pila* | 1 | | | |
| | | *ta* | 2 | 1 | 3 | |
| | | *to/te* | | 1 | | |
| | | *uva* | 1 | | | |
| | | *ya* | 7 | | | |
| | | *yuma* | 1 | | | |
| IV 4 Kalitaiga | Description | *ke* | | 1 | | |
| | | *kwe* | | 1 | | |
| IV 5 Tolivalu | Public speech | *gula* | | 1 | | |
| V 1/49 Vadomna | Description | *ke* | | 1 | | |
| | | *kwe* | | | 1 | |
| V 2/50 Sogeya | Description | *ke* | | 1 | | |
| | | *kudu* | 2 | | | |
| | | *kwe* | | | 1 | |
| | | *to/te* | | 1 | | |
| V 3/51 Kadawaya | Public speech | *buda* | | 1 | | |
| | | *kwe* | 1 | 1 | | |
| | | *to/te* | | 1 | | |
| | Description | *kwe* | | | 3 | |
| | | *na* | | | 2 | |
| V 4/53 Sibwesa | Interview | *bubwa* | | 1 | | |
| | | *ke* | 2 | 2 | | |
| | | *kova* | | 1 | | |
| | | *kwe* | 4 | 5 | 1 | |
| | | *na* | | 20 | 3 | |
| | | *to/te* | 10 | 5 | 2 | |
| | | *ya* | | 1 | | |
| V 5/55 Weyei | Public speech | *kwe* | | 2 | | |
| | | *na* | | 1 | | |
| | | *to/te* | | 1 | | |
| | Magic | *kwe* | | 1 | 14 | |

**Table** *(continued)*

| Age group, consultant no., name | Text category | CP type | CP tokens[†] N | D | A | IP |
|---|---|---|---|---|---|---|
| V 6/56 John Bomyoyeva | Description | *ke* | 3 | | | |
| | | *kwe* | 2 | 1 | 3 | |
| V 7/60 Vapalaguyau | Interview | *gula* | | 2 | | |
| | | *ke* | | 1 | 1 | |
| | | *kwe* | 19 | 1 | 1 | |
| | | *kwela* | | 3 | 4 | |
| | | *na* | | 1 | | |
| | | *tolte* | 1 | 1 | | |
| V 8 Bomesa | Songs | *ke* | 1 | | | |
| | | *na* | | 2 | | |
| V 9 Bwema'utila | Public speech | *ke* | | 1 | | |
| V 10 Ata-Gerubara | Public speech | *ke* | 2 | | 1 | |
| | | *kwe* | 1 | | 1 | |
| | | *tolte* | 1 | | | |
| | Myth | *na* | | 2 | 1 | |
| | | *tolte* | | 1 | | |
| | Prayer | *tolte* | | 2 | | |
| V 11 Kilagola | Public speech | *kwe* | 5 | 2 | 2 | |
| | | *na* | 3 | 1 | | |
| | | *tolte* | | 1 | | |
| | | *ya* | | 1 | | |
| | Public speech | *buda* | 4 | 5 | | |
| | | *gula* | | 1 | | |
| | | *kada* | | 1 | | |
| | | *ke* | | 1 | | |
| | | *kwe* | 5 | 8 | 3 | |
| | | *na* | | 1 | 1 | |
| | | *tolte* | 9 | 11 | | |
| | Myth | *buda* | 2 | 3 | | |
| | | *ke* | 1 | 2 | 7 | |
| | | *kudu* | | 1 | | |
| | | *kwe* | 5 | 20 | 9 | |
| | | *kweya* | | 1 | | |
| | | *na* | | 10 | | |
| | | *pila* | | | 3 | |
| | | *tolte* | 8 | 30 | 8 | 2 |
| | | *ya* | | 4 | 2 | |
| | Joke | *ke* | 1 | | 3 | |
| | | *na* | | 1 | | |
| | | *palpila* | | 2 | | |
| | | *tolte* | 2 | 14 | 4 | |
| | | *ya* | 3 | 3 | 1 | |
| | Magic | *kwe* | 1 | 1 | 1 | |
| | Description | *ke* | | | 2 | |
| | | *kwe* | 5 | | | |
| | Description | *ke* | 1 | 12 | 9 | 1 |
| | | *kwe* | 1 | 2 | 1 | |
| | | *na* | 1 | 25 | | |

**Table** *(continued)*

| Age group, consultant no., name | Text category | CP type | CP tokens[†] N | D | A | IP |
|---|---|---|---|---|---|---|
| | | *palpila* | | 2 | | |
| | | *tolte* | 1 | 4 | 7 | |
| | | *utu* | 1 | | | |
| V 12 Katubai | Public speech | *kwe* | 2 | 4 | | |
| V 13 Mokeilobu | Public speech | *ke* | | 4 | | |
| | | *kwe* | 3 | 1 | 1 | |
| | | *na* | | 1 | | |
| | | *tolte* | 6 | 11 | | |
| | Description | *ke* | | 1 | | |
| | | *kwe* | 3 | 1 | | |
| | | *tolte* | | 2 | | |
| | | *ya* | 1 | 6 | 2 | |
| V 14 Mokopei | Myth | *gudi* | 1 | | 1 | |
| | | *kali* | 1 | | | |
| | | *ke* | 1 | 1 | | |
| | | *kwe* | 2 | 19 | | |
| | | *kweya* | 1 | | | |
| | | *na* | | 15 | 6 | |
| | | *palpila* | | 1 | | |
| | | *sisi* | | 1 | | |
| | | *tolte* | 7 | 8 | 11 | |
| V 15 Tokunupei | Description | *kauya* | 2 | 2 | | |
| | | *kwe* | | | 1 | |
| | | *tolte* | 2 | | | |
| | Description | *ke* | | 3 | | |
| | | *kwe* | 3 | 3 | | |
| | | *ta* | 2 | | | |
| | Interview | *buda* | 1 | | | |
| | | *gudi* | 1 | 1 | | |
| | | *ke* | 1 | | | |
| | | *kwe* | 2 | 13 | 1 | |
| | | *na* | 2 | 36 | 3 | |
| | | *tolte* | 21 | 14 | | |
| V 16 Tomalala | Public speech | *kwe* | | 7 | 4 | |
| | Public speech | *kabulo* | 1 | | | |
| | | *kadalkeda* | 1 | 2 | 1 | |
| | | *ke* | 2 | 5 | 1 | |
| | | *kwe* | 10 | 10 | 2 | |
| | | *kwela* | 1 | | | |
| | | *na* | | 4 | | |
| | | *palpila* | | 8 | | |
| | | *tolte* | 9 | 39 | 3 | 2 |
| | | *ya* | | 1 | | |
| | Description | *ka* | 3 | 2 | | |
| | | *kwe* | | 1 | 2 | |
| V 17 Tosulala | Description | *bililo* | 4 | | | |
| | | *bwa* | 2 | | | |
| | | *kwabila* | | 1 | | |

**Table** *(continued)*

| Age group, consultant no., name | Text category | CP type | CP tokens[†] N | D | A | IP |
|---|---|---|---|---|---|---|
| | | kai | | 6 | | |
| | | ke | 4 | 35 | 2 | |
| | | kabulu | 1 | | | |
| | | kwe | 2 | 2 | 1 | |
| | | liku | | 2 | | |
| | | tolte | 4 | 6 | 1 | |
| | | uva | 5 | | | |
| | | ya | 8 | 5 | | |
| | Description | bubwa | 3 | | | |
| | | kasa | 1 | | | |
| | | ke | 3 | 3 | 3 | |
| | | kova | | 3 | | |
| | | kwe | 2 | 1 | 2 | |
| | | tolte | | 4 | | |
| | | yeni | 1 | | | |
| V 18 Yaurabina | Public speech | kwe | 2 | 4 | 1 | |
| | | tolte | | 3 | 1 | |
| | | utu | 1 | | | |
| | Public speech | kwe | 2 | 9 | 1 | |
| | | tolte | 1 | 1 | | |

CPs produced but not assignable to individual consultants

| | Text category | CP type | N | D | A | IP |
|---|---|---|---|---|---|---|
| | Nursery rhymes | ke | 6 | 1 | 2 | |
| | | kwe | 5 | 4 | 2 | |
| | | tolte | | | 5 | |
| | | bubwa | 1 | | | |
| | | kasa | 2 | | | |
| | | na | 1 | | 2 | |
| | | sam | 7 | | | |
| | | ya | 3 | | | |
| | | 0 | 2 | | | |
| | Songs | buda | | 1 | | |
| | | ke | 1 | | | |
| | | kwe | | | 1 | |
| | | na | 1 | | 6 | |
| | | pila | 1 | | | |
| | | tolte | | | 7 | |
| | | ya | | 2 | | |
| | Interview Background | kwe | 4 | | | |
| | | na | | 3 | | |
| | | tolte | 3 | 1 | | |
| | Public speech | kwe | | 3 | 2 | |
| | | na | | 1 | | |
| | | tolte | | 1 | 1 | |
| | | ya | | | 1 | |
| | Prayer | buda | | 1 | | |
| | | kai | | | 13 | |
| | | kwe | 2 | 1 | 1 | |
| | | tolte | 1 | 1 | 8 | |

# Appendix

# C

## Consultants: 1989 Restudy

*Restudy Question: Do Kilivila native speakers accept the weighting and ordering of the semantic domains as expressed by the hierarchy index in Table 3.4.22?*

| Age group (years) | Consultant name | Sex | Age (years) | Clan |
|---|---|---|---|---|
| II (8–14) | Igiobibila | f | 12 | Malasi |
| | Ebutu | f | 9 | Lukwasisiga |
| | Kalibokio | f | 10 | Malasi |
| | Dudauwelu | m | 13 | Malasi |
| | Mokeimeku | m | 11 | Malasi |
| | Moyadoga | m | 10 | Malasi |
| III (15–20) | Senubesa | f | 20 | Lukuba |
| | Payaya | f | 15 | Malasi |
| | Namyogai | f | 18 | Malasi |
| | Gumsakapu | m | 20 | Lukwasisiga |
| | Morakum | m | 17 | Malasi |
| | Dauya | m | 15 | Malasi |
| IV (21–35) | Kapudokoya | f | 26 | Malasi |
| | Dakevau | f | 34 | Lukulabuta |
| | Yebwaku | f | 33 | Malasi |
| | Kalitaiga | m | 34 | Malasi |
| | Tolivalu | m | 34 | Malasi |
| | Tova'ula | m | 30 | Malasi |
| V (36–75) | Igiova | f | 70 | Malasi |
| | Nakivila | f | 36 | Lukulabuta |
| | Inadila | f | 48 | Malasi |
| | Motaesa | m | 62 | Malasi |
| | Vapalaguyau | m | 54 | Malasi |
| | Vasopi | m | 58 | Malasi |

*Restudy Question: Do Kilivila native speakers accept the semantic domains constituted by the CP types proposed in section 3.3.4.2?*

| Age group (years) | Consultant name | No. | Sex | Age (years) | Clan |
|---|---|---|---|---|---|
| I (4–7) | Bokarawana | — | f | 4 | Lukulabuta |
| | Nakilim | — | f | 6 | Lukulabuta |
| | Vadomna | — | f | 4 | Malasi |
| | Mobiliuya | — | m | 4 | Malasi |
| | Yaurabina | — | m | 4 | Malasi |
| | Mopili | — | m | 5 | Lukwasisiga |
| II (8–14) | Kwelubituma | 1 | f | 11 | Malasi |
| | Igiobibila | 2 | f | 12 | Malasi |
| | Olopola | 3 | f | 14 | Lukwasisiga |
| | Towesei | 4 | m | 12 | Lukuba |
| | Tonakola | 5 | m | 10 | Malasi |
| | Tomdoya | 6 | m | 11 | Lukulabuta |
| III (15–20) | Iluboku | 7 | f | 20 | Lukwasisiga |
| | Namyogai | 8 | f | 18 | Malasi |
| | Emi | 9 | f | 17 | Malasi |
| | Kwelava | 10 | m | 20 | Lukwasisiga |
| | Dukuta'isi | 11 | m | 15 | Lukulabuta |
| | Tom | 12 | m | 18 | Lukwasisiga |
| IV (21–35) | Bomsamesa | 13 | f | 22 | Malasi |
| | Itakeda | 14 | f | 23 | Malasi |
| | Kapudokoya | 15 | f | 26 | Malasi |
| | Gayoboda | 16 | m | 25 | Malasi |
| | Moagawa | 17 | m | 26 | Lukwasisiga |
| | Gumadaka | 18 | m | 23 | Lukuba |
| V (36–75) | Sogeya | 19 | f | 50 | Lukwasisiga |
| | Vadomna | 20 | f | 62 | Malasi |
| | Kadawaya | 21 | f | 54 | Malasi |
| | Kilagola | 22 | m | 69 | Malasi |
| | Bwetadou | 23 | m | 36 | Lukulabuta |
| | Mwasei | 24 | m | 51 | Malasi |

*Restudy Question: Do Kilivila native speakers accept, reject, or modify the variable rules formulated in section 3.3.4.2?*

| Age group (years) | Consultant name | No. | Sex | Age (years) | Clan |
|---|---|---|---|---|---|
| II (8–14) | Igiobibila | 1 | f | 12 | Malasi |
| | Bomtula | 2 | f | 10 | Malasi |
| | Bomlisi | 3 | f | 13 | Malasi |
| | Moyadoga | 4 | m | 10 | Malasi |
| | Toyogima | 5 | m | 12 | Lukwasisiga |
| | Baigaega | 6 | m | 14 | Lukwasisiga |
| III (15–20) | Imkubula | 7 | f | 17 | Malasi |
| | Iluboku | 8 | f | 20 | Lukwasisiga |
| | Ilitula | 9 | f | 19 | Malasi |
| | Mwelabusi | 10 | m | 16 | Malasi |
| | Tosuelebu | 11 | m | 15 | Malasi |
| | Dauya | 12 | m | 15 | Malasi |
| IV (21–35) | Bwetagava | 13 | f | 35 | Malasi |
| | Ibonoma | 14 | f | 25 | Malasi |
| | Bokarawana | 15 | f | 30 | Malasi |
| | Moagawa | 16 | m | 26 | Lukwasisiga |
| | Tova'ula | 17 | m | 30 | Malasi |
| | Kalitaiga | 18 | m | 34 | Malasi |
| V (36–75) | Inoma | 19 | f | 39 | Lukwasisiga |
| | Inadila | 20 | f | 48 | Malasi |
| | Kadawaya | 21 | f | 54 | Malasi |
| | Gerubara | 22 | m | 45 | Lukwasisiga |
| | Tokunupei | 23 | m | 62 | Malasi |
| | Kilagola | 24 | m | 69 | Malasi |

*Restudy Question: Do Kilivila native speakers accept, reject, or modify the variable rules formulated in section 3.3.4.2?*

| Domain | Concept | Phrases presented in language evaluation test[†] | Gloss |
|---|---|---|---|
| 1a | Persons Children | *O davalusi esisusi tomanabweta tauwau namanabweta vivila gudimanabweta gugwadi. O davalusi esisusi tomanabweta tauwau tomanabweta vivila tomanabweta gugwadi.* | In our village live CP-beautiful men, CP-beautiful women, (and) CP-beautiful children. |
| | Corpse Spirit | *minana tomata*<br>*minana kosi* | this-CP-this corpse<br>this-CP-this spirit |
| 1b | Limb | *makweyana imitabogu*<br>*makwena imitabogu*<br>*makena imitabogu* | this-CP-this my finger |
| | Hand | *mayamna yamala*<br>*makweyana yamala*<br>*makwena yamala*<br>*mtona yamala*<br>*mayana yamala* | this-CP-this her/his hand |
| | Tooth | *maka'ina kudula*<br>*makuduna kudula*<br>*makwena kudula*<br>*makena kudula* | this-CP-this her/his tooth |
| 2 | Animal Shell | *minana mauna*<br>*makwena vigoda*<br>*\*minana vigoda* | this-CP-this animal<br>this-CP-this shell |
| 3a | Group/team | *makwena boda*<br>*mabudana boda* | this-CP-this group |
| | Group move | *madelina deli*<br>*makwena deli*<br>*mtona deli*<br>*minana deli*<br>*makasana deli* | this-CP-this group on the move |

| | Phrases | Gloss |
|---|---|---|
| Shoal | *mabudana boda bodavakaveaka*<br>*makwena boda bodavakaveaka*<br>*mayuvana boda bodavakaveaka*<br>*makena boda bodavakaveaka*<br>*makasana boda bodavakaveaka* | this-CP-this big shoal |
| Batch/fish | *masuyana yena budubadu esisusi*<br>*minasina yena budubadu esisusi*<br>*mawelana yena budubadu esisusi* | this-CP-this batch of fish-many are there |
| Fish/strings | *minasina yena isuisi*<br>*mawelana yena isuisi*<br>*maoylana yena isuisi* | this/these-CP-this/these fish they are on strings |
| 3b Heap | *makwena gugula*<br>*magulana gugula*<br>*matamna gugula*<br>*mabudana gugula* | this-CP-this heap |
| Plantation | *makwena po'ula*<br>*mapo'ulana po'ula*<br>*magulana po'ula* | this-CP-this plantation |
| Fruit cluster | *makena kavailuva*<br>*mayana kavailuva*<br>*mabukwana kavailuva*<br>*makwena kavailuva*<br>*masana kavailuva*<br>*mapo'ulana kavailuva*<br>*maluvana kavailuva* | this-CP-this (cluster of) fruit |
| Cluster/bundle | *madulina duli*<br>*makwena duli*<br>*makena duli* | this-CP-this cluster/bundle |
| Bundle/wrapped | *malubana duli elubisi*<br>*makapwana duli elubisi*<br>*makwena duli elubisi* | this-CP-this bundle they wrapped (it) up |

† In general, phrases are presented here with demonstrative pronouns only. I present these phrases to give the reader a better understanding of the language evaluation test. For the glosses of these phrases CPs are not translated.

**Table** (continued)

| Domain | Concept | Phrases presented in language evaluation test† | Gloss |
|--------|---------|-----------------------------------------------|-------|
|  | Small bit | *ma'utuna tobaki pikekita*<br>*masina tobaki pikekita*<br>*mavilina tobaki pikekita*<br>*makwena tobaki pikekita*<br>*mabwana tobaki pikekita*<br>*makena tobaki pikekita* | this-CP-this little (bit of) tobacco |
|  | Bit/piece | *magumna gum*<br>*makwena gum*<br>*makena gum*<br>*mayana gum*<br>*makasana gum*<br>*ma'utuna gum* | this-CP-this small piece |
|  | Part/piece | *mapilana sitana*<br>*mayana sitana*<br>*makena sitana*<br>*makwena sitana*<br>*mavilina sitana*<br>*ma'utuna sitana* | this-CP-this part |
|  | Scrap | *ma'utuna sitana ebwabusi*<br>*makena sitana ebwabusi*<br>*mabwana sitana ebwabusi*<br>*mabubwana sitana ebwabusi* | this-CP-this part (which) they cut off |
|  | Cluster/bananas | *makena usi duli galayomala*<br>*makilana usi duli galayomala*<br>*makwena usi duli galayomala* | these-CP-these bananas many bundles |
|  | Conical bundle | *mammwana uli duli bwena*<br>*makena uli duli bwena*<br>*magubana uli duli bwena* | these-CP-these taro (a) good bundle |

| No. | Category | | Gloss |
|---|---|---|---|
| | Nut bunch | *makwena uli duli bwena* | these-CP-these betelnuts many (of them) |
| | | *maluvana uli duli bwena* | |
| | | *mabudana uli duli bwena* | |
| | | *masana buva budubadu* | |
| | | *makena buva budubadu* | |
| | | *makwena buva budubadu* | |
| | | *maluvana buva budubadu* | |
| | | *mapo'ulana buva budubadu* | |
| | Sheaf | *masipuna sipu* | this-CP-this sheaf |
| | | *makwena sipu* | |
| | | *mayana sipu* | |
| | | *makena sipu* | |
| | Bundle of four things | *makwena vavagi makala kwevasi uk* | this-CP-this thing (looking) like CP-four hooks |
| | | *makena vavagi makala kevasi uk* | |
| | | *mayulaina vavagi makala yulaivasi uk* | |
| 4 | Handful | *mayenina pwaka* | this-CP-this lime |
| | Anything | *makwena vavagi avaka avaka* | this-CP-this thing whatever (it may be) |
| | | *makena vavagi avaka avaka* | |
| 5 | Span | *ma'uvana kuvi* | this-CP-this "kuvi" (-type of) yams |
| | | *makena kuvi* | |
| | | *makwena kuvi* | |
| | | *matamna kuvi* | |
| | Length | *mayumana pepe'u* | this-CP-this small basket |
| 6 | Night | *makwena bogi* | this-CP-this night |
| | | *mabogina bogi* | |
| | Day | *makwena yam* | this-CP-this day |
| | | *makalana yam* | |
| | | *matutana yam* | |
| | | *mayamna yam* | |
| | Time | *makwena tuta* | this-CP-this time |
| | | *matutana tuta* | |

**Table** *(continued)*

| Domain | Concept | Phrases presented in language evaluation test[†] | Gloss |
|---|---|---|---|
| 7 | | | |
| | Day/part | masivana tuta | this-CP-this part of the day |
| | | ma'utuna tuta | |
| | | matutana tuta | |
| | | mapilana tuta | |
| | Village sector | mameilana yam | this-CP-this village sector |
| | | makabulona kabuluyuvela | |
| | | makena kabuluyuvela | |
| | | makwena kabuluyuvela | |
| | | ma'utuna kabuluyuvela | |
| | Place/area | makwena valu | this-CP-this place |
| | | mavilona valu | |
| | Sea portion | makwena bwalita | this-CP-this part of the sea (where this man only has the right to fish) |
| | | (mtona wala magila epola) | |
| | | mabwalitana bwalita (. . .) | |
| | | ma'utuna bwalita (. . .) | |
| | | masiwana bwalita (. . .) | |
| | Land plot | makubilana kwabila | this-CP-this land |
| | | makwena kwabila | |
| | | makena kwabila | |
| | | mapilana kwabila | |
| | Corner/garden | manununa numula bagula | this-CP-this corner of the garden |
| | | makwena numula bagula | |
| | | makabulona numula bagula | |
| | | ma'utuna numula bagula | |
| | Mountain | makoyana koya | this-CP-this mountain |
| | | makwena koya | |

| | | |
|---|---|---|
| Swamp | *madumiana dumia* | this-CP-this swamp |
| Moon | *minana tukukona* | this-CP-this moon |
| Star | *minana manova* | this-CP-this big star |
| Area/authority | *malikuna kabulupuvela guyau esisu* | this-CP-this village sector (where) the chief lives |
| River/creek | *mavasina yeyela, vaya, bwalita* | this-CP-this small creek, river, sea |
| Cut | *magiwina giwi* | this-CP-this cut |
| | *makena giwi* | |
| | *makwena giwi* | |
| | *makasana giwi* | |
| Punctured | *maponana pwanina* | this-CP-this hole |
| | *makwena pwanina* | |
| | *manigwana pwanina* | |
| Cut off | *mabubwana sitana avaka ebwabusi* | this-CP-this part that they cut off |
| | *makena sitana avaka ebwabusi* | |
| | *mabwana sitana avaka ebwabusi* | |
| | *ma'utuna sitana avaka ebwabusi* | |
| | *makwena sitana avaka ebwabusi* | |
| Cut across | *mabubuna bobu ebwabusi* | this-CP-this log they cut off |
| | *makwena bobu ebwabusi* | |
| | *makena bobu ebwabusi* | |
| | *mabwana bobu ebwabusi* | |
| | *mayana bobu ebwabusi* | |
| | *mabubwana bobu ebwabusi* | |
| Flexible/thin | *miyana yoyu* | this-CP-this palm branch |
| | *masisina yoyu* | |
| | *makena yoyu* | |
| | *masina yoyu* | |
| | *mapilana yoyu* | |
| Untwisted | *mavilina tobaki dualilia* | this-CP-this (bit of) straight (stick of) tobacco |
| | *makena tobaki dualilia* | |
| | *ma'utuna tobaki dualilia* | |
| | *makwena tobaki dualilia* | |
| | *mabwana tobaki dualilia* | |

8

| Domain | Concept | Phrases presented in language evaluation test[†] | Gloss |
|--------|---------|--------------------------------------------------|-------|
| 9 | Protuberances | *makabulona matala peni*<br>*makena matala peni*<br>*ma'utuna matala peni*<br>*mabwana matala peni* | this-CP-this tip of the pencil |
| | Row/line | *makasana kasa*<br>*makwena kasa*<br>*makena kasa* | this-CP-this line |
| | Row | *magilina vakala*<br>*mayana vakala*<br>*makwena vakala*<br>*mavilina vakala*<br>*makasana vakala*<br>*mavakalana vakala* | this-CP-this belt of spondylus shell discs (in a row) |
| | Kneaded/dot/drop | *manotuna notu*<br>*makwena notu* | this-CP-this dot |
| 10 | Wood | *makena kai*<br>*mabwana kai* | this-CP-this (piece of) wood |
| | Trees | *makesina nuya, buva, seda, veva*<br>*mabwasina nuya, buva, seda, veva* | these-CP-these palm-, betelnut-, nut-, and mango-trees |
| | Bough/cut off | *masisina sisila*<br>*miyana sisila* | this-CP-this (cut off) branches |
| | Bough/branch | *makena keyala deli kelima kotolu*<br>*matilana keyala deli kelima ketolu* | this-CP-this spear with CP-five CP-four (= nine) heads |
| | Wooden dishes | *makena kaboma*<br>*maluvana kaboma*<br>*makwena kaboma* | this-CP-this wooden dish |

| | | | |
|---|---|---|---|
| 11 | Carving/human | *minana tokwalu odabala lagim* | this-CP-this carving on top of the canoe board |
| | Tool | *makavina kavi*<br>*makena kavi*<br>*makwena kavi*<br>*mapilana kavi* | this-CP-this tool |
| | String | *makena wela*<br>*makwena wela*<br>*mapilana wela*<br>*maoylana wela* | this-CP-this string of fish |
| | Basket | *matana/mapetana peta*<br>*makwena peta*<br>*mayana peta* | this-CP-this basket |
| | Pot/potlike | *makwelana kwena*<br>*makwena kwena*<br>*makena kwena* | this-CP-this pot |
| | Fish trap | *makauyana kivaya* | this-CP-this fish trap |
| 12 | Yams/basketful | *makwena tetu*<br>*tala tetu*<br>*matamna tetu*<br>*matetuna tetu* | this-CP-this yams |
| 13 | Compartment/foodhouse | *makabisina liku*<br>*makena liku*<br>*makwena liku*<br>*mabwana liku*<br>*ma'utuna liku*<br>*mapilana liku* | this-CP-this foodhouse |
| | Compartment/canoe/foodhouse | *malikusina waga kena liku*<br>*makwesina waga kena liku*<br>*makesina waga kena liku* | this-CP-this (part of a) canoe or foodhouse |
| | Compartment/creel | *malipuna kivaya* | this-CP-this (part of a) fish trap |

**Table** (continued)

| Domain | Concept | Phrases presented in language evaluation test[†] | Gloss |
|---|---|---|---|
| 14 | Door/entrance | maduyana taboda | this-CP-this door |
| | | mavayana taboda | |
| | | makadana taboda | |
| | | mayana taboda | |
| | | makwena taboda | |
| | | makena taboda | |
| 15 | Fire/oven | makovana kova | this-CP-this fire |
| | | makena kova | |
| | | makwena kova | |
| | Earth oven | makumlana kumkumla | this-CP-this earth oven |
| | | makwena kumkumla | |
| 16 | Road/track | makadana keda | this-CP-this road |
| | Walk/journey/trip | malilona lola | this-CP-this journey |
| | | makwena lola | |
| | | mayana lola | |
| | | makadana lola | |
| | | makena lola | |
| | | mabililona lola | |
| | Paddle strike | makalina kaikela baolaola | (with) this-CP-this paddle I will paddle |
| 17 | Part/song | maninana wosi | this-CP-this song |
| | | mapilana wosi | |
| | | makwena wosi | |
| | | mamegwana wosi | |
| | | ma'utuna wosi | |
| | | makasana wosi | |

| | | | |
|---|---|---|---|
| | Part/song/magic | mameilasina wosi deli megwa | these-CP-these songs and magical formulae |
| | | mapilasina wosi deli megwa | |
| | | mavosisina wosi deli megwa | |
| | | makesina wosi deli megwa | |
| | | makasasina wosi deli megwa | |
| | | makwesina wosi deli megwa | |
| | | ma'utusina wosi deli megwa | |
| | Division/magic | masisina megwa | this-CP-this (piece of) magic |
| 18 | Stone blade | makaina beku | this-CP-this stone blade |
| | | mabekuna beku | |
| | | makwena beku | |
| | Ginger | masamna neya | this-CP-this ginger |
| 19 | Band/fibers | makwena doba | this-CP-this grass-skirt |
| | | makuduna doba | |
| | | madobana doba | |
| | | mavakalana vakala | |
| | Belt/shells | ma'igana yegila | this-CP-this belt |
| 20 | Name | makwena yegila | this-CP-this name |

351

# Appendix

# D

## Some Speculations on the Origin of Classifers

Most linguists who study the phenomenon of classifiers cannot refrain from speculating on the origin of these formatives. Adams (1989:193–194) gives an excellent general account of the most interesting hypotheses proposed to date (see also Asmah 1972; de León 1988:128, 134–136, 141–142, 168–170; Seiler 1983; Unterbeck 1990a:8; 1990b:86, 90). On the basis of my research on Kilivila, I speculate in this appendix on the origin of the Kilivila classifiers. I assume that probably most, if not all, Kilivila CPs are traceable to nouns (see G. Senft 1993). This is a rather obvious hypothesis, considering that quite a few CPs are "repeaters". A repeater is a form that can function as a CP as well as a noun, or one might say, a repeater is a noun that functions as its own classifier. Repeaters are found in many classifier languages,[1] and the idea that CPs have evolved from nominals is far from original.[2] Nevertheless, let me develop this hypothesis briefly.

If we look again at Table 3.3.1 in section 3.3.1 and compare the CPs there with the lexical entries given in G. Senft (1986:185–430), we find the following:

The CPs or CP variants *beku, bogi, boda, bwalita, doba, duli, dumia, gula, yegila, keda, kasa, kova, kwena, koya, megwa, nigwa, peta, po'ula, siva, tetu, tuta, vaya, vakala, vosi,* and *yam* are repeaters. These 25 repeaters represent 28% of the 88 CPs discussed in detail in this book.

The CP *gudi* is a shortened form of the noun *gwadi*; the CP variant *iga* is a shortened form of the noun *yegila* (note that we also documented the CP variant *yegila*); the CP *ke* is a shortened form of the noun *kai* (note that in highly formal situations the CP variant *kai* is produced); the CP *kumla* is a shortened form of the noun *kumkumla*; the CP variants *kwoila/kwela/kway/ kwaila/kwaikwa* are modified forms of the noun *kwena* (note that we also

---

[1] See, for example, Asmah (1972:88–90); Barz and Diller (1985:168, 174); and the references in section 1.2 of the present volume.

[2] See also Carpenter (1986:18; 1992:139) and Lee (1987:404). Of course, classifiers may also originate in other word classes. Seiler (1986:17) argues that in Imonda, a Nonaustronesian language of the Trans-New Guinea phylum," erstwhile full verbs were semantically depleted and reanalysed as classifiers". See also Seiler 1983. The influence of classifier systems on other classifier systems and the consequences for CP systems of borrowing from other languages are discussed by Adams (1991).

documented the CP variant *kwena*); the CP *na* in its meaning 'person of female gender' is probably a shortened and modified form of the noun *vivila* (in the *biga galanani* variety of Kilivila, the noun is realized as *vivina*); the CP variants *pwanina/pona/ponina/ponu/polu/pwana* are shortened or modified forms of the noun *pwanana*; the CP *te/to* is a shortened form of the noun *tau* (note that in highly formal situations the CP variant *tau* is produced); and the CP *vilo* is a modified form of the noun *valu*. These nine cases cover seven more CP types that can be traced back to nouns; these seven CP types represent another 8% of the 88 CPs described in detail in this book.

The CP *kabulo/kabulu* in its meanings 'protuberances' and 'cape, point' can be traced back to the nouns *kabulula* 'point, ledge', *kabunu* 'point', and *kabulu*-PP IV 'nose'; the CP *kauya* can be traced back to the noun *kauya* 'woven basket' (however, the CP has a more specific meaning than the original noun); the CP *kudu* in its meaning 'tooth' can be traced back to the noun *kudu*-PP IV; the CP *liku* can be traced back to the noun *liku* 'big foodhouse' (however, the CP has a more specific meaning than the original noun); and the CP *yuma, yam* in its meaning 'hand' can be traced back to the noun *yama*-PP IV. These five CPs represent another 6% of the 88 CPs described in detail here.

In summary, 37 of the 88 CPs described in detail in this book can be readily traced to nouns. Thus, the hypothesis presented here seems to be highly plausible for 42% of the described CPs.

Malcolm Ross, in discussing this aspect of my research with me, suggested that I reconstruct the protoforms for the Kilivila CPs to find more evidence for this hypothesis (Ross 1989: personal communication). This is a very interesting proposal. However, I have some further evidence to support my hypothesis. Examination of the tables in section 3.3.4.2, which present the dynamic processes within the semantic domains, shows the following: the CP *kweya/kwaya/keya* supersedes the CP *yam/yuma/yama* and the CP *ka'i* supersedes the CP *kudu* (see Table 3.4.1.2a); the repeater *peta* is superseded by its shortened variant *ta* and the repeater *yegila* is superseded by its shortened variant *iga*; the CPs *bogi, koya, po'ula, siva, yam*, and to a certain extent the CP *boda*, are superseded by the general CP *kwe*; the CP *liku* and to a certain extent the CP *duli*, are superseded by the general CPs *ke* and *kwe*; the CP *kabulo* is superseded by the CP *ke*; the position of the CP *gula* is affected by the CPs *tam* and *kwe*; and the CPs *beku, bwalita, doba, dumia, megwa, nigwa, tetu, tuta, vaya, vakala, vosi*, and *kauya* play only a marginal role within the system of Kilivila CPs. These additional observations for 26 of the 37 CPs that could be traced to noun forms lead me to draw the following conclusion. I assume that most, if not all, Kilivila CPs originate in nouns (for a more general formulation of this idea, see Lee 1988:212, 225, 235). Originally, the CP system contained repeaters only. Over time, these repeaters were changed and modified, usually by processes of phonological reduction. Finally, CPs that can be easily traced to nouns have been superseded by the general CPs or by CPs that have undergone so many changes that their nominal origin is difficult or perhaps impossible to trace.

# References

Adams, Karen L. 1986. Numeral classifiers in Austroasiatic. In *Noun classes and categorization*, ed. Colette Craig, 241–262. Amsterdam: John Benjamins.

Adams, Karen L. 1989. *Systems of numeral classification in the Mon-Khmer, Nicobarese and Aslian subfamilies of Austroasiatic*. Pacific Linguistics, Series B, No. 101. Canberra: Australian National University.

Adams, Karen L. 1991. The influence of non-Austroasiatic languages on numeral classification in Austroasiatic. *Journal of the American Oriental Society* 111(1):62–81.

Adams, Karen L. 1992. A comparison of the numeral classification of humans in Mon-Khmer. *Mon-Khmer Studies* 21:107–129.

Adams, Karen L., and Nancy F. Conklin. 1973. Toward a theory of natural classification. In *Papers from the Ninth Regional Meeting, Chicago Linguistic Society*, eds. Claudia Corum, T. Cedric Smith-Stark, and Ann Weiser, 1–10. Chicago Linguistic Society, University of Chicago, Chicago, Ill.

Adams, Karen L., and Nancy F. Conklin. 1974. On the numeral classifier in Thai. Paper presented at the 7th International Conference on Sino-Tibetan Language and Linguistic Studies, Atlanta, Ga, October 19, 1974.

Adams, Karen L., Alton L. Becker, and Nancy F. Conklin. 1975. *Savoring the differences among classifier systems*. Paper presented at the 8th International Conference on Sino-Tibetan Languages and Linguistics, Berkeley, Calif., October 1975.

Adorno, Theodor W., Ralf Dahrendorf, Harald Pilot, Hans Albert, Jürgen Habermas, and Karl R. Popper, eds. 1969. *Der Positivismusstreit in der deutschen Soziologie*. Darmstadt, Germany: Hermann Luchterhand.

Allan, Keith. 1977. Classifiers. *Language* 53:285–311.

Alungum, John, Robert J. Conrad, and Joshua Lukas. 1978. Some Muhiang grammatical notes. In *Workpapers in Papua New Guinea languages*, ed. Richard Loving, 89–130. Ukarumpa, Papua New Guinea: Summer Institute of Linguistics.

Aristotle. 1976. *The Ethics of Aristotle. The Nicomachean Ethics.* Translated by J. A. K. Thomson. Harmondsworth, England: Penguin.

Asmah, Jaji Omar. 1972. Numeral classifiers in Malay and Iban. *Anthropological Linguistics* 14(3): 87–96.

Austen, Leo. 1939. The seasonal gardening calendar of Kiriwina, Trobriand Islands. *Oceania* 9:237–253.

Austen, Leo. 1949/50. A note on Dr. Leach's "Primitive calendars." *Oceania* 20:333–335.

Baldwin, Bernard. No date. *Biga Boyowa*, Catholic Mission Gusaweta, Papua New Guinea. Ms.

Barron, Roger. 1982. Das Phänomen klassifikatorischer Verben. In *Apprehension: das sprachliche Erfassen von Gegenständen*, part 1: *Bereich und Ordnung der Phänomene*, eds. Hansjakob Seiler and Christian Lehmann, 133–146. Tübingen, Germany: Narr.

Barron, Roger, and Fritz Serzisko. 1982. Noun classifiers in the Siouan languages. In *Apprehension: das sprachliche Erfassen von Gegenständen*, part 2: *Die Techniken und ihr Zusammenhang in Einzelsprachen*, eds. Hansjakob Seiler and Franz-Josef Stachowiak, 85–105. Tübingen, Germany: Narr.

Barz, R. K., and A. V. N. Diller. 1985. Classifiers and standardisation: Some South and South-East Asian comparisons. In *Papers in South-East Asian linguistics*, No. 9, ed. Daniel Bradley, 155–184. Canberra: Australian National University.

Bechert, Johannes. 1982. Grammatical gender in Europe: An areal study of a linguistic category. *Papiere zur Linguistik* 26: 23–34.

Bechert, Johannes. 1988. *The structure of the noun in European languages*. Paper presented at the Workshop on Typology of Languages in Europe. Rome, Italy, January 1988.

Becker, Alton L. 1975. A linguistic image of nature: The Burmese numerative classifier system. *Linguistics* 165: 109–121.

Becker, Alton L. 1986. The figure a classifier makes: Describing a particular Burmese classifier. In *Noun classes and categorization*, ed. Colette Craig, 327–343. Amsterdam: John Benjamins.

Bell-Krannhals, Ingrid. 1987. Nahrung aus dem Meer: Fischfang an den Küsten Neuguineas. In *Neuguinea: Nutzung und Deutung der Umwelt*, ed. Mark Münzel, vol. 1, 239–261. Frankfurt am Main, Germany: Museum für Völkerkunde.

Benton, Richard A. 1968. Numeral and attributive classifiers in Trukese. *Oceanic Linguistics* 7:104–146.

Berlin, Brent. 1968. *Tzeltal numeral classifiers: A study in ethnographic semantics*. The Hague: Mouton.

Berlin, Brent, and A. Kimball Romney. 1964. Descriptive semantics of Tzeltal numeral classifiers. *American Anthropologist* 66(3):79–98.

Berlin, Brent, Dennis E. Breedlove, and Peter H. Raven. 1969. Folk taxonomies and biological classification. In *Cognitive Anthropology*, ed. Stephen A. Tyler, 60–66. New York: Holt, Rinehart and Winston.

Berlin, Brent, Dennis E. Breedlove, and Peter H. Raven. 1973. General principles of classification and nomenclature in folk biology. *American Anthropologist* 75:214–242.

Berry, J. W., and Pierre R. Dasen, eds. 1974. *Culture and cognition. Readings in cross cultural psychology*. London: Methuen.

Biersack, Aletta. 1982. The logic of misplaced concreteness: Paiela body counting and the nature of the primitive mind. *American Anthropologist* 84:811–829.

Blust, Robert. 1988. Sketches of the morphology and phonology of Bornean languages, 2: Mukah (Melanau). In *Papers in Western Austronesian Linguistics*, no. 3, ed. Hein Steinhauer, Pacific Linguistics, Series A, No. 78:151–216. Canberra: Australian National University.

Bloomfield, Leonard. 1933 *Language*. London: Allen and Unwin.

Böhme, Karin. 1983. *Children's understanding and awareness of German possessive pronouns*. Doctoral dissertation, Katholieke Universiteit, Nijmegen, The Netherlands.

Bousfield, John. 1979. The world seen as a colour chart. In *Classifications in their social context*, eds Roy Ellen and David Reason, 195–220. London: Academic Press.

Bright, Jane O., and William Bright. 1969. Semantic structures in Northwestern California and the Sapir-Whorf hypothesis. In *Cognitive Anthropology*, ed. Stephen Tyler, 66–78. New York: Holt, Rinehart and Winston.

Broadfield, A. 1946. *The philosophy of classification*. London: Graffon and Co.

Brown, Roger W., and Eric H. Lenneberg. 1958. Studies in linguistic relativity. In *Readings in social psychology*, eds. Eleanor Maccoby, Theodore M. Newcomb, and Eugene L. Hartley, 9–18. New York: Holt, Rinehart and Winston.

Bruner, Jerome S., Jacqueline J. Goodnow, and George A. Austin. 1962. *A study of thinking, with an appendix on language by Roger Brown*. New York: Science Editions.

Bühler, Karl. 1978 [1934]. *Sprachtheorie: Die Darstellungsfunktion der Sprache*. Frankfurt am Main, Germany: Ullstein.

Burling, Robbins. 1965. How to choose a Burmese numeral classifier. In *Context and meaning in cultural anthropology*, ed. Melford E. Spiro, 243–264. New York: Free Press.

Bussmann, Hadumod. 1983. *Lexikon der Sprachwissenschaft*. Stuttgart, Germany: Kröner.

Capell, Arthur. 1969. *A survey of New Guinea languages*. Sydney, Australia: Sydney University Press.

Capell, Arthur. 1971. The Austronesian languages of Australian New Guinea. In *Current Trends in Linguistics*, vol. 8: *Linguistics in Oceania*, ed. Thomas A. Sebeok, 240–340. The Hague: Mouton.

Capell, Arthur. 1976. General picture of Austronesian languages, New Guinea area. In *New Guinea area languages and language study, vol. 2: Austronesian languages*, ed. Stephen A. Wurm, 5–52. Canberra: Australian National University.

Carpenter, Kathie. 1986. Productivity and pragmatics of Thai classifiers. In *Proceedings of the Twelfth Annual Meeting of the Berkeley Linguistic Society*, eds. Vassiliki Nikifaridou, Mary Van Clay, Mary Niepokuj, and Deborah Fedev, 14–25. University of California, Berkeley.

Carpenter, Kathie. 1991. Later rather than sooner: Extralinguistic categories in the acquisition of Thai classifiers. *Journal of Child Language* 18: 93–113.

Carpenter, Kathie. 1992. Two dynamic views of classifier systems: Diachronic change and individual development. *Cognitive Linguistics* 3:129–150.

Carroll, John B., and Joseph B. Casagrande. 1958. The function of language classification in behavior. In *Readings in social psychology*, eds. Eleanor Maccoby, Theodore M. Newcomb, and Eugene L. Hartley, 18–31. New York: Holt, Rinehart and Winston.

Chin, Ng Bee. 1989. *The acquisition of numeral classifiers in Hokkien, a Southern Min language*. Doctoral dissertation, La Trobe University, Bundoora, Victoria, Australia.

Cholodovic, A. A. 1954. *Ocerk grammatiki korejskogo jazyka*. Moscow, Russia, Izdatel'stvo literatury na inostrannych jazykach.

Clark, Eve V. 1976. Universal categories: On the semantics of classifiers and children's early word meanings. *Linguistic studies offered to Joseph Greenberg: Studia linguistica et philologica*, ed. Alphonse Juilland, 449–462. Saratoga, Calif.: Anma Libri.

Clark, Herbert, H., Patricia A. Carpenter, and Marcel A. Just. 1973. On the meeting of semantics and perception. In *Visual information processing*, ed. William G. Chase, 311–381. New York: Academic Press.

Cole, Michael, John Gay, Joseph A. Glick, and Donald W. Sharp. 1971. *The cultural context of learning: An exploration in experimental anthropology.* New York, Basic Books.

Cole, Michael, and Sylvia Scribner. 1974. *Culture and thought: A psychological introduction.* New York: John Wiley.

Collins, Allan M., and M. R. Quillian. 1969. Retrieval time from semantic memory. *Journal of Verbal Learning and Verbal Behavior* 8:240–247.

Conklin, Harold C. 1962. Lexicographic treatment of folk taxonomies. Problems in lexicography. *International Journal of American Linguistics* 28(4):119–141.

Corum, Claudia, T. Cedric Smith-Stark, and Ann Weiser, eds. 1973. *Papers from the Ninth Regional Meeting, Chicago Linguistic Society.* Chicago Linguistic Society, University of Chicago, Chicago, Ill.

Craig, Colette. 1986. Jacaltec noun classifiers: A study in language and culture. In *Noun classes and categorization,* ed. Colette Craig, 263–293. Amsterdam: John Benjamins.

Craig, Colette. 1992. Classifiers in a functional perspective. In *Layered structure and reference in a functional perspective,* eds. Michael Fortescue, Peter Harder, and Lars Kristoffersen, 277–301. Amsterdam: John Benjamins.

Delancey, Scott. 1986. Toward a history of Tai classifier systems. In *Noun classes and categorization,* ed. Colette Craig, 437–452. Amsterdam: John Benjamins.

Demuth, Katherine. 1988. Noun classes and agreement in Sesotho acquisition. In *Agreement in natural language: Approaches, theories, descriptions,* eds. Michael Barlow and Charles Ferguson, 305–321. Chicago, Ill.: University of Chicago Press.

Demuth, Katherine. 1992. The acquisition of Sesotho. In *The cross-linguistic study of language acquisition,* vol. 3, ed. Dan Slobin, 557–638. Hillsdale, N.J.: Lawrence Erlbaum.

Demuth, Katherine, Nicolas Faraclas, and Lynell Marchese. 1986. Niger-Congo noun class and agreement systems in language acquisition and historical change. In *Noun classes and categorization,* ed. Colette Craig, 453–471. Amsterdam: John Benjamins.

Denny, J. Peter. 1976. What are noun classifiers good for? In *Papers from the Twelfth Regional Meeting, Chicago Linguistic Society,* eds. Salikoko S. Mufwene, Carol A. Walker, and Sanford B. Steever, 122–132. Chicago Linguistic Society, University of Chicago, Chicago, Ill.

Denny, J. Peter. 1979. The "extendedness' variable in classifier semantics: Universal features and cultural variation. In *Ethnolinguistics: Boas, Sapir and Whorf revisited,* ed. Madeleine Mathiot, 97–119. The Hague: Mouton.

Denny, J. Peter. 1986. The semantic role of noun classifiers. In *Noun classes and categorization,* ed. Colette Craig, 297–308. Amsterdam: John Benjamins.

Diller, A. V. N. 1985. High and low Thai: Views from within. In *Papers in South-East Asian Linguistics,* ed. David Bradley, 51–76. Canberra: Australian National University.

Dixon, Robert M. W. 1968. Noun classes. *Lingua* 21:104–125.

Dixon, Robert M. W. 1972. *The Dyirbal language of North Queensland.* Cambridge: Cambridge University Press.

Dixon, Robert M. W. 1982. *Where have all the adjectives gone and other essays in semantics and syntax.* Berlin: Mouton.

Dixon, Robert M. W. 1986. Noun classes and noun classification in typological perspective. In *Noun classes and categorization,* ed. Colette Craig, 105–112. Amsterdam: John Benjamins.

Dolby, R. G. A. 1979. Classification of the sciences. The nineteenth century tradition.

In *Classifications in their social context*, eds. Roy F. Ellen and David Reason, 167–193. London: Academic Press.

Downing, Pamela. 1986. The anaphoric use of classifiers in Japanese. *Noun classes and categorization*, ed. Colette Craig, 345–375. Amsterdam: John Benjamins.

Durkheim, Emile, and Marcel Mauss. 1970 [1903]. *Primitive classification*. Translated by Rodney Needham. London: Routledge and Kegan Paul. (De quelques formes primitives de classification. *Année Sociologique* 1901–02.)

Eibl-Eibesfeldt, Irenäus. 1984. *Die Biologie des menschlichen Sozialverhaltens. Grundriß der Humanethologie*. München, Germany: Piper.

Eibl-Eibesfeldt, Irenäus, Barbara Senft, and Gunter Senft. 1987. Trobriander (Ost-Neuguinea, Trobriand Inseln, Kaile'una) Fadenspiele "ninikula". In *Publikationen zu Wissenschaftlichen Filmen*, Sektion Ethnologie, Serie 15, Nummer 25. Göttingen, Germany: Institut für den Wissenschaftlichen Film.

Eibl-Eibesfeldt, Irenäus, and Gunter Senft. 1986. Trobriander (Ost-Neuguinea, Trobriand Inseln, Kaile'una) Fadenspiele "ninikula". Film Nr. E 2958. Göttingen, Germany: Institut für den Wissenschaftlichen Film.

Ellen, Roy F. 1979. Introductory Essay. In *Classifications in their social context*, eds. Roy F. Ellen and David Reason, 1–32. London: Academic Press.

Ellen, Roy F., and David Reason. 1979. Preface. In *Classifications in Their Social Context*, eds. Roy F. Ellen and David Reason, vii–viii. London: Academic Press.

Erbaugh, Mary S. 1986. Taking stock: The development of Chinese noun classifiers historically and in young Children. In *Noun classes and categorization*, ed. Colette Craig, 399–436. Amsterdam: John Benjamins.

Ezard, Bryan. 1978. Classificatory prefixes of the Massim cluster. In *Second International Conference on Austronesian Linguistics: Proceedings*, Fascicle 2, eds. Stephen A. Wurm and Lois Carrington, 1159–1180. Pacific Linguistics, Series C, No. 61. Canberra: Australian National University.

Fellows, S. B. 1901. Grammar of the Kiriwina dialect (together with a vocabulary). In *Annual Report on British New Guinea 1900–1901*, appendix N2, 171–177; appendix O2, 177–196. Brisbane, Australia: G. A. Vaughan.

Fischer, Gero. 1972. Die syntaktischen und semantischen Eigenschaften der Numeralklassifikatoren im Thai. *Archiv Orientalni* 40:65–78.

Foley, William A. 1968. *The Papuan languages of New Guinea*. Cambridge: Cambridge University Press.

Foucault, Michel. 1980 [1966]. *Die Ordnung der Dinge. Eine Archäologie der Humanwissenschaften*. Frankfurt am Main, Germany: Suhrkamp. (*Les Mots et les choses*. Paris: Gallimard.)

Fox, James J. 1975. On binary categories and primary symbols. Some Rotinese perspectives. In *The interpretation of symbolism*, ed. Roy Willis, 99–132. London: Malaby Press.

Fox, James J. 1989. Category and complement: Binary ideologies and the organization of dualism in Eastern Indonesia. In *The attraction of opposites: Thought and society in the dualistic mode*, eds. David Maybury-Lewis and Uri Almagar, 33–56. Ann Arbor: University of Michigan Press.

Frake, Charles O. 1969. The ethnographic study of cognitive systems. In *Cognitive anthropology*, ed. Stephen A. Tyler, 28–41. New York: Holt, Rinehart and Winston.

Freilich, Morris, ed. 1970. *Marginal natives: Anthropologists at work*. New York: Harper and Row.

Friedrich, Paul. 1970. Shape in grammar. *Language* 46:379–407.

Gandour, Jack, Saranee H. Petty, Rochama Dardarananda, Suralee Dechongkit, and

Sunee Mukngoen. 1984. The acquisition of numeral classifiers in Thai. *Linguistics* 22:455–479.

Gipper, Helmut. 1972. *Gibt es ein sprachliches Relativitätsprinzip? Untersuchungen zur Sapir-Whorf-Hypothese.* Frankfurt am Main, Germany: S. Fischer.

Givón, Talmy. 1986. Prototypes: Between Plato and Wittgenstein. In *Noun classes and categorization,* ed. Colette Craig, 77–102. Amsterdam: John Benjamins.

Goffman, Erving. 1974. *Frame analysis. An essay on the organization of experience.* New York: Harper and Row.

Gohlke, Paul, ed. 1972. *Aristoteles—Kategorien und Hermeneutik.* Paderborn, Germany: Schöningh.

Gomez-Imbert, Elsa. 1982. *De la forme et du sens dans la classification nominale in Tatuyo (langue Tukano Orientale d'Amazonie Colombienne).* Doctoral dissertation, Université Sorbonne, Paris IV, Ecole Pratique des Hautes Etudes, IVe section.

Goodenough, Ward H. 1969. Rethinking "status" and "role": Toward a general model of the cultural organization of social relationships. In *Cognitive Anthropology,* ed. Stephen Tyler, 311–330. New York: Holt, Rinehart and Winston.

Goral, Donald A. 1978. Numeral classifier systems: A South-East Asian cross-linguistic analysis. *Linguistics in the Tibeto-Burman Area* 4:1–72.

Greenberg, Joseph H. 1972. Numerical classifiers and substantival number: Problems in the genesis of a linguistic type. *Working Papers in Language Universals* 9:1–39.

Greenberg, Joseph H. 1975. Numeral classifiers and substantival number: Problems in the genesis of a linguistic type. In *Proceedings of the 11th International Congress of Linguistics,* ed. Luigi Heilmann, 17–37. Bologna, Italy: Mulino.

Greenberg, Joseph H. 1978. How does a language acquire gender-markers? In *Universals of human language,* vol. 3, *Word structure,* ed. Joseph H. Greenberg, 47–82. Stanford, Calif.: Stanford University Press.

Haas, Mary R. 1942. The use of numeral classifiers in Thai. *Language* 18:201–205.

Hallpike, Christopher R. 1979. *The foundations of primitive thought.* Oxford: Clarendon Press.

Harweg, Roland 1987a. Stoffnamen und Gattungsnamen. *Zeitschrift für Phonetik, Sprachwissenschaft und Kommunikationsforschung* 40:792–804.

Harweg, Roland. 1987b. Zähleinheitswörter und Weltbild. *Archiv Orientalni* 55:253–270.

Haugen, Einar. 1977. Linguistic relativity: Myths and methods. In *Language and thought: Anthropological issues,* ed. William McCormack and Stephen A. Wurm, 11–28. The Hague: Mouton.

Heeschen, Volker. 1972. *Die Sprachphilosophie Wilhelm von Humboldts.* Doctoral dissertation, Ruhr-Universität, Bochum, Germany.

Heine, Bernd. 1982. African noun-class systems. In *Apprehension: das sprachliche Erfassen von Gegenständen,* Teil 1: *Bereich und Ordnung der Phänomene,* ed. Hansjakob Seiler and Christian Lehmann, 189–216. Tübingen, Germany: Narr.

Herder, Johan Gottfried 1978 [1770]. Über den Ursprung der Sprache. In *Herders Werke in fünf Bänden.* Band 2, 91–200. Berlin: Aufbau Verlag.

Hiranburana, SamAng. 1979. A classification of Thai classifiers. *South-East Asian Linguistic Studies.* vol. 4, ed. Dang Liem Nguyen, 39–54. (Pacific Linguistics, Series C, No. 49.) Canberra: Australian National University.

Hla Pe. 1965. A Re-examination of Burmese "classifiers". *Lingua* 15:163–185.

Hoa, Ngyen Dinh. 1957. Classifiers in Vietnamese. *Word* 13:124–152.

Hopper, Paul J. 1986. Some discourse functions of classifiers in Malay. In *Noun classes and categorization*, ed. Colette Craig, 309–325. Amsterdam: John Benjamins.

Humboldt, Wilhelm von. 1968 [1836]. *Über die Verschiedenheit des menschlichen Sprachbaues und ihren Einfluß auf die geistige Entwicklung des Menschengeschlechts.* Bonn, Germany: Dümmler.

Hundius, Harald, and Ulrike Kölver. 1983. Syntax and semantics of numeral classifiers in Thai. *Studies in Language* 7:165–214.

Hutchins, Edwin. 1980. *Culture and inference. A Trobriand case study.* Cambridge, Mass.: Harvard University Press.

Jackendoff, Ray S. 1968. Quantifiers in English. *Foundations of Language* 4:422–442.

Jacob, Judith M. 1965. Notes on numerals and numeral co-efficients in Old, Middle and Modern Khmer. *Lingua* 15:143–162.

Jensen, Hans. 1952. Die sprachliche Kategorie des Numerus. *Wissenschaftliche Zeitschrift der Universität Rostock* 1(H3):1–21.

Jones, Robert B. 1970. Classifier constructions in Southeast Asia. *Journal of the American Oriental Society* 90:1–12.

Juilland Alphonse, and Hans Heinrich Lieb. 1968. *Klasse und Klassifikation in der Sprachwissenschaft.* The Hague: Mouton.

Kaden, Klaus. 1964. *Der Ausdruck der Mehrzahlverhältnisse in der modernen chinesischen Sprache.* Berlin: Akademie Verlag.

Kantor, Rebecca. 1980. The acquisition of classifiers in American Sign Language. *Sign Language Studies* 28:193–208.

Kasaipwalova, John. 1980. *Sail the midnight sun.* Port Moresby, Papua New Guinea: National Arts School.

Katz, Elisabeth. 1982. Zur Distribution von Kompositum und Nominalgruppe im Deutschen. In *Apprehension: das sprachliche Erfassen von Gegenständen*, part 1: *Bereich und Ordnung der Phänomene*, ed. Hansjakob Seiler and Christian Lehmann, 112–129. Tübingen, Germany: Narr.

Kegl, Judy, and Sara Schley. 1986. When is a classifier no longer a classifier? In *Proceedings of the 12th Annual Meeting of the Berkeley Linguistic Society*, 425–441. Berkeley, Calif.: Berkeley Linguistic Society.

Kendon, Adam. 1988. *Sign languages of Aboriginal Australia: Cultural, semiotic and communicative perspectives.* Cambridge: Cambridge University Press.

Kessel, Frank S., ed. 1988. *The development of language and language researchers: Essays in honor of Roger Brown.* Hillsdale, N.J.: Lawrence Erlbaum.

Klaus, Georg, ed. 1968. *Wörterbuch der Kybernetik.* Berlin: Dietz.

Klein, Harriet E. Manelis. 1979. Noun classifiers in Toba. In *Ethnolinguistics: Boas, Sapir and Whorf revisited*, ed. Madeleine Mathiot, 85–95. The Hague: Mouton.

Klein, Wolfgang. 1974. *Variation in der Sprache.* Kronberg, Germany: Scriptor.

Klein, Wolfgang. 1984. *Zweitspracherwerb. Eine Einführung.* Königstein, Germany: Athenäum.

Klein, Wolfgang. 1986. *Second language acquisition.* Cambridge: Cambridge University Press.

Klein, Wolfgang, and Norbert Dittmar. 1979. *Developing grammars.* Berlin: Springer.

Klima, Edward S., and Ursula Bellugi. 1979. *The signs of language.* Cambridge, Mass.: Harvard University Press.

Koch, Gerd. 1984. *Malingdam. Mensch, Kultur und Umwelt im zentralen Bergland von West-Neuguinea*, vol. 15. Berlin: Reimer.

Koch, Walter A. 1986. *Genes vs. memes: Modes of integration for natural and cultural evolution in a holistic model ("ELPIS").* Bochum, Germany: Brockmeyer.

Koestler, Arthur. 1983. *Janus: A summing up*. London: Pan Picador.

Kölver, Ulrike. 1978. On Newari noun phrases. In *Language universals*, ed. Hansjakob Seiler, 277–300. Tübingen, Germany: Narr.

Kölver, Ulrike. 1979. Syntaktische Untersuchung von Numeralklassifikatoren im Zentralthai. *Akup*, 34, ed. Hansjakob Seiler. Cologne, Germany: Universität zu Köln.

Kölver, Ulrike. 1982a. Zu den Techniken Numerus, Kollektion und Numeral-klassifikation in der Bahasa Indonesia. In *Apprehension: das sprachliche Erfassen von Gegenständen*, part 2: *Die Techniken und ihr Zusammenhang in Einzelsprachen*, ed. Hansjakob Seiler and Franz-Josef Stachowiak, 107–122. Tübingen, Germany: Narr.

Kölver, Ulrike. 1982b. Interaktion von nominalen Kategorien am Beispiel der Entwicklung des modernen Bengali. In *Apprehension: das sprachliche Erfassen von Gegenständen*, part 1: *Bereich und Ordnung der Phänomene*, ed. Hansjakob Seiler and Christian Lehmann, 244–251. Tübingen, Germany: Narr.

Kölver, Ulrike. 1982c. Klassifikatorkonstruktion in Thai, Vietnamesisch und Chinesisch—Ein Beitrag zur Dimension der Apprehension. In *Apprehension: das sprachliche Erfassen von Gegenständen*, part 1: *Bereich und Ordnung der Phänomene*, ed. Hansjakob Seiler and Christian Lehmann, 160–185. Tübingen, Germany: Narr.

Kölver, Ulrike. 1983. The notion of scalarity in language comparison. In *Language invariants and mental operations*, ed. Hansjakob Seiler and Gunter Brettschneider, 53–57. Tübingen, Germany: Narr.

Koschmieder, Erwin. 1945. Zur Bestimmung der Funktion grammatischer Kategorien. In *Abhandlungen der Bayerischen Akademie der Wissenschaften: Philosophisch-historische Abteilung*, NF25:1–64.

Labov, William. 1972a. *Language in the inner city: Studies in the black English vernacular*. Philadelphia: University of Pennsylvania Press.

Labov, William. 1972b. *Sociolinguistic patterns*. Philadelphia: University of Pennsylvania Press.

Lakoff, George. 1986. Classifiers as a reflection of mind. *Noun classes and categorization*, ed. Colette Craig, 13–51. Amsterdam: John Benjamins.

Lakoff, George. 1987. *Women, fire, and dangerous things*. What categories reveal about the mind. Chicago: University of Chicago Press.

Lawton, Ralph. 1980. *The Kiriwinan classifiers*. Masters thesis. Canberra: Australian National University.

Leach, Edmund. 1972 (1964). Anthropologische Aspekte der Sprache: Tierkategorie und Schimpfwörter. In *Biologische Grundlagen der Sprache*, ed. Eric Lenneberg, 32–73. Frankfurt am Main, Germany: Suhrkamp (*Biological Foundations of Language*. New York: John Wiley).

Leach, Jerry W. 1949/50. Primitive calendars. *Oceania* 20:254–262.

Leach, Jerry W. 1981. A Kula folktale from Kiriwina. *Bikmaus* 2(1):50–92.

Lean, G. A. 1986. *Counting systems of Papua New Guinea—Research bibliography*. Lae, Papua New Guinea: Mathematics Education Centre, PNG University of Technology.

Lee, Michael. 1987. The cognitive basis of classifier systems. *Berkeley Linguistic Society, Proceedings of the 13th Annual Meeting*, 395–407. Berkeley, Calif.: Berkeley Linguistic Society.

Lee, Michael. 1988. Language, perception and the world. In *Explaining language universals*, ed. John Hawkins, 211–246. Oxford: Basil Blackwell.

Lehmann, F. K. 1979. Aspects of a formal theory of classifiers. *Studies in Language* 3:153–180.

Lenneberg, Eric H. 1953. Cognition in ethnolinguistics. *Language* 29:463–471.

Lenneberg, Eric H., ed. 1972 *Neue Perspektiven in der Erforschung der Sprache.* Frankfurt am Main, Germany: Suhrkamp (*New Directions in the Study of Language.* Cambridge, Mass.: MIT Press).

Lenneberg, Eric H. 1977 (1967). *Biologische Grundlagen der Sprache.* Frankfurt am Main: Suhrkamp (*Biological Foundations of Language.* New York: John Wiley).

de León, Lourdes. 1988. *Noun and numeral classifiers in Mixtec and Tzotzil: A referential view.* Doctoral dissertation, University of Sussex, Linguistics Division of the Graduate School, Sussex, England.

Lenz, Jakob Michael Reinhold. 1909 [1774]. Der neue Menoza oder Geschichte des kumbanischen Prinzen Tandi. Eine Komödie. In *Jakob Michael Reinhold Lenz, Gesammelte Schriften.* Herausgegeben von Franz Blei, vol. 2. Munich, Germany: Georg Müller.

Levelt, Willem J. M. 1980. On-line processing constraints on the properties of signed and spoken language. In *Signed and spoken language: Biological constraints on linguistic forms*, ed. Ursula Bellugi and Michael Studdert-Kennedy, 141–160. Weinheim, Germany: Verlag Chemie.

Levinson, Stephen C. 1983. *Pragmatics.* Cambridge: Cambridge University Press.

Lithgow, David. 1976. Austronesian languages: Milne Bay Province and adjacent islands (Milne Bay Province). In *New Guinea area languages and language study*, vol 2: *Austronesian Languages*, ed. Stephen A. Wurm, 441–523. Pacific Linguistics, Series C, No. 39. Canberra: Australian National University.

Löbel, Elisabeth. 1986. Apposition in der Quantifizierung. In *Pragmantax*, eds. Armin Burkhardt and Karl-Hermann Körner, 47–59. Tübingen, Germany: Niemeyer.

Lonning, Jam Tare. 1987. Mass terms and quantification. *Linguistics and Philosophy* 10:1–52.

Lorenz, Konrad. 1973. *Die Rückseite des Spiegels: Versuch einer Naturgeschichte menschlichen Erkennens.* Munich, Germany: Piper.

Lorenz, Konrad. 1977: *Behind the mirror: A search for a natural history of human knowledge.* Translated by Ronald Taylor. New York: Harcourt Brace Jovanovich.

Luke, K. K., and Godfrey Harrison, 1986. Young children's use of Chinese (Cantonese and Mandarin) sortal classifiers. In *Linguistics, psychology and the Chinese language*, eds. S. R. Henry Kao and Rumjahn Hoosain, 125–147. Centre of Asian Studies. Hong Kong: University of Hong Kong.

Lyons, John. 1977a. *Semantics I.* Cambridge: Cambridge University Press.

Lyons, John. 1977b. *Semantics II.* Cambridge: Cambridge University Press.

MacLaury, Robert E. 1991. Prototypes revisited. *Annual Review of Anthropology* 20:55–74.

Malinowski, Bronislaw. 1920. Classificatory particles in the language of Kiriwina. *Bulletin of the School of Oriental Studies* I(IV):33–78.

Malinowski, Bronislaw. 1978 [1922]. *Argonauts of the Western Pacific.* London: Routledge and Kegan Paul.

Malinowski, Bronislaw. 1982 [1929]. *The sexual life of savages in North Western Melanesia.* London: Routledge and Kegan Paul.

Malinowski, Bronislaw. 1966 [1935]. *Coral gardens and their magic*, 2 vols. London: Allen and Unwin.

Malinowski, Bronislaw. 1974. *Magic, science and religion and other essays.* London: Souvenir Press.

Malmberg, Bertil. 1987. Wilhelm von Humboldt und die moderne Sprachwissenschaft. In *Preprints of the Plenary Session Papers of the XIVth International Congress of Linguists organized under the Auspices of CIPL, Berlin, 10–15. August 1987*, 3–25. Berlin: Editorial Committee.

Martens, Michael. 1988. How big is your rice? Units of measurement among the Uma people. *Papers in Western Austronesian Linguistics*, No. 4, 257–261. Pacific Linguistics, Series A. No. 79. Canberra: Australian National University.

Matsumoto, Yo. 1985. Acquisition of some Japanese numeral classifiers: The search for convention. *Papers and Reports in Child Language Development*, Stanford University, 24:79–86.

Miller, George A. 1956. The magical number seven, plus or minus two: Some limits on our capacity for processing information. *Psychological Review* 63(2):81–96.

Miller, George A., and Philip N. Johnson-Laird. 1976. *Language and perception*. Cambridge, Mass.: Harvard University Press.

Milner, George B. 1963. Oceanic linguistics. In *Trends in modern linguistics*, eds. Christine Mohrmann, F. Norman, and Alf Sommerfelt, 62–94. Utrecht, The Netherlands: Spectrum Publishers.

Miram, Helga-Maria. 1983. *Numeral classifiers im yukatekischen Maya*. Hannover, Germany: Verlag für Ethnologie.

Mithun, Marianne. 1986. The convergence of noun classification systems. In *Noun classes and categorization*, ed. Colette Craig, 379–397. Amsterdam: John Benjamins.

Moerman, Michael. 1969. A little knowledge. In *Cognitive Anthropology*, ed. Stephen A. Tyler, 449–469. New York: Holt, Rinehart and Winston.

Mufwene, Salikoko S. 1980a. Number, countability and markedness in Lingala LI-/MA-noun class. *Linguistics* 18:1019–1052.

Mufwene, Salikoko S. 1980b. "Prototype" and "Kin-Class". *Anthropological Linguistics* 22:29–41.

Mufwene, Salikoko S. 1980c. Bantu class prefixes: Inflectional or derivational? In *Papers from the Sixteenth Regional Meeting, Chicago Linguistic Society*, 246–258. Chicago Linguistic Society, University of Chicago, Chicago, Ill.

Mufwene, Salikoko S. 1981. Noun individuation and the count/mass distinction. In *Papers from the Seventeenth Regional Meeting, Chicago Linguistic Society*, 221–238. Chicago Linguistic Society, University of Chicago, Chicago, Ill.

Mufwene, Salikoko S. 1983. Investigating what the words *Father* and *Mother* mean. *Language and Communication* 3:245–269.

Mufwene, Salikoko S. 1984. The count/mass distinction and the English lexicon. In *Papers from the parasession on lexical semantics, Chicago Linguistic Society*, 200–221. Chicago Linguistic Society, University of Chicago, Chicago, Ill.

Newport, Elissa, and Ted Supalla. 1980. Clues from the acquisition of signed and spoken language. In *Signed and spoken language: Biological constraints on linguistic form*, eds Ursula Bellugi and Michael Studdert-Kennedy, 187–212. Weinheim, Germany: Verlag Chemie.

Ohta, Itaru. 1987. Livestock individual identification among the Turkana: The animal classification and naming in the pastoral livestock management. In *African Study Monographs*, vol. 8, no. 1: 1–69. Kyoto, Japan: Kyoto University.

Parsons, Terence. 1970. An analysis of mass terms and amount terms. *Foundations of Language* 6: 362–388.

Plank, Frans. 1984. Verbs and objects in semantic agreement: Minor differences between English and German that might suggest a major one. *Journal of Semantics* 3:305–360.

Posner, Michael. 1986. Empirical studies on prototypes. In *Noun classes and categorization*, ed. Colette Craig, 53–61. Amsterdam: John Benjamins.

Powell, Harry A. 1957. *An analysis of present day social structure in the Trobriand Islands*. Doctoral dissertation, University of London, London, England.

Powell, Harry A. 1960. Competitive leadership in Trobriand political organization. *Journal of the Royal Anthropological Institute* 90:118–148.

Pribram, Karl H. 1987. *Brain and meaning*. Mimeo, Stanford University, Stanford, Calif.

Pullum, Geoffrey K. 1991. *The great Eskimo vocabulary hoax and other irrelevant essays on the study of language*. Chicago: University of Chicago Press.

Raible, Wolfgang. 1981. Von der Allgegenwart des Gegensinns (und einiger anderer Relationen): Strategien zur Einordnung semantischer Information. *Zeitschrift für romanische Philologie* 97:1–40.

Rausch, P. J. 1912. Die Sprache von Südost-Bougainville, Deutsche Salomonsinseln. *Anthropos* 7:105–134, 585–616, 964–994.

Ray, Sidney H. 1907. *Reports of the Cambridge Anthropological Expedition to Torres Straits*, vol. 3: *Linguistics*. Cambridge: Cambridge University Press.

Ray, Sidney H. 1938. The languages of the Eastern Lousiade Archipelago. *Bulletin of the School of Oriental Studies* 9:363–384.

Romaine, Suzanne. 1985. Variable rules, O.K.? Or can there be sociolinguistic grammars? *Language and Communication* 5:53–67.

Rosch, Eleanor. 1977. Human categorization. *Studies in Cross-Cultural Psychology*, vol. 1, ed. Neil Warren, 1–49. London: Academic Press.

Rosch, Eleanor. 1978. Principles of categorization. In *Cognition and Categorization*, eds. Eleanor Rosch and Barbara B. Lloyd, 27–48. Hillsdale, N.J.: Lawrence Erlbaum.

Rosch, Eleanor. 1988. Coherence and categorization: A historical view. In *The development of language and language researchers: Essays in honor of Roger Brown*, ed. Frank S. Kessel, 373–392. Hillsdale, N.J.: Lawrence Erlbaum.

Ross, Malcolm D. 1988. *Proto Oceanic and the Austronesian Languages of Western Melanesia*. Pacific Linguistics, Series C, No. 98. Canberra: Australian National University.

Royen, Gerlach. 1929. *Die nominalen Klassifikations-Systeme in den Sprachen der Erde: Historisch-kritische Studie, mit besonderer Berücksichtigung des Indogermanischen*. Anthropos Linguistische Bibliothek, vol. IV. Vienna: Anthropos.

Rude, Noel. 1986. Graphemic classifiers in Egyptian hieroglyphics and Mesopotamian cuneiform. In *Noun classes and categorization*, ed. Colette Craig, 133–138. Amsterdam: John Benjamins.

Sanches, Mary 1977. Language acquisition and language change: Japanese numeral classifiers. *Sociocultural dimensions of language change*, eds. Ben G. Blount and Mary Sanches, 51–62. New York: Academic Press.

Saul, Janice E. 1965. Classifiers in Nung. *Lingua* 13:278–290.

Schafer, Edward H., Jr. 1948. Noun classifiers in classical Chinese. *Language* 24:408–413.

Schiefenhövel, Wulf, and Ingrid Bell-Krannhals. 1986. Wer teilt hat teil an der Macht: Systeme der Yams-Vergabe auf den Trobriand Inseln, Papua-Neuguinea. *Mitteilungen der Anthropologischen Gesellschaft in Wien* 116:19–39.

Schieffelin, Bambi B., and Elinor Ochs. 1986. Language socialization. *Annual Review of Anthropology* 15:163–191.

Schleiermacher, Friedrich D. E. 1977 [1838]. *Hermeneutik und Kritik mit besonderer Beziehung auf das neue Testament*. Aus Schleirmachers handschriftlichem Nachlasse und nachgeschriebenen Vorlesungen herausgegeben und eingeleitet von Manfred Frank. Frankfurt am Main, Germany: Suhrkamp.

Schmidt, Arno. 1975. *Ansichten aus dem Leben eines Lords*. Frankfurt am Main, Germany: Fischer.

Schöne, Hermann. 1983. *Orientierung im Raum: Formen und Mechanismen der Lenkung des Verhaltens im Raum bei Tier und Mensch*. Stuttgart, Germany: Wissenschaftliche Verlagsanstalt.

Scoditti, Giancarlo M. G. 1985. *Kitawa: Iconografia e semantica in una società melanesiana*. Milan, Italy: Franco Angeli Libri.

Seiler, Hansjakob. 1973. Das Universalienkonzept. In *Linguistic Workshop I: Vorarbeiten zu einem Universalienprojekt*, ed. Hansjakob Seiler. Mimeo, Munich, Germany.

Seiler, Hansjakob. 1978. *Language Universals*. Tübingen, Germany: Narr.

Seiler, Hansjakob. 1982. Das sprachliche Erfassen von Gegenständen Apprehension. In *Apprehension: das sprachliche Erfassen von Gegenständen*, part 1: *Bereich und Ordnung der Phänomene*, eds. Hansjakob Seiler and Christian Lehmann, 3–11. Tübingen, Germany: Narr.

Seiler, Hansjakob. 1986. *Apprehension. Language, object, and order*, part III: *The universal dimension of apprehension*. Tübingen, Germany: Narr.

Seiler, Walter. 1983. The acquisition of a noun classification system by a language. *Language and Linguistics in Melanesia* 14:76–97.

Seiler, Walter. 1986. From verb serialisation to noun classification. In *Papers in New Guinea Linguistics*, No. 24, 11–19. Pacific Linguistics, Series A, No. 70. Canberra: Australian National University.

Senft, Barbara. 1985. *Kindheit in Tauwema. Die ersten 7 Jahre im Leben der Kinder auf den Trobriand-Inseln, Papua-Neuguinea*. Mimeo, Seewiesen, Germany: Forschungsstelle für Humanethologie.

Senft, Barbara, and Gunter Senft. 1986. Ninikula—Fadenspiele auf den Trobriand Inseln, Papua Neuguinea. Untersuchungen zum Spiele-Repertoire unter besonderer Berücksichtigung der Spiel-begleitenden Texte. *Baessler-Archiv, Beiträge zur Völkerkunde* NF 34(1):93–235.

Senft, Gunter. 1982. *Sprachliche Varietät und Variation im Sprachverhalten Kaiserslauterer Metallarbeiter: Untersuchungen zu ihrer Begrenzung, Beschreibung, und Bewertung*. Bern, Switzerland: Peter Lang.

Senft, Gunter. 1983. *The system of classificatory particles in Kilivila reconsidered—First results on its inventory, its acquisition, and its usage*. Paper presented at the Annual Meeting of the Linguistic Society of Papua New Guinea, Port Moresby, University of PNG, July 1983.

Senft, Gunter. 1985a. Klassifikationspartikel im Kilivila—Glossen zu ihrer morphologischen Rolle, ihrem Inventar und ihrer Funktion in Satz und Diskurs. *Linguistische Berichte* 99:373–393.

Senft, Gunter. 1985b. Kilivila—die Sprache der Trobriander. *Studium Linguistik* 17/18:127–138.

Senft, Gunter. 1985c. Weyeis Wettermagie—eine ethnolinguistische Untersuchung von fünf wettermagischen Formeln eines Wettermagiers auf den Trobriand Inseln. *Zeitschrift für Ethnologie* 10(1):67–90; (H2):erratum.

Senft, Gunter. 1985d. Trauer auf Trobriand—Eine ethnologisch/linguistische Fallstudie. *Anthropos* 80:471–492.

Senft, Gunter. 1985e. How to tell—and understand—a "dirty" joke in Kilivila. *Journal of Pragmatics* 9:815–834.

Senft, Gunter. 1985f. Emic or etic or just another catch 22? A repartee to Hartmut Haberland. *Journal of Pragmatics* 9:845.

Senft, Gunter. 1986. *Kilivila. The language of the Trobriand Islanders.* Mouton Grammar Library, 3. Berlin: Mouton de Gruyter.

Senft, Gunter. 1987a. The system of classificatory particles in Kilivila reconsidered— First results on its inventory, its acquisition, and its usage. *Language and Linguistics in Melanesia* 16:100–125.

Senft, Gunter. 1987b. Kilivila color terms. *Studies in Language* 11:315–346.

Senft, Gunter. 1987c. Rituelle Kommunikation auf den Trobriand Inseln. *Zeitschrift für Literaturwissenschaft und Linguistik* 65:105–130.

Senft, Gunter. 1987d. Nanam'sa Bwena—Gutes Denken: Eine ethnolinguistische Fallstudie über eine Dorfversammlung auf den Trobriand Inseln. *Zeitschrift für Ethnologie* 112:181–122.

Senft, Gunter. 1989. Apropos the whole and its parts: Classificatory particles in Kilivila language. In *Das Ganze und seine Teile—The Whole and its Parts*, ed. Walter A. Koch, 142–176. Bochum, Germany: Brockmeyer.

Senft, Gunter. 1991a. Bakavilisi Biga—We can "turn" the language—Or: What happens to English words in Kilivila language? In *Proceedings of the XIVth International Congress of Linguists (held in Berlin/GDR, 1987). Organized under the Auspices of CIPL*, eds Werner Bahner, Joachim Schildt; and Dieter Viehweger, vol. II, 1743–1746. Berlin: Akademie Verlag.

Senft, Gunter. 1991b. Prolegomena to the pragmatics of "situational-intentional" varieties in Kilivila language. In *Levels of linguistic adaptation: Selected papers from the 1987 International Pragmatics Conference*, vol. II, ed. Jef Verschueren, 235–248. Amsterdam: John Benjamins.

Senft, Gunter. 1991c. Network models to describe the Kilivila classifier system. *Oceanic Linguistics* 30:131–155.

Senft, Gunter. 1991d. Mahnreden auf den Trobriand Inseln—Eine Fallstudie. *Verbale Interaktion—Studien zur Empirie und Methodologie der Pragmatik*, ed. Dieter Flader, 27–49. Stuttgart, Germany: J. B. Metzler.

Senft, Gunter. 1992a. Bakavilisi Biga—Or: What happens to English words in the Kilivila language? *Language and Linguistics in Melanesia* 23:13–49.

Senft, Gunter. 1992b. What happened to "the fearless tailor" in Kilivila: A European fairy tale from the South Seas. *Anthropos* 87:407–421.

Senft, Gunter. 1992c. *Body and mind in the Trobriand Islands.* Paper presented at the 91st Annual Meeting of the American Anthropological Association, San Francisco, December 2–6, 1992. Mimeo, Nijmegen, Max-Planck-Institute, The Netherlands.

Senft, Gunter. 1993. A grammaticalization hypothesis on the origin of Kilivila classificatory particles. *Sprachtypologie und Universalienforschung* 46:100–112.

Senft, Gunter. In press. Zeichenkonzeptionen in Ozeanien. *Semiotics: A handbook on the sign-theoretic foundation of nature and culture*, eds. Roland Posner, Klaus Robering, and Thomas A. Sebeok. Berlin: de Gruyter.

Serzisko, Fritz. 1980. Sprachen mit Zahlklassifikatoren Analyse und Vergleich. In *Akup* Nr. 37, ed. Hansjakob Seiler. Cologne, Germany: Universität zu Köln.

Serzisko, Fritz. 1982a. Temporäre Klassifikation. Ihre Variationsbreite in Sprachen mit Zahlklassifikatoren. In *Apprehension: das sprachliche Erfassen von Gegenständen, part 1: Bereich und Ordnung der Phänomene*, eds. Hansjakob Seiler and Christian Lehmann, 147–159. Tübingen, Germany: Narr.

Serzisko, Fritz. 1982b. Gender, noun class, and numeral classification: a scale of classificatory techniques. In *Issues in the theory of universal grammar*, eds. Rene Dirven and Günter Radden, 95–123. Tübingen, Germany: Narr.

Silverstein, Michael. 1986. Classifiers, verb classifiers, and verbal categories. In *Proceedings of the 12th Annual Meeting of the Berkeley Linguistic Society*, 497–514. Berkeley, Calif.: Berkeley Linguistic Society.

Sinclar, Anne, Robert J. Jarvella, and Willem J. M. Levelt. 1978. *The child's conception of language*. Heidelberg, Germany: Springer.

Slobin, Dan I. 1991. Learning to think for speaking: Native language, cognition, and rhetorical style. *Pragmatics* 1:7–25.

Smith, Kenneth D. 1979. *Sedang Grammar*. Pacific Linguistics, Series B, No. 50. Canberra: Australian National University.

Spitulnik, Debra. 1988. Levels of semantic structuring in Bantu noun classification. In *Current approaches to African linguistics*, vol. 5, eds. Paul Newman and Robert D. Botne, 207–220. Dordrecht, The Netherlands: Foris.

Stern, Clara, and William Stern. 1981 [1928]. *Die Kindersprache*. Darmstadt, Germany: Wissenschaftliche Buchgesellschaft.

Stolz, Thomas 1991. *Die aztekischen Numeralklassifikatoren*. Mimeo, Ruhr-University Bochum, Germany.

Strawson, P. F. 1950. On referring. *Mind* 59:320–344.

Supalla, Ted. 1986. The classifier system in American Sign Language: Numeral classifiers in Austroasiatic. In *noun classes and categorization*, ed. Colette Craig, 181–214. Amsterdam: John Benjamins.

Tversky, Barbara. 1986. Components and categorization. *Noun classes and categorization*, ed. Colette Craig, 63–75. Amsterdam: John Benjamins.

Tyler, Stephen A. 1969. Introduction. *Cognitive anthropology*, ed. Stephen A. Tyler, 1–23. New York: Holt, Rinehart and Winston.

Unterbeck, Barbara. 1990a. *Thesen zur Dissertation: Kollektion, Numeralklassifikation und Transnumerus— Überlegungen zur Apprehension im Koreanischen und zu einer typologischen Charakteristik von Substantiven*. Zentralinstitut für Sprachwissenschaft, Akademie der Wissenschaften der DDR, Berlin.

Unterbeck, Barbara. 1990b. *Kollektion, Numeralklassifikation und Transnumerus— Überlegungen zur Apprehension im Koreanischen und zu einer typologischen Charakteristik von Substantiven*. Doctoral dissertation. Zentralinstitut für Sprachwissenschaft, Akademie der Wissenschaften der DDR.

Vachek, Joseph. 1976. Linguistic typology and linguistic characterology. In *Linguistic studies offered to Joseph Greenberg: Studia Linguistica et Philologica*, ed. Alphonse Juilland, 223–226. Saratoga, Calif.: Anma Libri.

Vater, Heinz. 1991. *Einführung in die Raum-Linguistik*, Klage 24. Cologne, Germany: Gabel Verlag.

Verhaar, John. 1986. Information structure and noun phrases. *Sophia Linguistica: Working Papers in Linguistics* 20/21:1–6.

Verhaar, John. 1987. Book review of Morton Benson et al. (1986). *The BBI combinatory dictionary of English: A guide to word combination. Studies in Language* 11:503–504.

Verhaar, John. 1988. Phrase syntax in contemporary Indonesian: Noun phrases. In *Towards a description of contemporary Indonesian: Preliminary studies, part III*, ed. Bambang Kaswanti Purwo, 1–45. Jakarta: Nusa.

Vollmer, Gerhard. 1988a. *Was können wir wissen?* vol. 1: *Die Natur der Erkenntnis*. Stuttgart, Germany: Hirzel.

Vollmer, Gerhard. 1988b. *Was können wir wissen?* vol. 2: *Die Erkenntnis der Natur*. Stuttgart, Germany: Hirzel.

Vollmer, Gerhard. 1989. Auf der Suche nach der Ordnung—Naturphilosophische Überlegungen zur Entwicklung von Weltbildern. In *Das Ganze und seine Teile—The Whole and its Parts*, ed. Walter A. Koch, 194–221. Bochum, Germany: Brockmeyer.

Wallace, Anthony F. C. 1962. Culture and cognition. *Science* 135:351–357.

Wallace, Ron. 1989. Cognitive mapping and the origin of language and mind. *Current Anthropology* 30:518–526.

Wassmann, Jürg, and Pierre R. Dasen. 1994. Yupno Number System and Counting. *Journal of Cross-Cultural Psychology* 25(2):78–94.

Watson-Gegeo, Karen Ann, and David W. Gegeo. 1986. The social world of Kwara'ae children: Acquisition of language and values. In *Children's world and children's language*, eds. Jenny Cook-Gumperz, William Corsaro, and Jürgen Streeck, 109–127. Berlin: Mouton de Gruyter.

Weiner, Annette B. 1976. *Women of value, men of renown: New perspectives in Trobriand exchange*. Austin: University of Texas Press.

Weiner, Annette B. 1982. Ten years in the life of an island. *Bikmaus* 3:64–75.

Weiner, Annette B. 1983. From words to objects to magic: Hard words and the boundaries of social interaction. *Man* 18:690–709.

Weiner, Annette B. 1988. *The Trobrianders of Papua New Guinea*. New York: Holt, Rinehart and Winston.

Weinreich, Uriel, William Labov, and Marvin I. Herzog. 1968. Empirical foundations for a theory of language change. In *Directions for historical linguistics*, eds W. P. Lehmann and Yakov Malkiel, 95–195. Austin: University of Texas Press.

Whorf, Benjamin Lee. 1958. Science and linguistics. In *Readings in social psychology*, eds. Eleanor Maccoby, Theodore M. Newcomb, and Eugene L. Hartley, 1–9. New York: Holt, Rinehart and Winston.

Whorf, Benjamin Lee. 1940. Science and linguistics. *Technology Review* 44:229–231, 247, 248.

Whorf, Benjamin Lee. 1963. Grammatische Kategorien. *Sprache, Denken, Wirklichkeit*, ed. Benjamin Lee Whorf, 133–139. Reinbek, Germany: Rowohlt.

Wittgenstein, Ludwig. 1971 [1922]. *Tractatus logico-philosophicus: Logisch-philosophische Abhandlung*. Frankfurt am Main, Germany: Suhrkamp.

Wittgenstein, Ludwig. 1977 [1958]. *Philosophische Untersuchungen*. Frankfurt am Main, Germany: Suhrkamp.

Wittgenstein, Ludwig. 1980 [1958]. *Das Blaue Buch: Eine Philosophische Betrachtung Das Braune Buch*. Frankfurt am Main, Germany: Suhrkamp.

Worsley, P. M. 1954. Noun-classification in Australian and Bantu: Formal or semantic? *Oceania* 24:275–288.

Wurm, Stephen A. 1981. The possessive class systems in AIWO, Reef Islands, Solomon Islands. *Papers in New Guinea Linguistics*, No. 21 Pacific Linguistics, Series A, No. 61:181–209. Canberra: Australian National University.

Zubin, David, and Klaus Michael Köpcke. 1986. Gender and folk taxonomy: The indexical relation between grammatical and lexical categorization. In *Noun classes and categorization*, ed. Colette Craig, 139–180. Amsterdam: John Benjamins.

# Index